AREAS OF RESPONSIBILITY

CODE
NAMES

Operation Iraqi Freedom: 22 Historic Days in Words and Pictures (with Marc Kusnetz, Gen. Montgomery Meigs [ret.], and Neal Shapiro)

The US Military Online: A Directory for Internet Access to the Department of Defense

Encyclopedia of the U.S. Military (with Joshua M. Handler, Julie A. Morrissey, and Jacquelyn M. Walsh)

Nuclear Weapons Databook: Volume IV: Soviet Nuclear Weapons (with Thomas B. Cochran, Robert S. Norris, and Jeffrey I. Sands), also published in Russia

Nuclear Weapons Databook: Volume III: U.S. Nuclear Warhead Facility Profiles (with Thomas B. Cochran, Milton M. Hoenig, and Robert S. Norris)

Nuclear Weapons Databook: Volume II: U.S. Nuclear Warhead Production (with Thomas B. Cochran, Milton M. Hoenig, and Robert S. Norris)

Nuclear Weapons Databook: Volume I: U.S. Nuclear Forces and Capabilities (with Thomas B. Cochran and Milton M. Hoenig)

Nuclear Battlefields: Global Links in the Arms Race (with Richard W. Fieldhouse)

SIOP: The Secret US Plan for Nuclear War (with Peter Pringle)

Research Guide to Current Military and Strategic Affairs

CODE NAMES

Deciphering US Military Plans, Programs, and Operations in the 9/11 World

WILLIAM M. ARKIN

STEERFORTH PRESS
HANOVER, NEW HAMPSHIRE

For more information visit www.codenames.org.

Library of Congress Cataloging-in-Publication Data
Arkin, William M.
Code names : deciphering US military plans, programs, and operations in the 9/11 world /
William M. Arkin.— 1st ed.
p. cm.
ISBN 1-58642-083-6 (alk. paper)
1. United States—Armed Forces—Organization. 2. Military planning—United States. 3. United
States—Defenses. 4. Civil defense—United States. 5. War on Terrorism, 2001– I. Title.

UA23.A689 2005
973.931—dc22

2004025039

FIRST EDITION

CONTENTS

ACKNOWLEDGMENTS

Collecting US code names has been a multidecade labor of love, and a seeming never-ending and wonderful time-waster that finally got a jump start with the events of 9/11 and the government subsequently resorting to its own brand of Cold War secrecy. I finally was spurred to turn my scribbling into a book by my friend Tom Powers, who is also conveniently a partner at Steerforth Press. Tom understood the project immediately and was a constant cheerleader. The rest of the crew at Steerforth — Chip Fleischer, Kristin Sperber, Helga Schmidt, Pia Needham, Laura Jorstad, Janet Jesso, and Peter Holm — all worked with the kind of friendly commitment that only comes from a small publisher. A book project with no problems and no complications. What could be better?

None of the work could have been concluded without the kibitzing of my cherished friends and colleagues: Tom Cochran, Sy Hersh, Matthew McKinzie, Stan Norris, Dana Priest, John Robinson, Sarah Sewall, and Bob Windrem. I have particularly been edified by the previous works of Jeffrey Richelson, and John Pike's hard work on the Web served as a baseline to understand what was already in the public domain. As always on matters of government secrecy, I received the good advice of Steve Aftergood. Hans Kristensen particularly stands out for individual mention, having spent many hours scouring his stockpile of declassified military documents for new code names. Finally to my attorney, Jeff Smith, thanks as always for the now more than two-decade association.

There are others I would like to mention, but their positions in or near the US government demand that discretion be the better part of valor. I am particularly indebted to the network of retired generals and admirals who have always been generous in sharing their wisdom and insights about the US military. To other friends and colleagues in the Defense Department and Air Force who prefer not to be mentioned: Thank you.

Throughout the writing of this book, I also worked with NBC News and MSNBC, and wrote for the *Los Angeles Times*, and I owe a particular note of thanks and gratitude to Steve Capus, Dick Cooper, Phil Griffin, Sue Horton, Doyle McManus, Jim Miklaszewski, Elena Nachmanoff, and Bill Wheatley.

On a personal note, thanks to Chuck Gundersen, Hannah Nichols and Steve Johnson, Peter Pringle, Julia Sweig and Reed Thompson, and Philene Taormina. Nanc wonderfully tolerated the long hours and obsessive behavior and was a source of enormous support. I dedicate this book to my daughters, Rikki and Hannah.

INTRODUCTION

Polo Step is a Pentagon code word for a security classification above Top Secret. The program requires that anyone with access to Polo Step material be "read into" the compartment and sign a nondisclosure pledge. Any discussions about Polo Step activities have to take place in specially cleared and "swept" rooms, and Polo Step documents must be hand carried or transmitted over approved and restricted communications circuits. Because the existence of Polo Step is itself classified, the clearance and program are referred to outside the world of those in the know simply by the digraph *PS*.

Before 9/11, Polo Step was used to confine highly sensitive Iraq and counter-terrorism war planning to a small circle. Starting in the mid-1990s, the Clinton administration tasked the navy with maintaining attack submarines capable of firing long-range Tomahawk cruise missiles on call in the Indian Ocean south of Pakistan should there be an immediate need for a strike against Osama bin Laden or other terrorist targets. The compartment itself related to the operation, the cruise missile technologies, and other "special" classified weapons and capabilities of the US military. After 9/11, Polo Step was used by the Pentagon and other parts of the American national security community to control access to, and circulation of, Top Secret contingency planning for Afghanistan and Iraq.

I referred to Polo Step in a June 23, 2002, column for the *Los Angeles Times,* the first public reference to the code name. Noting the revelation, my friend Eric Schmitt, a *New York Times* Pentagon correspondent, called me to follow up with his own story, which the *Times* published on its front page on July 5.

News articles are written about "war plans" and "secret" programs all the time, and leaking from the top sometimes seems like a way of life in Washington. But an article that includes a never-before-published code name adds a rare authenticity, because it suggests not only sourcing close to real secrets but also a source involved in internal government deliberations who is courageous (or reckless) enough to make an unauthorized revelation to the media.

Inside the Pentagon, the compromise of a code name that was itself classified and closely controlled set off alarm bells. Gen. Tommy Franks, commander of

Central Command and the officer responsible for Iraq war planning, wrote in his autobiography, *American Soldier,* that he called Secretary of Defense Donald Rumsfeld. "I'd like everyone in OSD [the office of the Secretary of Defense] and the JCS [joint chiefs of staff] who knows the details of our planning process to be polygraphed — and prosecuted if they're discovered to have leaked Top Secret information."

"I think it is so egregious, so terrible, that I decided to have an investigation," Rumsfeld said at a July 22 press conference referring to compromise of war planning for Iraq. "Anyone who has a position where they touch a war plan has an obligation to not leak it to the press or anybody else."

The Air Force Office of Special Investigations (OSI), working for Rumsfeld, set about determining how the tightly controlled Polo Step material had been compromised. Investigators interviewed, friends tell me, more than 1,000 Pentagon officials, military officers, and defense contractors, many of whom didn't even have Polo Step clearances, many more than once. Military officers were threatened with being "red lined" — that is, losing their own security clearances. The message inside the Pentagon was clear: Only Rumsfeld would speak for the vast department. There would be no discussion or debate about assumptions behind the looming Iraq war. By the time the investigation was winding down at the end of 2003 (after the Iraq "war" had already been fought), OSI had spent well over $1.5 million trying to uncover the Polo Step leak. It was all to protect a code name, and a well-worn national security habit, threatened by open information and debate.

At the time the initial Iraq war plans stories were published — just nine months after 9/11 — the fact that the Bush administration was preparing for a war in Iraq was probably the worst-kept secret in Washington. The news media were filled with speculation as to who was "next" after Afghanistan in the war on terror. For those who followed the national security establishment, it was fairly transparent that much of the military machine that had been activated to topple the Taliban in Afghanistan continued to buzz with activity: Military units, active and reserve, were still being shipped out to classified "Southwest Asia" nations and obscure Central Asian "Stans" almost every day, ships called at ports throughout the Arabian Gulf region, new task forces were being activated, generals and other senior military officers were quietly leaving their stateside posts to augment activities overseas, construction was being hurried, contractors were scurrying to new Middle East assignments.

Because of the sensitivity associated with war plans, and because American lives were potentially at stake, both Eric and I touched base with the Pentagon media apparatus to discuss our Iraq stories. When I asked the Central Command public affairs officer in Florida whether the command overseeing war planning had any reason to object to my revealing the actual code name, I got the robotic answer: "We don't comment on war plans."

After Schmitt let on that he was working from the same Polo Step information, officials from the highest level of the US government launched into frenzied negotiations about what they didn't want printed in the New York Times. Ironically, even though the Los Angeles Times had already mentioned it in print, the New York Times chose not to mention the Polo Step code name itself. But what the government really prevailed on the Times to exclude from its story (at least for a few days, at which point it came out anyway) was any mention of the country of Jordan.

From a low point in relations when Jordan's King Hussein tilted toward Baghdad after the Iraq invasion of Kuwait in 1990, King Abdullah II had repaired bilateral relations with the United States and opened a course of intimate intelligence and military cooperation. Abdullah, who had been the head of Jordan's own military commando force before becoming king, opened the door for US special operators to train and operate on Jordanian soil. He allowed US eavesdroppers from the National Security Agency and army intelligence to set up covert positions near the Iraqi and Syrian borders. He increased liaison with CIA case officers to assist in exploiting the sizable Iraqi community inside the country. After 9/11, Jordanian security services did much dirty work for the US in the war on terror, working closely with the supersecret Gray Fox organization and other covert intelligence and special operations units of the American government.

The overt side of US–Jordanian relations — arms sales, joint military exercises, unit exchanges, and routine deployments for desert and familiarization "training" — provided cover for a quiet American buildup toward war in Iraq. The US constructed storage bunkers to pre-position munitions and other military equipment. The facilities at two large expeditionary air bases were improved in the eastern desert near Iraq.

As planning for the 2003 war unfolded, the "western front" anchored in Jordan was a key element in the military strategy to attack from three sides: south, north, and west. Jordan was particularly important at the national level because it stood between Iraq and Israel, and planners believed that access was needed to interdict Iraqi missile firings (or air attacks) on Israel.

The public problem associated with all of this was that like many of its Arab neighbors, the Amman government also had to cater to public sentiment that strongly opposed a US war against Iraq and even more adamantly opposed Jordan's involvement in any American operation whose purpose was to defend Israel. So despite the obvious presence of American troops, and the buildup of more than 5,000 foreign troops on Jordanian soil, Amman continued to proclaim that there were no agreements with the United States, no military presence, no bases, and no arrangements.

This is where the code names and secrecy kick in. All through 2002 and 2003, a series of seemingly innocent military exercises took place with Jordanian forces. The ones that leaked out or were publicly acknowledged had code names such as Desert Thunderclap, Eager Light, Eager Tiger, Early Victor, Infinite Anvil, and Saffron Sands. As US (and British) forces built up east of Amman, the two American air bases in a "classified country" were code-named West Wing so that even in internal military documents the deployments could be referred to without ever having to mention Jordan.

In this way, covert intelligence operatives and commandos from the US, Britain, and later Australia arrived in country. "Black" special operations helicopters and gunships deployed to the Jordanian desert. Patriot surface-to-air missile batteries showed up in Amman, the nation's capital. A unit of the Rhode Island Air National Guard was activated and shipped to Jordan to set up a communications infrastructure. Infantry from the Florida and Indiana National Guards took up positions around American facilities to provide force protection. The very same deployments were being publicly announced in less sensitive Kuwait to the south. But the deployments in Jordan were officially secret. This condition was imposed by a Jordanian government that chose to publicly lie to its own people, and the United States manufactured secrets as payment.

And so it goes for dozens of Jordans around the globe. The war on terrorism and wars in Iraq and Afghanistan have led to a secrecy explosion, both at home and abroad. More than 20 countries such as Jordan are secretly or quietly providing bases and facilities — as of early 2004, 76 have granted permission for US military planes to land at their airfields and airports, and 89 have granted overflight rights. US Navy ships and submarines refuel and provision at 251 ports and foreign naval bases in scores of countries around the world. To conduct Operation Enduring Freedom (OEF, the war to topple the Taliban and disperse al Qaeda in Afghanistan), the United States established facilities in Kyrgyzstan, Pakistan, Tajikistan, and Uzbekistan, and secured overflight rights in Kazakhstan and Turkmenistan. To fight in Iraq, the US built up forces in

Bahrain, Jordan, Kuwait, Oman, Qatar, Saudi Arabia, Turkey, and the United Arab Emirates. Djibouti and Kenya have become forward military bases in Africa. In Asia, new military activity has started in India, Malaysia, Singapore, and Thailand. The US has a major counter-terrorism operation in the Philippines (where Freedom Eagle, Balance Piston/Vector Balance Piston, and OEF–Philippines are being waged), supported by US bases in Guam, Japan, and Southeast Asia. Even in our own hemisphere, relationships that were already dominated by military cooperation in the "war on drugs" have transformed into operations against "narco-terrorism."

Why This Book Is Needed

Most of these activities and relations hide behind a veil of secrecy, their long-term implications are unknown, and the wisdom of any of this is barely discussed or debated here at home. Every Jordan constitutes a set of compromises and quiet arrangements and secret agreements. We cooperate with foreign countries in trading secret information. We supply lethal hardware and train anyone who is willing in the arts of intelligence, counter-terrorism, and "counterinsurgency." We build up intimate relationships with countries that we are critical of in other realms, and we curry favor with many who are highly critical of us, even in public. We professionalize foreign military, security, police, and intelligence services even though we know in many cases that they will be used to monitor or round up dissidents, that they will torture and "disappear," that they ultimately are state agents to squelch democracy.

I don't question the theoretical underpinnings of government secrecy: that it is justified to prosecute military operations and the war on terrorism, to protect American military and intelligence capabilities, and to preserve American lives. But far too much secrecy merely exists "at the request of the host government" — that is, in order to gain American access or coalition cooperation with the hope (seemingly always fruitless) that a covert relationship also can be kept from the press and public and later denied.

When the host nation's interests are not being held as paramount, it is the bureaucracies' own interests that also account for much government secrecy. This secrecy is more often than not simply born of habits that have nothing to do with national security. If the subject is intelligence or special operations or space or nuclear weapons or submarines or cyber-warfare or homeland security — and on and on — the assumption is that it is secret. Secrecy is used to erect a wall around a budget or to make a segment of an agency or service seem more special. Secrecy is used in internal bureaucratic battles. Secrecy is employed by policy makers to avoid debate or oversight. The more controversial the program, weapon, or operation, the higher the classification and the narrower the access restrictions.

In other words, secrecy is hardly only about hiding capabilities from the "enemy" or protecting national security. In the case of Jordan, it was obvious to the Iraqi regime and to any other military power watching that thousands of American and coalition soldiers were arriving to prepare for war. Though the government "doesn't comment on war plans," in the case of Iraq less secrecy and more debate may have revealed some of the flaws and oversights in planning that became apparent only after the fall of Saddam Hussein's regime.

In the ways of the national security establishment, every secret also has a code name (even the leak investigation of the Polo Step compromise had a code name, which I believe may have been Seven Seekers). I started to seriously collect code names in the mid-1990s when it appeared to me that despite the end of the Cold War, government secrecy was only increasing. Code names seemed a good way to try to organize and understand the range and breadth of American military activity in the world. The code names themselves tend to be unclassified, even if their true meaning and exact implications are secret. Each code name tells a story of some expenditure of tax dollars and is tangibly connected to some activity with a complex institutional history and significance. Gathering them together seemed a good way to produce an anatomy, a sort of DNA map of American national security. The task became even more pressing and important with the events of 9/11, and with the war in Iraq.

For many, the immediate reaction to this compendium will be anger — *You're exposing secrets and endangering America!* — but frankly, I've been here before. When I co-authored the first volume of the five-volume *Nuclear Weapons Databook: U.S. Forces and Capabilities* in 1984, the Reagan administration launched a feverish protest stating that it would "not be in the national interest" to publish a book detailing the history and characteristics of nuclear weapons. A year later, when I co-authored *Nuclear Battlefields* about the worldwide spread of the American (and Soviet) nuclear weapons infrastructure, again the government denounced the revelation of official secrets. Conservative commentators opined about the dangers such information would incite: that it would provoke terrorism, that nuclear security would be compromised.

By the mid-1980s, I had already lost one job for revealing the location of US nuclear weapons in West Germany, and I had clashed with government lawyers and investigators trying to convince them that what they thought was highly classified was actually openly contained in telephone books and other publicly available budget, contracting, and programmatic documents. What is more, much of what was held to be highly secret dealing with nuclear weapons was obvious to the "enemy" or anyone else who cared to pry. Finally, like the US soldiers in Jordan in 2002–2003, physical security and force protection wasn't dependent on secrecy. Hundreds of millions of dollars were spent to guard nuclear sites and prepare counter-terrorist plans because of the very assumption that in an increasingly transparent world, both locals and foreign intelligence services knew where nuclear weapons were.

In retrospect, none of the predictions of certain damage to national security was even close to the mark. Secrecy was effectively and legitimately being used to protect the workings of nuclear warheads and to safeguard American military capabilities against technical counter-measures, but it was also shielding a nuclear infrastructure that had steadily taken on a dangerous, illegal, and questionable life of its own. Behind a shield of secrecy were plans for destabilizing first strikes and protracted nuclear wars. The United States had nuclear deployments and war plans that violated its treaty obligations. The US was lying to many of its closest allies, even in NATO, about its nuclear designs. Tens of thousands of nuclear weapons, hundreds of bases, and dozens of ships and submarines existed in a special secret world of their own with no rational military or even "deterrence" justification. The situation had become so incoherent that even the Reagan and Bush administrations undertook to eliminate thousands of nuclear weapons and scores of bases before the end of the Cold War.

The cumulative effect, then, of bringing the range and magnitude of American nuclear activities to public attention was to help focus and inform an ongoing public debate. We had simply accumulated too many nuclear weapons, and public debate about unintentional or accidental nuclear war highlighted that these weapons and their configurations threatened to undermine the very security they were intended to guard. Nuclear weapons were an increasing irritant to US foreign relations. The cost associated with the voracious infrastructure needed to support nuclear weapons ate into conventional military capabilities.

Many insiders had been questioning for years why so many nuclear weapons and bases were scattered about, many in highly vulnerable locations. But stripped of the secrecy that impeded public scrutiny, technical and arms control and institutional changes became easier to visualize. The nuclear problem could be more easily discussed with everyone on the same page.

Then, as now, my motivation in writing the *Databook* and *Nuclear Battlefields* wasn't fear of Armageddon or some other disaster revealed by flaws or weaknesses in the system. I was merely fearful that the government wasn't serving the public interest; that the right decisions weren't being made; that the nuclear priesthood and a cabal of faceless bureaucrats pursued questionable policies and activities shielded by illegitimate secrecy; and that the public's interest and collective wisdom were lost in the maze.

Fast-forward to the post-9/11 world. The threat of terrorism again justifies a sort of modern-day arms race and an explosion of new government secrecy. The same priesthood and the same bureaucrats and the same institutions assert that the danger from global terrorism is so dire that it demands extraordinary actions, expenditures, and compromises. The view of the government is that if we hesitate or question the war on terrorism, something even more destructive and deadly than 9/11 will occur at home. Because fear of another 9/11 is so palpable at home and because Americans are in harm's way in Iraq and all around the globe, extraordinary secrecy seems justified. The public is largely co-opted into accepting the government's view that a national security emergency exists.

Yet we live in a world in which the professionals charged with our security have again and again been unsuccessful at preventing 9/11s. Our Intelligence Community is constantly being surprised by events in the world and misreads what is happening. Our military fights spectacular and successful battles in places like Afghanistan and Iraq, yet we consistently seem to lose the bigger wars, the very wars that are the responsibility of the secret world of "special operators" and intelligence personnel. We have legions of psychological and information warriors, and perception managers and influence peddlers, and yet are losing the battle for hearts and minds and peaceful relations. Policy makers and the national security establishment can provide no particular guarantee that the counter-terrorism actions out there are being successful in forestalling an attack at home. The government readily admits that it is not doing enough to dry up the swamps that breed terrorists. We have invested billions in the "war" on drugs, but we have not reduced drug supply or use.

September 11, 2001, was one of the greatest failures of the American national security establishment in the history of our country, and yet not one official responsible for counter-terrorism, intelligence, law enforcement, immigration, or airline security has been fired. A mind-boggling bureaucratic archipelago of self-interested agencies didn't share or cooperate or even communicate before

9/11, and we are to believe that these same agencies, many with the same leaders, can now administer all this secrecy and all these code names.

In a perfect world, all this secrecy would protect legitimate secrets from prying foreign eyes. But in the real world, many of the individual secrets and much of the accumulated secrecy merely serve to keep a permanent system and a singular assumption of American national security from public debate and congressional oversight. My solution is simple: Democracy works better, and a brighter and safer future is more likely to be achieved, when the people understand what is being done in their name. You either believe in openness or you don't.

All the information in *Code Names* is derived from documents in the public domain or was revealed to me by government and industry sources in the course of my journalistic duties. In preparing this book, I was always mindful of my responsibilities as a citizen and carefully weighed the public value of a revelation against the potential harm that might be done to the United States. I recognize that some of these disclosures will cause anxiety and anguish to some in government and that some may argue that the accumulation of so much information in one place is itself damaging. But I relied on my judgment as a longtime military analyst and observer of the government to avoid revelations that could directly damage the military or Intelligence Community and tapped the wisdom and judgment of government officials and military officers, as well as other well-informed counselors, to ensure that nothing that is revealed is damaging. I can say with confidence that nothing in this book could compromise the identity of a US agent or a sensitive intelligence source or method. There is no information that could compromise an ongoing military operation.

A final question obviously arises from this compendium: Is there anything new here? Hasn't US national security policy always included intelligence collection and secret operations and covert action and convoluted relationships? Haven't there always been notorious programs such as Chaos, Condor, ECHELON, Mongoose, and Phoenix? Haven't mistakes with secret programs been made dozens, if not hundreds, of times in the past?

The answer is partly that a national security policy dominated by secrecy and covert relations has long-lasting impact. For example, during the Iran–Iraq war in the 1980s, when the national security professionals decided that it was more important to side with Iraq than Iran, the US provided Top Secret intelligence to Saddam Hussein (under Druid Leader, Elephant Grass, and Surf Fisher). By providing Iraq with secret assistance, we not only helped it defeat Iran but also demonstrated to Baghdad that nation-states can say one thing in public and do another in private. Of course, it didn't take the United States to teach Saddam Hussein to tell a lie or be evil, but as part of the US covert relationship, our message was that national interest justifies compromises in principles and values, or even lawbreaking. When Iraq used chemical weapons against its own citizens and on the battlefield against Iran during the same time period, because of our covert relationship and convoluted compromises born of those secret programs, we were conflicted in our condemnation, perhaps conveying the message to the Iraqis that we had to publicly condemn their illegal act while secretly wishing them well.

Later, the legacy of secrecy and covert relations would play out in Iraq's invasion of Kuwait in 1990 and even in the emergence of al Qaeda. Though Jordan openly opposed the coalition military response to Iraq during Desert Shield, most of Iraq's neighbors consented to American action and forward basing — provided, that is, that the details of their cooperation with the United States remained classified. Most sensitive to them were offensive military operations, intelligence collection, or special operations being launched from their soil. The US found itself in the ridiculous position, for instance, of operating a fleet of enormous and highly observable B-52 bombers from Jeddah in Saudi Arabia but having to maintain (even today) that the location was classified. No one doubts that "host nation sensitivity" is important; the United States should not throw its weight around the world insensitive to where it is operating. But that is also a far cry from operating under the conditions imposed by the duplicitous nondemocracies of the Arabian Gulf region, countries that the US is ostensibly in a partnership to defend.

In 1990, Saudi Arabia demanded not only secrecy but also a pledge that the United States would leave the kingdom once the war was over. Of course the war with Iraq didn't really end with Iraq's ejection from Kuwait, and the US didn't leave. Not coincidentally, then, as Saudi-born Osama bin Laden's al Qaeda organization grew, a significant ingredient of the jihadist call to arms was the presence of the infidel troops in the land of the "holy places" (Mecca and Medina). Again, my argument is not that the United States is responsible for al Qaeda. It is to merely make the observation that the continued US military presence in Saudi Arabia, facilitated by secrecy, had a far-reaching impact.

Over the years, the Saudis did hardly anything to stop the growth of the al Qaeda organization, and the kingdom placed enormous constraints on what the US could do on its soil. The Saudis treated US service members — particularly women — with contempt, they stonewalled US intelligence and law enforcement agencies, they even failed to cooperate with the US investigation after the deadly Khobar Towers terrorist attack on US forces in 1996. And yet the US military stayed, and it continued to operate under the public fig leaf that it was merely defending Saudi Arabia from potential Iraqi aggression. Through Arabian Gauntlet, Blackshark, Camel Hump, Earnest Leader, Grecian Firebolt, the Indigo series, Nautical Swimmer, Phoenix Scorpion, Red Reef, Silent Assurance, and countless American military "show of force" deployments under the Desert and Vigilant series, over the years the US and Saudi governments and militaries interacted, built things, wrote rules, planned, and negotiated. But in the end, the web of cooperative military operations and shared secrets suggested a better relationship and a stronger alliance than was actually the case. I can't help but mention that 15 of the 9/11 suicide bombers were Saudi citizens.

One could argue that after 9/11, the capabilities built up in Saudi Arabia proved priceless in fighting in Afghanistan and Iraq. But the truth of the matter is that though the Afghanistan air campaign was directed from the convenient, supermodern Combined Air Operations Center at Prince Sultan air base in Saudi Arabia, the Saudis were so uncomfortable with the US presence that they pressured the US to move activities to another command center, which was rapidly built in Qatar. When the second war with Iraq eventually came, the US military once again secretly operated from Saudi Arabia, flying some 300 US aircraft, including early warning, reconnaissance, special operations, aerial refueling, and transport aircraft, from Prince Sultan, Tabuk, and Ar Ar. But as soon as "major combat operations" were over in May 2003, the Saudis wasted no time in showing the US the door.

Of course, once again, the US has not really completely left. Saudi Arabia has become just another storehouse for continuing American secrets, another base without oversight, another presence without consideration for the long-term cost. In the ways of the Middle East, we have helped communicate a message to the enemies of the United States — a message that we will probably have to pay for later: The Saudi regime does as it pleases playing both sides of the fence, the royal family only looks out for itself, Saudi Arabia attacked an Arab neighbor and bowed to American pressure, and the voracious American empire shows no bounds in its worldwide spread, even in the land of the holy places. Meanwhile Saudi Arabia, despite an increasing number of its own domestic terrorism incidents, continues to provide only lip-service support to American counter-terrorism fighters on the ground.

On the other side of the Middle East, secret US–Israeli military and intelligence relations have flourished since the 1990 invasion. The very close communication and cooperation during Desert Storm led to a robust program of joint US–Israeli military operations and exercises under the code names Juniper Stallion, Juniper Cobra, other Juniper variations, Noble Shirley, and Shining Presence. Juniper Stallion 99 represented the high point, with US Air Force munitions specialists based in Italy quietly deploying to officially nonexistent sites in Israel where they inspected the $500 million worth of ammunition the US keeps in Israel. The American bases, called Sites 51, 53, and 54, don't appear on any map. Their specific locations are classified and highly sensitive. And it's not just munitions that the US pre-positions on Israeli soil; there are also vehicles, military equipment, even a 500-bed hospital for US Marines, all antiseptically described as "US–Israeli strategic cooperation."

Military cooperation such as this may or may not enhance American security, and may or may not be yet another sign of prudent planning by an ever-ready military. The reason for much of the secrecy, though, is clear: All around Israel, in Jordan, Saudi Arabia, Egypt, and the Gulf States, the US would be further constrained in its operational flexibility if it had to tell the truth. Here is the web we weave: In 2000, the US 22nd Fighter Squadron deployed from its base in Germany to Israel during exercise Juniper Stallion and also deployed to Saudi Arabia for a 90-day tour conducting Southern Watch no-fly-zone patrols over Iraq. The "defensive" Saudi deployment warranted a press release and a couple of stories in local military newspapers. But the squadron's foray into Israel to practice supersecret contingency plans was — and is — "classified." If the air force issued a press release about the deployment to Israel for Juniper Stallion, the 22nd might not be allowed back into Saudi Arabia. One could argue that secrecy ironically allows Riyadh to ignore the US–Israeli relationship, thus weakening any American protection.

American government secrecy has become so ingrained and obtuse that members of the public cannot know what its military is doing, or even how much of their tax dollars is spent by the Intelligence Community; it is estimated to be far more than $40 billion annually. But $40 billion is only the tip of the iceberg. To concoct all the code names and administer the vast secrecy system, to "clear" and keep an eye on the more than 2.5 million service members, government employees, and contractors with access to classified material and provide for physical security, we spend more than $7.5 billion annually. In 2003 alone, the government cost associated with secrecy increased by 14 percent over the previous year.

On top of intelligence and counter-intelligence and internal security spending, there are additional billions in the Pentagon's nonintelligence "black" budget, the so-called special access programs (SAPs) and special operations that are almost impossible to penetrate. The suggestion always is that what is "special" is sacred. Unfortunately, though, the SAPs that actually represent some revolutionary new stealth airplane are few and far between. Over the years, most supersecret "special" compartments have been used to overclassify mundane imagery and signals intelligence products. And many compartments are merely used to shield the politically sensitive or controversial from public view. Heck, even the Hebrew linguists and communications intercept activities of the US Intelligence Community directed against Israel are described in internal documents with the euphemism "special Arabic" to obscure the fact that the United States spies on one of its closest allies.

Beyond the ridiculous, though, there is a rapidly growing army of secret "special mission units" that are beyond scrutiny and increasingly a law unto themselves. SAPs, moreover, include a fair share of weapons and capabilities that are secret only because they might be perceived as repugnant (high-powered microwaves or blinding lasers), illegal (domestic programs that obscure the lines restricting what the military and Intelligence Community can do inside the United States), or downright dangerous (capabilities being developed to go beyond nuclear weapons in cyber-warfare and directed-energy weaponry to nullify enemy weapons — perfectly logical on the one hand, but potentially destabilizing if Russia or some other nuclear power ever perceived that they were part of a "first strike" program).

As I have learned in compiling this directory, most genuine secrets ironically remain secret. Enormous segments of the activities of the military and Intelligence Community remain safely under wraps and represent an even more staggeringly complex secret world. The thousands of code names covered in this compendium are in many ways only inadvertent secrets. The vast majority of the names here are perfectly in the open. But as with the case of Jordan, each name individually suggests much more that goes on beneath the surface in the world of warfare and espionage. In aggregate, the compendium suggests a scale that might be the only accurate means to determine how American resources are really used, what our true relationships and commitments are, and what importance or value a program or activity really has in the national security establishment.

When the Abu Ghraib prison scandal broke in 2004, we learned that some of those involved were neither government nor military personnel. They were "contractors." Others who were also implicated in the ranks of special operations units or the CIA evaded the exposure and public display that the hapless army reservists suffered. And third-country intelligence and special operations services, from Jordan and Britain and elsewhere, quietly slinked off. We learned that the interrogation program may have existed under a special access program called Copper Green. We learned that Abu Ghraib filled up in late 2003 after Operation Victory Bounty began. As the scandal unfolded, the Bush administration claimed complete transparency and candidness and asked for the forbearance of the American people as well as support for the troops.

Yet Abu Ghraib is like every other national security surprise: We cannot know who the players are or what they are up to until after disaster strikes. When the destroyer USS *Cole* was attacked in Yemen in 2000, when the navy EP-3 reconnaissance plane was attacked off Hainan Island in China, we were similarly educated about the underground activities of the US government. Add to Abu Ghraib, the *Cole*, the EP-3, and all the *Pueblo*s and U-2s and other US reconnaissance aircraft shot down inside Soviet airspace, the Iran–Contras and Iraq-gates, the Khobar Towers and Lebanon barracks bombings, the assassination plots, the coups, the covert programs, domestic spying operations, illegal weapons developments, and human experimentation. Faceless contractors, secret operations, unnamed accomplices, under-the-table agreements, quiet deployments, fake exercises, patrols, port calls, and constant movement — taken individually, each country may be a Jordan or a Saudi Arabia or an Israel with a special story and a justification. But when one adds it all up, it becomes apparent that US national security is increasingly everywhere and nowhere. Thus *Code Names* is just a small contribution to the beginning of the American education.

Naming Names

The naming of US military operations began with World War II (before then, operations were generally named for colors, such as Operation Indigo). The primary objective was operational security, but as the complexity of the war expanded, code word lists of some 10,000 common words were compiled to use in uniquely identifying a multitude of operations and projects. Blocks of code names were assigned to different commands (such as *Market* to Europe, *Olympic* to the Pacific), and words were randomly selected to create code names. Over time, a set of rules evolved: Avoid reference to living persons, do not trivialize military activity or be too triumphalistic, do not be insulting or vulgar. Code names were also selected with an eye toward inspiration of the fighting men.

With the end of the war and the creation of a permanent military and intelligence establishment, naming conventions continued to follow the same basic wartime principles. The major difference postwar was that code names now were for public consumption, to marshal support for the Cold War. Unclassified names, known as nicknames, were used for public relations purposes. Classified code words were used for operations, plans, and programs.

With Operation Just Cause in 1989, code names began to be used consistently to shape public opinion, and catchy, inspirational, or media-friendly nicknames came into vogue. After the 1990 Iraqi invasion of Kuwait, Gen. Norman Schwarzkopf chose the name Peninsula Shield, but the name suggested a war to protect Saudi oil rather than to liberate Kuwait and so was changed to Desert Shield (followed by Desert Storm). Just before the Afghanistan war began in 2001, the code name Infinite Justice was changed to Enduring Freedom after concerns were raised that only God had the power to dispense infinite justice.

Officially, there are three distinct types of code names:

+ **Nicknames:** A combination of two separate unassociated and unclassified words (say, *Polo* and *Step*) assigned to represent a specific program, activity, exercise, or special access program.
+ **Code words:** A single classified word (such as *BYEMAN*) assigned to represent a specific special access program or portion.
+ **Exercise terms:** A combination of two words, normally unclassified, used exclusively to designate a test, drill, or exercise.

In 1975, the Joint Chiefs of Staff introduced the computerized Code Word, Nickname, and Exercise Term System (NICKA), which automated the assignment of names. NICKA assigns each Defense Department organization a series of two-letter alphabetic sequences, requiring each "first word" of a nickname to begin with a letter pair. Some of the known assignments:

AG through AL: Joint Forces Command
AM through AR: North American Aerospace Defense Command
AS through AZ: European Command
CG through CL: Navy
CS through CZ: Marine Corps
EA through FF: North American Aerospace Defense Command
FG through FL: European Command
GS through GZ: Navy

HG through HL: Marine Corps

JG through JL: Joint Forces Command

JM through JR: North American Aerospace Defense Command

JS through JZ: European Command

LG through LL: Navy

LS through LZ: Marine Corps

NM through NR: European Command

OS through OZ: Navy

PG through PL: Marine Corps

QA through QF: Joint Forces Command

RA through RF: Navy

RS through RZ: Navy

SG through SL: European Command

SM through SR: Joint Forces Command

UM through UR: Joint Forces Command

VG through VL: North American Aerospace Defense Command

Under this system, for example, NORAD uses *Amalgam*, *Amazon*, and *Fencing* as first words, spawning Amalgam Virgo, Amazon Condor, and Fencing Brave.

The military is but one of the institutions within the national security community, and with the emergence of the Central Intelligence Agency, the National Security Agency, and other intelligence organizations, additional naming conventions also emerged to designate agents, sources, operations, and technologies. Internal to those organizations are complex sets of cryptonyms used to describe organizations, projects, and sources. The CIA uses cryptonyms based on a two-character digraph to designate covert operations in a country, region, or sector of the agency. The digraph is added to a random word to form the cryptonym (DB/ROCKSTARS, for instance, to designate the group of Iraq agents reporting to a CIA team in northern Iraq prior to Operation Iraqi Freedom). Some CIA digraphs known to have existed at different times include:

AE: Former Soviet Union

BE: Poland

DB: Iraq

DI: Former Czechoslovakia

DM: Former Yugoslavia

FU: Chile

PB: Guatemala

SM: United Kingdom

The Pentagon and all government agencies use the same security classification system of Top Secret, Secret, and Confidential, which designates "national security information," the protection of which the government deems necessary. But these three simple classification categories are supplemented by additional "compartments" and "special categories" where strict "need-to-know" and access controls are maintained beyond those normally needed for access to standard classified information.

Some of these compartments are as old as the Cold War. "Restricted Data," for instance, was established by the Atomic Energy Act of 1947 to segregate nuclear weapons design information. "National programs," such as those relating to the protection of the president, continuity of government operations, and covert action, are also long standing and generally controlled by the Executive Office of the President. The US intelligence gathering apparatus also generates a seemingly endless variety of compartments and code words, most themselves classified, to designate various types of espionage projects and communications intercepts.

The growth of US secret intelligence in the early days of the Cold War led to the introduction of distinctions among collateral information, sensitive compartmented information (SCI), and special intelligence (SI):

+ **Collateral information:** Nonsensitive noncompartmented information classified Confidential, Secret, or Top Secret.
+ **Sensitive compartmented information (SCI):** Information concerning or derived from intelligence sources, methods, or analytical processes, which is required to be handled exclusively within formal access control systems established by the Director of Central Intelligence (DCI), and additionally designated with a code word.
+ **Special intelligence (SI):** A classified category of SCI referring to signals intelligence and satellite or "national" derived imagery, also designated with a code word.

Each category of SCI and SI information is represented by a distinct code word, and these code words are further divided into various "compartments." Prior to 9/11, there were roughly 300 SCI compartments within the CIA and NSA, compared with an estimated 800 in the late 1980s. The most venerable of these code words, familiar to almost anyone who has served in government or the military, were Umbra, Spoke, and Moray, used for 40 years before they were eliminated in May 1999 to designate sensitive communications intercepts. As these were eliminated, some information was merely designated Top Secret/COMINT for communications intelligence, but other code words for more sensitive compartments (projects or collection methods) took their place, including two — ECI and H — so secret that national security experts outside government do not know what they stand for. *Code Names* identifies the following compartments and special categories of information, many for the first time:

> Archlane, Atomic Artificer, Atomic Music Principle, BYEMAN (B), Conifer, Credible Wolf (CW), ECI, Endseal, Focal Point (FP), Gamma (G), H, HCS, Hollow Tile (HT), ICS, Loma, NASP, Pearl, PH/ZH, Principal, Ragtime, RODCA, Sigma, SIOP-ESI, Spectre, Talent Keyhole (TK), Telephone Booth (TB), TESON, Theorem, Utah, VRK.

There are also additional categories "above" Top Secret called "special access programs" that are used to protect presidential, military, intelligence, anti-terrorism, counter-drug, special operations, and "sensitive activities," as well as classified research and development efforts where it is deemed that extraordinary secrecy is needed to protect capabilities and vulnerabilities. Special access programs are regulated by statute and are defined as deliberately designated programs where "need-to-know" or access controls beyond those normally provided to classified information are created. The clearance and access requirements are identical to, or exceed, those required for access to sensitive compartmented information, and SAPs require special (and expensive) security, access, and communications measures.

Publicly acknowledged SAPs are distinct from unacknowledged programs, with the latter colloquially referred to as "black" programs because their very existence and purpose are classified. Among black programs, further distinction is made for "waived" programs — SAPs considered so sensitive that they are exempt from standard reporting requirements to Congress. There are thus four different types of SAPs:

> + **Acknowledged SAPs:** Special access programs the existence of which is unclassified. Acknowledged SAPs are generally identified as at least existing in the defense budget and are reported to Congress in the form of an annual report.
> + **Unacknowledged SAPs:** Special access programs whose existence is classified. Though unacknowledged SAPs are not identified in unclassified documents, they are reported to Congress in the same form as acknowledged SAPs.
> + **Waived programs:** Classified special access programs specially designated by the secretary of defense and so sensitive they are only orally

briefed to the chairs and ranking minority members of the Armed Services and Defense Appropriations Committees.

+ **Alternative or Compensatory Control Measures (ACCMs):** SAP-like programs using alternative or compensatory control measures to provide protection similar to that of SAPs. ACCMs are created only to protect operations, intelligence, and support, and can be created by military service officials and agency heads.

Prior to 9/11, there were approximately 150 Defense Department-approved SAPs, down from 200 in the late 1980s. These numbers, however, do not include the many subcompartments, perhaps best termed "SAPs within SAPs." Subcompartments are often created to limit knowledge of extremely sensitive aspects of SAPs, particularly an operational SAP having to do with special operations and special mission units.

Code Names identifies the following special access programs and ACCMs:

Adobe, Antemate, Bell Weather, Bernie, Black Light, Blue Mail, Blue Zephyr, Cavalry, Centennial, Chalk series, Channel series, Citadel, Cloud Gap, Compass Link, Constant Help, Constant Pisces, Constant Star, Copper Coast, Copper Green, Coronet Phoenix, Distant Phoenix, Elegant Lady, Fireant, Footprint, Galaxy, Gentry, Giant Cave/Giant Dodge, Grass Blade, Greater Slope, Greyhound, Gulf, Gusty series, Gypsy series, Have Djinn, Have Flag, Have Trump, Have Void, Island Sun, LEO, Link series, Mallard, Meridian, Milkyway, Mustang, Olympic, Omega, Osprey series, Overtone, Oxide/Ozone, Panther series, Pave Runner, Pirate Sword, Polo Step, Procomm, Project 19, Project 643, Project 9000, Radius, Raven, Retract series, Reward, Rosetta Stone, Ruby, Scathe series, Science series, Sea Bass, Seek Clock, Senior Needle, Senior Nike, Sierra, SIT-II, Softring, Spear, Suter, Steel Puma, Talon Radiance, Tapestry, Theme Castle, Thermal Vicar, Thirst Watcher, Thirsty Saber, Tiger Lake, Titrant Ranger/Capacity Gear, Tractor series, Umbrella, White Knight.

There are additionally a number of words in *Code Names* representing programs, exercises, or operations where the exact meaning or country involved is or may be classified:

Acer Gable, Accurate Test, Bastion Bridge, Brave series, Castglance, Cedar Deck, Cobra Talon, Coral series, Credible series, Creditable Dove, Crystal Fog, Dark Tea, Eelpot, Forest Green, Gable Shark,

Gumdrop, Honor Guard, Icthus Nickel, Indigo Response, Irish series, Ketchum, Kodiak, Krimson Sword, Linebacker, Marshland, Mensa, Misty, Nautical Fire/Nautical Sentry, Pacer series, Picket Fence, Project 9GH, Project 9GI/GK, Radiant series, ROMO II, Saga, Sayers, Sensor Fir/Flam, Straight Arrow, Tempo, Trinity, Trojan Footprint, Western Response, Zhardem.

Three additional "special" programs deserve to be mentioned:

+ **SPECAT:** Special category projects or subjects that require special handling procedures in addition to the security classification. The SPECAT caveat is used in classified messages for three types of controlled information: SIOP-ESI information (that is, information dealing with the nuclear war Single Integrated Operational Plan and "extremely sensitive information"); exclusive for, which designates a backchannel or nonrecord communication between general officers and senior officials; and SPECAT (code word), which designates a communication as controlled by the access restrictions of the code word, which may or may not be SCI or a SAP. Emergency Action Messages (EAMs), which direct immediate military action, including the use of nuclear weapons, also are protected by SPECATs.

+ **Special Technical Operations (STO):** Classified SAPs and other compartmented programs, weapons, and operations associated with the CIA and "other government agencies." Entire separate channels of communication and clearances exist to compartment these military versions of clandestine and covert operations involving special operations, paramilitary activity, covert action, and cyber-warfare. A STO "cell" exists in the Joint Chiefs of Staff and at most operational military commands to segregate STO activity from normal operational activity, even highly classified activity.

+ **Special plans:** Once used solely to describe "deception" operations, special plans now refer to any "offline" compartmented activity. After 9/11, for instance, an "office of special plans" was established in the Office of the Secretary of Defense to oversee preparations for war with Iraq and became an Oliver North–like "operational" unit engaged in its own intelligence collection and activities.

The definition of "national" systems and capabilities has, since 9/11, been expanded to include nonsatellite "sensors" such as Predator and Global Hawk unmanned aerial vehicles (UAVs) and human resources such as special operations teams employed in reconnaissance and clandestine intelligence collection missions, most of which then become SAPs or SPECAT programs handled in STO channels only.

It is this complex system of names, classifications, and compartments that separate what is commonly known as a "white" program from a "black" program. *Black* generally refers to those activities and operations that are protected by SAPs or other compartments and are not acknowledged, such as much of the so-called Delta Force, the Gray Fox intelligence organization, and the associated special operations of the Joint Special Operations Command.

After the Vietnam War, there was a spurt of efforts within the military to get "behind the green door," as they used to say — to give normal soldiers and commanders access to compartmented intelligence information and weaponry. The situation certainly improved in the 1970s and 1980s with the advent of "all-source" intelligence and the move to provide more and more tactical and staff officers with access to SI information. In the 1980s and 1990s, there was also an explosion of SAPs and other compartmented programs. After the Allied Force campaign in the former Yugoslavia in 1999, the air force instituted the Coal Warfighter program to move more and more SAP and STO information into the open. Yet as we have seen again and again with excessive classification, the institutional interests associated with secrecy (information is power, after all) thwart the best efforts at efficiency and openness. If information can't move even internally to military and intelligence organizations and officers with Top Secret clearances who need it, of course, the internal and external mechanisms of oversight (Congress, auditors, inspector generals, legal counsel, and so on) couldn't be expected to keep up.

So is Polo Step an SCI classification compartment, a SAP, or merely a SPECAT designation? Sources tell me it is an ACCM. But the whole business of special controls is so complex, I still can't really answer the question with any confidence. Throughout this book, I have generally decided to use the phrase *code name* to describe a term, avoiding the official nickname and code word terminology except when it is specifically applicable.

How to Use This Book

Code Names is divided into four parts: a cast of characters, a country-by-country directory, a code names dictionary, and a glossary.

Part 1, Cast of Characters, includes a brief description of the main departments, agencies, commands, and organizations mentioned in the code names dictionary. For each, there is a brief discussion of its mission, roles, and activities, along with a list of their contingency plans (as much as is known) as well as information about its more obscure or secret activities and bases. The focus, obviously, is as much as possible on what is not readily known, and the emphasis is as well on the more obscure organizations (White House Communications Agency, NSA, DIA, Gray Fox, special operations, the military unified commands). Code names associated with particular organizations are categorized in this section.

Part 2, the country-by-country directory, highlights worldwide US military and intelligence relations. For each country, there is a brief description of cooperation (or discord) with the US in the war on terrorism and military operations, a listing of recent or important agreements relating to cooperation, and a description of US basing and activity in country. Again, code names associated with particular countries are categorized in this section.

Part 3, the code names dictionary, is an alphabetical listing of more than 3,000 code names. Not all code names could be included, not by a long shot, so the emphasis is on names that are current since the end of the Cold War, those that are of historical importance, and those that are not otherwise readily available in the public domain. Code names for weapons (Blackbird, Hornet, Orion, and so forth) are generally not included, because they are readily available elsewhere; call signs are also not included. As much as possible, specific names, dates, locations, and the like are given. A healthy dose of official acronyms and abbreviations is found in part 3, both to save space and to speak the language of the national security community. Part 4 is a combination acronym list and extended glossary.

Because this book is its own index, I have highlighted the major categories of code names below (programs associated with individual countries and regions are indexed in part 3):

+ Presidential support, continuity of government, and continuity of operations activities of the military and government to preserve constitutional government, and to prepare for catastrophic loss of government authority after a nuclear war (or, more recently, after a terrorist attack):

  Adobe, Blue Light, Cartwheel, Constant Blue, Crown Helo, Excalibur, Fig Leaf, Forward Challenge, High Point, Iron Gate, JEEP, Log Tree, Mystic Star, Nationwide, Night Blue, Nine Lives, Northstar, Page One, PH/ZH, Phoenix Copper/Banner/Silver, Pine Ridge, Pioneer, Polo Hat, Positive Response, Rebound Echo,

Roadrunner, Royal Crown, Sage Brush, Scope Command, Ski Jump, Snow series, Southern Pine, Surf Board, Swarmer, Timber Line, Title Globe, Tophat, Treetop, Trojan, Vanguard, Volant Banner/Silver, Wheelhouse, Yankee, Yankee/Zulu, Yankee White.

+ Nuclear war preparations and programs:

Able series, Apex Effort, Blue Light, Bulwark Bronze, Buoyant Force, Bust Out, Busy series, Buzzsaw, Central Harmony, Credible Journey, Crown Vigilance, Crystal Monarch, Crystal Nugget, Ellipse series, Flaming Arrow, Giant series, Global series, Gangbusters, Little Picture, Mighty Guardian, Olympic series, Pacer Crag, Pacer Mole, Pacer Stable, Phoenix, Phoenix Jewel, Pine Cone, Polo Hat, Positive Response, Praetorian Guard, Prime Directive, Ragtime, Regency Network, Saber series, Salty Script, Scope Force, Seek Clock, Sheepskin, Skybird, Skyking, Skymaster, STAFFEX, Stone Ax, Sun City, Toolchest, Toy Chest.

+ Nuclear weapons accident preparations and response:

Bowline, Broken Arrow, Diagonal Glance, Dial Flinty, Diamond Flame, Digger Shift, Dimming Sun, Display Select, Dull Sword, Faded Giant, Hammer Ace, Pinnacle series, Senator, Tier III.

+ Offensive counter-proliferation and countering enemy weapons of mass destruction operations:

Advanced Notice, Athena, Crashpad, Discrete series, Dipole series, Divine series, Dragon Fury.

+ Homeland security, domestic weapons of mass destruction terrorist use response, military support to civil authorities, extraordinary powers, and martial law:

Amalgam series, Ambient Breeze, Ardent Sentry, AWI, Blue Advance, Brave Knight, Calypso Wind, Capital Reaction, Clear Skies, Consequence series, Crucial Player, CUSEC, Dark Winter, Dangerous Wind, Determined Promise, Direct Focus, Equus Red, Garden Plot, Grown Tall, Impending Storm, Joshua Junction, Keystone, Launch Relief, Lincoln Gold, Lost Source, Measured Response, Mirrored Image, Olympic Charlie, Orbit Comet, Pacific Horizon, Pale Horse, Positive series, Rio Grande, Rubble Pile, Seven Hunters, Shaker Support, Silent Vector, Solid Citizen, Solid Curtain, Terminal Breeze, TOPOFF, Trilogy, Unified Defense, Vigilant Shield, West Wind, WISE.

+ War on terrorism, including special operations, as well as clandestine and covert activities of American commandos:

> Able Warrior, Activation Leap, Active Endeavour, Apex Gold, Arctic Breeze, Aztec Silence, Babylon, Balikatan, Blackhat, Blue Sky, Bronze Arrow, Condor, Constant Gate, Copper Green, Desert Sprint, Elaborate Crossbow, Elegant Lady, Eligible Receiver, Enduring Freedom, Epic Fury, Footprint, Forest Green, Freedom Eagle, Genesis II, Genoa, Global Lynx, Global Mercury, Goal Keeper, Gray Fox, Grecian Firebolt, Green Quest, Grenadier Bay, Iceberg, Jackel Cave, Joint Anvil, Kedge Hammer, Knob Key, Known Warrior, Krimson Sword, Link Acorn, Maraton, Night Fist, Picket Fence, Poise Talon, Project 9GH, Project 9GI/GK, Project 46, Project 12108, Project 24428, Project 42134, Project 42135, Project 42562, Project 47119, Project 50348, Project 53520, Project 53527, Prominent Hammer, SEACAT, Sly series, Symphony, Tempo, Terminal, THREADS, Topsail, Trinity, Underseal, Utopian Angel.

+ Missile defense programs:

> Ardent Shield, Coherent Defense, Coherent Joint Fires, Gatekeeper, Have Star, Juniper Cobra, Optic Windmill, Overwatch, Radiant Gold, Raptor Talon, Red Tigress, Shining Presence, Timber Wind, Topic 700/Topic 900, Total Defender, Zenith Star, Zodiac Beauchamp.

+ Submarine and anti-submarine programs:

> Baltops, Baracuda, Beartrap, Caesar Sword, Clarinet Merlin, Classic series, Cluster series, Cooperative Poseidon, Dogfish, EXTENDEX, Ghost, Giant Shadow, Gryphon, Jolly Roger, Lungfish, Manta, Phoenix cooperative, Ragtime, Saber, Sea Star, SHAREM, Shin Kame, Silent Hammer, Silent Knight, Silent Pearl, Sorbet Royale, Swamp Fox, TAMEX, TAPON, VERITAS II.

+ General intelligence programs and activities, intelligence technologies, particularly the ability to intercept communications and electronics:

> Aboveboard, Anchory, Astonish, Avalanche, Backhome, Badge Finder/Badge Keeper, Beyond Duty, BGE/SGF, Big Safari, Binocular, Blackknight, Blue Horizon, Breeze, Brite/Brite Knight, Broadsword, Capsule Jack, CELTIC, Challenge Athena, Clove, Cobra series, Combat series, Comfy series, Conga, Constant series,

Copper Cap, Cornerstone, Creek series, Crossfire, Crutch, Direct
Support, Docklamp, Eagerness, Eaglepipe, ECHELON, Edge,
Eidolon Lance, Enlarger, Fastner, Forest Green, Friartuck, Fulcrum,
Future Look/Have Bridge, Genesis II, Grandslam, Guidepost,
Gumdrop, Project Harmony, Have Sound, Hombre, Host, IBIS,
Isaiah, Jaguar, Lakota, Longroot, Marlock, Martcs, Matchlitc,
Mercury, Messiah, Monticello, Moon Smoke, Musketeer, Night
series, Nocona, Ocean Arium, Outboard, Pathfinder, Peace
Krypton, Peace Pioneer, Platinum Rail, Portal, Power Hunter,
Proud Flame, Quicksilver, Quidditch, Raindrop, Rivet series,
Roadwarrior, Rosetta Stone, Royal series, Sable Tent, Scattered
Castles, Semester, Senior series, Sensor series, Sentinel series,
Silverfish, Spiderweb, Starhouse, Starquake, Steamroller, Superbad,
Tabler, Tapestry, Taters, TIMBUKTU, Trojan series, Tumbril,
Warlord, Warstock, Wiley, Wolfers/Rocketeer, Wrangler.

+ Spy satellites:

Aquacade, Argon, Canyon, Chalet, Corona, Crystal, Gambit,
Indigo, Jumpseat, Kennan, LaCrosse, Lanyard, Littar, Magnum,
Mercury, Omni, Onyx, Orion, Parcae, Poppy, Ramrod, Rhyolite,
Trumpet, Vega, Vortex.

+ Clandestine and low-profile intelligence operations:

Crazy series, Grazing Lawn, Grisly Hunter, Keen Sage, Quasar
Talent, Scathe Mean, Scathe View, Seaspray, Senior Scout.

+ Naval (and Marine Corps) intelligence:

ARIES II, Apex Gold, Batrack, Binnacle, BRIGAND, Cast
Glance/Cluster Ranger, CERCIS, Charade, Cherry,
Chipped/Chocolate, Cinnamon, Cluster series, Cobra, Dark Eyes,
Deepwell, Direct Support, Emerald, Fireboat, Friar/Desperado,
Guestmaster, Guilder, Hairy Buffalo, Hardlook, Holystone,
Hyperwide/Deltawing, Iron Clad, Ivy Bells, Lightning, Musketeer,
Northstar, Orestes Bravo, Outboard, Outlaw series, Porthole,
Prairie series, Privateer, Rabbit, Radiant Mercury, Reef, Regal,
Seawatch, Sensor Pacer, Spotlight, Storm Jib, Story series, Top
Hunter, Windjammer.

+ Unmanned air and undersea vehicles:

Amber, Aurora, BAMS, Cobra, Compass series, Condor, Crossbolt,
Cyclops, Darkstar, Desert Predator, Desert Scimitar, Eagle Eye,

Firescout, Global Hawk, Have Gold, Hunter, Irish Straw, Lofty View, Nomad Vigil, Pave series, Perseous, Pioneer, Predator, Rover, Shadow, Spartan, Stingray, Talon Radiance, Tier series.

+ Human intelligence programs:

Creek Cab, Dragon Warrior, Formica, Gold Sword, Gray Fox, Have Cook, Modern Age, Modern Eagle, Rover, Southern Knight, Tonal Key, Tyne Tease, Vigilant.

+ Counter-intelligence programs:

Athena, Chambered Round, Cornerstone, Crystal Breakers, Hidden Treasure, Imminent Horizon, Ontario Water, Portico, Seek Gunfighter, Sensor Guard, Seven Acres, Seven Doors, Seven Phoenix, Slammer, Tight Door, Toltec Spear.

+ Foreign materiel procurement and exploitation involving acquiring equipment from former Warsaw Pact nations and manufacturers and evaluating it for intelligence value and counter-measures:

Cadmic Frame, Carob series, Casaba Hound, Coral Mat/Sensor Ghost, Dissent, Dole series, Dome Street, Gardenia, Grand Falcon, Grandma Beguile, Granite series, Gray Pan, Gypsy Wagon, Have Sabre, Have Whip, Heart Ache, Ibis series, Icon series, Ictus series, Mobcap Apex, Mountain series, Opinion series, Optic series, Opus Willow, Ordinary Farm, Orient Express, Rodent series, Root Cellar, Round Gopher, Royal Holiday, Sensor Eyes, Stadium Clock, Stock Deal, Strain Drum, Suspect Stole/Suspect Runaway, Tin Shield, Torpid Suction, Tossing series, Touted series, Toy series, Trophy, Twin Ears, Volant Sierra, Willow series.

+ War crimes investigations and related operations:

Amber Star, Blackbird, Buckeye, Fervent Archer, Justice Assured, Torn Victor.

+ Information warfare and cyber-warfare:

Adversary, Arena, Big Crow, Bobcat, Brazen Tsunami, Classic Troll, Cluster Robin, Compass Call, Constant Web, Crucial Player, Diamond, Digital Demon, Dockmaster, Dragon Lightning, Eligible Receiver, Evident Sunrise, Excalibur, Glacier, Iron Hare, Legation Quarter, Little Picture, Livewire, Midnight Stand/Idaho Hunter, Panther series, Phoenix Challenge, Lungfish, Prophet/Cassandra, Quick Draw, RIGEL, Rubicon, Saratoga Thunder, Senior

Keystone, Sensor series, Space 7, Steel Puma, Tel-scope, Thundercloud.

+ Deception operations:

Combat Hammer, Credible Wolf, Crested Dove, Project 9A, Project 33, Project 999, Project 8407.

PART I

CAST OF
CHARACTERS

The President and Continuity of Government

The president is assisted in his duties as the ultimate constitutional authority for the national defense by the National Security Council (NSC) and its staff, the new Homeland Security Council (HSC) and its staff, and the other agencies and elements of the Executive Office of the President (including the Office of Management and Budget, the Office of National Drug Control Policy, the Office of Science and Technology Policy, and the Office of the US Trade Representative). The president's national security adviser oversees the operations of the NSC and its staff. The assistant to the president for homeland security has responsibility for developing and coordinating the implementation of a national strategy for protecting the nation from terrorist threats or attacks.

The most secret national security element of the presidency is the continuity of government (COG) program to ensure survival of the president and constitutional government. Though the US Secret Service is responsible for all aspects of facilitating the protection of the president, the White House Military Office (WHMO) tends to the day-to-day workings of presidential command and control of the US government and military forces, and to COG. The White House Communications Agency (WHCA), a Defense Department element under the control of the WHMO, provides telecommunications and audiovisual support to the president, the vice president, the White House staff, the NSC and HSC, and the Secret Service through a variety of presidential and command facilities:

+ The White House ("18 Acres" complex), the White House Situation Room, and the Presidential Emergency Operations Center (PEOC).
+ Old and New Executive Office Buildings.
+ Presidential facilities at Anacostia Naval Station and Naval Annex, Washington, DC.
+ Presidential facilities at Andrews Air Force Base (AFB), MD.
+ Camp David, MD.
+ Communications towers and facilities at 18 Acres, the Bethesda Naval Hospital, the Capitol Building, the CIA, the Federal Aviation Administration (FAA) headquarters in Washington, DC, Fort Belvoir, VA, Fort Detrick, MD, Fort Meade, MD, the Pentagon, Quantico, VA, the State Department annex (Beltsville, MD), the US Naval Observatory (the vice president's home), the Manassas Radio Site, the Kennedy Center Radio Site, the Silver Hill FAA Radio Site,

the Tysons Radio Site, the Wang Radio Site, the Washington Hilton Radio Site, and Luke AFB, AZ.

+ Communications facilities at the continuity-of-government-related facilities at Mount Weather, Site C, Site D, Site M, and Site R (the latter being Department of Defense facilities serving the president).

The Federal Emergency Management Agency (FEMA), an agency of the Department of Homeland Security, oversees less secretive executive branch Continuity of Operations (COOP) planning. The FEMA Special Facility ("Mount Weather"), located 13 miles southeast of Berryville, VA, is the last of the main civil government bunkers built during the Cold War to survive a nuclear war. The Congressional Emergency Relocation Site (located under the Greenbriar Hotel in West Virginia) was closed in 1994. Since 9/11, COG and COOP planning within the US government has again increased in intensity, and new relocation sites have been established in the Washington, DC, area and in federal regions and state capitals. The various federal COOP and COG sites tend to be labeled with letters (for instance, Site A). Known active facilities include:

+ Site A: Washington, DC, Veterans Affairs Readiness Operations Center.
+ Site B: Veterans Administration Medical Center, Martinsburg, WV.
+ Site C: Veterans Administration Medical Center, Richmond, VA. Site C also provides microwave relays to Mount Weather and the DOD Site C.
+ Site C (DOD): Located atop Quirauk Mountain, north of Fort Ritchie, MD. Site C is a microwave and communications outpost of Site R.
+ Site Creed (DOD): Underground building complex on the west side of Site R (Raven Rock), a former autonomously operated hardened facility within the Site R complex.
+ Site D (DOD): Microwave relay, near Damascus, MD, part of the Site R complex.
+ Site D: Classified site in the DC area, operating 24/7 using employees detailed from other locations.
+ Site E: Veterans Administration Medical Center, Bay Pines, FL. A COOP mirror site that became operational on 8 Mar 2002.
+ Site E: Possibly located in Denver, CO.
+ Site M: Classified National Military Command Center (NMCC) facility located in the national capital region.

+ Site R (Raven Rock): Presidential and Department of Defense/Joint Chiefs of Staff emergency relocation site located on the PA–MD border just north of Sabillasville, MD, near Blue Ridge Summit, PA (Boyers, PA). Site R is the "undisclosed location" used by Vice President Dick Cheney since 9/11, containing the Pentagon's Alternate National Military Command Center (ANMCC), the Alternate Joint Communications Center (AJCC), and military service emergency operations centers.
+ Site RT (DOD): Communications relay site located atop Raven Rock Mountain.
+ Site X-ray: Army facility.
+ Site Yankee: Army facility.
+ Alternate National Warning Center (ANWC), Riggs Road, Olney, MD.
+ Federal Relocation Centers of the Department of Homeland Security: Bothell, WA; Denton, TX; Thomasville, GA; Olney, MD; and Maynard, MA.
+ Operations Systems Center (OSC), Martinsburg, WV.

CURRENT WAR PLANS: The Top Secret Presidential Decision Directive 67 (PDD-67), Enduring Constitutional Government and Continuity of Government Operations (signed 21 Oct 1998), establishes policies relating to presidential COG and relocation. The presidential directive is implemented by a number of extremely secret White House and executive agency directives and plans, including Presidential Emergency Action Documents (PEADs), Federal Emergency Plan D, the COG Annex to the National Response Plan, and the Interagency Contingency Communications Plan (ICCP).

+ National Response Plan, 30 Sep 2003: The core federal government plan integrates federal domestic prevention, preparedness, response, and recovery plans into one all-discipline, all-hazards plan, including the National Contingency Plan (oil and hazardous materials), the Federal Radiological Emergency Response Plan (FRERP), the United States Government Interagency Domestic Terrorism Concept of Operations Plan (CONPLAN), the Mass Immigration Emergency Plan, and the National Oil and Hazardous Substances Pollution Contingency Plan (NCP). Annexes cover emergency support functions such as transportation, emergency management, urban search and rescue, and public safety and security. "Incident annexes" include terrorism, nuclear and radiological incidents, biological warfare incidents, cyber-warfare response, and food security. The Terrorism Annex was added to the earlier Federal Response Plan during the 1997 update to respond to the consequences of terrorism within the US.

FEMA Federal Preparedness Circulars (FPC) also implement the national-level COG and COOP programs:

+ Continuity of the Executive Branch of the Federal Government at the Headquarters Level During National Security Emergencies, FPC 60, 20 Nov 1990.
+ Emergency Succession to Key Positions of the Federal Departments and Agencies, FPC 61, 2 Aug 1991.
+ Delegation of Authorities for Emergency Situations, FPC 62, 1 Aug 1991.
+ Federal Executive Branch Continuity of Operations (COOP), FPC 65, 15 Jun 2004.

Code names: Adobe, Blue Light, Cartwheel, Cirrus Wind, Constant Blue, Crown Helo, Distant Shore, Excalibur, Fig Leaf, Forward Challenge, Green Quest, High Point, Iron Gate, JEEP, Log Tree, Mystic Star, Nationwide, Night Blue, Nine Lives, Northstar, Omar Response, Page One, PH/ZH, Phoenix Banner, Phoeniz Copper, Phoeniz Silver, Pine Ridge, Pioneer, Polo Hat, Positive Response, Rebound Echo, Roadrunner, Royal Crown, Sage Brush, Scope Command, Silent Vector, Ski Jump, Snow series, Solid Citizen, Southern Pine, Surf Board, Swarmer, Timber Line, Title Globe, Tophat, TOPOFF, Treetop, Trojan, Vanguard, Volant Banner/Silver, Wheelhouse, Yankee, Yankee/Zulu, Yankee White.

Executive Departments and Agencies

The executive departments with national security responsibilities include:

+ Department of Commerce (including the Bureau of Industry and Security, and the International Trade Administration).
+ Department of Defense.
+ Department of Energy (including the National Nuclear Security Administration; the Office of Nuclear Energy, Science, and Technology; the Office of Policy and International Affairs; and the National Laboratories).
+ Department of Homeland Security.
+ Department of Justice (including the Drug Enforcement Administration and the Federal Bureau of Investigation).

+ Department of State.
+ Department of the Treasury (including the Office of International Affairs and the Office of Foreign Assets Control).

What follows is a brief discussion of the Departments of Defense and Homeland Security, and the various agencies of the US Intelligence Community (IC).

Department of Homeland Security (DHS)

Established after 9/11 under the Homeland Security Act of 2002 and homeland security presidential directives, DHS has five major divisions:

+ Border and Transportation Security (BTS) Division: Includes new Transportation Security Administration (TSA), the former US Customs Service, the border security functions of the former Immigration and Naturalization Service (INS), the Animal and Plant Health Inspection Service, and the Federal Law Enforcement Training Center.
+ Emergency Preparedness and Response (EPR) Division: Includes the Federal Emergency Management Agency (FEMA).
+ Science and Technology (S&T) Division.
+ Information Analysis and Infrastructure Protection (IAIP) Division: The DHS element of the US Intelligence Community (see below).
+ Management Division.

DHS also incorporates several independent agencies:

+ Coast Guard: Upon declaration of war or when the president so directs, the Coast Guard operates as an element of the Department of Defense.
+ US Secret Service.
+ Bureau of Citizenship and Immigration Services/US Citizenship and Immigration Services.

The Homeland Security Operations Center (HSOC) is the DHS equivalent of the military's National Military Command Center (NMCC). It maintains and shares real-time domestic "situational awareness" to detect incidents, coordinates security operations, and facilitates response and recovery for all critical incidents and threats. As of Feb 2004, 26 federal and local law enforcement agencies and Intelligence Community members were represented in the HSOC.

Code Names: Amalgam series, Ambient Breeze, AWI, Blue Advance, Brave Knight, Calypso Wind, Capital Reaction, Clear Skies, Consequence series, Crucial Player, CUSEC, Dark Winter, Dangerous Wind, Determined Promise, Direct Focus, Equus Red, Garden Plot, Grown Tall, Impending Storm,

Joshua Junction, Keystone, Launch Relief, Liberty Shield, Lincoln Gold, Livewire, Lost Source, Measured Response, Mirrored Image, Olympic Charlie, Orbit Comet, Pacific Horizon, Pale Horse, Positive series, Rio Grande, Rubble Pile, Scarlet Cloud, Seven Hunters, Shaker Support, Silent Vector, Solid Citizen, Solid Curtain, Terminal Breeze, TOPOFF, Trilogy, Unified Defense, West Wind, WISE.

Federal Bureau of Investigation (FBI)

An element of the Department of Justice, the FBI is tasked with upholding the law through the investigation of violations of federal criminal statutes; protecting the United States from terrorists (counter-terrorism) and hostile intelligence efforts (counter-intelligence); and providing assistance to foreign and other US federal, state, and local law enforcement agencies. With respect to counter-terrorism, the FBI's mission is to identify and neutralize the threat in the US posed by terrorists and their supporters, whether nations, groups, or individuals. With respect to counter-intelligence, the FBI is responsible for detecting and counteracting foreign intelligence activity.

Code Names: Carnivore, Crucial Player, Digital Storm, Dominant Chronicle, Equus Red, Grand Slam, Joshua Junction, Launch Relief, MAXCAP 05, Olympic Charlie, Penttbom, Seven Seekers, Storm Cloud, Trilogy, West Wind, WISE.

Drug Enforcement Administration (DEA)

An element of the Department of Justice, the DEA enforces laws and regulations governing narcotics and controlled substances, chemical diversion, and trafficking. It is the lead agency overseas for counter-narcotics law enforcement activities and investigations, with extensive support provided by the US military. The DEA makes a contribution both to the homeland security and intelligence functions of the US government, given the close connection between narcotics trafficking and illegal alien and arms smuggling.

Code Names: Baker series, Blast Furnace, Caper Focus, Centra Spike, Central Skies, Classic Outboard, Classic Trump, Constant Vigil, Convoy, Corner Back, Coronet Griffin, Coronet Macaw, Coronet Nighthawk, Coronet Oak, Dominant Chronicle, Drug Market, Gatekeeper, Ghost Zone, Ghostrider II, Gondola, Green Clover, Green Sweep, Laser Strike, LIMS, Pacer Bandit, Pacer Coin, Peace Panorama, Phoenix, Project 6404/6415, RIGEL, Ringgold, Safe Border, Sandkey, Senior Scout, Spartan, Steady State, Succumbios, Support Justice, TESON, Throttle Car.

Department of Defense (DOD)

The DOD includes the office of the secretary of defense, the Joint Chiefs of Staff (JCS), the Joint Staff, the defense agencies and field activities, the military departments (Departments of the Air Force, Army, and Navy), and the military services within those departments (air force, army, Marine Corps, and navy), and the combatant commands. Civilian DOD positions established since 9/11 include a new undersecretary of defense for intelligence and an assistant secretary of defense for homeland defense.

CURRENT WAR PLANS: War planning of the US military is governed by a number of strategic policy directives of the secretary of defense, the most important of which are the National Military Strategic Plan for the War on Terrorism (Oct 2002), the Defense Planning Scenario: Homeland Defense, 2010–2012 (12 Aug 2003 draft), and the Strategic Guidance Statement for Homeland Defense Planning (1 Mar 2004 draft). The Defense Department Contingency Planning Guidance (28 Jun 2004) provides the overall direction to the JCS and combatant commands on the preparation of their war plans. As of 2004, there were 68 or 69 active "deliberate" plans of the US military that must be prepared, reviewed, and updated on a biennial basis. These are "numbered" plans, each with a permanent Plan Identification (PID) number that is associated with a contingency (5027, for example, which is the basic US war plan for defense of the Korean peninsula; see the glossary). There are also functional plans, such as Continuity of Operations plans, that fall outside of the PID system.

+ Office of the Secretary of Defense (OSD) Continuity of Operations Plan, 29 Jan 1997.
+ DOD Civil Disturbance Plan ("Garden Plot"), 1 Feb 1994.
+ DOD Operations Plan for Routine Explosive Ordnance Disposal Protective Support for the United States Secret Service and the United States Department of State for Very Important Persons, 27 Jun 1995.
+ DOD Postal Augmentation Plan ("Graphic Hand"), 25 Sep 1990.

Joint Chiefs of Staff (JCS)

The JCS consists of the chairman, the vice chairmen, and the senior military officers of the services. The chairman of the JCS serves as the principal military adviser to the president, the NSC, and the secretary of defense. His responsibilities include strategic and contingency planning and readiness of the armed forces. The chairman and vice chairmen oversee the Joint Staff. Within the Joint Staff, a post-9/11 deputy directorate for the war on terrorism within J-5 (Strategic Plans and Policy) oversees national military strategy relating to counter-terrorism.

CURRENT WAR PLANS: The JCS Joint Strategic Capabilities Plan (FY 2002, 1 Oct 2002) provides tasks and missions to the combatant commands, apportions major combat forces and strategic lifts, and provides guidance and assumptions for preparation of plans. There are more than a dozen annexes to the JSCP that provide separate guidance for intelligence, special operations, special technical operations, nuclear weapons, and more. The Unified Command Plan (17 Apr 2002), a presidentially approved document, establishes missions, responsibilities, and force structure, and delineates geographic area of responsibility and/or functional responsibility for combatant commanders. The Apr 2002 UCP was the most comprehensive revision of the UCP in a generation, establishing Northern Command, placing Russia in the European Command's area of responsibility, and changing the mission of Joint Forces Command. Change 1 (Jun 2002) merged Space Command and Strategic Commands. Change 2 (Jan 2003) gave new missions to Strategic Command, including global strike, integrated missile defense, and information operations.

+ JCS CONPLAN 0300-97, Counter-Terrorism Special Operations Support to Civil Agencies in the event of a domestic incident, 14 Jan 1997, Secret.
+ CJCS CONPLAN 0400, Counter-proliferation of Weapons of Mass Destruction, Sep 2003, Secret.
+ CONPLAN 0500-03, Military Assistance to Domestic Consequence Management Operations in Response to a Chemical, Biological, Radiological, Nuclear or High Yield Explosive (CBRNE) Situation or Event, Mar 2003.
+ Continuity of Operations Plan (COOP) for the Chairman of the Joint Chiefs of Staff, OPORDER 03-2, 11 Sep 2002.
+ Joint Emergency Evacuation Plan (JEEP): Emergency helicopter transportation of selected personnel to predesignated emergency sites.
+ National Airborne Operations Center (NAOC) Operations, CJCS OPORDER 1-98, 1 Mar 1998.
+ Survivable Mobile Command Center Operations (SMCC Operations), CJCS OPORDER 2-98, 1 Mar 1998.

Code Names: Crystal, Eidolon Lance, Elaborate Crossbow, Eligible Receiver, Ellipse series, Focal Point, Griffin, Jackpot, JOPREP JIFFY, NIEX, Night series, Night Blue, Night Fist, Nimble Vision, Pinnacle series, Polo Hat, Polo Step, Positive Series, Praetorian Guard, Predominant Challenge, Present Arms, Prime Directive, Prominent Hammer, Prompt Response, Proud, Steel Puma, Treetop, Trojan Footprint.

US Intelligence Community (IC)

The Intelligence Community officially includes the CIA, the National Security Agency (NSA), the Defense Intelligence Agency (DIA), the National Geospatial-Intelligence Agency (NGA), the National Reconnaissance Office (NRO), the counter-intelligence, cryptologic, and some of the foreign intelligence elements of the military services (army, navy, air force, and Marine Corps intelligence), and the foreign intelligence and/or counter-intelligence elements of the FBI, the Coast Guard, and the Departments of Energy, Homeland Security, and State.

The Director of Central Intelligence (DCI), who is also the director of the CIA, is a cabinet member who at least in theory oversees the IC. He oversees the IC, operating through the Deputy Director for Community Management (DDCI/CM) and the chairman of the National Intelligence Council (NIC). The DCI also oversees a number of specialized centers, such as the Counterterrorist Center (CTC) and the Center for Weapons Intelligence, Nonproliferation, and Arms Control (WINPAC). The NIC oversees IC production and analysis, including National Intelligence Estimates, the most authoritative written judgments of the Intelligence Community.

Central Intelligence Agency (CIA)
The CIA collects foreign intelligence information through clandestine and overt means, produces political and economic intelligence, and conducts covert action on behalf of the US government. In 2004, the CIA had three deputy directors: Deputy Director for Operations (DO), Deputy Director for Intelligence (DI), and the Deputy Director for Science and Technology (DST). The DO manages clandestine human intelligence (HUMINT). In 1992, the CIA created the Office of Military Affairs (OMA), under a three-star military associate director. OMA negotiates, coordinates, manages, and monitors all aspects of agency support for military operations and vice versa. The CIA's Special Activities Division of the DO is the paramilitary arm of the agency, though it is made up of only a few hundred staff and dependent on the Defense Department for support, such as movement and medical care. The DOD appears to have a clandestine unit attached to OMA, called the Special Intelligence Squadron, that augments CIA paramilitary operations. DI analysts, either country or regional specialists, or functional experts (terrorism, drug trafficking), review reporting of the CIA and other agencies to keep up with activity.

National Security Agency (NSA)

The NSA coordinates and performs foreign signals intelligence (SIGINT) and information security (INFOSEC) functions for the US government. As the Central Security Service, NSA/CSS oversees all the SIGINT activities of the US, intercepting, deciphering, and analyzing electromagnetic signals, from broadband satellite and Internet traffic to narrow cell phone and local communications. NSA's National Security Operations Center (NSOC) is the crisis management center that processes all incoming intelligence. NSA oversees a number of joint US government centers, including the Defense Special Missile and Astronautics Center (DEFSMAC), established in 1964; and the Special Collection Service, a joint CIA–NSA service with the mission to penetrate denied foreign targets. NSA also manufactures and controls all of the codes and keys for the US government, such as the authenticating devices in the president's nuclear "football." In 1997, the secretary of defense and the director of central intelligence established the Information Operations Technology Center (IOTC), the US government's national-level organization dedicated to computer network attack and cutting-edge defense technologies and practices.

Defense Intelligence Agency (DIA)

DIA is a DOD agency and the senior military intelligence component of the Intelligence Community. The DIA oversees all aspects of technical and non-technical intelligence on foreign military organizations and supports a variety of specific military missions and needs, such as targeting and battle damage assessment, counter-narcotics, and medical intelligence. The DIA produces intelligence at its Washington Defense Intelligence Analysis Center (DIAC) and through a shared production program (SPP) that taps the talents of different services and commands (including the National Ground Intelligence Center, the National Air and Space Intelligence Center, and the National Maritime Intelligence Center). On 11 Feb 2003, DIA announced a significant restructuring, creating directorates for analysis, human intelligence, and technical collection. The director, DIA, is the DOD HUMINT manager and manages all DOD non-SIGINT intelligence collection, including reconnaissance intelligence and measurements and signatures intelligence (MASINT). In a unique arrangement, the Joint Staff J-2 (intelligence) staff is a major component of the DIA, operating the National Military Joint Intelligence Center in the Pentagon. Since 9/11, the Joint Intelligence Task Force — Combating Terrorism (JITF-CT) directs collection, exploitation, analysis, and dissemination in support of DOD counter-terrorism operations and planning. Two other DIA centers are the Missile and Space Intelligence Center (MSIC), Redstone Arsenal, AL, and the Armed Forces Medical Intelligence Center (AFMIC), Fort Detrick, MD.

National Geospatial-Intelligence Agency (NGA)
Formerly the National Imagery and Mapping Agency (NIMA), NGA is a DOD agency headquartered in Bethesda, MD, that provides geospatial intelligence and mapping in support of the US government military and intelligence. NGA analyzes government and commercial reconnaissance to create intelligence products and maps, and supports military operations, including nuclear targeting, precision-guided weapons use, and oceanography, with technical geographic information.

National Reconnaissance Office (NRO)
The NRO is a DOD agency responsible for space-borne imagery and SIGINT collection. It oversees the development of satellites and sensors and the operations of intelligence collection satellites. The NRO operates some of its own facilities for controlling spy satellites, such as the Australian–NRO Joint Defense Facility Pine Gap near Alice Springs, and Site 58 (euphemistically called the Defense Communications Electronics Evaluation Testing Activity, or D-CEETA), Fort Belvoir, VA.

Department of State Bureau of Intelligence and Research (INR)
INR is the State Department's primary source for interpretive analysis of global developments, established in 1946.

Department of Homeland Security (DHS) Intelligence
DHS became a member of the IC on 1 Mar 2003. Its Directorate for Information Analysis and Infrastructure Protection (IAIP) analyzes the vulnerabilities of US critical infrastructure, assesses the scope of terrorist threats to the US homeland, and provides indications and warning to the Homeland Security Advisory System. The DHS Terrorist Threat Integration Center (TTIC), a joint activity of the IC, exploits all terrorist-threat-related information and provides threat analysis to the president and federal agencies. The DHS also conducts intelligence collection activities under the US Customs Service, which operates its own aerial surveillance arm and intelligence analysis centers.

Department of Energy (DOE) Intelligence

DOE's foreign intelligence program provides the US government with intelligence analyses and technical and analytic support relating to nuclear weapons and materials and weapons of mass destruction.

Department of the Treasury Office of Intelligence Support

Supports the secretary in his role as chief economic and financial adviser to the president.

Army Intelligence

The Deputy Chief of Staff for Intelligence (G-2) exercises staff supervision over the Army Intelligence and Security Command (INSCOM) and other elements of army intelligence. INSCOM provides intelligence support to strategic and operational level commanders in the areas of IMINT, MASINT, SIGINT, tactical HUMINT, counter-intelligence, information operations, and general military, scientific, and technical intelligence. INSCOM is the doctrinal and training component for army intelligence specialists, and it also commands military intelligence units that are not otherwise assigned to combat units or higher headquarters. INSCOM is also the Service Cryptologic Element (SCE) for NSA. The INSCOM Information Dominance Center (IDC) is the army's post-9/11 Tactical Operations Center (TOC) for counter-terrorism, counter-intelligence, counter-narcotics, and computer network operations.

The National Ground Intelligence Center (NGIC), located in Charlottesville, VA, is the army's federated producer of technical ground forces intelligence in support of DIA and DOD. The 902nd Military Intelligence (MI) Brigade performs the counter-intelligence function for the army. The 1st Information Operations Command, Fort Belvoir, VA (formerly the Land Information Warfare Activity), is responsible for army support to Strategic Command (STRATCOM) information operations, psychological operations, operations security, electronic warfare, computer network operations, and military deception.

Air Force Intelligence

The Air Force Director of Intelligence, Surveillance, and Reconnaissance (AF/XOI) exercises staff supervision for intelligence policy, planning, programming, evaluation, and resource allocation. Air force intelligence organizations include the Air Intelligence Agency (AIA) and its National Air and Space Intelligence Center (NAIC), the Air Force Information Warfare Center (AFIWC), and the Air Force Office of Special Investigations (AFOSI), which provides counter-intelligence.

AIA, located at Kelly Air Force Base (AFB) in San Antonio, TX, has the mission of monitoring and exploiting information relating to air and space intelligence, weapons, and information warfare. AIA includes all facets of intelligence and information operations collection and analysis, from the traditional intelligence activities in support of air operations (SIGINT, HUMINT, MASINT, IMINT, OSINT), as well as AIA's rapidly expanding roles to gain, exploit, defend, and attack (GEDA) the space and information domains. AIA is also the Service Cryptologic Element for NSA.

NAIC, located at Wright Patterson AFB, OH, is AIA's and DIA's primary producer of air- and space-related scientific and technical intelligence. NAIC produces about 90 percent of the original technical intelligence regarding foreign space and counter-space capabilities. NAIC also produces the electronic warfare integrated reprogramming (EWIR) and Links and Nodes databases, as well as conducting analyses on weapons system characteristics and performance, tactics and engagement, and multi-spectral signatures. AFIWC, co-located with the Joint Information Operations Center (JIOC) at Lackland AFB, TX, provides information-operations-related intelligence to forces and support for STRATCOM. AFIWC was originally activated as the 6901st Special Communication Center in July 1953, and later redesignated the Air Force Electronic Warfare Center (AFEWC) in 1975, before being activated in Sep 1993.

The 480th Intelligence Group at Langley AFB, VA, provides conventional mission planning support, targets materials, and offers operational intelligence. The 20th Intelligence Squadron, Offutt AFB, NE, and the 36th Intelligence Squadron, Langley AFB, VA, provide unique digital targeting support for Conventional Air Launched Cruise Missile (CALCM) B-2s and F-117s, point mensuration, munitions effectiveness analysis, geospatial/multi-spectral data, and collateral damage estimation for all air forces.

Naval Intelligence
The Director of Naval Intelligence (DNI) exercises staff supervision over the Office of Naval Intelligence (ONI), which provides the intelligence necessary to plan, build, train, equip, and maintain US maritime forces. ONI, located primarily in the National Maritime Intelligence Center (NMIC) in Suitland, MD, is the national production center for global maritime intelligence — from the analysis of the design and construction of foreign surface ships to the collection and analysis of acoustic information on foreign sensor systems, ocean surveillance systems, submarine platforms, and undersea weapons systems. ONI is the principal source for intelligence on global merchant activities and

nontraditional maritime issues such as counter-narcotics, fishing, ocean dumping of radioactive waste, technology transfer, and counter-proliferation. The NMIC consists of ONI, a detachment of the Marine Corps Intelligence Activity (MCIA), the Coast Guard Intelligence Coordination Center (ICC), representation from the Drug Enforcement Administration and the US Customs Service, and the Naval Information Warfare Activity (NIWA).

The Naval Security Group is the Service Cryptologic Element for NSA. The Fleet Information Warfare Center (FIWC), an element of the Naval Network Warfare Command, is the navy component that provides information warfare support to STRATCOM. The Naval Criminal Investigative Service (NCIS) additionally provides counter-intelligence services and intelligence on terrorist and unconventional warfare threats.

Marine Corps Intelligence

The Marine Corps Intelligence Activity (MCIA) provides intelligence on littoral areas and regions of potential instability to support the rapid introduction of Marine Expeditionary Forces. The MCIA is headquartered at Quantico, VA, but has elements in the NMIC and the National Ground Intelligence Center.

Coast Guard Intelligence

A component of the Department of Homeland Security, the Coast Guard operates as both an armed force and a law enforcement organization. Coast Guard Intelligence, located in the navy's National Maritime Intelligence Center, also has Atlantic and Pacific Maritime Intelligence Fusion Centers, which serve as central hubs for collection, fusion, analysis, and dissemination of maritime intelligence.

Combatant Commands

The Unified Command Plan (UCP) establishes combatant command missions, responsibilities, and force structure, as well as delineating geographic areas of responsibility (AOR). Under law, the chairman of the Joint Chiefs of Staff is to review the UCP every two years and submit recommended changes to the president through the secretary of defense. There are currently five geographic and four functional combatant commands.

Central Command (CENTCOM)

MacDill AFB, FL

Established in 1983, CENTCOM comprises the area of the Middle East extending east to Pakistan, the Horn of Africa, and Central Asian nations on the periphery of the Middle East. Under the 2003 change to the UCP, CENTCOM received responsibility for Syria and Lebanon, previously under EUCOM control. CENTCOM has no permanently assigned combat units, but has since 9/11 operated forward in Afghanistan and Iraq under a wartime organizational structure.

CENTCOM's peacetime components:

+ Army Forces Central Command (ARCENT)/Third US Army, Fort McPherson, GA (also Combined Force Land Component Commander, CFLCC).
+ Central Command Air Forces (CENTAF)/9th Air Force, Shaw Air Force Base (AFB), SC (also Coalition Forces Air Component Command, C/JFACC).
+ Marine Forces Central Command (MARCENT), Camp H. M. Smith, HI.
+ Naval Forces Central Command (NAVCENT), Manama, Bahrain, including the Fifth Fleet (Bahrain) (also Coalition Forces Maritime Component Commander, CFMCC).
+ Special Operations Command Central (SOCCENT), MacDill AFB, FL, with forward Joint Forces Special Operations Component Command in Qatar.

CENTCOM's operational structure for fighting in Afghanistan and Iraq includes Joint Task Force 7 (JTF-7, Iraq) and Joint Task Force 76 (JTF-76)/Combined Joint Task Force 180 (CJTF-180, Afghanistan).

Combined Joint Task Force — Horn of Africa (CJTF-HOA), Camp Lemonier, Djibouti, activated Dec 2002, is responsible for counter-terrorism and operations on the Horn of Africa. Initially embarked on the USS *Mount Whitney*, the command headquarters moved to Djibouti in May 2003. The HQ includes personnel from Djibouti, Ethiopia, France, Italy, Kenya, Romania, and Yemen. The 1,800 personnel at Camp Lemonier coordinate military operations in Kenya, Somalia, Sudan, Eritrea, Ethiopia, Djibouti, and Yemen. Combined Task Force 150 (CTF 150), comprising US, UK, French, Italian, Spanish, and German ships, conducts missions in support of Operation Enduring Freedom in conjunction with CJTF-HOA.

CURRENT WAR PLANS: Prior to 9/11, CENTCOM was responsible for one Operations Plan (OPLAN), seven Operation Plans in Concept Form (CONPLANs), and two Functional Plans. The OPLAN, CENTCOM OPLAN 1003V-03 (officially dated 30 Jan 2003), was the campaign plan for Operation Iraqi Freedom. CENTCOM now has CONPLANs for Iran and some states of the former Soviet Union and recently inherited war planning relating to Syria from European Command.

+ CENTCOM OPORDER 97-01, Force Protection.
+ SOCEUR SUPPLAN 1001-90, 9 May 1989.
+ CENTCOM CONPLAN 1010, Jul 2003.
+ CENTCOM CONPLAN 1015-98, Major Theater War support possibly to OPLAN 5027 for Korea, 15 Mar 2001.
+ CENTCOM 1017, 1999.
+ CONPLAN 1020.
+ CENTCOM CONPLAN 1025, Iran?, Aug 2003.
+ CONPLAN 1067, Biological Warfare Response?
+ CENTCOM CONPLAN 1100-95, 31 Mar 1992.

Code Names:[1] Accurate Test, Arabian Gauntlet, Arid Farmer, Balance series, Brave, Bright Star, CATEX, Celtic series, Cobra, Coronet Scabbard, Desert series, Eager series, Eagle series, Early series, Earnest series, Eastern series, Echo Mountain, Ellipse Foxtrot, Enduring Freedom, Epic Mantle, Gallant series, Gentle Plan, Golden Spear, GULFEX, HyCAS, Impelling Victory, Indigo series, Inferno Creek, Infinite series, Inherent Fury, Initial Link, Inner Passage, Inspired series, Internal Look, Iraqi Freedom, Irish, Iron series, Lucky series, MEDFLAG, Native series, Natural Fire, Nautical series, Nectar Bend, Nemean Lion, Neon series, Neon Spear, Nimble Archer, Noble Piper, Pacer Camel, Phoenix Gauntlet, Regional Cooperation, Reliant Rescue, Rugged series, Safe Passage, Seven Acres, Southern Focus, Southern Watch, Ultimate Resolve, Vigilant Sentinel, Vigilant Warrior, Warrior Bravo, Western Response, Zhardem.

European Command (EUCOM)
Patch Barracks, Stuttgart-Vaihingen, Germany

EUCOM's area of responsibility includes 93 nations in Europe, Africa, and the Middle East, stretching from South Africa's Cape of Good Hope to Norway's North Cape and from Iceland to Russia. The EUCOM commander also serves as NATO's senior operational commander, Supreme Allied Commander Operations (formerly SACEUR), and is located in Belgium. The deputy commander of EUCOM is the overall commander of US forces in Europe on a day-to-day basis.

In July 1961, EUCOM gained responsibilities for military assistance in sub-

---

1. Country-specific code names are listed in part 2, Activities by Country.

Saharan Africa, having already been assigned responsibility for the Algerian department of France, hence its foothold in Africa. EUCOM lost its mission in sub-Saharan Africa in 1963, but in 1972 it gained responsibility for the entire Mediterranean littoral, the Middle East, the Red Sea, the Persian Gulf, and Iran. In 1983, with the newly established CENTCOM, EUCOM was given responsibility of the African countries in sub-Saharan Africa west of Sudan and the countries of Eastern Europe. Israel remained in EUCOM's orbit. The 2002 Unified Command Plan placed the previously unassigned areas of the Russian Federation and the Caspian Sea within EUCOM and expanded EUCOM's area to absorb elements of the Joint Forces Command's (JFCOM) former theater, including Iceland, Greenland, the Azores (Portugal), and more than half of the Atlantic Ocean — to nearly 500 miles off the East Coast of the United States.

The EUCOM intelligence structure consists of the headquarters J-2 staff (including the Survey Division located at Mons, Belgium) and the large all-source Joint Analysis Center (JAC) at RAF Molesworth, UK, EUCOM's Joint Intelligence Center (JIC). The EUCOM Plans and Operations Center (EPOC), opened in 2003, acts as the "standing joint force headquarters" core. The Joint Interagency Coordination Group handles information sharing and logistical support to non-DOD components.

EUCOM component commands:

+ US Air Forces in Europe (USAFE), Ramstein Air Base (AB), Germany, consisting of the 3rd Air Force (RAF Mildenhall, UK) and 16th Air Force (Aviano AB, Italy).
+ US Army, Europe (USAREUR), Heidelberg, Germany.
+ US Naval Forces Europe (NAVEUR), London, UK, consisting of the Sixth Fleet (Italy).
+ Marine Forces, Europe (MARFOREUR), Boeblingen, Germany.
+ Special Operations Command, Europe (SOCEUR), Stuttgart-Vaihingen, Germany.

EUCOM Sub-unified Commands and JTFs:

+ US Forces Azores (USFORAZORES).
+ Iceland Defense Force (ICEDEFOR).

CURRENT WAR PLANS: Prior to 9/11, EUCOM was responsible for nine CONPLANs and three Functional Plans. With the 2002 changes of the UCP, the command picked up additional CONPLANs from JFCOM for Iceland and the

Azores and has developed new post-9/11 counter-terrorism plans for Africa and the southern states of the former Soviet Union.

+ USAREUR OPLAN 4101.
+ EUCOM OPLAN 4102, Defense of Western Europe.
+ EUCOM CONPLAN 4110.
+ EUCOM CONPLAN 4122-98, Africa?, 1 Feb 2000.
+ EUCOM CONPLAN 4132, Jul 2003.
+ EUCOM CONPLAN 4217.
+ EUCOM CONPLAN 4220-95, 25 Feb 1993.
+ EUCOM CONPLAN 4221.
+ EUCOM CONPLAN 4222.
+ EUCOM CONPLAN 4265, 2004.
+ EUCOM CONPLAN 4269-96, Humanitarian Assistance and Disaster Relief Operations.
+ EUCOM CONPLAN 4285.
+ USAFE OPLAN 4286, Nuclear Weapons.
+ EUCOM OPLAN 4295.
+ EUCOM CONPLAN 4302.
+ EUCOM CONPLAN 4305.
+ USAREUR OPLAN 4310.
+ EUCOM CONPLAN 4348.
+ EUCOM CONPLAN 4349.
+ EUCOM OPLAN 4360.
+ EUCOM CONPLAN 4367.
+ EUCOM OPLAN 4375.
+ USAFE Plan 4405-97, USAFE Air Expeditionary Force (S/NF).
+ EUCOM OPLAN 4999-98, Defense of Western Europe in General War.

Code Names:[2] Able series, Action Express, Adriatic Phiblex, Adventure Exchange, African Lion, Agile series, Allied Action, Ardent Ground, ARRcade Fusion, Assured series, Atlantic Resolve, Atlas series, Auburn Endeavor, Azure Haze, Baltops, Blue Game, Blue Harrier, Brave Knight, Burning Harmony, Cactus Juggler, Cannon Cloud, Caravan Guard, Clean Hunter, CMX, Combined Endeavor, Cooperative series, Cornerstone, Creek series, Destined Glory, Distant Thunder, Dragon Lightning, Ellipse Bravo, Enable Freedom, Endrun, Eugenie, Excalibur, Exercise 48 Hours, Flexible Leader, Flintlock, Forward Warrior, Frisian Flag, Immediate Response, Juniper series, Kaleidescope, Keen Sage, Knotted Whip, Matador, MEDFLAG, Midget Thrust, Mountain Eagle, Noble Shirley, Noble Suzanne, Northern Viking, Northern Watch, Optic Windmill, Peaceshield, Phoenix Partner, Power Hunter, Project 9GI/GK, Provide series, Rescuer/MEDCEUR, Salty series, Scope Force, SCWS, Sea

2. Country-specific code names are listed in part 2, Activities by Country.

Breeze, Shared Endeavor, Sharp Reply, Shining series, Silent series, Silver Eagle, Skilled Anvil, Tactical Fighter Weaponry, Talon Radiance, Trojan Footprint, Union Flash, Urban Encounter, Urgent Resolve, Urgent Victory, Victory series, West Africa Training Cruise.

Joint Forces Command (JFCOM)
Norfolk, VA

JFCOM was established on 1 Oct 1999 from the former US Atlantic Command (LANTCOM). In 2002, JFCOM's geographic mission in North America was transferred to NORTHCOM, and its geographic missions in Northern Europe and the Atlantic were transferred to EUCOM. JFCOM was thus designated a functional combatant command effective 1 Oct 1992, focusing on transformation, joint experimentation, joint training, joint doctrine development, joint force providing, and joint interoperability. The commander, JFCOM, was also designated NATO's Allied Commander Transformation (ACT) on 19 Jun 2003.

JFCOM components:

+ Army Forces Command (FORSCOM), Fort McPherson, GA.
+ Air Combat Command (ACC), Langley AFB, VA.
+ Marine Corps Forces, Atlantic (MARFORLANT), Norfolk, VA.
+ Atlantic Fleet (LANTFLT), Norfolk, VA.
+ Special Operations Command, US Joint Forces Command (SOCJFCOM), Norfolk, VA.

The Joint Warfare Analysis Center (JWAC) special access program, located at the Naval Surface Warfare Center in Dahlgren, VA, is also subordinate to JFCOM. JWAC assists the Joint Chiefs of Staff and the combatant commanders in analysis of weapons effectiveness, systems analysis, and targeting of infrastructure (oil, electrical, transportation).

CURRENT WAR PLANS: Prior to 9/11, JFCOM was responsible for six CONPLANs and three Functional Plans. The 2002 UCP made changes to JFCOM's mission, resulting in the transfer of war plans to NORTHCOM and EUCOM. Some of the joint NORTHCOM/JFCOM plans will fully transition to NORTHCOM upon rewriting.

+ NORTHCOM/JFCOM CONPLAN 2100-98, Noncombatant Evacuation Operations.
+ EUCOM/JFCOM CONPLAN 2222-98, 1 Mar 2001.
+ JFCOM OPLAN 2307-95, 1 Oct 1993.
+ NORTHCOM/JFCOM FUNCPLAN 2500-98, Military Support to the Department of State and Office of Foreign Disaster Assistance (OFDA) for Humanitarian Assistance and Disaster Relief Operations, 15 Jun 2001.

+ NORTHCOM/JFCOM FUNCPLAN 2503-97, Military Support to the Department of Justice (DOJ) and Immigration and Naturalization Service (INS) During a Mass Immigration into the United States ("Legacy Freedom"), 30 Nov 1997.
+ NORTHCOM/JFCOM FUNCPLAN 2504-00, Response to CBRNE Incidents/Accidents, 1 May 2000.
+ USJFCOM FUNCPLAN 2508-98, Integrated Mobilization of CONUS Medical Assets and the Reception of Patients, 15 Jun 1998.
+ NORTHCOM/JFCOM FUNCPLAN 2707-00, Military Operations in Support of Counter Drug Operations, 17 Aug 2000.

Code Names: ASCIET, Capable Warrior, CJTFEX, Coherent series, Cooperative Nugget, Cooperative Ocean, Cooperative Osprey, Cooperative Support, Cooperative Telos, Cooperative Tide, Cooperative Zenith, Ellipse Alpha, Eloquent Nugget, Evident Surprise, JTFEX, Joint Spirit, Millennium Challenge, Northern Light, Ocean Venture, Pinnacle Impact, Quick Force, Roving Sands, Unified Endeavor, Unified Vision.

Northern Command (NORTHCOM)
Colorado Springs, CO
Proposed in Apr 2002 and activated 1 Oct 2002, NORTHCOM is the post-9/11 combatant command with a primary mission to defend the land, sea, and air approaches to the US, assuming missions previously assigned to Joint Forces Command (JFCOM) and the North American Aerospace Defense Command (NORAD), specifically the air, land, sea, and space defense of the US. NORTHCOM provides force protection for domestic US military forces and bases, air monitoring and interdiction, sea-lane security, and counter-mine sensing. NORTHCOM supports the Department of Homeland Security in maritime homeland security and is tasked with identifying and intercepting maritime threats as far from US shores as practical. NORTHCOM's area of responsibility includes the continental United States, Alaska, Canada, Mexico, and the surrounding waters out to approximately 500 nautical miles (including northern Caribbean nations within that area, such as Cuba). Northern Command has a Combined Intelligence and Fusion Center (CIFC) that coordinates the acquisition, analysis, and fusion of intelligence, counter-intelligence, and law enforcement information and shares that information with organizations at the national, state, and local levels. The commander of NORTHCOM is also the commander of NORAD.

Under normal peacetime conditions, NORTHCOM provides military assistance to civil authorities to mitigate the results of disasters and catastrophes, including those resulting from a WMD attack. Though NORTHCOM is not a law enforcement mechanism and its authority does not supersede the civil "first responder" emergency institutions in a domestic emergency, the homeland function includes contingencies to transition from homeland security to homeland defense when a crisis might demand a level of force or scope of operations outside civil law enforcement. "Lead federal agency" status then shifts from Department of Homeland Security to DOD for the conduct of combat operations within the US and emergency powers associated with nuclear weapons recovery and "consequence management" relating to terrorist attacks.

NORTHCOM subordinate task forces:

+ Standing Joint Force Headquarters North (SJFHQ-North), Colorado Spring, CO, activated in 2004 and replacing the provisional Joint Force Headquarters Homeland Security. SJFHQ-North is a full-time joint command and control element focused on domestic crisis response.

+ JTF — Civil Support (JTF-CS), Fort Monroe, VA. Activated in 1999 and transferred from JFCOM to respond in support of chemical, biological, radiological, nuclear and conventional high yield explosive emergencies. JTF-CS prepares to conduct primary missions in support of CONPLAN 0500.

+ JTF — 6 (JTF-6): Briggs Army Airfield, Fort Bliss, TX. DOD counter-drug support to civil agencies in the US. JTF-6 is transforming into Joint Interagency Task Force North (JIATF-North) to align with the JIATFs in PACOM and SOUTHCOM.

+ JTF National Capital Region, Fort McNair, Washington, DC, activated in Feb 2004 in support of the US Capitol Police to respond to suspected ricin poison contamination within the US Capitol complex and to oversee the air defense support to the national capital region.

CURRENT WAR PLANS: With the establishment of NORTHCOM, many former JFCOM and SOUTHCOM plans were shifted to the new command. Some plans remain joint because of cross-command responsibilities.

+ CONPLAN 2002, Homeland Defense, Oct 2003.
+ NORTHCOM/JFCOM CONPLAN 2100-98, Noncombatant Evacuation Operations.

- NORTHCOM/JFCOM FUNCPLAN 2500-98, Military Support to the Department of State and Office of Foreign Disaster Assistance (OFDA) for Humanitarian Assistance and Disaster Relief Operations, 15 Jun 2001.
- NORTHCOM FUNCPLAN 2501-97, Military Support to Civil Authorities (MSCA) in Responding to Natural or Man-made Disasters, 2 Feb 1998.
- NORTHCOM FUNCPLAN 2502, Civil Disturbance Plan ("Garden Plot"), Aug 2003.
- NORTHCOM/JFCOM FUNCPLAN 2503-97, Military Support to the Department of Justice (DOJ) and Immigration and Naturalization Service (INS) During a Mass Immigration into the United States ("Legacy Freedom"), 30 Nov 1997.
- NORTHCOM/JFCOM FUNCPLAN 2504-00, Response to CBRNE Incidents/Accidents, 1 May 2000.
- NORTHCOM CAMPAIGN PLAN 2525-02, Operations to Support Homeland Security and Civil Support (Campaign Plan for Homeland Security), 1 Oct 2002.
- NORTHCOM/JFCOM FUNCPLAN 2707-00, Military Operations in Support of Counter Drug Operations, 17 Aug 2000.
- NORTHCOM Combined Defense Plan, 14 Dec 200 (binational Concept Plan that provides for the combined defense and security of Canada and the US).
- NORTHCOM CONPLAN 3500, Jan 2004.
- NORTHCOM CONPLAN 3800-00, Mobile Consolidate Command Center Operations, 12 Apr 2000.
- NORTHCOM CONPLAN 3900, Dec 2002.
- NORTHCOM CONPLAN 6435 (transferred from SOUTHCOM 1 Oct 2003), Cuba?

Code Names: Determined Promise, Unified Defense, Unified Endeavor.

Pacific Command (PACOM)
Camp H. M. Smith, Honolulu, HI

Established on 1 Jan 1947, the Pacific Command area of responsibility includes 43 countries, 20 territories and possessions, and 10 US territories making up more than 50 percent of the earth's surface and nearly 60 percent of the world's population. Despite activation of NORTHCOM for homeland security in 2002, the defense of Hawaii and US territories and possessions in the Pacific remains the responsibility of PACOM. The 2002 UCP also tasked PACOM with supporting EUCOM's Russian responsibilities in the Far East. A post-9/11 Joint Interagency Coordination Group for Counter Terrorism (JIACG-CT) was activated at PACOM headquarters.

PACOM is typical of other regional commands in holding a series of formal and informal meetings with regional nations to bolster military-to-military relations:

+ Chiefs of Defense Conference (CHOD): Annual meeting of Asian defense chiefs.
+ Military Law and Operations Conference (MILOPS): Annual Judge Adjutant General (JAG) meeting.
+ Multinational Planning Augmentation Team (MPAT): Quarterly.
+ Pacific Area Senior Logistician Seminar (PASOLS): Annual.
+ Pacific Area Special Operations Conference (PASOC): Annual.
+ Pacific Senior Communications Meeting (PSCM): Annual midlevel meeting focusing on computer, spectrum management, and frequency issues.

PACOM component commands:

+ Army Pacific (ARPAC), Fort Shafter, HI, consisting primarily of the I Corps (WA) and 25th Infantry Division (Light) (HI, WA).
+ Marine Forces, Pacific (MARFORPAC), Camp H. M. Smith, HI, consisting of the I Marine Expeditionary Force (CA) and III Marine Expeditionary Force (Japan).
+ Pacific Fleet (PACFLT), Pearl Harbor, HI, consisting of the Third Fleet (CA) and Seventh Fleet (Japan).
+ Pacific Air Forces (PACAF), Hickam AFB, HI, consisting of 5th Air Force (Japan), 7th Air Force (South Korea), 11th Air Force (AK), and 13th Air Force (Guam).
+ Special Operations Command Pacific (SOCPAC), Camp H. M. Smith, HI. Joint Task Force (JTF) 510 is PACOM's crisis response, rapid deployment JTF.

PACOM Sub-unified Commands and JTFs:

+ Alaskan Command (ALCOM), Elmendorf AFB, Anchorage, AK.
+ US Forces Japan (USFJ), Yokota AB, near Tokyo, Japan.

+ US Forces Korea (USFK)/Eighth US Army, Yongsan Army Garrison, Seoul, South Korea.
+ Joint Interagency Task Force West (JIATF-West), Alameda, CA.

CURRENT WAR PLANS: Prior to 9/11, PACOM was responsible for two OPLANs, ten CONPLANs, and two Functional Plans. United Nations Command (UNC)/Combined Forces Command (CFC) Korea also had one OPLAN and one CON-PLAN. A non-numbered special access plan ("Project 19") also exists for Taiwan.

+ "Project 19," US–Taiwanese OPLAN.
+ PACOM CONPLAN 5002, Hawaii?, Oct 2003.
+ PACOM CONPLAN 5005, 2004.
+ PACOM CONPLAN 5026, US–Japan Operations Against North Korea, Aug 2003.
+ PACOM OPLAN 5027-98, Major Combat Operations on the Korean Peninsula, 18 Jan 2001.
+ PACOM CONPLAN 5028-98, support to CENTCOM OPLAN 1003?, 28 Nov 2000.
+ PACOM CONPLAN 5029, North Korea related?, 2004.
+ PACOM CONPLAN 5030, North Korea related?, Jun 2003.
+ PACOM CONPLAN 5055, Joint operations with Japanese Self-Defense Force, 2004.
+ PACOM CONPLAN 5060, Feb 2003.
+ PACOM CONPLAN 5070-96, Peacekeeping, Peace Enforcement, Foreign Humanitarian Assistance/Disaster Relief, Domestic Support Operations, and Other Small Scale Contingencies, Apr 2003.
+ PACOM OPLAN 5077, Jul 2003.
+ PACOM CONPLAN 5083, 2004.
+ PACOM CONPLAN 5100, Mar 2003.
+ PACOM OPLAN 5123-02, 31 Mar 2003.
+ PACOM CONPLAN 5150-96, Contingency Operations in the US Pacific Command Area of Responsibility.
+ PACOM CONPLAN 5200, May 2003.
+ PACOM CONPLAN 5304, Sep 2003.
+ PACOM CONPLAN 5305, 2004.

Code Names:[3] Arctic SAREX, Bachelor, Back, Bacon, Badge, Badger, Bag, Balance series, Bale, Balikatan, Ballistic, Balm, Banjo, Banner, Banyon, Basic, Bastion series, Baton, Beach series, Bean,

---

3. Country-specific code names are listed in part 2, Activities by Country.

Bear, Beard, Bearer, Bearing, Beauty, Beaver, Bed, Beef, Beggar, Begonia, Behavior, Beige, Belfry, Bell series, Belt, Beverly Morning, Blue Eagle, Brazen Tsunami, Capex, Cobra Gold, Commando series, Cope series, Distant Star, Elder Brave, Ellipse Charlie, FLEETEX, Foal Eagle, Formation, Fortify Freedom, Fortress, Fracture, Frame, Freedom series, Freemont, Freeze, Freighter, Frequent Storm, Fresh, Friday, Fried, Fringe, Frontier series, Gunslinger, Heavy series, Hong Kong SAFREX, Iron Hare, Kayo, Keen Edge, Keen Sword, Keens World, Kennel series, Kent, Kerosene, Key, Kingfisher, NOLES, Northern Edge, Omar Response, Overwatch, PACEX, Pacific series, Patriot Thunder, Sentry Strike, Project 9G/H, Project 19, Proper Lady, RIMPAC, Roll Call, RSO&I, SAGIP, Saratoga Thunder, Sea Angel, SEACAT, SEAL Orea, SPECWAR SUBEX, Talisman Saber, Tandem series, Tapioca, Tarpaulin, Tartan, Taxi, Teacher, Teak series, Team series, Tempest Express, Tempo Bravo, Temper, Tempest Express, Tennis, Terminal Fury, Terrace, Terrier, Thermal series, Ulchi-Focus Lens, Vacant, Vagabond, Valentine, Valid Shot, Valient Usher, Varsity, Vaudeville, Venture.

Southern Command (SOUTHCOM)

Miami, FL

SOUTHCOM focuses on developing modern militaries in the South and Central American regions, on the conduct of counter-narcotics operations, and increasingly on counter-terrorism. A Caribbean realignment under the 2002 UCP gave Cuba and other near Caribbean island nations to NORTHCOM.

SOUTHCOM component commands:

+ Army South (ARSO), Fort Buchanan, Puerto Rico.
+ Southern Air Force (SOUTHAF), Davis-Monthan AFB, AZ.
+ Naval Forces Southern Command (NAVSO), Mayport, FL.
+ Marine Forces South (MARFORSOUTH), Camp Lejeune, NC.
+ Special Operations Command South (SOCSOUTH), Homestead Air Reserve Base, FL.

SOUTHCOM Sub-unified Commands and JTFs:

+ Joint Interagency Task Force East (JIATF-East), Key West, FL. Counter-narcotics task force that also houses the Joint Southern Surveillance and Reconnaissance Operations Center (JSS-ROC), which fuses and disseminates intelligence gathered by aerial, ground-based, and other systems.
+ Joint Task Force — Bravo (JTF-B), Soto Cano AB, Honduras. In 1995, JTF-B expanded its primary mission from Honduras to a seven-nation geographic operations area comprising the Central American countries of Belize, Costa Rica, El Salvador, Guatemala, Honduras, Nicaragua, and Panama.

Cast of Characters

+ Joint Task Force — Guantanamo (JTF-GTMO), Cuba. Detainee
operations at Naval Station Guantanamo Bay.

CURRENT WAR PLANS: Prior to 9/11, SOUTHCOM was responsible for seven
CONPLANs and three Functional Plans. At least one of those CONPLANs has
been transferred to NORTHCOM, and additional CONPLANs have been established for support of homeland security and more aggressive counter-terrorism
operations.

+ SOUTHCOM CONPLAN 6100-95.
+ SOUTHCOM CONPLAN 6103-90.
+ SOUTHCOM CONPLAN 6115, Defense of the Southern US
and Caribbean (incorporates elements of former CONPLANs
2002 and 5002).
+ SOUTHCOM CONPLAN 6120-04, Jan 2004.
+ SOUTHCOM CONPLAN 6150-04, Feb 2004.
+ SOUTHCOM CONPLAN 6222.
+ SOUTHCOM CONPLAN 6225, Jan 2004.
+ SOUTHCOM CONPLAN 6300-97, 1 Oct 1994.
+ SOUTHCOM CONPLAN 6400, Aug 2003.
+ SOUTHCOM CONPLAN 6601-98, 1 Oct 1999.
+ SOUTHCOM OPORDER 6800, Sensitive Reconnaissance
Operations.

Code Names:[4] Ahuas Tara, Armistad, Blue Advance, Blue Spoon, Cabañas, Cedar Deck, Constant
Vigil, Distant Haven, Eagle, Ellipse Echo, Formica, Fuertes Caminos, Fuertes Defensas, Fuerzas
Aliadas, Fuerzas Commando, Fuerzas Defensas, Laser Strike, MEDRETE, New Horizons, Nimrod
Dancer, PKO, Southern Warrior, Tradewinds, Unitas.

Special Operations Command (SOCOM)
MacDill AFB, FL

SOCOM is a unique combatant command in that it exercises command
authority over all special operations forces (SOF), civil affairs, psychological
operations, and special counter-terrorism and reconnaissance forces and units
in the United States, and it oversees the training and equipping of SOF in a role
similar to the military services. The command was originally established as the
JCS Joint Special Operations Agency in Jan 1984; Congress mandated a unified command under PL 99-661 of Nov 1986, and SOCOM was established
on 16 Apr 1987. In 1989, SOCOM was given full program and budget

---

4. Country-specific code names are listed in part 2, Activities by Country.

authority. After 9/11, the role of SOCOM changed from being solely a "supporting" command to acting as a "supported" command. For certain counterterrorism missions, authorities were granted for the secretary of defense to direct SOCOM to exercise command over special operations overseas for campaigns against terrorist organizations whose cells, support networks, or activities are spread across several geographic combatant commander boundaries or when the mission parameters (available time, national risk, political sensitivity) demand SOCOM assets. These operations are primarily within the domain of SOCOM "special mission units" of the Joint Special Operations Command.

Internally, SOCOM has gone through an elaborate realignment to beef up the staff to be able to direct combat operations. The second phase was complete 1 May 2004, and all intelligence, operations, and planning functions were consolidated within the Center for Special Operations (CSO), replacing the Center for Intelligence and Information Operations and two other staff centers. The CSO has a subordinate Intelligence Support Group (J-2), Operations Support Group (J-3), and Campaign Support Group (J-5). A Special Operations Joint Interagency Collaboration Center has also been created. The third phase of realignment was completed in summer 2004 and included the establishment of a deployable, standing joint task force headquarters embedded within the CSO.

The SOCOM component commands and elements include:

+ Army Special Operations Command (ARSOC), Fort Bragg, NC.
+ Air Force Special Operations Command (AFSOC).
+ Naval Special Warfare Command (NAVSPECWARCOM).
+ Joint Special Operations Command (JSOC), Fort Bragg, NC. Established in 1980, JSOC is the equivalent of a joint task force made up of standing units (special mission units) and specialized task forces responsible for counter-terrorism (JTF-626, JTF-121, JTF-11, JTF-20), hostage rescue, offensive counter-proliferation, and nuclear weapons recovery. JSOC is, by secret executive orders, exempt from the *Posse Comitatus* statutes in the conduct of certain duties. Subordinate elements include:
  + Campaign Support Group, Fort Bragg, NC.
  + Combat Applications Group (CAG), Fort Bragg, NC, popularly known as the 1st Special Forces Operational Detachment — Delta (SFOD-D) or "Delta Force" and known internally as "CAG" or by the color green. Delta is organized into squadrons, each identified by a letter: A, B, C, and D.

+ Army 75th Ranger Regiment, known internally by the color red.
+ Naval Special Warfare Development Group (DEVGRU), Virginia Beach, VA, popularly known as SEAL Team 6 and internally as "devs" or by the color blue. DEVGRU is organized into combat assault teams, each identified by a color: red, gold, and blue.
+ 24th Special Tactics Squadron, Pope AFB, NC.
+ 66th Air Operations Squadron, Fort Bragg, NC.
+ JSOC Air Component. The 1st Battalion, 160th Special Operations Air Regiment (SOAR), Fort Campbell, KY, is dedicated to the direct support of CAG.
+ Army Tactical Support Team (Tactical Coordination Detachment?), Fort Belvoir, VA. Reponsible for operational preparation of the battlefield — characterizing buildings, bunkers, aircraft, and so on — for special missions, hostage rescue, or counter-terrorism. Known colloquially as "the secret army of northern Virginia," it is also known by the color orange.
+ Intelligence Support Activity (Gray Fox), Fort Belvoir, VA (see below).
+ Joint Communications Unit, MacDill AFB, FL.

The clandestine Intelligence Support Activity (informally known as Gray Fox and controlled under the Titrant Ranger special access program) was assigned to SOCOM in Jul 2002. The organization originated as a clandestine surveillance operation called the Foreign Operating Group (FOG) in 1979–1980. FOG and later ISA was under the administrative control of the Army Intelligence and Security Command (INSCOM). Its initial mission was to conduct "red team" surveillance of security at US embassies, similar to missions conducted by SOF at nuclear weapons storage sites. It soon became involved in a wide variety of human intelligence missions in support of special operations and the CIA, including hostage rescues, foreign materials acquisition, and support for growing US covert operations in Central America. The unit was publicly revealed in 1982 after it provided illegal support to a private venture to "rescue" POWs still thought to be in Vietnam. Today, Gray Fox is made up of intelligence and special operations personnel operating under civilian cover. The operators conduct clandestine surveillance and human intelligence operations, including close-in signals intelligence collection in support of special operations, hostage rescue, and counter-terrorism, as well as specialized support for foreign intelligence services and leaders. ISA was originally under the cover of the Army Tactical Concept Activity. In 1990, Gray

Fox was formally chartered under the Capacity Gear program, which established rules for its operations.

CURRENT WAR PLANS: Little is known about current SOCOM war plans (in the 7000–7999 numbering scheme).

Code Names: Able Warrior, Action Express, Activation Leap, Advanced Notice, Amber Star, Blackhat, Bright Knight, Bronze Arrow, Buckeye, Capacity Gear, Castle Hellion, Cemetery Wind, Centra Spike, Centurian Crusader, Cobb Ring, Condor, Constant Gate, Copper Green, Coral Fox, Desert Sprint, Dissent, Elegant Lady, Epic Goal, Focus Relief, Gable series, Global Lynx, Goal Keeper, Granite Rock, Granter Shadow, Grazing Lawn, Great Falcon, Green Light, Grenadier Bay, Heavy Shadow, Inspired Venture, Jackel Cave, Knob Key, Krimson Sword, Link Acorn, Night Fist, Orlon Drum, Patriot Excalibur, Poor Debtor, Powder Keg, Project 43, Project 6404, Project 6415, Project 12108, Project 24428, Project 42134, Project 42135, Project 42562, Project 47119, Project 50348, Project 53520, Project 53527, Queen's Hunter, Quick Thrust, Quiet Knight, Robin Court, Royal Cape, Royal Duke, Royal Patrol, Silent Shield, Silent Viper, Sly series, Sundowner, Swamp Fox, Sympton Odin, Tempo, Thor's Hammer, Titrant Ranger, Torn Victor, Trinity, Utopian Angel, Winter Harvest.

Strategic Command (STRATCOM)
Offutt AFB, Bellevue, NE

STRATCOM was originally formed 1 Jun 1992, merging navy and air force strategic nuclear forces under a single unified command and eliminating the Air Force Strategic Air Command. It is the single US military command responsible for the day-to-day readiness of nuclear forces; it prepares nuclear war plans and keeps the nuclear command and control system in constant readiness in accordance with the Nuclear Supplement to the Joint Strategic Capabilities Plan (JSCP).

On 1 Oct 2002, Space Command (SPACECOM) merged with STRATCOM under the revised Unified Command Plan (UCP) 2002, adding joint space operations and centralized command and control of the nation's space-based assets to the STRATCOM portfolio. Change 2 to the UCP (10 Jan 2003) further tasked STRATCOM with four previously unassigned responsibilities: global strike, integrated missile defense, information operations, and C4ISR (command and control, communications, computers, intelligence, surveillance, and reconnaissance). STRATCOM thus supports the US military worldwide with space support, intelligence communications, weather information, navigation, and ballistic missile attack warning. Additionally STRATCOM plans, commands, and controls extended-range precision global (nuclear and conventional) strikes directed by national authorities; oversees missile defense operations and support to worldwide combatant commands and NORAD; and integrates DOD computer network attack and defense, electronic warfare, operations security

(OPSEC), psychological operations (PSYOP), and military deception. With its global strike assignment, STRATCOM, like SOCOM, is now approved to act as a supported command in specific situations relating to US preemptive attacks worldwide.

STRATCOM also prepares nuclear options for theater command war plans and provides counter-proliferation support to regional commanders (specifically CENTCOM, EUCOM, and PACOM) under the provision of Change 4 to JSCP Annex C, issued in May 1994. STRATCOM also provides federated intelligence, planning, and conventional targeting support to regional commands, particularly as it relates to foreign missile forces and underground bases.

STRATCOM operates through service components (Air Force Space Command, Army Space and Missile Defense Command, Marine Forces Strategic Command, and Naval Network Warfare Command) and task forces (TFs):

+ TF Strategic Bomber and Reconnaissance Aircraft.
+ TF Aerial Refueling/Tankers.
+ TF Intercontinental Ballistic Missiles.
+ TF Ballistic Missile Submarines Atlantic.
+ TF Ballistic Missile Submarines Pacific.
+ TF Airborne Communications (E-6B aircraft and National Airborne Operations Center).
+ Joint Forces Headquarters — Information Operations (JFHQ-IO).

Three headquarters-level centers support STRATCOM's growing information operations missions:

+ **Joint Integrated Analysis and Planning Center** (JIAPC), Offutt AFB Bellevue, NE. Information operations targeting center specializing in integrating technical and human factors in high-value target analysis and precision influence targeting.
+ **Joint Information Operations Center** (JIOC), Lackland AFB, San Antonio, TX. Created in Sep 1999, JIOC is the principal DOD agency for non-service-specific IO support to operational commanders, including OPSEC, PSYOP, military deception, electronic warfare, physical destruction, and computer network attack. The JIOC's mission is to assist in both planning and executing information operations. JIOC was redesignated from the Joint Command and Control Warfare Center (JC2WC), which was formed from the nucleus of the former Joint Electronic Warfare Center (JEWC). The

JIOC is comprised of specialists from all four military services and three allied nations (presumably Australia, Canada, and the UK).

+ **Joint Task Force — Computer Network Operations** (JTF-CNO), Arlington, VA. Operational computer network defense component. The JTF-CNO integrates defensive capabilities into the operations of all DOD computers, networks, and systems.

CURRENT WAR PLANS: Prior to 9/11, STRATCOM was responsible for one OPLAN. A new CONPLAN (8022) has been written since 9/11.

+ STRATCOM CONPLAN 8022, Global Strike, Nov 2003.
+ STRATCOM OPLAN 8044, formerly called the Single Integrated Operational Plan (SIOP), Apr 2003.

Code Names: Apollo Force, Apollo Fury, Apollo Guardian, Apollo Leader, Apollo Look, Bulwark Bronze, Buoyant Force, Bustout, Busy series, Combat Sent, Crystal Nugget, Giant series, Giant Shadow, Global Archer, Global Guardian, Gypsy Wagon, Little Picture, Looking Glass, Midnight Stand, Night Blue, Olive series, Olympic series, Perseous, Polo Hat, Praetorian Guard, Sensor Heart, Skybird, Skyking, Skymaster, STAFFEX, Sun City, Thor's Hammer.

Transportation Command (TRANSCOM)

Scott AFB, IL

The command provides strategic air, land, and sea transportation for the DOD through three military commands:

+ Air Mobility Command (AMC), Scott AFB, IL. Operation of airlift aircraft and the Civil Reserve Air Fleet (CRAF).
+ Military Surface Deployment and Distribution Command (formerly Military Traffic Management Command), Alexandria, VA. Operation of military surface transportation and primary traffic management.
+ Military Sealift Command (MSC), Washington, DC. Operation of government-owned and commercial ships manned by civilians, including Fast Sealift Ships, the Afloat Pre-positioning Force, and the Ready Reserve Force.

Code Names: Atlantic Thunder, Phoenix series, Purple, Southern Breeze, Turbo series, Ultimate Caduceus, Unified Charger, Volant series.

International Commands

North American Aerospace Defense Command (NORAD)
Colorado Springs, CO

The binational US–Canadian North American Aerospace Defense Command is charged with the missions of detection and warning of attacks from hostile aircraft, missiles, and space vehicles, as well as the aerospace control for North America. The warning mission includes the monitoring of human-made objects in space. Aerospace control includes ensuring air sovereignty and air defense of the airspace of Canada and the US. Since 9/11, NORAD has moved to adapt its traditional outward-looking focus to threats posed by terrorists to the interior of North America, particularly domestic airspace threats. After an Exchange of Diplomatic Notes in Dec 2002, NORAD is also evolving to focus on maritime surveillance, maritime mine warfare, coastal operations, port security, and merchant ship control and protection. Comprehensive Enhanced Military Cooperation Plans are also being formulated to encompass combined aerospace, maritime, and land warning, as well as employment of military forces, to include support of or assisting civil authorities. NORAD operates from direction provided by the Military Cooperation Committee (MCC) and the Permanent (US–Canadian) Joint Board on Defense (PJBD). In Dec 2002, the US and Canada established the Bi-national Planning Group (BPG) to improve defenses against maritime and land-based threats to North America.

CURRENT WAR PLANS: Prior to 9/11, NORAD was responsible for two CONPLANs. Those same two plans have undergone major revision since 9/11.

+ NORAD OPORDER 3199, Air Defense of the US and Canada.
+ NORAD CONPLAN 3310-03.
+ NORAD CONPLAN 3349-04.

Code Names: Amalgam series, Amazon series, Ambush, Anchor, Angry, Anthem, Antler, Apron, Aqua, Bust Out, Clear Skies, Corner Back, Fabric, Factor, Faculty, Falcon, Falling, Feathered, Federal, Felix, Fencing series, Fertile, Feudal, Granite Sentry, Jockey, Joke, Jolly, Joplin, Jordan, Jorum, Northern Challenge, Olympic Shot, Vigilant Guardian, Vigilant Overview, Vigilant Skies.

North Atlantic Treaty Organization (NATO)

On 12 Jun 2003, NATO adopted a new streamlined military command structure.

+ Allied Command Operations: HQ, Mons, Belgium. Commanded by the Supreme Allied Commander Europe (SACEUR), ACO is the only NATO command with operational responsibilities, incorporating Allied Command Europe and Allied Command Atlantic. SACEUR continues to be dual-hatted as Commander, US EUCOM.

+ Allied Command Transformation: HQ, Norfolk, VA. Commanded by SACT (the Supreme Allied Commander Transformation), this is the command overseeing transformation of alliance forces and capabilities. SACT is dual-hatted as Commander, US JFCOM.

Allied Command Operations is organized with two standing Joint Force Commands (JFCs) — one in Brunssum, the Netherlands, and one in Naples, Italy. A more limited standing Joint Headquarters (JHQ) is located in Lisbon, Portugal. Each of the JFCs has subordinate component commands similar in design to US "joint forces."

+ JFC Brunssum (formerly AFNORTH).
  + Air Component Command, Ramstein, Germany, including Combined Air Operations Centres (CAOCs) at Uedem, Germany, and Finderup, Denmark.
  + Maritime Component Command, Northwood, UK.
  + Land Component Command, Heidelberg, Germany.
+ JFC Naples (formerly AFSOUTH). On 15 Mar 2004, AFSOUTH was deactivated and Joint Force Command Naples was activated.
  + Air Component Command, Izmir, Turkey (formerly AIRSOUTH), including CAOCs at Poggio Renatico, Italy, and Larissa, Greece.
  + Maritime Component Command, Naples, Italy (formerly NAVSOUTH).
  + Land Component Command, Madrid, Spain.

There is a difference between the NATO Command Structure and the NATO Force Structure. The Command Structure has a strategic scope, primarily intended to command and control the alliance's joint operations (operations in which more than one service is involved). The NATO Force Structure is tactical in scope and provides additional command and control capabilities at the single-service level, including land forces, maritime forces, and air forces. On 15 Oct 2003, Allied Command Operations inaugurated the new NATO Response Force (NRF), a joint, multi-national, advanced force able to deploy in 5 days and remain sustainable for 30 days.

Land forces:

+ The Allied Command Europe Rapid Reaction Corps (ARRC) HQ in Rheindalen, Germany, with the UK as framework nation.

+ The Rapid Deployable German–Netherlands Corps HQ based on the 1st German–Netherlands Corps HQ in Munster, Germany.
+ The Rapid Deployable Italian Corps HQ based on the Italian Rapid Reaction Corps HQ in Solbiate Olona, close to Milan, Italy.
+ The Rapid Deployable Spanish Corps HQ based on the Spanish Corps HQ in Valencia, Spain.
+ The Rapid Deployable Turkish Corps HQ based on the 3rd Turkish Corps HQ near Istanbul, Turkey.
+ The EUROCORPS HQ in Strasbourg, France, sponsored by Belgium, France, Germany, Luxembourg, and Spain. The EURO-CORPS HQ — which has a different international military status based on the Strasbourg Treaty — has signed a technical arrangement with Allied Command Operations and can also be committed to NATO missions.
+ The Multinational Corps HQ North-East in Szczecin, Poland, sponsored by Denmark, Germany, and Poland.
+ The Greek "C" Corps HQ near Thessaloniki, Greece.
+ The II HQ Polish Corps in Krakow, Poland.

Maritime forces:

+ HQs Commander Italian Maritime Forces on board Italy's INS *Garibaldi*.
+ HQs Commander Spanish Maritime Forces on board SNS *Castilla*.
+ HQs Commander UK Maritime Forces on board HMS *Ark Royal*.

PART II

ACTIVITIES BY COUNTRY

Afghanistan

On 11 Aug 2003, NATO took over command and coordination of the International Security Assistance Force (ISAF) in Afghanistan, NATO's first mission beyond the Euro-Atlantic area. Independently of ISAF, US military forces continue to operate in the mountains of southern and eastern Afghanistan against al Qaeda, anti-coalition militias, and Taliban insurgents under Operation Enduring Freedom (OEF).

Austria, Canada, Denmark, Finland, France, Germany, Greece, Italy, New Zealand, the Netherlands, Norway, Portugal, Romania, Spain, Sweden, Turkey, and the UK signed a joint memorandum of understanding (MOU) on 10 Jan 2002 formalizing their contributions to ISAF. Belgium subsequently also signed the MOU, and Bulgaria is also contributing personnel. On 14 Mar 2002, the Czech Republic signed the MOU, offering to contribute a military field hospital. Other countries participating in ISAF or coalition operations include Albania, Azerbaijan, Croatia, Estonia, Hungary, Iceland, Ireland, Latvia, Lithuania, and Macedonia. Non-US partners have deployed nearly 4,000 troops to Afghanistan and provide 95 percent of the ISAF.

Despite the enormous effort, anti-government violence targeting Afghan security forces, civic leaders, and international aid workers has increased, there has been a resurgence of poppy cultivation and the drug trade since 9/11, and recruiting and retention of the new Afghan National Army has been disappointing. In 2003, the UN even suspended operations in the southern provinces of Helmand, Oruzgan, Khandahar, and Zabol. Domestically, an Emergency Loya Jirga (Grand Assembly) in Jun 2002 established a Transitional Administration to govern until elections in 2004. The new Afghan constitution was agreed on 4 Jan 2004.

On 30 Dec 2003, ISAF expanded its mission and assumed command of the German-led Provincial Reconstruction Team (PRT) in Konduz in northern Afghanistan to expand ISAF outside the Kabul area and establish a nationwide presence. Thirteen PRTs are planned.

The US has provided well over $1 billion in humanitarian assistance and reconstruction aid to Afghanistan, and the Afghanistan Freedom Support Act, approved by Congress, authorizes $3.47 billion for Afghanistan for FYs 2003–2006. In FYs 2002 and 2003, the US provided more than $900 million annually in aid to Afghanistan. The US is also the lead nation in establishing, training, and equipping the new Afghan National Army, committing more than $400 million, and is involved in the creation of a Presidential Protective Service to take over from US and coalition special operations forces, which are providing security as an interim measure.

US COMMAND: Coalition militaries operating under OEF are under the overall US command of Combined Forces Command — Afghanistan (CFC-A) (formerly Combined Task Force Afghanistan), also known as CJTF (Combined Joint Task Force) 180, headquartered at Bagram air base, north of Kabul. CFC-A includes military forces from some 20 partner countries. The overall US command for US forces is JTF-76. Combined Joint Special Operation Task Force — Afghanistan (CJSOTF-A) is the special operations component of CJTF–180/JTF-76. CJSOTF-A nominally controls special operations forces and CIA paramilitary groups involved in the hunt for "high-value targets" under a special Joint Task Force 626/121. An army brigadier general commands the Joint Interagency Task Force at Bagram air base to coordinate CIA, DOD, and coalition special operations.

AGREEMENTS: Acquisition and Cross-Servicing Agreement, Article 98 Agreement.
A US–Afghan–Pakistani Tripartite Commission deals with cross-border conflict.

US ASSISTANCE: Receives Foreign Military Financing program grants, International Military Education and Training aid, eligible to receive grant Excess Defense Articles, receives aid for humanitarian demining efforts, receives peacekeeping operations (PKO) funding, participates in National Defense University Near East South Asia (NESA) Center seminars, receives International Narcotics Control and Law Enforcement funding, participates in the Terrorist Interdiction Program.

BASES AND ACCESS: Bagram air base, north of Kabul, is the hub of the US headquarters (CJTF 180). ISAF, Task Force Kabul, and the Coalition Joint Civil Military Operations Task Force are all in the capital city. Kandahar International Airport, first occupied by marines 25 Nov 2001, serves as the main southern base. Dozens of additional additional camps and forward operating bases are maintained, and the US has regularly used Faizabad, Heart, Mazar-i-Sharif, and Shindand airfields.

Code Names: Al Miwan, Alamo Sweep, Allied Sweep, Anaconda, Athena, Avalanche, Buzzard, Carpathian Lightning, Champion Strike, Condor, Crackdown, Crashpad, Crescent Wind, Damask, Desert Lion, Devil Shock, Divine Kingfisher, Dragon Fury, Eagle Fury, Enduring Freedom, Fingel, Full Throttle, Ginger, Harpoon, Haven Denial, Iceberg, Infinite Reach, IWER, Mongoose, Mountain series, Polar Harpoon, Ptarmigan, Resolute Strike, Sensor Harvest, Slipper, Snipe, Swift Freedom, Torii, Tri-City Sweep, Unified Resolve, Valiant Strike, Veritas, Vigilant Guardian, Viper, Warrior Sweep.

Albania

Prior to 9/11, Albania was firmly in the US orbit, participating in peacekeeping and humanitarian operations with US forces, providing support for regular port visits by US Navy ships and submarines, and hosting US intelligence collection assets. During Allied Force, some 9,000 NATO troops were deployed in

Albania before crossing into Kosovo. A residual NATO force of around 1,000 remained in Albania as part of the initial Kosovo Force (KFOR) mission.

Since 9/11, Albania has supported the war on terrorism by extending blanket landing and overflight clearances, opening ports for refueling and maintenance support, sharing intelligence on terrorist-related groups and activities, freezing terrorist assets, improved financial transaction monitoring, shutting down suspect Islamic NGOs, and expelling Islamic extremists. Albania joined NATO's Partnership for Peace (23 Feb 1994) and Membership Action Plan, established in 1999 to help countries prepare for entry into the alliance.

US COMMAND: EUCOM.

AGREEMENTS: Treaty on the Prevention of Proliferation of Weapons of Mass Destruction and the Promotion of Defense and Military Relations (May 2003), Reciprocal SOFA, PfP SOFA (8 Jun 1996), Acquisition and Cross-Servicing Agreement (8 Nov 2000), Article 98 Agreement (2 May 2003), MOU on Defense Cooperation (1993).

US ASSISTANCE: Receives Foreign Military Financing program grants, International Military Education and Training aid, participates in the EUCOM Joint Contact Team Program, National Guard partner with SC, receives Support for East European Democracy (SEED) funds for anti-trafficking, counter-narcotics, and anti-organized-crime training, participates in George C. Marshall Center conferences and seminars.

BASES AND ACCESS: On 17 Jun 2002, NATO transformed the former KFOR Communication Zone West into a NATO Headquarters in Tirana (NHQT). NHQT facilitates coordination between Albania and NATO.

US intelligence collection positions are reported at Durres, Shkoder, and Tirana. Under the 1993 MOU, the US began operations at the Albanian military base at Perlat, 35 miles southwest of Tirana. The CIA and air force also began operating the Gnat 750 and Predator unmanned aerial vehicles (UAVs) from Albania for surveillance operations over Bosnia and the former Yugoslavia.

FORCES DEPLOYED: Albania has provided peacekeepers for SFOR in Bosnia, has provided a "kommando" detachment under Turkish command to the International Security Assistance Force (ISAF) in Afghanistan, and has served with the 101st Airborne Division as part of Operation Iraqi Freedom (OIF) in northern Iraq.

Code Names: Adriatic Phiblex, Adventure Express, Allied Harbor, Artisan, Combined Endeavor, Cooperative Assembly, Cooperative Dragon, Cooperative Osprey, Cooperative Zenith, Cornerstone, Crystal Water, Dacia, Eagle, Eloquent Nugget, Esperia, Joint Forge, MEDCEUR, Nomad Vigil, Peaceful Eagle, Prometheus, Rescue Eagle, Salvation Eagle, SAREX, Security Force, Silver Knight, Silver Wake, Sustain Hope/Shining Hope, Uje Krystal, Viking.

Algeria

The US military maintains cordial relations with its Algerian counterpart, a relationship that predates 9/11, but one that intensified and broadened to counterterrorism cooperation after the World Trade Center attacks. In Jul 2001, Abdelaziz Bouteflika became the first Algerian president to visit the White House in 16 years. The visit was followed by a second meeting in Nov 2001 and a meeting with President Bush in New York in Sep 2003. In Jun 2004, Algeria was designated a full-fledged partner in the NATO Mediterranean Dialogue.

The Sixth Fleet flagship, the USS *Mount Whitney,* visited Algeria in Sep 1999, becoming the first navy ship to moor pierside in Algeria since 1962. The rescue and salvage ship USS *Grasp* (ARS 51) visited Algeria in 2000, and the destroyer USS *Mitscher* (DDG 57) visited in 2001, conducting joint anti-submarine-warfare (ASW) training with the attack submarine USS *Norfolk* (SSN 714) and the Algerian navy, including the Algerian Soviet-made *Kilo*-class attack submarine *El Hadj Slimane.* In Jun 2001, the commander of US Air Forces Europe (USAFE) and the chief of the Algerian Air Force also held staff-to-staff talks. USAFE then sent a delegation to Algiers in Nov 2001 in preparation for Jan 2002 joint training. Algeria also participated in a Mar 2004 EUCOM counterterrorism chiefs of defense conference in Stuttgart, Germany, with Chad, Mali, Mauritania, Morocco, Niger, Senegal, Tunisia, and the US.

During Feb and Mar 2003, an Algerian terrorist group, the Salafist Group for Call and Combat (GSPC), kidnapped 32 European tourists in Algeria. Fourteen of the hostages were transported into northern Mali. By 20 Aug 2003, one had died in captivity, and all others had been released. On 11 Sep 2003, the GSPC issued a statement declaring allegiance to several jihadist causes and leaders, including al Qaeda and Osama bin Ladin. Members of the GSPC are believed hiding in the Sahel region, crossing among Chad, Mali, Mauritania, Niger, and Algeria. A London-based Middle East newspaper has reported that Algeria and the US have created a joint security commission for the surveillance and pursuit of GSPC and other armed Islamic groups, and there were numerous operations in the other Sahel countries in 2003–2004 to pursue GSPC.

US COMMAND: EUCOM.

AGREEMENTS: The US and Algeria were reported working on a "mini SOFA," the first draft of which was produced in Mar 2001.

US ASSISTANCE: Receives International Military Education and Training aid, participates in National Defense University Near East South Asia (NESA) Center seminars, participates in Africa Center for Strategic Studies conferences and seminars.

BASES AND ACCESS: Algiers International Airport hosts Air Mobility Command transit and supply operations.

Code Names: Active Endeavour, Cooperative Best Effort, Cooperative Poseidon, Cooperative Support, Eloquent Nugget.

Angola

More than three decades of internal conflict have left Angola with one of the world's most serious land mine problems, covering nearly 50 percent of the country. The US has trained and equipped deminers and focused on humanitarian demining and civic action programs. The External Intelligence Services of Angola (SIE) hosted a meeting of 17 other African intelligence and security services in Apr 2004 to discuss coordination on mercenary activities and international terrorism.

US COMMAND: EUCOM.

US ASSISTANCE: Receives modest International Military Education and Training aid, eligible to receive grant Excess Defense Articles, receives aid for humanitarian demining efforts, participates in Africa Center for Strategic Studies conferences and seminars.

BASES AND ACCESS: The US has negotiated access to Angolan airstrips for transit, for refueling, and to position troops and equipment.

Code Names: High Flight, Provide Transition.

Anguilla (UK Overseas Territory)

The UK is responsible for Anguilla's external relations, defense, and internal security. Anguillan police receive training at the US Coast Guard Training Center at Yorktown, VA.

US COMMAND: SOUTHCOM.

Antigua and Barbuda

Prior to 9/11, Antigua and Barbuda hosted regular port visits by US Navy ships and participated in counter-narcotic efforts. The former US Naval Support Facility, turned over to Antigua in 1995, is being developed as a regional Coast Guard training facility. The US also maintains a space tracking facility on Barnes Hill and a Trident missile Portable Impact Location System (PILS) operating location to monitor Atlantic Ocean missile testing. Communications and instrumentation systems in Antigua have been upgraded under the Jun 1993 Range Standardization and Automation (RSA) contract.

US COMMAND: SOUTHCOM.

AGREEMENTS: SOFA, Acquisition and Cross-Servicing Agreement eligible (20 Apr 1993), Article 98 Agreement (30 Sep 2003).

Antigua was one of six initial ratifiers of the Inter-American Convention Against Terrorism (2003).

US ASSISTANCE: Receives International Military Education and Training aid, participates in Center for Hemispheric Defense Studies conferences and seminars. The US provided an 82-foot patrol boat in 1998.

Code Names: Fuerzas Aliadas, New Horizons, PKO, Tradewinds.

Argentina

Argentina has actively supported US counter-terrorism and counter-narcotics activities and has played a leading role in international peacekeeping. Argentina has cooperated with the US in counter-terrorism activity centered on the tri-border area (TBA) with Brazil and Paraguay. Argentina is vice chair of the Inter-American Committee Against Terrorism (the US is chair). Argentina has also been cooperative in responding to US requests related to blocking terrorist financial assets, and is a member of the Financial Action Task Force.

In Dec 2002, a high-level US interagency delegation attended a special meeting in Buenos Aires of the Tripartite Commission of the Triple Frontier, the mechanism established by the three TBA countries in 1998. This "Three Plus One" meeting (the three TBA countries plus the US) serves as the counter-terrorism forum to open the way for US operations, and the four countries agreed to establish a permanent working group on counter-terrorism. At US insistence, the first issue on the working group's 2003 agenda was terrorist fund-raising on behalf of Hezbollah and Hamas in the TBA. In 2003, the US proposed to establish a joint regional intelligence center and deepen border security cooperation to counter the Islamic threat, but was thwarted by the three TBA countries, which argued that "available information" did not substantiate reports of operational activities by terrorists in the TBA.

US COMMAND: SOUTHCOM.

AGREEMENTS: Acquisition and Cross-Servicing Agreement (15 Jan 1999); granted Major Non-NATO Ally status.

The Office of the Secretary of Defense and the Argentine Ministry of Defense hold an annual Bilateral Working Group Meeting, alternating between Argentina and Washington, DC.

US ASSISTANCE: Receives Foreign Military Financing program grants, International Military Education and Training aid, eligible to receive grant Excess Defense Articles, participates in Center for Hemispheric Defense Studies conferences and seminars.

BASES AND ACCESS: US Navy ships conduct port visits and receive fuel service at Ingeniero White, Puerto Belgrano, and Ushuai.

FORCES DEPLOYED: Argentina has contributed to UN peacekeeping missions in East Timor, Western Sahara, Ethiopia–Eritrea, Iraq–Kuwait, Cyprus, Bosnia, and Kosovo.

Code Names: Cabañas, Dogu Akdeniz, Eagle, Fleetex, Fluvial, Fuerzas Aliadas, Ghost, Gringo-Gaucho, Joint Forge/Joint Guardian, New Horizons, Oceanic, PKO, River Operation, SAR 2000, Transoceanic Exercise, Trilateral War Game, Unitas.

Armenia

Armenia has supported the war on terrorism, Operation Enduring Freedom, and Operation Iraqi Freedom by offering "unreserved assistance" including overflight and landing rights, medical assistance, and information sharing. Armenia joined the NATO Partnership for Peace on 5 Oct 1994 and hosted Cooperative Best Effort in Jun 2003, the first Partnership for Peace exercise hosted by Armenia and the first time Russia participated in such a NATO exercise.

Relations between Armenia and Azerbaijan have been strained since the two countries clashed in 1988 over the Nagorno-Karabakh enclave, a disputed territory. The conflict left some 30,000 killed and created some 1 million refugees. A cease-fire declared in 1994 still holds, but occasional exchanges of gunfire continue along the cease-fire line. The Organization for Security and Cooperation in Europe (OSCE) imposed an arms embargo on both Armenia and Azerbaijan in 1992, and US assistance takes in consideration constraints that do not disturb the military balance with Azerbaijan.[5] Armenia's borders with Azerbaijan and Turkey also remain closed.

US COMMAND: EUCOM, effective 1 Oct 1998.

AGREEMENTS: Acquisition and Cross-Servicing Agreement (27 Apr 2004), Article 98 Agreement (26 Jan 2004).

---

5. Section 907 of the Freedom Support Act previously prohibited most US assistance to Azerbaijan, and, as part of a policy of evenhandedness, the US extended this prohibition to Armenia as well. Congress then gave the president the authority to issue a renewable one-year waiver of the Section 907 restrictions on assistance to Azerbaijan, which was used to permit fuller cooperation between the US and Armenia.

Armenia was one of six parties to the Commonwealth of Independent States (CIS) Treaty of Collective Security signed in Tashkent in May 1993. There is a Russian division stationed in Armenia, as well as Russian border guards. An Armenian–Russian treaty was signed on 16 Mar 1995 establishing the legal status of the base. In Aug 1997, Russia and Armenia also signed a Friendship Treaty. Azerbaijan strongly criticized the treaty on the grounds that it contained provisions on military cooperation.

US ASSISTANCE: Receives Foreign Military Financing program grants (initiated in FY 2002), modest International Military Education and Training aid, eligible to receive grant Excess Defense Articles, National Guard partner with KS (established 2003), participates in the Export Control and Related Border Security Assistance program, Border Interdiction Training is provided to Armenian customs and border guards, participates in George C. Marshall Center conferences and seminars.

FORCES DEPLOYED: On 5 Aug 2003, Armenia offered to send a team of military doctors and deminers to Iraq to contribute to the coalition's stabilization efforts.

Code Names: Combined Endeavor, Cooperative Associate, Cooperative Best Effort, Cooperative Determination, Cooperative Zenith, Dacia, Eloquent Nugget, Prometheus.

Aruba

US–Aruba cooperation focuses on counter-narcotics and organized crime. In Oct 2001, the US and the Netherlands signed a 10-year agreement for the establishment of forward operating locations on Aruba and Curaçao. The Reina Beatrix IAP Cooperative Security Location (CSL; formerly forward operating location) has hosted US Customs P-3 and other surveillance aircraft since 1 May 99. Air-force-owned Cessna Citation 550 and other aircraft also operate from the airport. US ships regularly call and fuel at Organjestad.

US COMMAND: SOUTHCOM.

Ascension Island (UK Overseas Territory)

During World War II, the US established an airstrip on Ascension, located 500 miles south of the equator in the middle of the Atlantic Ocean, and the island serves as a missile and satellite tracking station. The air force operates communications, radar, and satellite tracking equipment on 4,000 leased acres to monitor space launches and space objects, as well as a GPS satellite control station. The navy operates the Portable Impact Location System (PILS), a Trident missile tracking system for tests in the Atlantic Ocean. Ascension was a staging post for the transport of troops and equipment to and from the Falklands during the conflict in 1982, and the RAF continues to have a base there to support resupply of the Falklands.

US **command:** SOUTHCOM.

Agreements: Reciprocal SOFA (with the UK).

Bases and access: US–UK negotiations, concluded in Oct 2003, allow air charter access to the US-controlled Wideawake airfield on Ascension.

Code Names: Atlantic Drive, Mercury, Mystic Star, Turtle Heritage, Turtle Truss.

Australia

In the wake of 9/11, Australia invoked the 1951 ANZUS Treaty for the first time in its history and has fully cooperated in the war on terror, deploying forces to Afghanistan and Iraq, and fully participating in US military operations. Special Air Service (SAS) troops have been intimately involved in US special operations throughout the Middle East and Asia. Additionally, Australia has been a leader in pursuing multi-lateral counter-terrorism initiatives in Southeast Asia and has signed numerous counter-terrorism MOUs. Australia is also a member of the Financial Action Task Force and the Proliferation Security Initiative. Australia hosts significant US intelligence collection and communications facilities and was a first-tier intelligence partner with US military and civil agencies well before 9/11. The US and Australia have an extensive Joint/Combined Exchange Training special operations program.

US **command:** PACOM.

Agreements: Security Treaty Between Australia, New Zealand, and the US (ANZUS Treaty; 1 Sep 1951); SOFA, Acquisition and Cross-Servicing Agreement (9 Dec 1998); Agreement on Establishment of a Joint Defence Space Research Facility ("Pine Gap"; 9 Dec 1966, amended 4 Jun 1998); granted Major Non-NATO Ally status.

In 1985, the nature of the ANZUS alliance changed after New Zealand refused port calls by US nuclear-weapons-capable and nuclear-powered ships. The US suspended defense obligations to New Zealand, and annual bilateral meetings between the US secretary of state and the Australian foreign minister replaced annual meetings of the ANZUS Council of Foreign Ministers. The first bilateral meeting was held in Canberra in 1985. At the second, in San Francisco in 1986, the US and Australia announced that the US was suspending its treaty security obligations to New Zealand pending the restoration of port access. Subsequent bilateral Australian–US Ministerial (AUSMIN) meetings have alternated between Australia and the US. The 15th AUSMIN meeting took place in Washington, DC, on 28 Oct 2002.

Australia has broadened its network of bilateral counterterrorism arrangements in Southeast Asia, signing MOUs on cooperation to combat international terrorism with Singapore, the Philippines, Fiji, Cambodia, East Timor, Indonesia, and India during 2003, bringing Australia's network of MOUs to eight. These MOUs are umbrella arrangements that set out a framework for bilateral cooperation in law enforcement, defense, intelligence, customs, and immigration. In Jun 2003, Australia and Singapore co-hosted a seminar on managing the consequences of a major terrorist attack, which focused on practical measures that governments can take to recover from such an incident.

BASES AND ACCESS: The only "official" US military base in Australia is a semi-active Naval Communications Station at North West Cape, near Exmouth. The largest facility by far, though, is the Australian–CIA–National Reconnaissance Office Joint Defense Facility "Pine Gap" near Alice Springs, which serves as a major ground station for intelligence, early warning, and communications satellites. Pine Gap took over control of the Defence Support Program (DSP) satellite function from the Defence Facility Nurrungar (Woomera Air Station), which formally closed on 12 Oct 1999. Royal Australian Air Force (RAAF) Richmond serves as the main US airlift terminal. US Navy ships make port visits to Brisbane, Bunbury, Cairns, Darwin, Fremantle, Geraldton, Hobart (Tasmania), Mackay, Perth, Stirling, Sydney, and Townsville. In Jan 2004, US and Australian officials announced that they were considering building a joint ground training area in northern Australia.

FORCES DEPLOYED: The Australian Defence Force (ADF) has deployed approximately 2,000 personnel on two distinct operations in the Middle East. These are known as Slipper (support to the war on terrorism and Operation Enduring Freedom) and Bastille/Falconer (support for US operations in Iraq). For Slipper, Australia deployed more than 1,500 military personnel, including Special Air Service (SAS) troops, who performed the full spectrum of SOF missions. F-18 fighter aircraft deployed to Diego Garcia to perform combat air patrol (CAP) missions, and two KB-707 aircraft were stationed in Manas, Kyrgyzstan (until Sep 2002), supporting US and French aircraft. Australia also deployed surface ships and conducted maritime interdiction operations in the Arabian Gulf, and deployed P-3 Orion aircraft to the Arabian Gulf.

For Bastille/Falconer (Operation Iraqi Freedom), Australia initially deployed about 2,000 military personnel, including SAS troops in Jordan and Kuwait. SAS entered Iraq with the first groups in western and southern Iraq; F-18 fighter aircraft were involved in offensive operations, and navy divers and mine clearance specialists operated in southern Iraq.

Code Names: Aces North, Albatross Ausindo, Anaconda, Aurora, Ausina, Axolotl, Bastille, Beachcomber, Bel Isi, Bell Buoy, Bell Thunder, Bullseye, Burbage, Busy Boomerang, Cascade Peak, Cassowary, Celesta, Celtic, Chapel Gold, Churinga, Citadel, Commando Sling, Cooperative

Thunder, Cope Boomerang, Cope Thunder, Cope Tiger, Crocodile, Croix Du Sud, Cygnet Globe, Damask, Dawn Panther, Dawn Seagull, Day Anchor, Dugong, ECHELON, Elang Ausindo, EXTENDEX, Falconer, Fincastle, Flaming Arrow, Flying Fish, Freedom Banner, Gateway, GI Joe, Global Guardian, Gold Eagle, Goodwill, Griffin, Haringaroo, Helicon Luk, Hunter, Husky, IADS ADEX, Imminent Horizon, Kangaroo, Kernel Blitz, Kerry, Longlook, Longreach, Lumbus, Lungfish, Mallee Bull, Marcot, Mellin, Merino, Mistral, MTX, New Horizon, Night series, NOLES, Northern Trilogy, Nugget, Oak Tree, Ocean Wave, Osreal, Pacific Bond, Pacific Look, Pacific Protector, Pacific Reserve, Paradise, Peace Reef, Penguin, Pirap Jabiru, Pitchblack, Platypus Moon, Pomelo, Premier Gunner, Prominent Hammer, Prowler, Rainbow Serpent, Rajawali Ausindo, Red Snake, Relex, RIMPAC, Sandgroper, Sanso, Sea Eagle, Sea Saber, Short Haul, Silent Pearl, Singaroo, Slipper, Slow Walker, Solania, Southern Frontier, Southern Tiger, Star Eagle, Star Leopard, Stardex, Starfish, Suman Warrior, Taa Nok In Sii, Talisman Saber, TAMEX, Tanager, Tandem Thrust, Tasman, Tasmanex, Team Challenge, Temple Jade, Thai Boomerang, Tri-Crab, Trident Eagle, Trisetia, Vigilant, Wantok Warrior, Westpac MCMEX, Willoh, Wyvern Sun.

Austria

Though a neutral country, Austria is a full participant in the Euro-Atlantic Partnership Council (EAPC) and joined NATO's Partnership for Peace 10 Feb 1995. After 9/11, Austria established an interdepartmental counter-terrorism working group that incorporates its departments of interior, finance, and justice, and created a financial intelligence unit. It is a member of the Financial Action Task Force. Austria did not take part in Operation Enduring Freedom, but offered the use of its airspace, contributed $330 million to EU operations in Afghanistan, and increased intelligence sharing with US and European countries. Austria also participated in the International Security Assistance Force in Afghanistan, contributing about 60 troops.

US COMMAND: EUCOM.

AGREEMENTS: Reciprocal SOFA, PfP SOFA (2 Sep 1998), Acquisition and Cross-Servicing Agreement (15 Mar 2000).

FORCES DEPLOYED: Austria contributes forces for Kosovo (KFOR) and has contributed to SFOR in Bosnia.

Code Names: Baltlink, CMX, Combined Endeavor, Concordia, Cooperative Associate, Cooperative Aura, Cooperative Best Effort, Cooperative Chance, Cooperative Determination, Cooperative Dragon, Cooperative Jaguar, Cooperative Key, Cooperative Safeguard, Cooperative Support, Dacia, Eloquent Nugget, Esperia, Hexagrant, Joint Forge, Joint Guardian, Mothia, Viking.

Azerbaijan

Azerbaijan joined the NATO Partnership for Peace on 4 May 1994 and attended its first NATO summit in Apr 1999. Cooperation between Azerbaijan and the US on counter-terrorism is long standing and has intensified since

9/11. Azerbaijan offered to provide "whatever necessary." The focus of US cooperation has been on financial intelligence and preventing terrorists from transiting Azerbaijani territory. Azerbaijan deployed a platoon with the Turkish International Security Assistance Force in Afghanistan in Nov 2002, and in Aug 2003, 150 Azerbaijani soldiers joined the international contingent in Iraq. Under Operation Caspian Guard, the US is helping Azerbaijan build air and sea surveillance capabilities in the Caspian Sea.

Relations with Azerbaijan are complicated by the continuing friction between Azerbaijan and Armenia over the Nagorno–Karabakh enclave, a disputed territory. A cease-fire declared in 1994 still holds, but occasional exchanges of fire continue along the cease-fire line. The Organization for Security and Cooperation in Europe (OSCE) imposed an arms embargo on both Armenia and Azerbaijan in 1992, and the US continued it own suspension of aid until a presidential waiver of Section 907 of the Freedom Support Act (FSA) in 2002 opened the door to greater US involvement and engagement. New assistance in 2003 by the Departments of State and Treasury and US Customs Service focused on training for police and legal institutions, development of law enforcement data information management systems, counter-narcotics, and development of a modern forensics laboratory system. US military assistance focuses on military reform and strengthening of civil society, counter-terrorism, and the prevention of the proliferation of weapons of mass destruction.

US COMMAND: EUCOM, effective 1 Oct 1998.

AGREEMENTS: Reciprocal SOFA, PfP SOFA (2 Apr 2000), Article 98 Agreement.

US–Azerbaijan Bilateral Defense Consultations focus on three primary areas of military cooperation: maritime security, airspace management, and interoperability with NATO and international forces. The first bilateral working group met 26–27 Mar 2002.

US ASSISTANCE: Receives Foreign Military Financing program grants, International Military Education and Training aid, eligible to receive grant Excess Defense Articles, National Guard partner with Oklahoma (established 2002), receives aid for humanitarian demining efforts, participates in George C. Marshall Center conferences and seminars, participates in the Export Control and Related Border Security Assistance program.

Code Names: Centrasbat, Combined Endeavor, Cooperative Adventure Exchange, Cooperative Associate, Cooperative Banners/Chance, Cooperative Best Effort, Cooperative Determination, Cooperative Dragon, Cooperative Key, Cooperative Partner, Cooperative Zenith, Dacia, Eloquent Nugget, Joint Guardian, MEDCEUR, Peaceshield, Regional Cooperation, Rescue Eagle, Viking.

Azores

See Portugal.

Bahamas

US national security policy in the Bahamas focuses on counter-narcotics and illegal immigration, and — since 9/11 — combating money laundering, increased support for asset forfeiture investigations and prosecutions, and stopping financial support for terrorism. The combined counter-drug law enforcement effort Operation Bahamas and Turks and Caicos (OPBAT) includes Bahamian and Turks and Caicos police and US DEA, Coast Guard, and Army personnel. In 2001–2002, the US provided three fast patrol boats to the Bahamas.

US COMMAND: The Bahamas falls under the jurisdiction of NORTHCOM, created in 2002.

AGREEMENTS: US–UK–Bahamas–Turks and Caicos Islands OPBAT MOU (1990), SOFA, Acquisition and Cross-Servicing Agreement eligible (29 Aug 2000).

US ASSISTANCE: Receives International Military Education and Training aid.

BASES AND ACCESS: The US Navy Atlantic Undersea Test and Evaluation Center (AUTEC), centered on Andros Island, has operated an underwater research facility in the Atlantic Ocean and Berry Islands for more than 30 years. The range supports submarine and sensor operations, torpedo and weapons testing, electronic warfare, and special operations. Seven participating NATO member nations — Canada, Denmark, Germany, Greece, Italy, Norway, and the UK — use the Naval Forces Sensor and Weapon Accuracy Check Site (FORACS). OPBAT operates from Nassau, Great Exuma, and Great Inagua, and a SOUTHCOM Tactical Analysis Team, staffed by DOD and Coast Guard intelligence specialists, is located in Nassau.

Code Names: Giant Shadow, Mercury, New Horizons, PKO, Tradewinds.

Bahrain

Bahrain has provided port facilities to US naval forces for 50 years, furnishes bases for pre-positioned equipment, and serves as the headquarters and home-port for the US Naval Forces Central Command (since 1 Apr 1993) and the Fifth Fleet (since 1 Jul 1995). Bahrain supported US operations against Iran in the 1980s. Bahraini pilots flew strikes against Iraq during Desert Storm, and the island was used as a base for military operations in the Arabian Gulf. Bahrain's partnership with the US intensified after 1991. Bahrain provided logistical and basing support to international maritime interdiction operations efforts to enforce UN sanctions and prevent illegal smuggling of oil from Iraq in the 1990s. Starting in 1995, Bahrain hosted several deployments in support of Southern Watch.

After 9/11, Bahrain became an active supporter of the war on terrorism, becoming the only Gulf Cooperation Council (GCC) country to provide a ship to the maritime interdiction effort. During Operation Enduring Freedom, Bahrain was a hub for the US presence in the Arabian Gulf, providing basing and extensive overflight clearances. In 2002, an estimated 185 US Navy ships docked in Bahrain, including four homeported minesweepers, making it the US Navy's busiest overseas port. Bahrain responded positively to Kuwait's request to deploy the GCC collective defense force, Peninsula Shield, during the buildup and execution of Operation Iraqi Freedom (OIF) in 2003. Bahrain also cooperates with the US on criminal investigations in support of the war on terrorism; the Bahrain Monetary Agency has particularly moved to restrict terrorists' transfer of funds through Bahrain's financial system.

US COMMAND: CENTCOM.

AGREEMENTS: Defense Cooperation Agreement (DCA; Oct 1991), classified SOFA, granted Major Non-NATO Ally status (25 Oct 2001), Acquisition and Cross-Servicing Agreement (20 Jan 1994), Article 98 Agreement

Bahrain is a member of the GCC. The Defense Cooperation Agreement grants US forces access to Bahraini facilities and ensures the right to pre-position military materiel for future crises.

US ASSISTANCE: Receives Foreign Military Financing program grants (initiated in 2002), International Military Education and Training aid, eligible to receive grant Excess Defense Articles. US military sales to Bahrain currently total $1.6 billion. Principal US military systems purchased by the Bahrain Defense Forces (BDF) include F-16C/D aircraft, Apache and Cobra helicopters, M60A3 tanks, and the TPS-59 radar system. Bahrain has received $200 million in US Excess Defense Articles since 1995.

BASES AND ACCESS: Prior to 9/11, the US had seven controlled facilities in Bahrain and utilized an additional 110 Bahrain-controlled facilities. The Naval Support Activity Bahrain in Manama — comprising 65 acres of facilities — hosts most US headquarters and more than 40 commands. Bahrain International Airport (Muharraq) serves as the main gateway; Sheikh Isa air base is the main US military airfield in Bahrain, regularly hosting EP-3 and other intelligence and surveillance aircraft. The minehunter USS *Ardent* was forward deployed to Manama on 1 Mar 2000, the first US Navy ship to be homeported in the Arabian Gulf. The Mina al-Sulman port facility provides homeporting and fuel service.

Code Names: Arabian Gauntlet, Bell Buoy, Blue Flag, Desert Sailor, Eagle Resolve, Early Victor, Gateway, Inherent Fury, Initial Link, Neon series, Peace Crown, Peninsula Shield, Purple Star, Rugged Charly, Seek Gunfighter, Sensor Pacer, SHAREM, Vigilant Sentinel, Vigilant Warrior.

Bangladesh

US–Bangladeshi relations were boosted in Mar 2000 when President Clinton visited Bangladesh, the first visit ever by a sitting US president. After 9/11, Bangladesh granted overflight rights and the use of airports and ports. Secretary of State Colin Powell visited Bangladesh in Jun 2003. Bangladesh is a major player in international peacekeeping, and hosts a regional Peacekeeping Center. An extensive Joint/Combined Exchange Training (JCET) special operations program also exists between the US 1st Special Forces Group and 1st Para-commando Battalion and Bangladesh naval commandos (Isha Khan-Chitagong and Haji).

US COMMAND: PACOM.

AGREEMENTS: Activity-specific SOFA, Acquisition and Cross-Servicing Agreement eligible (6 Feb 1996), Article 98 Agreement (17 Aug 2003).

US ASSISTANCE: Receives International Military Education and Training aid, eligible to receive grant Excess Defense Articles, participates in National Defense University Near East South Asia (NESA) Center seminars, participates in Asia Pacific Center for Security Studies executive courses, participates in the Terrorist Interdiction Program. A centerpiece of the bilateral relationship is a large US economic aid program. The US gave the Bangladesh air force four C-130 transport aircraft in 2001 under Excess Defense Articles. US economic and food aid programs, which began as emergency relief following the 1971 war for independence, now concentrate on long-term development. In total, the US has provided more than $4.3 billion in food and development assistance to Bangladesh.

FORCES DEPLOYED: A 2,300-member Bangladesh army contingent served with coalition forces during Desert Storm. As of Jun 2003, Bangladesh was the third leading contributor to UN peacekeeping operations, with some 2,650 deployed. Bangladeshi troops have served or are serving in Sierra Leone, Somalia, Rwanda, Mozambique, Kuwait, Ethiopia–Eritrea, Kosovo, East Timor, Georgia, Congo, Côte d'Ivoire and Western Sahara, Bosnia, and Haiti.

Code Names: Light of Hope (Ashar Alo), NOLES, Sea Angel, Shant Boot, Shanti Path, Sumo Tiger.

Barbados

The US and Barbados cooperate on counter-narcotics assistance and other forms of transnational crime, and hosted CTSIMEX 1, an Inter-American

Committee Against Terrorism exercise, 16–18 Jun 2004. Barbados is the headquarters of the Regional Security System (RSS), which involves Caribbean Coast Guards. It also hosts a Trident missile testing Portable Impact Location System (PILS) operating location.

US COMMAND: SOUTHCOM.

AGREEMENTS: Acquisition and Cross-Servicing Agreement eligible (22 Mar 1999).

Code Names: PKO, Tradewinds.

Belarus

Belarus is is not eligible to receive US-funded security assistance, and in 2002 the UT National Guard dissolved its State Partnership with Belarus due to the country's inability to comply with security cooperation requirements. After an illegal electoral referendum in 1996, the US adopted a limited aid policy focusing on humanitarian and health assistance. In Feb 1997, the Clinton administration further decertified Belarus under the Cooperative Threat Reduction (CTR) program. In Aug 1998, US training operations in Belarus were suspended. After 9/11, the government of Belarus expressed its willingness to provide assistance in the war on terrorism. However, intelligence information indicating the transfer of arms and dual-use equipment to Iraq and other countries hampered any such efforts.

On 11 Jan 1995, Belarus signed NATO's Partnership for Peace Agreement. However, President Lukashenko continued as a critic of NATO enlargement, and after Belarus shut down the Organization for Security and Cooperation in Europe (OSCE) office in Minsk in 2002, NATO indicated that Lukashenko's presence at its summit in Prague in Nov 2002 would be unwelcome. The Czechs subsequently refused him a visa.

US COMMAND: EUCOM, effective 1 Oct 1998.

AGREEMENTS: The US and Belarus signed a government-to-government umbrella agreement on CTR assistance in 1992, seven agency-to-agency CTR-implementing agreements, and one MOU; the umbrella agreement was extended for one year in Oct 1997, but has now expired.

In Jan 2000, Belarus and Russia signed a Union Treaty, which would allow the creation of a confederation. However, continuing negotiations between Presidents Putin and Lukashenko have been strained. Russia has made it clear that it would only proceed with integration on its own terms and conditions, which could include the creation of a "single state" or the formation of an EU-style arrangement, while Belarus does not want to cede its sovereignty. Despite three meetings between Putin and Lukashenko in Sep 2003, no firm commitments were made by either side toward closer union.

US ASSISTANCE: Participates in George C. Marshall Center conferences and seminars.

Code Names: Cooperative Zenith, Dacia, Peaceshield, Provide Hope.

Belgium

Belgium is a core NATO member, hosting the headquarters for the alliance in Brussels, as well as Supreme Headquarters Allied Powers Europe (SHAPE) and Allied Command Operations (formerly Allied Command Europe) near Mons. The country also hosts US nuclear weapons (at Kleine Brogel AB) and numerous US military support bases.

After 9/11, the Belgian General Intelligence and Security Service and law enforcement authorities increased intelligence sharing with the US on terrorist threats, and Belgium's Financial Intelligence Unit provided the US Treasury Financial Crimes Enforcement Unit with information on individuals and entities with suspected ties to terrorist groups. Intelligence sharing and collaboration with the US is long standing. In 1999, for instance, Belgian military intelligence co-sponsored the first-ever NATO-wide, multi-national counter-intelligence and HUMINT exercise in a Kosovo-like scenario.

US COMMAND: EUCOM.

AGREEMENTS: NATO SOFA (16 Jun 1951), classified Pine Cone Technical Agreement (nuclear weapons), Reciprocal SOFA, PfP SOFA (9 Nov 1997), Acquisition and Cross-Servicing Agreement (6 May 1982).

BASES AND ACCESS: US nuclear weapons are stored at Kleine Brogel AB, the main Belgian F-16 base. Chievres AB, between Mons and Ath, and Daumerie Caserne in Ath are the centers of US military support for NATO operations in Belgium. The 650th Military Intelligence Group handles NATO counter-intelligence. Most Cold War US military bases in Belgium have been closed; some minor communications sites exist. Army Pre-positioned Stocks (APS) at Zutendaal were withdrawn in 1999; Both Vriezenveen and Brunssum bases were closed in Feb 2004. Antwerp continues to be an important transshipment point for US materiel. In 2003, thousands of tons of cargo belonging to the US Army's V Corps and 4th Infantry Division were loaded at Antwerp, Belgium, for shipment to the Middle East.

FORCES DEPLOYED: Belgium led the largest multi-national humanitarian assistance mission to Afghanistan 6–29 Oct 2001. It later airlifted food aid, medical supplies, and humanitarian aid in support of Romania and Egypt and in collaboration with the UK, France, Italy, and Greece. Belgium air force C-130/A-310 aircraft delivered aid to Dushanbe, Tajikistan. A Belgian C-130 transport deployed to Karachi, Pakistan, on 10 Apr 2002, flying dedicated relief missions on one-month rotations in cooperation with the Portuguese air force. Belgium also participated in International Security Assistance Force in Afghanistan, providing security at Kabul International Airport.

Code Names: Able series, Adventure Express, Allied Action, Allied Response, Ample Train, Arabian Gauntlet, Ardent Ground, Bright Horizon, Brilliant Foil, Cannon Cloud, Central Enterprise, Clean Hunter, Combined Endeavor, Constant Harmony, Cooperative Adventure Exchange, Cooperative Assembly, Cooperative Banish, Cooperative Light, Coronet Dart, Dacia, Distant Thunder, Dynamic Impact, Dynamic Mix, Harvest Partner, JTFEX, Mothia, Neo Tapon, Orient Express, Peaceshield, Phoenix Partner, Pine Cone, Sacred Company, SAREX, Strong Resolve, Sunny Hope/Sunny Relief, Trident D'Or, Unified Charger, Volant Partner, West Eagle.

Belize

US–Belize relations center on counter-narcotics and other transnational crimes. Belize and the US signed stolen vehicle, extradiction, and mutual legal assistance treaties between 2001 and 2003. The US is the largest provider of economic assistance to Belize, most of which is administered by the US Military Liaison Office. The UK continues to maintain the British Army Training Support Unit Belize (BATSUB) to assist in the administration of the Belize Jungle School. The US 7th and 20th Special Forces Groups conduct regular Joint/Combined Exchange Training (JCET) at San Ignacio. A SOUTHCOM Tactical Analysis Team (TAT) is stationed in Belize.

US COMMAND: SOUTHCOM. Belize is located in the Joint Task Force — Bravo (JTF-B) geographic operations area.

AGREEMENTS: Acquisition and Cross-Servicing Agreement eligible (29 Aug 2000), Article 98 Agreement (2003).

US ASSISTANCE: Receives Foreign Military Financing program grants, International Military Education and Training aid, eligible to receive grant Excess Defense Articles, National Guard partner with LA and NH, receives modest International Narcotics Control and Law Enforcement funding.

FORCES DEPLOYED: Belize Defense Force troops serve with the Caribbean Community (CARICOM) Battalion during peacekeeping operations in Haiti and participate in regional training exercises with US, UK, and Caribbean forces.

Code Names: Bushmaster, Cygnet Goose, Fuerzas Aliadas, Mercury, Native Trail, New Horizons, Panther Cub, PKO, Sailfish, Thirsty Panther, Tradewinds.

Benin

US–Benin military cooperation focuses on civil–military relations, law enforcement and corruption, promoting good governance, and the rule of law. In early 2003, Benin provided a peacekeeping contingent to the Economic Community of West African States (ECOWAS) stabilization force in Côte d'Ivoire.

US COMMAND: EUCOM.

US ASSISTANCE: Receives International Military Education and Training aid, eligible to receive grant Excess Defense Articles, participates in the African Contingency Operations Training and Assistance program and earlier African Crisis Response Initiative, participates in Africa Center for Strategic Studies conferences and seminars.

AGREEMENTS: SOFA (28 Jul 1998), Acquisition and Cross-Servicing Agreement eligible (26 Jan 1998).

Code Names: MEDFLAG.

Bermuda (UK Nonsovereign Territory)

Since the US closed its Cold War military bases in Bermuda, the relationship has focused on maritime control, search and rescue, and counter-narcotics support. US assistance allows students from Bermuda to attend the US Coast Guard Training Center at Yorktown, VA. Since 9/11, Bermuda has collaborated with the US by assuring that Bermuda is not offering physical or financial hiding places for terrorism.

US COMMAND: With the creation of NORTHCOM in 2002, Bermuda no longer falls under JFCOM (and earlier Atlantic Command).

AGREEMENTS: Reciprocal SOFA (with the UK).

BASES AND ACCESS: Bermuda hosts US Navy ships at Ferry Reach and Penno's Wharf. The US military base at Kindley Field, established in World War II, was closed down in 1995, and the formal termination of the lease was completed in 2003.

Bhutan

The US and Bhutan do not have diplomatic relations, and there is no foreign assistance program. A few Bhutanese military officers have attended courses at the Asia-Pacific Center for Security Studies.

US COMMAND: PACOM.

AGREEMENTS: Article 98 Agreement.

Bolivia

US–Bolivian relations are dominated by counter-narcotics, with the US increasingly pushing for military, customs, immigration, financial, and cooperation in policing Bolivia's long, sparsely inhabited border to keep it from becoming a transit point for international terrorists. Bolivia's financial investigations unit has cooperated with the US in sharing information about possible terrorist-linked financial transactions. The US is providing equipment and training for the Bolivian army's new counter-terrorism unit. Special Bolivian counter-narcotic forces and special military units are also active participants with the US in the drug war and are increasingly being trained in counter-terrorism tasks. There have been numerous violent controntations in which government security forces have used lethal force, raising human rights concerns. An extensive Joint/Combined Exchange Training (JCET) special operations program takes place among the Bolivian Tocopillo Battalion, Victoria Battalion (CITE), Jordan Battalion, Special Forces Command, Condor School, Mendez Arcos Battalion, Manchego Battalion and 1st Battalion, 20th Special Forces Group, 16th Special OperationsWing, 720th Special Tactics Group, and 25th Intelligence Squadron at El Paso, Cochanbamba, Sandanita, and Ororu Province.

US COMMAND: SOUTHCOM.

AGREEMENTS: Acquisition and Cross-Servicing Agreement eligible (29 Aug 2000), Article 98 Agreement.

US ASSISTANCE: Receives Foreign Military Financing program grants, International Military Education and Training aid, National Guard partner with MS (established in Oct 1999).

BASES AND ACCESS: The Army Corps of Engineers is involved in an upgrade program at Chimore airfield.

FORCES DEPLOYED: Bolivia is heavily involved in international peacekeeping, including in the Congo, Guatemala, Cyprus, Kosovo, Kuwait, Sierra Leone, and East Timor. Bolivia has also committed a reinforced battalion to the UN's "standby" force.

Code Names: Blast Furnace, Cabañas, Fuerzas Aliadas, Fuerzas Unidas, Ghost Zone, Green Sweep, JTFEX, New Horizons, PKO.

Bosnia–Herzegovina

The Bosnia–Herzegovina Stabilization Force (SFOR) has transitioned from three divisions to three brigades to three task forces and from a force of 33,000 in 1999 to 16,000 in 2002 and 7,000 in 2004. The General Framework for Peace, known as the Dayton Peace Agreement, signed in Dec 1995, ended almost three and a half years of fighting, creating a 60,000-strong NATO-led Implementation Force (IFOR) for one year, which was then followed by SFOR. The agreement provided a new constitution for Bosnia, and two "entities" — the Federation of Bosnia and Herzegovina, and the Republika Srpska (RS) — were established underneath the umbrella of the state-level government. As the Bosnians have made progress toward military reform and disarmament, SFOR has drawn down its forces. The SFOR mission is drawing to a conclusion, to be replaced by an EU police force.

A US "warm base" (Task Force Eagle) will continue to pursue Persons Indicted for War Crimes in support of the International Criminal Tribunal for Yugoslavia. The US has donated hundreds of millions of dollars to help with reconstruction, humanitarian assistance, economic development, and military reconstruction in Bosnia and Herzegovina. US military assistance has gone toward efforts to train and equip the defense forces of the Muslim–Croat Federation, a program that concluded in Nov 2002.

Two scandals in 2002–2003 involved discovery of arms exports to Iraq by the Republika Srpska–based company VZ Orao and espionage by RS military intelligence against international organizations in Bosnia.

US COMMAND: EUCOM.

AGREEMENTS: SOFA (respecting IFOR/SFOR), Article 98 Agreement.

US ASSISTANCE: Receives Foreign Military Financing program grants, International Military Education and Training aid, eligible to receive grant Excess Defense Articles, receives aid for humanitarian demining efforts.

BASES AND ACCESS: Camp Butmir in Sarajevo serves as headquarters for the NATO SFOR. Tuzla AB is the primary support base for the Joint Forge and Task Force Eagle mission in the US Sector of Bosnia–Herzegovina. Three multi-national brigades/task forces make up SFOR: North in Tuzla, Southeast in Mostar, and Northwest in Banja Luka. US forces are assigned to the North.

Code Names: Aladdin, Amber Star, Blackbird, Blue Sword, Daring Lion, Decisive series, Deliberate series, Deny Flight, Disciplined Guard, Dynamic Response, Eagle, Falcon, Fervent Archer, Green Light, Hatchet, Joint Endeavor, Joint Forge, Joint Guard, Joint Guardian, Mountain Shield, Palladium, Provide Promise, Radiant Cirrus, Sharp Guard.

Botswana

Botswana has been active in the war on terrorism, especially in financial matters, and hosts an International Law Enforcement Academy, established in Jul 2000.

The Otse academy, located outside Gaborone, is internationally financed, managed, and staffed and provides training to police and government officials from southern Africa. The US has been the largest single contributor to the development of the professional Botswana military, and a large segment of its officer corps has received US training. Joint/Combined Exchange Training (JCET) special operations training also takes place between the US 3rd Special Forces Group and civil affairs units and the Botswana Commando Squadron.

US COMMAND: EUCOM.

AGREEMENTS: SOFA (13 Feb 2001), Acquisition and Cross-Servicing Agreement in negotiation (2004).

US ASSISTANCE: Receives Foreign Military Financing program grants, International Military Education and Training aid, eligible to receive grant Excess Defense Articles, participates in Africa Center for Strategic Studies conferences and seminars.

BASES AND ACCESS: The US International Board of Broadcasters operates a major Voice of America (VOA) relay station in Botswana, serving most of the African continent.

Code Names: Diamond Cutter, Flintlock, MEDFLAG, Shared Endeavor, Silver Eagle.

Brazil

Brazil is the only country that borders on all three of the major coca-producing nations in the world and is an important transit country for illegal narcotics flows to the US and Europe; it faces a growing domestic drug abuse problem. The relationship between the US and Brazil has been warm since 1995, and President Bush met with President Henrique Cardoso within three months of his inauguration. President Bush then invited President-elect Lula to Washington in Dec 2002, and President Lula again visited Washington on 20 Jun 2003.

US–Brazilian military relations have focused on counter-narcotics, and since 9/11 Brazil has cooperated with the US in counter-terrorism activity centered on the tri-border area (TBA) with Argentina and Paraguay. In 2002, the TBA countries established a regional counterterrorism mechanism. Brazil is a member of the Financial Action Task Force.

US COMMAND: SOUTHCOM.

AGREEMENTS: Acquisition and Cross-Servicing Agreement eligible, Master Information Exchange Agreement (MIEA; post-9/11). A General Security of Military Information Agreement (GSOMIA), which would allow the exchange of classified information, has been in negotiation for some time.

US ASSISTANCE: Receives International Military Education and Training aid for military training, participates in Center for Hemispheric Defense Studies conferences and seminars.

BASES AND ACCESS: The US has no bases in Brazil, but the country hosts an operating location of the Trident missile testing Portable Impact Location System (PILS). Rio de Janeiro also hosts US Navy port visits and provides fuel service. A SOUTHCOM Tactical Analysis Team (TAT) is stationed in Brazil. At the end of Oct 1995, the 156th Fighter Wing, Puerto Rico National Guard, became the first air force unit to deploy to Brazil since the end of World War II, conducting air-to-air and air-to-ground missions.

FORCES DEPLOYED: The Brazilian military actively participates in international peacekeeping and other multi-lateral efforts.

Code Names: Cabañas, Eagle III, JTFEX, Oceanic, PKO, Transoceanic Exercise, Trilateral War Game, Unitas.

British Virgin Islands (BVI) (UK Overseas Territory)

The US and UK cooperate with regard to counter-narotics and maritime surveillance of the BVI; the UK has provided a police launch, and jointly funds police surveillance aircraft and other anti-narcotics equipment. The BVI closely cooperates with US law enforcement agencies. Legislation passed in 2003 addresses money laundering.

US COMMAND: The BVI falls under the jurisdiction of NORTHCOM, which was created in 2002.

Code Names: Cygnet Virgin.

Brunei Darussalam

Brunei has forged close military and intelligence ties with Australia, the UK, and the US, supporting international military forces in the region and the war on terrorism. Brunei has a defense agreement with the UK, under which a British Gurkha battalion (1,500 men) is permanently stationed in Seria, near the center of Brunei's oil industry.[6] In May 1999, Australia and Brunei signed an MOU on defense cooperation, and inaugural bilateral defense talks took place in Nov 1999

---

6. Gurkhas are an integral and extremely important part of the UK army. They are highly regarded around the world for their bravery and professionalism. The brigade has a current strength of 3,300 divided into two infantry battalions and support units. The bulk of the brigade is based in the UK, with one battalion in Brunei. Gurkhas' terms and conditions of service are governed by the 1947 Tri-Partite Agreement on Gurkha recruitment signed by the UK, India, and Nepal.

in Canberra, followed by intelligence cooperation talks in Nov 2001. The US and Brunei signed a Nov 1994 MOU on Defense Cooperation, setting the stage for joint exercises, training programs, and other military exchanges.

US COMMAND: PACOM.

AGREEMENTS: MOU on Defense Cooperation (29 Nov 1994), SOFA, Acquisition and Cross-Servicing Agreement eligible.

Code Names: CARAT Brunei, Cooperative Thunder, Cope Thunder, Mallee Bull, Night Leopard, NOLES, Penguin, SEACAT, Star Leopard, Ulu Rajah, Westpac MCMEX.

Bulgaria

Bulgaria became a member of NATO on 29 Mar 2004, and has been fully supportive of international military operations since it provided support for operations in Kosovo in 1999. After 9/11, Bulgaria hosted the deployment of six US KC-135 aerial refueling aircraft at Burgas, the first stationing of foreign forces in Bulgaria since World War II. Bulgaria has since offered additional bases and training ranges for US use, and deployed forces to Iraq. With a significant organized crime problem (money laundering and drug transit), the US has made law enforcement assistance its top priority in US–Bulgarian relations, stationing full-time Secret Service and DEA representation in country, along with a permanent FBI office. The US is also assisting in the development of the Bulgarian rapid reaction force to combat terrorism.

Bulgaria is a member of the South East European Peace-Keeping Force (SEEBRIG), and has hosted its headquarters in Plovdiv. It is undertaking a major reorganization of its defense establishment (Defense Reform 2004), supported by US military aid and training.

US COMMAND: EUCOM.

AGREEMENTS: NATO SOFA (16 Jun 1951), PfP SOFA (28 Jun 1996), NATO–Bulgaria Transit Agreement (signed 21 Mar 2001), Reciprocal SOFA, Acquisition and Cross-Servicing Agreement.

US ASSISTANCE: Receives Foreign Military Financing program grants, International Military Education and Training aid, eligible to receive grant Excess Defense Articles, National Guard partner with Tennessee, receives Enhanced International Peacekeeping Capabilities (EIPC) grants for training, participates in George C. Marshall Center conferences and seminars.

BASES AND ACCESS: During Allied Force, Bulgaria granted access to its airspace, and later provided ground transit permission for NATO forces and equipment entering Kosovo under Joint Guardian. The US has been operating aerial refueling aircraft from Sarafovo Air Base/Camp Sarafovo, near Burgas, since Nov 2001. On 22 Dec 2003, the Bulgarian parliament approved the establishment of permanent US and NATO military bases in Bulgaria. There have been rumors that the US would move C-130 transport aircraft from Ramstein, Germany, or U-2 and RC-135 aircraft currently in the UK, to Bulgaria. Bulgaria has identified the upgrade of three air bases, located at Graf Ignatievo (Plovdiv), Kamenetz, and Bezmer, as a priority for NATO and US use, and is seeking external funding to upgrade them. Bezmer is near the Koren and Novo Selo maneuver areas, already being used by French, Italian, and UK forces.

FORCES DEPLOYED: Bulgaria provided an NBC decontamination unit to Afghanistan as part of International Security Assistance Force, and in Sep 2003 deployed a battalion to Iraq as part of the Polish-led Multi-National Division in Karbala. In Jun 2004, Bulgaria rotated its battalions. Bulgaria has sent peacekeepers to Bosnia (SFOR) and Kosovo (KFOR), and was the only NATO Partnership for Peace state to participate with its own contingent in Bosnia.

Code Names: Black Sea Partnership, Briz, Bulwark, Combined Endeavor, Cooperative Adventure Exchange, Cooperative Associate, Cooperative Banners/Chance, Cooperative Best Effort, Cooperative Chance, Cooperative Determination, Cooperative Dragon, Cooperative Key, Cooperative Mermaid/Classica, Cooperative Osprey, Cooperative Partner, Cooperative Poseidon, Cooperative Zenith, Cornerstone, Dacia, Eloquent Nugget, Esperia, Joint Forge, Joint Guardian, MEDCEUR, Peaceful Eagle, Peaceshield, Prometheus, Rescue Eagle, Sea Breeze, Ursa Minor, Viking, Yolkos.

Burkina Faso

US International Military Education and Training for Burkina Faso has been halted because of the country's activities to destabilize its neighbors. Burkina Faso participates in Africa Center for Strategic Studies conferences and seminars (permission was granted in 2002).

US COMMAND: EUCOM.

Burma (Myanmar)

Official relations between the US and Burma have been cool since the 1988 military coup and violent suppression of pro-democracy demonstrations, and the US has imposed broad sanctions against Burma. However, the US government measures Burma by its position against international terrorism; the military government has sought to portray insurgent attacks as international terrorism to curry favor with the US.

US COMMAND: PACOM.

Burundi

A transitional government continues to struggle to reach final agreement with rebel factions and conduct local and national elections. The US has provided financial support for the peace process, but US bilateral aid — with the exception of humanitarian assistance — was ended following the 1996 coup. The US has supported the South African Special Protection Unit in Burundi to protect political figures.

US COMMAND: EUCOM.

US ASSISTANCE: Receives International Military Education and Training aid, participates in Africa Center for Strategic Studies conferences and seminars (resumed in 2003). Authorization to receive grant Excess Defense Articles is dependent on a successful peace process and cease-fire.

Code Names: Agile Lion, Distant Runner, Golden Spear, Neon Spear.

Cambodia

The US seeks closer cooperation with Cambodia in counter-terrorism and border security, legal reform, and anti-corruption; developing a smaller, more professional military; and supporting a credible Khmer Rouge Tribunal. But the US suspended indefinitely its $30 million aid program in Jul 1997 until progress toward free and fair elections was made. After 9/11, Cambodia made efforts to curry favor with the US, providing flyover and landing facilities to US aircraft on Operation Enduring Freedom missions. Since then, the US pledged $28 million to Cambodia at a Donors' Consultative Group meeting in Jun 2002, including health assistance and direct support to NGOs. In Jun 2003, the UN and Cambodia signed an agreement to establish a credible Khmer Rouge Tribunal to try former Khmer Rouge leaders responsible for the genocide carried out 1975–1979. The government has received international assistance to upgrade its counter-terrorism programs, instituting a computerized immigration system at Phnom Penh's international airport and supporting US requests to monitor terrorists and terrorist entities listed as supporters of terrorist financing.

US COMMAND: PACOM.

AGREEMENTS: SOFA, Article 98 Agreement (27 Jun 2003).

US ASSISTANCE: Receives aid for humanitarian demining efforts, participates in the Terrorist Interdiction Program. Public Law 108-199 for FY 2004 restricts assistance to the central government, with limited exceptions. International Military Education and Training aid and Excess Defense Articles are dependent on the lifting of current restrictions.

Code Names: Bevel Edge, Full Accounting.

Cameroon

Cameroon's political stability, central location in Africa, and excellent airport facilities make it ideal as a staging area for humanitarian assistance programs, or for evacuation operations necessitated by conflict in the region. The US seeks access to Cameroonian air and port facilities.

US COMMAND: EUCOM.

AGREEMENTS: SOFA (24 Feb 2000), Acquisition and Cross-Servicing Agreement eligible (26 Jan 1998).

US ASSISTANCE: Receives International Military Education and Training aid, eligible to receive grant Excess Defense Articles, participates in Africa Center for Strategic Studies conferences and seminars.

Code Names: Brilliant Lion, MEDFLAG.

Canada

US defense arrangements with Canada are more extensive than with any other country, and intelligence and law enforcement cooperation is also more intimate. The US and Canada share NATO mutual security commitments. In addition, US and Canadian military forces have cooperated since 1958 on continental air defense within the framework of the North American Aerospace Defense Command (NORAD). Response to the terrorist hijackings on 9/11 tested and strengthened military cooperation. In Dec 2002, the two countries established a Bi-national Planning Group to develop joint plans for maritime and land defense and for military support to civil authorities in times of emergency. Canada has participated in joint military actions in Afghanistan and, in 2004, assumed command of the International Security Assistance Force in Kabul.

The US and Canada have unrivaled cooperation on domestic terrorism. A Bilateral Consultative Group on Counter-terrorism Cooperation, established in 1988, reviews international terrorist threats to North America and plans joint approaches to intensify counter-terrorism efforts. The US attorney general and Canadian solicitor general coordinate policy at the US–Canada Cross-Border Crime Forum. The forum met in 2003 and established a counter-terrorism subgroup to enhance cooperation in law enforcement and prosecutions. Canada is an active participant in the Top Officials (TOPOFF) terrorist incident response exercise. Canada is one of three international partners with cooperative R&D agreements with the counter-terrorism Technical Support Working Group Program. Canada is also a member of the Counter-Terrorism Action Group, created by the G-8 countries in 2003, was one of six original countries to ratify the OAS Inter-American Committee Against Terrorism

(CICTE) agreement (2003), and is a member of the Proliferation Security Initiative and the Financial Action Task Force.

US command: NORTHCOM.

Agreements: NATO SOFA (16 Jun 1951), NORAD Agreement (12 May 1958), PfP SOFA (1 Jun 1996), Reciprocal SOFA, Acquisition and Cross-Servicing Agreement (11 Feb 1983, 22 Oct 1999), Agreement Concerning the Establishment of a Jointly Staffed Undersea Surveillance Facility in Halifax, Nova Scotia (Exchange of Notes, 23 Mar 1994), Global Hawk UAV Sensor Characterization, Interoperability and Airspace Management Project Agreement (7 Mar 2002).

The Permanent Joint Board on Defense, established in 1940, provides policy-level consultation on defense matters. The US–Canada Defense Space Cooperation Working Group overseas cooperative protects relating to space and ballistic missile defense.

The NORAD Agreement was first signed by US and Canada on 12 May 1958, and has been renewed eight times. The basic text of the agreement was revised substantially in 1975, 1981, and 1996.

Bases and access: The Canadian NORAD region has an underground complex located at Canadian Forces Base (CFB) North Bay, Ontario, with the headquarters at CFB Winnipeg. Eleven of 15 long-range North Warning System (NWS) radars and 36 of 39 short-range radars are located in Canada (the others are in Alaska) along the northern edge of North America. CFB Cold Lake, Alberta, and CFB Bagotville, Quebec, provide support to Canadian NORAD CF-18s and support AWACS aircraft when they deploy. Most Cold War US bases have been closed, though the navy continues to operate an important submarine and weapons testing facility at Nanoose Bay, British Columbia (BC). The US maintains a presence for liaison at Canadian Security Establishment (Canadian NSA) monitoring stations at Gander, Newfoundland, Leitrim near Ottawa, Massett in BC, and CFS Alert at the tip of Ellesmere Island. Though the US closed its main submarine monitoring station at Argentia, Newfoundland, in May 1995, the Canadian Forces Integrated Undersea Surveillance System Centre was opened at Trinity, Halifax, as an integral part of the Integrated Undersea Surveillance System (IUSS). The Air Force Technical Application Center (AFTAC) maintains nuclear monitoring stations at Flin Flon, Manitoba, and Alert.

Forces deployed: During Operation Enduring Freedom (Operation Apollo) and International Security Assistance Force (Operation Athena) in Afghanistan, Canada contributed the first coalition Task Group to arrive in theater and became a full partner in the war on terror, deploying special operations forces of its own clandestine JTF-2. Some 3,500 total personnel served from Oct 2001 through the end of 2003 in Kandahar as well as on seven ships in the Arabian Gulf, and with

CP 140 Aurora (P-3C) maritime surveillance aircraft (through Jun 2003 as part of US Task Force 57). As of 2004, Canada had 2,100 personnel in the CENTCOM (1,100 land, 200 air, and 800 naval). On 9 Feb 2004, a Canadian lieutenant general assumed command of the NATO-led peacekeeping mission in Afghanistan from his German counterpart. Canada also fully supports international peacekeeping operations, including SFOR.

Code Names: Amalgam series, Amazon, Anaconda, Apollo, Arctic SAREX, Ardent Ground, Artisan, Athena, Aurora, Bass Rock, Bell Buoy, Big Photo, Blue Flag, Blue Game, Bright Horizon, Bullseye, Caravan, Caravan Guard, Central Enterprise, Clean Hunter, Coalition Flag, Combined Endeavor, Constant Harmony, Cooperative series, Cross Check, Cygnet Globe, Dacia, Defense Challenge, Dogfish, Dynamic Mix, ECHELON, Fabric/Factor/Faculty, Fincastle, Fingals Cave, Frisian Flag, GI Joe, Global Cruise, Global Shadow, Global Mercury, Green Flag, Griffin, Hard Flint, Harpoon, Iceshelf, Jolly Roger, JTFEX, Kernel Blitz, Linked Seas, MACE, Maple Flag, MARCOT, Medicine Man, MTX, Neo Tapon, Northern Pike, Palladium, Peaceshield, Pond Jump West, Purple Caduceus, RIMPAC, Sapphire, Scope Command, Sea Breeze, Shant Doot, SHAREM, Skybird, Snow Shoe, Spinnaker, Strong Resolve, Tandem Thrust, TOPOFF, Torii, Tradewinds, Trial, Trilateral War Game, Unified Defense, Vigilant series, Western Vortex.

Cape Verde

Cape Verde has been an enthusiastic supporter of the war on terrorism and is a regular recipient of US food aid. Military assistance focuses on increasing the Cape Verde Coast Guard's ability to patrol territorial waters, and counterterrorism assistance works to develop a rapid reaction anti-terrorism force for the international airport.

US COMMAND: EUCOM.

AGREEMENTS: Acquisition and Cross-Servicing Agreement (post-9/11).

US ASSISTANCE: Receives International Military Education and Training aid, eligible to receive grant Excess Defense Articles, participates in Africa Center for Strategic Studies conferences and seminars.

Cayman Islands (UK Overseas Territory)

In Jun 2000, Cayman Islands was listed by multi-lateral organizations as a tax haven and a noncooperative territory in fighting money laundering. The listing led to the Caymans enacting laws limiting banking secrecy, introducing requirements for customer identification and record keeping, and cooperative programs for foreign investigators. Caymans was removed from the list of noncooperative territories in Jun 2001.

US COMMAND: SOUTHCOM.

Code Names: Mercury.

Central African Republic (CAR)

The US and CAR enjoy generally good relations, although concerns over continued reports of arbitrary detainment, torture, and extrajudicial killings affects US aid and assistance. In the late 1990s, France withdrew its forces stationed in the CAR.

US COMMAND: EUCOM.

US ASSISTANCE: Receives International Military Education and Training aid, eligible to receive grant Excess Defense Articles, participates in Africa Center for Strategic Studies conferences and seminars.

Code Names: Quick Response, Shepherd Sentry.

Chad

Chad is a participant in the Pan Sahel Initiative (PSI), a multi-year effort to wage war on terrorism and enhance regional security in the Sahel. A US-led Chad–Niger operation against the Algerian Salafist Group (GPSC) in early 2004 reportedly killed 43 terrorists, and there is ongoing Joint/Combined Exchange Training (JCET) special operations training by 3rd Special Forces Group to assist Chad in countering the small-scale insurgency in the north. Chad also participated in a Mar 2004 EUCOM counter-terrorism chiefs of defense conference in Stuttgart, Germany, with Algeria, Mali, Mauritania, Morocco, Niger, Senegal, Tunisia, and the US.

US COMMAND: EUCOM.

AGREEMENTS: Classified SOFA (Agreement on the Status of US Military Personnel in Chad), Acquisition and Cross-Servicing Agreement eligible (26 Jan 1998).

US ASSISTANCE: Receives Foreign Military Financing program grants, International Military Education and Training aid, eligible to receive grant Excess Defense Articles, receives peacekeeping operations (PKO) funding, receives aid for humanitarian demining efforts, participates in Africa Center for Strategic Studies conferences and seminars.

Code Names: Arid Farmer, Coronet Lightning, MEDFLAG.

Chile

Chile is a key military partner in the Western Hemisphere and is heavily involved in multi-national naval activities and international peacekeeping. As the fourth largest user of the Panama Canal behind the US, Japan, and China, Chile takes an active leadership role in exercises designed to guarantee the security of the canal. An extensive Joint/Combined Exchange Training (JCET) special operations program exists among Buzos Tacticos De Le Armada De Chile and SEAL Team 4, 8th Special Operations Squadron, 16th Special Operations Wing, and 23rd Special Tactics Squadron at Iquique, Vina Del Mar, and La Serena. There are also regular port visits by US Navy ships at Punta Arenas and Valparaiso.

US COMMAND: SOUTHCOM.

AGREEMENTS: Acquisition and Cross-Servicing Agreement (17 Oct 2000).

US ASSISTANCE: Receives Foreign Military Financing program grants, International Military Education and Training aid, eligible to receive grant Excess Defense Articles, receives Enhanced International Peacekeeping Capabilities (EIPC) grants for training, receives International Narcotics Control and Law Enforcement funding.

FORCES DEPLOYED: Chile rapidly deployed a force to Haiti in 2004.

Code Names: Bell Buoy, Cabañas, CI Bilateral Exchange, Eagle, Fuerzas Aliadas, Fuerzas Unidas, MARCOT, Oceanic, PANAMAX, Peace Puma, PKO, RIMPAC, Salitre, Silent Pearl, Transoceanic Exercise, Unitas.

China

Relations between the US and China have weathered the bombing of the Chinese embassy in Belgrade in May 1999 and the collision by a Chinese F-8 fighter with a US EP-3 reconnaissance plane in international waters in Apr 2001, which forced the US plane to make an emergency landing on Hainan Island. Following 9/11, the US and China commenced a counter-terrorism dialogue. China actively participates in the Shanghai Cooperation Organization (SCO), established in 2001; assisted in the establishment of an SCO Counterterrorism Center in Tashkent, Uzbekistan; and participates in SCO joint counter-terrorism exercises. China offered strong public support for the war on terrorism, voting in favor of key UN Security Council resolutions supporting the US campaign in Afghanistan. China contributed $150 million in bilateral assistance to Afghan reconstruction.

The US and China have a small military-to-military relationship. The USS *Paul Foster* visited Qingdao in Nov 2002, and the PACOM commander visited China 13–17 Dec 2002. President Bush has met top Chinese leaders half a dozen times, and military-to-military relations have improved as overall normalization has moved forward. China is also an important partner with regard to the ongoing tensions over North Korea's nuclear weapons program.

US COMMAND: PACOM.

AGREEMENTS: Presidents Putin and Jiang signed a Treaty of Friendship and Cooperation in Jul 2001.

US ASSISTANCE: PL 106-65 (FY 2000 National Defense Authorization Act) limits the US to direct aid in the areas of humanitarian assistance/disaster relief (HA/DR) and other nonwarfighting venues. China participated in Asia-Pacific Center for Security Studies executive courses for the first time in 2003.

BASES AND ACCESS: In the 1970s, when China and the US made common cause against the Soviet Union, the Chinese agreed to cooperate with the US to establish two intelligence collection facilities along the Soviet border at Qitai and Korla in the Xinjiang Uighur autonomous region. After many years of delay, a basic agreement was signed in Jan 1980, and the CIA-run stations began joint operation later that year. Later, seismic stations were also established to monitor Soviet/Russian nuclear testing. In the mid-1990s, a drug intelligence collection station monitoring Burma was reportedly set up in Ruili.

Code Names: Cobra Joe, Cope Thunder, Peace Pearl.

Colombia

Colombia is the source of most of the cocaine and heroin consumed in the US and the centerpiece of the US counter-narcotics effort. In 1999, Colombia developed Plan Colombia to fight the drug war, promote a peace process, and revive the economy. US assistance supported achievement of that plan through 2002, incorporating cooperation with Colombia's neighbors and interdiction of drug movements in the Caribbean and Central America. Since 2002, US training has refocused on assisting the Colombian military in a new campaign against "narco-terrorists." In 2003 and 2004, Congress provided Expanded Authority to use counter-drug funds for counter-terrorism missions in Colombia, accepting the US government's assertion that there was no distinction between narco-trafficker and terrorist activity, hence the term *narco-terrorist*. Expanded Authority also permits greater intelligence sharing and allows Colombia to use US-funded equipment for counter-terrorism missions. In Mar 2004 testimony before Congress, SOUTHCOM commander Gen. James T. Hill stated that he had been to Colombia 23 times since he took command.

Long-term effects of progress in the war on drugs/terror are difficult to assess. In 2004, the US reported that homicides, kidnappings, robberies, and thefts were down, and cocaine eradication was up. US intelligence is tracking an elevated rate of desertion from Colombian narco-terrorist ranks, and the United Self-Defense Forces of Colombia (Autodefensas Unidas de Colombia;

AUC) declared a cease-fire in Dec 2002. In Jul 2003, the AUC and government of Colombia agreed to formal peace talks.

With expanded US assistance, the Colombian military has become more aggressive in operations against the Revolutionary Armed Forces of Colombia (Fuerzas Armadas Revolucionarios de Colombia; FARC), the National Liberation Army (Ejército de Liberación Nacional de Colombia; ELN), and the AUC. There have been fewer terrorist attacks on the electrical grid, pipeline, and other civilian infrastructure. Colombia has resumed a robust Air Bridge Denial Program to monitor air traffic. The US also claims that none of the Colombian units that US forces have vetted and trained has been found to have committed human rights abuses. US military units have trained and worked with Colombian helicopter units, riverine combat elements, and the Counter Narcotics Brigade and the 1st Counterdrug Battalion. US special operations forces (SOF) from the 7th Special Forces Group, Navy SEALs, and 6th Special Operations Squadron have also established a close working relationship with the Colombian Special Operations Command, the 1st Commando Battalion, the Lancero Battalion, and the Colombian urban counter-terrorist unit. At any one time, there are about 600–1,000 US military and intelligence personnel in country. US intelligence organizations work with their Colombian counterparts. In Jan 2004, the Joint Interagency Task Force — South in Key West, FL, hosted an interagency counter-narcotics trafficking conference that included high-level Colombian participation and set the course for future operations.

US COMMAND: SOUTHCOM.

AGREEMENTS: SOFA, Acquisition and Cross-Servicing Agreement eligible (28 Jan 2000), Article 98 Agreement (Sep 2003).

In 1997, the US and Colombia signed a maritime ship-boarding agreement to allow for search of suspected drug-running vessels.

US ASSISTANCE: Receives Foreign Military Financing program grants, receives International Military Education and Training aid, participates in Center for Hemispheric Defense Studies conferences and seminars. During the period 1988–1996, the US provided about $765 million in assistance to Colombia. In 1999, US assistance exceeded $200 million annually for the first time. A $1.3 billion FY 2000 Plan Colombia emergency supplement was approved in Jul 2000, in addition to previously programmed assistance of nearly $300 million for FY 2000.

BASES AND ACCESS: The US has built up an extensive surveillance and intelligence collection network in Colombia, at Araracurara, Cerro Maco, Leticia, Marandua,

Rio Hacha, San Andres Island, San José del Guarviare, and Tolemaida. US intelligence analysts and planners staff the Joint Task Force South Intelligence Center, located at the Tres Esquines military base, and the SOUTHCOM Tactical Analysis Team at Baranquilla. US military operations also take place from Apiay, a Colombian air force base, and Mariquita, home of the Colombia national police counter-narcotics air arm.

Code Names: Centra Spike, Constant Vigil, Majestic Eagle, Peace Panorama, Southern Warrior, Unitas.

Comoros

The Comoros, a Muslim country with historic trade ties to the Middle East, condemned the 9/11 attacks, but an Apr 1999 military coup had resulted in a suspension of US assistance to the country, and there has been little follow-up. France maintains a small maritime base and a foreign legion contingent on Mayotte.

US COMMAND: PACOM.

Congo, Democratic Republic of (DRC) (Congo-Kinshasa, formerly Zaire)

The UN Organization Mission in the Democratic Republic of the Congo (MONUC), established on 30 Nov 1999 in response to the Lusaka Ceasefire Agreement of Jul 1999, has expanded in size and mandate, particularly after the assassination of Laurent Kabila on 16 Jan 2001. By the end of 2002, all Angolan, Rwandan, Namibian, and Zimbabwean troops had withdrawn from the DRC, and Ugandan troops withdrew in May 2003. As of Jan 2004, 10,866 total uniformed personnel, 115 civilian police, and more than 600 international civilian personnel made up MONUC. A transitional government is slated to last until elections, slated for 2005 or 2006.

US COMMAND: EUCOM.

AGREEMENTS: SOFA (22 Jul 1994 Exchange of Letters), Article 98 Agreement.

US ASSISTANCE: There is no current US direct aid to the DRC. Participates in Africa Center for Strategic Studies conferences and seminars.

Code Names: Autumn Shelter, Golden Spear, Quick Lift, Neon Spear.

Congo, Republic of (ROC) (Congo-Brazzaville)

With a new 2001 constitution, presidential elections in Mar 2002, and a peace accord with the remaining armed anti-government group, the Ninjas, the ROC has achieved some measure of stability. Relations between the US and the government of President Denis Sassou-Nguesso are strong and cooperative.

US COMMAND: EUCOM.

US ASSISTANCE: Receives International Military Education and Training aid, eligible to receive grant Excess Defense Articles, participates in Africa Center for Strategic Studies conferences and seminars.

Code Names: Firm Response.

Costa Rica

Costa Rica is one of two countries in Latin America that does not have a military, relying on its Public Security Forces (PSF) for defense. It has become a close partner in the counter-narcotics war and the fight against international crime, complementing US law enforcement efforts. A Maritime Counter-Drug Agreement signed in 1999, the first of its kind in Central America, permits cooperation on stopping drug trafficking through Costa Rican waters. Joint/Combined Exchange Training (JCET) special operations training takes place between Costa Rican PSF and the 20th Special Forces Group at Murcielago.

US COMMAND: SOUTHCOM. Costa Rica is located in the Joint Task Force — Bravo (JTF-B) geographic operations area.

US ASSISTANCE: Receives International Military Education and Training aid, eligible to receive grant Excess Defense Articles, receives International Narcotics Control and Law Enforcement funding, participates in Center for Hemispheric Defense Studies conferences and seminars.

Code Names: Central Skies.

Côte d'Ivoire (Ivory Coast)

On 24 Dec 1999, a military coup ousted the duly elected president, followed by flawed elections that resulted in Section 508 of the Foreign Operations Appropriations Act sanctions and the suspension of US military assistance. An armed rebellion further erupted 19 Sep 2002, provoking the Security Council to create the UN Mission in Côte d'Ivoire (MINUCI) on 13 May 2003 to complement operations of Economic Community of West African States (ECOWAS) peacekeeping force and French troops.

After the Sep 2002 events, the Ivoirian government criticized the French for failing to uphold commitments under the 1961 mutual defense treaty by helping government forces to recapture rebel-held areas. France did send additional forces, reaching a total of around 4,000 troops by the end of 2003, in addition to some 3,000 ECOWAS troops.

US COMMAND: EUCOM.

AGREEMENTS: SOFA (2 Nov 1998), Acquisition and Cross-Servicing Agreement in negotiation (2004), Article 98 Agreement.

BASES AND ACCESS: Imminent Danger Pay was authorized for US forces in Feb 2003.

A 1961 mutual defense treaty with France provides for the stationing of French forces in Côte d'Ivoire. The 43rd Marine Infantry Battalion is based in Port Bouet adjacent to the Abidjan Airport and has normally more than 500 troops assigned.

US ASSISTANCE: Sanctions will remain in place until the president either waives them or a democratically elected government has taken office. By exercising post-9/11 waivers to Section 508, the US has provided some some small-scale efforts in the country and provided Africa Regional Economic Support Funds (ESF) to undertake counter-terrorism cooperation. Abidjan is host to a large and wealthy community of Lebanese merchants whose relations with questionable charities or possibly Hezbollah are areas of concern for US intelligence.

Code Names: Aspiring Falcon, Assured Lift, Autumn Return, Flintlock, MEDFLAG.

Croatia

On 2 May 2003, the US joined Croatia, Albania, and Macedonia in signing the Adriatic Charter, in which the three NATO aspirants pledged their commitment to NATO values. Croatia joined NATO's Partnership for Peace on 25 May 2000 and became an aspirant for NATO membership on 14 May 2002. Failure to fully cooperate with the International Criminal Tribunal for the Former Yugoslavia (ICTY) has stood in the way of movement forward on NATO membership and in ratification of Croatia's EU Stabilization and Association Agreement.

The US is working with the Croatian military to create an Air Sovereignty Operations Center and integrate into the NATO air defense structure. Joint/Combined Exchange Training (JCET) special operations training takes place among 3rd Battalion, 10th Special Forces Group, and the 350th Military Intelligence Battalion in Zagreb, and among missile boats (PTGS) *Kresimir* and *Sibenik, Mirna*-class PC, combat swimmer unit and submarine rescue ship *Faust Vranic,* and US Navy SEALs at Split.

US COMMAND: EUCOM.

AGREEMENTS: PfP SOFA (10 Feb 2002), SOFA (respecting IFOR), Acquisition and Cross-Servicing Agreement (2002).

US ASSISTANCE: Receives Foreign Military Financing program grants, receives International Military Education and Training aid, participates in EUCOM Joint Contact Team Program, eligible to receive grant Excess Defense Articles (eligible in FY 2002), National Guard partner with Minnesota, receives aid for humanitarian demining efforts, receives peacekeeping operations (PKO) funding.

BASES AND ACCESS: The 16th Air Expeditionary Wing, located in Zagreb, Croatia, worked as part of Joint Guardian to monitor Bosnia–Herzegovina airspace. NATO controllers successfully completed handover of Bosnia-Herzegovina airspace at 10,000–28,000 feet to Croatia Control Limited on 27 Dec 2001. Regular port visits by US Navy ships take place in Dubrovnik, Split, and Zadar.

FORCES DEPLOYED: Croatia has contributed troops to UN operations in Sierra Leone, Ethiopia–Eritrea, and Kashmir. It also sent a military police unit to support the International Security Assistance Force in Afghanistan.

Code Names: Adriatic Phiblex, Combined Endeavor, Cooperative series, Croatian Phiblex, Dacia, Deny Flight, Eagle, Eloquent Nugget, Quick Lift, Resolute Barbara, Slunj, Taming the Dragon, Viking.

Cuba

Joint Task Force — Guantanamo (formerly JTF 160) at the US naval complex at Guantanamo Bay, was established in Jan 2002 to oversee the US detention and interrogation facility (Camp Delta, originally Camp X-Ray) for al Qaeda, Taliban, and other terrorist personnel who come under US control as a result of the ongoing war on terrorism. It also serves as the military's focal point for interrogation operations in support of Operation Enduring Freedom. Intelligence operations at Guantanamo have provided information regarding terrorist organizations, leadership, finances, and planned and potential attacks. Guantanamo also hosts military commissions established to try terror suspects.

US COMMAND: With the creation of NORTHCOM in 2002, Cuba no longer falls under SOUTHCOM, but is under the jurisdiction of US homeland security organizations.

BASES AND ACCESS: The naval complex at Guantanamo Bay is on long-term lease from Cuba and houses significant fair-weather and open-water training areas, a naval air station, marine barracks, an intelligence collection station, radar supporting counter-narcotics missions, as well as the Camp Delta/X-Ray Guard and Security Force.

Code Names: Able Manner, Able Vigil, Marathon, Present Haven, Safe Passage, Sea Signal, Sentinel Lifeguard, Standoff Four, Uphold Democracy.

Cyprus

In 1974, Turkish troops landed in northern Cyprus following a Greek-backed coup on the island, effectively partitioning the country, with approximately 36 percent of the territory of the Republic of Cyprus not under the control of the government. A "Green Line" — a buffer zone — is patrolled by the UN Peacekeeping Force in Cyprus (UNFICYP). As of 31 Jan 2004, 1,262 total unifomed personnel are deployed. The Turkish Cypriot "Turkish Republic of Northern Cyprus," established in 1983, is not internationally recognized.

The US and Cyprus work closely on the war on terrorism, and Cyprus has offered the US use of its airspace and airport facilities. A Mutual Legal Assistance Treaty, which has been in force since 18 Sep 2002, facilitates bilateral cooperation.

US COMMAND: EUCOM.

AGREEMENTS: Cyprus Diplomatic Note (1 Mar 2002), Acquisition and Cross-Servicing Agreement eligible (20 Apr 1993).

BASES AND ACCESS: The Sovereign Base Areas (SBAs) are sovereign UK territory and cover 98 square miles of the island of Cyprus. They are run by the SBA Administration and have their own legislation, police force, and courts; they are in a customs and currency union with the Republic of Cyprus. US forces have been on RAF Akrotiri in the SBA for more than 25 years, originally in support of UN Security Council resolutions and the 1973 Arab–Israel accords, and now supporting U-2 (and other) intelligence collection and CIA activities in the Mediterranean and Middle East. US military personnel enter on a regular flight from RAF Brize Norton, UK. An NSA SIGINT station has been mentioned at Episkopi SBA (annex to Akrotiri), and another listening post is reported at Ayios Nikolaos.

Code Names: Cobra Shoe, Creek Dragon, Cygnet Vine, Lion Sun, Lion's Pride, Olive Harvest.

Czech Republic

The Czech Republic, along with Poland and Hungary, joined NATO on 12 Mar 1999, and the first NATO summit held in a former Warsaw Pact member country took place in Prague on 21–22 Nov 2002. Since 9/11, the Czech Republic has provided basing and overflight permission for all coalition and US forces, continuing its integration into the Western military system and making a significant contribution to the war on terrorism relative to its size. The Czech Republic initially deployed an NBC defense unit in support of Operation Enduring Freedom (OEF) and a field hospital in support of the International Security Assistance Force (ISAF) in Afghanistan. In 2003, it moved the field hospital from Afghanistan to Basra, Iraq, and deployed an NBC unit to Kuwait. After their return home in Dec 2003, the Czechs deployed a civilian–military cooperation unit and approximately 150 military police to Iraq. The Czechs also trained Iraqi diplomats in Prague and assisted in the effort to train Iraqi police in Jordan. In 2004, the Czech Republic deployed 120 special operations troops to OEF in Afghanistan.

The Czech Republic has been assigned to lead the NATO Multinational Chemical, Biological, Radiological and Nuclear (CBRN) Defense Battalion, including Belgium, Canada, Hungary, Italy, Norway, Poland, Portugal, Romania, Spain, Turkey, the UK, and the US. Activated 1 Dec 2003, the battalion reached final operational capability at Liberec in Jul 2004.

US COMMAND: EUCOM.

AGREEMENTS: NATO SOFA (16 Jun 1951), PfP SOFA (26 Apr 1996), Reciprocal SOFA, Acquisition and Cross-Servicing Agreement (19 Nov 1996).

US ASSISTANCE: Receives Foreign Military Financing program grants, International Military Education and Training aid, eligible to receive grant Excess Defense Articles, National Guard partner with Texas and Nebraska.

FORCES DEPLOYED: The Czech Republic operated a field hospital in Kabul in support of ISAF during 2002 and deployed a special forces unit to Afghanistan. Prior to Operation Iraqi Freedom (OIF), it maintained an NBC defense unit at Camp Doha, Kuwait, to provide theaterwide coalition consequence management support. The Czech Republic later deployed a military police company and field hospital as part of the headquarters of Multi-National Division (South-East) in Iraq. The Czech Republic has also contributed to peacekeeping efforts in Bosnia (SFOR) and Kosovo (KFOR).

Code Names: Allied Response, Ardent Ground, Cannon Cloud, Cathode Emission, Centurian Crusader, Clean Hunter, Combined Endeavor, Constant Harmony, Cooperative series, Dacia, Distant Thunder, Dynamic Mix, Esperia, Iron Dragon, Strong Resolve, Summit Cap.

Denmark

Since 9/11, NATO member Denmark has been proactive in the war on terrorism, contributing substantially to ISAF in Afghanistan and neighboring countries. In 2003, Denmark was among the first countries to join the "coalition of the willing," supplying a submarine, *Corvette*-class ship, and military personnel to the effort in Iraq to enforce UN Security Council Resolution 1441. Denmark has participated in the military operation Operation Iraqi

Freedom (OIF) as an active member of the US-led coalition together with Australia, Poland, and the UK, contributing personnel and equipment.

US command: EUCOM.

Agreements: NATO SOFA (16 Jun 1951), PfP SOFA (7 Aug 1999), Reciprocal SOFA, Acquisition and Cross-Servicing Agreement (8 Jan 1998).

Forces deployed: Some 100 Danish special operations forces deployed to Afghanistan as part of a multi-national task force under US command in 2002. A Danish Air Force C-130 deployed to Manas, Kyrgyzstan, in Apr 2002 to form a joint airlift detachment with the Netherlands and Norway. In Oct 2002, the three nations deployed 18 F-16s to form the European Participating Air Forces (EPAF) at Manas, flying combat missions over Afghanistan in relief of the French Mirage 2000 unit. Danish ground forces also contributed a small element to International Security Assistance Force.

For initial operations in support of OIF, Denmark contributed two surface ships and the submarine "The Seal" in the Arabian Gulf, as well as a surgical team in Jordan. A Danish infantry battle group then deployed to Iraq in 2003 as part of the Multi-National Division (South-East), incorporating a Lithuanian detachment, and including SOF. Danish peacekeepers also support SFOR in Bosnia.

Code Names: Action Express, Allied Response, Ample Train, Baltic series, Baltlink, Baltops, Bikini, Blue Game, Blue Harrier, Brave Eagle, Bright Horizon, Cathode Emission, Central Enterprise, Clean Hunter, Combined Endeavor, Constant Harmony, Cooperative series, Coronet series, Courageous Bat, Distant Thunder, Dynamic Mix, Harvest Partner, Joint Endeavor, JTFEX, Lark Song/Foxtrot, Linked Seas, MACE, Peaceshield, Sea Saber, SHAREM, Strong Resolve, Tactical Fighter Weaponry, Thor/Odin, Trial, Trident D'Or, Viking.

Diego Garcia (British Indian Ocean Territory)

Diego Garcia, a British-controlled island in the Indian Ocean, serves as a major military base for the US, hosting B-2 and B-52 bombers for Operation Enduring Freedom and Operation Iraqi Freedom, P-3 and other surveillance aircraft, aerial refueling and airlift, Australian F-18s, and a host of munitions and pre-positioned equipment-related activities. Heavy use in support of operations in Afghanistan and Iraq led to plans to build a more capable en route port to support PACOM and CENTCOM naval operations. Construction projects and other services in support of the US military in Diego Garcia are carried out by UK and US military personnel and civilian contract employees, mostly recruited from Mauritius and the Philippines. Maritime Prepositioning Ship Squadron Two and Afloat Prepositioning Ship Squadron Four are normally forward deployed at Diego Garcia in the Indian Ocean. In Jan 2003, both squadrons off-loaded their equipment in Kuwait prior to the commencement of major combat operations.

US COMMAND: CENTCOM.

AGREEMENTS: Reciprocal SOFA (with the UK).

A series of UK–US agreements regulate matters relating to the use of the territory for defense purposes, such as jurisdiction over US military and other personnel.

Code Names: Busy Lobster, Native Fury, Vigilant Sentinel.

Djibouti

The tiny East African country of 650,000 is considered a "front-line state" in the war on terrorism, has strong historic military ties to France, and hosts the only US military base in sub-Saharan Africa. Prior to 9/11, Djibouti had become an important refueling point for US military aircraft and a training area for US military personnel as well as ships and aircraft, and was a coalition member extending back to Desert Storm. In Nov 2002, the CIA used Djibouti to launch a Predator Unmanned Aerial Vehicle (UAV) over Yemen during the operation to kill an al Qaeda leader. Djibouti is a member of the Eastern Africa Counterterrorism Initiative.

US COMMAND. CENTCOM. Combined Joint Task Force — Horn of Africa (CJTF-HOA).

AGREEMENTS: Acquisition and Cross-Servicing Agreement, Article 98 Agreement (Jan 2003).

Djibouti has signed agreements securing overflight, landing, seaport, and basing rights and has signed contractual agreements for the establishment of medium-wave and FM Voice of America broadcasts, scheduled for completion at the end of 2004.

US ASSISTANCE: Receives Foreign Military Financing program grants, International Military Education and Training aid, eligible to receive grant Excess Defense Articles, participates in Africa Center for Strategic Studies conferences and seminars.

Djibouti receives about $90 million in US aid, the largest recipient of US aid in sub-Saharan Africa.

BASES AND ACCESS: Djibouti was designated a combat zone as of 1 Jul 2002. The first US forces arrived at Camp Lemonier, a former foreign legion post, in Jun 2002. In Oct 2002, the US established the CJTF-HOA, which coordinates coalition counter-terrorism operations in six East African countries and Yemen. Since the stand-up of CJTF-HOA, Djibouti has hosted rotating detachments of marines, the 10th Mountain Division, various helicopter and fixed-wing transport detachments, civil affairs, MPs and security police, and engineers. There is close cooperation between CJTF-HOA and French forces on such matters as force protection, force security, and air defenses. US forces also use Ambouli International Airport.

Some 2,700 French troops are stationed in Djibouti under agreements signed at independence, and constitute France's largest military base overseas. The French foreign legion keeps a brigade in Djibouti, and French Mirage jets regularly deploy along with Atlantique aircraft, which participate daily in coalition intelligence missions. Bouffard French military hospital is a key trauma care center in the area and helped stabilize victims after the terrorist attack on the USS *Cole* in Yemen in Oct 2000.

Djibouti also is the headquarters for the Combined Task Force — 150 multinational Indian Ocean task force, consisting additionally of forces from Germany, Italy, Spain, and the UK. There are two German Sea King helicopters based in Djibouti.

Code Names: Ebony Flame, Golden Spear, Neon Spear.

Dominica

The US and Dominica work together in counter-narcotics. In 1995, the US and Dominica signed a maritime law enforcement agreement, and in 1996 they signed mutual legal assistance and extradition treaties.

US COMMAND: SOUTHCOM.

AGREEMENTS: Activity-specific SOFA.

US ASSISTANCE: Receives International Military Education and Training aid.

Code Names: New Horizons, PKO, Tradewinds.

Dominican Republic

The close US–Dominican Republic relationship was underscored when President Hipolito Mejia visited President Bush at the White House in early 2003. The Mejia government supported the US in Iraq and has improved counter-narcotics and counter-terrorism cooperation, particularly efforts to control contraband and illegal immigration from Haiti. Joint/Combined Exchange Training (JCET) special operations training among Dominican air force special forces units and the US 7th and 20th Special Forces Groups takes place at Santo Domingo and Puerto Plaza.

US COMMAND: SOUTHCOM.

AGREEMENTS: SOFA, Acquisition and Cross-Servicing Agreement eligible (29 Aug 2000).

In 2002, the Dominican Republic became the first country in the Western Hemisphere to sign an Article 98 agreement exempting US military personnel from the jurisdiction of the International Criminal Court.

US ASSISTANCE: Receives Foreign Military Financing program grants, International Military Education and Training aid, eligible to receive grant Excess Defense Articles.

BASES AND ACCESS: US counter-drug naval operations reportedly have access to La Romana, Puerto Plata, San Isidro AB, and Sosua.

Code Names: Able Manner, Able Response, Frontier Lance, Fuerzas Aliades, New Horizons, PKO, Tradewinds.

East Timor
See Timor-Leste.

Ecuador
Ecuador's military relations with the US are dominated by counter-narcotics and US efforts to instill respect for civilian government. The US is one of the four guarantor nations (along with Argentina, Brazil, and Chile) of the peace agreement between Ecuador and Peru over undemarcated sections of the border. Since 1995, the Military Observers Mission to Ecuador Peru (MOMEP) has monitored the zone. Ironically, much more effort is expended on the northern Colombian border, which the US has pushed to secure, drawing most of Ecuador's best troops and alleviating any tensions with Peru. Ecuador also hosts one of SOUTHCOM's Cooperative Security Locations (CSL) in Manta.

US COMMAND: SOUTHCOM.

AGREEMENTS: Acquisition and Cross-Servicing Agreement (18 Oct 2000).

Both Ecuador and the US are signatories of the Rio Treaty of 1947, the Western Hemisphere's regional mutual security treaty. Although there are problems with money laundering, border controls, and illegal alien immigration, Ecuador shares US concerns over narco-trafficking and international terrorism and has energetically condemned terrorist actions, whether directed against government officials or private citizens. The government has maintained Ecuador virtually free of coca production since the mid-1980s and is working to combat money laundering and the transshipment of drugs and chemicals essential to the processing of cocaine.

Ecuador and the US agreed in 1999 to a 10-year arrangement whereby US military surveillance aircraft could use the air base at Manta, Ecuador, as a forward operating location to detect drug trafficking flights through the region.

US ASSISTANCE: Receives Foreign Military Financing program grants, International Military Education and Training and E-International Military Education and Training aid, eligible to receive grant Excess Defense Articles, National Guard partner with Kentucky, receives Andean Counterdrug Initiative (ACI) funds, participates in Center for Hemispheric Defense Studies conferences and seminars, receives aid for humanitarian demining efforts along the Peruvian border.

BASES AND ACCESS: In Nov 1999, Ecuador and the US concluded a 10-year agreement for access and use of Manta AB as a forward operating location for US aircraft monitoring drug trafficking flights through the region and in the Pacific zone. US operations from Manta began 1 May 1999. The bed down program developed facilities, ramps, and taxiways for four large (E-3 AWACS and KC-135 aerial refueling) and seven medium (P-3, Senior Scout, Army Reconnaissance Low) aircraft. With completion of the plan, Manta supports multi-faceted 24/7 all-weather flight operations.

Code Names: Cabañas, DFT, MEDRETE, New Horizons, Oceanic, PKO, Safe Border, Succumbios, Transoceanic Exercise, Unitas.

Egypt

Egypt is one of quiet Arab partners of the US, discreetly hosting US forces, cooperating with the US military and intelligence establishment, and almost always supporting US action. Egypt was a coalition partner in Desert Storm (but then, so was Syria), Egypt consistently supported US military action against Iraq during the 1990s, a close "liaison" relationship grew between Egyptian intelligence services and the CIA, and President Mubarak was the first head of an Arab state to make a public statement of support for the strikes on Afghanistan in Operation Enduring Freedom, providing Suez Canal access and security as well as overflight clearances.

Following 9/11, Egypt became a key supporter of the war on terrorism, cooperating in attempting to put greater control on financing of terrorist entities, and improving coordination on law enforcement and intelligence sharing. The first US–Egypt Counterterrorism Joint Working Group meeting was held in Washington in Jul 2003. In Jun 2004, Egypt was designated a full-fledged partner in the NATO Mediterranean Dialogue.

A central pillar of the US–Egypt bilateral relationship is the enormous program of security and economic assistance to Egypt, which expanded significantly in the wake of the Egyptian–Israeli Peace Treaty in 1979. US military aid to Egypt totals more than $1.3 billion annually. US military cooperation has helped Egypt modernize its armed forces. Under foreign military sales programs, the US has provided F-4 and F-16 jet fighters, M-60A3 and M1A1 tanks, armored personnel carriers, Apache helicopters, anti-aircraft missile batteries, aerial surveillance aircraft, and other equipment. The US and Egypt also participate in combined military exercises, including deployments of large numbers of US troops to Egypt. Every other year, Egypt hosts Bright Star, a multi-lateral military exercise with the US, and the largest military exercise in the world.

US COMMAND: EUCOM.

AGREEMENTS: SOFA (26 Jul 1981), granted Major Non-NATO Ally status, Acquisition and Cross-Servicing Agreement in negotiation (2004).

US ASSISTANCE: Receives more than a billion dollars annually in Foreign Military Financing program grants, International Military Education and Training aid, eligible to receive grant Excess Defense Articles, participates in Africa Center for Strategic Studies conferences and seminars.

BASES AND ACCESS: Prior to 9/11, the US had two CENTCOM-controlled facilities in Egypt and utilized an additional 20 Egyptian controlled facilities. Pre-positioned equipment was quietly stored for US forces, and a number of air and naval bases were kept in top shape for US use, particularly Cairo (East) and Cairo (West) air bases, and Wadi Kena. In 2001, Egypt granted clearances for more than 6,250 military overflights and for 53 US Navy ship passages. Regular port visits by US Navy ships and submarines took place in Alexandria/Ras El Tin, Hurghada, Port Said, and El Suez. The Multinational Force and Observers (MFO), established by the Egyptian–Israeli Peace Treaty, provides monitors and a liaison system between the Israeli and Egyptian defense forces in the Sinai.

FORCES DEPLOYED: Egypt continues to contribute regularly to UN peacekeeping missions, most recently in East Timor, Sierra Leone, and Liberia.

Code Names: Bright Star, Coronet Aspen, Coronet Scabbard, Eagle Arena, Eagle Resolve, Eagle Salute, Early Call, Eastern Castle, Eloquent Nugget, Golden Spear, Infinite Shadow, Iron Cobra, Neon Spear, Pacer Chariot, Pacer Forge, Pacer Lightning, Pacer Reed, Peace Luxor, Peace Pharaoh, Peace Reed, Peace Vector, Sand Eagle, Shant Doot, Ultimate Resolve.

El Salvador

Military assistance to El Salvador has dramatically declined since the end of the civil war in 1992. As a transit point for illegal immigration and drugs to the US, the US focuses assistance on counter-narcotics and border control, as well as training the El Salvador military in disaster relief and reconstruction. El Salvador is home to one of the three Cooperative Security Locations (CSL;

formerly forward operating locations, FOL) that support US counter-narcotic operations in the Pacific corridor and Colombia. The Salvadoran legislative assembly ratified the FOL agreement in Aug 2000. El Salvador was chair of the Organization of American States (OAS) anti-terrorism coordinating body, the Inter-American Committee Against Terrorism (CICTE), 2002–2003. Joint/Combined Exchange Training (JCET) special operations training among the US 7th and 20th Special Forces Groups, 16th Special Operations Wing, Special Operations Group (GOE), 4th Infantry Brigade, and 4th Infantry Brigade Detachment 4 takes place in San Salvador and Illopango.

US COMMAND: SOUTHCOM. El Salvador is located in the Joint Task Force — Bravo (JTF-B) geographic operations area.

AGREEMENTS: Acquisition and Cross-Servicing Agreement eligible (29 Aug 2000), Article 98 Agreement.

El Salvador is one of six nations to ratify the Inter-American Convention Against Terrorism (2003).

US ASSISTANCE: Receives Foreign Military Financing program grants, International Military Education and Training aid, eligible to receive grant Excess Defense Articles.

BASES AND ACCESS: The US CSL/FOL opened at Comalapa AB/San Salvador International Airport in Mar 2000. The El Salvador facility hosts navy P-3 (or similar-sized) surveillance aircraft on regular rotation. US Navy ships also regularly visit and fuel at La Union.

FORCES DEPLOYED: El Salvador sent a battalion-sized unit to Iraq in Jul 2003 for a one-year tour.

Code Names: Eagle, Fuertes Caminos, Fuerzas Aliados, PKO, Poplar Tree, Queens Hunter, Strong Support.

Equatorial Guinea

US military assistance (International Military Education and Training) is dependent on Equatorial Guinea taking steps to improve its human rights record. In the meantime, Equatorial Guinea participates in Africa Center for Strategic Studies conferences and seminars.

US COMMAND: EUCOM.

AGREEMENTS: Acquisition and Cross-Servicing Agreement eligible (26 Jan 1998), Article 98 Agreement (Sep 2003).

Code Names: MEDFLAG/MEDCAP.

Eritrea

Eritrea is a coalition partner in the war on terrorism, offering military assistance and use of facilities while at the same time struggling with a generally antagonistic relationship with the US over democratization and human rights. Since the cease-fire between Ethiopia and Eritrea in 2000, the UN Mission in Ethiopia and Eritrea (UNMEE) has established a 15.5-mile-wide Temporary Security Zone separating the two countries, bringing a large and diverse military presence. As of 31 Jan 2004, some 4,000 military personnel from 42 countries were deployed.

US military cooperation with Eritrea, which was suspended following the outbreak of hostilities with Ethiopia and a UN embargo on military coopera-tion with either side, has resumed on a modest basis. The US once operated its major Africa and Middle East monitoring station in Asmara, a station that continues to operate under Eritrean control with a US presence.

US COMMAND: CENTCOM. Combined Joint Task Force — Horn of Africa (CJTF-HOA).

US ASSISTANCE: Receives Foreign Military Financing program grants, International Military Education and Training aid, eligible to receive grant Excess Defense Articles, receives aid for humanitarian demining efforts, participates in Africa Center for Strategic Studies conferences and seminars.

BASES AND ACCESS. Imminent Danger Pay was authorized for US personnel oper-ating in Eritrea in Jul 2002. In 1953, the US signed a mutual defense treaty with Ethiopia. The treaty granted the US control and expansion of the UK-run Kagnew communications and eavesdropping base outside Asmara. In the 1960s, as many as 4,000 US military personnel were stationed at Kagnew Station. In 1974, Kagnew Station drastically reduced its personnel complement, while continuing as a remote collection station. In early 1977, the US informed the Ethiopian government that it intended to close Kagnew Station permanently by 30 Sep 1977. But in April, Ethiopia under the Mengistu regime abrogated the 1953 mutual defense treaty and ordered a reduction of US personnel in Ethiopia, including the closure of Kagnew Station. In the 1990s, it is believed that NSA and Air Force 26th Intelligence Group (Forward) personnel returned to Eritrea. An NSA–Israeli SIGINT station (called the 8200 site) also is reported on or near Dahlak Island.

Code Names: Golden Spear, Neon Spear, Safe Departure.

Estonia

Estonia became a member of NATO on 29 Mar 2004. Since 9/11, Estonia has supported the war on terrorism, Operation Enduring Freedom, the International

Security Assistance Force in Afghanistan, and the US-led war against Iraq. It approved unconditional overflight and landing rights for all US and coalition partners. US–Estonian Joint/Combined Exchange Training (JCET) special operations training take place among the Coastal Defense Company, US SEAL Team 2, and 7th Special Operations Squadron at Tallinn.

US COMMAND: EUCOM.

AGREEMENTS: NATO SOFA (16 Jun 1951), PfP SOFA (6 Sep 1996), Reciprocal SOFA, Acquisition and Cross-Servicing Agreement (21 Oct 1998).

Along with the other two Baltic states, Latvia and Lithuania, Estonia concluded the Baltic Charter with the US on 16 Jan 1998. Lithuania, Latvia, and Estonia have formed a joint peacekeeping battalion (BALTBAT), a joint navy unit (BALTRON), a joint system of airspace monitoring (BALTNET), and a joint military school (BALTDEFCOL).

US ASSISTANCE: Receives Foreign Military Financing program grants, International Military Education and Training aid, eligible to receive grant Excess Defense Articles, National Guard partner with Maryland.

FORCES DEPLOYED: In support of Operation Enduring Freedom, Estonia supplemented the Danish military contingent at Manas, Kyrgyzstan, Estonia's first foreign military operation. Subsequently, Estonia deployed two explosive ordnance disposal (EOD) units to Afghanistan. Estonia contributed a cargo handling team and an infantry platoon under US command for Operation Iraqi Freedom. Estonia further sent 45 peacekeepers to Iraq in Dec 2003. On 18 Jun 2004, Estonia deployed two small contingents of special operations forces. Estonia has contributed forces to the Stabilization Force (SFOR) in Bosnia and the Kosovo Force (KFOR) in Kosovo.

Code Names: Amber Hope, Amber Sea, BALTEX, Baltic Castle, Baltic Hope, Baltic Triangle, Baltic Venture, Baltlink, Baltops, Combined Endeavor, Cooperative series, Cornerstone, Dacia, Eloquent Nugget, Joint Endeavor, Joint Forge, Joint Guardian, MCOP-EST, MEDCEUR, Open Spirit, Partner Challenge, PASSEX, Peaceshield, Rescuer, Viking.

Ethiopia

Ethiopia is considered a "front-line state" in the war on terrorism, directly supporting CIA and Combined Joint Task Force — Horn of Africa (JTF-HOA) overt and clandestine efforts to apprehend terrorists in Ethiopia, and active in countering the Somalia-based Al-Ittihad Al-Islami (AIAI) in the region. After 9/11, Ethiopia has undertaken increased military efforts to control its lengthy and porous border with Somalia and has undertaken significantly enhanced counter-terrorism and military coordination with the US. Ethiopia has also shut down avenues of terrorist funding. Ethiopia is a member of the Eastern Africa Counterterrorism Initiative. The 10th Mountain Division worked with Ethiopian troops in 2003–2004, laying the groundwork for combat operations.

In Jul 2000, the UN Security Council set up the United Nations Mission in Ethiopia and Eritrea (UNMEE) to verifying the 2000 cease-fire and patrol the border. As of 31 Jan 2004, some 4,000 military personnel from 42 countries were deployed. Since the 1998–2000 war ended, some 150,000 of 350,000 soldiers have been demobilized, and the Ethiopian military is in the process of transitioning to an all-volunteer military force. In additional to professional military education and skills, US aid and training focus on peacekeeping operations and counter-terrorism.

US COMMAND: CENTCOM. CJTF-HOA.

AGREEMENTS: SOFA (27 and 31 May 1994), Acquisition and Cross-Servicing Agreement (post-9/11).

US ASSISTANCE: Receives Foreign Military Financing program grants, International Military Education and Training aid, eligible to receive grant Excess Defense Articles, receives aid for humanitarian demining efforts, participates in African Contingency Operations Training and Assistance program and earlier African Crisis Response Initiative (ACRI), participates in Africa Center for Strategic Studies conferences and seminars.

BASES AND ACCESS: Ethiopia has agreed to all requests for support to Operation Enduring Freedom, and offered access for basing, overflights, and site surveys. The US does not maintain permanent military bases in Ethiopia, though there have been consistent rumors of an intelligence collection station in Addis Ababa.

FORCES DEPLOYED: Ethiopia has a long history of participation in UN military efforts, dating back to the Korean War and including involvement in Rwanda (1996–1997) and the deployment of peacekeepers in Burundi and Liberia.

Code Names: Golden Spear, Nectar Bend, Neon Spear.

Fiji

Civilian governments in Fiji have been overthrown three times, most recently in May 2000, leading to suspensions of military aid and relations. Aug 2001 parliamentary elections, though judged free, have not reduced interethnic tensions, and there have been questions about the constitutionality of the composition of the cabinet.

Absent US relations, Fiji is a regional security partner of Australia, has an extensive Defense Cooperation Program (DCP) with Australia, and is linked in South Pacific initiatives to combat terrorism and transnational organized crime. Australia and Fiji signed a bilateral MOU on Counter-Terrorism in Mar 2003. Fijian–UK military links are also close, with a number of Fijian cadets training each year at the UK's Royal Military Academy at Sandhurst. A large number of Fijians exercise their right as commonwealth citizens to join the UK army.

US command: PACOM.

Agreements: Acquisition and Cross-Servicing Agreement (14 Apr 1998), Article 98 Agreement (2003).

US assistance: International Military Education and Training aid suspended. Eligible to receive grant Excess Defense Articles.

Forces deployed: Fiji's contributions to UN peacekeeping are unique for a nation of its size. It maintains about 550 soldiers overseas in peacekeeping missions, mainly with the Multinational Force and Observers (MFO) Sinai in the Middle East and the UN in East Timor. Fiji has also made an important contribution to regional assistance missions on Bougainville and the Solomon Islands.

Code Names: Bel Isi, Shanti Path.

Finland

Finland's 1994 decision to join NATO's Partnership for Peace (9 May 1994) and buy 64 F-18 fighter planes from the US signaled the abandonment of the country's Cold War policies. Finland became a full member of the EU in Jan 1995, acquiring observer status in the Western European Union. Since 9/11, Finland has been a solid partner with the US in military and intelligence cooperation, In Jan 2004, the Finnish security police created a special unit concentrating solely on fighting terrorism, the first of its kind in Finland.

All during the Cold War, the NSA cooperated with its Finnish partner, the VKL, in sharing SIGINT on the Soviet Union. It is assumed the exchanges continue. Joint/Combined Exchange Training (JCET) special operations training also takes place among the Utti Jager Regiment, Special Forces Command, and US SEAL Team 8 at Utti.

US command: EUCOM.

Agreements: Reciprocal SOFA, PfP SOFA (13 Jun 1997 with declaration), Acquisition and Cross-Servicing Agreement (25 Jul 1998).

US assistance: The US maintains a small foreign-military-sales-purchased training program with Finland.

FORCES DEPLOYED: Finland does not commit troops to military action but participates in humanitarian relief operations and peacekeeping. Finland provided the largest Civil–Military Cooperation (CIMIC) unit in Kabul in support of International Security Assistance Force. In 2003, Afghanistan was the single largest country recipient of Finland's foreign aid. Finland has also been actively engaged in the Balkans and has been a mainstay of other international peace-keeping efforts (such as the UN Interim Force in Lebanon, or UNIFIL, in south Lebanon, which ended in Dec 2001).

Code Names: Baltic Challenge, Baltic Eagle, Baltlink, Baltops, Brave Eagle, Combined Endeavor, Cooperative series, Eloquent Nugget, Frisian Flag, Joint Endeavor, Joint Forge, Joint Guardian, Lone Kestrel, Nordic Peace, Peaceshield, Viking.

France

Despite severe differences over the war in Iraq, US–French military and intelligence relations are actually quite strong. The French military is probably the second most active international force, after the US, with nearly 10 percent of the 435,000-strong military assigned outside metropolitan France for operations in Afghanistan, Iraq, the Horn of Africa, and elsewhere. As of 2004, more than 4,000 French military personnel were operating in CENTCOM countries alongside US forces. France has been particularly supportive of US operations in the Horn of Africa, contributing forces in support of the Combined Joint Task Force — Horn of Africa (CJTF-HOA) and Combined Task Force 150 and coordinating its own operations with US operations.

France is a founding member of NATO, announcing in Dec 1995 that it would increase its participation in NATO's military wing (France withdrew from NATO's military bodies in 1966 while remaining a full participant in the alliance's political councils). France also actively participates in international arms control and counter-terrorism activities, including G-8 activities, the Financial Action Task Force, and the new Proliferation Security Initiative.

US COMMAND: EUCOM.

AGREEMENTS: NATO SOFA (16 Jun 1951), PfP SOFA (2 Mar 2000), Reciprocal SOFA, Implementation Protocol (deployments to Air Base 125, Istres; 27 Nov 1997), Implementing Arrangement on Mutual Logistic Support (12 Jun 1995), Agreement on Airbases and Facilities (4 Oct 1952), Acquisition and Cross-Servicing Agreement (23 Feb 1987), US–France Agreement Concerning Technology Research and Development Projects (10 Jan 1994).

BASES AND ACCESS: Though the US does not deploy permanent military forces in France, since the breakup of the former Yugoslavia, the US has consistently operated from French soil, particularly at Istres (Air Base 125), where the 16th Expeditionary Operations Group has overseen aerial refueling and U-2 reconnaissance operations. US Navy ships and submarines regularly call at, and refuel at, Cannes, Lavera, Marseilles, Nice, Toulon, and Villefranche.

FORCES DEPLOYED: France has actively participated in peacekeeping and coalition efforts in Africa, the Middle East, and the Balkans. French military forces play a significant role in Africa, especially in former colonies. France maintains permanent military bases in Chad, Côte d'Ivoire, Djibouti, Gabon, and Senegal, and deployed crisis response forces to Côte d'Ivoire in 2002 and to the Central African Republic in 2003. France also led an international military operation to the Democratic Republic of the Congo in 2003.

France was the single largest non-US military contributor to Operation Enduring Freedom in Afghanistan. Twenty-five French naval vessels were deployed, representing a fifth of the entire French navy. France's only aircraft carrier, the *Charles de Gaulle,* operated in the northern Arabian Sea, flying 2,000 reconnaissance, strike, and electronic warfare missions. A detachment of six Mirage 2000 fighters and KC-135 tankers was based at Manas, Kyrgyzstan, supporting Anaconda and other operations until relieved in Oct 2002. France contributed marines, army mountain forces, and special operations forces in Afghanistan. Humanitarian assistance and airlift support was mounted out of Dushanbe, Tajikistan. After the fall of the Taliban, France deployed infantry to Mazar-i-Sharif, as well as engineers and a recon company.

Code Names: Air Brake, Allied Response, Amber Star, Arabian Gauntlet, Asterix, Balance Ultra, Baltops, Bell Buoy, Bright Horizon, Bright Star, Brilliant Foil, Cannon Cloud, Caravan Guard, Cathode Emission, Central Enterprise, Centrasbat, Clean Hunter, Combined Endeavor, Constant Harmony, Cooperative series, Coronet Star, Cossack Express, Counter Guard, Croix du Sud, Dacia, Destined Glory, Distant Thunder, Dogfish, Dogu Akdemiz, Dynamic series, Eagle Vision, Entgrou, Eugenie, European Mountaineer, Fancy, Frisian Flag, Global Mercury, Griffin, GULFEX, Jolly Roger, JTFEX, Mace, Majestic Eagle, Med Shark, MEDCEUR, Mothia, Neo Tapon, Neon, Northern Lights, Pacific Protector, Peace Armangnac, Peace Burgundy, Prairie Warrior, Rescue Eagle, RIMPAC, Sanso, Sea Breeze, Sea Saber, Sorbet Royale, Strong Resolve, Trial, Viking.

Gabon

In Sep 2002, Secretary of State Colin Powell made a brief visit to Gabon. The US had earlier negotiated access to Gabon airstrips for transit, refueling, and staging for operations in central and southern Africa. Joint/Combined Exchange Training (JCET) special operations training is conducted by the US 3rd Special Forces Group.

US COMMAND: EUCOM.

AGREEMENTS: SOFA (1 Dec 1999), Acquisition and Cross-Servicing Agreement eligible (6 Feb 1996), Article 98 Agreement.

US ASSISTANCE: Receives International Military Education and Training aid, eligible to receive grant Excess Defense Articles, participates in Africa Center for Strategic Studies conferences and seminars.

BASES AND ACCESS: The 3rd Air Force conducted a site survey at Libreville, Gabon, in 2001 and produced a Base Support Plan.

FORCES DEPLOYED: Gabon plays an important role in UN peacekeeping in the Central African Republic (MINURCA).

Code Names: Autumn Shelter, MEDFLAG, WATC.

Gambia

Sanctions imposed against Gambia in accordance with Section 508 of the Foreign Operations Appropriations Act as a result of the 1994 coup were lifted after presidential and legislative elections in Oct 2001 and Jan 2002. The president of Gambia, Yahya Jammeh, spoke out strongly in support of the war on terrorism and has instituted laws to block terrorist financing.

US COMMAND: EUCOM.

AGREEMENTS: Article 98 Agreement (Oct 2002), Article 98 Agreement.

US ASSISTANCE: Receives International Military Education and Training aid (recommenced in FY 2003), eligible to receive grant Excess Defense Articles, participates in Africa Center for Strategic Studies conferences and seminars.

FORCES DEPLOYED: Gambia has participated in the Economic Community of West Africa's Monitoring Group (ECOMOG) since 1990, deploying peacekeepers in Sierra Leone, Guinea–Bissau, and, in 2003, Liberia. Gambian forces have also participated in peacekeeping operations in Bosnia, Kosovo, Democratic Republic of Congo, Eritrea, and East Timor.

Georgia

The election of pro-Western Mikhail Saakashvili on 4 Jan 2004 solidified close US–Georgian military relations, and Georgia has expressed interest in joining NATO. Domestically, though, Georgia would need to resolve conflicts in Abkhazia, South Ossetia, and Adjara, and improve Georgian–Russian relations. Relations with Russia have been strained over accusations of Georgian support for Chechen fighters, the status of Ossetia and Abkhazia, and remaining Russian bases in Georgia. The United Nations Observer Mission in

Georgia (UNOMIG) was established in Aug 1993 to verify compliance with the cease-fire agreement with Abkhaz authorities.

Georgia has been a strong supporter in the war on terrorism, granting the US overflight rights and potential basing. Georgia joined the NATO Partnership for Peace on 23 Mar 1994. Since 9/11, US military operations and CIA activity have been focused on the reported presence of international terrorists and Chechen fighters in Georgia's Pankisi Gorge, near the border with Chechnya. Georgian officials said in 2002 that there were Afghan and Arab fighters in the area, and Russian defense minister Sergei Ivanov called the area "a mini-Afghanistan on Russia's doorstep." Starting in May 2002, the US Georgia Train and Equip Program (GTEP) provided training to Georgian military, interior ministry troops, and border guards to enhance Georgian control in the Pakisi Gorge and over the breakaway regions of Abkhazia and South Ossetia. In Dec 2002, the program transitioned from special operations forces (SOF) to Marine Corps Forces, Europe.

US COMMAND: EUCOM, effective 1 Oct 1998.

AGREEMENTS: SOFA (bilateral for specific activity), Agreement Concerning Cooperation in the Area of the Prevention of Proliferation of Weapons of Mass Destruction and the Promotion of Defense and Military Relations (17 Jul 1997), PfP SOFA (18 Jul 1997), Agreement on Humanitarian and Technical Economic Assistance (31 Jul 1992), Acquisition and Cross-Servicing Agreement eligible (26 Jan 1998). Article 98 Agreement.

A US–Georgia Bilateral Working Group on Defense and Military Cooperation oversees relations.

US ASSISTANCE: Receives Foreign Military Financing program grants, International Military Education and Training aid, eligible to receive grant Excess Defense Articles (received UH-1H helicopters in Oct 2001); receives aid for humanitarian demining efforts, particularly in the Abkhazian region; National Guard partner with Georgia; participates in the Export Control and Related Border Security Assistance program; participates in George C. Marshall Center conferences and seminars. The US provided Georgia approximately $1.2 billion in assistance through 2001, averaging about $100 million annually.

BASES AND ACCESS: Imminent Danger Pay was authorized for US forces in Georgia in Jul 2002. US Customs Service–Georgian border guard projects under construction include the Tbilisi Aviation Detachment, Poti Coast Guard Station, Red Bridge Border Guard Station, and Lilo Training Complex. US Navy ships make regular calls to Georgia.

FORCES DEPLOYED: Georgia contributed a small contingent to Iraq in Aug 2003. In 2004, it deployed a battalion-sized unit, including Georgian SOF.

Code Names: Atlas Drop, Auburn Endeavor, Black Sea Partnership, Centrasbat, Combined Endeavor, Cooperative series, Cornerstone, Eloquent Nugget, Joint Guardian, MEDCEUR, Peaceful Bridge, Peaceshield, Phazisi, Rescue Eagle, Rescuer, SAREX, Sea Breeze.

Germany

Close German–US military and intelligence cooperation derives from the Cold War, and the US continues to maintain some of its most critical intelligence and counter-terrorism bases on German soil. Since 9/11, Germany has made unprecedented military contributions overseas in Afghanistan and the Horn of Africa. NATO member Germany is fully involved in all international fora relating to arms control, nonproliferation, and counter-terrorism, including the new Proliferation Security Initiative and the Financial Action Task Force.

The US made significant reductions in its troop levels in Germany after the Cold War ended, through some 70,000 military personnel remain in the country, and Germany hosts the headquarters of the US European Command and many of its subordinate commands. Annually, Germany contributes almost a billion dollars to offset the costs of maintaining US military forces on its soil, representing about 20 percent of US nonpersonnel stationing costs in the country. Germany is one of six European nations to continue to host US nuclear weapons.

US COMMAND: EUCOM.

AGREEMENTS: NATO SOFA (16 Jun 1951), Toolchest Technical Agreement (nuclear weapons), SOFA (Supplemental Agreement 3 Aug 1959, updated and effective 29 Mar 1998), PfP SOFA (24 Oct 1998), 4 Plus 2 Implementing Notes (12 Sep 1994; US military activities in the territory of the former German Democratic Republic), Acquisition and Cross-Servicing Agreement (21 Jan 1983), High Altitude Long Endurance (HALE) Unmanned Aerial Vehicle Concept of Operations, Sensor Integration and Flight Demonstration Project Agreement (Global Hawk; Oct 2001).

BASES AND ACCESS: Germany ranks number one in hosting a permanent US overseas military presence, with some 70,000 military personnel at some 250 bases and facilities. One of the army's four corps and 2 of the army's 10 divisions are based in Germany (a total of four brigades in 2004). The greatest numbers of air force installations in Europe are located in Germany. Germany also hosts a number of important intelligence installations, particularly Bad Aibling station near Munich, as well as US special operations commands and units serving Europe and Africa.

Many of these intelligence and special operations commands directly support US military operations in Iraq and other locations even if Germany is not itself involved. An example is Task Force Firepower at Ramstein AB, which provided support to Joint Special Operations Task Force — North in Iraq. In 2003, thousands of containers of munitions and equipment for US forces were shipped from Nordenham, Germany, to Kuwait for Operation Iraqi Freedom (OIF).

The US continues to withdraw forces from Germany and consolidate its enormous Cold War infrastructure. US Air Force and German authorities signed an agreement 23 Dec 1999 to close Rhein Main AB (at Frankfurt IAP) and return the base to Germany by 31 Dec 2005. Efficient Basing Granfenwoehr is an initiative to restation a brigade combat team from 13 installations in central Germany to a single location at Grafenwoehr. In 2003, the US identified 13 installations in the Giessen and Freiberg area for closure. The DOD announced in Aug 2004 that the two heavy divisions currently stationed in Germany would be eventually redeployed to the US as a result of the "Global Posture Review." The divisions will be replaced with a light Army Stryker brigade, ending the Cold War deployment of US forces in Germany. An F-16 wing in Germany will also likely redeploy to southern Europe.

FORCES DEPLOYED: After 9/11, Germany deployed combat ships and maritime aircraft for operations outside Europe for the first time in more than 50 years, and the German parliament authorized deployment of ground forces in support of Operation Enduring Freedom (OEF) in Afghanistan in Nov 2001. Germany supported Anaconda with a special operations forces (SOF) unit under US command, and then continued to commit forces for OEF and the International Security Assistance Force (ISAF) in Afghanistan. Germany and the Netherlands were lead ISAF nations before NATO assumed command in 2003. A German air transport element operates out of Termez, Uzbekistan.

Germany has also been a major player in the multi-national maritime interdiction force in the Horn of Africa, Combined Task Force 150 based in Djibouti (Germany commanded Combined Task Force 150 Apr–Oct 2002). About 1,400 German personnel have been based in the Horn of Africa since Jan 2002. The German navy deployed frigates and patrol boats, as well as an intelligence ship operating out of Djibouti. German maritime patrol helicopters operate from Djibouti and aircraft fly missions in the Indian Ocean out of Mombasa, Kenya.

Germany ranked first among in personnel contributions to multi-national peace operations at the end of 2002, supplying almost 4,000 to the Kosovo Force in Kosovo, and another 1,300 for the Stabilization Force in Bosnia. Germany also made large financial contributions to UN peace operations, ranking fourth in absolute terms after the US, Japan, and France.

Code Names: Able Condor, Active Endeavour, Adventure Express, Agile series, Allied Response, Amber Star, Ample series, Arabian Gauntlet, Arcade series, ARRcade Fusion, Ardent Ground, Artful series, Assets, Astonish, Atlantic Resolve, Atlas Response, Austere Challenge, Avalanche, Azure Haze, Back Home, Baltic series, Baltlink, Baltops, Black Knight, Blue Game, Brave Knight, Breeze, Bright Horizon, Bright Star, Brilliant Foil, Burning Harmony, Cannon Cloud, Canyon, Caravan Guard, Cathode Emission, Celtic, Central Enterprise, Central Fortress, Centurion Crusader, Clean Hunter, Clove, Combat Track, Combined Endeavor, Conga, Constant Harmony, Cooperative series, Counter Guard, Crested Cap, Crested Eagle, Crutch, Cygnet Globe, Dacia, Desert Falcon, Destined Glory, Dimming Sun, Distant Thunder, Dogfish, Dogu Akdeniz, Dynamics series, Eagerness, Eagle Vision, Eagle Pipe, Ellipse Bravo, Enable Freedom, Fastener, Flying Rhino, Frisian Flag, Global Mercury, Golden Python, Grecian Firebolt, Green Flag, Griffin, Hawkeye, Hombre, Icon, Iron Dragon, Jaguar, Jolly Roger, JTFEX, Juniper Cobra, Kaleidoscope, Keen Sage, Lakota, Linked Seas, Mace, Majestic Eagle, Matador, Med Shark, MEDCEUR, MEDFLAG, Messiah, Millennium Falcon, Mothia, Mountain series, Musketeer, Neo Tapon, Nimble Lion, Open Spirit, Optic Windmill, Pacific Protector, Paper Chase, Peace Haven, Peace Tornado, Peaceshield, Phoenix Ark, Phoenix Over, Premier Link, Provide Promise, Provide Transition, Quicksilver, Quidditch, Reforger, Regional Cooperation, Rescue Eagle, Rhino, Sanso, Scope Sand, Sea Breeze, Sea Saber, Semester, Sentry Corsair, SHAREM, Sharp Eagle, Shining Hope, Silver Anvil, Silverfish, Skilled Anvil, Spartan Challege, Spiderweb, Starhouse, Starquake, Steel Box, Strong Resolve, Superbad, Swabian Crusade, Tabler, Toolchest, Trailblazer, Trial, Trident D'Or, Trojan Warrior, Tumbril, Unified Charger, Union Flash, Urgent Resolve, Urgent Victory, Victory Focus, Victory Scrimmage, Viking, Warstock, Wet Gap, Wiley.

Ghana

The US and Ghana have cooperated in numerous joint training exercises, culminating with Ghanaian participation in the African Crisis Response Initiative (ACRI) and the newer African Contingency Operations Training and Assistance (ACOTA) program.

The Ghanaian armed forces have a long record in peacekeeping operations, particularly in Liberia, Sierra Leone, and Côte d'Ivoire. Ghana also provides a platform for staging humanitarian operations (including Feb–Apr 2000 flood relief for Mozambique, and Sept 2002 EUCOM operation to extract Americans from civil unrest in Côte d'Ivoire) and regional peacekeeping training activities. The Kofi Annan International Peacekeeping Center, used to train regional armed forces in peace support operations, is supported by US assistance.

US COMMAND: EUCOM.

AGREEMENTS: SOFA (24 Feb 1998), Acquisition and Cross-Servicing Agreement eligible (6 Feb 1996), Article 98 Agreement.

US ASSISTANCE: Receives Foreign Military Financing program grants, International Military Education and Training aid, eligible to receive grant Excess Defense Articles, participates in African Contingency Operations Training and Assistance program and earlier ACRI (one of the first militaries to receive ACOTA training in early 2003), receives peacekeeping operations (PKO) funding, participates in Africa Center for Strategic Studies conferences and seminars. The Excess Defense Articles program has been used to supply deep-water patrol vessels for counter-smuggling, and several surplus naval transports have been supplied to support regional peacekeeping.

FORCES DEPLOYED: Ghana is the fifth largest contributor to UN operations. Military personnel have been deployed in Lebanon, Bosnia, Iraq and Kuwait, Western Sahara, Croatia, and Tajikistan. Ghana has also supplied troops for peacekeeping and peace monitoring operations in Liberia, Côte d'Ivoire, Democratic Republic of Congo, and Sierra Leone.

BASES AND ACCESS: The 3rd Air Force conducted a site survey at Accra, Ghana, in 2001 and produced a Base Support Plan.

Code Names: Focus Relief, MEDFLAG, WATC.

Gibraltar (UK Overseas Territory)

US COMMAND: EUCOM.

Code Names: Active Endeavour, Coronet Bat, Marble Tor, Neo Tapon, Power Drive, Rock Work, Royal Patrol.

Greece

NATO member Greece hosts US military bases and has been fully cooperative in the war on terrorism, offering unimpeded use of airspace, and more or less permanently stationing a Greek navy frigate in the Arabian Sea since 15 Mar 2003, Greece's most distant deployment ever.

Greece has a long history of dealing with domestic terrorism, and it scored a major victory in the summer of 2002 when Greek authorities captured numerous suspected members of "17 November," a terrorist group that had perpetrated numerous killings, including the 23 Dec 1975 assassination of CIA station chief Richard Welch, the death of four other US mission employees, and UK Defense Attaché Brigadier Stephen Saunders, killed in Athens on 8 Jun 2000. With its hosting of the Summer Olympic Games in 2004, Greece also received significant US and international support in security and counter-terrorism, as well as an upgrade of command, communications, and control facilities.

US COMMAND: EUCOM.

AGREEMENTS: NATO SOFA (16 Jun 1951), Sheepskin Technical Agreement (nuclear weapons), PfP SOFA (signed 9 Oct 1997), Mutual Defense Cooperation

Agreement (MDCA; 8 Jul 1990), Comprehensive Technical Agreement (13 Jun 2001), Acquisition and Cross-Servicing Agreement (8 May 1996).

In 1953, the first Greek–US defense cooperation agreement was signed, providing for the establishment and operation of American military installations on Greek territory. The current MDCA provides for the operation of a naval support facility at Souda Bay, Crete.

US ASSISTANCE: Receives International Military Education and Training aid, eligible to receive grant Excess Defense Articles. The US has provided Greece with more than $11.1 billion in economic and security assistance since 1946. By law, aid adheres to a 7:10 Greece:Turkey ratio.

BASES AND ACCESS: The Greek naval and air base at Souda, Crete, is used as a forward logistics site to support ships and aircraft in the eastern Mediterranen, and is the main remaining American base in country. The base hosted regular RC-135 and P-3 maritime patrol and intelligence collection missions.

The US closed three of its main bases in the 1990s (Nea Makri communications station, Hellenikon air base, and the intelligence station at Iraklion, Crete), as well as numerous remote communications sites, and withdrew the last nuclear weapons stored in Greece at Araxos air base in 2001. Pireaus, Corfu, Kalamata, Kerkira, Kithira, Piraeus, Rhodes, St. Theodore, and Thessaloniki are regularly used to support naval port calls and refueling

FORCES DEPLOYED: In support of Operation Enduring Freedom, Greece deployed one engineer company and staff officers in support of International Security Assistance Force in Afghanistan, donated material to the Afghan National Army, and deployed two C-130 transport aircraft and a support detachment to Karachi airport, Pakistan, for logistical support. During the period 1 Jan–20 Aug 2002, Greek aircraft transported Albanian, Croatian, Egyptian, Romanian, and Swiss aid. As part of NATO's Active Endeavour in the Mediterranean Sea, Greece also deployed ships and maritime patrol aircraft in support of Standing Naval Force Mediterranean (SNFM), and activated a comprehensive Advanced Surveillance System in the Aegean Sea. Greece has been an active participant in regional peacekeeping missions in Albania, Bosnia (Stabilization Force), and Kosovo (Kosovo Force).

Code Names: Adventure Exchange, Adventure Express, Agile Response, Alexander the Great/Alexandros, Allied Response, Ample Train, ARRcade Fusion, Ardent Ground, Breeze, Bright Star, Centrasbat, Combined Endeavor, Cooperative series, Cornerstone, Dacia, Damsel Fair, Destined Glory, Distant Thunder, Dogfish, Dynamic series, Eagle, Greek Knights, Hammerlock, Majestic Eagle, Med Shark, MEDCEUR, Megas Alexandros, Mothia, Neo Tapon, Peace Icarus, Peace Xenia, Peaceful Eagle, Peaceshield, Prometheus, Rescue Eagle, Sacred Company, Scope Axis, Sea Breeze, Sheepskin, Silent Guide, Strong Resolve, TAPON, Trident D'Or, Viking.

Greenland (Denmark self-governing terrority)

The US base at Thule, which currently provides early warning for the United States, represents an investment of $2.7 billion.

US COMMAND: EUCOM. Under the Apr 2002 Unified Command Plan, EUCOM gained responsibility for Greenland from JFCOM.

Code Names: Chrome Dome, Mystic Star, Pacer Goose, Pacer North, Volant Dew.

Grenada

Grenada and the US cooperate in counter-narcotics. In 1995, the US and Grenada signed a maritime law enforcement treaty. In 1996, they signed a mutual legal assistance treaty and an extradition treaty as well as an overflight/order-to-land amendment. Grenada receives modest International Military Education and Training aid.

US COMMAND: SOUTHCOM.

AGREEMENTS: Activity-specific SOFA.

Code Names: Island Breeze, New Horizons, Piercer, PKO, Tradewinds, Urgent Fury.

Guatemala

US–Guatemalan relations have been strained or impeded by continuing impunity in cases involving military participation in human rights abuses, concerns about military corruption, and a recent resurgence of abuses believed to be orchestrated by ex- and current military officials. US–Guatemalan military relations focus on counter-narcotics, disaster relief, and humanitarian operations. The US Military Group (USMILGP) represents SOUTHCOM and DOD in Guatemala. It is augmented by a Tactical Analysis Team (TAT) and Joint Planning Assistance Team (JPAT) element involved in the planning and coordination of all counter-narcotics-related activities.

US COMMAND: SOUTHCOM. Guatemala is located in the Joint Task Force — Bravo (JTF-B) geographic operations area.

AGREEMENTS: Activity-specific SOFA, Acquisition and Cross-Servicing Agreement eligible (29 Aug 2000).

US ASSISTANCE: Receives E-International Military Education and Training aid for military training, eligible to receive grant Excess Defense Articles, participates in Center for Hemispheric Defense Studies conferences and seminars. Because of continuing concerns regarding human rights, Guatemala is restricted by congressional mandate to receiving Expanded International Military Education and Training (E-International Military Education and Training) only.

Code Names: Fuertes Caminos, Fuerzas Aliades, New Horizons, PKO, Strong Support.

Guinea

Guinea has publicly supported the US war on terrorism, and in return the US maintains a modest military assistance program that provides military education, language training, and humanitarian assistance. Joint/Combined Exchange Training (JCET) special operations training is also conducted by the US 3rd Special Forces Group.

US COMMAND: EUCOM.

AGREEMENTS: Acquisition and Cross-Servicing Agreement eligible (26 Jan 1998).

US ASSISTANCE: Receives International Military Education and Training aid, eligible to receive grant Excess Defense Articles, participates in Africa Center for Strategic Studies conferences and seminars.

FORCES DEPLOYED: Guinea has participated in both diplomatic and military efforts to resolve conflicts in Liberia, Sierra Leone, and Guinea–Bissau, and contributed contingents of troops to peacekeeping operations in all three countries as part of the Military Observer Group of the Economic Community of West African States (ECOMOG) and UN peacekeeping efforts in Sierra Leone (UNAMSIL).

Code Names: Noble Obelisk.

Guinea–Bissau

Since suffering an army uprising in Jun 1998, a bloody civil war that created hundreds of thousands of displaced persons, and a military junta takeover in May 1999, Guinea–Bissau has been unable to establish a democratic government or the rule of law. On 12 Sep 2003, the president of the National Elections Commission announced that it would be impossible to hold elections. The army once again intervened on 14 Sep, and the president was placed under house arrest. Civilian rule was restored, but there were no elections until the Mar 2004 legislative elections, which were deemed free and fair. The US embassy suspended operations in Bissau on 14 Jun 1998, terminating military assistance.

US COMMAND: EUCOM.

US ASSISTANCE: Due to the Sep 2003 military coup, International Military Education and Training and other direct aid to Guinea–Bissau is prohibited by Section 508 of the Foreign Operations Appropriations Act. Sanctions can be lifted when the president reports to Congress that a democratically elected government has taken office in Guinea–Bissau.

AGREEMENTS: Acquisition and Cross-Servicing Agreement eligible (26 Jan 1998).

Code Names: Shepherd Venture.

Guyana

Guyana has strong links to the UK, and US–Guyana relations revolve around counter-narcotics and law enforcement. US military teams conduct civil projects and provide medical treatment in Guyana and hold a training exercise program with the Guyana Coast Guard. With US help, Guyana has established a Joint Information Coordination Center for counter-narcotics. Guyana purchased the former British minesweeper HMS *Orwell,* now known as the GDFS *Essiquibo,* in Mar 2001.

US COMMAND: SOUTHCOM.

AGREEMENTS: Acquisition and Cross-Servicing Agreement eligible (29 Aug 2000).

US ASSISTANCE: Receives Foreign Military Financing program grants, International Military Education and Training aid, eligible to receive grant Excess Defense Articles, participates in Center for Hemispheric Defense Studies conferences and seminars. In 2001, Guyana received four US Coast Guard patrol boats under Excess Defense Articles.

Code Names: New Horizons, PKO, Tradewinds.

Haiti

Haiti experienced continuing civil and political unrest in 2003, culminating in the flight of President Aristide on 29 Feb 2004 to the Central African Republic. Despite a constitutional transfer of power to the interim government and deployment of international peacekeepers in the Multinational Interim Force (MIF), many cities and towns continue to be controlled by rogue elements; police protection and central government services are either limited or unavailable. Peacekeepers from Canada, Chile, France, and the US deployed with the MIF. The UN assumed command 25 Jun 2004 when formal authority was handed over to the UN Stabilization Mission for Haiti (MINUSTAH). Led by Brazil, MINUSTAH is expected to be composed of 6,700 military and 1,600 police personnel from about 30 nations. All US military peacekeepers departed Haiti by Jul 2004.

Haiti is a major transshipment point for South American narcotics. Prior to the fall of the Aristide government, the US and Haiti signed a counter-narcotics letter of agreement 15 May 2002, and the US supported the counter-narcotics division of the Haitian national police and the Haitian Coast Guard, aid provided under a waiver on grounds of vital national security interest.

US COMMAND: SOUTHCOM.

AGREEMENTS: SOFA.

US ASSISTANCE: Receives International Military Education and Training aid, eligible to receive grant Excess Defense Articles.

Code Names: Able Manner, Agile Provider, Distant Haven, Fairwinds, Falcon, Frontier Lance, Maintain Democracy, New Horizons, Phoenix Shark, Restore Democracy, Sea Signal, Support Democracy, Tradewinds, Uphold Democracy, Victor Squared, West Eagle.

Honduras

Honduras has been a strong supporter in the war on terrorism, deploying a contingent to Iraq for Operation Iraqi Freedom (OIF), hosting the US military, and supporting counter-narcotics operations. The US Joint Task Force — Bravo (JTF-B) stationed at the Honduran Soto Cano AB supports counter-narcotics operations, intelligence collection, humanitarian deployments, and combined exercises.

US and Honduran forces conducted combined training as early as 1965. In 1983, the US began to increase the size and number of those exercises. In Jan 2004, Soto Cano supported the first deployment of the SOUTHCOM Standing Joint Force Headquarters (SJFHQ), conducting a two-week exercise with full connectivity to Southern Command headquarters in Miami. Joint/Combined Exchange Training (JCET) special operations training takes place among the US 7th and 20th Special Forces Groups, 16th Special Operations Wing, and 720th Special Tactics Group and the Honduran 115th Brigade and 16th Battalion in Juticalpa and Punuare; with the 4th Marine Infantry Battaliion in La Ceiba, La Venta, Soto Cano, and Trujillo.

US COMMAND: SOUTHCOM. JTF-B was established in Aug 1984 to exercise command and control of US forces in Honduras (it was previously known as JTF-11 and then JTF-Alpha).

AGREEMENTS: Acquisition and Cross-Servicing Agreement eligible (29 Mar 1988), Article 98 Agreement.

There does not appear to be a SOFA between Honduras and the US covering Soto Cano AB.

US ASSISTANCE: Receives Foreign Military Financing grants, International Military Education and Training aid, eligible to receive grant Excess Defense Articles,

National Guard partner with Puerto Rico, receives aid for humanitarian demining efforts, participates in Center for Hemispheric Defense Studies conferences and seminars, receives International Narcotics Control and Law Enforcement funding. Honduras's creation of a new combined military–police unit benefited from Excess Defense Articles boats, vehicles, and helicopters, including a 44-foot boat.

BASES AND ACCESS: The US presence at Soto Cano AB (previously known as Palmerola AB) in Comayagua, 747 miles northwest of Tegucigalpa, began in 1984. The base is primarily staffed by US military personnel from units in the US on temporary assignment. Soto Cano is the most capable C-5 airfield in all Central America. JTF-B commands approximately 190 military and about 730 permanent civilian personnel and provides command, communications, intelligence, and logistics support for US exercises and deployments. JTF-B also organizes and supports multi-national humanitarian, counter-narcotics, and disaster relief operations. Radars and surveillance teams are also operational at Cerro La Mole and on Swan Island. A SOUTHCOM Tactical Analysis Team is active at the US embassy.

FORCES DEPLOYED: The Honduran military contribution to OIF left Iraq in May 2004. Honduras contributed troops for the 1990s UN peacekeeping mission in Haiti and continues to participate in the UN Observer Mission in the Western Sahara.

Code Names: Ahuas Tara, Blazing Trails, Bold Eagle, Canvas Shield, Central Skies, Fuertes Caminos, Fuerzas Aliades, Golden Pheasant, Grazing Lawn, King's Guard, New Horizons, Peace Bonito, PKO, Poker Buff, Queen's Hunter, Strong Support, Support Sovereignty.

Hong Kong (Special Administrative Region of China)
Hong Kong is an active supporter of the war on terrorism, a participant in the Container Security Initiative, a member of the Financial Action Task Force, and an important partner in combating money laundering. Since the 1997 handover of Hong Kong to China, there have been few changes in borders, staffing, or technology export controls. The US has substantial economic and social ties with Hong Kong. About 50,000 American residents live in Hong Kong and more than 1,000 US firms are represented, accounting for two-way trade totaling $21.9 billion in 2002. Hong Kong regularly hosts US Navy ships.

US COMMAND: PACOM.

Code Names: Hong Kong SAREX, SHAREM, Westpac MCMEX.

Hungary
Hungary has been a NATO member since 12 Mar 1999, and has been slowly modernizing and downsizing its armed forces since it left the Warsaw Pact in

1990. Hungarian armed forces personnel are present in Bosnia (Stabilization Force; SFOR), Kosovo (Kosovo Force; KFOR), Afghanistan, and Iraq. Hungary made Taszar air base available to the US and NATO starting in 1995. After 9/11, Hungary provided basing and overflight access for US and NATO forces. Contributions since 9/11 have included expanded counter-terrorism training at the International Law Enforcement Academy (ILEA) in Budapest, equipment for the Afghan National Army and US Georgia Train and Equip Program (GTEP), and military and humanitarian equipment for Turkey. Hungary also provided a base to US forces for the purpose of training Iraq "opposition forces" associated with the Iraqi National Congress.

US COMMAND: EUCOM.

AGREEMENTS: SOFA, PfP SOFA (13 Jan 1996), Activities of US Forces in Hungary (4 May 1997), Acquisition and Cross-Servicing Agreement (9 Dec 1996).

US ASSISTANCE: Receives Foreign Military Financing program grants, International Military Education and Training aid, National Guard partner with OH.

BASES AND ACCESS: Taszar AB has hosted NATO and US forces since 1995 in support of operations in Bosnia and Kosovo. Ferihegy IAP in Budapest also hosted US operations during Allied Force in 1999.

FORCES DEPLOYED: In early Mar 2003, Hungary deployed a military medical unit to the International Security Assistance Force in Afghanistan. A small Hungarian unit operates in Iraq as part of the Polish brigade. Hungary also increased its presence in the Balkans (SFOR and KFOR) to replace other forces headed for Afghanistan.

Code Names: Ample Train, Ardent Ground, Brave Eagle, Carpathian Exchange, Combined Endeavor, Cooperative series, Dacia, Destined Glory, Distant Thunder, Dynamic Mix, Esperia, Imminent Horizon, Lariat Response, MEDCEUR, Nomad Vigil, PLANEX, Rescue Eagle, Strong Resolve.

Iceland

When Iceland became a founding member of NATO in 1949, it did so with the explicit understanding that it would not be expected to establish an indigenous force. Throughout the Cold War, Iceland's main contribution to the alliance was rent-free access to military facilities, the most important of which was the naval air station (NAS) at Keflavik. Since the end of the Cold War, Iceland has taken a more active role in NATO deliberations and planning. In 1997, Iceland began hosting Cooperative Safeguard, an exercise that attracts a large number of partner countries, including Russia. Iceland has also contributed uniquely to peacekeeping in Kosovo and Afghanistan, and offered the airport at Keflavik for any US operations in support of the war on terrorism.

US COMMAND: EUCOM. Under the Apr 2002 Unified Command Plan, EUCOM gained responsibility for Iceland from JFCOM.

AGREEMENTS: NATO SOFA (16 Jun 1951), PfP SOFA (signed 10 Mar 1997), Acquisition and Cross-Servicing Agreement eligible (25 Aug 1999).

BASES AND ACCESS: NAS Keflavik is still a major US base, and the Keflavik station represents the largest US military investment in Europe, with an estimated replacement value of $3.4 billion. Keflavik hosts permanently stationed personnel from Canada, Denmark, the Netherlands, Norway, and the UK. Dutch P-3 aircraft and crew deploy temporarily to Keflavik. US–Icelandic negotiations regarding implementation of a new "Agreed Minute" governing force structure and operations at Keflavik commenced in 2003. The US also operates surveillance radars in Iceland and intelligence collection equipment. In 1996, Naval Facility Keflavik, an ocean surveillance station, ceased operations after 30 years. The DOD announced in Aug 2004 that the US would consolidate main operating bases in Europe as a result of the "Global Posture Review." This will likely include significant reductions in the US presence in Iceland.

FORCES DEPLOYED: Building on its experience from running Pristina airport in Kosovo on behalf of NATO, Iceland took sole responsibility for the operation of the Kabul airport on 1 Jun 2004. Iceland also agreed in Feb 2004 to provide chartered airlift for Dutch military assets en route to Afghanistan.

Code Names: Cooperative Safeguard, Fan, Gatekeeper, Joint Endeavor, Northern Viking, West Axe.

India

The US and India have transformed their relationship since 9/11, putting aside differences over India's nuclear weapons programs. In late Sep 2001, President Bush lifted sanctions imposed under the terms of the 1994 Nuclear Proliferation Prevention Act following India's nuclear tests in May 1998. President Bush met Prime Minister Vajpayee in Nov 2001, continuing the bilateral series of high-level visits that began with President Clinton's visit to India in Mar 2000. An Indo-US Joint Working Group on Counterterrorism was established in 2000. The US–India Defense Policy Group (DPG) was revived in 2001. The US–India Joint Technical Group (JTG), a group established to discuss conditions for future cooperation, met 4–5 Mar 2002, four years since its last meeting. In May 2002, India and the US launched the Indo-US Cyber Security Forum. The US and India also began a DOD-led Security Cooperation Group (SCG), focused on the issues of nuclear weapons security and command and control. The US and India announced on 12 Jan 2004 the "Next Steps in the Strategic Partnership."

Since 9/11, the US and India have conducted a number of successful exercises — ranging from special operations exchanges to airborne operations and naval exercises. India's armed forces have become tangibly involved in the war on terrorism by escorting US and other ships transiting the Strait of Malacca, by sharing intelligence on terrorist training camps used by Osama bin Laden's supporters inside Afghanistan and Pakistan, through joint investigations, and through improved border security.

Despite unprecedented US involvement in India and Pakistan, tensions between the two countries continue. The UN Military Observer Group in India and Pakistan (UNMOGIP), established in 1949 to supervise the ceasefire in the states of Jammu and Kashmir, continues to function. More than one million troops are deployed along the "line of control" in Kashmir despite overtures by India in 2003 that resulted in normalizing of diplomatic relations and reestablished bus service.

The Indian military is one of the largest in the world, purchasing equipment primarily from Russia, Israel, the UK, and France. President Bush's Sep 2001 decision to waive sanctions opened the way for full resumption of defense cooperation. The two countries signed a General Security of Military Information Agreement in Jan 2002, and there were exchange visits by Defense Secretary Rumsfeld and Defense Minister Fernandes. The US is encouraging Indian use of US equipment, particularly in counter-terrorism and surveillance. A Joint/Combined Exchange Training (JCET) special operations program among the Indian Air Force 4th Wing and the US 2nd Battalion, 1st Special Forces Group, and 353rd SOG was initiated at Agra.

US COMMAND: PACOM.

AGREEMENTS: Acquisition and Cross-Servicing Agreement eligible (6 Feb 1996), Article 98 Agreement, General Security of Military Information Agreement (GSOMIA; Jan 2002).

US ASSSISTANCE: Foreign Military Financing program grants, International Military Education and Training aid, eligible to receive grant Excess Defense Articles, participated in Asia-Pacific Center for Security Studies executive courses for the first time in 2002.

BASES AND ACCESS: Following 9/11, India offered the use of its territory for US troops or equipment for military operations, made shipyards available for coalition ship repairs, and opened ports for naval ships. US Navy ships and submarines regularly call and fuel at Cochin, Mumbai, and Vizagapatam.

Code Names: Balance Iroquois, Cope India, Flash Iroquois, Geronimo Thrust, Malabar, NOLES, SAREX, Shant Doot, Shanti Path, Yudh Abyas.

Indonesia

Indonesia is the world's most populous Muslim country, but like Pakistan and Saudi Arabia it has had difficulty seeing the international dimensions of the internal Jemaah Islamiyah (JI) terrorist threat and has been conflicted in its pursuit of US counter-terrorism objectives. The Bali bombing on 12 Oct 2002, which killed 202, was a turning point, and after the bombing of a J. W. Marriott hotel in Jakarta on 5 Aug 2003, Indonesian authorities increased their pursuit of terrorists on their own soil. As in the other two countries, nonetheless, there are factions in the military and security services that do not want to aggressively investigate domestic groups sympathetic to al Qaeda, and they attribute international terrorism to US Middle East policy.

US counter-terrorism cooperation with Indonesia has focused on joint investigations, border control, and police, judicial, and financial training. After Bali, Indonesia issued emergency decrees, and invited Australian, British, and US counter-terrorism personnel to participate in the investigation. US assistance favors law enforcement in counter-terrorism, as the Indonesian military and special forces (KOPASSUS) have a history of excessive use of force and have been implicated in numerous hiuman rights scandals. US assistance has funded the National Police Counter-terrorism Task Force and a financial intelligence unit. On 4–5 Feb 2004, Indonesia and Australia co-chaired an international counter-terrorism conference in Bali. The conference launched the Indonesia Centre for Law Enforcement Co-operation (ICLEC), which will be jointly run by Australia and Indonesia.

US military interest in Indonesia prior to 9/11 focused on the country's location astride a number of international maritime straits. Frictions existed on a number of issues, particularly East Timor and human rights, and Indonesia struggles with separatist movements in Aceh, the Moluccas, and Papua. Congress cut off grant military training assistance to Indonesia in 1992 for three years over the conduct of Indonesian security forces in East Timor, and military assistance programs were again suspended following Indonesia's outbreak of violence after the 30 Aug 1999 independence referendum. The International Military Education and Training program was slow to develop because of congressional concerns about the human rights records of the Indonesia military, but language in the FY 2003 foreign appropriations bill authorized unrestricted International Military Education and Training.

US COMMAND: PACOM.

AGREEMENTS: Acquisition and Cross-Servicing Agreement (post-9/11), letter of agreement to purchase F-16s (Aug 1986).

US ASSISTANCE: Receives International Military Education and Training aid, receives aid for humanitarian demining efforts, receives Nonproliferation, Anti-terrorism, Demining, and Related (NADR) and Anti-Terrorism Assistance funds for the National Police Counter-terrorism Task Force and financial intelligence unit, participates in the Regional Defense Counter-terrorism Fellowship Program, participates in the DIA Fellows programs.

BASES AND ACCESS: The US has no military bases or facilities in Indonesia. US ships call and refuel at Bali, Jakarta, and Surabaya. Imminent Danger Pay was authorized for Indonesia in Oct 2002.

Code Names: Albatross Ausindo, Ausina, Balance Iron, Bevel Incline, CARAT Indonesia, Cassowary, Cooperative Thunder, Cope Tiger, Elang Ausindo, Fincastle, Kangaroo, New Horizon, NOLES, Nursery/Nutmeg, Peace Bima-Sena, Rajawali Ausindo, SEACAT, Trisetia, Westpac MCMEX.

Iran

After Iranian militants and students occupied the US embassy in Tehran on 4 Nov 1979, holding 52 Americans hostage for 444 days, the US broke diplomatic relations with Iran. Commercial relations between Iran and the US are restricted by US sanctions and consist mainly of Iranian purchases of food and medical products and US purchases of carpets and food. Obstacles to improved relations between the two countries include Iranian weapons of mass destruction efforts in violation of international legal obligations, support for and involvement in international terrorism, and a continuing dismal human rights record.

The US extended the Iran–Libya Sanctions Act for a further five years in Jul 2001, and in Jan 2002 President Bush referred to Iran as part of an "Axis of Evil." All factions in Iran, elected and unelected, conservative and reformist, condemned the president's remarks. After 9/11, President Khatami was quick to condemn the attacks, and his condemnations were followed up by other Iranian officials, including supreme leader Khamenei. Since then, the US and Iran have quietly cooperated to avoid conflict over US operations in Afghanistan, and there have even been rumors that Iran supported the deployment of US combat search and rescue elements. According to media reports, Iranian special unit forces worked with US and UK special operations forces (SOF) during Operation Enduring Freedom. Iran also closed the border with Afghanistan. Iran has pledged more than $500 million over five years to the reconstruction of Afghanistan.

The US and Iran have also worked together at a low level in counter-narcotics in the region, and in handling the large number of refugees from Iraq and

Afghanistan. President Khatami has visited a number of European countries, including Austria, France, Germany, Greece, Italy, and Spain, since 9/11. He also visited Russia in 2001 and has received a number of other leaders in Iran since 9/11, including the UK foreign secretary, who visited on 25 Sep 2001, the first visit by a British foreign minister since before the Iranian Revolution in 1979. After the fall of Saddam Hussein, Iran opened direct bilateral relations with the Iraqi Governing Council (and later the Iraqi government) and signed an MOU with Iraq on trade.

US COMMAND: CENTCOM.

AGREEMENTS: Activity-specific SOFA (TIAS 2295).

In Jan 2003, an Indo-Iranian defense cooperation agreement was signed in Tehran. Media reports state that the accord gives India the right to use Iranian military bases in the event of any war with Pakistan.

Code Names: Austere Challenge, Eagle Claw, Gray Pan, Nordic Thrust, Peace Station, Pony Express, Praying Mantis, Prime Chance, Rice Bowl, SHAREM 102, Unified Quest.

Iraq

The coalition returned legal sovereignty to a provisional Iraqi government on 28 Jun 2004, ending the reign of the Coalition Provisional Authority and the Iraqi Governing Council. At the time of turnover of sovereignty, the US had more than 115,000 troops in Iraq (and another 25,000 in Kuwait), supplemented by some 23,000 uniformed personnel from more than 30 countries. The international community has pledged well over $30 billion to Iraqi reconstruction.

The US implemented the rotation of "OIF 2" (Operation Iraqi Freedom 2) in Iraq between Dec 2003 and Apr 2004. Countries with forces deployed in Iraq during 2003–2004 included Albania, Australia, Azerbaijan, Bulgaria, the Czech Republic, Denmark, El Salvador, Estonia, Georgia, Hungary, Italy, Japan, Jordan, Kazakhstan, Latvia, Lithuania, Macedonia, Moldova, Mongolia, the Netherlands, New Zealand, Norway, the Philippines, Poland, Portugal, Romania, Singapore, Slovakia, South Korea, Thailand, Ukraine, the UAE, and the UK. Forces from the Dominican Republic, Honduras, Nicaragua, and Spain withdrew from Iraq in 2004.

US COMMAND: CENTCOM. Joint Task Force 7 remains the primary US military headquarters.

Code Names: Bayonet Lightning, Camel Hump, CBAT, Copper Green, Crashpad, Crescent Wind, Desert series, Display Deterrence, Druid Leader, Eager Glacier, Early Victor, Earnest Will, Elephant Grass, Grand Falcon, Imminent Horizon, Infinite Moonlight, Internal Look, Iron series, Isaiah, Ivy series, Juniper Cobra, Lucky Warrior, Mountain Hall, Night Camel, Northern Watch, NTEX, Pacific Haven, Peninsula Shield, Peninsula Strike, Planet X, Prominent Hammer, Provide Comfort, Quick Transit, Reef Point, Reindeer Games, Rifle Blitz, Roll-up, Scathe Mean, Seminole, Sidewinder, Slow Walker, Soda Mountain, Southern Focus, Southern Watch, Steel Box, Surf Fisher, Sweeney, Telic, Thirst Warrior, Victory series, Vigilant Sentinel, Vigilant Warrior.

Ireland

Ireland is a member of NATO's Partnership for Peace (1 Dec 1999) and participant in the European Union's security and defense policies. After 9/11, it offered to let US aircraft use Irish airfields.

US COMMAND: EUCOM.

AGREEMENTS: Acquisition and Cross-Servicing Agreement eligible (26 Jan 1998).

FORCES DEPLOYED: Ireland provides troops for peacekeeping in Eritrea–Ethiopia, East Timor, the Stabilization Force in Bosnia, and the Kosovo Force in Kosovo.

Code Names: Combined Endeavor, Eloquent Nugget, Joint Forge, Joint Guardian, Viking.

Israel

The US commitment to Israel's security has been a cornerstone of US policy in the Middle East since 1948. Israel and the US are close military and intelligence allies, a relationship that has stood the test of the Cold War and Arab Israeli wars, and has only strengthened since the Iraqi invasion of Kuwait in Aug 1990.

The Israel Defence Forces (IDF) comprise an army of 125,000 regulars, of whom 100,000 are conscripts, and an additional 460,000 reservists; an air force of 13 squadrons, staffed by 32,000 regulars, of whom 22,000 are conscripts, and an additional 5,000 reservists; and a navy staffed by 8,000 regulars, of whom 3,000 are conscripts, and an additional 2,000 reservists. There is also a paramilitary border police force of 6,000 responsible for control of frontiers and some security duties in the Occupied Territories. Israel spends more than 15 percent of its GDP on defense. The US has provided Israel with over $90 billion in economic and military assistance since 1949, and Israel continues to receive the largest share of US military assistance worldwide, well over $2 billion annually. The US also provides military support to implementation of cease-fire and disengagement agreements concerning the Sinai and the Golan Heights among Israel, Egypt, and Syria; and in support of the Egyptian–Israeli Peace Treaty and Camp David accords.

Israel is a strong supporter of the war on terrorism, fighting its own war with Palestinian terrorist groups, which conducted a large number of attacks in

Israel, the West Bank, and Gaza Strip in 2003–2004. In Jun 2004, Israel was designated a full-fledged partner in the NATO Mediterranean Dialogue. The US has designated Hamas, the Palestinian Islamic Jihad (PIJ), and the al-Aqsa Martyrs Brigades as foreign terrorist organizations. Israeli authorities have arrested individuals claiming allegiance to al Qaeda, but the organization does not appear to have ever established a foothold in Israel, the West Bank, or Gaza. On 15 Oct 2003, Palestinian militants attacked a US diplomatic convoy in Gaza with an improvised explosive device, killing three Americans.

Israel's counter-terrorism tactics and military operations, particularly its campaign of targeted killings, its destruction of family homes of suspected suicide bombers, and its extensive security fencing, have drawn much criticism. Though some claim that Israeli counter-terrorism measures appear to have reduced the frequency of attacks, there is no end in sight in the Israeli–Palestinian conflict.

The UN Truce Supervision Organization (UNTSO), the first peacekeeping operation established by the United Nations and set up in 1948, remains in the Middle East to monitor cease-fires and supervise armistice agreements. UNTSO maintains offices in Beirut and Damascus, and observers are attached to the UN Disengagement Observer Force (UNDOF) in the Golan Heights and the UN Interim Force in Lebanon (UNIFIL). Observers maintain a UN presence on the Sinai peninsula, in coordination with the Multinational Force and Observers (MFO).

US COMMAND: EUCOM.

AGREEMENTS: MOU on training, doctrine, and equipment development (13 Nov 2000), MOU between Israel and the United States (21 Apr 1988), SOFA (22 Jan 1991, with diplomatic note), granted Major Non-NATO Ally status, Acquisition and Cross-Servicing Agreement (10 Feb 98), Article 98 Agreement (4 Aug 2002).

In 1983, the US and Israel established the Joint Political–Military Group (JPMG), which meets twice a year to coordinate joint planning. In 1996, the two also established a Joint Counter-terrorism Group to enhance cooperation. The US and Israel participate in joint military planning and collaborate on a wide range of military research and weapons development projects. Israel is one of three international partners with cooperative R&D agreements with the US counter-terrorism Techical Support Working Group Program. A US–Israel Combined Logistics Committee (CLC) oversees US and Israeli planning and cooperation.

US ASSISTANCE: Israel receives more than $2.3 billion annually under the Foreign Military Financing program (representing about 20 percent of its defense budget), enabling procurement and upkeep of US-origin systems such as F-16I fighters and Apache Longbow attack helicopters; eligible to receive grant Excess Defense

Articles. Training for Israeli personnel includes Air, Naval, and Army War College courses and other professional military education classes, flight simulator training, and technical and maintenance training.

BASES AND ACCESS: Quietly, the US maintains pre-positioned equipment and munitions on Israeli soil for use by US and Israeli forces. The War Reserve Stocks for Allies — Israel (WRS-I) program includes ammunition owned by the US but intended for Israeli use, overseen by the army and Marine Corps. The navy store a number of medical units and medical stocks in Israel, including a fleet hospital, which was moved to Israel in 1998. The Air Force OL-A in Tel Aviv, part of 16th Air Force, headquartered at Aviano, Italy, manages its own set of munition and equipment storage sites, as well as standby air bases, in Israel.

The US facilities include:
+ Site 51: Air-force-managed munitions and equipment storage in earth-covered magazines.
+ Site 53: Air-force-managed munitions storage and war reserve vehicles on Israeli air bases.
+ Site 54: A 500-bed contingency hospital in or near Tel Aviv.
+ Site 55: A munitions storage site.
+ Site 56: A munitions storage site.

The locations include Ben Gurion IAP, Herzliya-Pituach, Nevatim airfield, and Ovda AB. US Navy ships and submarines also regularly call at Eilat and Haifa.

Code Names: Anatolian Eagle, Cooperative Safeguard, Ellipse Bravo, Eloquent Nugget, Hammer Rick, Have Nap, Infinite Moonlight, Juniper series, Mountain series, Nickel Grass, Noble series, Pacer Ship, Patriot Defender, Peace Dove, Peace Echo, Peace Fox, Peace Jack, Peace Marble, Peace Patch, Reliant Mermaid, Shining Presence, Trophy.

Italy

NATO member Italy is a consistent military and intelligence partner of the US, and has been a strong supporter of the war on terrorism. The relationship was strengthened during the Balkans wars in the 1990s, when the most crucial NATO and US planning and intelligence organizations were in Italy. Air bases in Italy were essential in the bombing campaign against Yugoslavia during Allied Forces, and they continue to provide staging and transportation points for peacekeeping missions in the Balkans. Italy is one of six foreign nations to host US nuclear weapons.

After 9/11, Italy actively supported coalition military operations in Afghanistan, the Horn of Africa, and Iraq. In 2002, it supported maritime surveillance and interdiction efforts in the Indian Ocean, Arabian Gulf, and Red

Sea. Italy's deployment of Task Force Nibbio to Afghanistan in Mar 2003 was its first major combat deployment overseas since World War II.

US command: EUCOM.

Agreements: NATO SOFA (16 Jun 1951), Mutual Defense Assistance Agreement (27 Jan 1950), classified Stone Ax Technical Agreement (nuclear weapons), Aviano Technical Agreement (1994), MOU Concerning Use of Installations by US Forces in Italy (2 Feb 1995; "The Shell Agreement"), PfP SOFA (23 Oct 1998), Acquisition and Cross-Servicing Agreement.

Bases and access: The US has about 16,000 military personnel stationed in Italy, and Italy hosts important US military forces at seven major bases in Vicenza and Livorno (army); Aviano (air force); and Sigonella, Gaeta, and Naples (navy). Vicenza is home to the 173rd Airborne Brigade, the only US combat unit in Southern Europe, a unit that was deployed to northern Iraq in Operation Iraqi Freedom (OIF). Gaeta is the homeport for the Sixth Fleet, one of five US fleets and one of three stationed overseas. Aviano AB in Pordenone is home to the headquarters of the 16th Air Force and 31st Fighter Wing, the only permanent air force combat units in Southern Europe. US Navy ships and submarines also call at, and refuel and reprovision at, Auga Bay, Sicily, Brindisi, Cagliara, Catania, Gaeta, Genoa, Livorno, Messina, Naples, Palermo, Porta Torres, San Remo, Taormina, Taranto, Trieste, and Venice. La Maddalena continues as the most important forward US submarine support base. Ghedi AB hosts US nuclear weapons. San Vito has hosted the 48th Expeditionary Intelligence Squadron for operations in the Balkans and Macedonia, providing a data link between U-2 aircraft and Beale Air Force Base, CA, and supporting Celtic Axe, Celtic Warrior, and Sentinel Torch missions.

The DOD announced in Aug 2004 that the US would consolidate main operating bases in Italy as a result of the "Global Posture Review." This will include consolidation of two naval headquarters in Europe in Naples, and likely result in moving Sixth Fleet headquarters from Gaeta to Naples as well.

Italy also hosts a number of important NATO commands. Joint Forces Command South in Naples (formerly Allied Forces Southern Europe) is one of two major NATO operational commands. A new headquarters facility is being built at Lago Patria, some 12 miles west of Naples, to house the command.

Forces deployed: After 9/11, Italy provided its only aircraft carrier battle group centered on the *Garibaldi* to support combat operations in the North Arabian Sea, deployed military personnel to Operation Enduring Freedom on 15 Jan 2002, and later deployed 1,000 Alpini ground troops (Task Force Nibbio) to International Security Assistance Force Mar–Sep 2003. It also flew C-130s from Abu Dhabi,

UAE. The 5th Air Detachment deployed to Manas, Kyrgyzstan, 22 Oct 2002 with two C-130J aircraft.

Italy contributed approximately 3,000 troops, including the "Sassari" mechanized brigade, marine company, and carabinieri detachment as part of the Multi-National Division (South-East) in Iraq starting in 2003. Despite bombing of the carabinieri headquarters in Nasiriyah on 2 Nov 2003, which killed 19 Italian citizens, Italy remained one of the four largest contributors of troops and personnel in Iraq. On 22 Jun 2004, Italy extended its military commitment in Iraq to 31 Dec 2004.

Italy ranks third (after Germany and France) in personnel contributions to multi-national peace support operations, with nearly 6,300 military and carabinieri troops deployed abroad. At the end of 2002, Italy had 4,300 troops deployed in Kosovo and Albania with the Kosovo Force (KFOR), and Italy took command of KFOR for a six-month period starting in Oct 2002. Italy had approximately 1,200 serving with the Stabilization Force (SFOR) in Bosnia. A further 200 personnel were deployed in Macedonia as part of NATO's Allied Harmony, and about 250 were serving in Albania under the auspices of bilateral military assistance programs. Italy has also made peacekeeping contributions in the West Bank, Congo, Kosovo, Lebanon, Somalia, Mozambique, East Timor, Western Sahara, and on the Iraq–Kuwait, India–Pakistan, and Eritrea–Ethiopia borders.

Code Names: Agile series, Air Brake, Ample Train, ARRcade Fusion, Ardent Ground, Atlas Response, Bright Horizon, Bright Star, Cathode Emission, Celtic Axe, Celtic Torch, Clean Hunter, Combined Endeavor, Comfy Cobalt, Constant Harmony, Cooperative series, Coronet Garrison, Coronet Independence, Coronet Soldier, Dacia, Damsel Fair, Decisive Endeavor, Destined Glory, Disciplined Warrior, Distant Thunder, Dogfish, Dogu Akdeniz, Dynamic series, Eagle, Esperia, Global Mercury, Green Flag, Iron Ram, JTFEX, Mace, Major Manar, Majestic Eagle, Matador, Med Shark, MED-CEUR, Mothia, Optic Windmill, Pacific Protector, Peace Caesar, Peaceful Eagle, Peaceshield, Phoenix Duke, Ponte Vecchio, Prometheus, Rescue Eagle, Sanso, Sea Breeze, Sea Saber, Sentinel Torch, SHAREM, Sorbet Royale, Stone Ax, Strong Resolve, Trial, Trident D'Or, Unified Charger, Urgent Resolve, Veneto Rescue, Viking, Volant Partner, Winter Harvest.

Ivory Coast
See Côte d'Ivoire.

Jamaica
Jamaica and the US have warm relations, and Jamaica cooperates with the US on a variety of international and regional issues, including contributing troops to the US-led multi-national force that intervened in Haiti in 1994. Jamaica is a major transit country for cocaine and the largest Caribbean producer and exporter of marijuana, and cooperates fully with US counter-narcotics efforts.

US funding also supports development of Jamaica's anti-money-laundering capabilities and effective anti-corruption mechanisms. Jamaica hosted an Inter-American Committee Against Terrorism Seminar, 12–14 Apr 2004. The US is also funding border control and port security efforts.

US COMMAND: SOUTHCOM.

AGREEMENTS: SOFA, Acquisition and Cross-Servicing Agreement eligible (20 Apr 1993).

US ASSISTANCE: Receives Foreign Military Financing program grants, International Military Education and Training aid, eligible to receive grant Excess Defense Articles, National Guard partner with Washington, DC. The US supplied three 42-foot patrol boats to Jamaica in 2003.

Code Names: New Horizons, PKO, Red Stripe, Tradewinds, West Eagle.

Japan

Since 9/11, Japan has been a significant player in the war on terrorism by providing logistical support for US and coalition forces in the Pacific and Indian Oceans, and by playing a leading role in funding Afghanistan and Iraq reconstruction, even by deploying token forces. Japan is an active participant in new counter-terrorism and arms control initiatives, including the Proliferation Security Initiative and the Financial Action Task Force.

Revised 2001 Defense Guidelines and historic Jun 2003 legislation expanded Japan's noncombat role in a regional contingency and allowed Japan's Self-Defense Forces (SDF) to participate in reconstruction and humanitarian missions abroad. In Oct 2002, SDF transport aircraft delivered humanitarian aid to Islamabad, Pakistan. In Nov 2002, the Japanese government decided that the SDF could transport materials, including heavy construction equipment belonging to Thailand, to Afghanistan. The JASDF flew its first humanitarian mission into Iraq on 3 Mar 2004; by mid-2004, nearly 1,000 SDF troops were operating in the south.

Despite extremely close relations, the majority of Japanese citizens — about 70 percent — say they would like to see a reduction in the US presence in the country. The US–Japan Special Action Committee on Okinawa (SACO) led to a program to consolidate the US Marine Corps presence, and there are numerous other initiatives to reduce operational, noise, and environmental impact. Nonetheless, on 17 Jan 2003, Japan agreed to allow a nuclear-powered US aircraft carrier to be based at Yokosuka, an inconceivable event in anti-nuclear Japan during the Cold War.

US COMMAND: PACOM. US Forces Japan (Yokota AB) is the sub-unified command.

AGREEMENTS: Mutual Legal Assistance Treaty (Aug 2003; cooperation in investigations and prosecution of terrorists), Treaty of Mutual Cooperation and Security, Agreement on Host Nation Support (2001), SOFA, Acquisition and Cross-Servicing Agreement (28 Apr 1998), granted Major Non-NATO Ally status

BASES AND ACCESS: The US maintains roughly 40,000 troops in Japan, approximately half of whom are stationed in Okinawa, and some 6,000 of whom are forward-deployed naval personnel. Japan provides bases and financial and material support to US forces to the tune of more than $4.5 billion in annual host nation support, the most generous of any US ally.

The US Navy bases at Yokosuka — home to the Seventh Fleet and the aircraft carrier USS *Kitty Hawk* — are considered the navy's largest and most important overseas installations. The Seventh Fleet operates throughout Asia and the Indian Ocean. The base at Sasebo hosts an amphibious squadron, and the navy has its only overseas shore-based carrier wing in Japan. US Navy ships and submarines also regularly call at Buckner Bay and Naha, Okinawa; Hachinohe, Kagoshima, Kure, Maizuru, Muroran, Numazu, Ominato, Otaru, and Yokohama.

The Marine Corp's only division-sized unit overseas — the III Marine Expeditionary Force (MEF) — has been based on Okinawa since 1971. Marine forces in Okinawa and on mainland Japan provide support for counter terrorism operations in the Philippines, staging from bases in Okinawa.

The 5th Air Force, headquartered at Yokota AB near Tokyo, supports air operations at Yokota, Kadena AB on Okinawa, and Misawa AB in northern Japan. Japan hosts US F-15 fighters, an airlift unit, tankers, and reconnaissance and surveillance aircraft, including P-3s and EP-3s.

The 9th Theater Army Area Command supports an infrastructure of pre-positioned equipment, ammunition, and fuel in support of US war plans to defend Japan. The 1st Battalion, 1st Special Forces Group in Okinawa is the only army ground combat unit in the country. Japan also hosts numerous US intelligence, reconnaissance, and ocean surveillance units.

The DOD announced in Aug 2004 that the US would consolidate main operating bases in Japan as a result of the "Global Posture Review." The size of US forces in Japan will likely remain fairly stable.

FORCES DEPLOYED: The remaining 140 troops of the first Japanese contingent to Iraq arrived back in Japan on 31 May 2004.

Code Names: ANNUALEX, ARGEX, ASWEX, Beach Crest, Beverly Morning, Black series, Cobra Ball, Comet, Commando, Cooperative Thunder, Cope Angel, Cope India, Cope Jade, Code North, Cope Thaw, Cope Thunder, Coral Rice, Credible Partner, DIESELEX, Forage, Forest Light, Ford,

Formal, Frown, Frugal, Giant series, Global Mercury, Goodwill, Keen Edge, Keen Sword, Ladylove, MINEX/EODEX, Mystic Star, North Wind, Orient Shield, Pacific Protector, Pacific Reach, Peace Eagle, RIMPAC, Sanso, Scope Dial, Sea Eagle, Sea Saber, Shant Doot, SHAREM, Shin Kame, Silent Fury, Silent Shield, Terminal Fury, Trident Arch, Wild Cherry, Westpac MCMEX, Yama Sakura.

Johnston Island

Johnston Atoll airfield Chemical Agent Disposal System (US Army Chemical Activity, Pacific).

US COMMAND: PACOM.

Jordan

US–Jordanian military and intelligence relations have fully recovered from 1991, when King Hussein opposed the US efforts in Desert Shield/Desert Storm. Since then, King Abdullah II, himself a former commander of Jordan's special operations force, has forged close ties, even if enormous efforts are made to keep them classified. A variety of US rewards are offered for the ostensibly Western-oriented regime. In Sep 1999, as an example, King Abdullah II piloted a US Navy helicopter from the USS *John F. Kennedy* (CV 67), the first US Navy aircraft ever flown by a foreign king. On a more serious note, the US provides virtual protection of Jordan from (former) Iraq and Israeli attack. The US and Jordan have an active combined exercise program, including fairly large-scale training activities involving special operations forces (SOF), air defense, communications, fighter aircraft, and other military units, together with the annual monthlong Infinite Moonlight exercise with navy and marine units. There is a robust (and classified) Joint/Combined Exchange Training (JCET) special operations program with the 5th Special Forces Group. UK–Jordanian military relations are also quite close; annual joint military exercises have taken place since 1993, and RN ships pay regular visits to Aqaba.

In the war on terrorism, Jordan has worked closely with US intelligence and SOF, providing access for operations and HUMINT support. The CIA has long-established and very intimate ties with the Jordanian GID, the civilian intelligence service. There have been reliable reports that Jordanian secret services and intelligence personnel have done some of the "dirty work" for their US counterparts, including interrogations and targeted killings. In early 2002, Jordan reportedly began a training program for Yemeni counter-terrorism forces. In 2003, Jordan signed an MOU with the Coalition Provisional Authority in Iraq to train Iraqi police cadets. Jordan was also the only Arab country to contribute to Operation Enduring Freedom in Afghanistan, and it deployed mine clearance and medical personnel to Afghanistan in 2002. In

Jun 2004, Jordan was designated a full-fledged partner in the NATO Mediterranean Dialogue.

US COMMAND: CENTCOM.

AGREEMENTS: SOFA, Acquisition and Cross-Servicing Agreement (29 Feb 2000), granted Major Non-NATO Ally status (13 Nov 1996).

A US–Jordanian Joint Military Commission was set up in 1974.

US ASSISTANCE: Receives Foreign Military Financing program grants for modernization and sustainment of US-origin F-16 fighters and other equipment, and to purchase Blackhawk helicopters, has one of the largest International Military Education and Training aid programs in the world, eligible to receive grant Excess Defense Articles, National Guard partner with CO (established in Mar 2004). Under the State Partnership agreement, Jordan has sent army helicopter pilots to train at Colorado's High Altitude Army Aviation Training Site at Eagle County Airport. Jordan also carries out exchanges with the 162nd Fighter Wing in Tucson, AZ. Pilots in the 162nd delivered the first F-16s Jordan purchased from the US in Jan 2003.

BASES AND ACCESS: Jordan was designated a combat zone for US personnel on 19 Sep 2001, and the country has provided basing and overflight permission for all US and coalition forces. The era of modern US–Jordanian military relations dates from Mar 1995, when almost 1,200 personnel and 34 F-15s and F-16s set up camp at two air bases near Azraq for almost three months as AEF II, flying Southern Watch and other missions. The majority of planes flew from Shaheed Mwaffaq AB (Muaffaq-as Salti), while aerial refuelers operated from H-5 (Prince Hassan AB). This would be the first of a number of deployments to the two bases, which would be code-named West Wing during Operation Iraqi Freedom (OIF) to obscure the presence of US forces in the country. The US military has also established permanent SIGINT monitoring stations in Jordan.

Soon after 9/11, US special operations forces established a permanent presence in Jordan. Six RC-12s of the army's 15th MI Battalion from Fort Hood, TX, deployed on 22 Apr 2002 to eavesdrop on Iraqi communications. As part of Early Victor in Oct, more than 1,000 SOF deployed, and the US Special Operations Command — Jordan was established in Nov 2002. The command included a core of 5th Special Forces Group, Army Rangers, elements of 160th SOAR, JSOC, UK, and Australian special operations forces, and other government agency (OGA) contingents.

On 30 Jan 2003, Jordan granted blanket overflight rights. This facilitated aircraft carrier strikes on Iraq from the eastern Mediterranean. The 282nd Combat Communications Squadron, RI ANG, arrived in Jan to enlarge the communications infrastructure, and five Patriot missile fire units were airlifted starting 13 Feb 2003, the equipment arriving at the port of Aqaba on 17 Mar. Personnel from Marine Air Control Squadron 2 provided air traffic control at H-5. By the beginning of OIF, Jordan hosted more than 5,000 US and coalition troops and had transformed into Joint Task Force — West under Maj. Gen. Jonathan S. Gration. One of the first missions of OIF was breaching of the Iraq–Jordan border berms to allow SOF to drive through as part of the campaign to control western Iraq. The UK deployed Harrier Jump jets to support Special Air Service (SAS) operations in western Iraq, and Australia deployed helicopters of the 5th Aviation Regiment.

Code Names: Blue Flag, Bright Star, Cooperative Support, Coronet Orion, Eager Light, Eager Tiger, Eagle Resolve, Early Victor, Eloquent Nugget, Encased Sword, Falconer, Golden Sands, Infinite Acclaim, Infinite Anvil, Infinite Courage, Infinite Moonlight, Infinite Shadow, Joint Guardian, Peace Flame, Peace Range, Peace Ultra, Phoenix Scirocco, Regional Cooperation, Reliant Mermaid, Safe Departure, Saffron Sands, Seminole, Shadow Hawk, Sunny Hope/Sunny Relief, Vigilant Sentinel, West Wing.

Kazakhstan

Kazakhstan became a de facto nuclear weapons state when the Soviet Union dissolved and the initial US relationship focused on elimination of the former Soviet weapons of mass destruction infrastructure, particularly the SS-18 ballistic missiles. The US has assisted Kazakhstan in the removal of nuclear warheads and weapons-grade materials. In 1994, Kazakhstan transferred more than half a ton of weapons-grade uranium to the US. In 1995, Kazakhstan removed its last nuclear warheads, and in May 2000 it completed the sealing of 181 nuclear test tunnels.

Kazakhstan is a member of NATO's PfP (27 May 1994) and an active US military partner, hosting 22 joint military-to-military engagement events (from information exchanges to military exercises) with CENTCOM in 2002. After 9/11, Kazakhstan provided overflight rights and allowed for the trans-shipment of supplies to US forces based in Central Asia. The country stressed that there would be no "permanent" US military presence. Kazakhstan is also a member of the Shanghai Cooperation Organization (SCO) along with China, Russia, Tajikistan, Uzbekistan, and Kyrgyzstan.

From fiscal year 1993 to 2001, the US obligated about $586 million in assistance to Kazakhstan. Of this amount, $193 million was for security assistance, including $180 million for cooperative threat reduction. In FY 2002, budgeted aid totaled about $58 million. Requested assistance for FYs 2003 and 2004 totaled $100 million. US assistance focuses on training programs in border security, immigration procedures, and counter-proliferation awareness, as well as professional military skills, particularly to enhance Kazakhstan's peacekeeping battalion (KAZBAT). Joint counter-terrorism activity includes training and operating with special operations and internal security forces.

US–Kazakhstani Consultative Group Meetings were also held at CENTCOM in MacDill Air Force Base, FL, in Jun 2000. During 2003–2004, the emphasis in exchanges was emergency response, noncommissioned officer professional development, and tactical maintenance and logistics. In Nov 2003, two officials from the Kazakhstan Emergency Situations Agency attended the Bio-Terrorism and National Pharmaceutical Stockpile exercise in Tucson, AZ.

Kazakhstan continues to participate in the Cooperative Threat Reduction (CTR) program to eliminate the former Soviet WMD infrastructure. Joint DOD–FBI and DOD–customs counter-proliferation programs in Kazakhstan, which began in the 1990s, focus on the development of enforcement mechanisms as well as institutional development.

US COMMAND: CENTCOM.

AGREEMENTS: MOU on Use of Almaty Airport (10 Jul 2002), Reciprocal SOFA, MOU on Cooperation on Defense and Military Relations (14 Feb 1994), Cooperative Threat Reduction Agreement, PfP SOFA (10 Aug 1997), Acquisition and Cross-Servicing Agreement eligible, Article 98 Agreement (22 Sep 2003).

The US–Kazakhstan Joint Commission which first met in Almaty, Kazakhstan, includes a Defense Bilateral Working Group that promotes defense cooperation and defense conversion.

US ASSISTANCE: Receives Foreign Military Financing program grants to train and equip the peacekeeping battalion, to refurbish a military base at Atyrau near the North Caspian Sea for counter-terrorism training, and to purchase communications, night vision, and other equipment; receives International Military Education and Training aid, eligible to receive grant Excess Defense Articles; National Guard partner with Arizona (established in 1995); receives Nonproliferation, Anti-terrorism, Demining, and Related (NADR) and Anti-Terrorism Assistance funds to secure nuclear materals and spent fuel at the stand-by BN-350 breeder reactor in Aktau, to improve security, and to employ scientists in peaceful research; participates in the Export Control and Related Border Security Assistance program; receives Anti-Crime Training and Technical Assistance support.

BASES AND ACCESS: The 2002 agreement permits US military aircraft to use Almaty airport for emergency landings and allows transshipment of supplies to US forces in Uzbekistan and Kyrgyzstan. Kazakhstan also allows the use of two other airfields, in Djambyl and Shymkent, as emergency landing strips for endangered US and coalition aircraft taking part in missions over Afghanistan. Kazakhstan allowed more than 1,100 US overflights in support of Operation Enduring Freedom from Dec 2001 through the end of 2003. Non-US coalition aircraft have also been allowed to use Kazakh bases and airspace.

A 1997 Seismic Monitoring Agreement provides for the establishment and operation of a seismic monitoring station.

Prior to 9/11, US Foreign Military Financing assistance was being used for reconstruction of a maritime base in Atyrau. After 9/11, the project was transformed to develop a Special Forces Training Center for Counterterrorism. The center will be used for joint and multi-lateral exercises and to follow on with KAZBAT.

FORCES DEPLOYED: In the summer of 2003, Kazakhstan sent a 27-member military engineering and ordnance disposal contingent to Iraq, stationed with Ukraine in Kut. After the violence in Iraq in Apr 2004, Kazakhstan stated that it would withdraw its forces after the normal rotation in 2004.

Code Names: Balance Kayak, Centrasbat, Combined Endeavor, Cooperative series, Eloquent Nugget, Ferghana, IWER, Peace Shield, Provide Hope, Regional Cooperation, Zhardem.

Kenya
Kenya has been targeted by terrorist groups (including al Qaeda cells) and has been hit twice by terrorist attacks: the 1998 bombing of the US embassy in Nairobi, which killed more than 200 Kenyans, and the Mombasa attacks on 28 Nov 2002. After Djibouti, Kenya is a principal point of access for US military operations in the Horn of Africa, and has been a supporter of the war on terrorism since 1998. Following 9/11, Kenya began intelligence sharing on suspected terrorists, and improved law enforcement cooperation on domestic matters. The focus has since shifted to supporting Combined Joint Task Force — Horn of Africa (CJTF-HOA) operations and US special operations and CIA missions against Somalian, Yemeni, and other terrorist groups in the Horn of Africa. CJTF-HOA has trained Kenyan special operations, ground, and naval forces. Extensive US–Kenyan training took place at Embakasi air base in Nairobi, 21 Jul–15 Aug 2003. Kenya is also a member of the Eastern Africa Counterterrorism Initiative.

US COMMAND: CENTCOM. CJTF-HOA.

AGREEMENTS: Classified SOFA (1980), Acquisition and Cross-Servicing Agreement (eligible 5 Sep 2000).

BASES AND ACCESS: The US staged forces from Kenya during Somalia operations in 1992–1993, and has used Kenyan bases for operations in Congo and Sudan.

During Operation Enduring Freedom, Kenya provided access, overflight, basing, and support for maritime interdiction in the eastern Indian Ocean. Kenya also regularly allows US military ships to use the port at Mombasa. Imminent Danger Pay was authorized for US forces in Kenya in Jul 2002.

US ASSISTANCE: Receives Foreign Military Financing program grants, International Military Education and Training aid, eligible to receive grant Excess Defense Articles, receives peacekeeping operations (PKO) funding, participates in African Contingency Operations Training and Assistance (ACOTA) program and the earlier African Crisis Response Initiative (ACRI), participates in Africa Center for Strategic Studies conferences and seminars, participates in the Terrorist Interdiction Program.

FORCES DEPLOYED: The Kenyan military is an active participant in international peacekeeping in Democratic Republic of Congo, Sierra Leone, Eritrea–Ethiopia, and East Timor.

Code Names: Continue Hope, Crab Apple, Delenda, Eastern Castle, Edged Mallet, Golden Spear, Grand Prix, Infinite Reach, Mercury, Mono Prix, Natural Fire, Neon Spear, Noble Piper, Noble Response, Oak Apple, Pine Apple, Provide Relief, Resolute Response, Sharp Point.

Kiribati

Participates in Asia-Pacific Center for Security Studies executive courses.

US COMMAND: PACOM.

Kosovo

See Serbia and Montenegro, Kosovo.

Kuwait

Kuwait has been the single most important US ally in the war against Iraq since the invasion on 2 Aug 1990 and the multi-national coalition under Desert Storm to eject it. Throughout the 1990s, Kuwait hosted (and financed) a growing and more capable US military presence, supported Southern Watch and a profusion of US military operations against Iraq, pre-positioned materiel and ammunition, and hardened its country for war. Kuwait has been especially supportive of the Multinational Interception Force (MIF) and all efforts aimed at enforcing UN Security Council–declared sanctions against the Saddam-led Iraqi government.

After 9/11, Kuwait hosted the CENTCOM headquarters for US military ground operations in Afghanistan, and served as an unlimited staging base for the US. As tensions with Iraq grew in 2002–2003, Kuwaiti officials heightened security along their border with Iraq to prevent infiltration, and Kuwait worked with Jordan, Syria, and Iran to develop procedures to increase intelligence sharing and enhance customs and border monitoring cooperation.

During the 2002–2003 buildup to and execution of Operation Iraqi Freedom (OIF), Kuwait was the central coalition partner, reserving a full 60 percent of its total landmass for use by coalition forces and donating upward of $350 million in assistance in kind (primarily fuel) to the war effort. In the aftermath of OIF, Kuwait has been consistently involved in reconstruction efforts in Iraq, pledging $1.5 billion at the Oct 2003 international donors' conference in Madrid.

US COMMAND: CENTCOM.

AGREEMENTS: Classified SOFA, Acquisition and Cross-Servicing Agreement eligible (20 Apr 1993), granted Major Non-NATO Ally status (17 Feb 2004).

Kuwait is a member of the Gulf Cooperation Council (GCC).

US ASSISTANCE: US military sales to Kuwait total $6.8 billion since 1992. The US provides military and defense technical assistance to Kuwait from both foreign military sales (FMS) and commercial sources. All transactions are made by direct cash sale. Principal US military systems currently purchased by the Kuwait Defense Forces are Patriot missile systems, F-18 Hornet fighters, the M1A2 main battle tank, and the Apache helicopter.

BASES AND ACCESS: Prior to 9/11, the US had six CENTCOM-controlled facilities in Kuwait, and utilized an additional 21 Kuwaiti-controlled facilities. In 2002, Kuwait hosted greatly increased contingents of US ground and air forces deployed both to support of ongoing operations in Afghanistan and to prepare for possible operations against Iraq. Kuwait contributed more than 50 percent of US nonpersonnel stationing costs prior to 2001 at the main bases at Arifjan, Camp Doha, Ahmed al Jaber AB, Ali al-Salem AB, Kuwait City, Mina al Ahmadi, and Kuwait IAP. After 9/11, Kuwait provided basing and overflight permission for all US and coalition forces. Prior to OIF, Kuwait hosted a pre-positioned US Army heavy brigade equipment set.

Code Names: Arabian Gauntlet, Bell Buoy, Blue Flag, Bright Star, Desert series, Eager series, Early Victor, Earnest Will, Grecian Firebolt, Hammer Handle, Inherent Fury, Initial Link, Internal Look, Intrinsic Action, Iris Gold, Lucky Sentinel, Lucky Warrior, Native Fury, Pacific Wind, Peninsula series, Phoenix Scorpion, Provide Cover, Rolling Thunder, Rugged Nautilus, Sunny Hope, Turbo Cads, Ultimate Resolve, Unified Orbit, Vigilant series.

Kwajalein Atoll
See Marshall Islands.

Kyrgyzstan

The Kyrgyz Republic joined NATO's Partnership for Peace program on 1 Jun 1994, when it began regular participation in PfP exercises and regional and multi-lateral fora. Following 9/11, the Kyrgyz government immediately offered assistance and allowed US and coalition combat and support aircraft to operate from a base adjacent to the Manas International Airport in Bishkek (named Ganci air base for Chief Peter J. Ganci Jr., chief of the New York City Fire Department, who died on 9/11). In 2003, Russia also opened an air base in Kyzgyzstan, only 19 miles from Ganci. Though the Kyrgyz government and Moscow take the position that Ganci only supports humanitarian missions for Operation Enduring Freedom (OEF) in Afghanistan, the US states that the base will exist "as long as necessary."

As the Kyrgyz–US strategic relationship has grown stronger, the country's domestic stability has markedly deteriorated. President Askar Akayev continued to wield autocratic power after a rigged 2000 election. The government clamped down on independent media and intimidated and arrested opposition political figures. In Mar 2002, Kyrgyz authorities opened fire on demonstrators in the southern Ak-Sui, killing civilians. In a Feb 2003 constitutional referendum, President Akayev achieved overwhelming backing to remain in office until 2005. The conduct of the referendum, which abolished the upper house and granted immunity to Akayev, was criticized by international organizations and opposition groups. Also in 2003, there were protests throughout Kyrgyzstan against US military action in Iraq.

The political opposition is primarily based in southern Kyrgyzstan, and leaders there accuse Akayev of neglecting their region at the expense of the north. There is also opposition to the US military presence and resentment that the US has muted its criticism of the central government since Kyrgyzstan became a military base. There are suspicions that Akayev and his family are personally profiting from the strategic alliance with the US. (In 2002, Kyrgyzstan's deputy prime minister praised the economic benefits of Manas, saying that coalition forces had spent up to $35 million, about 15 percent of Kyrgyzstan's yearly budget.) In May 2002, after the Kyrgyz government resigned en masse, President Akayev appointed an ethnic Russian prime minister, further angering the opposition.

Insurgent and terrorist activity in Kyrgyzstan has also provided the backdrop for government repression. In Dec 2002, a bombing occurred at the Dordoi Bazaar, a market frequented by locals and foreigners. And in May 2003, a bank in Osh was bombed. The Kyrgyz government blamed the Islamic Movement of Uzbekistan (IMU) for both bombings. Al Qaeda and other militant Islamic groups are also suspected of operating in the country. Since 2000, after a kidnapping incident involving US citizens, travel in the republic has been restricted south and west of Osh and in rural areas along the Kyrgyz–Uzbek border.

Since 9/11, the US has invested substantial capital in Kyrgyzstan. From FY 1993 to 2001, the US obligated about $317 million in assistance, about $309 million of which was economic aid. In FY 2002, budgeted assistance totaled about $85 million. Requested assistance for FYs 2003 and 2004 totaled about $92 million. The US conducts a variety of forms of military cooperation with Kyrgyzstan, and provides counter-terrorism, security, and law enforcement aid for intelligence, border guards, customs, and the Ministry of Interior. Recent efforts have focused on special operations, mountain survival, and training of airborne and related unit leaders. The State Department has also funded research grant proposals to redirect former Soviet weapons scientists to peaceful, civilian research. With the fall of the Taliban, Kyrgyzstan has increasingly become a transshipment point for drugs. Growing anti-crime training and technical assistance programs provide training and infrastructure to enhance Kyrgyz counter-narcotics capabilities.

US COMMAND: CENTCOM. US operations are under the command of Combined Joint Task Force 180 (CJTF-180).

AGREEMENTS: US–Kyrgyz Manas basing agreement (SOFA), Acquisition and Cross-Servicing Agreement eligible (6 Feb 1996).

Kyrgyz has signed Status of Forces Agreements with each coalition country deploying forces to Ganci air base, including South Korea, Italy, Spain, Denmark, Norway, and the Netherlands.

Prior to 9/11, the MT National Guard and Kyrgyzstan had a full year of exchanges. In mid-Feb 2001, Kyrgyz armed forces personnel traveled to Montana for training in cold-weather tactics, techniques, and procedures in mountain rescue. Kyrgyz and MT medical specialists conducted summer training in Helena. Kyrgyz personnel conducted infantry exchanges and Military Support to Civil Authorities training. After 9/11, the exchanges flourished, capped off by a visit by the commanding general of the Kyrgyzstan National Guard to Montana in 2002.

Kyrgyzstan is a member of the Shanghai Cooperation Organization (SCO) with China, Russia, Kazakhstan, Tajikistan, and Uzbekistan.

US ASSISTANCE: Receives Foreign Military Financing program grants, International Military Education and Training aid, eligible to receive grant Excess Defense Articles, National Guard partner with Montana, receives Nonproliferation, Anti-terrorism, Demining, and Related (NADR) and Anti-Terrorism Assistance funds for counter-terrorism training to law enforcement and other security personnel, participates in George C. Marshall Center conferences and seminars, participates in the Export Control and Related Border Security Assistance program, receives Anti-Crime Training and Technical Assistance support.

BASES AND ACCESS: Kyrgyzstan was designated a combat zone as of 1 Oct 2001, and Imminent Danger Pay was authorized for US military personnel in Feb 2002. Manas International Airport (Peter Ganci AB), located 19 miles from Bishkek, is the main military base for US and coalition aircraft, established in Dec 2001. The base was transformed from a "bare base" to an operational facility within 74 days in 2001–2002. Between 15 and 25 attack sorties were then launched daily in support of OEF, including Marine Corps F/A-18s and French Mirage 2000s. French Mirage and tanker aircraft actively supported the coalition during Operation Anaconda in Mar 2002. In early Oct 2002, French forces at Manas completed their mission and withdrew. They were replaced by Norwegian, Danish, and Dutch F-16 aircraft. As of 2004, troops from Australia, Denmark, France, Italy, the Netherlands, New Zealand, Norway, South Korea, and Spain had been deployed to Manas. The Kyrgyz government, under pressure from Moscow, turned down plans by Estonia, Latvia, and Lithuania to send forces to Manas. Manas is also a US transit hub for Bagram and Mazar-i-Sharif in Afghanistan and Karshi-Khanabad, Uzbekistan.

A British Royal Marines team visited Kyrgyzstan in Dec 2001 on a scoping mission to assess the potential to help start a new Kyrgyz Mountain Warfare Training Unit. Turkey has also provided training to Kyrgyz mountain troops. In Oct 2002, China and Kyrgyzstan conducted a joint military exercise aimed at coordinating their response to terrorism.

In 1994 Kyrgyzstan agreed to permit Russian army border troops to guard Kyrgyzstan's border with China. Prior to 9/11, Akayev pushed for even more Russian military presence, hinting broadly that if Russia was not interested in managing Soviet air bases in the republic, perhaps other powers, such as the US or North Atlantic Treaty Organization, might be. The Russian military presence remained modest until Jun 2003, when a Russian military air base was established at Kant, near Bishkek and only 30 miles from Manas. The base was constructed under the auspices of the Collective Security Treaty Organization (CSTO), involving Russia, Armenia, Belarus, Kazakhstan, Kyrgyzstan, and Tajikistan. Kant is expected to house more than 20 Russian aircraft, including Su-25 and Su-27 fighters.

Code Names: Centrasbat, Combined Endeavor, Cooperative series, Eloquent Nugget, Ferghana, IWER, Regional Cooperation.

Laos

Since the restoration of full diplomatic relations in 1992, progress in accounting for Americans missing in Laos from the Vietnam War has been a principal measure of improving relations. Counter-narcotics activities are also an important part of the bilateral relationship. In the 1990s, humanitarian demining and efforts to eradicate enormous amounts of unexploded ordnance from the war was added to the mix.

Following 9/11, the Lao government approved a long-standing US request to post a regional security officer at the US embassy. Laos has also issued an assets freeze order, has publicly supported US actions in the war on terrorism, and has passed eight international anti-terrorism conventions.

US COMMAND: PACOM. Joint Task Force Full Accounting.

AGREEMENTS: Article 98 Agreement (24 Dec 2003).

US ASSISTANCE: Receives International Military Education and Training aid, eligible to receive grant Excess Defense Articles, receives aid for humanitarian demining efforts, participated in its first executive course at the Asia Pacific Center for Security Studies in FY 2002 . Grant Excess Defense Articles items, including communications equipment and transportation assets to support counter-narcotics goals, accounting of missing personnel from the war in Southeast Asia, and demining.

Code Names: Full Accounting.

Latvia

Latvia became a member of NATO on 24 Mar 2004. Following 9/11, Latvia declared its support for the war on terrorism and approved blanket overflight clearance and use of airfields and ports. It has sent modest forces to Afghanistan and Iraq. The country subsequently adopted an counter-terrorism action plan, including amendments to the country's criminal law holding individuals responsible for both participating in and providing financial support to terror operations.

Latvia is involved in the full program of NATO and Baltic regional military activities and exercises. Estonia, Latvia, and Lithuania have formed a joint peacekeeping battalion (BALTBAT), a joint navy unit (BALTRON), a joint system of airspace monitoring (BALTNET), and a joint military school (BALTDEFCOL). US special operations forces have also conducted Joint/Combined Exchange Training (JCET) special operations training with the Special Tasks Unit *(Special Uzdevumu)* Vieniba at Riga.

US COMMAND: EUCOM.

AGREEMENTS: NATO SOFA (16 Jun 1951), PfP SOFA (18 May 1996), Acquisition and Cross-Servicing Agreement (30 Mar 1998).

US ASSISTANCE: Receives Foreign Military Financing program grants, International Military Education and Training aid, eligible to receive grant Excess Defense Articles, National Guard partner with MI, participates in the Export Control and Related Border Security Assistance program.

FORCES DEPLOYED: For Operation Enduring Freedom, Latvia deployed a small team as part of the Danish contingent in Manas, Kyrgyzstan. Latvia contributed a medical team in support of the International Security Assistance Force in Afghanistan. For Operation Iraqi Freedom, Latvia contributed an infantry company under the Polish-led Multi-National Division. Latvia deploys forces in Bosnia (Stabilization Force) and Kosovo (Kosovo Force), doubling its contributions to compensate for NATO forces deployed elsewhere.

Code Names: Amber Hope, Amber Sea, Baltic series, Baltlink, Baltops, Bikini, Centrasbat, Combined Endeavor, Cooperative series, Cornerstone, Eloquent Nugget, Joint series, MEDCEUR, Open Spirit, Partner Challenge, Peaceshield, Rescuer, Viking.

Lebanon

Lebanon is host to numerous US-designated terrorist groups, including Lebanese Hezbollah, the Palestinian Islamic Jihad (PIJ), the Popular Front for the Liberation of Palestine — General Command (PFLP-GC), the Abu Nidal organization (ANO), and Hamas. Lebanon's counter-terrorism efforts generally ignore or exempt organizations that target Israel from money laundering and terrorism financing laws, and Lebanese security forces are unwilling to enter Palestinian refugee camps. Syria and Iran additionally support Hezbollah activities in Lebanon, and provide training and assistance to Palestinian rejectionist groups. There are some counter-terrorism activities in Lebanon, particularly against Sunni extremists in the north who have attacked Lebanese interests and soldiers, and Asbat al-Ansar, which has been linked to al Qaeda.

Israel withdrew its troops from southern Lebanon in May 2000, ending 22 years of occupation. An estimated 16,000 Syrian troops remain deployed in Lebanon and, despite an agreement in 1992, did not leave Greater Beirut until mid-2001. The Israeli–Lebanese border is monitored by the United Nations Interim Force in Lebanon (UNIFIL), created in 1978. UNIFIL is supported by UN Truce Supervision Organization (UNTSO) observers. As of 31 Jan 2004, some 2,000 troops were deployed with UNIFIL.

US **command**: Under change 3 to the Unified Command Plan signed by President Bush on 10 Mar 2004, Lebanon was moved from European to Central Command's area of responsibility.

US **assistance**: Receives International Military Education and Training aid (reinstated in 1993), eligible to receive grant Excess Defense Articles (resumed in 1991), receives aid for humanitarian demining efforts.

Lesotho

US **command**: EUCOM.

US **assistance**: Receives International Military Education and Training aid, participates in Africa Center for Strategic Studies conferences and seminars.

Agreements: Acquisition and Cross-Servicing Agreement eligible (26 Jan 1998).

Liberia

Civil war in 2002 spread throughout Liberia and to the outskirts of the capital, Monrovia, with the Movement of Democracy for Liberia (MODEL) emerging from the Krahn ethnic group in eastern Liberia, and joined by disaffected Liberians, mercenaries, and former fighters of the Guinea-based Liberians United for Reconciliation and Democracy (LURD). By Jun 2003, LURD was 10 miles outside of Monrovia and MODEL controlled most of eastern Liberia. The US deployed Special Operations Command Europe to Liberia as a Joint Special Operations Task Force with 300 special operations personnel to coordinate and assist with the evacuation of 133 American citizens and 32 third-country nationals. The US then responded to the worsening humanitarian crisis by deploying JTF Liberia, a sea-based Joint Task Force (JTF) of more than 3,800 commanded by the army's Southern European Task Force (SETAF) headquarters. The American presence both offshore and on the ground supported the introduction of the peacekeeping force from the Economic Community of West African States (ECOWAS).

Peace talks among all sides, sponsored by ECOWAS and the members of the International Contact Group on Liberia, began in Accra, Ghana, in Jun. This coincided with the announcement by the Special Court for Sierra Leone of its indictment of President Charles Taylor for war crimes and crimes against humanity committed since 1996 in the Sierra Leonean civil war. On 4 Aug, Nigerian forces arrived in Monrovia as the vanguard of the ECOWAS international force (ECOMIL) mandated by UN Security Council Resolution 1497, and on 14 Aug President Taylor went into exile in Calabar, Nigeria. A

Comprehensive Peace Agreement was signed by all parties to the conflict on 18 Sep 2003. The National Transitional Government of Liberia (NTGL) is made up of representatives from LURD, MODEL, the former Taylor government, civil society, and political parties. On 19 Sep 2003, the UN Security Council authorized a 15,000-strong peacekeeping force (United Nations Mission in Liberia, UNMIL) to provide security. As of 31 Jan 2004, 11,453 total uniformed personnel are deployed.

US COMMAND: EUCOM.

AGREEMENTS: Article 98 Agreement (Oct 2003).

Code Names: Assured Lift, Assured Response, Liane, MEDFLAG, Shadow Express, Sharp Edge, Shining Express.

Libya

Though Libya officially remains on the US government's State Sponsors of Terrorism list, the US opened a Liaison Office in Tripoli on 28 Jun 2004 and is well on the way to normalizing relations in the wake of Libya's decision to repudiate weapons of mass destruction and cooperate with international legal bodies on holding Libyans responsible for international terror incidents.

On 21 Dec 1988, Pan Am Flight 103 was blown up over Lockerbie, Scotland. All 259 passengers and crew were killed, as were 11 residents of Lockerbie. In 1999, the Libyan government surrendered two Libyans suspected of involvement in the bombing. The Lockerbie trial, which began on 3 May 2000, found one Libyan guilty, and trilateral talks began on 13 Feb 2001 to discuss how Libya could meet the remaining requirements of the UN Security Council. These talks culminated in the UK tabling a resolution on 15 Aug 2003 recommending that the Security Council lift UN sanctions. Libya accepted responsibility for the actions of its officials and agreed to payment of appropriate compensation to the victims' families. UN sanctions were lifted on 12 Sep 2003.

On 13 Nov 2001, a German court additionally found four persons, including a former employee of the Libyan embassy in East Berlin, guilty in connection with the 1986 La Belle disco bombing, in which two US servicemen were killed. The court also established a connection to the Libyan government.

US COMMAND: EUCOM.

Code Names: Arid Farmer, Coronet Lightning, Creek series, Eagle Look, Early Call, El Dorado Canyon, Prairie Fire.

Lithuania

Lithuania became a member of NATO on 24 Mar 2004. On 26 Sep 2001, Lithuania granted blanket overflight rights to the US and 10 NATO members in support of the war on terrorism and operations in Afghanistan, an offer that was renewed on 1 Jan 2003. With NATO membership, Lithuania is transforming its military to focus more on contributing to international operations, rather than territorial defense. It has participated in 11 international operations, including Afghanistan and Iraq.

Lithuania is involved in the full program of NATO and Baltic regional military activities and exercises. Estonia, Latvia, and Lithuania have formed a joint peacekeeping battalion (BALTBAT), a joint navy unit (BALTRON), a joint system of airspace monitoring (BALTNET), and a joint military school (BALTDEFCOL). US special operations forces (SOF) have also conducted Joint/Combined Exchange Training (JCET) special operations training with YPT-40 at Klaipeda.

US COMMAND: EUCOM.

AGREEMENTS: NATO SOFA (16 Jun 1951), PfP SOFA (14 Sep 1996), Acquisition and Cross-Servicing Agreement (30 Apr 1996).

US ASSISTANCE: Receives Foreign Military Financing program grants, International Military Education and Training aid, eligible to receive grant Excess Defense Articles (eligible in FY 2004), National Guard partner with PA, receives Nonproliferation, Anti-terrorism, Demining, and Related (NADR) and Anti-Terrorism Assistance funds for border security.

FORCES DEPLOYED: Since Nov 2002, a small Lithuanian SOF unit has participated in Operation Enduring Freedom in Afghanistan under US command. Lithuania deployed a small detachment as part of Danish contingent deployed to Manas, Kyrgyzstan, and provided medical support to a Czech medical unit in the International Security Assistance Force. Lithuania deployed a detachment as part of the Danish infantry battalion group in the Multi-National Division (South-East) in Iraq. Lithuanian forces have also participated in peacekeeping missions in Bosnia (Stabilization Force) and Kosovo (Kosovo Force).

Code Names: Adventure Express, Amber series, Baltic series, Baltlink, Baltops, Combined Endeavor, Cooperative series, Cornerstone, Eloquent Nugget, Empire Med, Joint series, MEDCEUR, Open Spirit, Partner Challenge, SAREX, Strong Resolve.

Luxembourg

NATO member Luxembourg has participated in the European Corps (EUROCORPS) since 1994 and is now integrated into the Multinational

Belurokas Force under Belgian command. Luxembourg has contributed peacekeeping troops to the UNPROFOR, IFOR/SFOR (Bosnia), and KFOR (Kosovo) missions in the former Yugoslavia. It has also participated in the NATO International Security Assistance Force mission in Afghanistan. Luxembourg has financially supported international peacekeeping missions during Desert Storm, in Rwanda, and in Albania, and has provided humanitarian aid to Iraq.

US COMMAND: EUCOM.

AGREEMENTS: NATO SOFA (16 Jun 1951), Reciprocal SOFA, PfP SOFA (signed 18 Feb 1997), Acquisition and Cross-Servicing Agreement (12 Jun 1996).

BASES AND ACCESS: The US has long stored pre-positioned equipment in Luxembourg for use in an emergency at Bettembourg site, Dudelange, and Sanem Site, Esch-s-Alzette.

Code Names: Clean Hunter, Cooperative series.

Macedonia (former Yugoslav Republic of Macedonia)

Since independence in 1991, Macedonia has struggled to achieve territorial integrity and security, and has worked to strengthen its ties with NATO and the US. With the end of the EU Concordia military mission on 15 Dec 2003, Macedonia for the first time was left without an international military presence. As a NATO aspirant and Partnership for Peace member (11 Nov 1995), Macedonia continues to use the Kosovo Force's presence to familiarize itself with NATO procedures. Macedonia has supported the US in Afghanistan and Iraq, deploying a small special operations forces (SOF) contingent to Iraq.

Prior to the Allied Force bombing in 1999, the number of NATO troops in Macedonia peaked at 17,000. The 2001 Ohrid Framework Agreement ended the National Liberation Army (NLA) armed ethnic Albanian insurgency in northwestern Macedonia. Task Force Essential Harvest deployed in 2001 to collect weapons from the NLA and implement the Ohrid Agreement. Successive task forces (Amber Fox, Allied Harmony) provided security until 31 Mar 2003, when the duty was passed over to the first EU military mission, Concordia, which was terminated on 15 Dec 2003.

US COMMAND: EUCOM.

AGREEMENTS: NATO SOFA (respecting transiting IFOR), SOFA (Jun 1996), PfP SOFA (19 Jul 1996), NATO–Macedonia Basic Agreement (24 Dec 1998), Acquisition and Cross-Servicing Agreement (23 Sep 1998), Article 98 Agreement (2003).

US ASSISTANCE: Receives Foreign Military Financing program grants, International Military Education and Training aid, National Guard partner with Vermont, participates in George C. Marshall Center conferences and seminars. Bilateral assistance provided to Macedonia under the Southeast Europe Economic Development (SEED) Act totaled more than $378 million 1990–2003.

BASES AND ACCESS: The US closed its Camp Able Sentry base in Skopje, Macedonia, in Dec 2002. The Predator Unmanned Aerial Vehicle (RQ-1B) was based in Skopje for operations over Kosovo, and withdrew in Jul 2001. NATO Headquarters Skopje (NHQS) was created in Apr 2002 to amalgamate existing organizations in Macedonia, including Kosovo Force Rear. Macedonia continues to be the main conduit for assistance and logistics for international forces and the UN administration in Kosovo.

Code Names: Able Sentry, Allied Effort, Allied Harbor, Amber Fox, Arcade Guard, Brave Eagle, Combined Endeavor, Concordia, Cooperative series, Cornerstone, Eagle, Eloquent Nugget, Essential Harvest, Esperia, Hazarfend, Joint Endeavor, MEDCEUR, Open Road, Peaceful Eagle, Peaceful Oriole, Prometheus, Rescuer, Saber, Strong Resolve, Viking.

Madagascar

Madagascar has supported the war on terrorism through law enforcement cooperation and implementation of financial sector counter-terrorism measures. US military assistance focuses on counter-drug maritime activities and coastal security.

US COMMAND: EUCOM? PACOM.

AGREEMENTS: SOFA (13 Mar 2000), Acquisition and Cross-Servicing Agreement eligible, Article 98 Agreement.

US ASSISTANCE: Receives International Military Education and Training aid, eligible to receive grant Excess Defense Articles, participates in Africa Center for Strategic Studies conferences and seminars.

Code Names: Cathode Emission, SAREX, Shant Doot.

Malawi

Malawi was the only southern African country to receive peacekeeping training under the US-sponsored African Crisis Response Initiative (ACRI). It has an active slate of military-to-military programs, including Joint/Combined Exchange Training (JCET) special operations training between the Malawi Army Parachute Battalion and the US 3rd Special Forces Group. The national police also receives US assistance.

US COMMAND: EUCOM.

AGREEMENTS: Activity-specific SOFA (28 Jul 1997), Acquisition and Cross-Servicing Agreement eligible (26 Jan 1998), Article 98 Agreement (20 Sep 2003).

US ASSISTANCE: Receives International Military Education and Training aid, eligible to receive grant Excess Defense Articles, participates in African Contingency Operations Training and Assistance program and the earlier ACRI, participates in Africa Center for Strategic Studies conferences and seminars.

FORCES DEPLOYED: Malawi has deployed ACRI-trained observers in Kosovo and the Democratic Republic of the Congo.

Code Names: Silver Eagle.

Malaysia

Predominantly Muslim, Malaysia has quietly supported the war on terrorism and US forward presence in Asia. But Malaysia opposed military action in Iraq on the basis that it did not have UN backing and declined to contribute to the International Security Assistance Force in Afghanistan because it was not a UN force. Still, Malaysia signed a bilateral counter-terrorism agreement with the US in May 2002, and has approved all requests for overflight clearance since 9/11, welcoming US ships under the cover of joint military activities. Malaysia also increasingly shares intelligence and law enforcement information with US authorities, and has become a center for counter-terrorism training.

In Aug 2003, Malaysia opened the Association of Southeast Asian Nations (ASEAN) Southeast Asia Regional Center for Counterterrorism (SEARCCT), which will train police and security personnel from 15 nations in South and Southeast Asia. SEARCCT's first training was sponsored by the US Treasury's financial intelligence unit and involved 15 nations. The US and Malaysia also co-hosted the ASEAN Regional Forum (ARF) Intersessional Meeting on Counter-Terrorism and Transnational Crime in Mar 2003.

Australia remains Malaysia's major source of military assistance and training, but the US–Malaysia Bilateral Training and Consultative Group (BITACG) is the longest-standing bilateral exchange that US PACOM has. In the early 1990s, Malaysia undertook a major program to expand and modernize its armed forces, including procurement of US F/A-18 and C-130 aircraft. Joint/Combined Exchange Training (JCET) special operations training also is conducted with 4th Troop Yankee Squadron, 21st Commando Regiment, and 21st Special Services Group at Camp Sungai Udang (Malaka) Subang. The US regularly sends forces to receive jungle survival training at Malaysia's Jungle

Warfare Training Center in Pulada. The Malaysian army also sends a team of jungle trainers to Hawaii each year to run a jungle tracking and survival course for US military based there.

US COMMAND: PACOM.

AGREEMENTS: Classified SOFA, Declaration of Cooperation to Combat International Terrorism (May 2002), Acquisition and Cross-Servicing Agreement (18 Mar 1997).

Malaysia is a member of the Five Power Defence Agreement (FPDA — Australia, Malaysia, New Zealand, Singapore, and the UK), originally intended to replace the former defense role of the UK in the Singapore–Malaysia area. In Aug 2002, Australia and Malaysia signed an additional agreement on counter-terrorism cooperation.

US ASSISTANCE: Receives International Military Education and Training aid, eligible to receive grant Excess Defense Articles, receives Nonproliferation, Anti-terrorism, Demining, and Related (NADR) and Anti-Terrorism Assistance funds to improve export controls, participates in Asia-Pacific Center for Security Studies executive courses, participates in Container Security Initiative.

BASES AND ACCESS: Imminent Danger Pay for Malaysia was authorized in Oct 2001. US ships and submarines visit and refuel at Kota-Kinabulu, Kuantan, Lumut, Penang, and Port Klang. Australia also maintains a presence at Butterworth AB.

FORCES DEPLOYED: Malaysia has contributed to UN peacekeeping in Angola, East Timor, the former Yugoslavia, Kuwait, Western Sahara, and Liberia. Malaysia also provided humanitarian and medical support to help Afghan refugees in Pakistan.

Code Names: Baker Mint, Baker Mint Lens, Balance Mint, CARAT Malaysia, Churinga, Cooperative Thunder, Cope Taufan, Cope Thunder, Cope Tiger, Cope West, Flying Fish, Haringaroo, IADS ADEX, Kangaroo, Keris Strike, Paskal, SEACAT, Shant Doot, Shanti Path, Southern Tiger, Stardex, Starfish, Suman Warrior, Unified Shield, Vector Balance Mint, Westpac MCMEX.

Maldives

The Maldives supports the war on terrorism, and offered blanket overflight and ship clearances for Operation Enduring Freedom. Airport access provided in Desert Storm was again offered for the Afghanistan operation. US vessels regularly call at Male, and the US funds training in airport management, customs, and counter-narcotics. The US also trains a small number of Maldivian military personnel annually. Absent a US mission in the Maldives, relations are managed by the US embassy in Sri Lanka.

US COMMAND: PACOM?

AGREEMENTS: Article 98 Agreement, Acquisition and Cross-Servicing Agreement eligible.

US ASSISTANCE: Receives International Military Education and Training aid, participates in Asia-Pacific Center for Security Studies executive courses.

Code Names: NOLES, SAREX, Shant Doot.

Mali

Mali is active in the war on terrorism and key recipient of the Pan Sahel Initiative and EUCOM North Africa counter-terrorism program attention. In Oct 2003, Mali sponsored a pan-Sahel regional counter-terrorism seminar in Bamako. Mali also participated in a Mar 2004 EUCOM counter-terrorism chiefs of defense conference in Stuttgart, Germany, with Algeria, Chad, Mauritania, Morocco, Niger, Senegal, Tunisia, and the US.

In Feb 2003, 14 of 32 European hostages of the Algeria-based Salafist Group for Preaching and Combat (GSPC) were taken to northern Mali before being released in Aug 2003. The Malian military reportedly chased up to 100 GSPC members out of Mali in Jan 2004 and continued thereafter to quietly work with US special operations forces (SOF) in joint counter-terrorism initiatives.

An active Joint/Combined Exchange Training (JCET) special operations program among the Malian 33rd Parachute Regiment, the 512th Motorized Infantry Company, and the 3rd and 10th Special Force Groups has resulted in numerous trainings and exercises. In Mar 2004, the 1st Battalion, 10th Special Forces Group and the 352nd Special Operations Group trained with the 33rd Regiment and 5th Military Region in Timbuktu, and conducted counter-terrorism operations in Gao, Bamako, and Timbuktu. Air operations included two standard air-drop training bundles and one army personnel drop.

US COMMAND: EUCOM.

AGREEMENTS: SOFA (Exchange of Notes, 30 Jul 1997, 22 Aug 1997, and 30 Sep 1997), Acquisition and Cross-Servicing Agreement in negotiation (2004).

US ASSISTANCE: Receives International Military Education and Training aid (one of the largest such programs in Africa on a per capita basis), eligible to receive grant Excess Defense Articles, participates in the Regional Defense Counter-terrorism Fellowship (RD Combined Task Force) program, receives peacekeeping operations (PKO) funding, participates in African Contingency Operations Training and Assistance (ACOTA) program and earlier African Crisis Response Initiative (ACRI), participates in Africa Center for Strategic Studies conferences and seminars.

BASES AND ACCESS: US forces have reportedly negotiated access to Gao airport.

Code Names: Flintlock, MEDFLAG.

Activities by Country

Malta

After an earlier period of frosty relations, in 1992 US Navy ships started paying regular liberty calls in Malta. The US focus for Malta is stemming illicit trafficking in the Mediterranean Sea, which is accomplished through Active Endeavour.

US COMMAND: EUCOM.

US ASSISTANCE: Receives Foreign Military Financing program grants and International Military Education and Training aid.

BASES AND ACCESS: US navy ships and submarines regularly call at Valetta.

Code Names: SAREX.

Marshall Islands (Kwajalein)[7]

The US has full authority and responsibility for security and defense of the Marshall Islands. The DOD, under a subsidiary government-to-government agreement, has use of the lagoon and several islands on Kwajalein Atoll, the largest in the world. The original agreement allows the use of the US Army Kwajalein Atoll (USAKA) missile test range until 2016, and subsequent amendments and options extend rights until 2086. Another major subsidiary agreement of the original compact provides for settlement of all claims arising from US nuclear tests conducted at Bikini and Enewetak Atolls 1946–1958. Kwajalein is used to support missile testing, missile defense, and intelligence collection.

US COMMAND: PACOM. The US Army Pacific (USARPAC) is the joint commander for homeland defense, civil support, and consequence management.

AGREEMENTS: Compact of Free Association (25 Jun 1983, with amendments entered into force 21 Oct 1986), Article 98 Agreement.

Mauritania

US–Mauritania relations reached a low point in 1991, first because of Mauritania's support for Iraq, and then because of the Mauritanian military's role in widespread human rights abuses and reports of continued slavery. All assistance was halted. By the late 1990s, Mauritania was rehabilitated and military cooperation and training resumed. Mauritania opened diplomatic relations with Israel in 2000 and remains one of only three Arab League member nations to have done so.

---

7. The Republic of the Marshall Islands is a self-governing country in a Compact of Free Association with the US. It comprises 34 atolls and coral islands stretching in two parallel chains across thousands of miles of the western Pacific.

After 9/11, Mauritania agreed to block all terrorist-related financial assets. Mauritania is a participant in the Pan Sahel Initiative, a multi-year effort to wage war on terrorism and enhance border control in the Sahel region of Mali, Niger, Mauritania, and Chad. Mauritania participated in a Mar 2004 EUCOM counter-terrorism chiefs of defense conference in Stuttgart, Germany, with Algeria, Chad, Mali, Morocco, Niger, Senegal, Tunisia, and the US. In Mar 2004, the US 1st Battalion, 10th Special Forces Group, and 352nd Special Operations Group trained with the 1st Commando Battalion in Atar airport and the surrounding area. In Jun 2004, Mauritania was also designated a full-fledged partner in the NATO Mediterranean Dialogue.

US COMMAND: EUCOM.

AGREEMENTS: Acquisition and Cross-Servicing Agreement eligible (26 Jan 1998), Article 98 Agreement.

US ASSISTANCE: Receives International Military Education and Training aid (initiated in FY 2002), eligible to receive grant Excess Defense Articles, receives aid for human-itarian demining efforts, receives regional peacekeeping operations (PKO) funding, participates in Africa Center for Strategic Studies conferences and seminars.

Code Names: Eloquent Nugget, MEDFLAG.

Mauritius

Since 9/11, Mauritius has consistently supported the war on terrorism, passing counter-terrorism legislation and responding to US requests for financial inter-diction of terrorist resources. With the support of the Department of the Treasury, Mauritius established a financial intelligence unit. The US also pro-vides training to the Mauritian Coast Guard in maritime law enforcement and coastal security.

US COMMAND: PACOM?

AGREEMENTS: Article 98 Agreement (26 Jun 2003).

US ASSISTANCE: Receives International Military Education and Training aid, eligible to receive grant Excess Defense Articles, participates in Asia-Pacific Center for Security Studies executive courses, participates in Africa Center for Strategic Studies conferences and seminars.

Code Names: SAREX, Shant Doot.

Mexico

US–Mexican national security relations are dominated by counter-narcotics and, since 9/11, additional border control measures to fight terrorism and transnational crime, including the US–Mexico Smart Border Accord — a 22-point border action plan signed in 2002 that aims to improve border infrastructure. The US conducts extensive training in the counter-narcotics area.

US COMMAND: With the creation of NORTHCOM in 2002, Mexico no longer falls under SOUTHCOM.

AGREEMENTS: Since 1981, the management of US–Mexican relations has been formalized in the US–Mexico Binational Commission, which holds annual plenary meetings overseeing many subgroups including counter-narcotics and border affairs. Other mechanisms for cooperation include the Senior Law Enforcement Plenary (SLEP), the Bilateral Interdiction Working Group (BIWG), and the US–Mexico Committee on Transborder Critical Infrastructure Protection.

Mexico is one of six nations to ratify the Inter-American Convention Against Terrorism (2003).

US ASSISTANCE: Receives International Military Education and Training aid, eligible to receive grant Excess Defense Articles, National Guard partner with Kentucky, participates in Center for Hemispheric Defense Studies conferences and seminars.

BASES AND ACCESS: US Navy ships and submarines regularly call at Acapulco, Cabo San Lucas, and Puerto Vallarta.

Code Names: Amalgam Virgo, ASCIET, Cabañas, Dimming Sun, Ghostrider, Global Mercury, Mercury, Unified Defense.

Micronesia (Federated States of Micronesia)[8]

The US has full authority and responsibility for security and defense of Micronesia.

US COMMAND: PACOM. The US Army Pacific (USARPAC) is the joint commander for homeland defense, civil support, and consequence management.

AGREEMENTS: Compact of Free Association (1986, renegotiated 14 May 2003), Article 98 Agreement.

Moldova

Moldova has generally supported the war on terrorism since 9/11, offering overflight rights and the use of an airport as well as deploying a small contingent to Iraq. Moldova joined the NATO Partnership for Peace on 16 Mar 1994, and has a cooperative security relationship with the US. US assistance

8. The Federated States of Micronesia is an independent country in a Compact of Free Association with the US. It consists of 607 volcanic islands spread over 1.2 million square miles of ocean just north of the equator.

focuses on developing a special operations capability within Moldova's armed forces in order to handle a low-level terrorist threat, preventing weapons proliferation, and combating transnational crime.

Moldova continues to have conflicts with Russia and separatist forces in the Transnistrian region. As of 2004, Russia had not removed the weapons and munitions for its forces in Transnistria, a pledge it had made in 1999.

US COMMAND: EUCOM, effective 1 Oct 1998.

AGREEMENTS: Reciprocal SOFA, PfP SOFA (31 Oct 1997), Acquisition and Cross-Servicing Agreement eligible (26 Jan 1998).

On 10 Oct 1997, the US signed an agreement with Moldova to purchase 21 MiG-29 Fulcrum fighter aircraft and associated air-to-air weapons equipment. The Moldovan MiGs were delivered from Markulesht AB, Moldova, to the National Air Intelligence Center, Wright-Patterson Air Force Base, OH, for exploitation.

US ASSISTANCE: Receives Foreign Military Financing program grants, International Military Education and Training aid, eligible to receive grant Excess Defense Articles, National Guard partner with North Carolina, participates in George C. Marshall Center conferences and seminars, participates in the Export Control and Related Border Security Assistance program for monitoring the secessionist region of Transnistria and establishing the Moldovan Department of Civil Defense "first response unit" for weapons of mass destruction.

BASES AND ACCESS: Moldova allows the use of Moldovan airspace for the war on terrorism and has offered the use of Chisinau airport.

FORCES DEPLOYED: Moldova sent a contingent of deminers and peacekeepers to participate in post-conflict humanitarian assistance in Iraq.

Code Names: Combined Endeavor, Cooperative series, Cornerstone, Dacia, Eloquent Nugget, MEDCEUR, Peaceshield, Provide Hope, Rescue Eagle.

Mongolia

US–Mongolian military relations focus on training for Mongolian special forces, peacekeeping, medical, and civil affairs units at the Mongolian Armed Forces Training Center. US special operations forces (SOF) have also conducted Joint/Combined Exchange Training (JCET) special operations training with the Peacekeeping Battalion at Ulaanbaatar and Tsetserleg.

US COMMAND: PACOM.

AGREEMENTS: Article 98 Agreement.

US ASSISTANCE: Receives Foreign Military Financing program grants, International

Military Education and Training aid, eligible to receive grant Excess Defense Articles, receives Enhanced International Peacekeeping Capabilities (EIPC) grants for training, participates in Asia-Pacific Center for Security Studies executive courses.

FORCES DEPLOYED: In 2002, Mongolia began participating in international peace-keeping operations with the deployment of observers to the UN Mission in the Congo. Mongolia also sent a peacekeeping contingent for Operation Iraqi Freedom.

Code Names: Baker Mondial, Baker Mongoose, Balance Magic, Centrasbat, Cobra Gold, Regional Cooperation, Shant Doot, Shanti Path.

Morocco

Morocco was among the first Arab and Islamic states to denounce the 9/11 terrorist attacks, just as it was the first Arab state to condemn Iraq's invasion of Kuwait in 1990. In Jun 2002, Morocco took into custody al Qaeda operatives plotting to attack US and NATO ships in the Strait of Gibraltar, and US assistance since 9/11 has focused on improving Morocco's coastal surveillance and security in the strait and on its northern coast. An ongoing Joint/Combined Exchange Training (JCET) special operations program exists among the US 10th Special Forces Group and numerous US special operations squadrons and the Moroccan 2nd and 5th Royal Air Forces Bases, 1st and 2nd Parachute Brigades. Morocco participated in a Mar 2004 EUCOM counter-terrorism chiefs of defense conference in Stuttgart, Germany, with Algeria, Chad, Mali, Mauritania, Niger, Senegal, Tunisia, and the US. In Jun 2004, Morocco was designated a full-fledged partner in the NATO Mediterranean Dialogue. Morocco also hosted the large multi-national exercise and show of force Med Shark/Majestic Eagle in Jul 2004.

Morocco's continued claim to Western Sahara has strained Algerian relations for several decades. The Polisario independence movement is based in Tindouf, Algeria, and, despite a 1991 cease-fire, final resolution of the conflict remains elusive. The UN, under the lead of the secretary general's envoy James Baker, continues to explore a final political settlement.

US COMMAND: EUCOM.

AGREEMENTS: SOFA (with classified supplement and Exchange of Letters, 27 May 1982), Mohammedia Port Agreement (Jul 1987), Acquisition and Cross-Servicing Agreement eligible (20 Apr 1993).

US ASSISTANCE: Receives Foreign Military Financing program grants, International Military Education and Training aid, eligible to receive grant Excess Defense

Articles, National Guard partner with Utah (established in 2003), participates in Africa Center for Strategic Studies conferences and seminars.

BASES AND ACCESS: In addition to US Navy port visits to Tangiers, Morocco considers on a case-by-case basis requests from US forces to enter Moroccan airspace. In the past, Morocco has allowed NASA the use of Ben Guerir airfield as an emergency landing site for space shuttles. A $200 million International Board of Broadcasters (IBB) transmitter in Morocco is one of the world's largest. The US previously operated communications facilities at Boukandel and Sidi Yahia, and has recently constructed facilities at Sidi Slimane AB to support US forces exercising in Morocco.

FORCES DEPLOYED: Morocco provided troops in Desert Storm, Somalia, Bosnia (SFOR), and Kosovo (KFOR).

Code Names: Aferdou, African Eagle, African Falcon, African Fox, African Lion, Blue Sands, Burning Bush, Eloquent Nugget, Flank Thrust, Joint Forge, Joint Guardian, Majestic Eagle, Med Shark, MEDFLAG, Outigui, Peace Chellah, Peace Menara.

Mozambique

Post-9/11 US–Mozambican military relations focus on fighting money laundering. A Joint/Combined Exchange Training (JCET) special operations program among the 3rd Special Forces Group and civil affairs specialists and the Mozambique 1st Special Forces Platoon and Graciano Antinio Navila takes place at Boquisso Barracks. In Sep 2002, Mozambique hosted a weeklong conference for southern African countries focused on security cooperation, sponsored by the Africa Center for Strategic Studies.

US COMMAND: EUCOM.

AGREEMENTS: SOFA (3 Mar 2000), Acquisition and Cross-Servicing Agreement eligible (26 Jan 1998).

US ASSISTANCE: Receives International Military Education and Training aid, eligible to receive grant Excess Defense Articles, receives aid for humanitarian demining efforts, participates in Africa Center for Strategic Studies conferences and seminars, receives International Narcotics Control and Law Enforcement funding.

FORCES DEPLOYED: In Apr 2001, with US assistance, Mozambique activated a Quick Reaction Demining Force that can deploy worldwide. The force deployed to Sri Lanka in Apr 2002, and has made subsequent emergency deployments to Sudan and Iraq.

Code Names: Atlas Response, Brilliant Lion, MEDFLAG, Silent Promise.

Namibia

The US military supports Namibia's peacekeeping and demining activities and conducts Joint/Combined Exchange Training (JCET) special operations training among Namibia's 12th and 26th Brigades and US 3rd Special Forces Group in Windhoek.

US COMMAND: EUCOM.

AGREEMENTS: SOFA pending as of 2004, Acquisition and Cross-Servicing Agreement eligible (6 Feb 1996), Exchange of Notes for recovery operations following C-141 crash (Sep 1997). The US does not have an Article 98 agreement with Namibia.

US ASSISTANCE: Receives International Military Education and Training aid, eligible to receive grant Excess Defense Articles, receives aid for humanitarian demining efforts, participates in Africa Center for Strategic Studies conferences and seminars.

Code Names: High Flight, WATC.

Nauru

US COMMAND: PACOM.

AGREEMENTS: Article 98 Agreement.

Nepal

Nepal strongly supports the war on terrorism, though it has been focused on a Maoist insurgency since Feb 1996 and internal stability since Crown Prince Dipendra shot and killed his father, King Birendra, and other members of his family before committing suicide on 1 Jun 2001. Since 2002, Nepal has been under a state of emergency; the House is dissolved, and the king retains full control of the military and government.

The US provides aid to the Royal Nepal Army (RNA) to battle the Maoist insurgents, including counter-terrorism, Ranger, and special operations training, counter-intelligence training, and equipment for the military and police. A Joint/Combined Exchange Training (JCET) special operations program exists between RNA Infantry School at Nagarkot and the US 1st Special Forces Group.

US COMMAND: PACOM.

AGREEMENTS: Anti-terrorism assistance program agreement (25 Apr 2003), Acquisition and Cross-Servicing Agreement eligible (24 Aug 1998), Article 98 Agreement.

US ASSISTANCE: Receives Foreign Military Financing grants, International Military Education and Training aid, receives Enhanced International Peacekeeping Capabilities (EIPC) grants for training, participates in Asia-Pacific Center for Security Studies executive courses, participates in the Terrorist Interdiction Program and the Counter-terrorism Fellowship program.

FORCES DEPLOYED: Nepalese units have served alongside US forces in Haiti, Iraq, and Somalia and have contributed more than 40,000 peacekeepers to missions in Lebanon (UNIFIL), the former Yugoslavia (UNPROFOR), and East Timor (UNTAET), as well as current missions in Sierra Leone and the Democratic Republic of the Congo. Approximately 3,400 Nepalese Gurkhas serve in the UK army, and 40,000 serve in the Indian army. The UK Brigade has one battalion in Brunei.

Code Names: Himalayan Bluebell, Mercury, NOLES, Shant Doot, Shanti Path.

Netherland Antilles

US Customs Service and military aircraft have been operating from Curaçao's Hato International Airport since 1 May 1999. The Curaçao site hosts ANG F-16s, navy P-3 and E-2 airborne early warning planes, air force E-3 AWACS aircraft, and intelligence aircraft. There is close US–Netherlands cooperation on joint counter-narcotics operations in the Caribbean. A 10-year forward operating location (FOL) agreement between the US and the kingdom became effective in Oct 2001 (the base is now called a Cooperative Security Location, or CSL).

US COMMAND: SOUTHCOM.

Code Names: Coronet Nighthawk, Senior Scout, Tradewinds.

The Netherlands

NATO member the Netherlands fully supports the US in the war on terror, hosts US nuclear weapons on its soil, and has been a consistent partner with the US in military operations, intelligence cooperation, and counter-narcotics. The Netherlands was an active partner in Operation Enduring Freedom, and in 2003 took over joint command of the International Security Assistance Force in Afghanistan with Germany. The Netherlands deployed a significant ground force in Iraq; Dutch navy vessels and maritime patrol aircraft also participated in coalition operations in the Indian Ocean and Arabian Gulf regions starting in 2002.

US COMMAND: EUCOM.

AGREEMENTS: NATO SOFA (19 Jun 1951), Exchange of Notes on Stationing of US Armed Forces in the Netherlands (13 Aug 1954), Reciprocal SOFA, Toy Chest Technical Agreement (nuclear weapons), PfP SOFA (25 Jul 1997), Acquisition and Cross-Servicing Agreement (21 Jan 1999).

The first meeting of the bilateral US–Netherlands Aviation Security Working Group was held in Apr 2003, and the inaugural meeting of the Port and Maritime Security Working Group was held in May 2003.

BASES AND ACCESS: The Netherlands still hosts US nuclear weapons at Volkel air base, and serves as a major transshipment point for US military equipment. The US announced in Feb 2000 that it would cease dispersal operations at Soesterberg AB, a former US F-15 base.

In 1999, the US turned over control of pre-positioned equipment stocks in the Netherlands to the Netherlands Pre-positioned Organizational Materiel Sets (NL-POMS), a Dutch national command. The storage and administration sites are at Brunssum, Coevorden, Eygelshoven, and Vriezenveen (Almelo). Rotterdam is the main US military port for shipments. In 2003, thousands of tons of cargo belonging to the Army's V Corps and 4th Infantry Division heading for Iraq were loaded at Rotterdam for shipment to the Middle East. As part of port security measures in the war on terrorism, radiological monitors are being installed in the port of Rotterdam in 2004.

The new NATO Joint Headquarters North has been established in Brunssum (replacing AFNORTH)

FORCES DEPLOYED: The Netherlands deployed six F-16 aircraft and a KDC-10 tanker/transport to Manas, Kyrgyzstan, in Oct 2002 as part of the Danish–Dutch–Norwegian European Participating Air Forces (EPAF) unit. The F-16s flew combat missions over Afghanistan in relief of the French Mirage 2000 unit. Earlier, in Apr 2002, Denmark, the Netherlands, and Norway had established a joint airlift detachment at Manas.

For Operation Iraqi Freedom, in the summer of 2003, the Netherlands sent a contingent of 1,100 troops in a mechanized battalion group as part of the Multi-National Division (South-East) in Iraq, and a KDC-10 was deployed to al Udeid, Qatar. On 11 Jun 2004, the Netherlands extended the deployment of its Iraq forces through at least Mar 2005.

Dutch navy vessels also participated in coalition maritime operations in the Indian Ocean and Arabian Gulf during 2002, and a navy P-3C maritime patrol aircraft deployed to Fujairah in the UAE to conduct surveillance. Other Dutch naval ships, along with Dutch P-3s, also relieved US units in the Caribbean during 2004 to conduct counter-narcotics missions. As part of NATO's contribution to the war on terrorism, Dutch Patriot missiles were deployed in Turkey in 2003, and Dutch frigates and maritime patrol aircraft also participated in Active Endeavour in the Mediterranean Sea. The Netherlands contributed forces to NATO peacekeeping in Bosnia (the Stabilization Force) and Kosovo (the Kosovo Force).

Code Names: Active series, Adventure Express, Amber Star, Arabian Gauntlet, Ardent series, Artful Issue, Baltic series, Baltops, Bartisan Hinge, Battle Griffin, Bright Horizon, Bright Star, Brilliant Foil, Cannon Cloud, Cathode Emission, Central Enterprise, Centurion Crusader, Clean Hunter, Combined Endeavor, Constant Harmony, Cooperative series, Coronet Havoc, Coronet Volunteer, Counter Guard, Destined Glory, Distant Thunder, Dogfish, Dogu Akdeniz, Dynamic series, Frisian Flag, Harvest Partner, Jolly Roger, JTFEX, Linked Seas, Mace, MEDFLAG, Mothia, Optic Windmill, Pacific Protector, Prometheus, Rolling Deep, Sanso, Sea Breeze, SHAREM, Sorbet Royale, Southern Knight, Strong Resolve, Tartan Venture, Toy Chest, Tradewinds, Trial, Unified Charger.

New Zealand

US–New Zealand relations are still officially strained by 1984 Labour government decision to bar nuclear-armed and nuclear-powered ships from New Zealand ports, which led to the US suspending its ANZUS security obligations to New Zealand in Aug 1986. Even after President Bush announced in 1991 that US ships would no longer carry nuclear weapons, New Zealand's legislation prohibiting visits of nuclear-powered ships continues to preclude a bilateral security alliance.

Despite continued suspension, New Zealand has been an active participant in the war on terrorism, is one of the core intelligence partners of the US, and has deployed forces to Afghanistan and Iraq.

US COMMAND: PACOM.

AGREEMENTS: Security Treaty Between Australia, New Zealand and the US (ANZUS Treaty; 1951), SOFA, granted Major Non-NATO Ally status, Acquisition and Cross-Servicing Agreement (2 Nov 2000).

Notwithstanding the suspension of its US–New Zealand element of ANZUS, the formal expression of the bilateral security partnership between New Zealand and Australia is found in the ANZUS Treaty, the 1944 Canberra Pact, and the 1991 Australia–New Zealand Closer Defence Relations (CDR) agreement.

US ASSISTANCE: After winning the 1999 election, the Labour government canceled a lease-to-buy agreement with the US for 28 F-16 aircraft, announcing in May 2001 that it was scrapping its combat air force. In 2001, New Zealand contracted to purchase 105 US armored vehicles, and in 2002 it announced planned upgrades of its P-3 maritime patrol and C-130 transport aircraft, as well as plans to purchase a number of patrol vessels.

FORCES DEPLOYED: For Operation Enduring Freedom, New Zealand Special Air Service (SAS) troops work alongside coalition special operations forces (SOF) under US command. New Zealand provided C-130 logistics and humanitarian airlift in Afghanistan (Operation Tui), and deployed staff officers to the International Security Assistance Force. New Zealand also participated in the Multilateral Interception Force in the Arabian Gulf, deploying a frigate to the Canadian-led Coalition Task Group (Operation Tiki) and a P-3K Orion (Operation Troy) in Apr 2003. New Zealand later deployed an engineer task force (TF Rake) as part of the Multi-National Division (South-East) in Iraq. In Apr 2004, it announced that it would withdraw its engineers.

New Zealand participates in sharing training facilities, personnel exchanges, and joint exercises with the Philippines, Thailand, Indonesia, Papua New Guinea, Brunei, Tonga, and South Pacific states. It also exercises with its Five Power Defence Agreement partners — Australia, the UK, Malaysia, and Singapore.

New Zealand is an active participant in peacekeeping and has taken a leading role in the Solomon Islands and the neighboring island of Bougainville. New Zealand maintains a contingent in the Sinai Multinational Force and Observers and has contributed to UN peacekeeping operations in Angola, Cambodia, Somalia, the former Yugoslavia, and East Timor (where it initially dispatched almost 10 percent of its entire defense force).

BASE AND ACCESS: The US uses Christchurch to support military activities in Antarctica.

Code Names: Bel Isi, Bell Buoy, Bullseye, Churinga, Croix du Sud, Cygnet Globe, ECHELON, Fincastle, Flying Fish, GI Joe, Griffin, IADS ADEX, Longreach, Mercury, Night Kiwi, Pacific Kukri, Sea Eagle, Short Haul, Stardex, Starfish, Suman Warrior, TAMEX, Tasman, Tasmanex, Westpac MCMEX, Willoh.

Nicaragua

US–Nicaraguan military relations focus on counter-narcotics and transborder crime. The 1991 Maritime Agreement allows US Coast Guard and Nicaraguan law enforcement elements to conduct interdiction operations in Nicaraguan waters.

US COMMAND: SOUTHCOM. Nicaragua is located in the Joint Task Force — Bravo (JTF-B) geographic operations area.

AGREEMENTS: Counternarcotics Maritime Agreement (Nov 2001), Acquisition and Cross-Servicing Agreement eligible, Article 98 Agreement (Jun 2003).

Nicaragua is one of six nations to ratify the Inter-American Convention Against Terrorism (2003).

US ASSISTANCE: Receives Foreign Military Financing program grants (initiated in FY 2002), International Military Education and Training aid, eligible to receive grant Excess Defense Articles, receives aid for humanitarian demining efforts, participates in Center for Hemispheric Defense Studies conferences and seminars, receives International Narcotics Control and Law Enforcement funding.

FORCES DEPLOYED: Nicraragua deployed a small force with Spain in Iraq until 2004.

Code Names: Ahuas Tara, Elephant Herd, Fuerzas Aliades, Golden Pheasant, MEDRETE, New Horizons, PKO, Quadrant Search, Queen's Hunter, Rook's Landing, Strong Support.

Niger

Niger is the poorest Muslim country, ringed by unstable neighbors and encompassing vast territories that are difficult to police. It is a member of the Pan Sahel Initiative, a multi-year effort to wage the war on terrorism and enhance security in the Sahel region of Africa. PSI aims to assist the countries of the Sahel — Chad, Niger, Mauritania, and Mali — in controlling their borders. In 2003, the US provided initial equipment training to Nigerien soldiers as part of the initiative. A US-led Chad–Niger operation against the Salafist Group (GPSC) in early 2004 reportedly killed 43 associated terrorists. Niger also participated in a Mar 2004 EUCOM counter-terrorism chiefs of defense conference in Stuttgart, Germany, with Algeria, Chad, Mali, Mauritania, Morocco, Senegal, Tunisia, and the US. The US is concerned that Niger's uranium production not be diverted.

US COMMAND: EUCOM.

US ASSISTANCE: Receives International Military Education and Training aid, eligible to receive grant Excess Defense Articles, receives peacekeeping operations (PKO) funding, participates in Africa Center for Strategic Studies conferences and seminars. France provides the largest share of military assistance to Niger, and the Nigerien armed forces are equipped mainly with French materiel. Morocco, Algeria, China, and Libya have also provided military assistance.

FORCES DEPLOYED: Niger deployed a company of troops to Côte d'Ivoire as part of the Economic Community of West African States (ECOWAS) stabilization force in Jan 2003. Niger sent a 400-man military contingent to join the coalition in Desert Storm in 1991.

Code Names: MEDFLAG.

Nigeria

Nigeria, home of Africa's largest Muslim population, has supported the war on terrorism, actively sharing intelligence with the US since 9/11 about radical Islamic activity. However, Nigeria has only limited capacity to combat terrorist financing and monitor porous borders, and widespread corruption and Nigerian crime syndicates hamper effective law enforcement. US law enforcement assistance focuses on improving financial, immigration, and security sectors to stem drug trafficking, international crime, and terrorism.

US COMMAND: EUCOM.

AGREEMENTS: SOFA (7 Sep 2000), Acquisition and Cross-Servicing Agreement eligible (20 Dec 2000).

US ASSISTANCE: Receives Foreign Military Financing program grants, International Military Education and Training aid, eligible to receive grant Excess Defense Articles, receives International Narcotics Control and Law Enforcement funding, receives peacekeeping operations (PKO) funding, participates in the African Contingency Operations Training and Assistance (ACOTA) program and the earlier African Crisis Response Initiative (ACRI), participates in Africa Center for Strategic Studies conferences and seminars. US efforts in Focus Relief, Aug 2000–Dec 2001, played a major role in professionalizing the Nigerian army and enhancing its ability to plan an effective regional peacekeeping role with the United Nations Mission in Sierra Leone (UNAMSIL).

FORCES DEPLOYED: Nigeria has played a leadership role in peacekeeping in West Africa, notably Sierra Leone and Liberia. It has sent peacekeepers to Angola, Burundi, Congo, Rwanda, Somalia, and the former Yugoslavia.

Code Names: Avid Recovery, Focus Relief, MEDFLAG, WATC.

Norway

Throughout the Cold War, NATO member Norway had a special relationship with the US because of its close proximity to the former Soviet Union, and its hosting of intelligence collection stations and pre-positioned military material for US and NATO reinforcements. Since 9/11, Norway has provided support for Operation Enduring Freedom (OEF) and the International Security Assistance Force (ISAF) in Afghanistan, and contributed forces for Operation Iraqi Freedom (OIF) in Iraq.

US COMMAND: EUCOM.

AGREEMENTS: NATO SOFA (16 Jun 1951), Reciprocal SOFA, Exchange of Notes on Mutual Defense Assistance (13 Apr 1954), PfP SOFA (3 Nov 1997), Acquisition and Cross-Servicing Agreement (20 Aug 1982).

BASES AND ACCESS: Norway hosts the Have Stare radar at Vardo and other joint intelligence and surveillance systems focused on the Arctic and Russia. Norway continues to serve as a storage site for Marine Corps equipment under the Norway Air Landed Marine Expeditionary Brigade program, for army pre-positioned stocks (APS) and War Reserve Stocks for Allies (WRSA) — which also includes equipment for Canada and Germany — and for navy pre-positioned medical assets; it activately maintains air force co-located operating bases (COBs). The US–Norwegian COB Agreement was renegotiated in 1994 and now includes five airfields: Andoya, Bodo, Sola, Evenes, and Bardufoss.

FORCES DEPLOYED: In Oct 2001, Norway deployed special operations forces (SOF) as part of the coalition task force under US command in Afghanistan, subsequently conducting exploitation missions and providing leadership transport with 21 hardened vehicles. The first SOF contingent redeployed home in Jun 2002, replaced by SOF II. Norwegian explosive ordnance disposal (EOD) and demining personnel also supported OEF and ISAF. On 1 Sep 2002, as part of the Danish–Dutch–Norwegian European Participating Air Forces (EPAF) detachment, Norway deployed six F-16s to Manas, Kyrgyzstan, relieving French Mirage 2000s and flying combat operations until 31 Mar 2003. Norwegian C-130s have provided airlift support from Manas as well. Elements of the "Telemark Task Force," a mechanized infantry company, deployed to Afghanistan in Dec 2003. The unit provided security for the Loya Jirga proceedings and conducts security missions in and around Kabul as part of the ISAF. For Operation Iraqi Freedom (OIF), Norway deployed an engineer company as part of the Multi-National Division (South-East) in southern Iraq.

The Norwegian navy has maintained a near-continuous presence in Active Endeavour with frigates, submarines, or torpedo boats in the Mediterranean. Norway also contributes to the Stabilization Force (Bosnia) and other peacekeeping missions.

Code Names: Adventure Express, Affirmative Alert, Allied Response, Anorak Express, Arctic Express, Ardent Ground, Baltic Eagle, Baltlink, Barents Peace, Battle Griffin, Blue Flag, Blue Game, Bright Horizon, Brilliant Foil, Clean Hunter, Combined Endeavor, Constant Harmony, Cooperative series, Creek Chart, Dacia, Dogfish, Frisian Flag, Gemini, Glacier Enigma, Globus, Hairspring, Hard Fall, Have Stare, Joint series, JTFEX, Mace, Neo Tapon, Nordic Peace, North Star, Peceshield, Snow Falcon, Sorbet Royale, Strong Resolve, Trial, Trident Arch, Veritas, Viking.

Oman

Since the US concluded a bilateral agreement for access to military bases with Oman in 1980, relations have been close. Oman maintained its diplomatic relations with Iraq throughout Desert Storm even while sending a contingent of troops to join coalition forces and allowing US pre-positioning of weapons and supplies. Throughout the 1990s, Oman served as an important base and forward storage location for ongoing operations against Iraq and Iran. After 9/11, Oman allowed its bases to be used for Operation Enduring Freedom (OEF), and it provided access to naval facilities for US and coalition ships and maritime patrol aircraft. The Joint Special Operations Command and CIA use Oman as a main base in the Middle East.

Oman participates in joint military exercises with US and coalition forces, and Navy SEALs from Naval Special Warfare Unit 3 conduct a full program of Joint/Combined Exchange Training (JCET) special operations training with the Royal Oman Coast Guard and the Royal Omani Police Coastal Response Team. Oman also has significant military ties to the UK, and allowed UK troops to conduct a large military exercise in Nov 2001, the largest deployment of UK forces since Desert Storm.

US COMMAND: CENTCOM.

AGREEMENTS: Military Cooperation Agreement (1980, revised and renewed in 2000), classified SOFA, Facilities Access Agreement (renewed in 1990), Acquisition and Cross-Servicing Agreement.

Oman is a member of the Gulf Cooperation Council (GCC).

US ASSISTANCE: Receives Foreign Military Financing program grants, International Military Education and Training aid, eligible to receive grant Excess Defense Articles.

BASES AND ACCESS: Prior to 9/11, the US had five CENTCOM-controlled facilities in Oman housing significant caches of pre-positioned US equipment, munitions, and supplies, and utilized an additional 24 Omani-controlled facilities. Oman offset 79 percent of US stationing costs in 2001. After 9/11, the sultan of Oman reiterated permission for the US to use the facilities and airfields at Seeb, Thumrait, and Masirah Island. US special operations forces (SOF), including "black" SOF engaged in the war on terror, operate from Oman. Seeb became a central airlift hub for clandestine flights to Jacobabad and Shamsi-Bandari, Pakistan, and later for Kandahar and Bagram, Afghanistan. Predator Unmanned Aerial Vehicles (UAVs) operated from Seeb during OEF, and B-1 bombers operated from Thumrait. Naval ships utilized Muscat for port and fuel service. P-3 Orion and intelligence aircraft operated from Masirah AB. Goat Island, Khasab, and Masirah Island have all been mentioned as US surveillance bases.

Code Names: Accurate Test, Arabian Gauntlet, Argonaut/Saif Sareea II, Beacon Flash, Blue Flag, Boron Mercury, Circuit Mayflower, Desert Warrior, Destined Glory, Early Victor, Eastern Castle, Eastern Valor, Inferno Creek, Jade Tiger, Magellan, Magic Carpet, Magic Roundabout, Phoenix Oasis, Rocky Lance, Saif Sareea, Sea Soldier, SHAREM, Turbo Cads, Vigilant Warrior.

Pakistan

The events of 9/11 led the US to waive 1990 sanctions imposed on Pakistan for its development and testing of nuclear weapons and in response to the 1999 military coup that brought General Musharraf to power. Since the Soviet invasion of Afghanistan in 1979, the CIA had been running covert operations from Pakistan through Pakistan's intelligence service — the Inter-Services Intelligence (ISI) — but in the late 1990s, as the CIA increased its Pakistan-based activities against Osama bin Laden, the relationship with ISI became more strained. The target wasn't the Soviet Union on the Pakistani doorstep any longer, and ISI had close relations with the Taliban and the infrastructure of Arab and foreign fighters who had originally come to the area during the Soviet war.

After 9/11, President Musharraf had to choose between supporting US operations in Afghanistan and maintaining support for the Taliban. He granted permission for the US to use Pakistani military bases in Operation Enduring Freedom (OEF), and the US, particularly law enforcement agencies, increased pressure on Pakistani agencies to apprehend al Qaeda and Taliban members openly operating on Pakistani soil, particularly in the border areas with Afghanistan. Pakistan captured and turned over more than 500 al Qaeda members. But by late 2002, when US focus shifted to Iraq, much of the pressure in Pakistan dissipated, and the border areas again became a refuge. Pakistan established a greater government presence along the Pakistani–Afghan border and undertook operations in the autonomous Federally Administered Tribal Areas, but it also imposed significant constraints on US operations on its soil. Among those captured were Abu Zubayda — considered number two man in al Qaeda — and Ramzi Bin al-Shaiba, suspected of being directly involved in the 9/11 attacks. In 2003, Khalid Shaykh Muhammad — the mastermind of the 9/11 attacks — and Walid Bin Attash (Khallad Ba'Attash), a prime suspect in the attack on the USS *Cole* in Oct 2000, were also apprehended in Pakistan. Through 2003 and into 2004, President Musharraf himself became the target of numerous asassination attempts.

Pakistan has the world's eighth largest armed forces, utilizing a mix of Chinese, French, UK, and US equipment. Until 1990, the US provided significant military aid to Pakistan — the third largest program behind Israel and Egypt. Military assistance resumed in 2001 and has provided spare parts and equipment. US–Pakistani military cooperation focuses on equipment requirements for border control and counter-terrorism.

For OEF, International Security Assistance Force (ISAF), and the war on terrorism, Pakistan quietly provided basing and overflight permission for all US and coalition forces. After the fall of the Taliban, Pakistan continued to work with the CIA, FBI, and special operations forces (SOF) to hunt for al Qaeda and Taliban remnants. In 2003, there were consistent rumors that the newly reorganized JTF-121 (now JTF-626), the "black" counter-terrorism SOF task force, had moved elements to western Pakistan.

US COMMAND: CENTCOM.

AGREEMENTS: Granted Major Non-NATO Ally status (Mar 2004), Acquisition and Cross-Servicing Agreement, Article 98 Agreement (21 Jul 2003)

In 2002, the US and Pakistan established the Working Group on Counterterrorism and Law-Enforcement Cooperation. The Tripartite Commission consisting of the US, Afghanistan, and Pakistan concluded its fifth session in Dec 2003, establishing a sub-committee on cross-border rules of engagement. The UK–Pakistan Defence Cooperation Forum (DCF) provides the framework to discuss security, military contacts, cooperation, and equipment sales.

US ASSISTANCE: Pakistan's International Military Education and Training program was renewed in Oct 2001 after Section 508 of the Foreign Operations Appropriations Act sanctions against Pakistan was waived. Receives Foreign Military Financing program grants to purchase C-130s, Cobra and Huey helicopters, P-3 surveillance aircraft, communications, for fighter training, high-mobility vehicles, and for other equipment and training; International Military Education and Training aid; eligible to receive grant Excess Defense Articles; participates in National Defense University Near East South Asia (NESA) Center seminars; participates in Asia-Pacific Center for Security Studies executive courses; receives Nonproliferation, Anti-terrorism, Demining, and Related (NADR) and Anti-Terrorism Assistance funds to train a dedicated counter-terrorism civilian investigative unit; receives International Narcotics Control and Law Enforcement funding; participates in the Terrorist Interdiction Program. FY 2001 Emergency Response Funds contributed toward development of a new forward operating location in Peshawar to reach into the North West Frontier Province (NWFP).

In FYs 1993–2001, the US obligated about $384 million in total assistance to Pakistan, all of which was economic assistance. In FY 2002, budgeted assistance totaled about one billion dollars. Requested assistance for FYs 2003 and 2004 totaled another $686 million. During President Musharraf's visit to the US in 2003, President Bush announced that the US intended to provide Pakistan three billion dollars in economic and military aid over five years.

BASES AND ACCESS: Prior to 9/11, Pakistan cooperated with US intelligence agencies in electronic intelligence gathering near the Soviet Union (at Peshawar). But after sanctions were imposed in 1990, even the covert US presence diminished. Pakistan was designated a combat zone as of 19 Sep 2001. After 9/11, Pakistan granted logistics support and overflight rights to support OEF, provided access to five air bases, and accommodated more than 1,000 American personnel on its soil.

Pakistan provided a landing facility and access to the Pasni naval facility, curtailing its own navy activities to accommodate coalition naval operations. The Marine Corps operations at Pasni were the largest amphibious operations in size, duration, and depth since the Korean War. In all, 8,000 marines, 330 vehicles, and more than 1,350 tons of equipment were off-loaded at the beach and flown to Kandahar, Afghanistan, from Pasni. At Shabaz AB in Jacobabad, SOF and combat search and rescue forces deployed for OEF under the 438th Air Expeditionary Group, to be followed by Predator Unmanned Aerial Vehicles (UAVs) with the 15th Expeditionary Reconnaissance Squadron. In Nov 2001, elements of the 1st Battalion, 187th Infantry Regiment of the 101st Airborne Division deployed to Jacobabad, conducting airfield security and numerous cross-border "sensitive site exploitations." On 8 Mar 2002, Marine Corps KC-130T tankers deployed to Jacobabad to support Anaconda and other operations. Other bases used by the US include Shamsi-Bandari forward operating base and "Site 24," an unknown location. To facilitate the International Security Assistance Force in Afghanistan, the Karachi airport and port facilities have been used. Through the end of 2003, a total of 57,800 sorties had been generated from Pakistan's soil or through its airspace.

Code Names: Al Miwan, Anaconda, Arabian Gauntlet, Avalanche, Buzzard, Celtic Straw, Eager Dancer, Gambol Venture, Impressive Lift, Inspired series, IWER, Mountain Resolve, Pacer Storage, Peace Gate, Peace Pack, Regional Cooperation, Restore Hope, United Shield, Valiant Strike.

Panama

Following transfer of the Panama Canal to Panama on 31 Dec 1999 and withdrawal of US forces from Panama bases, the US and Panama continue a close working relationship relating to security of the canal and counter-narcotics interdiction. Not only is Panama a crossroads for illegal trafficking in drugs, arms, and money laundering, but it also has been affected by Colombia's ongoing civil conflict. Panama remains one of three Latin American nations without a standing military, and US assistance focuses on border security.

US COMMAND: SOUTHCOM. Panama is located in the Joint Task Force — Bravo (JTF-B) geographic operations area.

AGREEMENTS: Article 98 Agreement (2003).

The 1977 Panama Canal Treaties entered into force on 1 Oct 1979, replacing the 1903 Hay/Bunau-Varilla Treaty and all other US–Panama agreements concerning the canal. The treaties comprise a basic treaty governing the operation and defense of the canal until 31 Dec 1999 (Panama Canal Treaty) and a treaty guaranteeing the permanent neutrality of the canal (Neutrality Treaty).

US ASSISTANCE: Receives Foreign Military Financing program grants to purchase and sustain mobility equipment, riverine patrol craft, and communications, for technical training and maintenance of the National Air Service, and to enhance Panama's counter-terrorism forces; eligible to receive grant Excess Defense Articles; National Guard partner with Michigan.

BASES AND ACCESS: The Southern Regional Operations Center in Panama continues as part of the Caribbean Basin Radar Network. In Mar 1999, property was returned to Panama under the Panama Canal Treaty, which mandated the full departure of the US military. Facilities included Albrook, Balboa, Balboa Summit, Colon, Corozol, Farfan, Fort Clayton, Fort Davis, Fort Kobbe, Fort Sherman, Galeta Island, Howard Air Force Base, Quarry Heights, and Rodman.

Code Names: Acid Gambit, Amalgam Virgo, Bell Buoy, Blade Jewel, Blind Logic, Blue Advance, Blue Spoon, Bushmaster, Constant Vigil, Coronet Cove, Coronet Guard, Coronet Nighthawk, Coronet Oak, Elaborate Maze, Eloquent Banquet, Fuerzas Aliades, Fuerzas Defensas, Gable Adder, Grecian Firebolt, Grisly Hunter, Just Cause, Kindle Liberty, Klondike Key, New Horizons, Nifty Package, Nimrod Dancer, Prayer Book, Promote Liberty, Purple Storm, Safe Haven, Safe Passage, Senior Scout, Volant Oak.

Papua New Guinea

The US military and Papua New Guinea defense force maintain cordial relations, and the US provides police and other training courses to enhance Papua New Guinea's ability to patrol its border. A peace agreement with rebel forces on Bougainville Island was signed in Aug 2001, leading to establishment of a UN observer mission.

US COMMAND: PACOM.

AGREEMENTS: SOFA.

US ASSISTANCE: Receives International Military Education and Training aid, eligible to receive grant Excess Defense Articles, receives aid for humanitarian demining efforts, participates in Asia-Pacific Center for Security Studies executive courses.

Code Names: Balance Passion, Helicon Luk, Kangaroo, Night Falcon, Paradise, Wantok Warrior.

Paraguay

Since 9/11, the US has focused its national security attention in Paraguay to combating terrorism financing activity in the tri-border area (TBA) of Argentina–Brazil–Paraguay. The US–Paraguay partnership on counter-narcotics cooperation, anti-money-laundering, and other illicit cross-border activities has refocused on Islamic fund-raising and suspected support for international terrorist organizations.

In 2002, Argentina, Brazil, Paraguay, and the US established a regional counter-terrorism mechanism built on the framework of the 1998 Tripartite Commission of the Triple Frontier to focus on practical steps to strengthen financial and border controls, and enhance law enforcement and intelligence sharing. In Dec 2003, a high-level US delegation attended a special meeting in Asuncion to discuss counter-terrorism cooperation. The US proposed to establish a joint regional intelligence center and deepen border security cooperation to counter the Islamic threat, but the Latin American parties successfully argued that "available information" did not substantiate reports of operational activities by terrorists in the TBA.

US military assistance focuses on assisting the Paraguayan military to refocus its democratic mission and organize peacekeeping efforts. Joint/Combined Exchange Training (JCET) special operations training exists between the US 7th Special Forces Group and Paraguayan SENAD and Marine Commando.

US command: SOUTHCOM.

Agreements: Acquisition and Cross-Servicing Agreement eligible (29 Aug 2000).

US assistance. Receives International Military Education and Training aid, eligible to receive grant Excess Defense Articles, participates in Center for Hemispheric Defense Studies conferences and seminars, receives International Narcotics Control and Law Enforcement funding.

Code Names: Cabañas, Eagle, Fuerzas Aliades, New Horizons, Oceanic, PKO, Transoceanic Exercise, Unitas.

Peru

The US and Peru are focused on counter-narcotics, and Peru remains the second largest producer of coca leaf in the world, with some 200,000 Peruvians engaged in the production, refining, or distribution of cocaine. Peru, Colombia, and Brazil signed a three-way agreement on 10 Feb 2004 to combat drug trafficking in the Amazonian region.

The US Air Bridge Denial Program was suspended in Apr 2001 after a CIA-contracted plane accidentally shot down a civilian plane, killing Baptist missionary Veronica Bowers and her seven-month-old daughter, but was reinstated in Colombia in Aug 2003. The US is working with Peru to establish a coordination center that could allow resumption in Peru.

Sendero Luminoso remains an ongoing problem and has adopted some of the

Revolutionary Armed Forces of Colombia (Fuerzas Armadas Revolucionarios de Colombia; FARC) model of protecting narcotics traffickers in exchange for funding. Joint/Combined Exchange Training (JCET) special operations training exists among US SEAL Team 2 and 7th Special Forces Group and the Peruvian Fuerzas De Operacines Especiales.

US COMMAND: SOUTHCOM.

AGREEMENTS: Activity-specific SOFA, Acquisition and Cross-Servicing Agreement.

US ASSISTANCE: Receives Foreign Military Financing program grants to support and maintain C-130s, to improve the ability of security units to operate in remote areas, and to equip Peru's dedicated counter-terrorism unit with body armor, night vision goggles, and small arms; receives International Military Education and Training aid; eligible to receive grant Excess Defense Articles; National Guard partner with WV; receives aid for humanitarian demining efforts; receives Andean Counterdrug Initiative (ACI) funds.

Peru is one of six nations to ratify the Inter-American Convention Against Terrorism (2003).

BASES AND ACCESS: The Air Bridge Denial Program, suspended in Apr 2001, involved aircraft owned by DOD, flown by DynCorp (a CIA contractor), and maintained by Aviation Development Corporation, a CIA aviation proprietary company, operating from Santa Lucia. The US operates radars in Peru at Andoas, Iquitos, Pucallpa, and Yurimaguas, and reportedly has a number of low-level SIGINT sites in the country.

Code Names: Cabañas, Green Clover, JTFEX, MEDRETE, Oceanic, PKO, RIMPAC, Safe Border, Steady State, Support Justice, Transoceanic Exercise, Unitas.

Philippines

The Philippines is a key player in the war on terrorism, and the Philippine government has committed its full support to the US, offering intelligence sharing, unconditional overflight permission, use of military facilities, logistical support, food, medicine, and medical personnel. President Gloria Macapagal-Arroyo met with President Bush in an official working visit in Nov 2001 and made a state visit to Washington on 19 May 2003. Secretary of State Colin Powell also visited the Philippines in Aug 2002, and President Bush visited on 18 Oct 2003.

The US has listed four indigenous Philippine groups as foreign terrorist organizations — the Abu Sayyaf Group (ASG), the Communist Party of the Philippines/New People's Army (CPP/NPP), the Alex Boncayo Brigade, and the Pentagon Gang. Additionally, the US has designated Jemaah Islamiya (JI), with cells throughout Southeast Asia, including the Philippines, as a foreign terrorist organization.

President Gloria Macapagal-Arroyo has pursued a military response to the ASG, a kidnap-for-ransom group suspected of having providing some logistics support to al Qaeda and other terrorist organizations. In May 2001, ASG kidnapped several Americans, beheading one of them in Jun 2001. About 1,000 US troops deployed to the southern island of Basilan starting on 31 Jan 2002, including the US 1st Special Forces Group and Army 160th Special Operations Aviation Regiment, to assist Filipino forces in their counter-insurgency operations against ASG. Ostensibly, the US forces deployed to conduct a six-month Balikatan (shoulder-to-shoulder) "exercise," and the US and Philippines insisted that US forces do not engage in direct combat, which is prohibited under the Philippine constitution. Nonetheless, US surveillance aircraft provided direct intelligence, US "advisers" accompanied Philippine forces on combat patrols, and US forces were authorized to use force in self-defense. Efforts to track down ASG fighters met with some success in 2002. On 21 Jun 2002, members of ASG were captured and its leader, Abu Sabaya, was killed. Another ASG leader — "Commander Robot" — was captured in Dec 2003.

Following conclusion of Balikatan 02-1 in Jul 2002, several hundred US soldiers remained in the Philippines under Special Operations Command Pacific (JTF 510) to assist with infrastructure projects and continue counter-terrorism training. JTF 555 Operation Enduring Freedom — Philippines (OEF-P) was later activated to oversee the US war on terrorism in the Philippines, with the subordinate Joint Special Operations Task Force — Philippines (JSOTF-P) providing assistance to the Philippines Southern Command headquarters. Though Presidents Bush and Macapagal-Arroyo had agreed to hold Balikatan 03-1 as a follow-on, continuing controversy delayed a second major operation until Balikatan 04, which opened 23 Feb 2004 and involved a force of 2,500 marines operating with their Philippine counterparts in a three-part exercise far away from Baslan, with training on the island of Palawan and in central Luzon, to include Clark AB in Pampanga, Fort Magsaysay in Nueva Ecija, and Marine Base Ternate in Cavite.

Since the withdrawal of US military bases in 1991, domestic nationalist sentiments have opposed strengthening of US–Philippine military links. But since 9/11, the US pledged to provide $100 million in security assistance to the Philippines. The International Military Education and Training program is the largest in Asia and the second largest in the world. At $148 million, the Philippines is also the number one recipient in Asia of Excess Defense Articles. The US has also committed significant military equipment, including 30 helicopters and spare parts, under presidential drawdown authority.

Beyond operations against ASG, the US and the Philippines have embarked on a comprehensive military-to-military program focusing on counter-terrorism. The major US training effort in place in the Philippines during the 1990s involved Joint/Combined Exchange Training (JCET) special operations training exercises known as Balance Piston. Starting in the mid-1990s, there were two to four exercises annually, generally conducted with the Philippine Army Special Operations Command. Since 9/11, Balance Piston exercises have expanded to include direct counter-terrorism training and a new Vector Balance Piston counter-terrorism operation.

US COMMAND: PACOM. OEF-P (JTF 555) oversees the US war on terrorism operation in the Philippines. JSOTF-P provides counter-terrorism and counter-insurgency support.

AGREEMENTS: Mutual Defense Treaty (MDT; 1952), Visiting Forces Agreement (1 Jun 1999), Mutual Logistics Support Agreement or MLSA (incorporated an Acquisition and Cross-Servicing Agreement; 21 Nov 2002, Acquisition and Cross-Servicing Agreement eligible 29 Mar 1988), SOFA, granted Major Non-NATO Ally status, Article 98 Agreement.

In Feb 1998, the US and the Philippines concluded the Visiting Forces Agreement, paving the way for increased military cooperation under the MDT. The agreement was approved by the Philippine senate in May 1999. Under the VFA, the US conducts ship visits to Philippine ports and resumed large combined military exercises with Philippine forces. The US–Philippine Mutual Defense Board, which meets quarterly, is the current intergovernmental direct liaison mechanism on military matters.

In May 2002, the Philippines signed a Trilateral Agreement on Terrorism and Transnational Crimes with Indonesia and Malaysia to fight terrorism in Southeast Asia. In Mar 2003, Australia and the Philippines signed an MOU on Cooperation to Combat International Terrorism.

US ASSISTANCE: Receives Foreign Military Financing program grants, largest International Military Education and Training aid program in Asia and second largest in the world, eligible to receive grant Excess Defense Articles (equipment provided since 9/11 includes one C-130 transport, UH-1H helicopters, two-and-a-half-ton trucks, and thousands of M16 rifles), National Guard partner with Hawaii and Guam, receives International Narcotics Control and Law Enforcement funding, receives Nonproliferation, Anti-terrorism, Demining, and Related

(NADR) and Anti-Terrorism Assistance funds for counter-terrorism and law enforcement assistance, participates in Asia-Pacific Center for Security Studies executive courses, participates in the Terrorist Interdiction Program.

BASES AND ACCESS: Until Nov 1992, pursuant to a 1947 Military Bases Agreement, the US maintained and operated major facilities at Clark AB, Subic Bay Naval Complex, and several smaller subsidiary installations in the Philippines. In 1983 and 1988, the US and the Philippines completed successful reviews and extensions of the Military Bases Agreement. In Aug 1991, negotiators from the two countries reached agreement on a draft treaty providing for use of Subic Bay by US forces for 10 years. The draft treaty did not include use of Clark AB, which had been so heavily damaged by the 1991 eruption of Mount Pinatubo that the US decided to abandon it (it was closed 26 Nov 1991). In Sep 1991, however, the Philippine senate rejected the bases treaty. The Philippine government informed the US on 6 Dec 1991 that it would have one year to complete withdrawal, and the last US forces departed on 24 Nov 1992. The Philippines was designated a combat zone as of 9 Jan 2002.

FORCES DEPLOYED: The Philippines has sent around 100 personnel to Iraq as part of a civil affairs and humanitarian assistance team operating in the Polish sector.

Code Names: ARGEX, Baker Piston Lens, Balance Piston, Balikatan, CARAT Philippines, Cascade Warrior, Cobra Gold, Commando Cope Thunder, Fiery Relief, Fiery Vigil, Flush Piston, Freedom Eagle, Giant, Handa, Kalamazoo, Kale, Kansas, Kedge Hammer, Lumbus, MARSEAEX, MARSURVEX, MTWS, Mystic Star, NOLES, PALAH, PIX (Philippine marine interoperability exercise), Project 9GH, SAGIP, SEACAT, Shant Doot, Shanti Path, Talon Vision, Tasty, Teak Piston, Team Challenge, Unified Quest, Vector Balance Piston, Westpac MCMEX.

Poland

Poland became a member of NATO in Mar 1999, and is one of the closest US allies in Europe, supportive of the war on terrorism, the war in Afghanistan, and US efforts in Iraq. Poland is fully involved in the international community on the war on terrorism, including membership in the new Proliferation Security Initiative.

The Poles have embarked upon a serious multi-year military modernization program focusing resources on ensuring that the one-third of their forces designated for NATO missions are fully interoperable by 2006. Members of Poland's special forces took part in Operation Iraqi Freedom (OIF), and on 3 Sep 2003 a Polish-led Multi-National Division assumed control of the Central-South security zone in Iraq, including more than 2,000 Polish soldiers. In Afghanistan, some 100 Polish military personnel are involved in mine clearing operations.

Poland also provided weapons and ammunition to the Afghan National Army and the US Georgia Train and Equip Program (GTEP).

US COMMAND: EUCOM.

AGREEMENTS: SOFA, PfP SOFA (4 May 1997), Acquisition and Cross-Servicing Agreement (22 Nov 1996).

US ASSISTANCE: Receives Foreign Military Financing program grants, International Military Education and Training aid, eligible to receive grant Excess Defense Articles, National Guard partner with Illinois.

BASES AND ACCESS: Poland approved basing and unrestricted overflight for forces participating in Operation Enduring Freedom (OEF).

FORCES DEPLOYED: Polish military forces have served in both OEF in Afghanistan and OIF in Iraq, first contributing vessels to coalition maritime operations in the Indian Ocean, Arabian Gulf, and Red Sea, and then deploying engineer and logistics units in Afghanistan in Mar 2002. The elite Polish "GROM" special operations forces (SOF) unit also deployed to the Arabian Gulf in 2002, and became fully engaged in maritime interception operations in the northern Arabian Gulf and then later in leadership interception operations inside Iraq. Poland was one of four countries (including Australia and the UK) to send toops to the gulf as part of "the coalition of the willing" for combat operations during OIF. On 3 Sep 2003, Poland officially assumed command of a Multi-National Division of stabilization forces in Iraq (MDN-CS), deployed in the central southern zone. In Jul 2003, four US-chartered ships loaded elements of Poland's 12th Mechanized Division (more than 2,400 Polish soldiers) at Szczecin for transport to Iraq — the nation's largest equipment move since World War II, and the first deployment overseas. On 31 May 2004, Poland announced that the number of troops in Iraq would be cut following domestic elections.

Poland is also an active contributor to NATO, UN, and Organization for Security and Cooperation in Europe (OSCE) peacekeeping operations and observer missions, with more than 1,500 personnel deployed in 15 peacekeeping missions, including southern Lebanon. After joining NATO, Poland shifted participation away from the traditional focus of UN-led operations. It has maintained significant forces in support of the Stabilization Force (Bosnia) and Kosovo Force (Kosovo).

Code Names: Allied Effort, Allied Response, Amber Hope, Amber Sea, Ardent Ground, Baltic series, Baltlink, Baltops, Brave Eagle/Eagle Talon, Cannon Cloud, Carbon Gap, Cathode Emission, Celestial Fire, Central Enterprise, Clean Hunter, Combined Endeavor, Constant Harmony, Challenging Husar, Cooperative series, Cossack Steppe, Double Eagle, Dual Eagle, Eagle's Talon,

Esperia, Iron Dragon, Joint series, Pacific Protector, Peaceshield, PLANEX, Sanso, Sentry White Eagle, Strong Resolve, Ulan Eagle, Victory Strike, Viking.

Portugal

Portugal has been a supporter of the war on terrorism, supporting operations in Afghanistan and Iraq. Portugal was a founding member of NATO and host to NATO's newly renamed Joint Headquarters West (JHQW; formerly South Atlantic Command, or SOUTHLANT), located near Lisbon, one of three joint headquarters activated in Mar 2004. Portuguese military modernization includes an ongoing effort to create an all-volunteer military (conscription is scheduled to end in 2004).

US COMMAND: EUCOM. Under the Apr 2002 Unified Command Plan, EUCOM gained responsibility for the Azores from JFCOM.

AGREEMENTS: NATO SOFA (16 Jun 1951), Agreement on Cooperation and Defense (1995; provides US forces continued access to the Lajes AB in the Azores), Technical Agreement (1 Jun 1995), PfP SOFA (5 Mar 2000), Technical Agreement (1 Jun 1995), Acquisition and Cross-Servicing Agreement (14 Jan 1998).

US ASSISTANCE: Receives International Military Education and Training aid.

BASES AND ACCESS: Lajes AB at Terceira in the Azores is the centerpiece of US–Portuguese relations and has played an important role in supporting US military aircraft engaged in counter-terrorism and humanitarian missions, including operations in Afghanistan and Iraq. Lajes earlier served as a staging point for the US during NATO military operations in Kosovo, Desert Storm, and Desert Fox, and it supports ongoing operations in Bosnia and Kosovo. In 2001, Portugal provided blanket overflight and landing rights at Lajes; it also provides the US and NATO allies access to Montijo AB and a number of ports.

FORCES DEPLOYED: Portugal provided a C-130 at Karachi, Pakistan, and a small medical team in Afghanistan in support of the International Security Assistance Force. For Operation Iraqi Freedom, Portugal deployed a security company as part of the Italian brigade in the Multi-National Division (South-East) in Iraq. Portugal contributes troops to both the Stabilization Force (Bosnia) and the Kosovo Force (Kosovo).

Code Names: Air Brake, Combined Endeavor, Cooperative series, Dacia, Destined Glory, Distant Thunder, Dogfish, Dynamic series, Linked Seas, Jupiter, Majestic Eagle, Med Shark, Molico, Mystic Star, Neo Tapon, Orion, Pacific Protector, Peace Atlantis, Peace Corsair, PHIBEX, Roller Derby, Sanso, Sea Saber, Strong Resolve, Trial, Trident D'Or.

Qatar

Qatar hosts the CENTCOM forward headquarters and the newly built Combined Air Operations Center (CAOC), which moved from Saudi Arabia in 2002–2003, and the most impressive military infrastructure in the Middle East. The al Udeid AB features one of the longest and most capable runways in the region, and hosts the CAOC facility. Qatar has spent more than $400 million to upgrade al Udeid and other bases in exchange for US military protection. The close US relationship was confirmed when President Bush visited Qatar in Jun 2003.

Beginning in 1995, Qatar hosted several Air Expeditionary Force deployments in support of Southern Watch. Thoughout the 1990s, Qatar hosted one of the largest stocks of pre-positioned military equipment in the region and constructed a 27-building complex to store US military vehicles and personnel in case of a war with Iraq. The forward headquarters of CENTCOM Special Operations Command (SOCCENT) moved to al Saliyah, Qatar, in 2001, followed by CENTCOM's deployable forward headquarters in 2002, established at al Saliyah under the guise of the exercise Internal Look, which practiced the war plan and procedures for Operation Iraqi Freedom (OIF).

US COMMAND: CENTCOM.

AGREEMENTS: Classified SOFA, Acquisition and Cross-Servicing Agreement, Implementing Agreement (2002).

Qatar is a member of the Gulf Cooperation Council (GCC).

BASES AND ACCESS: Prior to 9/11, the US had four CENTCOM-controlled facilities in Qatar, and utilized an additional 24 Qatari-controlled facilities. Prior to OIF, a heavy combat brigade set of material was stored in Qatar at two separate sites, Site One (al Saliyah) and Site Two (531 miles southwest of Doha). The US has major activities at Camp Snoopy — Doha International Airport, Camp al Saliyah, al Udeid AB, Logistics Support Station Umm Saeed (Said), and the Falcon-78 Ammunition Storage Point. Doha International and al Udeid have hosted a wide variety of fighter, transport, and tanker aircraft, as well as E-8C JSTARS. Doha serves as a US airlift hub for Djibouti; Dushanbe, Tajikistan; Masirah, Oman; Kandahar, Afghanistan; and Shamsi, Pakistan.

Code Names: Arabian Gauntlet, Blue Flag, Eastern series, Falcon, Falconer, Impelling Victory, Indigo, Initial Link, Initiate Response, Internal Look, Native Atlas, Native Fury, Rugged Nautilus, Silent Assurance, Turbo Cads, Vigilant Warrior, Warrior Bravo.

Romania

Romania became a member of NATO on 29 Mar 2004, having been the first country to enroll in the NATO Partnership for Peace program, and by far the country with the largest armed forces of all the NATO expansion nations. Since 9/11, Romania has been fully supportive of the war on terrorism and Iraq, including overflight rights and use of ports and military facilities. President Bush visited Bucharest in Nov 2002; Romanian President Iliescu paid a return visit to the US in Dec 2003. In 2004, about 1,200 Romanian troops served in Iraq and Afghanistan, and Romania pledged to maintain its commitment of troops through sovereignty.

US Europe-based special operations forces (SOF) have a full Joint/Combined Exchange Training (JCET) program with Romanian forces in Bucharest, Otopeni, and Predeal, and at number 57, 86, and 90 air bases. Romania also served as a staging and organizing base for US SOF before Operation Iraqi Freedom (OIF).

Bucharest is host of the 12-member Southeast European Cooperation Initiative, a regional center that provides law enforcement training and intelligence sharing on terrorism and law enforcement. The multi-national Southeast European Brigade (SEEBRIG) rotates headquarters to Constanta, and Romania contributes to the multi-national naval patrol in the Black Sea.

US COMMAND: EUCOM.

AGREEMENTS: SOFA (supplementary agreement to the PfP SOFA; 30 Oct 2001), PfP SOFA (5 Jul 1996, with supplemental agreement 30 Oct 2001), Acquisition and Cross-Servicing Agreement, Article 98 Agreement (1 Aug 2002).

In 1996, Romania signed and ratified a basic bilateral treaty with Hungary that settled outstanding issues. This was followed in Jun 1997 by a bilateral treaty with Ukraine that resolved territorial and minority issues. Romania also signed a basic bilateral treaty with Russia in Jul 2003. In 1997, Presidents Clinton and Constantinescu declared a "Strategic Partnership" between the US and Romania.

US ASSISTANCE: Receives Foreign Military Financing program grants, International Military Education and Training aid, eligible to receive grant Excess Defense Articles, National Guard partner with AL, participates in George C. Marshall Center conferences and seminars. In 1993, the US military began training of Romanian military and civilian officials through International Military Education and Training and other exchange programs.

BASES AND ACCESS: On 19 Sep 2001, the Romanian parliament made its airspace, ground infrastructure, and naval facilities available to US and NATO forces engaged in the global war against terrorism. The US made extensive use of Mihail Kogalniceanu air base ("MK air base") near Contanta, Romania, which became a staging base for Joint Special Operations Task Force — Viking before it entered northern Iraq for OIF. Craiova AB was used by US forces during Allied Force/Noble Anvil in 1999.

Forces deployed: Romania's initial contribution to Operation Enduring Freedom and the International Security Assistance Force included an MP platoon and a C-130. In Jun 2002, Romania deployed a motorized infantry battalion and a national intelligence cell to Afghanistan. For OIF, Romania initially deployed an NBC defense unit to Kuwait for support in the event Iraq used chemical or biological weapons. Romania later attached a mechanized infantry battalion to the Italian brigade in the Multi-National Division (South-East) in Iraq, and dispatched a SIGINT and Shadow Unmanned Aerial Vehicle (UAV) unit in support of coalition operations. Romania has also supported US and NATO through its military presence in Bosnia (Stabilization Force) and Kosovo (Kosovo Force).

Code Names: Black Sea Partnership, Briz, Carpathian Lightning, Combined Endeavor, Cooperative series, Cornerstone, Dacia, Eloquent Nugget, Imminent Horizon, Joint series, MEDCEUR, Peaceful Eagle, Peaceshield, Poseidon, Prometheus, Rescue, Rescue Eagle, Rescuer, Sacred Company, Sea Breeze, Strong Resolve, Viking.

Russia

Russia has been a strong supporter of the war on terrorism, granting overflight rights, sharing intelligence, law enforcement information and expertise, and political support. Russia provided support for US (and Northern Alliance) operations in Operation Enduring Freedom (OEF) in 2001, drawing on its long and unhappy experience in Afghanistan. Russia quietly agreed to the US and coalition military presence in the former Soviet republics of Central Asia. It was the first to deploy medical support to Kabul after the fall of the Taliban. Russia helped Germany build a pontoon bridge from Tajikistan into Afghanistan and opened the Salang tunnel enabling transport between northern and southern Afghanistan.

Though Russia's opposition to US military action in Iraq in the first half of 2003 soured US–Russian relations, the war seems not to have had a long-term effect. In Mar 2003, Russia hosted a meeting of representatives from the intelligence services of 39 countries to discuss the war on terrorism. New cooperation between the Russian Federal Security Service (FSB) and the FBI on operational information was demonstrated with the arrest of Hermant Lahkani in New Jersey in Aug 2003 for attempting to sell a shoulder-fired missile to an undercover operative posing as an al Qaeda terrorist. Russia provided much of the original information in the case. Russia is also a member of the Financial Action Task Force.

The major irritant of US–Russian national security relations is the conduct of Russian forces in Chechnya. Fighting continues daily, with substantial civilian casualties. In Oct 2002, the conflict affected Moscow when Chechens seized the Dubrovka Theatre and some 760 hostages. When Russian special forces stormed the theater, about 170 hostages and terrorists died. Since the Dubrovka siege, suicide attacks and bombings against "soft" targets have grown. Russia has attempted to describe its use of force in Chechnya as an anti-terrorist operation, stressing linkages between Chechen fighters and al Qaeda.

Presidents Bush and Putin announced in Nov 2001 in Washington that they would work together to improve the relationship between NATO and Russia, and a new NATO–Russia Council was established. Since Russia joined the NATO Partnership for Peace on 22 Jun 1994, Warsaw Initiative funding for PfP exercises has provided opportunities for Russian officers to interact with their NATO counterparts.

US COMMAND: EUCOM/PACOM. Under the Unified Command Plan approved by President Bush on 30 Apr 2002, Russia and the Caspian Sea were assigned to European Command. Pacific Command was assigned responsibilities for "certain activities" in eastern Russia. In the past, Russia was under the purview of the chairman of the Joint Chiefs of Staff.

AGREEMENTS: SOFA (nuclear-specific agreement), Acquisition and Cross-Servicing Agreement eligible (31 Dec 1995).

The Working Group on Counterterrorism co-chaired by Deputy Secretary of State Richard Armitage and Russian First Deputy Foreign Minister Vyacheslav Trubnikov facilitates counter-terrorism cooperation between the two nations. Russia has also established bilateral counter-terrorism working groups with France, Germany, India, and the UK.

The Russia–China Friendship and Amity Agreement (Jul 2001) paved the way for establishment of the Shanghai Cooperation Organization (SCO), which groups the two countries with Kazakhstan, Kyrgyzstan, Tajikistan, and Uzbekistan.

US ASSISTANCE: As of 24 May 2001, the State Department suspended Foreign Military Financing and International Military Education and Training programs in accordance with legal limitations on assistance due to Russian arms transfers to nations listed as sponsoring international terrorism. In Nov 2002, suspension was partially lifted to allow English-language training and equipment. Freedom Support Act (FSA)–funded programs seek to improve Russia's capacity to combat transnational crime, focusing on counter-narcotics, border security, alien smuggling/trafficking, and export controls. Under the State Partnership Program, the IA and AK National Guards executed three contact events with the Russian military during 2000 and six events for 2001.

The US and Russia continue a large Cooperative Threat Reduction (CTR) program that provides Russia aid in dismantling weapons of mass destruction and preventing the proliferation of weapons and materials. The FY 2003 budget for CTR programs in Russia was $288.3 million, up from $262.7 million in FY 2002.

FORCES DEPLOYED: Soon after 9/11, Russia demonstrably reversed the drawdown of its military presence in Central Asia, increasing troops in Tajikistan and signing new military accords with Kyrgyzstan. Kyrgyzstan agreed that its Kant airfield outside Bishkek could be used as a base for the Russian-led Central Asian rapid reaction forces. Russian forces have participated in Stabilization Force operations in Bosnia and Kosovo Force operations in Kosovo.

Code Names: Arctic SAREX, Balance Ultra, Baltlink, Baltops, Black Sea Partnership, Briz, Centrasbat, Combined Endeavor, Cooperative series, Cope Thunder, Eloquent Nugget, Falcon, Gifted Eagle, GULFEX, Joint series, Ladylove, Moonlight Maze, Peacekeeper, Peaceshield, Russian BILAT, Sea Breeze, Sensor Flower, Sun City, Viking, Westpac MCMEX.

Rwanda

Rwanda is still recovering from the war and genocide of 1994 (which claimed some 800,000 lives) and from military conflicts with the Democratic Republic of the Congo, which it invaded, along with Uganda, in 1998. During 2003, Rwanda aggressively pursued the Democratic Forces for the Liberation of Rwanda, formerly known as the Army for the Liberation of Rwanda, an armed rebel force composed of former soldiers that orchestrated the genocide in 1994. The group continues to operate in the DRC.

US military cooperation with Rwanda was suspended in Jun 2000 after clashes between Rwandan and Ugandan forces in Kisangani, DRC. After the Rwandan withdrawal from the DRC in Oct 2002, Rwanda launched an ambitious plan to demobilize thousands of soldiers, transforming to a 25,000-strong well-equipped army. The US then announced that it would consider reviving assistance to focus on developing the professionalism of the Rwandan military.

US COMMAND: CENTCOM.

AGREEMENTS: SOFA (17 Jan 1992 and Dec 1997), Acquisition and Cross-Servicing Agreement eligible (26 Jan 1998), Article 98 Agreement (4 Mar 2003).

US ASSISTANCE: Since 1995, the US has been the principal donor for Rwanda's humanitarian demining program. Rwanda participates in Africa Center for Strategic Studies conferences and seminars.

Code Names: Distant Runner, Falcon, Golden Spear, Guardian Assistance, Neon Spear, Phoenix Tusk, Provide Assistance, Support Hope.

St. Helena
See Ascension Island.

St. Kitts and Nevis
St. Lucia
St. Vincent and the Grenadines
The Caribbean island nations of St. Kitts and Nevis, St. Lucia, and St. Vincent and the Grenadines receive counter-narcotics assistance and benefit from US military exercises and humanitarian civic action construction projects. All concluded various bilateral treaties with the US in the 1990s, including maritime law enforcement agreements, overflight and order-to-land argreements, mutual legal assistance agreements, and extradition agreements.

US COMMAND: SOUTHCOM.

AGREEMENTS: SOFA (St. Kitts, St. Lucia), Acquisition and Cross-Servicing Agreement eligible (St. Kitts, 29 Aug 2000).

Code Names: New Horizons, PKO, Tradewinds.

Saipan, Northern Marianas Islands[9]
Saipan hosts pre-positioned equipment stored for US forces, naval port visits, and occasional aircraft on transit and in exercises.

US COMMAND: PACOM.

Samoa
Samoan police participated in the UN-sponsored peacekeeping force in East Timor in 2000, the first time Samoa made a contribution to a peacekeeping force. US assistance seeks to improve Samoan maritime law enforcement capability and enhance interoperability with the Coast Guard.

US COMMAND: PACOM.

AGREEMENTS: SOFA.

US ASSISTANCE: Receives International Military Education and Training aid, eligible to receive grant Excess Defense Articles, participates in Asia-Pacific Center for Security Studies executive courses.

Sao Tome and Principe
Sao Tome and Principe — a potentially oil-rich archipelago 186 miles off the coast of Africa — is being eyed as a potential US base. In 1992, Sao Tome signed a long-term agreement with the Voice of America (VOA) for the establishment

---

9. The Commonwealth of the Northern Mariana Islands (CNMI) is a self-governing territory in political union with the US. Its chain of 16 islands marks the divide between the Pacific Ocean and the Philippines Sea.

of a $50 million relay transmitter station; VOA currently broadcasts to much of Africa from the facility. More recently, the US initiated feasibility studies on building a deep-water seaport and developing the airport. An extended runway, US military officials said, would facilitate US deployments.

US COMMAND: EUCOM.

US ASSISTANCE: Receives International Military Education and Training aid, eligible to receive grant Excess Defense Articles, participates in Africa Center for Strategic Studies conferences and seminars.

Saudi Arabia

Despite its public stance as independent and standoffish toward the US in military and counter-terrorism matters, since the 1990 Iraqi invasion of Kuwait, Saudi Arabia has quietly assisted the US by hosting a variety of semi-permanent military bases and providing more than 50 percent of US nonpersonnel stationing costs for operations focused on Baghdad. It has, at the same time, placed enormous restrictions on US operations and imports, and has also stonewalled attempts to establish deep intelligence ties or law enforcement cooperation.

Throughout the 1990s, though, military-to-military cooperation over enforcement of the Iraq southern no-fly zone (Southern Watch) did deepen, paving the way for many of the post-9/11 operations. The Combined Air Operations Center (CAOC) at Prince Sultan air base (al Kharj), built in the 1990s as the nerve center for Southern Watch, quickly (though not without Saudi restrictions) retooled for Operation Enduring Freedom (OEF) and Operation Iraqi Freedom (OIF). US aircraft operated from Saudi bases during OEF. Saudi Arabia provided overflight rights and even hosted combat search and rescue elements during OIF, and US and coalition special operations forces (SOF) staged from northern Saudi Arabia into Iraq.

The presence of the US military forces in the "holy places" in Saudi Arabia has been one of al Qaeda's main grievances, and 15 of the 9/11 suicide bombers were Saudi citizens. One of the first spectacular international terrorist attacks was a Jun 1996 suicide bombing by Saudi Hezbollah of the US military Khobar Towers housing compound near Dhahran AB, in which 19 Americans died.[10] On 12 May 2003, suicide bombers killed 35 people, including 9 Americans, in attacks at three housing compounds in Riyadh. On 8 Nov 2003, another compound housing foreign workers from mainly Arab countries was attacked, killing 18, and bombings and kidnappings steadily increased into 2004.

---

10. An earlier attack on the headquarters of the US training program for the Saudi National Guard in Riyadh occurred on 13 Nov 1995, killing seven (including five US citizens).

US officials claim that after the 12 May 2003 attack, counter-terrorism cooperation with Saudi Arabia increased significantly. On the surface, joint counter-terrorist components were established (including a US–Saudi Joint Task Force on Terrorist Financing in Riyadh, established in Aug 2003), information sharing improved, and Saudi security forces arrested scores of al Qaeda facilitators and suspected terrorists. But long-standing tensions continued over US intelligence and investigative operations on Saudi soil. Despite decades of operations with the Saudi General Intelligence Department (GID) and Interior Ministry, the CIA still had not fashioned an authentic day-to-day working relationship with the Saudi security services. From the Khober Towers investigation on, the Saudi regime was largely uncooperative. Though some in the US government craved access to the closed kingdom for joint investigations and operations against terrorists, Saudi behavior never really changed after 9/11. Despite offers of joint covert action throughout the 1990s to kill or depose Saddam Hussein, little ever came of Saudi action, and US officials have always suspected that the Saudi GID and other security services were feeding the US useless intelligence as part of their "liaison" relationship.

The US military presence in Saudi Arabia originated with a training mission established at Dhahran in 1953. Over the years, the US has sold Saudi Arabia military aircraft (F-15s, AWACS aircraft, and UH-60 Blackhawks), air defenses (Patriot and Hawk missiles), armored vehicles (M1A2 Abrams tanks and Bradley fighting vehicles), and other equipment. Based on decades of cooperation, military-to-military relations are thus close and positive. There is a full program of training, joint exercises, Saudi attendance at US military schools, and activities relating to administering the multi-billion-dollar arms sales program.

The Saudi military currently enjoys diminished funding from its oil-rich days, and, to US consternation, has sought less expensive — and what the US thinks is less effective — military training from other countries. The long-term impact of reduced interoperability worries those involved in the extensive US–Saudi program, but in wake of the fall of Saddam Hussein in Iraq, it probably has an inconsequential impact of US national security.

US COMMAND: CENTCOM.

AGREEMENTS: Classified SOFA, Acquisition and Cross-Servicing Agreement eligible (29 Mar 1998).

> The US and Saudi Arabia are not linked by a formal defense treaty. Saudi Arabia is a member of the Gulf Cooperation Council (GCC).

US ASSISTANCE: Receives International Military Education and Training aid (allows Saudi military students to attend training in the US at a discount), eligible to receive grant Excess Defense Articles.

BASES AND ACCESS: On 29 Apr 2003, Secretary of Defense Donald Rumsfeld announced that US forces would discontinue enforcing the no-fly zones and withdraw from Saudi Arabia. The CAOC had already moved Afghanistan and Horn of Africa operations to Qatar by 2003, and the Iraq cells moved after the fall of the Baghdad regime. In Aug 2003, the US formally withdrew most of its forces stationed in Saudi Arabia, though significant elements remain.

During Desert Storm, the US staged its ground invasion force in northern Saudi Arabia, operated an enormous logistical network from Saudi and Gulf State ports, and flew aircraft from at least 13 Saudi bases: al Jouf, al Kharj (Prince Sultan), Ar Ar, Dhahran (King Abdul Aziz AB and King Fahd International Airport), Jeddah, Khamis Mushayt, King Khalid Military City, Rafha, Riyadh (Riyadh AB and King Khalid International), Taif, Tabuk. US Navy ships and submarines regularly called at the Saudi ports of ad Damman, Jeddah, al Jubayl, and Yanbu.

After the 1991 Gulf War, US aircraft and selected forces continued to operate from the modern facilities. Ground-based intelligence monitoring continued (including reported SIGINT stations at Araz and Khafji and the "Park Place" NSA intelligence operation), and Saudi Arabia hosted U-2 and RC-135 reconnaissance aircraft. The US had planned to leave about one armored division's worth of tanks and heavy equipment in place near the King Khalid Military City, but the Saudi government balked, fearful that the pre-positioned stocks would give the appearance of the establishment of an American base. Most of the army's pre-positioned stocks were shifted instead to nearby gulf countries.

After Khobar Towers, Operation Desert Shift transitioned the headquarters of Joint Task Force — Southwest Asia and other exposed US forces to the more remote Prince Sultan AB. By 9/11, the US had 13 CENTCOM-controlled facilities in Saudi Arabia, and utilized an additional 66 Saudi-controlled facilities. Prince Sultan became the hub of US activity, hosting fighter aircraft flying in support of the no-fly-zone mission, as well as U-2 spy planes. Other bases regularly used by US forces included Dhahran (King Abdul Aziz AB), Khamis Mushayt, Riyadh (King Khalid IAP), Tabuk, and Taif. Some 300 US aircraft, including E-3 AWACS aircraft, RC-135s, JSTARs, F-16s, and special operations, aerial refueling, and transport aircraft flew from Prince Sultan, Tabuk, and Ar Ar during OIF, and special operations forces reportedly staged operations from al Jouf.

Code Names: Arabian Gauntlet, Black Shark, Blue Flag, Camel Hump, Desert Falcon, Defense Focus, Desert Shift, Desert Warrior, Earnest Leader, Elf One, Giant Voice, Grecian Firebolt,

GULFEX, Indigo series, Mighty Guardian, Nautical series, Pacer Parts, Pacer Sentinel, Peace Hawk, Peace Pulse, Peace Sentinel, Peace Shield, Peace Sun, Peninsula Shield, Phoenix Scorpion, Provide Cover, Red Reef, Southern Watch, Steel Box, Turbo Cads, Vigilant Sentinel, Vigilant Warrior, Warrior Bravo.

Senegal

Senegal took a strong position against terrorism in the wake of 9/11 and hosted a conference establishing an African Pact Against Terrorism in Oct 2001. The Senegalese military receives most of its training, equipment, and support from France. Senegal hosted the inaugural Africa Center for Strategic Studies seminar in Dakar, 31 Oct–12 Nov 1999, and the first brigade-level African Contingency Operations Training and Assistance (ACOTA) — known at that time as African Crisis Response Initiative (ACRI) — training in Oct 2000. A Joint/Combined Exchange Training (JCET) special operations program exists between Senegal's Commando Battalion and the US 3rd Special Forces Group at Camp Thies. Senegal participated in a Mar 2004 EUCOM counter-terrorism chiefs of defense conference in Stuttgart, Germany, with Algeria, Chad, Mali, Mauritania, Morocco, Niger, Tunisia, and the US.

US COMMAND: EUCOM.

AGREEMENTS: SOFA (11 Jan 2001), Acquisition and Cross-Servicing Agreement (14 May 2001), Article 98 Agreement.

US ASSISTANCE: Receives Foreign Military Financing program grants, International Military Education and Training aid, eligible to receive grant Excess Defense Articles, participates in ACOTA and the earlier ACRI, participates in Africa Center for Strategic Studies conferences and seminars.

FORCES DEPLOYED: Senegal's professional armed forces have been active in peace-keeping in Bosnia, the Central African Republic, the Democratic Republic of Congo, Lebanon, Liberia, Rwanda, Sierra Leone, and the Sinai. Senegal has agreed to lead the Economic Community of West African States (ECOWAS) force in Côte d'Ivoire. It was the only sub-Saharan nation to send a contingent to participate in Desert Storm.

Code Names: Assured Response, Focus Relief, MEDFLAG, Midget Thrust, Shepherd Venture, Silver Anvil.

Serbia and Montenegro (former Republic of Yugoslavia)

Since 9/11, the federal government and its two constituent republics, Serbia and Montenegro, have cooperated with the US by implementing financial sanctions against terrorist groups, by establishing an anti-terrorism task force and a financial intelligence unit, and by investigating links between weapons exporters and states of concern, including Iraq.

Since Oct 2000, Serbia and Montenegro has moved forward on a less nationalistic course, strengthening bilateral relationships with neighboring countries, resolving its long-standing border dispute with Macedonia, and establishing full diplomatic relations with Croatia. Serbia and Montenegro has established a working relationship with the United Nations Interim Administration Mission in Kosovo (UNMIK) and released all disputed ethnic Albanian prisoners from Kosovo.

After Serbian Prime Minister Djindjic was assassinated on 12 Mar 2003, the newly formed union government of Serbia and Montenegro declared a state of emergency. Presidential elections on 16 Nov 2003 were declared invalid. The US announced 31 Mar 2004 that it was suspending assistance to Serbia and Montenegro because Belgrade had not cooperated sufficiently with efforts to apprehend persons indicted by the International Criminal Tribunal for the Former Yugoslavia (ICTY).

US COMMAND: EUCOM.

US ASSISTANCE: Prior to the suspension of aid in Apr 2004, Serbia and Montenegro received International Military Education and Training aid, participated in George C. Marshall Center conferences and seminars, and participated in the Export Control and Related Border Security Assistance program. Support for East European Democracy (SEED) funds were also used to fund efforts to investigate, prosecute, and try war crimes.

Code Names: Able Sentry, Adventure Exchange, Allied Force, Allied Harbor, Amber Star, Ample Train, ARRcade Fusion, Arcade Guard, Ardent Ground, Balkan Calm, Brilliant Foil, Calm Support, Central Enterprise, Cobalt Flash, Cossack Steppe, Courageous Bat, Crown Eagle, Cygnet Spear, Cygnet Vine, Dacia, Decisive Guardian, Deliberate Falcon, Determined Falcon, Devil's Hat, Dimming Sun, Distant Thunder, Dynamic Response, Eagle Eye, Falcon, Flexible Anvil, Gaulish, Glow Worm, Gobi Dust, Iron Ram, Joint series, Lark Song, Lion Sun, Mountain Hawk, Nimble Lion, Noble Anvil, Peaceshield, Provide Refuge, Rapid Cheetah, Rapid Guardian, Shining Hope, Sky Anvil, Stoney Run, Sustain Hope, Unified Charger, Western Vortex, Winged Star.

Serbia and Montenegro, Kosovo

Kosovo, a province of Serbia, has been under the administrative control of the United Nations Interim Administration Mission in Kosovo (UNMIK) since Jun 1999. NATO's Kosovo Force (KFOR) entered Kosovo on 12 Jun 1999, and provides security. KFOR troop strength was reduced to 17,730 in 2003 and has included military personnel from more than 30 countries (including 2,000 from the US). Continuing violence in the province has led to a number of emergency deployments, and undermined the US effort in 2002–2003 to reduce the US presence in the Balkans in order to redeploy forces to Iraq and Afghanistan.

US COMMAND: EUCOM.

US ASSISTANCE: Receives peacekeeping operations (PKO) funding, receives Support for East European Democracy (SEED) funds to support the UNMIK International Police Force, and to train and equip the Kosovo police service.

BASES AND ACCESS: The Multi-National Brigade (East) (NMB-E), referred to as the American Sector and also called Task Force Falcon, includes the base camps of Bondsteel (near Pristina) and Monteith and remote sites staffed by Falcon forces. Other military bases are controlled by Multi-National Division West (Italian), Multi-National Brigade South (German), Multi-National Brigade North (French), and Multi-National Brigade Center (UK).

Code Names: *See* Serbia, above.

Seychelles

The Seychelles supports the US in the war on terrorism and has offered facilities to the US military allowing US naval vessels to make several port calls a year at Mahe. The US, through the Kenya–US Liaison Office in Nairobi, support the Seychelles's counter-narcotics maritime activities and coastal security efforts.

US COMMAND: PACOM?

AGREEMENTS: Acquisition and Cross-Servicing Agreement eligible (5 Sep 2000), Article 98 Agreement.

US ASSISTANCE: Receives modest International Military Education and Training aid, eligible to receive grant Excess Defense Articles, participates in Africa Center for Strategic Studies conferences and seminars.

BASES AND ACCESS: The official US presence in the Seychelles began in 1963 when an air force tracking station was built on Mahe. The station officially closed 30 Sep 1996.

Code Names: Golden Spear, Neon Spear.

Sierra Leone

Elections in May 2002 have led to a reduction in the UN Mission in Sierra Leone (UNAMSIL), established on 22 Oct 1999 to implement the Lome Peace Agreement and assist in disarmament and demobilization. In Nov 2002, UNAMSIL began a gradual reduction from a peak strength of 17,500 personnel. As of 31 Jan 2004, 11,615 total uniformed personnel, including 11,500 troops and military observers, were deployed from 31 countries.

US COMMAND: EUCOM.

AGREEMENTS: Article 98 Agreement.

US ASSISTANCE: Receives International Military Education and Training aid, eligible to receive grant Excess Defense Articles, participates in Africa Center for Strategic Studies conferences and seminars.

Code Names: Assured Response, Dynamic Mix, Focus Relief, Hard Flint, Jagged Course, MED-FLAG, Midget Thrust, Noble Obelisk, Shadow Express, SHAREM, Silver Anvil, Snow Falcon, Tartan Eagle, Unified Spirit.

Singapore

Singapore is one of the strongest counter-terrorism partners of the US and a strong supporter of the US military presence in Asia. Since 9/11, Singapore has stepped up intelligence, law enforcement, and counter-terrorism cooperation with the US, disrupted terrorist plots targeting the US, and made a number of high-profile arrests of suspected Jemaah Islamiyah (JI) members. In Mar 2003, Singapore became the first Asian port to begin operations under the Container Security Initiative. It is also a member of the Proliferation Security Initiative.

The Singapore armed forces engage in training with Association of Southeast Asian Nations (ASEAN) and with Australia, New Zealand, Taiwan, India, and the US. A program of Joint/Combined Exchange Training (JCET) special operations training instructs the 1st Commando Battalion at Camp Hendon, Changi Point, and Coney Island.

US COMMAND: PACOM.

AGREEMENTS: MOU on access to bases (1990, amended in 1999), Implementing Arrangement with the Republic of Singapore Navy (20 Apr 2000), classified SOFA, Acquisition and Cross-Servicing Agreement (1 Apr 2000).

Singapore is a member of the Five Power Defence Agreement (FPDA — Australia, Malaysia, New Zealand, Singapore, and the UK), concluded originally to replace the former defense role of the UK in the Singapore–Malaysia area. The arrangement obligates members to consult in the event of external threat and provides for stationing commonwealth forces in Singapore.

In Oct 2003, the US and Singapore announced their intention to negotiate a "Strategic Framework Agreement" on defense and security. The US–Singapore Defense Cooperation Committee coordinates and manages cooperative activities between the two countries.

US ASSISTANCE: Participates in Asia-Pacific Center for Security Studies executive courses. Approximately 85 percent of Singapore's military equipment come from the US.

BASES AND ACCESS: With the closure of US bases in the Philippines, Singapore became a key US forward deployment base. The 1990 MOU allowed access to Singapore facilities at Paya Lebar air base and the Sembawang wharves. Under the MOU, a US Navy logistics unit of approximately 160 people was established at Changi Naval Base in 1992 to facilitate more than 100 US ship visits per year. In Mar 2001, Singapore inaugurated a pier at Changi Naval Base to accommodate US aircraft carriers.

US fighter aircraft deploy regularly to Paya Lebar and Sembawang for exercises. After 9/11, Singapore granted blanket overflight clearance and tanker fueling in support of Operation Enduring Freedom. The National Guard also maintains a special relationship with the Singapore armed forces. The 162nd Fighter Wing of the AZ Air National Guard provides training for Singapore F-16 pilots in Arizona, while the TX Army National Guard trains Singapore's helicopter pilots in the CH-47 "Chinook" helicopter at Peace Prairie. The National Guard will also train Singapore's pilots in the AH-64 Apache Longbow when the country takes delivery.

FORCES DEPLOYED: Singapore has participated in UN peacekeeping missions in Angola, Cambodia, East Timor, Kuwait, and Namibia, providing the peacekeeping force commander in East Timor Aug 2002–Aug 2003. After Operation Iraqi Freedom, Singapore provided a unit to train Iraqi police. In Nov 2003, a Singapore amphibious ship deployed to Iraq, and Singapore pledged a C-130. In Apr 2004, Singapore's 200 military personnel returned from Iraq with no plans to send more troops.

Code Names: Axolotl, Bell Buoy, CARAT Singapore, Churinga, Coalition Flag, Cobra Gold, Commando Sling, Cope Taufan, Cope Thunder, Cope Tiger, Coronet Bat, Dawn Seagull, Flaming Arrow, Flying Fish, Hunter, IADS ADEX, Kangaroo, Mercury, Mergate, Merlion, Merlynx, MTX, Night Lion, NOLES, Paradise, Peace Carvin, Peace Guardian, Pitch Black, Sea Saber, SEACAT, Singaroo, Southern Tiger, Spartan, Stardex, Starfish, Suman Warrior, Tandem Thrust, Team Challenge, Tiger Balm, Tri-crab, Valiant Mark, Westpac MCMEX.

Slovak Republic

Slovakia became a member of NATO on 29 Mar 2004, and has supported the war on terrorism, Operation Enduring Freedom (OEF) in Afghanistan, and Operation Iraqi Freedom (OIF) in Iraq. During Allied Force, Slovakia provided overflight and transit rights for NATO deployments, and has continued these rights for Afghanistan and Iraq.

US COMMAND: EUCOM.

AGREEMENTS: Reciprocal SOFA, PfP SOFA (13 Jan 1996), Acquisition and Cross-Servicing Agreement (15 Dec 1998).

US ASSISTANCE: Receives Foreign Military Financing program grants, International Military Education and Training aid, participates in the EUCOM Joint Contact Team Program, National Guard partner with Indiana.

BASES AND ACCESS: On 18 Sep 2001, Slovakia notified the US that it would grant blanket overflight and basing rights to all coalition partners in OEF.

FORCES DEPLOYED: Slovakia deployed an engineering unit to Afghanistan under the International Security Assistance Force and has offered a special forces regiment. Slovakia sent an NBC contingent, integrated into the Czech NBC unit, during the preparations for OIF, and later sent an engineering unit deployed to the Polish sector inside Iraq.

Slovakia has one of the largest per capita peacekeeping contingents. Slovak troops have participated in UN peacekeeping missions in Bosnia, Cyprus, the Golan Heights, Ethiopia and Eritrea, and East Timor. Slovaks soldiers are deployed in the joint Czech–Slovak mechanized battalion assigned to Kosovo Force (KFOR). Slovakia markedly increased its commitment to KFOR and to the Stabilization Force (SFOR) in 2002.

Code Names: Combined Endeavor, Cooperative series, Dacia, Eloquent Nugget, Esperia, Joint series, Lone Eagle, MEDCEUR, Motion, Peaceshield, PLANEX, Rescue Eagle, Slovak Express, Strong Resolve.

Slovenia

Slovenia became a member of NATO on 29 Mar 2004, and has modestly supported US operations in Afghanistan and Iraq. Then–Prime Minister Drnovsek met again with President Bush in Washington in May 2002; Secretary of Defense Donald Rumsfeld visited Ljubljana in Nov 2002.

Left virtually without military equipment or infrastructure after its 10-day war for independence in 1991, Slovenia has striven to model its small volunteer armed forces on those of the US and NATO, focusing on peacekeeping rather than territorial defense. Slovenia announced its intention to deploy a special forces contingent to Afghanistan in 2004 and has made modest humanitarian contributions to Iraq. A Joint/Combined Exchange Training (JCET) special operations program is conducted among US SEAL Team 2 and 21st Special Operations Squadron and the Special Brigade *(Specialna Brigada)* at Ljubljana. Slovenia hosted its first Partnership for Peace exercise — Cooperative Adventure Exchange 98 — a disaster preparedness command post exercise involving almost 6,000 troops from 19 NATO and PfP member nations.

US command: EUCOM.

Agreements: Reciprocal SOFA, PfP SOFA (17 Feb 1996), Acquisition and Cross-Servicing Agreement.

US assistance: Receives Foreign Military Financing program grants, International Military Education and Training aid, participates in the EUCOM Joint Contact Team Program, National Guard partner with Colorado, participates in George C. Marshall Center conferences and seminars.

Forces deployed: Slovenia's elite units have trained with and were integrated into NATO operations, particularly the Stabilization Force in Bosnia, where Slovenia has provided a military police platoon for the Italian-led Multinational Specialized Unit (MSU) in Sarajevo since Jan 1999, one motorized rifle company deployed in Jan 2003, and provides VIP support helicopter and light transport aircraft missions, as well as the use of an air base in southern Slovenia.

Code Names: Combined Endeavor, Cooperative series, Dacia, Dobodan Lena, Eloquent Nugget, Joint series, PASSEX, Peaceful Eagle, Strong Resolve, Veneto Rescue.

Soloman Islands

US military forces carry out annual bilateral meetings as well as small-scale exercises with the Solomon Islands Police Border Protection Force. The US also provides training in coastal surveillance and seaborne law enforcement.

US command: PACOM.

Agreements: SOFA.

US assistance: Receives International Military Education and Training aid, eligible to receive grant Excess Defense Articles, participates in Asia-Pacific Center for Security Studies executive courses.

Somalia

Somalia's lack of a functioning central government, its protracted state of violent instability, and its porous borders make it a "front-line state" in the war on terrorism. The US does not have official relations with any entity in Somalia. The Somalia-based Al-Ittihad Al-Islami (Islamic Unity), originally formed in the early 1990s with a goal of creating an Islamic state in Somalia, has committed terrorist acts, primarily in Ethiopia. At least one faction is sympathetic to al Qaeda and has provided assistance to its members.

Djibouti, Egypt, Kenya, and Yemen, together with former colonial power Italy, have all been involved in mediation and reconciliation efforts to establish a national government. Meanwhile, various Arab states and Eritrea and Ethiopia have also been providing political support to clan groups and warlords.

US command: CENTCOM. Combined Joint Task Force — Horn of Africa (CJTF-HOA).

Agreements: Classified SOFA (1980).

Code Names: Continue Hope, Eastern Exit, Gothic Serpent, Impressive Lift, Phoenix Onyx, Provide Relief, Quick Draw, Ranger, Red Reef, Restore Hope, United Shield.

South Africa

South Africa has become a close military partner of the US, active in the war on terrorism, taking a military leadership in southern Africa and the southern Atlantic and Indian Oceans. The country has shared law enforcement and intelligence information, and has been active on financial tracking since a new financial intelligence center was establishment.

Regular port visits by US Navy ships and submarines to Durban and other ports facilitate low-level training and interoperability. An active Joint/Combined Exchange Training (JCET) special operations program, together with a major special operations exercise series, builds close ties between US and South African special operations forces (SOF). In 2003, South Africa became the first African nation to participate in the National Guard State Partnership Program, and on 22 Aug 2003, NY Adjutant General Maj. Gen. Thomas P. Maguire Jr. and Lt. Gen. Godfrey N. Ngwenya, South African National Defence Forces chief of joint operations, exchanged flags to initiate their partnership.

US command: EUCOM.

Agreements: SOFA (11 Jun 1999), Acquisition and Cross-Servicing Agreement (8 May 2001), Seismic Monitoring Agreement, Master Exchange Agreement.

The South Africa–US Defense Committee Meeting (DEFCOM) held its seventh annual meeting 4–6 Jun 2003 in Annapolis, MD. The committee includes an Acquisition and Technology Working Group (A&TWG).

US assistance: Receives International Military Education and Training aid, participates in the Export Control and Related Border Security Assistance program, participates in Africa Center for Strategic Studies conferences and seminars.

Code Names: Atlas Response, Blue Crane, Combined Endeavor, Flintlock, MEDFLAG, Oceanic, Silent Promise, Trailblazer, Transoceanic Exercise, WATC.

South Korea (Republic of Korea)

The threat from North Korea remains one of the few classic conventional military confrontations from the Cold War, and South Korea ranks third (behind Germany and Japan) in terms of a permanent US overseas military presence, with 37,000 personnel at some 80 bases and facilities.

The US–South Korean relationship, despite its ups and downs, remains extremely strong in the military field, and the Korean armed forces have deployed to support US military operations in the war on terrorism, from Guam to Central Asia to Afghanistan and Iraq. With the dispatch of 3,000 troops to Iraq, South Korea made the third largest contributing force there, after the US and the UK. Since 9/11, South Korea has also supported the war on terrorism by sharing intelligence, creating a new financial intelligence unit.

Though there was an outcry by many over the 2004 announcement that US forces in Korea would serve a rotation in Iraq, the US and South Korea have been discussing for some time reforms of the military posture, with the South taking a greater role in its own defense. A reduction of US forces takes into consideration a view that US forces were deployed too close to the DMZ, as well as improvements in military technology that would make smaller military forces more effective in defeating any North Korean offensive.

As part of the reform of military relations, the US–South Korea Land Partnership Plan, agreed to in Mar 2002, proposes to reduce the number of major US installations by 18 (from 41 to 23), primarily by closing and consolidating facilities north of Seoul. US forces will now consolidate around key hubs, relocate the Seoul-based garrison at Yongson, and move south of the Han River by 2007. The plan also significantly enhances training and combined warfighting to continue to move South Korean military forces from the supporting to the leading role on the peninsula. South Korea has also agreed to pay a larger portion of US force's stationing costs.

An extensive Joint/Combined Exchange Training (JCET) special operations program involves army special forces, air force special operations squadrons, and Navy SEALs training with their South Korean counterparts at Camp 6525 in Byupyong, Osan AB, the Maesanri DZ, Pilsung Range, in Seoul, Sungnam, Jeungpyong, and Inchon.

Following North Korea's Oct 2002 admission that it had a covert highly enriched uranium program, relations became particularly tense. Multi-lateral talks with China, Japan, and Russia participating opened in Apr 2003. On 25 Feb 2004, all six parties sat down in Beijing to attempt to find a way to achieve complete, verifiable, and irreversible elimination of North Korea's nuclear weapons programs.

US COMMAND: PACOM. A Combined Forces Command (CFC) was established in 1978 to coordinate operations between US and South Korean armed forces. The head of the CFC also serves as commander of the United Nations Command

(UNC) and US Forces Korea (USFK, which is also co-located with the Eighth US Army). The air force command and infrastructure is centered on Osan AB, where there is an active Combined Air Operations Center (CAOC). The US Navy command is headquartered in Chinhae.

AGREEMENTS: US–ROK Mutual Defense Treaty (1954), Special Review of the US/R.O.K. Status of Forces Agreement (SOFA; 1989–1991), Special Measures Agreement (SMA; 1991), Acquisition and Cross-Servicing Agreement (7 Jun 1988), granted Major Non-NATO Ally status.

US ASSISTANCE: Participates in Asia-Pacific Center for Security Studies executive courses.

BASES AND ACCESS: The 2nd Infantry Division has been stationed in South Korea since the 1950s, when the Korean War ended. Some 13,000 army soldiers rotate to South Korea on one-year unaccompanied tours to staff the division. The 8th US Army (EUSA) supports the infrastructure of camps and forward bases, communications and intelligence stations (many isolated and small), as well as the training areas, firing ranges, and depots supporting US forces. There is an extensive intelligence collection infrastructure on the peninsula, and numerous special operations components. Signficant pre-positioned equipment, ammunition, and fuel stocks are stored for US forces.

The DOD announced in Aug 2004 that the 2nd Infantry Division forces deployed to Iraq would not return to Korea and that a total reduction of 12,500 US service members would be undertaken under the "Global Posture Review." The department noted that some of the US bases needed to be updated and moved, given that many were in the same places they were when the fighting stopped in the Korean War in 1953.

FORCES DEPLOYED: South Korea announced on 18 Jun 2004 that it would deploy 3,660 troops to northern Iraq, supplementing the 600 engineers and military medical personnel in the south.

Code Names: Balance Knife, Bell Buoy, Cooperative Thunder, Cope Jade, Coral Lease, Coronet Extent, Coronet Regatta, Courageous Channel, CSOFEX, DISELEX, EODEX, Falconer, Flash Knife, Foal Eagle, Foam, Focus, Fog, Freedom Banner, Grecian Firebolt, Indy, Intelex, MINEX, MTX, Neptune Thunder, Pacific Nightingale, Peace Krypton, Peace Pheasant, Peace Pioneer, Peace Spectator, Phanton Saber, Prairie Warrior, Rapid Thunder, RIMPAC, Rook Knight, RSO&I, SALVEX, SEALEX, Seek Smoke, SHAREM, Skivvy, Spartan, SUBEX, Tandem Thrust, Team Spirit, Trident Arch, Turbo Cads, Turbo Intermodel Surge, Ulchi Focus Lens, War Steed, Westpac MCMEX.

Spain

After terrorists bombed four commuter trains coming into Madrid on 11 Mar 2004, causing 191 deaths and more than 1,400 injuries, internal Spanish politics and Spain's support for the war on terrorism were transformed. The Popular Party of President Jose Maria Aznar was voted out of office, and Spain announced plans to withdraw its combat forces from Iraq.

Spain has been a member of NATO since 1982, and has participated in the full panoply of military operations in the former Yugoslavia. Because of its own experience with Euskadi Ta Askatasuna (ETA — Basque Homeland and Liberty) terrorism, after 9/11 Spain became an unserving ally in the war on terrorism, backing Operation Enduring Freedom (OEF) in Afghanistan and Operation Iraqi Freedom (OIF) in Iraq. As part of Operacion Datil since Nov 2001, Spanish police have detained 17 al Qaeda suspects in Madrid and Castellon.

Spain is also active in NATO operations to boost the protection of merchant shipping in the Mediterranean and Strait of Gibraltar. Spain continues to focus attention on North Africa, especially Morocco. In 2002, Spanish forces evicted a small contingent of Moroccans from a tiny islet off Morocco's coast following that nation's attempt to assert sovereignty over the Spanish island.

US COMMAND: EUCOM.

AGREEMENTS: Joint Declaration (11 Jan 2001), Agreement on Defense Cooperation (1988, amended 10 Apr 2002), PfP SOFA (6 Mar 1998), Acquisition and Cross-Servicing Agreement (11 May 1999).

   Bilateral defense and security relations between the US and Spain are regulated by the Agreement on Defense Cooperation. The 2001 Joint Declaration lays out a road map for expanded cooperation in six areas, including defense and combating new threats.

BASES AND ACCESS: Spain authorized the US use of military bases at Naval Station Rota and Moron AB in support of military operations in Afghanistan. Rota also supports US intelligence collection and surveillance operations, including EP-3 operations. The Spanish government offered to make available Rota and the Tarifa control center, as well as reconnaissance planes and helicopters, in support of NATO operations in the western Mediterranean. In Mar 2003, Military Sealift Command (MSC) Europe organized the movement of an entire navy fleet hospital — 79,000 square feet in total — from storage in Bogen Bay, Norway, to Rota to treat wounded US service personnel returning from the war in Iraq. Fleet Hospital 8 eventually treated more than 1,000 wounded service personnel.

FORCES DEPLOYED: Spain has supported OEF in Afghanistan and OIF in Iraq, NATO's Active Endeavour, and operations in the Horn of Africa. As part of OEF, Spain contributed C-130s for transport at Manas, Kyrgyzstan, as well as an airborne detachment and medical unit in Afghanistan. Two Spanish search and rescue helicopters deployed to Manas in support of OEF and the International Security Assistance Force (ISAF) in Apr 2003. One battalion-sized task force also deployed to Kabul as part of ISAF.

From Oct 2002, the Spanish navy commanded Combined Task Force 150, the multi-national maritime interdiction force based in Djibouti, contributing two vessels and 400 sailors and marines. A Spanish P-3 is deployed to Djibouti in support of maritime surveillance and reconnaissance operations. Spanish forces participating in Combined Task Force 150 were responsible for the interdiction and search of the North Korean cargo ship *So San,* which was found to be carrying Scud missiles.

In Aug 2003, Spain deployed 1,300 troops to southern Iraq, increasing the number to 1,800 by Apr 2004, when the announcement of their withdrawal was made. On 27 Apr, Spain began the withdrawal of its forces. Spain has also contributed forces to the Stabilization Force in Bosnia and to the Kosovo Force.

Code Names: Adventure Exchange, Adventure Express, Air Brake, Allied Response, Ample Train, Ardent Ground, Betacom, Bright Horizon, Bright Star, Britannia Way, Cathode Emission, Clean Hunter, Coalition Flag, Combined Endeavor, Common Energy, Constant Harmony, Cooperative series, Destined Glory, Distant Thunder, Diving, Dogfish, Dogu Akdeniz, Dynamic series, Esperia, Green Flag, Link Seas, Lisa Azul, Mace, Majestic Eagle, Matador, Med Shark, Mothia, One Way, Pacific Protector, Peaceshield, Poised Eagle, Sanso, Sea Saber, Shadow Express, Strong Resolve, TAPON, Trial, Trident D'Or, Unified Charger, Volant Partner.

Sri Lanka

The government of Sri Lanka and the Liberation Tigers of Tamil Eclam (LTTE) declared unilateral cease-fires in Dec 2001, signed a cease-fire accord in Feb 2002, and began negotiations toward internal autonomy within a federal Sri Lankan state. Though the US designated the LTTE a foreign terrorist organization in Oct 1997, in 2002 it established working-level contacts to facilitate humanitarian aid. In Apr 2003, the LTTE withdrew from the ongoing talks, but the cease-fire continued. There was also a split within the LTTE in early Mar 2004.

Sri Lanka has been completely cooperative in allowing overflights, husbanding of ships and aircraft, and supporting operational missions since Desert Storm. US Navy ships and submarines have made regular visits to Columbo, and in Mar 2003 the US announced the transfer of the US Coast

Guard cutter *Courageous* to the Sri Lankan navy. The US and Sri Lanka have a small military-to-military relationship. In 2000, Sri Lanka requested National Guard subject matter expertise in managing media relations. An extensive Joint/Combined Exchange Training (JCET) special operations program has taken place among US special operations forces and the Sri Lankan Special Boat Squadron, Fast Attack Flotilla, and 1st and 2nd Commando Regiments, at Dakshana and Rahuna naval bases, at Columbo, Dakshina, Ganemulla, Hambantota, Kaluthra, Kudo Oya, Minneriya, Tangalle, and Wirawila. The US also operates an International Broadcast Bureau (formerly Voice of America) transmitting station in Sri Lanka.

US COMMAND: PACOM.

AGREEMENTS: SOFA, Article 98 Agreement, Acquisition and Cross-Servicing Agreement (post-9/11 agreement).

US ASSISTANCE: Receives Foreign Military Financing program grants, receives International Military Education and Training aid, eligible to receive grant Excess Defense Articles, participates in National Defense University Near East South Asia (NESA) Center seminars, participates in Asia-Pacific Center for Security Studies executive courses. Peacekeeping funds were requested in 2004 to support any peacekeeping mission resulting from a peace settlement.

CODE NAMES: Balance Style, Becker Serum, Cooperative Thunder, Flash Style, NOLES, SAREX, Shant Doot, Shanti Path.

Sudan

Sudan took a pro-Iraqi stance in Desert Storm, was home to Osama bin Laden 1991–1996, and had earlier hosted Carlos the Jackal, Abu Nidal, and other terrorist leaders. Throughout the 1990s, Sudan not only was a terrorist safe haven but also supported insurrections in Algeria, Egypt, Eritrea, Ethiopia, Tunisia, and Uganda. It was designated a state sponsor of terrorism in 1993; in Oct 1997, the US imposed comprehensive sanctions against Sudan. In Aug 1998, the US attacked the al Shifa Pharmaceutical Plant in Khartoum, based on intelligence that it was involved with both Iraq and Osama bin Laden in the production of chemical weapons.

The US and Sudan entered into a dialogue on counter-terrorism in May 2000, and since 9/11 Sudan has provided intelligence and law enforcement cooperation to the FBI and CIA. The end of the Sudan civil war in the south in 2002 opened the way for improving relations and border controls, though throughout 2004 the domestic situation in Sudan continued to decline. A Combined Joint Task Force — Horn of Africa (CJTF-HOA) C-130 aircraft landed in Khartoum on 17 May 2003, the first time a US military airplane had landed in Sudan since 1993. Sudan is also the second largest recipient of general US aid in sub-Saharan Africa, after Djibouti.

US COMMAND: CENTCOM. CJTF-HOA.

AGREEMENTS: SOFA (12 Nov and 7 Dec 1981).

US ASSISTANCE: All US military assistance was terminated following the coup of 1989. Sudan receives most of its military equipment from China, Russia, and Libya (and previously Iraq).

Code Names: Arid Farmer, Coronet Lightning, Delenda, Eagle Look, Early Call.

Suriname

With a vast, sparsely populated interior and unpoliced border, Suriname is considered a favored transshipment point for narcotics and weapons to and from the US and Europe. Suriname receives military assistance from the US and the Netherlands, and Brazil, China, France, and India all provide professional development for the Surinamese armed forces. In the mid-1990s, China also began donating military equipment.

The US counter-narcotics security relationship increasingly operates under the "counter-terrorism" banner. In 2003, the US completed renovation of Suriname's National Emergency Operations Center. The Special Forces Company of the Surinamese armed forces trains with Navy SEALs at Ayoko Kaserne, Concordia, and Paramaribo under the Joint/Combined Exchange Training (JCET) special operations program. The ninth in a series of Medical Readiness (MEDRETE) exercises concluded on 19 Apr 2004.

US COMMAND: SOUTHCOM.

US ASSISTANCE: Receives Foreign Military Financing program grants, International Military Education and Training aid, eligible to receive grant Excess Defense Articles (signed an Excess Defense Articles agreement Dec 2002), receives International Narcotics Control and Law Enforcement funding.

Code Names: Distant Haven, New Horizons, PKO.

Swaziland

Swaziland receives International Military Education and Training aid for civil–military relations, peacekeeping, and professional military leadership training; it participates in Africa Center for Strategic Studies conferences and seminars. A pre-9/11 Joint/Combined Exchange Training (JCET) special operations program brought together US and Swazi military personnel in special operations and peacekeeping training.

US COMMAND: EUCOM.

AGREEMENTS: Acquisition and Cross-Servicing Agreement eligible (26 Jan 1998).

Sweden

Sweden is an active participant in the NATO Partnership for Peace program (9 May 1994), a leader in Baltic security and international peacekeeping, and a partner with the US in intelligence technologies and the war on terrorism. Combined training under the Joint/Combined Exchange Training (JCET) special operations program has taken place between Sarskilda Syddes Group (SSG) and Navy SEALs at Shovde. In 2004, Sweden assumed the chairmanship of the Financial Action Task Force.

US COMMAND: EUCOM.

AGREEMENTS: Reciprocal SOFA, PfP SOFA (13 Dec 1996), Agreement Concerning Technology Research and Development Projects (1997).

FORCES DEPLOYED: Sweden has participated in the International Security Assistance Force (ISAF) in Afghanistan since its inception with rotating intelligence, special forces, and engineering personnel. Sweden also deployed two C-130 transport aircraft in support of ISAF, contributed a Civil–Military Cooperation (CIMIC) unit, and provided logistics support for humanitarian aid and reconstruction. Sweden actively assists the three Baltic nations (Estonia, Latvia, and Lithuania) with military aid and training. As of the end of 2003, Sweden had about 1,000 troops deployed in peacekeeping operations in the Balkans, Congo, and Afghanistan.

Code Names: Baltic series, Baltlink, Baltops, Combined Endeavor, Cooperative series, Dacia, Eloquent Nugget, Frisian Flag, Imminent Horizon, Joint series, Nordic Peace, Peaceshield, Sorbet Royale, Strong Resolve, Viking.

Switzerland

Despite neutrality, since Switzerland joined NATO Partnership for Peace activities on 11 Dec 1996 it has increasingly integrated into peacekeeping and humanitarian assistance operations, as well as joint military exercises. In Jun 2001, Swiss citizens approved new legislation allowing deployment of armed Swiss troops for international peacekeeping missions and international military training. In 2002, Switzerland planned participation in 27 NATO courses and exercises, 14 put on by the Swiss armed forces and 13 in other European countries. Switzerland's three centers — the Geneva Center for Humanitarian Demining, Geneva Center for Security Policy, and Geneva Center for the Democratic Control of Armed Forces — all are fully involved in international military training.

Swiss participation in the war on terrorism focuses on financial controls. A US–Swiss Joint Economic Commission, established in 2000, oversees bilateral ties on anti-money-laundering efforts and counter-terrorism. Since Nov 2001, Swiss authorities have blocked more than 70 accounts totaling more than $22 million.

US COMMAND: EUCOM.

AGREEMENTS: SOFA (relating to arms control delegations), Acquisition and Cross-Servicing Agreement.

Code Names: Allied Action, Combined Endeavor, Cooperative Associate, Dacia, Eloquent Nugget, Joint Guardian, Open Road, Peace Alps, Viking.

Syria

Syria has gone from military ally in Desert Storm, where it provided a division to the Arab sector against Iraq, to uneasy neighbor of US-occupied Iraq. Imminent Danger Pay was authorized for US military personnel in Jul 2003. The US military suspects that Syria shields some components of weapons of mass destruction shipped prior to Operation Iraqi Freedom (OIF) and that Syria provides sanctuary for former Iraqi regime leaders and insurgents and terrorists fighting the US in Iraq. On the other hand, the US and Syria have been able to cooperate on a low level since the fall of Saddam; US forces in northern Iraq, for instance, negotiated for use of Syrian electrical power, Syria serves as a transshipment point for Iraqi oil, and Syria has also supplied food and other goods.

Politically, the US relationship with Syria is dominated by Syria's role in Middle East peacemaking and by the continued presence of Syrian forces in Lebanon. Syria has also been on the US list of state sponsors of terrorism since 1979. In Oct 2003, following a suicide bombing in Haifa that killed 20 Israelis, Israel Defence Forces attacked a suspected Palestinian Islamic Jihad camp 9 miles north of Damascus, the first such Israeli attack deep inside Syrian territory since 1973. Syria also provides landing rights at Damascus International Airport for the Iranian Revolutionary Guard Corps and Lebanese Hezbollah, key to Iran's influence in Lebanon.

The United Nations Disengagement Observer Force (UNDOF) on the Golan Heights, established in 1974, continues to maintain the local cease-fire. As of 31 Jan 2004, 1,000 peacekeepers and military observers were deployed from Austria, Canada, Japan, Poland, and the Slovak Republic.

US COMMAND: CENTCOM. Under change 3 to the Unified Command Plan signed by President Bush 10 Mar 2004, Syria was moved from European to Central Command's area of responsibility.

Code Names: Ultimate Resolve.

Taiwan

After the US recognized the government of the People's Republic of China as the sole legal government of China in 1979, the US began to conduct unofficial relations with Taiwan under the Taiwan Relations Act (TRA). The Mutual Defense Treaty with Taiwan was terminated, but the US continues a close military relationship with the Taipei government, providing "defensive" military equipment to equip and sustain US weapons and Taiwan's large military establishment.

Taiwan operates one of the busiest container ports in the world, and in 2003 it agreed to participate in the Container Security Initiative, which aims to protect containerized shipping from exploitation by terrorists. Regular port visits by US Navy ships and submarines take place in Chilung and Kaohsiung.

US COMMAND: PACOM.

AGREEMENTS: Under PL 107-228, Taiwan is treated as though it was designated a Major Non-NATO Ally.

Code Names: Battery, Dragon's Thunder, Fond, Food, Former, Frost, Frozen, Peace Approach, Peace Edge, Peace Fenghuang, Peace Stallion, Project 19.

Tajikistan

Tajikistan is the poorest of the former Soviet republics, and the country is heavily dependent on Russia and international aid for economic support. During the late 1990s, the CIA established some covert operations and safe houses in Tajikistan for its anti-Taliban and anti–Osama bin Laden operations (the Northern Alliance also maintained rear-area facilities). But with the largest Russian military presence in Central Asia, Tajikistan can do very little without Moscow's permission. Tajikistan condemned the 9/11 attacks, and the Tajik president offered overflight and basing rights to coalition (that is, non-US) forces. Airports at Dushanbe and Kulyab were selected for possible use, and coalition forces established a presence at Dushanbe airport in 2001 to facilitate shipment of humanitarian aid to Afghanistan.

Because of its cooperation, Tajikistan was removed from the International Traffic in Arms (ITAR) list in Dec 2001, and it has become eligible for military assistance.[11] Tajikistan also became a member of NATO's Partnership for Peace (20 Feb 2002), and it participates in counter-terrorism initiatives as a member of the Shanghai Cooperation Organization (SCO) and Commonwealth of Independent States (CIS).

---

11. Since 1993, Tajikistan had been included on a list in the International Traffic in Arms Regulations, which implements the Arms Export Control Act, prohibiting the licensing or export of defense articles and services to countries on the list.

Tajikistan borders Afghanistan, Pakistan, China, and Kyrgyzstan, and its porous borders make it highly vulnerable as a transit point for the movement of terrorist and insurgents, narcotics, and weapons. Prior to 9/11, Tajikistan was used by the Islamic Movement of Uzbekistan (IMU) as a staging ground for insurgency against the government of Uzbekistan. One of the by-products of Operation Enduring Freedom (OEF), nonetheless, was that the IMU suffered heavy casualties while fighting in Afghanistan on the side of the Taliban and al Qaeda. Not by coincidence, in 2002 assassinations and outbreaks of violence declined in Tajikistan, and Tajik–Uzbek relations improved.

US military aid focuses on strengthening an independent Tajik border guard, English-language education, and expansion of direct military-to-military relations. Tajikistan has committed to cooperating with the US on countering terrorism, the proliferation of weapons of mass destruction, weapons technology, and other illicit arms and drug trafficking. In May 2003, the US provided uniforms and communications equipment to the State Border Protection Committee, and US Customs personnel began training in Tajikistan. In Jul 2003, a delegation of civil engineers from the Army Corps of Engineers visited Tajikistan to conduct a site survey for the proposed Tajik–Afghan bridge, a project to reopen a historic trade route and increase economic integration in the region. The VA National Guard also hosted the first official visit by Tajik military officers on 15 Jan 2004 at the Army Aviation Support Facility in Sandston. On 3–6 May 2004, a NATO Civil Emergency Planning Workshop was held in Tajikistan.

US COMMAND: CENTCOM. US forces in Tajikistan are under the command of Combined Joint Task Force 180 (CTJF-180).

AGREEMENTS: NATO PfP (20 Feb 2002), Article 98 Agreement (27 Aug 2002).
   Consultative talks between the DOD and Tajik Ministry of Defense prior to 9/11 in 2001 explored ways to improve bilateral security cooperation.
   A 1993 bilateral mutual assistance treaty between Tajikistan and Russia confirms that Tajikistan's borders are in effect Russian borders, and that they have to be protected against the import of arms, drugs, and Islamic extremism. On 14 Nov 2003, Tajikistan and India also created a bilateral counterterrorist working group.

US ASSISTANCE: Receives Foreign Military Financing program grants, International Military Education and Training aid, National Guard partner with VA (established in 2003), participates in the Export Control and Related Border Security Assistance program, participates in George C. Marshall Center conferences and seminars, participates in DOD–FBI–customs counter-proliferation programs.
   In FYs 1993–2001, the US obligated about $195 million in total assistance, of

which about $193 million was economic assistance. In FY 2002, budgeted assistance totaled about $94 million. Requested assistance for FYs 2003 and 2004 totaled about $68 million.

BASES AND ACCESS: Tajikistan was designated a combat zone as of 19 Sep 2001. The government announced in Nov 2001 its agreement to the basing of US and coalition troops and aircraft in Tajikistan, and throughout 2002 US, French, and UK aircraft were permitted to carry out refueling operations at Dushanbe International Airport. The US also has access to additional military facilities in Khujand, Kulyab (Kuliab), and Kurgan-Tyube. Military transports from the US, France, and Italy have used Kulyab airfield to transport troops, munitions, and various other materiel to Afghanistan since 2002.

India also uses Tajikistan to transport supplies into Afghanistan, and India and Tajikistan held a joint military exercise in Aug 2003. India media report that an Indian base at Farkhor was established in May 2002 after Pakistan and India imposed bans on overflights in Dec 2001.

Some 23,000 Russian troops are deployed throughout the country, including 11,000 frontier troops along the Tajik–Afghan border. The 201st Motorized Infantry Division is stationed in Kulyab.

Code Names: Eloquent Nugget, IWER, Provide Hope.

Tanzania

After the al Qaeda attack on the US embassy in Dar es Salaam on 7 Aug 1998, the US and Tanzania established a close working relationship on the investigation, one that broadened after 9/11 to include civil aviation security, anti-money-laundering initiatives, border control, and police training. Tanzania has offered assistance including intelligence information to the war on terrorism effort, and is a member of the Eastern Africa Counterterrorism Initiative. As part of increased cooperation, a Joint/Combined Exchange Training (JCET) special operations exchange program is planned with Tanzania.

US COMMAND: EUCOM.

AGREEMENTS: SOFA pending as of 2004, Acquisition and Cross-Servicing Agreement eligible (26 Jan 1998).

US ASSISTANCE: Receives International Military Education and Training aid, eligible to receive grant Excess Defense Articles, participates in Africa Center for Strategic Studies conferences and seminars.

Code Names: Delenda, Golden Spear, Infinite Reach, MEDFLAG, Natural Fire/Native Fury, Neon Spear, Resolute Response, Shard Accord.

Thailand

Thailand is one of the closest US allies in Southeast Asia, fully engaged in military, intelligence, and counter-terrorism cooperation. After al Qaeda leader Abu Zubaydah was captured in Pakistan in Apr 2002, the CIA shipped him to Thailand, where he was interrogated at a secret facility. After the Bali, Indonesia, bombing in Oct 2002, Thailand intensified its own counter-terrorism efforts, capturing a top Jemaah Islamiyah (JI) leader with ties to al Qaeda, Nurjaman Riduan bin Isomuddin ("Hambali"), in Aug 2003. Others implicated in conspiracies to attack Western embassies were also captured.

After 9/11, Thailand, a treaty ally of the US, offered unimpeded access to training facilities, ports, and airfields, involving itself in all aspects of the war on terror. President Bush met with Prime Minister Thaksin of Thailand on 19 Oct 2003 and announced the granting of Major Non-NATO Ally status. Joint US–Thai training, culminating in the large-scale annual Cobra Gold exercise, shifted toward cooperation on counter-narcotics, disaster response, and peace-keeping in the 1990s. Counter-terrorism was added in 2001, and in 2002 four US–Thai bilateral military exercises had significant counter-terrorism components. Thailand also deployed military engineers and medical personnel in support of Operation Enduring Freedom (OEF) and Operation Iraqi Freedom (OIF). Thailand's contributions to peacekeeping include significant contributions in Timor-Leste and Aceh, Indonesia.

In the war on terrorism, Thailand has cooperated closely on information sharing, building on the long-standing formal SIGINT partnership. Thailand is most interested in combating narco-terrorism, while the US has been more interested in the broader aspects of the global war on terrorism. Thailand is joining the Container Security Initiative, and cooperates with US agencies to curtail terrorist finances. Thailand is a major recipient of the Anti-Terrorism Assistance program, with numerous Thai police and security officials participating in US-sponsored training courses.

Thailand is a route for Golden Triangle heroin trafficking, bordering two of the world's three largest opium producers (Burma and Laos). Thai and US law enforcement and military units work together on counter-narcotics assistance, improving border security, fighting police and military corruption, and stopping money laundering. The International Law Enforcement Academy (ILEA) in Bangkok, a cooperative US–Thai undertaking, trains regional countries. Since 9/11, ILEA has included training in techniques to disrupt terrorist financing.

Thailand has received US military equipment, supplies, training, and assistance since 1950. The US military advisory group in Thailand oversees the delivery of equipment and training of Thai military personnel. Thailand and the US have a vigorous joint military exercise program, averaging some 40 joint exercises per year. US training concentrates on operational interoperability, officer leadership, airborne, aviation and aircraft maintenance, engineering, field artillery, intelligence, Ranger, munitions, and Marine Corps courses.

A full Joint/Combined Exchange Training (JCET) special operations program exists between US special operations forces and Thai Task Force 399, the Special Operations Regiment, the 5th Long Range Recon Patrol Special Forces Team, 4th Army Area Special Forces Training Company, and RTAF Squadrons 102, 103, 106, 403, and 601 at Camp Mai Rim, Camp Maraie, Chiang Mai, Lop Buri, Sichon, Korat AB, and Utapao NAS. The JCET provides cover for US special operations forces to work with the new Task Force 399 on counter-terrorism and counter-narcotics operations.

State Partnership exchanges between WA and Thailand since Apr 2002 have focused on emergency and disaster response, and sharing tactics, techniques, and procedures for both narco-terrorism and weapons of mass destruction consequence management. National Guard personnel have participated in a US Joint Interagency Coordinating Group/Counterterrorism (JIACG/CT) exercise in Bangkok in 2003, and a Thai Air Force Special Operations Team participated in a Drug Demand Reduction Camp in Washington.

US COMMAND: PACOM.

AGREEMENTS: Acquisition and Cross-Servicing Agreement (20 Sep 1993), granted Major Non-NATO Ally status (20 Sep 2003), Article 98 Agreement.

The US and Thailand are among the signatories of the 1954 Manila pact of the former Southeast Asia Treaty Organization (SEATO) and still operate under Article IV(1), which obligates the US to "act to meet the common danger in accordance with its constitutional processes" in the event of armed attack in the treaty area. Despite the dissolution of SEATO in 1977, the Manila pact remains in force and, together with the Thanat-Rusk communiqué of 1962, constitutes the basis of US security commitments to Thailand.

Military-to-military policy with Thailand is managed through annual Thai–US consultations.

US ASSISTANCE: Receives Foreign Military Financing program grants, International Military Education and Training aid, eligible to receive grant Excess Defense Articles, National Guard partner with Washington (established in 2002), receives aid for humanitarian demining efforts, participates in Asia-Pacific Center for Security Studies executive courses, participates in the Export Control and Related

Border Security Assistance program, receives International Narcotics Control and Law Enforcement funding to train and equip the Anti-Money Laundering Office and fund the ILEA, participates in the Terrorist Interdiction Program.

BASES AND ACCESS: After 9/11, the Thai government granted blanket overflight permission and opened up its military facilities to US planes for refueling and logistical support. US Navy ships and submarines continued to call and refuel at Laem Chabang, Pattaya, Phuket, and Sattahip, as they had prior to 9/11. Aircraft used Thai airfields, particularly U'Tapao, where Operation Joint Task Force — Full Accounting (JTF-FA) has been located. The US also pre-positioned equipment and ammunition for US forces in Thailand under the War Reserve Stockpile — Thailand (WRS-T) program. There have been numerous reports of US intelligence collection stations in Thailand, including at Khon Kaen.

Code Names: Baker Tepid, Baker Torch, Baker Torch Lens, Balance Tandem, Balance Torch, Bevil Edge, CARAT Thailand, Chapel Gold, Cobra Ball, Cobra Gold, Colt, Cope Thunder, Cope Tiger, Coronet Knight, Dawn Panther, Eligible Receiver, Foil, Folder, Folio, Follow, Freedom Banner, Frequent Storm, Hunter, Known Warrior, MARSEAEX, NOLES, Peace Chakri, Peace Meadow, Peace Narusuan, Pirap Jabiru, SEACAT, SEASURVEX, Shant Doot, Shanti Path, Taa Nok In Sii, Tassel, Teak Torch, Team Challenge, Thai Boomerang, Underseal, Urgent Response, Vector Balance Torch, Westpac MCMEX, Wyvern Sun.

Timor-Leste (East Timor)

On 20 May 2002, East Timor became an independent country, changing its name to Timor-Leste. The United Nations Mission of Support in East Timor (UNMISET) was established to replace the UN Transitional Administration in East Timor (UNTAET) and oversee transition before a scheduled phaseout in 2004. As of 31 Jan 2004, just over 2,000 uniformed personnel and military observers from 25 countries were deployed with UNMISET. The US Support Group East Timor (USGET), which conducted monthly ship visits and undertook a full humanitarian and civic action program, deactivated on 17 Dec 2002.

US COMMAND: PACOM.

AGREEMENTS: Article 98 Agreement (2002).

US ASSISTANCE: Receives Foreign Military Financing program grants, modest International Military Education and Training aid, eligible to receive grant Excess Defense Articles (presidential determination in 2002), receives peacekeeping operations (PKO) funding, participated in Asia-Pacific Center for Security Studies executive courses.

Code Names: Citadel, Stabilise, Tanager.

Togo

Togo led the UN peacekeeping mission in Guinea–Bissau and contributed to peacekeeping efforts in the Central African Republic and Rwanda, while helping to broker a cease-fire in Sierra Leone and resolve successive crises in Côte d'Ivoire. US aid, however, has been cut off because of a fraudulent election in Jun 2003, the country's poor human rights record, and failure to service its external debt.

US COMMAND: EUCOM.

AGREEMENTS: Article 98 Agreement.

US ASSISTANCE: Receives modest International Military Education and Training aid, participates in Africa Center for Strategic Studies conferences and seminars.

Code Names: WATC.

Tonga

Tonga is primarily tied to Australia and New Zealand by defense cooperation agreements, and receives only a small amount of military training from the US. Tonga joined Australia, New Zealand, Vanuatu, and Fiji in 1999 in providing unarmed peace monitors in Papua New Guinea's Bougainville Island Province, and in 2002 deployed peacekeepers to the Solomon Islands. A Joint/Combined Exchange Training (JCET) special operations program is planned to contribute to Tonga's peacekeeping and maritime law enforcement capabilities.

US COMMAND: PACOM.

AGREEMENTS: SOFA, Acquisition and Cross-Servicing Agreement (11 Jun 1997), Acquisition and Cross-Servicing Agreement, Article 98 Agreement.

US ASSISTANCE: Receives International Military Education and Training aid, eligible to receive grant Excess Defense Articles, participates in Asia-Pacific Center for Security Studies executive courses.

Code Names: CARAT Tonga, Croix du Sud, Shanti Path.

Trinidad and Tobago

US–Trinidad and Tobago military relations focus on counter-narcotics and international crime, particularly money laundering. Joint/Combined Exchange Training (JCET) special operations training has been held among Navy SEALs, the 720th STF, and the Special Operations Group at Port of Spain, Chaguaramas, and Isla Chacachacare. The local government's interagency coordination center cooperates with US military and civil intelligence and law enforcement agencies. Trinidad and Tobago hosted CFATF XIX, an Inter-American Committee Against Terrorism seminar, on 19–22 Apr 2004.

US COMMAND: SOUTHCOM.

AGREEMENTS: SOFA, Acquisition and Cross-Servicing Agreement eligible (22 Mar 1999).

US ASSISTANCE: International Military Education and Training and Foreign Military Financing programs were suspended in Jul 2003 under the terms of the American Service Members Protection Act because Trinidad and Tobago, a member of the International Criminal Court, had not concluded a bilateral nonsurrender, or Article 98, agreement with the US. Trinidad and Tobago is otherwise eligible to receive grant Excess Defense Articles, participates in Center for Hemispheric Defense Studies conferences and seminars, and receives International Narcotics Control and Law Enforcement funding. The US has donated five 82-foot patrol boats, two C-26 transports, and two Piper-Navajo aircraft to improve the country's air and sea surveillance.

Code Names: Mercury, New Horizons, PKO, Tradewinds.

Tunisia

US–Tunisian ties have improved since Tunisia objected to US intervention after the Iraq invasion of Kuwait in 1990. Prior to 9/11, the US and moderate Tunisia had an active schedule of military exercises and exchanges, and since 9/11 Tunisia has been supportive of the war on terrorism, even offering access to Tunisian bases in support of Operation Enduring Freedom. The first major al Qaeda attack to occur after the fall of the Taliban occurred in Tunisia in Apr 2002, increasing cooperation with the US.

Joint training exercises are an important feature of the US–Tunisian relationship, and there are 10–12 combined exercises with US forces annually. Joint/Combined Exchange Training (JCET) special operations training also take place between the 3rd Special Forces Group and the Group Des Forces Speciale. Tunisia participated in a Mar 2004 EUCOM counter-terrorism chiefs of defense conference in Stuttgart, Germany, with Algeria, Chad, Mali, Mauritania, Morocco, Niger, Senegal, and the US. In Jun 2004, Tunisia was designated a full-fledged partner in the NATO Mediterranean Dialogue.

US COMMAND: EUCOM.

AGREEMENTS: SOFA (signed 26 May 1993), Acquisition and Cross-Servicing Agreement (29 Apr 1994), Article 98 Agreement (2003).

The US–Tunisian Joint Military Commission meets annually to discuss military cooperation and other security matters, and has been active since 1981. It met 15–17 Mar 2004 in Washington. Tunisia attended a NATO Mediterranean Dialogue conference at RHQ AFSOUTH in Oct 2002, along with Algeria, Jordan, Mauritania, and Morocco.

US ASSISTANCE: Receives Foreign Military Financing program grants, International Military Education and Training aid, participates in National Defense University Near East South Asia (NESA) Center seminars, participates in Africa Center for Strategic Studies conferences and seminars. More than 70 percent of Tunisian military equipment is of US origin, and US assistance and training focuses on maintenance and logistical shortfalls.

FORCES DEPLOYED: Tunisia is active in international peacekeeping, with troops deployed in UN peacekeeping missions in the Democratic Republic of the Congo, Eritrea, and Kosovo.

BASES AND ACCESS: US Navy ships make regular port visits to Bizerte, Sfax, Sousse, and Tunis.

Code Names: Atlas series, Eloquent Nugget, Major Manar, MEDFLAG, Poised Eagle, Shared Accord.

Turkey

Turkey is a NATO member, hosts major US bases (and nuclear weapons), and was a strong ally of the US throughout the Cold War. Turkey hosted Northern Watch, enforcement of the northern no-fly zone in Iraq, until the operation ceased in May 2003. Throughout the 1990s, the CIA regularly used Turkey to stage agents in northern Iraq (sometimes with Turkish escorts), and those operations continued after 9/11.

Soon after 9/11, the Turkish prime minister backed a parliamentary resolution permitting the government to send Turkish troops abroad and to allow foreign troops to be stationed on Turkish soil. Turkey was one of the first countries to demonstrate strong support for Operation Enduring Freedom (OEF) in Afghanistan, and it has deployed forces and taken command of the International Security Assistance Force (ISAF). The Turkish parliament voted in Feb 2003 to provide initial military support for the US in Iraq, but then decided on 1 Mar not to let the army 4th Infantry Division stage from Turkey. Incirlik air base (and other air bases in eastern Turkey) continued to quietly support US special operations, intelligence, and combat search and rescue in northern Iraq, and Turkish bases later provided support for the rotation of American troops out of Iraq, but the decision was a blow to the US war plan at the time. Under Display Deterrence, two NATO AWACS early warning aircraft were deployed to Konya air base on 26 Feb 2003 to provide surveillance and early warning should Iraq attack the NATO country. NATO also assumed control of three Dutch Patriot air defense batteries that were deployed to Diyarbakir and Batman. Two additional US Patriot batteries were deployed to Turkey as well.

After the fall of Saddam Hussein, Turkey committed $50 million in aid to reconstruction efforts in Iraq, and has established a coordination committee to promote and develop bilateral trade. In Jul 2003, after an incident in which US forces detained 11 members of Turkey's special forces in the town of al Suleimaniyah in northern Iraq, it became clear that Turkish special operations forces (SOF) had also been long operating inside Iraq.

The US has designated the Kurdistan Workers Party (PKK) — now known as the Kurdistan Freedom and Democracy Congress (KADEK) — a terrorist organization, and there were clashes between PKK/KADEK forces and the Iraqi border police and US forces in northern Iraq in 2003.[12] Through 2003–2004, the US and Turkey met several times to discuss cooperation against KADEK, and in Oct 2003 Secretary Powell reiterated the US commitment to assist Turkey in eliminating the organization.

US COMMAND: EUCOM.

AGREEMENTS: NATO SOFA (19 Jun 1951), PfP SOFA (20 May 2000), Defense Cooperation Agreement (DECA; 29 Mar 1980, and paper relating to US forces in Turkey, 3 Feb 1999), Acquisition and Cross-Servicing Agreement (12 Aug 1996), MOU on bilateral missile defense architecture analysis (6 Jun 2001).

A US–Turkish MOU on modernization of bases and ports in Turkey was signed in Feb 2003.

US ASSISTANCE: Turkey is a major recipient of US military aid, and utilizes mostly US-made equipment. By law, aid adheres to a 7:10 Greece:Turkey ratio. Turkey has agreed to purchase Boeing E-3 AWACS aircraft, and the US and Turkey signed an MOU on 11 Jul 2002 formalizing Turkish participation in the F-35 Joint Strike Fighter program. US training and exchanges are focused on Turkey's efforts to modernize its armed forces, and improve disaster relief and search and rescue equipment in support of participation in the war on terrorism, peacekeeping, humanitarian, and other operations.

BASES AND ACCESS: US bases in Turkey are long standing and fall under the 1951 SOFA and numerous bilateral agreements. The last US nuclear weapons in Turkey are located at Incirlik, the main US facility, and the US operates half a dozen other

---

12. In Oct 2003, KADEK made yet another name change, to the Kurdistan People's Congress (KHK or Kongra-Gel).

facilities, most notably in Izmir and Diyarbakir. Most Cold War intelligence collection activity has been shut down or significantly reduced in staffing. The Pirinclik, Turkey, "cooperative radar" activated in 1955, and used to track Iraqi Scud launches in Desert Storm, was closed on 30 Sep 1997. Outside major bases, more than 1,000 additional US military personnel are assigned to NATO, Office of Defense Cooperation, Military Traffic Management Command (at Iskenderun and Izmir), and other facilities in the country.

The DOD announced in Aug 2004 that the US would consolidate main operating bases in Europe as a result of the "Global Posture Review." This includes the possible move of a permanent F-16 wing to Incirlik and negotiations for "more flexible use" of Turkish bases in Middle East contingencies.

After 9/11, Turkey offered overflight and use of Incirlik, Afyon, and Yenisehir air bases, Istanbul–Sabiha Gokcen and Trabzon airports, Aksaz Naval Base (Mamaris), and Antalya, Izmir, and Istanbul ports. Aksaz and Antalya support Active Endeavour, NATO's counter-terrorism maritime operation. US special operations forces and the CIA have also utilized Batman and Diyarbakir air bases for operations in Iraq and elsewhere.

Incirlik in Adana is a high-performance base, well equipped to service and refuel planes en route to other destinations, a function currently carried out by about 1,400 US troops stationed at the base (Turkish KC-135 refuelers are also stationed at the base). Incirlik has the infrastructure to temporarily house large numbers of forces, having hosted 1,500 additional US military personnel involved in Northern Watch. Incirlik was designated a combat zone as of 21 Sep 2001.

FORCES DEPLOYED: After 9/11, Turkey provided KC-135 aerial refueling support during OEF, and contributed five ships to NATO counter-terrorism operations in the Mediterranean, including Active Endeavour. Turkey also offered 90 SOF troops for deployment to Afghanistan in 2002.

After OEF, Turkey provided troops for Phase I of the ISAF under British command, and then assumed leadership of ISAF-II on 20 Jun 2002. In Jun–Feb 2003, the Turkish contribution to ISAF was approximately 1,400 personnel (of the 2,600 total from 22 countries). In addition to its patrols and projects in the Kabul area, ISAF provided training to almost 800 bodyguards for Afghan ministers and the former king. When Germany and the Netherlands could not take over command in Dec 2002, the Turks agreed to stay on until 10 Feb 2003. Turkey then contributed to ISAF-III with a reinforced company team incorporating an Azerbaijani and an Albanian platoon of 23 personnel each.

Turkey participates in UN peacekeeping operations, contributing police to the UN Transitional Administration for East Timor and deploying forces in the Stabilization Force (Bosnia).

Code Names: Allied Action, Allied Response, Ample Train, Anatolian Eagle, Anvil Ghost, ARRcade Fusion, Ardent Ground, Aurora Express, Avid Response, Balance Ultra, Black Sea Partnership, Centrasbat, Clean Hunter, Constant Harmony, Cooperative series, Cornerstone, Coronet Freedom, Coronet Rambler, Dacia, Damsel Fair, Deprem, Destined Glory, Disciplined Warrior, Display Determination, Display Deterrence, Distant Thunder, Dogfish, Dogu Akdeniz, Dynamic series, Hazarfend, Joint series, Majestic Eagle, Med Shark, MEDCEUR, Mothia, Mystic Star, Neo Tapon, Northern Watch, Pacer Console, Peace Diamond, Peace Djem, Peace Onyx, Peace Ranger, Peace Remo, Peace Vector, Peaceful Bridge, Peaceful Eagle, Peaceshield, Prometheous, Proven Force, Provide Comfort, Regional Cooperation, Reliant Mermaid, Rescue Eagle, Scope Axis, Scope Sand, Sea Breeze, Sea Saber, Snow Eagle, Strong Eagle, Trident D'Or, Viking.

Turkmenistan

The former Soviet republic of Turkmenistan's declaration of "permanent neutrality" was formally recognized by the United Nations in 1995, and it has not provided formal military assistance in the war on terrorism. However, on 24 Sep 2001, the Turkmenistan president gave his consent for ground transport and overflights to deliver humanitarian aid to Afghanistan.

A 25 Nov 2002 assassination attempt on President Saparmurat Niyazov, and the crackdown on the political opposition that followed, led to a marked downturn in bilateral relations. Niyazov is essentially president for life, and the single-party state has been severely criticized by the international community for its human rights practices, corruption, and sham political trials. In Feb 2003, Turkmenistan instituted a strict exit visa regime (for all Turkmenistan and foreign citizens).

Turkmenistan, which shares a long border with Afghanistan, has been the second largest conduit for international aid into Afghanistan. Since 9/11, there has been a growing cross-border trade with the regime in Afghanistan, and significant commercial relationships with Turkey, Russia, and Iran. The country faces problems with drug trafficking and environmental disputes with its neighbors.

In FYs 1993–2001, the US obligated about $153 million in assistance, about $149 million of which was economic aid. In FY 2002, budgeted assistance totaled about $20 million. Requested assistance for FYs 2003 and 2004 totaled about $20 million.

The US seeks to enhance Turkmenistan's ability to secure its borders to control the movement of narcotics, weapons, and terrorists. US priorities are also focused on encouraging internal reform and promoting energy development (Turkmenistan has the world's fifth largest natural gas reserves). As a member of NATO Partnership for Peace (10 May 1994), Turkmenistan is also encouraged to engage in Euro-Atlantic security institutions.

US COMMAND: CENTCOM. US military operations are under the command of Combined Joint Task Force 180 (CJTF-180).

AGREEMENTS: PfP SOFA (signed 10 May 1994), Acquisition and Cross-Servicing Agreement eligible (6 Feb 1996).

US ASSISTANCE: Receives Foreign Military Financing program grants, International Military Education and Training aid, National Guard partner with NV (established in 2002), eligible to receive grant Excess Defense Articles. Hosted Coast Guard Mobile Training Teams and received an 82-foot Coast Guard cutter.

BASES AND ACCESS: The US obtained approval to refuel aircraft at the Ashgabat airport soon after 9/11, and C-17 humanitarian flights carrying goods for Afghanistan began to regularly arrive in Ashgabat on 10 Dec 2001. During the first few months of Operation Enduring Freedom, Turkmenistan facilitated the transfer of some 40 percent of the humanitarian aid into Afghanistanin. In Jan 2002, the media reported that Turkmenistan turned down a German request to use military bases to support operations in Afghanistan.

Code Names: Eloquent Nugget, IWER, Peaceshield, Regional Cooperation.

Turks and Caicos Islands (UK Overseas Territory)

US military relations with the Turks and Caicos are dominated by counter-narcotics through Operation Bahamas and Turks and Caicos (OPBAT). US Army helicopter operations at Providenciales relocated to Georgetown in 1991.

US COMMAND: With the creation of NORTHCOM in 2002, Turks and Caicos no longer falls under SOUTHCOM.

AGREEMENTS: US–UK–Bahamas–Turks and Caicos Islands OPBAT Memorandum of Understanding (MOU; 1990), Reciprocal SOFA (with the UK).

Code Names: Mercury.

Tuvalu

Tuvalu participates in Asia-Pacific Center for Security Studies executive courses and has signed an Article 98 Agreement with the US.

US COMMAND: PACOM.

Uganda

Uganda has faced armed opposition by the Allied Democratic Front (ADF) and the Lord's Resistance Army (LRA), the former of which was virtually destroyed as a group in 2003. The LRA continues to kill and abduct local children, plunder villages, and ambush vehicles in northern Uganda, where the number of displaced person living in refugee camps is estimated at more than one million. Uganda has maintained ties with North Korea and Libya, has invaded the Democratic Republic of the Congo, and has had strained relations with Sudan because of alleged support for the LRA. In Mar 2002, Uganda and Sudan agreed that the Ugandan military could cross into southern Sudan to pursue the LRA (Iron Fist). Uganda withdrew its troops from the DRC in Jun 2003. Uganda has provided support for coalition efforts in the war on terrorism and cooperated with the US in law enforcement and financial monitoring. Uganda is a member of the Eastern Africa Counterterrorism Initiative.

US COMMAND: EUCOM.

AGREEMENTS: SOFA (US Diplomatic Note 223/97, 15 Jul 1997), Acquisition and Cross-Servicing Agreement eligible (6 Feb 1996), Article 98 Agreement.

US ASSISTANCE: Receives International Military Education and Training aid, eligible to receive grant Excess Defense Articles, participates in the African Contingency Operations Training and Assistance (ACOTA) program and earlier African Crisis Response Initiative (ACRI), participates in Africa Center for Strategic Studies conferences and seminars. US military assistance was terminated in 2000 as a result of the Ugandan incursion into the DRC. Following Jun 2003, the US restarted limited nonlethal military assistance.

BASES AND ACCESS: US forces have negotiated access to Entebbe, Uganda, for stopovers and refueling, maintaining permanent spots to park and refuel planes. The 3rd Air Force conducted a site survey at Entebbe in 2001 and produced a Base Support Plan.

FORCES DEPLOYED: Prior to 2000, US military forces participated with Uganda in training activities under ACRI, and Uganda has played a role in the Sudan, Congo, and Burundi peace processes.

Code Names: Golden Spear, MEDFLAG, Natural Fire, Neon Spear, Support Hope.

Ukraine

Ukraine is an original member of NATO's Partnership for Peace program (joining 8 Feb 1994), contributes troops to the Kosovo Force (KFOR), and supports both Operation Enduring Freedom (OEF) and Operation Iraqi Freedom (OIF). Still, US–Ukrainian military relations suffer from unrealistic expectations about Ukrainian capabilities, and corruption and bureaucratic difficulties with a still-Soviet-style defense structure. Overall relations suffered a setback in Sep 2002 after US intelligence authenticated a recording of President Kuchma's Jul 2000 decision to transfer a Kolchuga air defense early warning system to Iraq, in violation of sanctions, and during active US (and UK) air operations to enforce no-fly zones.

After 9/11, Ukraine provided overflight permission for all US and coalition forces, and has been one of the largest coalition troop providers in Iraq, with a nuclear, biological, and chemical remediation unit in Kuwait and a 1,650-member brigade serving in the Polish-led Multi-National Division around Kut. Ukraine provided airlift assets for some coalition forces.

Ukraine's primary bilateral relationship remains with Russia. The two countries ratified a friendship treaty in 1999 under which Ukraine has committed itself not to join any military blocs for the duration of Russia's 20-year lease on the naval base in Sevastopol on the Black Sea. Nevertheless, integration of Ukraine into NATO continues to move forward. NATO foreign and defense ministers meeting in Brussels in Dec 2003 publicly recognized Ukraine's progress in implementing its Membership Action Plan. Ukraine has peacekeepers in the US sector of Kosovo and participated in SFOR in Bosnia and Herzegovinia.

Through 2003, the US provided more than $675 million to Ukraine under the Cooperative Threat Reduction (CTR) program to eliminate former Soviet strategic nuclear delivery systems in Ukraine. CTR activities eliminated, removed, or rendered inoperable SS-19 and SS-24 ballistic missiles and associated silos and launch control centers, heavy bombers, and air-launched cruise missiles of the Soviet 43rd Rocket Army. The US assisted in funding the closure of the nuclear reactor at Chernobyl, which took place in Dec 2000, and continues to contribute funding toward the construction of the sarcophagus to contain radioctivity. Ongoing work continues to safeguard nuclear materials and prevent biotechnology proliferation. Ukraine has agreed to install US-funded nuclear portal monitors at 20 border crossings, airports, and ports to detect nuclear materials.

Under the 1992 Freedom Support Act and other aid programs, total US assistance since independence has been more than three billion dollars. US–Ukrainian bilateral military activity, begun in 1993, has included exchanges, major combined exercises, and port call visits. US military training and assistance focuses on crisis response operations, participation in exercises, peacekeeping, and military reform. Joint/Combined Exchange Training (JCET) special operations training has taken place with the A1594 Special Operations Unit at Odessa.

US COMMAND: EUCOM, effective 1 Oct 1998.

AGREEMENTS: Reciprocal SOFA, PfP SOFA (ratified 26 May 2000 after years of delay), Acquisition and Cross-Servicing Agreement (19 Nov 1999), Memorandum of Understanding and Cooperation (Jul 1993).

The 1993 MOU establishes the basis for military exchanges and exercises and the US–Ukraine Defense Cooperation Plan. The US–Ukraine Joint Working Group on Bilateral Defense and Military Cooperation annually establishes the program. The NATO–Ukraine Commission established in 1997 oversees improved interoperability, agreements, and exercises.

US ASSISTANCE: Receives Foreign Military Financing program grants, International Military Education and Training aid, eligible to receive grant Excess Defense Articles, receives Freedom Support Act (FSA) assistance, National Guard partner with California and Kansas, participates in George C. Marshall Center conferences and seminars.

BASES AND ACCESS: Ukraine has provided overflight permission for all US and coalition forces, allowing more than 5,000 overflights through 2003, and has offered access to three air bases for US forces.

In 1999, the Yavoriv training area was designated the first NATO Partnership for Peace training center in the territory of the former Soviet Union. Yavoriv had previously been used for large-scale exercises, but since Cooperative Neighbor in 1997 excessive Ukrainian fees stymied additional activity. Five US construction projects to facilitate future training were completed in 2001 in support of Peaceshield.

FORCES DEPLOYED: Ukraine deployed elements of the 6th Mechanized Brigade to Iraq in 2003 and announced plans to replace the brigade with the 7th Mechanized Infantry Brigade in mid-2004.

Code Names: Black Sea Partnership, Brave Eagle, Centrasbat, Combined Endeavor, Cooperative series, Cossack Steppe, Dacia, Eloquent Nugget, Joint series, Partnership Guard, Peaceshield, PLANEX, Regional Cooperation, Rough and Ready, Sea Breeze, Ulan Eagle, Viking.

United Arab Emirates[13]

US military relations with the UAE developed significantly during the Iran–Iraq war when shipping in the Arabian Gulf was threatened. In the run-up to the 1990 Iraqi invasion of Kuwait, US aerial refuelers deployed to the UAE as a "deterrent," and the UAE subsequently hosted US offensive forces, even sending troops to liberate Kuwait as part of the Peninsula Shield force. During the 1990s, the UAE became increasingly involved in US military and covert operations directed against Iraq and Afghanistan. The CIA established "liaison" relations

---

13. The UAE is a federation of seven emirates (Abu Dhabi, Dubai, Sharjah, Ras al Khaimah, Ajman, Umm al Qawain, and Fujairah) that joined together in Dec 1971 after the UK's withdrawal from the gulf.

with its UAE counterparts and put pressure on them to cut ties to the Taliban. US aircraft flying Southern Watch no-fly-zone missions originated from UAE bases. Joint/Combined Exchange Training (JCET) special operations training took place among US Navy SEALs, Naval Special Warfare Unit 3, and the UAE Special Operations Command at Arizanah Island and other locations. US CIA and special operations forces (SOF) also operated from UAE soil on regional intelligence collection and counter-terrorism missions.

In Mar 2000, the UAE ordered 80 of the most sophisticated versions of the US F-16 aircraft (nicknamed Desert Falcon) — 55 single-seaters and 25 dual-seaters — for eight billion dollars, investing almost three billion dollars in research and development. The sale marked the first time that the US sold a better aircraft overseas than its own forces were flying. The first planes were scheduled to be delivered in 2004.

US–UAE relations have become especially close and mutually supportive since the beginning of Operation Enduring Freedom (OEF). The UAE provides access to US forces and hosts more US Navy ships than any port outside the US. In 2002, UAE bases hosted greatly increased contingents of US ground and air forces supporting operations in Afghanistan and preparing for operations against Iraq. The UAE again deployed forces to Kuwait in Feb 2003 as part of Peninsula Shield. After the defeat of Saddam Hussein, the UAE also became host to a regional Office of Foreign Disaster Assistance (AID) storage and distribution facility in the Jebel Ali Free Trade Zone in Dubai.

The UAE has also participated in peacekeeping, with forces in Lebanon since 1992. UAE Apache and Puma helicopters were deployed to Kosovo, and UAE C-130s supported humanitarian assistance in Afghanistan and Iraq.

US COMMAND: CENTCOM.

AGREEMENTS: Classified SOFA, Acquisition and Cross-Servicing Agreement eligible (20 Apr 1993).

   UAE is a member of the Gulf Cooperation Council (GCC). The US and UAE have defense cooperation agreements permitting access and pre-positioning of military equipment and munitions. The US and UAE signed an agreement in Jul 2003 to create a permanent cantonment site at al Dhafra. The UK–UAE Defence Cooperation Agreement represents Britain's largest defense commitment outside NATO; more than 35,000 British citizens live and work in the UAE. Because of its small population base, UAE relies on British and Pakistani contract pilots and officers to operate its air force.

BASES AND ACCESS: Prior to 9/11, the US had eight CENTCOM-controlled facilities in the UAE, and utilized an additional 38 UAE-controlled facilities. The US

Navy used a highly valuable dedicated deep-water berthing space in the Jebel Ali port complex, and ships and submarines regularly utilized Abu Dhabi and Fujairah. The UAE also provides hangar and ramp space for US aircraft at al Dhafra air base and Fujairah. Al Dhafra has become a main operating base for refueling and intelligence and surveillance aircraft in the theater. Pre-positioned equipment was stored in the UAE long before 9/11.

Code Names: Arabian Gauntlet, Bell Buoy, Blue Flag, Bright Star, Desert Falcon, Early Victor, Eastern Castle, Initial Link, Iron Falcon, Iron Fist, Iron Magic, Iron Siren, Joint Guardian, Peninsula Shield, Sea Dagger, Solar Sunrise, Southern Watch, Vigilant Warrior.

United Kingdom

The United Kingdom is the closest military and intelligence ally of the US and has demonstrated its like-mindedness with the US since 9/11 by its full participation in Operation Enduring Freedom (OEF), its command of International Security Assistance Force I (ISAF-I) in Afghanistan, its unlimited support for the war on terrorism, its unique involvement in using offensive air power to enforce the northern and southern no-fly zones over Iraq prior to the war in Iraq, and its complete integration in Operation Iraqi Freedom (OIF). Britain also plays major roles in NATO's conventional and nuclear force structures.

In Jun 2003, the British government established an interagency Joint Terrorism Analysis Center (JTAC) — a counterpart to the US Terrorist Threat Integration Center — responsible for assessing and disseminating information about the terrorist threat to UK domestic and overseas interests. The US and UK have a major program of joint training and exercising on nuclear weapons, weapons of mass destruction, and counter-terrorism. The UK is also fully involved in the panoply of multi-lateral intelligence and law enforcement initiatives to fight terrorism, drug trafficking, and proliferation.

US COMMAND: EUCOM.

AGREEMENTS: NATO SOFA (16 Jun 1951), Cost Sharing Arrangement (classified; 1973), Reciprocal SOFA, PfP SOFA (22 Jul 1999), Acquisition and Cross-Servicing Agreement (11 Oct 1984).

The UK is one of three international partners with cooperative research and development agreements with the counter-terrorism Technical Support Working Group Program.

BASES AND ACCESS: The US base structure in the UK, though diminished from its Cold War peak, provides unique intelligence, special operations, and offensive air power support for US operations. The EUCOM Joint Analysis Center (JAC) at RAF Molesworth is the premier intelligence fusion center of the US military, and additional joint US–UK intelligence collection and analysis stations are operated at Digby, RAF Menwith Hill, Morwenstow, RAF Oakhanger, and other locations. The US Air Force maintains major bases at RAF Lakenheath and Mildenhall, as well as dispersal and contingency bases that accommodate rotational aircraft from the US. The US pre-positions materiel and munitions in the UK and has an extensive communications and early warning infrastructure. Regular port visits by US Navy ships and submarines take place at Glasgow, Killingholme, London, Portland, Portsmouth, and Southhampton.

The DOD announced in Aug 2004 that the US would consolidate main operating bases in the UK as a result of the "Global Posture Review," closing Naval Forces Europe headquarters in London (and consolidating functions with another naval command in Naples, Italy) and redeploying aircraft from RAF Lakenheath to bases nearer to the Middle East.

FORCES DEPLOYED: The UK supported OEF with a variety of forces, including special operations forces (SOF). UK submarine-launched Tomahawk cruise missiles struck targets alongside their US counterparts, and UK aircraft flew numerous combat missions over Afghanistan. The UK deployed its largest naval task force since Desert Storm. A naval task force of a dozen warships built around the aircraft carrier HMS *Illustrious* deployed Sep 2001–early 2002, when the helicopter carrier HMS *Ocean* relieved it. The RAF contributed tanker, AWACS, Nimrod, and Canberra PR9 reconnaissance and surveillance aircraft, along with transport aircraft. A ground task force comprising a 1,700-person Infantry Battle Group, built around 45 Royal Marine Commando with artillery, helicopter, and engineering support, deployed into Afghanistan in 2002. Royal Navy frigates also participated in maritime interdiction operations (MIOs) in the Indian Ocean.

The UK contributed about 5,500 personnel to NATO operations in the Balkans for most of 2002, declining to roughly 4,900 at year's end: 1,900 in Bosnia (Stabilization Force) and 3,000 in Kosovo (Kosovo Force). British forces served in UN peace operations in Cyprus, on the Iraq–Kuwait and Eritrea–Ethiopia borders, in Georgia, Sierra Leone, the Democratic Republic of the Congo, and East Timor. British forces independently deploy around the world in pursuit of national and international commitments.

The UK also commanded the first operational rotation of ISAF-I Jan–20 Jun 2002 (Operation Fingal), with about 1,800 infantry, headquarters, engineer, medical, logistics, military police, and air transport support troops at peak strength, in addition to SOF personnel in Afghanistan. After it relinquished control to Turkey, it continued to support ISAF-II and ISAF-III with about 500 soldiers.

For OIF (Operation Telic), the UK initially contributed some 45,000 personnel.

UK SOF operated along the Iraqi coast, in Basra and southern Iraq. The amphibious force numbered some 4,000 and included 40 and 42 Commando Royal Marines. The land force numbered some 26,000, centered on the 1 (UK) Armoured Division. The RAF provided 66 Tornado, Jaguar, and Harrier fighter aircraft, 14 tanker aircraft, 41 helicopters, 10 reconnaissance aircraft, 4 AWACS aircraft, and 4 aircraft for airlift. The UK deployed the largest number of coalition vessels in support of OIF, with a maximum of 31. These forces again included the HMS *Ark Royal* and the HMS *Ocean*, destroyers, frigates, supply ships, mine counter-measure forces, and submarines. With the conclusion of major combat operations, the 1 (UK) Division was replaced by the 3 (UK) Division, which formed the headquarters of the Multi-National Division (South-East) with UK, Italian, Norwegian, Romanian, Danish, Dutch, Czech, Portuguese, Lithuanian, and New Zealand troops under its command.

Code Names: Able Condor, Action Express, Active Improvement, Adventure Express, Air Warrior, Allied Response, Amber Star, Anvil Ghost, Arabian Gauntlet, ARRcade Fusion, Arcade series, Ardent Ground, Argonaut, Artificer, Artful Image, Artful Issue, ASCIET, Asterix, Atlantic Drive, Atomic Music Principle, Auburn Endeavor, Aurora, Avid Recovery, Baltic series, Baltlink, Baltops, Barracuda, Bartisan Hinge, Bass Rock, Battle Griffin, Beady Eye, Bell Buoy, Big Red, Black Hat, Blue Flag, Blue Harrier, Blue Hungwe, Blue Tiger, Boron Mercury, Bowline, Brave Heart, Bright Horizon, Bright Star, Brilliant Foil, Britannia Way, Bullseye, Burmese Chase, Burning Bush, Buzzard, Cajun Combat, Cape Petrel, Carpathian Exchange, Central Enterprise, Centrasbat, Chalet, Churinga, Circuit Mayflower, Classic Owl, Clean Hunter, Cobb Ring, Combined Endeavor, Condor, Conifer, Constant Harmony, Cooperative series, Cope Thunder, Coronet East, Coronet Nova, Coronet Regatta, Coronet Yankee, Cossack Express, Cossack Steppe, Counter Guard, Courageous Bat, Crab Apple, Cross Check, Cross Ski, Cygnet series, Datex, Delphin, Desert series, Destined Glory, Devil's Hat, Diagonal Glance, Diamond Cutter, Dimming Sun, Distant Frontier, Distant Thunder, Dogfish, Dogu Akdeniz, Druid's Dance, Dynamic series, Eager Sentry, Early Victor, Eastern Sailor, ECHELON, Elder Forest, Entgrou, European Mountaineer, Excalibur, Extract, Falcon Sound, Final Nail, Fincastle, Fingel, Fingel's Cave, Flying Fish, Flying Rhino, Frisian Flag, Full Moon, Gardenia, Gaulish, GI Joe, Giant, Glacial Enigma, Global series, Glow Worm, Gobi Dust, Golden Sands, Granby, Grand Prix, Green Flag, Griffin, GULFEX, Hairpsring, Hard Flint, Have Eagle, High Court, Himalayan Bluebell, IADS ADEX, Ince, Infinite Courage, Initial Link, Interpret, Iron series, Island Spell, Istar, Jackel Cave, Jagged Course, Joint Winter, Jolly Roger, JTFEX, Jumbo, Juniper Cobra, Kangaroo, Kelp, Kingfisher, Lark Song, Linked Seas, Lion Sun, Lion's Pride, Lone Eagle, Lone Kestrel, Lone Star, Long Look, Looking Glass, Lucky Sentinel, Mace, Magic Carpet, Magic Roundabout, Magestran, Majestic Eagle, Mallet Blow, Maple Flag, Maple Tour, MARCOT, MCOP, Med Shark, MEDFLAG, Medicine Man, Mercury, Mono Prix, Moon Penny, Mothia, Mulberry Tree, Mystic Star, Native Trail, Neo Tapon, Neon, Neop Spark, Neptune's series, Nightjar, Northern Light, Northern Lights, Northern Watch, Oak Apple, Odette, Oracle, Orient Express, Pacific Kukri, Pacific Protector, Panther Cub, Peaceshield, Pet Worth, Pine Apple, Pinemartin, Pitch Black, Pond Jump West, Power Drive, Prairie Warrior, Principal, Premier Link, Prominent Hammer, Provide Hope, Ptarmigan, Purple Star, Purple Strike, Quick Lift, Quick Stand, Red Stripe, Raynard Chase, Rhino,

RIMPAC, Rock Work, Rocky Lance, Rolling Deep, Roving Sands, Royal Patrol, Rutley, Saffron Sands, Saif Sareea, Sailfish, Sandy Coast, Sanso, Scope Sand, Sea series, Senator, Sensor Pacer, Shant Doot, SHAREM, Sharp Point, Silver Weed Ruckus, SIT, Slovak Express, Snipe, Snow Falcon, Snow Shoe, Snow Drop, Soothsayer, Sorbet Royale, Southern Crusade, Southern Knight, Southern Watch, Spirochaete, Spontex, Stardex, Starfish, Starwindow, Steeplebush, Stoney Run, Strong Resolve, Suman Warrior, Suriot, Swabian Crusade, Sweeney, TAPON, Tartan Eagle, Tartan Venture, Telic, Temple Jade, Thirsty Panther, Thor/Odin, Tier III, Tiger Lake, Timbuktu, Torpedo Focus, Totaliser, Tradewinds, Trailblazer, Trial, Trident D'Or, Troutman, Turtle Heritage, Turtle Truss, Tyne Tease, Ulan Eagle, Ultrapure, Ulu Rajah, Unified Charger, Unified Spirit, United Shield, Urban Encounter, Ursa Minor, Utah, Vampire, Vigilant, Viking, Warlord, Western Vortex, Westpac MCMEX, Wet Gap, Winged Star.

Uruguay

The US and Uruguay maintain strong bilateral relations, and Uruguayan armed forces conduct a robust program of confidence and security building exercises and professional exchanges with the US and with its neighbors. Among Latin American nations, Uruguay is the largest per capita contributor of personnel for international peacekeeping missions. In 2003, Uruguay had peacekeepers deployed on missions in 11 countries. The largest group is in the Congo, where 1,500 Uruguayan troops control one sector of the country. US Joint/Combined Exchange Training (JCET) special operations training takes place between the 7th Special Forces Group and 14th Battalion of the Uraguayan army, among other units.

US COMMAND: SOUTHCOM.

AGREEMENTS: Acquisition and Cross-Servicing Agreement (29 Mar 2000).

US ASSISTANCE: Receives Foreign Military Financing program grants, International Military Education and Training aid, eligible to receive grant Excess Defense Articles, participates in Center for Hemispheric Defense Studies conferences and seminars, receives International Narcotics Control and Law Enforcement funding.

Code Names: Cabañas, Eagle, Fuerzas Aliades, Fuerzas Unidas, Oceanic, PKO, Unitas.

Uzbekistan

The Operation Enduring Freedom (OEF) bombing campaign began just hours after Uzbekistan formally agreed that the US could carry out search and rescue missions from Karshi-Khanabad air base (nicknamed "K2" by the US) on 7 Oct 2001. It was not the beginning of US–Uzbek cooperation, however, because the US had provided 16 military transport vehicles to the Uzbek military in Feb 2000, its first sizable transfer of military equipment to any Central Asian state, and the CIA and NSA had been operating from the country since

1999, with Uzbekistan also heavily involved in supporting the Northern Alliance opposition to the Taliban. Uzbekistan became the initial base for clandestine US Predator Unmanned Aerial Vehicle (UAV) operations against al Qaeda. Of 11 successful Predator flights sent across the mountains from Uzbekistan to Afghanistan in Sep and Oct 2000, 3 spotted a person whom several US intelligence analysts concluded was bin Laden. The sightings were the major impetus for development of an armed Predator.

Since 2001, K2 has since grown to a major US military base, providing blanket overflight permission for US and coalition forces, routinely voting with the US at the UN, and the first country worldwide to bring into force an Article 98 agreement exempting US servicemen from the jurisdiction of the International Criminal Court. Uzbekistan possesses the largest and most competent military forces in the Central Asian region, facilitating joint military exercises and exchanges. The military has also been largely freed of a significant mission with the disruption of the Islamic Movement of Uzbekistan (IMU), which fought on the Taliban and al Qaeda side in Afghanistan. The remnants of the IMU remain important, as does increased drug trafficking.

After the fall of the Taliban, Uzbek authorities reopened the country's Termez bridge border crossing with Afghanistan. The bridge streamlines the transport of food assistance and avoids a lengthy trip through Turkmenistan. Uzbekistan has also renewed deliveries of electric power and liquefied gas to Afghanistan.

Though Uzbekistan remains an authoritarian state, US aid has consistently increased. In FYs 1993–2001, the US obligated about $208 million in assistance for Uzbekistan, about $188 million in economic aid. After 9/11, the US Export–Import Bank granted Uzbekistan a $55 million credit guarantee, and the US tripled annual foreign aid in FY 2002 to $160 million. Requested assistance for fiscal years 2003 and 2004 totaled about $100 million. US military priorities include enhancing Uzbekistan's capability to combat terrorist insurgents and cells in Central Asia, improving border controls, and preventing proliferation of weapons of mass destruction and materials. Cooperative Threat Reduction (CTR) programs predate 9/11, and include demilitarization and cleanup of former Soviet facilities, shipping spent nuclear fuel back to Russia, improved nuclear material protection, control and accounting, and grant efforts to keep Uzbek weapons scientists employed in peaceful research.

Uzbekistan sees itself in a leading role in Central Asia, is an active participant in NATO's Partnership for Peace (13 Jul 1994), was a partner in the original

Central Asian Peacekeeping Battalion (CENTRASBAT) program, and is involved in joint peacekeeping initiatives with Kazakhstan, the Kyrgyz Republic, and NATO. Uzkbekistan is also an active member of the Shanghai Cooperation Organization (SCO); in Aug 2003, Tashkent was designated the location for an SCO Regional Anti-Terrorism Center.

Uzbekistan also supports an active demilitarization program by the Defense Threat Reduction Agency in its western region (the former chemical weapons facility in Nukus and the biological weapons facility on Vozrozhdeniye Island in the Aral Sea).

US command: CENTCOM. US military operations are under the command of Combined Joint Task Force 180 (CJTF-180).

Agreements: US–Uzbekistan Declaration of Strategic Partnership (12 Mar 2002), MOU on Economic Cooperation (7 Nov 2001), agreement to clean up the former Soviet biological weapons test range on Vozrozhdeniya (22 Oct 2001), SOFA (7 Oct 2001), PfP SOFA (1 Mar 1997), Acquisition and Cross-Servicing Agreement eligible, Article 98 Agreement.

On 26 Sept 2001, the Uzbek president permitted US use of Uzbek airspace against Afghanistan-based terrorists for "humanitarian and security purposes" if Uzbekistan's security was guaranteed. The US–Uzbekistan Declaration of Strategic Partnership includes a nonspecific security guarantee. The US affirms that "it would regard with grave concern any external threat" to Uzbekistan's security and would consult with Uzbekistan "on an urgent basis" regarding a response. The two states pledge to intensify military cooperation, including "re-equipping the Armed Forces" of Uzbekistan, and the US offers to support setting up a Partnership for Peace Training Center in Uzbekistan and to help Uzbekistan introduce NATO standards, equipment, and training.

US assistance: Foreign Military Financing program grants, International Military Education and Training aid, eligible to receive grant Excess Defense Articles, National Guard partner with Louisiana, participates in George C. Marshall Center conferences and seminars, receives Nonproliferation, Anti-terrorism, Demining, and Related (NADR) and Anti-Terrorism Assistance funds for counter-terrorism training to Uzbek law enforcement agencies, receives Anti-Crime Training and Technical Assistance support.

Bases and access: US intelligence set up covert operations in Uzbekistan in 1999, both to conduct liaison with anti-Taliban forces in Afghanistan and to train Uzbek special operations forces (SOF). The NSA established listening posts. Uzbekistan was designated a combat zone as of 1 Oct 2001, and Imminent Danger Pay was also authorized for US personnel in Oct 2001. Post-9/11, the US military has access to military facilities in Chirchik, Khanabad, and Tuzel, and German units have access to Termez. Karshi-Khanabad (K2/Camp Stronghold Freedom) air base is the main US and coalition base. Joint Special Operations Task Force — Dagger operated from the airfield 6 Oct 2001–28 Feb 2002 during OEF, and the US deployed troops of the army's 10th Mountain Division there in 2001. AC-130 gunships also operated from K2 for combat missions in Afghanistan through 2002. The total of US and coalition personnel at K2 reached 5,000 at the peak. In 2004, the number had stabilized at about 1,750, including 450 civilian contractors.

Code Names: Balance Ultra, Balance Umbra, Balance Umpire, Balance Unity, Centrasbat, Combined Endeavor, Cooperative series, Dacia, Eloquent Nugget, Ferghana, IWER, Regional Cooperation, Viking.

Vanuatu

The US provides military training assistance to the Vanuatu Mobile Force, a paramilitary branch of the Vanuatu police, while the US Coast Guard trains Vanuatu in maritime law enforcement, supplementing Australian and New Zealand programs. A Joint/Combined Exchange Training (JCET) special operations program is also planned with Vanuatu.

US COMMAND: PACOM.

US ASSISTANCE: Receives International Military Education and Training aid, participates in Asia-Pacific Center for Security Studies executive courses.

Venezuela

Since Apr 2002, when President Hugo Chavez was temporarily taken into custody by military officers, Venezuela has experienced political crisis, instability, and disruption, culminating in efforts by the opposition to recall the president. US counter-narcotics and counter-terrorism assistance and activity has continued during this period.

US COMMAND: SOUTHCOM.

US ASSISTANCE: Receives International Military Education and Training aid, eligible to receive grant Excess Defense Articles, National Guard partner with Florida, participates in Center for Hemispheric Defense Studies conferences and seminars, receives Andean Counterdrug Initiative (ACI) and Economic Support Fund (ESF) aid for counter-narcotics and judicial reform.

AGREEMENTS: Acquisition and Cross-Servicing Agreement eligible (29 Aug 2000).

Bases and access: In the 1990s, Venezuela was integrated into the Counterdrug Surveillance and Control System and the Caribbean Basin Radar Network (CBRN), operated by the DOD and DEA. Radars were built at Baman, El Copay, Margarita Island, and Monte Cano (Punto Fijo). The radar sites also serve as protected SIGINT outposts. US ships and submarines call and refuel at La Guaira, Montevideo, and Puerto La Cruz.

Code Names: Armistad, Cabañas, Constant Vigil, DFT, Fundamental Response, Laser Strike, Pacer Griffin, Peace Delta, PKO, Transoceanic Exercise, Unitas.

Vietnam

Since political normalization in 1995, Vietnam has opened political and trade relations with the US and begun cooperation on regional security matters. Secretary of Defense William Cohen visited Vietnam in Mar 2000, and President Clinton visited to crowds of well-wishers in Oct 2000. Cooperation on recovery of Americans missing since the Vietnam War continues to dominate relations.

US military cooperation and aid remain limited. A team from PACOM visited Vietnam in 2001 to provide instruction on the use of US-provided demining equipment, and the US Coast Guard identified Vietnamese counter-narcotics requirements, but bilateral assistance and International Military Education and Training funding have been blocked by Vietnam's failure to conclude an agreement on end-user assurances. Japan thus remains Vietnam's major trading partner and bilateral aid donor. During a visit to Vietnam in Mar 2001 by President Putin (the first visit to Vietnam by a head of state from Moscow — Russian or Soviet), Vietnam and Russia also signed a strategic partnership agreement. Russia did not renew its lease on naval facilities at Cam Ranh Bay and was scheduled to withdraw from Vietnam in 2004, ending a 26-year military presence.

US command: PACOM.

US assistance: Receives International Military Education and Training aid, receives aid for humanitarian demining efforts, receives Nonproliferation, Anti-terrorism, Demining, and Related (NADR) and Anti-Terrorism Assistance funds, participates in Asia-Pacific Center for Security Studies executive courses.

Wake Island (US Unincorporated Territory)

A 1962 executive order designated the secretary of the interior responsible for the civil administration of the atoll; since 1 Oct 1994, the Ballistic Missile Defense Organization has funded Wake's actual administration. Wake Island airfield is the most important feature, important also as part of the Pacific Tanker Air Bridge to bases in Asia and the Pacific. The US initiated a major airfield renovation in 2003.

US COMMAND: PACOM.

Western Sahara

Following agreement between Morocco and the Frente Polisario, the United Nations Mission for the Referendum in Western Sahara (MINURSO) was deployed in Sep 1991 to monitor the cease-fire. As of 31 Jan 2004, some 350 civilian and military peacekeepers and observers were deployed from 24 countries.

US COMMAND: EUCOM.

Yemen

Warming US relations with Yemen in the late 1990s led to the visit of the destroyer USS *Cole* (and ultimately the al Qaeda attack in Aden port) in Oct 2000. The incident led to increased US–Yemeni intelligence and law enforcement cooperation and increased joint counter-terrorism training and cooperation. In late Nov 2001, Yemeni President Ali Abdullah Saleh visited Washington to strengthen US–Yemeni relations. After that visit, US special operations forces (SOF) began training Yemeni military forces, and the US worked to establish a professional Yemeni Coast Guard force (supplying seven 44-foot US-manufactured patrol boats, which arrived Feb 2004).

The culmination of US–Yemeni cooperation occurred 3 Nov 2002, when a combined operation resulted in the death of Abu Ali al-Harithi, an al Qaeda leader suspected of masterminding the attack on the USS *Cole*. A Predator drone launched from Djibouti was used to launch a Hellfire missile at the car al-Harithi was driving, which killed five others.

Since the stand-up of the Combined Joint Task Force — Horn of Africa (CJTF–HOE) in Djibouti in 2002, Yemeni SOF personnel have regularly trained with SOF and marine reconnaissance and security specialists, as well as CIA and FBI specialists in counter-terrorism and other efforts to close potential terrorist transit routes across the Bab al-Mandeb straits to East Africa. FBI Director Robert Mueller met President Ali Abdullah Saleh on 5 Nov 2003 for talks on combating terrorism.

US COMMAND: CENTCOM. CJTF-HOA.

AGREEMENTS: Acquisition and Cross-Servicing Agreement (post-9/11).

In the summer of 2000, Yemen and Saudi Arabia signed an International Border Treaty settling a 50-year-old dispute over the location of the desert border between the two countries. Yemen also settled its dispute with Eritrea over the Hanish Islands in 1998.

US ASSISTANCE: Receives Foreign Military Financing program grants, International Military Education and Training aid, eligible to receive grant Excess Defense Articles, participates in the Terrorist Interdiction Program.

BASES AND ACCESS: The US Navy began refueling operations in Aden in Jan 1999, and Yemen has seen regular US ship visits since 9/11. Yemen was designated a combat zone as of 10 Apr 2002. Socotra Island, a former Soviet base, is often mentioned as a US SIGINT facility, though there is no firm evidence to confirm these reports. US military advisers and combat units of CJTF-HOA have been permitted to maintain a more or less permanent prescence in the country to provide counter-terrorism training.

Code Names: Blue Sky, Determined Response, Peace Bell, Tiger Rescue.

Zambia

Zambia and the US have a cordial military-to-military relationship, including Joint/Combined Exchange Training (JCET) exchanges between Zambia's 1st Commando Battalion and the US 3rd Special Forces Group, military and peacekeeping training, and cooperation in humanitarian demining. Land mines in five provinces render an estimated 975-square-mile area inhospitable.

US COMMAND: EUCOM.

AGREEMENTS: Acquisition and Cross-Servicing Agreement eligible (26 Jan 1998), Article 98 Agreement.

US ASSISTANCE: Receives International Military Education and Training aid, eligible to receive grant Excess Defense Articles, receives aid for humanitarian demining efforts, participates in Africa Center for Strategic Studies conferences and seminars.

Code Names: MEDFLAG.

Zimbabwe

Zimbabwe is in the midst of interrelated political, economic, and humanitarian crises, with the economy in precipitous decline. The US imposed targeted measures on the government in 2002, including financial and visa sanctions, a ban on transfers of defense items and services, and a suspension of nonhumanitarian government-to-government assistance. There is still some limited cooperation on law enforcement and counter-terrorism matters, but there is no International Military Education and Training program, and no military training activities.

US COMMAND: EUCOM.

AGREEMENTS: Acquisition and Cross-Servicing Agreement eligible (26 Jan 1998).

Code Names: Blue Hungwe, Flintlock, MEDFLAG.

PART III

CODE NAMES

Able: NATO Allied Command Europe (ACE) and EUCOM nuclear weapons exercise first word. The Able first word has been used for more than two decades. Most notably, during exercise Able Archer 83 in Nov 1983, Soviet leaders reportedly were concerned that the Reagan administration was preparing a nuclear first strike and placed their nuclear forces on alert. "The world did not quite reach the edge of the nuclear abyss," says Oleg Gordievsky, a US agent within the KGB. "But during Able Archer 83 it had . . . come frighteningly close."

+ **Able Ally:** Annual highly classified command post exercise practicing command and staff procedures involving escalation to hostilities involving nuclear weapons and attacks against enemy nuclear, biological, and chemical targets. Held in Nov–Dec. Includes Able Ally 04 (Nov–Dec 2004), Able Ally 03, Able Ally 01, Able Ally 00, Able Ally 98, Able Ally 97, Able Ally 94, and Able Ally 93.

+ **Able Crystal:** Nuclear-weapons-related exercise series.

+ **Able Effort:** Nuclear-weapons-related exercise, 1999.

+ **Able Fast:** Series of three quarterly nuclear weapons command and control exercises of the US liaison cell at ACE culminating in the annual Able Ally exercise, 1999 present.

+ **Able Gain:** Annual USAFE-led highly classified field training exercise focusing on contingency planning, operations plans, and cross-servicing procedures involving NATO nuclear air force capabilities. Ample Gain 04: mid-Mar 2004. Ample Gain 02.

+ **Able Staff:** Nuclear Status Control, Alerting and Reporting System (SCARS II) command post exercise, Apr–Sep 1997, practicing SACEUR's nuclear warning system and involving the nuclear-capable air forces of NATO.

Able: Coast Guard operation first word.

+ **Able Manner:** Patrols in the Windward Passage (the body of water between Haiti and Cuba) to interdict Haitian migrants, Jan 1993–Nov 1994. Followed by Sea Angel.

+ **Able Response:** Operation to intercept Dominican migrants, 1 Apr 1995–1 Oct 1997.

+ **Able Vigil:** Operation to intercerpt mass illegal migration from Cuba in the Straits of Florida, 1 Aug–16 Sep 1994. Able Vigil was the largest

Code Names

peacetime Coast Guard operation since the Vietnam War, involving 38 Coast Guard cutters as well as the USS *Vicksburg* (CG 69), USS *Gallery* (FFG 26), USS *Klakring* (FFG 42), USS *Oliver Hazard Perry* (FFG 7), USS *Stark* (FFG 31), and USS *Whidbey Island* (LSD 41). Followed by Sea Angel.

Able Condor: UK army signals command post exercise, Germany, May–Jun 2001.

Able Sentry (TF Able Sentry): Task force charged with observing and reporting violations of UN sanctions and assisting in maintaining stability along the Serbian–Macedonian border, 12 Jul 1993–31 Mar 1999.

Able Warrior: SOCOM global war on terrorism exercise series, the only SOCOM-sponsored large-scale exercise, to train the headquarters and component command staffs in "supported command" operations to lead offensive counter-terrorism actions.

Aboveboard/Above Board: NSA-developed software for message processing. Army intelligence used Aboveboard to receive intelligence data by many of the deployed divisions involved in Desert Storm and Restore Democracy.

Accurate Test: US–Oman biennial classified exercise series. Accurate Test 81-2, 13–23 Feb 1981, was the first-ever Rapid Deployment Joint Task Force deployment to Southwest Asia. Accurate Test 03. Accurate Test 01. Accurate Test 99. Accurate Test 97. Accurate Test 95.

Accrued Action: Joint Special Operations Command exercise involving a Personal Information Carrier Proof of Concept Test, 6–16 Dec 1999.

Acer Gable: Air force unknown project or weapon.

Aces North: Australian Air Force Fighter Weapons School graduation exercise, held every odd year, usually with US F-15 participation.

Acetone: Former Cold War navy covert submarine surveillance program.

Acid Gambit: Operation to free accused CIA Agent Kurt Meuse from a Panamanian prison. On 20 Dec 1989, during Just Cause, Joint Special Operations Command forces stormed the Carcel Modelo prison and freed Meuse.

Action Express: EUCOM special operations exercise held in Denmark each autumn and including UK forces. Action Express 93.

Activation Leap: Classified special operations exercise, Puerto Rico, Jan 1997.

Active Endeavour: NATO Allied Forces Southern Europe counter-terrorism TF activated after 9/11 on 26 Oct 2001. TF Endeavour is made up of Standing Naval Force Mediterranean deployed to the eastern Mediterrranean to patrol and monitor shipping. On 4 Feb 2003, the North Atlantic Council (NAC) decided to extend Active Endeavour to include escorting nonmilitary ships through the Strait of Gibraltar. On 10 Mar 2003, a second TF made up of Standing Naval Force Atlantic deployed to the Strait of Gibraltar. On 29 Apr 2003, TF Endeavour began boarding operations following an NAC decision. The naval TF visited Algiers, Algeria, in Oct 2003. In Dec 2001, EUCOM established a Joint Forces Maritime Component Commander (JFMCC), consisting of Sixth Fleet assets, to operate with Active Endeavour. In 2001–2004, JFMCC and NATO forces hailed 39,500 ships in order to ascertain specific information regarding the carrier, its cargo, and its destination; they conducted 45 boardings.

Active Improvement: NATO Multi-National Div (MND) command post exercise series. Active Improvement 01: Netherlands, May 2001. Active Improvement 00: Netherlands, May 2000. Another planned MND exercise is Active Improvement 05.

Adobe: FEMA continuity of government special access program designation, 1980s.

Adriatic Phiblex: NATO ISO/PfP maritime and amphibious landing and peace enforcement operations exercise, Adriatic Sea. Participants include Albania and Croatia. Adriatic Phiblex 05: Jun 2005. Adriatic Phiblex 04: 15 Apr–15 Jun 2004. Adriatic Phiblex 03.

Advanced Notice: Defense Threat Reduction Agency Advanced Concept Technology Demonstration to produce special-operations-focused capabilities for counter-proliferation operations against enemy biological warfare production, storage, and weaponization facilities.

Adventure: NATO Allied Mobile Force (Land), or AMF (L), first word.

+ **Adventure Exchange:** Command post exercise. Adventure Exchange 03. Adventure Exchange 01. Adventure Exchange 00: Romanelli Barracks, Kozani, Greece, 19–30 Sep 2000. Adventure Exchange 99 canceled because of Kosovo operations. Adventure Exchange 98. Adventure Exchange 95/Ardent Ground: Moron AB, Spain, Oct–Nov 1995.

+ **Adventure Express:** AMF (L) winter exercise series held on the northern and southern flanks of NATO. Goes back to at least Adventure Express 83. Participants include Albania, Belgium, Germany, Greece, Lithuania, the Netherlands, Norway, Spain, the UK, and the US. Adventure Express 03. Adventure Express 01: Albania and Greece, 25 Feb–10 Mar 2001. UK participation was canceled due to force protection concerns in Albania. Adventure Express 00/Affirmative Alert 00: Bardufoss, Norway, 1 Feb–20 Mar 2000. Adventure Express 97: Northern Norway, 6–13 Mar 1997. First full-scale cold-weather exercises of the NATO composite force (NCF). The 174th Fighter Wing deployed to Andoya, Norway. Adventure Express 96/Cooperative Adventure Express.

Adversary: 1. Air-force-developed command and control nodal analysis tool used for information warfare targeting. The tool is used to analyze the communications infrastructure of target countries and then report the results of the analysis in graphical form.

2. **Adversary:** Element of the Joint Deployable Intelligence Support System (JDISS).

Aferdou: US–Moroccan exercise series, 1980s.

Affirmative Alert: NATO composite force (NCF) exercise series held in Norway and designed to test Article 5 procedures in defense of NATO's northern boundaries against foreign incursions. Affirmative Alert 03. Affirmative Alert 01. Affirmative Alert 00/Adventure Express 01. Affirmative Alert 99: Feb 1999.

African: US–Moroccan EUCOM first word.

+ **African Eagle:** US–Moroccan biennial exercise that practices deployment, employment, and redeployment of Air Force assets to Morocco. Goes back to at least African Eagle 84. African Eagle 01: Sidi Slimane, Morocco, 21 Jan–9 Feb 2001. The exercise combined air-to-air scenarios with the Moroccan air force. African Eagle 98: Morocco, 4–19 Dec 1998. African Eagle 96: Air-defense-focused exercise, Dec 1996. Main US participant was the 31st Fighter Wing. The exercise created a daily air tasking order (ATO) in the 16th Air Force operations center, transferring it to flying units and a five-man Special Commander's Assessment Team, which acted as the eyes and ears of the USAFE commander on the scene. African Eagle 95: 22nd MEU. African Eagle 94: Morocco, 4 Dec 1993. Fifth exercise in the series. USS *Ponce* (LPD 15),

USS *Cape St. George* (CG 71), USS *Gunston Hall* (LSD 44), USS *L. Mendel Rivers* (SSN 686), 22nd MEU, and 48th Fighter Wing. Two B-1B bombers flew from the US to Morocco to conduct low-level bombing simulation. African Eagle 93.

+ **African Falcon 85:** Morocco, 9–21 Dec 1985.
+ **African Fox 85:** Morocco, 23 Jan–22 Feb 1985.
+ **African Lion:** Army SETAF-led bilateral computer-assisted exercise/command post exercise held in Morocco. African Lion 04. African Lion 03. African Lion 00. African Lion 99. African Lion 98: Dec 1998. The UT and LA ARNG provided French linguists in a real-world translation role in support of this exercise.

Agile: EUCOM Southern European JTF first word.

+ **Agile Leader:** JTF exercise. Agile Leader 05: Focus on the army's V Corps as a Joint Forces Land Component Commander HQ and Joint Forces Command headquarters in light of experience in Iraq as JTF-7. Agile Leader 04/Urgent Victory 04: V Corps JTF practice for certification in Urgent Victory 04. Agile Leader 03: Air operations center focus.
+ **Agile Lion:** US Army Europe JTF series. Union Flash 02, Agile Lion 02, and Warfighter Exercise (WFX) 02 were linked through a common scenario and planning process, resulting in a new JTF exercise named Urgent Resolve 02. Agile Lion 01. Agile Lion 00. Agile Lion 99: Jan 1999. Scenario involved Burundi embassy staff and US citizen noncombatant evacuation operation, and simultaneous humanitarian assistance mission. National Reconnaissance Office personnel participating in Italy supplemented with real-world imagery depicting worsening conditions in Burundi. Agile Lion 98: Grafenwohr, Germany, 15–30 Jan 1998.
+ **Agile Response:** JTF noncombatant evacuation operation exercise series. Agile Response 05: USAFE- and 3rd Air Force–led JTF exercise concentrating on foreign humanitarian assistance. Agile Response 04: 8–31 Mar 2004. The EUCOM priority exercise event of the year; focus was on SETAF as a core JTF headquarters in preparation for crisis management support to the Summer Olympics in Aug 2004. Held in conjuection with Silent Guide 04. Agile Response 03: Gaeta, Vicenza, and Longare, Italy; Ramstein AB, Germany; and distributed sites, 11–25 Nov 2002.

Agile Provider 94: Atlantic Command (now JFCOM) field training exercise, Apr–May 1994. Agile Provider practiced tactics and weapons that would be used in the invasion of Haiti. USS *Theodore Roosevelt* (CVN 71). Navy

Pioneer UAV video was broadcast from the USS *Mount Whitney* (LCC 20) to Norfolk, VA. *Cyclone*-class patrol craft, new to the SOCOM inventory, were also tested. Air force RC-135s of the 55th Wing also participated.

Aguila: *See* Eagle.

Ahuas Tara: SOUTHCOM Honduras-based operations and command post exercise series, initiated in 1983 and continued through Ahuas Tara 96, also known as Project 9AH. Ahuas Tara was the focus of a number of court battles regarding the rights of state governors to withhold National Guard forces. In 1986, Congress passed a National Defense Authorization Act amendment ("Montgomery Amendment") authored by Rep. Sonny Montgomery (D-MS) that prevented governors from refusing to support overseas training missions except where state troops were needed to support a state emergency. After much protest by governors, on 18 Apr 1989, the Supreme Court, without comment, supported a 1st US Circuit Court of Appeals ruling that upheld the constitutionality of this 1986 amendment.

Air Brake 04: Proliferation Security Initiative exercise held in the Mediterranean Sea, 18–19 Feb 2004. Participants included France, Italy, Portugal, Spain, and the US. The scenario involved interception of airplane simulated to be trafficking in WMD components. *See also* Pacific Protector.

Air Warrior/Air Warrior II: Air Combat Command exercise series designed to train aircrews, air liaison officers, tactical air controllers, battle management personnel, and weapons system operators in the planning and execution of close air support operations. Air Warrior I was held at National Training Center, Fort Irwin, CA, and Nellis AFB, NV. Air Warrior II was held at the Joint Readiness Training Center, Fort Polk, LA, and Barksdale AFB, LA. In Air Warrior II 96-7, May 1996, the scenario centered on the country of Cortinia, located on the southwestern portion of the mythical island of Aragon, between the West Indies and the Azores. The People's Democratic Republic of Atlantica (PDRA), to the east, was overwhelming the Cortinians, and they requested US help. After the PDRA joined forces with the Cortinian Liberation Front (CLF), the president of Cortinia requested US assistance. A JTF was formed and deployed, assisting the Cortinian government in repelling the opposition forces. Fort Polk served as the country of Cortinia. Participants include the UK.

Al Miwan: Pakistan military and security forces offensive against Taliban remnants and al Qaeda fighters in the Federally Administered Tribal Areas along the Afghanistan border, initiated in 2003.

Aladdin: Program to modify Navy S-3 Viking anti-submarine-warfare aircraft for general surveillance missions over Bosnia, 1990s.

Alamo Sweep: 82nd Airborne Div sensitive site exploitation, Khowst, Afghanistan, Sep 2002.

Alaskan Road: PACOM multi-year engineering effort to construct approximately 14.5 miles of mountainous and coastal roadway on Annette Island in southeastern Alaska. Road construction occurs primarily between Apr and Sep of each year.

Albatross Ausindo: Australian–Indonesian maritime air surveillance exercise series. Albatross Ausindo 98: Apr–Jun 1998. Albatross Ausindo 97: Dec 1997.

ALERT (Attack and Launch Early Report to Theater): 11th Space Warning Sqn theater event system deployed at Joint Tactical Ground Stations for receipt of real-time satellite data. *See also* Shield.

Alexander the Great/Alexandros (Alexander): Greek national Mediterranean Sea–based force-on-force amphibious exercise. Alexander the Great 01: USS *Kearsarge* (LHD 3). Alexander the Great 99. Alexander 98: 26–31 Jan 1998. Alexander the Great 97: 22nd MEU. Alexander the Great 96: 22nd MEU. Alexander the Great 95: 26th MEU with Greek marines. Alexander the Great 94.

Allied: NATO Allied Command Europe (ACE) first word.

+ **Allied Action:** Annual exercise to validate the CJTF and test NATO's ability to rapidly plan and launch a multi-national crisis response operation. Allied Action 05: Spring 2005. CJTF command post exercise for NATO Response Force (NRF) certification for NRF 5/6 and Joint Headquarters (JHF) West. Allied Action 04: 28 May–8 Jun 2004, including Switzerland. Allied Action 03: Istanbul, Turkey and Belgium, 3–18 Nov 2003. First NATO exercise involving the NBC Event Response Team and a Deployable NBC Laboratory.

+ **Allied Effort:** Command post exercise to practice staff procedures, including the planning and conduct of peacekeeping operation utilizing a CJTF HQ and component commands. Allied Effort 01: Wrowclow, Poland, 5–20 Nov 2001. Allied Effort 97: First trial of the NATO CJTF, Nov 1997. A CJTF HQ had to be prepared for a peace support operation in a fictional peninsula with rudimentary infrastructure (lack of modern road, airfield, and communications networks), little host nation support, and far from Europe's Central Region. The trial assessed the requirements for a land-based CJTF headquarters. The exercise was an accelerated effort built on the existing annual Central Region exercise series, Cooperative Guard.

+ **Allied Force:** Operation to stop Yugoslav "ethnic cleansing" campaign in Kosovo, 24 Mar–10 Jun 1999. The operation began when US military forces, acting with NATO allies, commenced air strikes against targets throughout the former Yugoslavia. For 78 days, the US and its NATO allies continued bombing to bring an end to Serbian activities in Kosovo. On 10 Jun 1999, NATO Secretary General Javier Solana announced that he had instructed Gen. Wesley Clark, SACEUR, to suspend NATO's air operations. Yugoslavia's withdrawal from Kosovo was in accordance with a Military–Technical Agreement concluded between NATO and the Federal Republic of Yugoslavia on the evening of 9 Jun 1999.

+ **Allied Harbor:** Humanitarian operation in Albania and Macedonia, 14 Apr 1999–1 Sep 1999. On 11 Apr 1999, the NATO Council at the ambassadorial level approved the Allied Harbor operational plan in Albania aimed at humanitarian assistance to Kosovo refugees. The operation was launched on 14 Apr. JTF Shining Hope was established by EUCOM on 4 Apr 1999. During its first 50 days of operation, JTF Shining Hope delivered more than 3,400 tons of food, equipment, and medical supplies.

+ **Allied Mix:** Allied Forces Southern Europe exercise series to prepare a NATO CJTF parent HQ. Allied Mix 00. Allied Mix 99: 22–30 Sep 1999.

+ **Allied Reach 04:** Special seminar designed to test the concepts behind NATO's new Response Force, 22–25 Jan 2004.

+ **Allied Response 03:** NATO Response Force (NRF) demonstration, Doganbey Military Training Range south of Izmir, Turkey, Nov 2003. Included elements of the first rotation of the NRF: the NATO Rapid Deployable Corps — Turkey, the Spanish High Readiness Force (Maritime), and Allied Air Forces Northern Europe. Participants included Belgium, the Czech Republic, Denmark, France, Germany, Greece, Norway, Poland, Spain, Turkey, and the UK.

Allied Sweep: 82nd Airborne Div–led operation launched in eastern Afghanistan to eliminate remnants of Taliban and al Qaeda, Oct 2002.

Amalgam: NORAD first word.

+ **Amalgam Brave 87:** Largest NORAD exercise ever held in Alaska, 10–18 May 1987.

+ **Amalgam Chief:** Alaskan NORAD Region binational exercise series, dating to the 1970s, and including Snowtime. Amalgam Chief 03/Northern Edge 03: Homeland security scenario involving a simulated stolen military aircraft flying over Alaskan airspace. Amalgam Chief 92, Goose Bay, Canada, 3–4 Jun 1992.

+ **Amalgam Fabric Brave:** Biennial. Region-scheduled field training exercise held in Canada. The primary purpose is to to periodically deploy fighter assets and conduct air operations from the region's deployed operating bases and forward operating locations. Amalgam Fabric Brave 03/02. Amalgam Fabric Brave 00: 5 Wing Goose Bay, Canada, Sep 2000. Amalgam Fabric Brave 98-1, off the west coast of British Columbia.

+ **Amalgam Falcon Brave:** Biennial field training exercise held in the US (counterpart to Amalgam Fabric Brave). Amalgam Falcon Brave 02/03.

+ **Amalgam Fencing Brave:** *See* Fencing Brave.

+ **Amalgam Mute:** Code word that designates an exercise as an actual operational evaluation.

+ **Amalgam Talent:** Support of William Tell exercises.

+ **Amalgam Virgo:** Multi-agency binational annual live-fly homeland security interagency exercise. Amalgam Virgo 04: 6–7 Aug 2004. Including the Nuclear Regulatory Commission in a counter-terror scenario. Amalgam Virgo 03. Amalgam Virgo 02: Exercise scenario involved an airborne terrorism scenario over the US and Canada, beginning 4 Jun 2002. The exercise was planned prior to the events of 9/11. Participants included the Vancouver Airport Authority and Delta Air Lines. The 1st AF and the Florida ARNG also tested a Surface Launched Advanced Medium Range Air to Air Missile fire unit and a Sentry command and control system, both developed by Raytheon Company, in homeland security play at the Venice Airport in Venice, FL, and at Tyndall AFB in Panama City, FL. Amalgam Virgo 01: 1–2 Jun 2001. First Amalgam Virgo to practice a counter-terrorism scenario, involving a Third World UAV launched off a rogue freighter in the Gulf of Mexico. Amalgam Virgo 99-2: Provided NORAD a sensor-to-shooter evaluation of critical Thin Line systems across all four major mission areas; missile warning, space warning, air warning, and aerospace control in preparation for

Y2K. Additional non-NORAD systems of Strategic Command and Space Command were also evaluated to properly evaluate the sensor-to-shooter linkage.

+ **Amalgam Warrior:** Large-scale live-fly air defense and air intercept field training exercise, held twice per year. Emphasis is placed on realistic surveillance, detection, tracking, air interception, rules of engagement, force generation, electronic warfare, penetration tactics, attack warning, attack assessment, counter-cruise-missile operations, counter-narcotics operations, and contingency plan implementation. In Amalgam Warrior 98-1, the largest NORAD exercise ever held, six B-1B bombers deployed to Eielson AFB, AK, to act as the "bad guy" threat by infiltrating the aerial borders of North America. Two B-52Hs also carried out a 34.3-hour mission with cruise missiles to simulate cruise missile employment. The exercise is sometimes combined with Global Guardian. Amalgam Warrior 04. Amalgam Warrior 03. Amalgam Warrior 02. Amalgam Warrior 01: 31 Oct–2 Nov 2000. Amalgam Warrior 98. Amalgam Warrior 96. Amalgam Warrior 95.

Amazon: NORAD Cheyenne Mountain first word.

+ **Amazon Condor:** Internal command post exercise focusing on Battle Staff and the Cheyenne Mountain Operations Center. The exercise is designed to train newly assigned personnel and to examine command and control and emergency procedures. One Amazon Condor exercise is scheduled each year (replaced Amazon Dolly).

+ **Amazon Dolly:** Now Amazon Condor.

Amber: DARPA-funded long-endurance reconnaissance UAV, 1980s.

Amber Fox: NATO Macedonia operation began on 26 Sep 2001 to provide security for international community monitors in the crisis areas, while government authorities had primarily responsibility for their security. NATO decided to bring the mission to an end on 15 Dec 2002, and started a new mission called Allied Harmony under NATO Headquarters Skopje.

Amber Hope: German, Polish, Baltic (Estonia, Latvia, Lithuania) annual peacekeeping exercise. Amber Hope 01: Latvia. Amber Hope 99. Amber Hope 97.

Amber Sea: NATO ISO/PfP annual Baltic (Estonia, Latvia, Lithuania) naval exercise series focused on coastal and harbor defence. Amber Sea 03. Amber

Sea 02: Three Baltic navies exercised to counter enemy forces and terrorist groups in Paldiski Harbor, Estonia, completed 6 Oct 2002. Amber Sea 00: Latvia. Amber Sea 98: Poland. Amber Sea 97: Poland.

Amber Star: NATO operation to apprehend "persons indicted for war crimes" in the former Yugoslavia, 1995–2001. CTF Amber Star, headquartered at EUCOM in Stuttgart, Germany, conducted the operations. Participants included Joint Special Operations Command, the CIA and the intelligence services, and SOF components of the US, UK, Germany, Netherlands, and France. A US-only Green Light effort focused on Radovan Karadzic, the former Bosnian Serb political leader, collecting intelligence under Buckeye. *See also* Fervent Archer.

Amber Valley 97: Lithuania.

Ambient Breeze: Counter-biological-weapons bioaerosol detection system large aerosol wind tunnel — the Ambient Breeze Tunnel (ABT) first built at Battelle's facility in West Jefferson, OH. The ABT development effort began in the latter part of 2000, culminating in a first operational test of several biodetection systems in Apr 2001. A second ABT was built by Battelle at Dugway Proving Grounds, UT, in 2001.

Ambush: NORAD first word.

Ample: NATO logistics-related first word.

+ **Ample Gain:** Operational aircraft cross-servicing (ACS) missions where aircrew maintain their ACS proficiency by flying to bases in other nations, allowing technicians and support facilities to validate recovery of the aircraft, mission planning, and weapons and launching procedures.
+ **Ample Support:** Rear Support Command annual study period to develop Reception, Staging and Onward Movement doctrine and procedures. Ample Support 03: Armed Forces Recreation Centre in Garmisch, Germany, 6–11 Jul 2003. Ample Support 02: Armed Forces Recreational Center, Chiemsee, Germany, 20–24 May 2002.
+ **Ample Train:** Aircraft cross-servicing exercise. Participants include Belgium, Germany, Greece, Hungary, Italy, and Turkey. Ample Train 02: Aalborg, Denmark, 29 Apr–3 May 2002. Ample Train 01: Nea Anchialos air base, Greece, 2–6 Apr 2001. Ample Train 99 was canceled because of Kosovo operations. Ample Train 97: Torrejon AB, Spain, 12–16 May 1997.

Code Names

Anaconda: US-led coalition force operation to search the mountainous Shahi Khot region south of the city of Gardez in eastern Afghanistan for al Qaeda and Taliban fighters, capture them, and destroy their shelters, 1–18 Mar 2002. Participants included the US, Canada, and Australia. Maj. Gen. Buster Hagenbeck of the 10th Mountain Div was the commander. The 10th Div and the 101st Airborne Div, along with Afghan forces, were inserted into an area covering some 60–70 square miles. Rough terrain, an altitude of 8,000–12,000 feet, and a temperature in the evenings between 15 and 20 degrees F, made for tough operating conditions. US SOF and counterparts from several nations set up observation posts.

Resistance ceased after 11 days of heavy fighting. The coalition force met with determined resistance, and the enemy demonstrated that they were well organized and well supplied. Taliban and al Qaeda fighters were pushed out of their defensive positions, but US and Canadian withdrawal from the Shahi Khot region on 20 Mar allowed many to escape through the loosely guarded Pakistani border. Afghanistan contributed about half of the 2,000 troops that participated in Anaconda.

Anatolian Eagle: US–Israel–Turkey annual low-level flying exercise conducted from Konya AB, Turkey. Anatolian Eagle 01: The 22nd Fighter Sqn deployed to Konya.

Anchor: NORAD first word.

Anchory: NSA textual database search engine, one of four major NSA military databases. Access to this single-site-based database allows the analyst to search and retrieve the full text of SIGINT products and data from other selected Intelligence Community databases. The system is being replaced by Ocean Arium.

Angel: Code name for *Air Force One.*

Angry: NORAD first word.

ANNUALEX: US–Japanese annual large-scale maritime exercise that tests the ability of the Seventh Fleet and elements of the Japan Maritime Self-Defense Force (JMSDF) to conduct coordinated bilateral operations in the defense of Japan. ANNUALEX 15G: 2003. More than 7,500 US sailors participated in Annualex 15G from USS *Kittyhawk* (CV 63) and Battle Force Seventh Fleet. About 80 Japanese ships, 170 aircraft, and 25,000 Japanese SDF troops also participated. ANNUALEX 14G: 11–22 Nov 2002, including the USS *Kitty Hawk* (CV 63), USS *John S. McCain* (DDG 56), USS *Curtis Wilbur* (DDG 54), USS *O'Brien* (DD 975), USS *Gary* (FFG 51), USS *Paul F. Foster* (DD 964), USS *Chicago* (SSN 721), and USS *Louisville* (SSN 724). ANNUALEX 12G: 2000, including USS *Kitty Hawk* (CV 63), USS *Chancellorsville* (CG 62), USS *Cowpens* (CG 63), USS *Gary* (FFG 51), USS *Cushing* (DD 985), USS *John S. MaCain* (DDG 56), USS *Honolulu* (SSN 718), USNS *Rappahannok* (TAO 204), and USNS *Victorious* (T-AGOS 19). ANNUALEX 11G: Nov 1999, including the USS *Kitty Hawk* (CV 63) operating in the East China Sea, near Nansei Islands, and in the Western Pacific. ANNUALEX 99/Keen Sword 99: Yokosuka, Japan, and the USS *Kitty Hawk* (CV 63) (embarking at Yokusuka), Nov 1998. ANNUALEX-11G/Foal Eagle 99.

ANNULET: Cryptologic maintenance system training course taught at Goodfellow AFB, TX.

Anorak Express: NATO Cold War exercise series held in northern Norway.

Antelope: Missile reentry vehicle/penetration aid for Polaris and Poseidon SLBMs, 1980s.

Antemate: Air Force Big Safari–managed special access program.

Anthem/Antler: NORAD first words.

Anvil: Neural network program for three-dimensional automated target recognition on multi-spectral imagery (MASINT related?), 1990s.

Anvil Ghost: UK–Turkish large-scale land warfare exercise, 2000–2001.

Apex Effort: NATO nuclear-weapons-related exercise, 1999.

Apex Gold: Navy "special projects aircraft" enhancements to baseline P-3 intelligence collection capabilities used in OEF and for the war on terrorism. Funds for Apex Gold were included in the FY 2003 Defense Emergency Readiness Fund.

Apollo: 1. STRATCOM exercise series (formerly US Space Command series), including Apollo Endeavor, Apollo Fury, Apollo Force 03/Look, Apollo Guardian/Brave, Apollo Knight, Apollo Lens, and Apollo Look. Apollo CND was the first-ever global computer network defense (CND) exercise, Apr 2000. The exercise tested the requirement of UCP 99 assigning the CND mission to SPACECOM.

2. **Apollo (Operation Apollo):** Canadian contribution to the war on terrorism, Oct 2001–Oct 2003.

Apple Juice: Exercise term for simulated Air Defense Warning Red.

Appliqu: Army battlefield visualization system for enhanced situational awareness.

Apron/Aqua: NORAD first words.

Aquacade: Code word for Rhyolite SIGINT geostationary satellite after Rhyolite was compromised by Soviet spies. Aquacade was succeded by the Magnum/Orion series.

Aquatone: Development code name for the U-2. Renamed Chalice.

Aquila: Army early RPV development program that emerged from the initial DARPA–Army collaboration on Praerie. After the cost of the Aquila development program increased almost 10-fold, the army abandoned it in 1987.

Arabian Gauntlet: CENTCOM and Fifth Fleet mine clearance and sea lines of communications exercise (SLOCEX) series held in the Arabian Gulf. Participants include Bahrain, Belgium, France, Germany, Kuwait, the Netherlands, Oman, Pakistan, Qatar, Saudi Arabia, UAE, the UK, and the US. Arabian Gauntlet 05: 23 Mar–4 Apr 2005. Arabian Gauntlet 03: Bahrain. Arabian Gauntlet 01: Oman and Bahrain, Mar–Apr 2001. Arabian Gauntlet 00/Neon Falcon 00. Arabian Gauntlet 99.

Aragon Lightning: Army I Corps exercise series, Fort Lewis, WA. Aragon V, Mar 2002, and Aragon IV, Mar 2001.

Arcade: NATO Allied Command Europe Rapid Reaction Corps (ARRC) exercise series related to preparations for deployments. Includes Arcade Azimuth, Arcade Bugle I/II, Arcade Deployex 03, Arcade Holdfast, Arcade Seizure, and Arcade Warrior 02.

+ **Arcade Falcon:** ARRC warfighting command post exercise, Jun 2001.
+ **ARRCade Fusion:** ARRC annual warfighting computer-assisted exercise/command post exercise, Germany. The exercise practices the deployment of divisional HQ and corps troops into the field, followed by a warfighting phase in a regional conflict setting. ARRCade Fusion 05 (linked with Constant Harmony 04): Nov 2004 (FY05). Participants include Germany, Italy, Turkey, the UK, and the multinational engineer brigade. ARRcade Fusion 03: Sennelager Training

Centre, near Paderborn, Germany, 3–14 Nov 2003. ARRCade Fusion 02. ARRCade Fusion 01: Oct 2001, including the 1st Armored Div. ARRCade Fusion 00: Germany, 13–26 Oct 2000. The scenario placed ARRC as the land component command of a high-intensity conflict. Involved 11 nations. ARRCade Fusion 99 canceled because of Kosovo operations. ARRCade Fusion 98: Included Greece.

+ **Arcade Globe 02:** ARRC exercise, Germany, Jul 2002, canceled by HQ ARRC.

+ **Arcade Guard:** ARRC validation exercises, Germany. Arcade Guard 03. Arcade Guard 02: Feb–Mar 2002. HQ ARRC achieved Supreme Headquarters Allied Powers Europe accreditation as a result of this exercise. Arcade Guard 01: 18–30 Mar 2001. UK forces canceled participation because of foot-and-mouth disease restrictions. Arcade Guard 99 was canceled because of Kosovo operations. Arcade Guard 95: Scenario involved a possible UN withdrawal from the former Yugoslavia, ended 28 Apr 1995. Arcade Guard 94: Macedonia?, Mar 1994.

Arch Angel 95: Military–civilian disaster exercise, St. Louis, MO, 1995.

Archlane: Reported CIA compartmented communications channel, 1990s.

Archway Express 85: Reagan-era exercise with NSC involvement, 1985.

Arctic Breeze 96: 2nd Bn, 1st SFG exercise in AK testing the newly adopted Lightweight Environmental Protection (LEP) suite, SOCOM's future uniform using state-of-the-art fabrics in a SOF configuration.

Arctic Express 94: NATO exercise, Andoya AB and Troms in northern Norway, 27 Feb–Mar 1994. Arctic Express was the first test of the US contribution to the NATO Composite Force (NCF), reinforcing northern Norway.

Arctic SAREX (Search and Rescue Exercise): Alaskan Command SAREX series initiated in 1993 with Russia and Canada. The exercise rotates from Alaska to Canada to Russia. Primary participants are the HH-60s and HC-130s of the 210th Rescue Sqn (Alaska ANG).

+ **Arctic SAREX 00:** Leningrad military district Levashovo airfield, Lake Khepoyarve, and Kasimovo airfield, Russia, 15–19 Aug 2000. The forces exercised crash site management, medical procedures, and patient handling.

+ **Arctic SAREX 96:** Khabarovsk airfield and Petropavlovskoye Lake, approximately 16 miles northeast of Khabarovsk, Russia, Sep 1996. The exercise included Canadian and US HC-130s flying to the airfield and involved the simulated crash of a Russian commercial passenger aircraft in a remote Arctic location.

Ardent: NATO first word, including Ardent Leader 03 and Ardent Response 03.

+ **Ardent Ground:** Allied Command Europe (ACE) Mobile Force (Land) annual live-fire rapid reaction exercise. Participants include Belgium, Canada, the Czech Republic, Germany, Greece, Hungary, Italy, the Netherlands, Norway, Poland, Spain, Turkey, the UK, and the US. Ardent Ground 03. Ardent Ground 02: northern Germany, 12–24 May 2002. The UK withdrew from the exercise. Ardent Ground 01: Scheduled for Powidz AB, Poland, 8–15 May 2001. The exercise was canceled by the host nation. Ardent Ground 00: Varpalota training area, Hungary, 29 Apr–13 May 2000. Ardent Ground 99: Canceled because of Kosovo operations, May 1999. Ardent Ground 98: Scotland, UK. Ardent Ground 97: Northwest Turkey, 23 Apr–19 May 1997. Ardent Ground 92/Allegiance Exchange: Jun 1992.

+ **Ardent Shield:** Theater Missile Defense exercise series.

Ardent Sentry: NORTHCOM high level homeland security field training exercise established in 2004, and merged with TOPOFF in odd numbered years (Apr 2005). For Ardent Sentry 06, planned for Apr/May 2006, the Department of Homeland Security is also planning a national level command post exercise.

Arena: Object-based modeling and simulation environment for performing information warfare analyses, evaluations, and decision making. Used by the Joint Information Operations Center to create country studies of electronic infrastructure characteristics, targeting analyses, operational information warfare plans, and support for exercises and real-world operations.

ARGEX (Blue/Green Workups): Seventh Fleet annual Marine Corps special operations capble (SOC) certification series, held every other year in conjunction with Blue/Green (BG) workups. BG/ARGEX 03: Subic Bay, Philippines, Sep 2003, including USS *Essex* (LHD 2) ARG and 31st MEU. ARGEX/SOCEX 02: Sep 2002, USS *Essex* (LHD 2) and 31st MEU. ARGEX 01: Okinawa, Japan, 21–27 Mar 2001, USS *Germantown* (LSD 42).

Argon: Former KH-5 imagery satellite.

Argonaut 01/Saif Sareea II: UK–Oman amphibious exercise, Aug–Nov 2001. The exercise provided cover for deployment of forces in support of OEF.

Argus: 1. SIGINT satellite that was to have replaced Rhyolite, canceled in the 1970s.

2. **ARGUS** (Advanced Remote Ground Unattended System): Ground-emplaced sensors providing seismic and acoustic detection of moving targets, a key element of the MASINT architecture. The sensors are delivered by F-16 aircraft and penetrate the ground before beginning operations.

3. **Argus:** National Target Signature Data System, the DOD-wide MASINT distributed data system.

4. **Argus:** C-135E optical imaging aircraft of 452nd Flight Test Sqn (NC-135?).

Arid Farmer: Deployments to Sudan as part of the US reaction to Libyan aggression in Chad, 2–23 Aug 1983. The operation included an RC-135, two KC-10s, two E-3A AWACS aircraft, and seven F-15 fighters to Sudan.

ARIES II (Airborne Reconnaissance Integrated Electronic System II): Navy EP-3E over-the-horizon SIGINT collection system consisting of synthetic aperture radar (ISAR), COMINT, and ELINT collectors. It is designed to provide intelligence, targeting, and BDA, especially in areas beyond the range of carrier-based assets. The 11 aircraft in the navy's inventory are based on the Orion P-3 airframe. There are 24 seating positions, of which 19 are crew stations. The ARIES II is capable of 12-plus-hour endurance and a 3,000-plus-nautical-mile range.

Armistad 99-01: SOUTHCOM exercise, 24 Apr–1 May 1999. The 71st Rescue Sqn deployed one aircraft and several personnel to Le Liberador AB, Venezuela.

Artemis: Naval Sea Systems Command chemical standoff detection system; formerly Joint Service Warning and Identification LIDAR (Light Detection and Ranging) Detector.

Artful Image: Germany-based exercise series. The UK canceled participation in the 12–16 Mar 2001 exercise because of foot-and-mouth disease restrictions.

Artful Issue: NATO Multi-National Div interoperability exercise. Artful Issue 02: Germany, Oct 2002. The UK withdrew from participation. Artful Issue 01: Netherlands, Sep 2001. Involved 16 Air Assault Bde, UK.

Artificer (UK Atomic Artificer): UK Secret or Top Secret information concerning hardness of Polaris/Trident missile systems.

Artisan: Canadian involvement in the Rinas Airfield Rehabilitation Project in Tirana, Albania.

ASCIET (All Service Combat Identification Evaluation Team): JFCOM exercise series to study the issue of combat ID and "friendly fire" (fratricide), including the UK. ASCIET 04. ASCIET 00: Nellis AFB, NV. ASCIET 95: Gulf of Mexico near Gulfport, MS, 4–15 Sep 1995.

Ashar Alo ("Light of Hope"): US–Bangladesh command post exercise on humanitarian assistance and disaster relief operations, Bangladesh, Oct 2002.

Aspiring Falcon: French peacekeeping operations in Abidjan, Côte d'Ivoire, 19 Nov 2002–.

Assets: Army SIGINT satellite-related system, Bad Aibling, Germany.

Assured: EUCOM first word.

+ **Assured Lift:** JTF operations in support of moving Economic Community of West African States Cease-Fire Monitoring Group (ECOMOG) troops into Liberia, 4 Feb–8 Mar 1997, from Abidjan, Côte d'Ivoire.

+ **Assured Response:** JTF in support of noncombatant evacuation operation from Monrovia, Liberia, 8 Apr–12 Aug 1996. SOCEUR evacuated 400 US citizens and 1,700 foreigners 9–20 Apr, using an intermediate staging base at Freetown, Sierra Leone, and a safe haven in Dakar, Senegal. The operation was supported by the USS *Guam* (LPH 9); 3rd Bn, 325th Airborne Infantry; 1st Bn, 10th SFG; 3rd Bn, 160th SOAR; and SETAF. 3/160th SOAR deployed four MH-47Ds to Freetown, Sierra Leone, Africa. An air force MC-130P provided air refueling for helicopters shuttling evacuees. The 16th SOS (AC-130) deployed to Dakar in support of the operation.

Asterix: UK–French exercise series. Asterix 4/02 was canceled in Oct 2002 because of a UK firefighters strike. Asterix Sapper 00 was canceled by France.

Astonish: Army intelligence system, Bad Aibling, Germany.

Athena: 1. The Defense Counter-Intelligence Information System (DCIIS), a national counter-intelligence automated database.

2. **Athena:** Active exercise series.

3. **Athena:** Counter-proliferation intelligence "information space" under development to support mission planning and operations. *See also* Dragon Fury.

4. **Athena:** AGEX II Los Alamos project.

5. **Athena (Operation Athena):** Canadian contribution to the ISAF in Afghanistan, complementing forces still deployed in support of Operation Apollo.

Atlantic Drive: UK exercise on Ascension Island, 2001.

Atlantic Resolve: EUCOM exercise, formerly called REFORGER (Return of Forces to Germany), the first global distributed training exercise. Atlantic Resolve 96. Atlantic Resolve 94: Grafenwohr/Hohenfels, Germany, Nov–Dec 1994. The first Advanced Warfighting Experiment was Atlantic Resolve 94. The EUCOM Joint Forces Air Component Commander concept was utilized for the first time during Atlantic Resolve, and the exercise provided insights about linking disparate virtual and live simulations in a synthetic theater of war.

Atlantic Thunder 03: Army reserve multi-modal transportation exercise, 06–20 Jun 2003.

Atlantis (Project Atlantis): Ocean surveillance.

Atlas: EUCOM US–Tunisian first word.

+ **Atlas Drop:** Annual live-fire ground and air exercise at the Cap Serrat training area. The series provides training for SETAF airborne forces that have a wartime and contingency mission in Africa. Atlas Drop 04 was canceled. Atlas Drop 03. Atlas Drop 02: 14–25 Jan 2002. Atlas Drop/ MEDLITE 01: Sidi Ahmed, Tunisia, 23 Oct–6 Nov 2001. Atlas Drop 00: Sep 2000, 26th MEU (SOC). Atlas Drop 98: Oct 1998. The exercise was designed to practice infiltration to seize an airfield, test desert survival, and provide jump training and exercise company maneuvers with the Tunisian airborne forces. The Georgia ARNG provided a long-range surveillance detachment in support of this exercise. Atlas Drop 97.

+ **Atlas Eagle 03:** Classified exercise.

+ **Atlas Gate:** Classified USAFE exercise. Atlas Gate 01. Atlas Gate 99.

+ **Atlas Hinge:** Naval field training exercise. Atlas Hinge 01: Included an amphibious landing by US Marines. Atlas Hinge 00: Cap Serat, Tunisia, Jul 2000, 26th MEU. Atlas Hinge 98: 22nd MEU. Atlas Hinge 97. Atlas Hinge 96: SEAL Team 8, Tunisian combat swimmers, and US Marine force reconnaissance elements. The USS *Firebolt* (PC 10) conducted insert and extraction operations for reconnaissance parties prior to an amphibious landing by troops from the USS *Saipan* (LHA 2) ARG. Atlas Hinge 95.

Atlas Response: EUCOM JTF Atlas Response relief effort following torrential rains and flooding in southern Mozambique and South Africa, 6 Mar–16 Apr 2000. USAFE personnel established airfield operations at Hoedspruit, South Africa, and Maputo and Beira, Mozambique. C-17s from Ramstein AB, Germany, picked up cargo from a US Agency for International Development facility in Pisa, Italy. US aircraft flew 29 airlift missions to transport 720 passengers and 910 short tons of cargo.

Atlas Shield: Classified special operation, 2003–2004.

Atomic Music Principle: UK nuclear information compartment used for sharing information with the US; goes back at least to the 1980s.

Attain Document: European operation, 1980s.

Auburn Endeavor: Joint Interagency TF and EUCOM operation to evacuate highly enriched uranium from a reactor in Tblisi, Georgia, to a disposal site in Scotland, UK, 25 Mar–30 Apr 1998.

Aurora: 1. Naval EW, ELINT, and COMINT platform, possibly cooperative with Canadian CP-140?.
   2. **Aurora:** Airborne hyperspectral sensor modified for placement on the Predator UAV.

Aurora 04: US–UK–Australian interoperability exercise that coincides with Joint Warfighter Interoperability Demonstration 04.

Aurora Express: NATO exercise involving deployments to eastern Turkey.

Ausina 97-1: Australian–Indonesian maritime passage exercise, Apr 1997.

Austere Challenge 04: USAFE Joint Forces Air Component Commander war planning computer-assisted exercise, Ramstein AB and the Warrior Preparation Center, Germany, 14–28 Apr 2004. The 16th Air Force–led exercise practiced a classified scenario for future warfare including an unnamed country, presumed to be Iran. Formerly called Urgent Victory.

Autumn Eagle 92: Emergency deployment readiness exercise, 101st Airborne Div.

Autumn Return: Security and evacuation operations in Côte d'Ivoire to prevent injury or loss of life to Americans and designated third-country nationals, 24 Sep–9 Oct 2002.

Autumn Shelter: Noncombatant evacuation operation (NEO), Democratic Republic of Congo/Gabon, Aug 1998. The operation included the USS *Saipan* (LHA 2) Amphibious Ready Group, 22nd MEU, SOF, and air force units, all on standby. The NEO was ultimately canceled.

Avalanche: 1. Series of OEF operations along the Afghanistan–Pakistan border, Dec 2003.
2. **Avalanche:** Army intelligence system, Bad Aibling, Germany.

Avid Recovery: US–UK explosive ordnance disposal support to Nigeria after an accident in Lagos, at the Ikeja Cantonment Area, 27 Jan 2902.

Avid Response: Earthquake relief operation in western Turkey, 20 Aug–12 Sep 1999. 26th MEU (SOC) and the USS *Kearsarge* (LHD 3).

AWI (Asymmetric Warfare Initiative): Interagency Technical Support Working Group exercise series led by the navy's Center for Asymmetric Warfare and devoted to countering an asymmetric homeland security threat in a maritime environment. Participants include the navy, Coast Guard, FBI, and local law enforcement. AWI-04 Tabletop Exercise, 12–16 Jan 2004. AWI-03: Nov 2003.

Axolotl: Australian–Singapore mine warfare diving exercise. Mar 1998, Mar 1997.

Aztec Silence: Classified special operation as part of the war on terrorism, 2003–present.

Azure Haze: EUCOM chemical and biological awareness training series. Azure Haze 99: Marine Corps. Azure Haze 97: Nov 1997.

– B –

Babylon: DARPA Terrorism Information Awareness project to develop rapid, two-way, natural language speech translation interfaces for use by soldiers in the field for force protection, refugee processing, and medical triage. The PDA-sized Babylon devices initially provided speech translation in Arabic, Chinese (Mandarin), Dari, and Pashto.

Bachelor/Back: PACOM first words.

Backhome: Army intelligence system, Bad Aibling, Germany.

Bacon/Badge: PACOM first words.

Badge Finder/Badge Keeper: Unknown military intelligence system or program.

Badger: Pacific Fleet first word.

Bag: PACOM first word.

Baker: US Army Pacific JCET counter-narcotics exercise series.

+ **Baker Blade:** Classified JCET series.
+ **Baker Mint:** US–Malaysian counter-narcotics JCET series. In Aug 1997, JIATF West conducted the first Baker Mint exercise with Malaysia. Forces provided combat lifesaving training to Malaysian counter-narcotics personnel. Baker Mint 99-1: Intelligence Preparation of the Battlefield and photographic surveillance technique training.
+ **Baker Mint Lens 99:** US–Malaysian program to develop a long-range training plan for Malaysian counter-narcotics law enforcement agencies.
+ **Baker Mondial V:** US Army Pacific medical team in Mongolia, 1997.
+ **Baker Mongoose II:** Mongolia deployment, May 1995. US Army Pacific and 176th Group, Alaska ANG mission — only the second time that US military members, other than embassy staff, visited the nation. The AK ANG crew flew a C-130 to Ulaanbaatar to transport a team from the 23rd Engineer Bde, Fort Richardson, AK. The 25-person army team of civil engineers remained in Mongolia for several months to expand and upgrade a schoolhouse in Ulaanbaatar.
+ **Baker Piston Lens 2000:** Program to develop a long-range training plan for Philippines counter-narcotics law enforcement agencies.
+ **Baker Tepid:** US–Thai JCET series. As of 1998, JIATF West was conducting eight Baker Tepid exercises annually in Thailand. The exercises provided training to Thai counter-narcotics forces in small-unit tactics, leadership, marksmanship, jungle navigation, and combat lifesaving.
+ **Baker Torch:** US–Thai JCET training series to combat cross-border drug trafficking, conducted by the 1st SFG, and initiated in 1998. Baker Torch 01: Exercise with Thai TF 399 at Chiang Mai and Mae Hong Son, coordinated with Cobra Gold 01, Apr 2001. Baker Torch 00: Exercise to improve host nation counter-narcotics interdiction capabilities. Baker Torch 99: Exercise in leadership and small-unit tactics.
+ **Baker Torch Lens:** US–Thai JCET series to provide officers with no navy diving experience the training necessary to manage and perform operational diving duties.

Balance: PACOM and CENTCOM JCET events that began in 1992.

+ **Balance Bars:** Classified series. Balance Bars 04, Balance Bars 03, Balance Bars 02.

+ **Balance Buffalo:** US–Bangladesh JCET SOF series, 13 Jul–15 Aug 2002, including disaster assistance response training conducted in Dhaka 20 Jul–1 Aug under the Bangladesh air force.

+ **Balance Iron:** US–Indonesian JCET series with Indonesian Kopassus (army special forces), Paskasau (air force special forces), and Pussenif (Infantry Training Center). Balance Iron 98-7: 1st Bn, 1st SFG conducted combat-sapper training (demolition safety, firing systems, calculation, placement, mine warfare, obstacle breaching, et cetera). Balance Iron 98-3: 17–21 Nov 1997, 1st Bn, 1st SFG. Balance Iron 98-2: 353rd SOG, 6th SOS with Paskasau and regular Indonesian army in foreign internal defense, ground air communications, outdoor survival, movement to contact, ambush, raids, fire support planning, area/zone reconnaissance. Balance Iron 98-1: 20 Oct–15 Nov 1997. Kodam Jaya (Jakarta Area Military Command), Pussenif MOUT training. Balance Iron 97-6A: 15 May–27 Jun 1997. Kopassus Group 1 special reconnaissance training. Balance Iron 97-6: 12 May–13 Jun 1997. Kopassus, Kostrad (army strategic command) special reconnaissance training. Balance Iron 97-5: 25 Jul–25 Aug 1997. Balance Iron 97-4: 2–21 Sep 1997, air force Kopaskasau special forces. Balance Iron 97-3: 23 Feb–28 Mar 1997. Kopassus Group 2 mortar training. Balance Iron 97-2: 6 Jan–15 Feb 1997. Kopassus military free-fall training. Balance Iron 97-1A: 4–20 Nov 1997. 3rd Bn, 1st SFG and Kopassus special reconnaissance training. Balance Iron 97-1: 1–18 Dec 1996. Kopassus, Kodam Jaya special operations and psychological operations training. Balance Iron 96-6: 8 Aug–1 Sep 1996. Kopassus special reconnaissance training. Balance Iron 96-5: 8 Aug–1 Sep 1996. Kopassus Group 5. Balance Iron 96-4: 5–19 Jul 1996. Pussenif marksmanship and demolition. Balance Iron 96-3: 4 Apr–15 May 1996. Kopassus, Kostrad, Penerbad (army aviation squadron), and Pussenif air assault leaders course. Balance Iron 96-2B: 11 Mar–5 Apr 1996. Pussenif recondo instructor training. Balance Iron 96-2A: 1 Jan–24 Feb 1996. Pussenif mortar training. Balance Iron 96-1: 5–22 Oct 1995. Kopassus, Pussenif peacekeeping operations. Balance Iron 95-5: 11–23 Sep 1995. Kopassus peacekeeping operations. Balance Iron 95-2: 1-30 Jun 1995. Kopassus Groups 1, 2, and 3 maritime operations. Balance Iron 95-1A: 3–30 Aug 1995.

Kopassus, Paspampres (Presidential Security Guards) EOD support for VIP protective operations. Balance Iron 95-1: 17 Jan–19 Feb 1995. Kopassus and air force military free-fall and advanced sniper techniques. Balance Iron 94-3: 10 Jun–1 Jul 1994. Kopassus, air force SOF. Balance Iron 94-2: 25 Apr–14 May 1994. Kopassus, Penerbad (army aviation). Balance Iron 94-1: 7 Jan–20 Feb 1994. Kopassus Groups 1, 2, and 3, Paspampres presidential security guards close-quarters combat and marksmanship. Balance Iron 93-2: 24 Aug–22 Sep 1993. Kopassus, 17th and 315th air force air operations and demolitions. Balance Iron 93-1: 26 Jun–3 Aug 1993. Kostrad, Kopassus, and Pusdikif (Infantry Training Center) infantry and sniper training.

+ **Balance Iroquois (Vajra Prahar):** US–Indian JCET series. Balance Iroquois 03-2: Guam, Jun 2003. Balance Iroquois 03-1: Silchar airfield and the Indian Counter-Insurgency Jungle Warfare School in Mizoram, 10–26 Apr 2003. Three-week counter-terrorism exercise held in northeastern India involving US and Indian SOF. Balance Iroquois officially ended with a mass airborne drop from An-32s, using Indian-army-supplied parachutes. Balance Iroquois 02-2/Geronimo Thrust: Alaska, Sep 2002. Balance Iroquois 02-1: SOF exercise in Agra, India, commencing 16 May 2002. The largest-ever airborne exercise between the US and India, itncluded US 2nd Bn, 1st SFG, and air force MC-130 of the 353rd SOW, and the 4 Para Bn of 50 Independent Para Bde of the Indian army.

+ **Balance Kayak:** US–Kazakhstan JCET series. Balance Kayak 00: 5th SFG deployment to Alamaty, Kazakhstan. Balance Kayak 98-1: Kazakhstan, 1–10 Aug 1998.

+ **Balance Knife:** Classified US–South Korean JCET series, including Balance Knife 04 and Balance Knifc 03.

+ **Balance Knight:** Classified JCET series. Balance Knight 04 and Balance Knight 03.

+ **Balance Magic:** US–Mongolian JCET series. The first JCET event in 1996 focused on training in humanitarian assistance/disaster relief operations, as did the 1997 event, which added medical training. Balance Magic 99-1, conducted in Feb 1999, involved medical cross-training and included training in search and rescue, survival, and aerial resupply. Balance Magic 98-1 involved medical cross-training and additional training in Pathfinder and aerial delivery operations.

+ **Balance Mint:** US–Malaysian JCET series. Balance Mint 03.

+ **Balance Passion:** US–Papua New Guinea JCET series.

+ **Balance Piston:** US–Philippine JCET series involving the Philippine Army Special Operations Command (PASOCOM) and Army Special Operations Command 1st SFG. The monthlong training events specialize in small-unit tactics. Balance Piston 03-5: Clark AB, Feb 2003. 353rd SOG, 320th STS, 1st Bn, 1st SFG, and E Co, 160th SOAR. Balance Piston 99-3: Fort Magsaysay, Philippines, Apr–May 1999. 1st Bn, 1st SFG.

+ **Balance Style:** US–Sri Lankan JCET series initiated in 1994. US and Sri Lankan forces participated in nine JCET exercises 1994–1999. During this time, some 115 US military personnel participated in JCET programs, training with about 700 personnel from the Sri Lankan armed forces. Sri Lankan units have included the army's Special Forces Bde, the Commando Bde, and the Air Mobile Bde. The navy's Special Boat Sqn (roughly equivalent to the US Navy SEALs) and Fast Attack Craft Crews have also participated in JCETs, as have helicopter pilots from the air force. *See also* Flash Style.

+ **Balance Tandem:** US–Thai? JCET series. Balance Tandem 04 and Balance Tandem 03.

+ **Balance Torch:** US–Thai JCET series. Balance Torch 96 involved SOCPAC, the 1st Bn, 19th SFG, and Utah ARNG, with 349th Air Mobility Wing involvement. Balance Torch 94: 349th Air Mobility Wing involvement.

+ **Balance Ultra:** US–Uzbek JCET series. Balance Ultra 04 and Balance Ultra 03. Began with Balance Ultra 96 in the Ferganskaya Valley. Uzbek armed forces participants were one platoon of a separate airborne battalion. The US contingent consisted of 13 soldiers. American instructors conducted training for tactical units on combat first aid and airborne training, including all elements of training for jumping with a parachute and an actual parachute jump. A tactical exercise with an airborne platoon made a combat jump under tactical conditions. The mission of the jumpers was to destroy an enemy communications hub and ammunition storage site. The final mission was to seize a mountain pass and hold it until the arrival of the main force. Participants included France, Russia, and Turkey.

+ **Balance Umbra:** US–Uzbek JCET series. Balance Umbra 04 and Balance Umbra 03. Balance Umbra 00: Chirchik, Uzbekistan, 4–6 Apr 2000.

+ **Balance Umpire:** US–Uzbek JCET series. Balance Umpire 04 and Balance Umpire 03.

Code Names

+ **Balance Unity:** US–Uzbek JCET series. Balance Unity 03/04 and Balance Unity 02.
+ **Balance Zhardem:** Classified JCET series.

Bale: PACOM first word.

Balikatan (Shoulder to Shoulder): US–Philippine annual exercise held in the Philippines, incorporating real-world counter-terrorism operations since 9/11. *Balikatan* refers to the operations and exercises with Philippine armed forces and national police but is also generally applied to rotations of US SOF into the Philippines. Through Balikatan 02 and 03, the Armed Forces of the Philippines (AFP) and US practiced interoperability in combating terrorism. The Defense Department concept for Balikatan 03-1 envisioned US combat support for an operation on Jolo Island led by the AFP, including Intelligence, Surveillance and Reconnaissance support; humanitarian and civic action projects; and US advisory teams operating at the battalion level. In Jun 2003, due to concerns of the Philippine government about constitutional obstacles to a US combat support role in this AFP-led mission, the plans were put on indefinite hold. Mindanao Balikatan 02-1 describes US–Philippine military operations against Abu Sayyaf, held on Basilan Island. Balikatan 00, 31 Jan–3 Mar 2000, was the first time since 1995 that the two countries participated in a large-scale military endeavor.

Balkan Calm: DOS-led Kosovo Diplomatic Observer Mission to provide US presence with observer teams, Jul 1998.

Ballistic: Pacific Fleet first word.

Balm: PACOM first word.

BALTEX (Baltimore Exercise): First responder and Law Enforcement Incident Management WMD exercise series. BALTEX XI: Poly/Western complex, Baltimore, MD, 23 Aug 2000. BALTEX X: Holiday Inn, Baltimore West, MD, 16 Mar 2000. BALTEX IX: Columbia, MD, 17 Nov 1999. BALTEX VIII: Harbor Hospital, Baltimore, MD, 29 Oct 1999. BALTEX VII: Aberdeen Proving Ground, MD, 18–19 May 1999. BALTEX VI: Essex Community College, MD, 20–21 Jan 1999. BALTEX V: Baltimore City Fire Academy, MD, 9–10 Sep 1998. BALTEX IV: Columbia, MD, 2–3 Jun 1998. BALTEX III: Rowing Club, Baltimore, MD, 24–25 Feb 1998. BALTEX II: Aberdeen Proving Ground, MD, 18–19 Nov 1997. BALTEX I: Aberdeen Proving Ground, MD, 9–10 Sep 1997.

Baltic: NATO PfP exercise series held in the Baltic states of Estonia, Latvia, and Lithuania.

+ **Baltic Castle 97.**
+ **Baltic Challenge:** Multinational Baltic Bn (BALTBAT) series, including Finland. Now called Partner Challenge. Baltic Challenge 98: Lithuania, 10–25 Jul 1998. Baltic Challenge 97: Estonia. Baltic Challenge 96: Latvia, summer 1996. Baltic Challenge 96 was the first of the annual ISO/PfP exercise to be conducted in the three Baltic states.
+ **Baltic Circle 96:** Slagelse, Denmark, 30 Sep–11 Oct 1996.
+ **Baltic Cooperation 00:** ISO/PfP exercise, Aug 2000.
+ **Baltic Eagle:** Baltic Eagle 02. Baltic Eagle 00: Adazi, Latvia, 9–20 Oct 2000. Participants from the Baltics, Denmark, Finland, Netherlands, Norway, Sweden, the UK, and the US.
+ **Baltic Endeavor:** Mine warfare exercise including Denmark, Germany, Poland, and Sweden.
+ **Baltic Eye:** Search and rescue (SAR) exercise and bilateral UK cooperation with Swedish SAR agencies. Baltic Eye/Lone Shark 01: Sweden, 8–19 May 2001.
+ **Baltic Game 02.**
+ **Baltic Hope:** Baltic ISO/PfP annual exercise. Baltic Hope 00: Adazi military range, Latvia, 7–13 Aug 2000. Baltic Hope 99: Lithuania, Jul–Aug 1999. Baltic Hope 98: Estonia. Baltic Hope 97: Latvia.
+ **Baltic Swift:** Biennial symposium and/or live exercise dealing with the employment of smaller-sized surface naval combatants, including Germany and Poland. Baltic Swift 02. Baltic Swift 00.
+ **Baltic Trainer 97:** Rukla training grounds, central Lithuania, Oct 1997.
+ **Baltic Trial:** Multi-national Baltic Bn (BALTBAT) graduation training series, held by the Command of the Eastern District of the Danish Army. Baltic Trial II (1997) and I.
+ **Baltic Triangle:** Multi-national Baltic Bn (BALTBAT) training exercise held by the Command of the Eastern District of the Danish Army, including Germany and Poland. Baltic Triangle 00: Aug 2000. Baltic Triangle 97.
+ **Baltic Venture:** Small-unit combat tactics exercise series begun in 1995. Baltic Venture 98: Latvia, mid-Jan 1998. Co A, 2nd Bn, 10th SFG, Fort Carson, CO, participated with approximately 70 soldiers of Estonia, Latvia, and Lithuania. Baltic Venture 97: Lithuania.

Baltlink (Baltic Link) 00: NATO ISO/PfP peacekeeping exercise, held in the airspace south of Gotland, Sweden, 14–25 Aug 2000. The exercise was conducted by Swedish Air Force Command. Participants included Austria, Denmark, Estonia, Finland, Germany, Latvia, Lithuania, Norway, Poland, Russia, and the UK.

Baltops: Naval Forces Europe–led annual invitational two-phase major Baltic Sea exercise to enhance interoperability with Northern European allies. Exercise activity includes anti-submarine-warfare techniques, ship boarding, maritime interdiction operations, cross-decking and replenishment-at-sea, fast patrol boat defense, and anti-air-defense methods. Baltops 04 was the 31st annual exercise. Participants include Denmark, Estonia, Finland, France, Germany, Latvia, Lithuania, Netherlands, Poland, Russia, Sweden, the UK, and the US. Baltops 05: Jun 2005. Baltops 04: 5–19 Jun 2004. Baltops 03/02. Baltops 01: 5–15 Jun 2001. Baltops 00: Sweden and Kiel Germany, 2–17 Jun 2000. The most open and encompassing Baltops exercise ever, including the largest visit of warships to Stockholm. Baltops 99: 7–18 Jun 1999. Baltops 98: 1 May–30 Jun 1998. Baltops 97: Gdynia, Poland, and Kiel, Germany, 16–27 Jun 1997. A 9th BS/7th BW and 37th BS/28th BW B-1B detachment from RAF Fairford, UK, participated. Baltops 96: Jun 1996. A 37th BS/28th BW B-1B and 96th BS/2nd BW B-52 detachment from RAF Fairford, UK, participated. Baltops 95. Baltops 93.

Bamboo: Air force Berlin-related first word, 1980s.

Banjo/Banner/Banyan: PACOM first words.

Baracuda: 1. Navy submarine-based ESM system.
 2. (**Operation Baracuda**): Coast Guard operation, 22–26 Apr 1991.

Barents Peace 99: NATO PfP exercise in Norway with Swedish participation, 7–18 Jun 1999.

Barnacle: Submarine clandestine reconnaissance program that replaced Holystone.

Barracuda: UK maritime SIGINT/ESM equipment used in OEF/OIF. *See also* Baracuda.

Bartizan Hinge: NATO North Sea maritime exercise involving the Netherlands, UK, and US. Bartizan Hinge 1999: US P-3s. Bartizan Hinge 97: 15–26 Sep 1997.

Basic: PACOM first word.

Bass Rock: UK–Canada exercise. Bass Rock 02 was canceled by Canada.

Bastion: Pacific Fleet first word.

+ **Bastion Bridge:** Marine Corps classified exercise, 1990s.

Baton: PACOM first word.

Batrack: EP-3 configuration replaced by ARIES II.

Battery: US–Taiwanese first word.

Battle Griffin: Norwegian biennial amphibious exercise practicing reception, staging, and operations of a MAGTF in defense of northern Norway, including the Netherlands, UK, and US. Battle Griffin 99: Vaernes Airfield, Norway. Battle Griffin 96: 12 Feb–22 Mar 1996.

BattleScape: Commercial software program used to create 2-D and 3-D views using digital maps, imagery, and elevation data. BattleScape is used in the National Military Command and Control Center, at the Joint Warfare Analysis Center, and was employed by CENTAF in the CAOC in OEF and OIF.

Bayonet Lightning: Army 173rd Airborne Bde and TF Ironhorse operation in Kirkuk, Iraq, completed on 3 Dec 2003.

Beach: Pacific Fleet first word.

+ **Beach Guard 84-2:** Reagan-era exercise with NSC involvement, 15–16 Jul 1984.
+ **Beach Crest:** Marine Corps air–ground exercise conducted in Okinawa, Japan. Beach Crest 98: Dec 98. Beach Crest 95. Beach Crest 94: USS *Constellation* (CV-64).

Beachcomber: Australian domestic land surveillance and the collection of military geographic information.

Beacon Flash: US–Oman dissimilar air combat training exercise going back to the 1970s. Beacon Flash 01: USS *Harry S. Truman* (CVN 75). Beacon Flash 97: USS *John F. Kennedy* (CV 67). Beacon Flash 95: USS *Constellation* (CV 64). Beacon Flash 91.

Beacon Sword: Seventh Fleet exercise.

Bead Crystal: Former Third Fleet command and control exercise, held in the Aleutian Islands.

Beady Eye: UK land-based SIGINT/ESM equipment used in OEF/OIF.

Beamformer: Compass Bright Beamforming Receiver Architecture classified project, 2003–2005.

Bean: Pacific Fleet first word.

Bear: Pacific Fleet first word.

   + **Bear Hunt:** III Marine Expeditionary Force (MEF) exercise. Bear Hunt 88. Bear Hunt 84.

Beard/Bearer/Bearing: Pacific Fleet first words.

Beartrap: Navy receiver and record laboratory, Patuxent River, MD, used to support the development, test, and evaluation of advanced air anti-submarine-warfare sonobuoy receivers and acoustic tape recording systems for P-3s and other maritime surveillance aircraft.

Beauty/Beaver: Pacific Fleet first words.

Becker Serum VII: US–Sri Lankan medical and humanitarian mission/exercise, 10–22 Aug 1997.

Bed/Beef/Beggar/Begonia/Behavior: Pacific Fleet first words.

BEELINE: Air force nickname for mandated report of any incident or event where headquarters, Department of the Air Force–level interest is indicated but not requiring a JCS Pinnacle-level OPREP-3 report.

Beige: Pacific Fleet first word.

Bel Isi II: Peace Monitoring Group activities in Bougainville, with Australia, Fiji, New Zealand, and Vanuatu.

Belfry: Pacific Fleet first word.

Bell: Pacific Fleet first word.

   + **Bell Buoy:** Naval control of shipping exercise series generally held in the Pacific and Indian Ocean regions. Participants include Australia, Canada, Chile, France, New Zealand, Panama, Singapore, South Korea, the UK, and the US. Bell Buoy 03: May–Jun 2003. Bell Buoy 01: Valparaiso, Chile, and Panama, 23 Apr–4 May 2001. Bell Buoy 00: Australia. Bell Buoy 99: Arabian Gulf, May 1999. Exercise participants established a plot of merchant shipping in the Arabian Gulf.

Participants included Bahrain, Kuwait, and the UAE. Bell Buoy 98: May 1998. Bell Buoy 97: Canada, Apr 1997.

+ **Bell Orca:** Navy and Marine Corps EOD and mine counter-measures exercise.

+ **Bell Thunder:** Navy and Marine Corps EOD exercise utilizing marine mammals in mine detection and since 9/11, with EOD mobile units to detect and track subsurface targets such as swimmers that might threaten port areas. Goes back at least to Bell Thunder 93. Bell Thunder 99: 19 Mar–4 Apr 1999. Participants included Australia. Bell Thunder 95: Jul 1995, associated with Keen Edge.

+ **Bell Volcano:** Former Hawaii based amphibious exercise series, 1980s.

Bell Weather: Former air force special access program.

Belt: Pacific Fleet first word.

Bench/Bend/Bendix: Pacific Air Forces first words.

Bent Pipe: Air force lead Advanced Concept Technology Demonstration (ACTD) to improve real-time precision targeting of short uptime (less than 10 second) RF emitters, Jan 2002–present. The system uses Rivet Joint capabilities and a self-forming wireless communications system developed for DARPA.

Beret: Pacific Air Forces first word.

Bernie: Air force space-based radar R&D special access program.

Berry: Pacific Air Forces first word.

Beryllium/Copper Gold Tin: Navy TENCAP project, 1996.

Best: Pacific Air Forces first word.

Betacom: US–Spanish naval amphibious exercise, held in the Mediterranean Sea. Betacom 97: 22nd MEU. Betacom 95: 16th Air Force. Betacom 94. Betacom 93.

Bevel: Pacific Air Forces first word.

+ **Bevel Edge:** JTF led by III Marine Expeditionary Force deployed to Utapao, Thailand, in Jul 1997 when fighting erupted between rival political factions in Cambodia. The 31st MEU (SOC) was deployed in preparation for a possible evacuation of American citizens.

+ **Bevel Incline:** Preparation for the possible evacuation of American citizens from Indonesia, May 1998. USS *Belleau Wood* (LHA 3) and 31st MEU (SOC).

Beverly Morning: Pacific Air Forces force protection and cyber-terrorism exercise, Yokota AB, Japan. Beverly Morning 2000: Aug 2000. Beverly Morning 98-05: May 1998. The scenario centered on a destabilized political environment in the region, with troops from Yokota and Misawa air bases deployed to Kadena AB, Japan, to support operations. While the troops were away, those left at Yokota had to take precautions against the "increased threat." One area tested was the security of their information exchange systems.

Beyond Duty: Unknown military intelligence system or program.

BGE/SGF (Project BGE/SGF): Army intelligence activity initiated 6 Sep 1984 (Project 922), Vint Hill Farms, VA, and also known as Salem.

Big: Air force electronic warfare first word, including Big Look (EA-3A/EP-3E), Big Tail (SR-71A), and Big Team (RC-135B/C). Big Crow is an NKC-135 aircraft configured to simulate hostile EW systems, part of the multi-service Electronic Warfare Vulnerability Assessment program used to provide ECM testing and training support. The Big Crow platform was used during OAF for an experimental information warfare jamming program, in OEF, and then again in OIF for information warfare. For OEF, Big Crow deployed from Kirtland AFB, NM, to a classified location with a classified contingency high-priority mission support kit (CHPMSK).

Big Bird: *See* Hexagon.

Big Noise: Exercise term for simulated Air Defense Emergency.

Big Photo: General call sign used to contact aircraft performing airborne electronic attack in the US and Canada.

Big Red: US–UK maritime and logistics over-the-shore (LOTS) exercise series. Big Red 99 and Big Red 99.

Big Safari: Air force special program office at Wright Patterson AFB, OH, responsible for providing current and advanced intelligence and reconnaissance technologies to DOD. The Big Safari office keeps abreast of initiatives and off-the-shelf products and evaluates their utility. Programs supported include the high-profile SR-71, Cobra Ball, Commando Solo, and Predator. Other programs currently supported include TRACS, SPEAR, Senior Nike,

Compass Call, Panther Vision, Antemate, Fireant, Mustang, Greyhound, Scathe Mean, Scathe View, Senior Suter, Panther Den, Distant Phoenix, Compass Link, and Peace Sentinel 6. Big Safari also supports a variety of other government agency technology assets, foreign programs, NATO programs, directed energy, and counter-narcotics programs, as well as the development of special-purpose weapons systems at Greenville, TX. The Big Safari office was established in 1953.

Bigfoot 90-1: Air Combat Command Operational Readiness Inspection, Alpena, MI, 2–8 Aug 1990.

Bigger Focus 84: Reagan-era exercise with NSC involvement, 18 Aug–15 Dec 1984.

Bikini: Baltic Sea region search and rescue exercise series. Participants include Denmark and Latvia.

Binacle: Former submarine intelligence collection program.

Binocular: NSA broadcast (now called Near Real Time Dissemination) of SIGINT intercepts.

Birdsnest: NSA high-performance, UNIX-based, desktop computer system.

Black: Air force special access program first word, used in the 1970s and 1980s, including Black Shield, A-12 (precursor of the SR-71) from Kadena AB, Japan; and Black Dome.

Black Demon: Air force network operations and cyber-warfare exercise modeled after the aerial combat Red Flag exercise. Black Demon's purpose is to develop day-to-day network operations tactics from the tactical level through full-scale warfare. Held in Mar 2004 and 2002.

Black Light (aka Blacklite?): Office of the Secretary of Defense and DARPA special access program, 2004–present.

Black List One: Saddam Hussein.

Black Sea Partnership: NATO ISO/PfP exercise by the Turkish Naval Forces Command. Participants include Bulgaria, Georgia, Romania, Turkey, Ukraine, and the US. Azerbaijan and Russia participated as observers. Black Sea Partnership 03: Western Black Sea, 8–15 Sep 2003. Black Sea Partnership 02: Istanbul and Eregli and in the western Black Sea, 9–12 Sep 2002. Black Sea Partnership 01. Black Sea Partnership 00. Black Sea Partnership 99:

20–25 Sep 1999. Black Sea Partnership 98: 21–26 Sep 1998. Black Sea Partnership 96.

Blackbird: HUMINT and counter-intelligence database developed by TF Eagle in Bosnia to file and store spot reports and debriefs, used to conduct link and pattern analysis and for building association matrixes. All raw reporting from local sources as well as theater, national, and open sources related to the Balkans is entered. The database is available at the sensitive compartmented information, Secret, and NATO releasable classification levels.

Blackcat (Project Blackcat): Air Intelligence Agency 33rd Information Operations Sqn, 2002.

Blacker: 1. NSA cryptographic device.
2. **Blacker:** Former navy anti-submarine-warfare system.

Blackhat: SOCOM air-to-ground network operations at RAF Mildenhall, UK.

Blackknight: Army intelligence system, Bad Aibling, Germany.

Blackshark: US–Saudi Arabian anti-submarine-warfare training, 2000.

Blade Jewel: Evacuation of US military dependents from Panama, 1989.

Blast Furnace: US–Bolivian counter-narcotics cocaine interdiction operation, Jul–Oct 1986. Blast Furnace provided US air and counter-insurgency training assistance and helicopter transportation to Bolivian forces to search out and destroy coca processing facilities. Six US Blackhawk helicopters and 160 US support personnel arrived in Bolivia on 14 Jul.

Blazing Trails: Road building operations in Honduras to support US deployments, 1983.

Blind Bat: Relay of Emergency Action Messages by the FAA.

Blind Logic: Panama operations plan to support a new government with US military assistance, late 1980s.

Bloodhound: Navy system for enhanced situational awareness of the battlespace.

Blowtorch (Project Blowtorch): Compartmented security clearance for personnel assigned to the NSA.

Blue: Coast Guard special operations first word. Blue Dawn, 10 Oct–5 Nov 1998. Blue Line, 1–31 Mar 1992. Blue Marble, 8 Jul–4 Aug 1988. Blue Pennant, 1 Jul 1987–30 Sep 1989. Blue Whale, 14–18 Aug 1991.

Blue Advance: SOUTHCOM-sponsored annual crisis action training focused on plans and procedures involving consequence management in response to biological terrorism and operations other than war. Blue Advance 04: 2–6 Feb 2004. Blue Advance 02/03: MacDill AFB, FL, 4–13 Sep 2002. Exercise scenario led by JTF-Civil Support focusing on a domestic biocontagious terrorist attack originating on a cruise ship in Puerto Rico. Blue Advance 01: Disaster preparedness exercise posited a level 3–4 hurricane that strikes an island national in the Caribbean. Blue Advance 97: Panama, Feb 1997.

Blue Bird: Former RC-135B/C ELINT aircraft.

Blue Blade 84: Reagan-era exercise with NSC involvement, 20 Aug–30 Sep 1984.

Blue Crab: Reserve/NG joint training exercise, Aberdeen Test Center and Lauderick Creek Training Area, MD, 4–6 Jun 1999.

Blue Crane: South Africa hosted peacekeeping exercise, 16–29 Apr 1999. Blue Crane was a follow-on subregional exercise to Blue Hungwe.

Blue Eagle: Former PACOM EC-135 airborne command post.

Blue Flag: Air Combat Command exercise designed to train the Numbered Air Force Commanders and their Air Operations Group staffs by providing operational-level, air component battle staff experience in a realistic training environment. The Air Force Command and Control Training and Innovation Group develops exercise scenarios that provide realistic replication of forces, plans, procedures, intelligence capabilities, and threats. Blue Flag, designed to be an eight-day computer-assisted exercise, is held at Hurlburt Field, FL. Participants include Bahrain, Canada, Jordan, Kuwait, Norway, Oman, Qatar, Saudi Arabia, UAE, and the UK. Blue Flag 01-2, Southwest Asia scenario, 4–8 Feb 2001. Blue Flag 00-3. Blue Flag 00-2: Southwest Asia scenario, 1–8 Mar 2000. One of the largest and most diverse exercises ever. Blue Flag 99-4: 20–28 Sep 1999. Blue Flag 98-1: South America scenario, 14–21 Nov 1997. Blue Flag 97-1: Southwest Asia scenario, 20–28 Feb 1997. Blue Flag 96-4: Caribbean scenario, 18–25 Sep 1996. Blue Flag 92-1: Desert Storm revisited, 15–16 Jan 1992.

Blue Game: NATO Allied Forces North annual mine counter-measures and surface naval exercise regularly including Norway, Germany, Denmark, and Canada. The exercise joined Blue Harrier and Bold Game by combining mine warfare and surface warfare under a common littoral warfare scenario.

Blue Game 05: North Sea, May 2005. Blue Game 04/Clean Hunter 04: Baltic Sea, 4–30 Apr 2004. Blue Game 03. Blue Game 02: Sixth Fleet area. Blue Game 01: Danish and Norwegian waters against mining and fast patrol boat threats, Apr–May 2001. Blue Game 99: EOD operations in Denmark and Norway, Apr 1999.

Blue Harrier: Former EUCOM major mining and counter-mining exercise, now incorporated into Blue Game. Blue Harrier 98. Blue Harrier/EURO-97: Denmark. On 23–24 Apr 1997, two Barksdale AFB, LA, B-52s conducted a 23-hour aerial mining as part of the exercise. Blue Harrier 96: Two B-52s arrived at RAF Fairford, UK, on 26 Apr 1996 to participate. Blue Harrier 95. Blue Harrier 93.

Blue Horizon: Air force intelligence related.

Blue Hungwe: First Africa-based peacekeeping exercise, held in Zimbabwe, 1997. Hosted by Zimbabwe and by the UK, 21 African, European, and North American countries participated. The US provided observers.

Blue Knight: E-3 AWACS nickname.

Blue Light: 1. Project Blue Light, a SIOP adaptive planning experiment undertaken in 1994.
    2. **Blue Light:** Navy code name.
    3. **Blue Light:** Continuity of government procedures associated with Site R (Raven Rock). *See also* Iron Gate.

Blue Lightning: NSA-related operations and control center.

Blue Mail: Former navy special access program.

Blue Raven: Air force continuity of operations exercise required to be held at least three times a year.

Blue Sands: US–Moroccan semi-annual training exercise initiated in 1996. Blue Sands 01-01: Ben Guerir airfield and Marrakech, Morocco, 16 Mar–8 Apr 2001. The largest Blue Sands exercise to date. Blue Sands 00: Ben Guerir airfield, Morocco, 9–21 Apr 2000. Air force and army troops teamed up with Moroccan army paratroopers. Blue Sands 98.

Blue Sky: Informal name of the CIA counter-terrorism center al Qaeda retaliation plan developed after the attack on the USS *Cole* (DDG 67) in Yemen in Oct 2000. The plan was sent to the NSC in Dec 2000, and recommended increased support to anti-Taliban groups and local proxies who might attack Osama bin Laden.

Blue Spoon: SOUTHCOM original OPLAN dealing with Panama contingencies, 1988–1989; became Just Cause upon implementation.

Blue Sword: Close air support operations for UN peacekeeping units in Bosnia, 1994.

Blue Tiger 04: UK–Bangladesh peacekeeping map exercise, held in Dhaka, 14–18 Feb 2004.

Blue Zephyr (Project Blue Zephyr): Former army special access program.
Bluemax: STRATCOM strategic nuclear weapons system software application.

Bobcat: Fleet Information Warfare Center information warfare program, 1999.

Bold Eagle: 1. Former US Readiness Command exercise series, Eglin AFB, FL, 1978–1988.
    2. **Bold Eagle:** Deployments to Soto Canto AFB, Honduras.

Bold Rapier: Joint navy, Marine Corps, and army exercise, 19–20 Dec 1996. A Sea Ferret prototype was successfully controlled by the USS *Asheville* (SSN /58), a marine recon team ashore, and an army aviation team during an operational demonstration at Camp Pendleton, CA. The Sea Ferret flew over the area of operations attached to a Cessna 206 test aircraft and received flight commands while tranmitting sensor data and serving as a communications node for exchange of e-mail among the three groups.

Bold Shift: Army operation to address reserve forces readiness and mobilization, 1992–.

Bold Standard 93: 263rd Combat Communications Sqn (North Carolina ANG) exercise, Fort Pickett, VA, 1993.

Bollard: Submarine clandestine reconnaissance program also known as Holystone.

Bonus Deal: Air-force-related nickname, 1980s.

Border Star: Reagan-era exercise with NSC involvement, Fort Bliss and Biggs Field, TX.

Boresight (Project Boresight): Navy network of high frequency/direction finding (HFDF) stations to intercept and fix the source of radio transmissions from surface ships and submarines.

Boron Mercury: UK–Oman exercise, 2000–2001.

Bowline: UK submarine nuclear weapons accident exercise. Bowline 00: Coulport, UK, May 2000. Bowline 98: Clyde Naval Base, UK, Nov 1998.

Bowspirit/Sail: Navy anti-submarine-warfare system, 1980s.

Brave: CENTCOM first word associated with classified reconnaissance operations, 2001–present, including Brave Emerald, Brave Wind (RC-135 operations during OEF), and Brave Warrior.

Brave Eagle: NATO ISO/PfP peacekeeping computer-assisted command post exercise. Participants included Denmark, Finland, Hungary, Poland, Ukraine, and the US. Brave Eagle 01. Brave Eagle 99: 28 Jul–8 Aug 1999. Brave Eagle 97: Drasko Pomorskie military training facility, Karwice, Poland, 8–19 Sep 1997.

Brave Knight: EUCOM WMD incident response command post exercise series, Stuttgart, Germany. Brave Knight 99 was a Presidential Decision Directive 56 (PDD-56), Managing Complex Contingency Operations training event linking interagency actors with the supported CINC. Most of the exercise occurred at the deputy assistant aecretary level. Brave Knight 01. Brave Knight 99: Spring 1999. Brave Knight 98: Planning conference for Brave Knight 99 to simulate recovery efforts following a terrorist-initiated nuclear explosion.

Braveheart: UK-based exercise, Apr 2000.

Brazen Deed: Baltic maritime exercise conducted by Air Force 79th Tactical Fighter Sqn, Jun 1990.

Brazen Tsunami: PACOM Joint Intelligence Center Pacific exercise to practice intelligence support for cyber-warfare, 1999.

Breeze: Army intelligence system, Bad Aibling, Germany.

Breeze 98: NATO PfP small-scale naval exercise, 18–25 Jul 1998. Included Greece.

Breeze/Crimson Jade Topaz: Navy TENCAP program, 1996.

Briar Patch: KC-135R ELINT configuration.

Bridge Sequel: Seventh Fleet US-only naval exercise, 2002–2003.

Bridget: ELINT "ferret" satellite nickname, 1970s. *See also* Farrah, Marilyn, and Raquel.

Bright Eye: NATO biennial live search and rescue exercise. Bright Eye 00: 8–12 Jun 2000.

Bright Future: NATO biennial naval control of shipping exercise. Bright Future 00: 7–13 Oct 2000.

Bright Horizon: NATO maritime surface, subsurface, and air training exercise in the North Sea. Northern Light/Bright Horizon 96: Sep 1996. Participants included Belgium, Canada, Denmark, France, Germany, Italy, the Netherlands, Norway, Spain, the UK, and the US. Bright Horizon 95.

Bright Star: US–Egyptian biennial coalition tactical air, ground, naval, and SOF field training exercise, held in Egypt. Bright Star conducts coalition warfare training for key battle staff element and prepares CENTCOM to rapidly deploy and employ forces to deter aggressors and, if necessary, fight side by side with Egypt and regional partners. The exercise is the largest in the CENTCOM area of responsibility and often involves more than 50,000 coalition forces, including France, Germany, Greece, Italy, Jordan, Kuwait, the Netherlands, Spain, the UAE, and the UK. Bright Star began in 1980 as a single-service, bilateral, ground maneuver event. Bright Star 81 was the first Rapid Deployment JTF exercise held outside the US, held 7–27 Nov 1980. Due to the growing numbers of participating troops and the logistical demands, Bright Star became a biennial event starting in 1983. With Bright Star 89, the exercise changed from summer to fall. Following Desert Storm, Bright Star 91/92 was canceled.

+ **Bright Star 03/04:** The US announced in early Aug 2003 that it would not be able to participate due to commitments in Iraq and Afghanistan.
+ **Bright Star 01/First Retort 01:** 10–26 Oct 2001.
+ **Bright Star 99/00:** Started 16 Oct 1999. The National Reconnaissance Office's (NRO) Synthetic Imagery Generation System (SIGS) provided unclassified simulations of NRO, U-2, and Predator images.
+ **Bright Star 98/99:** Mubarek Military City compound outside Cairo, Egypt, Oct 1997. Kuwait participated for the first time.
+ **Bright Star 96/97:** First exercise to add France, the UK, and Germany, as well as the UAE.

Brilliant Eyes: Air Force strategic defense initiative (SDI) program.

Brilliant Foil/Brilliant Invader: NATO air defense exercise series based in the UK. Participants include Belgium, Germany, France, the Netherlands, Norway, the UK, and the US. Brilliant Foil 99 was canceled because of Kosovo operations. Brilliant Foil 98: RAF St. Mawgan, UK. Brilliant Foil 97/Central Enterprise 97: 27–30 May 1997. B-1Bs crews flew low-level global power missions into France as part of the exercise. Brilliant Invader 96: RAF Leuchars, Aug 1996. Brilliant Foil/Invader 95: 20–23 Mar 1995.

Brilliant Lion: EUCOM Joint/Combined Exchange Training series in Africa, including Cameroon and Mozambique. Brilliant Lion 00-1: 86th AW and SOF deployment to Mozambique and Cameroon.

Brilliant Pebble: Air force strategic defense initiative and missile defense program.

Brilliant Quest: Air force 55th Wing EC/RC-135 exercise, 5–23 Apr 1996.

Brim Frost: AK-based Cold War–era multi-service exercise to defend against sabotage.

Britannia Way/Iberian Focus: UK exercise in Spain. The Sep 2002 exercise was canceled because of a UK firefighters strike. The 15–26 Oct 2001 exercise was canceled by Spain.

BRITE/Brite Knight: Imagery distribution system focused on providing imagery to austere operating locations. BRITE provides imagery collection notification and reachback for requesting and disseminating national imagery to special operations users in the field. Bright Knight is the Air Force special operations portion of the BRITE architecture.

Briz 96: Bulgaria-hosted exercise with Bulgarian, Russian, Romanian, Turkish, Greek, Italian, and US forces, 1996.

Broadsword: DIA Joint Worldwide Intelligence Communications System (JWICS) and SIPRNET search engine that allows users to broker their access to various intelligence databases.

Broadsword is composed of several Gatekeeper servers connected through a Global Map Manager known as a Keymaster. Data mined can be formatted to interoperate with automated intelligence and operations applications. It was initially fielded in 1999.

Broken Arrow: Nuclear weapons major accident. Broken Arrow exercises are also held to test the ability of bases and units to respond to a major accident. For instance, Broken Arrow 00 at Langley AFB, 8–9 Mar 2000, simulated a nuclear-armed plane crash on Langley AFB.

Bronze Arrow: Classified ongoing SOCOM exercise and training series. Bronze Arrow 03. Bronze Arrow 02. Bronz Arrow 01.

Bubble Girl: SAC exercise or operation, 1960s.

Buccaneer Sword: SAC Global Shield exercise special activity, 1980s.

Buckeye: Covert intelligence effort in support of Amber Star and Green Light and involving the Special Collection Service of the CIA and NSA and the former Army Intelligence Support Activity (Gray Fox, now a part of SOCOM) under the code name Torn Victor.

Buffalo: SAC exercise and operations term, 1970s, including Buffalo Grass (an FB-111 exercise) and Buffalo Horn (a designation for SAC OPLAN 8500, 1974).

Bug Bite: Alaska NG contingency plans for Y2K, based on Operations Plan BUG BITE 99-1.

Buggy: SAC first word, 1970s–1980s, including Buggy Ride (a SAC alert force launch from one or more bases under certain conditions such as disaster, civil disorder, and so on) and Buggy Whip.

Bugle Rag: U-2 photo-reconnaissance project, 1960s–.

Bullet: SAC-related first word, 1980s, including Bullet Blitz (a short-range attack missile (SRAM) live launch series) and Bullet Shot (a SAC operation).

Bulls Eye: Air force TENCAP project that integrated National Reconnaissance Office–developed "Validation of Integrated Points" and "Tactical Fusion Prototype" software into the Theater Battle Management Core Systems, providing better and faster targeting using imagery products.

Bullseye: 1. Network of huge circularly disposed antenna arrays (CDAA), including up to two rings of dipole antennas and two reflector screens to a diameter of 800 feet. The first of the CDAAs, installed at the Hybla Valley Coast Guard Station, Alexandria, VA, in 1957, was used to track the Soviet Sputnik's 20 MHz signal and determine its orbit. Today's Bullseye net control system training takes place at Skagg Island, CA. Formerly Bulldog and Boresight.

2. **Bullseye 97:** Tactical air transport competition. Bullseye 98: Jun 1998. Bullseye 97: CFB Trenton, Ontario, Canada, 25 May–11 Jun 1997. Participants included Australia, Canada, the UK, and New Zealand.

Bulwark 04: US–Bulgarian exercise, the first to take place after Bulgaria's NATO membership, Novo Selo, Jul–Aug 2004.

Bulwark Bronze: STRATCOM annual national-level nuclear war preparation exercise. Bulwark Bronze 94 was STRATCOM's first major exercise after its activation in 1992, and the first in the Clinton administration to include national-level participation. Bulwark Bronze 95: 2–9 Nov 1995. The first time the Air Combat Command participated fully in a nuclear exercise; it included a theater nuclear scenario with dual-capable aircraft and 5th BW theater tasking, and practiced responses to terrorism threats, cyber-warfare, and mobile command posts. Following the exercise, Lt. Gen. Arlen James, deputy commander of STRATCOM, said: "We're now pursuing a process to combine Bulwark Bronze with the major SPACECOM exercise, and, therefore, exercise offense and defense at the same time." Bulwark Bronze 94: May 1994.

Buoyant Force: STRATCOM nuclear C3 exercise, 2001–2002.

Burbage: Australian cyclical maritime surveillance operations in the Indian Ocean.

Burmese Chase: US–UK Marine Corps and Royal Commando exercise series. Burmese Chase 01: Jun–Jul 2001. UK forces did not participate because RAF Air Transport was unavailable due to other operational and exercise taskings. Burmese Chase 99, Burmese Chase 98, Burmese Chase 92.

Burning: RC-135 mission first word, first used in the 1970s, including Burning Candy, Burning Cigar, Burning Shield, Burning Star, and Burning Wind.

Burning Bush: UK–Moroccan exercise, 2000–2001.

Burning Harmony 98: EUCOM Joint Theater Level Simulation (JTLS) exercise, Warrior Preparation Center, Germany.

Burning Sentry: Air Combat Command exercise that tests the ability of fighter aircraft to protect high-value assets operating near enemy airspace. In Burning Sentry 92, F-15s protected E-3A AWACS and RC-135 Rivet Joint aircraft. Burning Sentry 89-1.

Burnt Orange: OPSEC threat warning code word, 1980s.

Bushmaster 99: Army field training exercise, San Antonio, TX, 11–19 Nov 1999.

Bushmaster 96: US Army South operation at Fort Kobbe, Panama, and the Salamanca Camp, Belize, site of the Belize Defense Force Jungle Warfare School.

Bustout: Unclassified nickname used to notify NORAD and STRATCOM of SIOP Positive Control Launch and dispersal of nuclear-loaded, aerial refueling, and reconnaissance aircraft.

Busy: STRATCOM (and formerly SAC) first word. The 1980s nickname and exercise term included Busy Boomerang (B-52 deployments to Australia), Busy Brewer (conventional B-52 support to NATO), and Busy Island (B-52H deployments to the Pacific). Busy Aim, Busy Bear, Busy Eagle, Busy Hawk, and Busy Knife are all aircraft spare parts programs related to SIOP support.

+ **Busy Lobster:** Aerial refueling operations at Diego Garcia.
+ **Busy Luggage:** Nuclear gravity bomb test drop series, 1990s. The operations occurred at the Tonopah Test Range, NV, or the UT Test and Training Range. Renamed Busy Mudbug in late 1990s.
+ **Busy Mudbug:** Nuclear gravity bomb test drop series.
+ **Busy Relay:** Rivet Joint missions, also flown by TC-135 aircraft of the 55th Wing.

Busy Observer: Pacific Fleet exercise, 1981.

Buy None: SAC operation, 1960–1980s.

Buzzard: UK 45 Commando Group operation along the Pakistani border in the Khowst region to interdict Taliban and al Qaeda fighters from returning to Afghanistan, 29 May–9 Jul 2002.

Buzzer: Nickname for electronic noise jamming or deception.

Buzzsaw: Legacy SIOP software program of unknown purpose.

BYEMAN: Classified sensitive compartmented information compartment for information relating to the workings and operations of US imaging and SIGINT satellites. At the unclassified level, *B, BRAVO,* and *BYE* are used interchangeably instead of *BYEMAN* to designate a person's security clearance level or the classification level (such as Top Secret/Bravo). Additional categories are and have been used to designate specific satellites or processes and are associated with BYEMAN data (Aquacade, Chalet, Corona, Gambit, Hexagon, Jumpseat, Kenna, LaCrosse/Vega, Magnum, Onyx, Oxcart, Rhyolite, and Vortex).

— C —

Cabañas: Special Operations Command South (SOCSOUTH) exercise series dating to the early 1980s. Participants include Argentina, Bolivia, Brazil, Chile, Colombia, Ecuador, Paraguay, Peru, and Uruguay. Cabañas 02: Santiago, Chile, 16–29 Oct 2002. 7th SFG. Cabañas 01: Salta, Argentina, 22 Aug–11 Sep 2001. Colombia, Mexico, and Venezuela participated as observers. Cabañas 00: Cordoba, Argentina, 6–21 Sep 2000. 1st Bn, 141st Infantry, TX ARNG, and 7th SFG. Cabañas 99. Cabañas Puerto Rico, 1–6 Jun and 12–20 Aug 1998.

Cactus: Nickname for the communications switch at Camp David, MD.

Cactus Juggler 92: US Army Europe exercise, 1992.

Cadence Brake: UK Royal Navy exercise planned for Nov 1999, canceled.

Cadmic Frame: Army Foreign Science and Technology Center foreign material exploitation, 1990.

Caesar: Unclassified nickname for the first Sound Surveillance System (SOSUS) hydrophone arrays, established in 1952.

Caesar Sword: Sixth Fleet attack submarine Tomahawk strike exercise series conducted in the Mediterranean Sea. Caesar Sword 03. Caesar Sword 98-1 north of Sicily included the USS *Boise* (SSN 764) as launch area coordinator (LAC) to evaluate a submarine's capability to perform with new EHF satellite communications. This was the first time a submarine assumed the LAC role in a major strike exercise. Firing units were the *Boise*, USS *City of Corpus Christi* (SSN 705), and USS *Toledo* (SSN 769). The USS *John Rodgers* (DD 983) acted as the alternate LAC. The scenario called for a two-salvo, multimission strike. The exercise demonstrated that attack submarines had the satellite connectivity to fulfill the LAC role in a no-notice situation.

Caesar's Fury: Sixth Fleet exercise series.

Cajun Kombat: Air combat training exercise with UK Tornado fighters, Eglin AFB, FL, 23 Mar–5 Apr 2002.

Call Forward: Army mobilization station exercise, the only exercise that simulates the actual mobilization of the Individual Ready Reserve (IRR). The exercise occurs annually in Apr, May, or Jun, and is two weeks in length. The exercise has been held since at least 1994. After the terrorist events of Sep 11, the exercise was canceled for FY 2002.

Calligram: Unknown NSA computer virus program, 1986.

Calm Support: EUCOM support to Kosovo Diplomatic Observer Mission, 1998–1999.

Calypso Wind: Exercise series involving WMD accident and incident response, 1997.

Camel Hump: U-2R reconnaissance operations from Taif AB, Saudi Arabia, monitoring Iraq after Desert Storm. The name was based on the informal designation of the Taif operating location (OL-CH for Camel Hump).

CAMEO 7: Software applications used to plan for and respond to domestic chemical emergencies. CAMEO 7 was developed by the EPA's Chemical Emergency Preparedness and Prevention Office and the NOAA to assist front-line chemical emergency planners and responders.

Cameo Bluejay: Helicopter-mounted laser weapon, a spin-off of the army's ALQ-169 Optical Warning Location/Detection (OWL/D) device. Technical problems led to cancelation in 1989.

Canasta Player: Army Foreign Counter-intelligence Activity–led investigation of spies Army Sgt. 1st Class Clyde Lee Conrad and Army Sgt. 1st Class Zoltan Szabo. In 1978, the CIA informed the army that NATO war plans for Europe were being compromised. Canasta Player, which included CIA and FBI investigators, continued until 1986, when Clyde Conrad was apprehended.

Cannon Cloud: NATO rapid reaction qualification command post exercise/computer-assisted exercise based on an Article 5 scenario. The exercise is held every four years and includes Germany, France, Belgium, Poland, the Netherlands, and the Czech Republic. Cannon Cloud 02: Baumholder, Germany and Poland, 3–15 Nov 2002. Cannon Cloud/Certain Benefit 99.

Cannon Iron Flow: Air Combat Command Support Plan 98-06.

Code Names

Canvas Shield: Operational security assessment of clandestine Grazing Lawn Army Intelligence Support Activity (Gray Fox) airborne reconnaissance operation conducted from Tegucigalpa, Honduras, 1983–1985.

Canyon: First SIGINT geostationary satellite, launched in Aug 1968. Canyon was controlled from a ground station at Bad Aibling, Germany. Seven Canyon satellites were launched 1968–1977.

Capable Warrior: JFCOM advanced warfighting experiment involving interactive planning, rapid decisive operations, common relevant operational picture, adaptive command and control, and forcible entry operations.

Capacity Gear: Special access program compartment code name for the Army Intelligence Support Activity (Gray Fox), designated 30 Mar 1990 and replacing Grantor Shadow. Capacity Gear was replaced by Titrant Ranger.

Cape Petrel: UK–Falklands exercise, 2000–2001.

Caper Focus: Counter-narcotics operation, 19 Mar–11 Jun 2001. Coordinated efforts by the USS *Rodney Davis* (FFG 60) and navy P-3s, the Coast Guard, customs, and DEA, plus host nations, focused on illegal drug movements in the eastern Pacific, Caribbean, and Central America transit zone regions.

Capex: Pacific Air Force annual service-level logistics field training exercise.

Capitol Reaction: Exercise involving response to accidents and incidents involving use of WMD, 1997. Capitol Reaction was the first such exercise to be conducted after the passage of the Defense Against Weapons of Mass Destruction Act of 1996. It addressed a local–state–federal response to terrorist use of WMD during the presidential inaugural. It focused on interagency cooperation and communication in the event of a real-world incident.

Capsule Jack: Unknown military intelligence system or program.

CARAT (Cooperation Afloat Readiness and Training): US–Association of Southeast Asian Nations (ASEAN) military training exercise series designed to enhance interoperability of naval services. The four-month series of annual exercises is conducted with Brunei, Philippines, Indonesia, Singapore, Thailand, Malaysia, and Tonga. CARAT began in 1995 with the concept of scheduling several previously existing bilateral exercises into one series of sequential exercises.

+ **CARAT 03:** Royal Brunei Land Force Berakas Garrison, Brunei, 23 Jun–Jul 2003.

+ **CARAT 02:** Sattahip, Thailand, began 10 Jun 2002. USS *Vincennes* (CG 49).
+ **CARAT Singapore 00:** Ended 22 Sep 2000. Five US ships and one submarine, led by the flagship USS *Germantown* (LSD 42).
+ **CARAT Singapore 99:** Brani naval base, Singapore, Jul 1999. First CARAT exercise to see the establishment of a combined headquarters of US and Singapore armed forces.
+ **CARAT Malaysia 99:** Ended 9 Jul 1999.
+ **CARAT Thailand 99:** Began 26 Jul 1999.
+ **CARAT Indonesia 99:** Began 11 Aug 1999.
+ **CARAT Singapore 98:** Sembawang Camp, Singapore, Jul 1998.
+ **CARAT 96:** Singapore, 22 Apr–12 Jul 1996. USS *Germantown* (LSD 42).

Caravan Guard: US Army Europe Joint Military Contact Program command post exercise series. Caravan Guard 95. Caravan Guard 92. Participants include Canada, Germany, and France.

Carnivore: FBI e-mail monitoring system that collects meta-data on the origins, size, and routing of Internet-based messages, but not the content.

Carob: Army intelligence foreign material exploitation, including Carob Standard (1991–1993) and Carob Teal (1991).

Carpathian Exchange 98: US–Hungarian exercise, Kesckemet and Szolnok, Hungary, 17–27 Mar 1998. The 352nd SOG, RAF Mildenhall, UK, deployed two aircraft.

Carpathian Lightning: US–Romanian unexploded ordnance detonation operation in Afghanistan, 23 Apr 2003.

Cartwheel: Mystic Star–related communications program.

Casaba Hound: Army foreign material exploitation program through at least 1992.

Casanova: Naval intelligence, 1980s–1990s.

Cascade: Army I Corps, Fort Lewis, WA, Pacific-oriented first word, including Cascade Command and Cascade Sage.

+ **Cascade Cudgel:** Cascade Cudgel 8, Mar 2001, Cascade Cudgel 7, Dec 2000, Cascade Cudgel 6, Feb 2000 (canceled because of an earthquake in Seattle, WA).

+ **Cascade Mist:** Deep operations exercise held every other year in Oct/Nov. Cascade Mist/Peak 02, Cascade Mist 99, Cascade Mist 96.
+ **Cascade Peak:** Battle Command Training Program computer-assisted exercise held every other year in Oct/Nov. Cascade Mist/Peak 02. Cascade Peak 99. Cascade Peak 96/Yama Sakura 96: Nov 1996, included participation of the Australian 1 Bde.
+ **Cascade Steel III:** Combat service support training exercise conducted by the 311th COSCOM. Cascade Steel III. Cascade Steel II, 22 Mar–5 Apr 1998.
+ **Cascade Warrior:** JTF-level command post exercise, Sep 2000. The scenario was templated over a map of the Philippines. The Republic of Blue, a US-allied country already dealing with an insurgency within its borders, was invaded by a hostile neighboring country. I Corps was the command element of the JTF called in to help Blue.

Cascade Fury II: Department of Transportation emergency transportation exercise, Wyoming, 24–27 May 2004.

Cascade Peak: Army I Corps warfighter exercise series.

Casino Gambit: Army 10th SFG emergency deployment readiness exercise, 1980s.

Cassandra: *See* Prophet/Cassandra.

Cassowary: Australian–Indonesian patrol boat exercise. Cassowary 98-1, May 1998. Cassowary 97-1, Apr 1997.

Cast Glance/Cluster Ranger: Naval P-3/NP-3 stabilized photographic and electro-optical sensor systems. Cast Glance provides high-resolution imagery of missile and space test operations. Cluster Ranger is the electro-optical portion. Castglance (*sic*) is also an Air Force Space Command classified project, Sep 2000.

Castle Hellion: Air force special operations exercise, Jul–Aug 1985.

CATEX-94: CENTCOM-sponsored joint humanitarian assistance field training exercise, Camp Pendleton, CA.

Cathode Emission: NATO deployable communications interoperability training exercise. Cathode Emission 03: Aalborg, Denmark, 9–20 Jun 2003. The scenario was based on the deployment of a CJTF into a very austere

Madagascar-type area of operations. Participants included the Czech Republic, Denmark, France, Italy, Germany, the Netherlands, Poland, and Spain.

Cavalry: Air force space-related special access program.

CBAT–Central Command: OPLAN 1003-96 (war with Iraq) seminar, gaming health service support operations under chemical and biological weapons conditions, Feb 1999.

Cease Buzzer: Unclassified term used to terminate electronic attack activities, including the use of EW expendables such as chaff. Suspension of EW activity is required for safety-of-flight reasons, in cases of harmful interference in the radio frequency spectrum, or for OPSEC reasons.

Cedar Deck (Project 9AK): SOUTHCOM classified program, 30 Nov 1984–present.

Cef-: Army intelligence letter block first word. Early Cef programs include Ceflien Lion (RP/AP-2E, former Navy Neptunes) and Cefish Person (airborne RU-6A/RU-8D missions).

+ **Cefirm Leader:** Consolidated airborne SIGINT collection system originally developed for the RU-21, evolved from the Crazy Dog program. The updated Cefirm Leader RU-21A/B/C aircraft were flown in Royal Duke and Ordway Grove clandestine operations in Central America during the 1980s. Cefirm Leader was also used during Desert Storm by six aircraft of the army 201st MI Bn. Replaced by Crazy Horse.
+ **Cefly (Communications and Electronics Forward Looking Flying) Lancer:** RU-21J ELINT platform deployed in the 1980s, part of the early Guardrail program.

Celesta: Australian operations to enforce an exclusive economic zone in the Heard Island–McDonald Island area, 2001–present.

CELTIC: 1. (Celtic II) Army intelligence system, Bad Aibling, Germany.
   2. **Celtic:** Navy EW, ELINT, or COMINT system.
   3. **Celtic:** Australia HF/DF system.

Celtic: CENTCOM first word.

+ **Celtic Axe:** Global Hawk airborne reconnaissance mission, 2001.
+ **Celtic Cross:** 622nd Aero-medical Evacuation Sqn, Macdill AFB, FL, deployment 1993.

+ **Celtic Emerald:** Airborne reconnaissance mission, Dec 2001.
+ **Celtic Straw:** Reconnaissance operation, probably Predator in Pakistan, 2001–present.
+ **Celtic Warrior:** Airborne reconnaissance mission, Dec 2001.
+ **Celtic Wind:** Rivet Joint airborne reconnaissance missions during OEF, Oct 2001.

Cemetery Wind: Army Intelligence Support Activity (Gray Fox) code name for operations in Central and South America in the late 1980s and early 1990s.

Centennial: Air force applied technology and integration special access program.

Center Lane: CIA remote viewing program.

Centerboard: Upgraded central processor computers for the navy HF/DF network (aka Unitary DF, or Crosshair).

Centra Spike: Army Intelligence Support Activity (Gray Fox) counter-narcotics operations in Colombia and the hunt for drug lord Pablo Escobar, 1989–1993 time frame.

Central: NATO first word associated with defense of NATO's Central Region.

+ **Central Enterprise:** Allied Air Forces Central Europe annual live large-scale exercise. Participants include Belgium, Canada, Denmark, France, Germany, the Netherlands, the UK, and the US. Central Enterprise 01. Central Enterprise/Clean Hunter 00: May 2000: US F-16s flew about 100 miles into Poland, where the Polish air force defended an airfield against simulated attack. Poland then sent eight MiG-21s to fight with the F-16s as they returned to Karup, Denmark. Central Enterprise 99 was canceled because of Kosovo operations. Central Enterprise 98/Baltops: RAF Fairford AB, UK, Interim Combined Air Operations Center (ICAOC) 1, Finderup, Denmark, and ICAOC 2 Kalkar, Germany, and at bases in Denmark, Germany, and the UK 7th Bomb Wing. Dyess AFB, TX, deployed six B-1Bs and 93rd Bomb Sqn, Barksdale AFB, LA, deployed four B-52s. The two wings combined to form the 7th Expeditionary Operations Group (EOG), 25 May–6 Jul 1998. 7th EOG also participated in the linked exercise Baltops. F-15Es deployed to Denmark. The USS *Vella Gulf* (CG 72) generated simulated theater ballistic missile and cruise missile threats for an army Patriot missile battery located in Germany. Central Enterprise 97: UK, Jun 1997. Largest-ever deployment of B-1Bs to RAF Fairford, UK.

Central Enterprise 96: Jun 1996. Central Enterprise 95. Central
Enterprise 93: Jun 1993. Eight F-117As were deployed to Gilzen Rijen,
the Netherlands. Central Enterprise 91: 10–14 Jun 1991.

+ **Central Fortress:** Germany, Jun 1992.

+ **Central Harmony:** Highly classified annual Supreme Headquarters
Allied Power Europe command post exercise focused on European theater nuclear weapons planning and execution.

Central Skies: Counter-narcotics operation involving military assets, Coast
Guard, customs, and DEA, plus host nations, in surveillance and interdiction
in the eastern Pacific, Caribbean, and Central America. The missions began
in Jun 1998 in Costa Rica and are run out of Soto Cano AB, Honduras.

Centrasbat (Central Asian Bn): Peacekeeping and humanitarian assistance operations field training exercise, originally the Central Asian Bn of Kazakhstan,
Kyrgyzstan, and Uzbekistan, formed in Dec 1995. The name of the exercise
series was changed to Regional Cooperation in 2001. Participants include
Azerbaijan, Georgia, Kazakhstan, Kyrgyzstan, Latvia, Mongolia, Russia, Turkey,
the UK, and Uzbekistan, with France and Ukraine as observers.

+ **Centrasbat 00:** Almaty, Kazakhstan, 10–18 Sep 2000. 5th SFG and
82nd Airborne Div. Two C-17s picked up approximately 160 paratroopers at Pope AFB, NC, and flew approximately 20 hours nonstop
to a drop zone in Kazakhstan.

+ **Centrasbat 99:** US, May 1999.

+ **Centrasbat 98:** Chirchik and Osh, Uzbekistan, Sep 1998. 10th
Mountain Div.

+ **Centrasbat 97:** Shymkent, Kazakhstan, and Chirchik, Uzbekistan,
15–21 Sep 1997. The exercise included the longest-distance airborne
operation in history and more than 900 military personnel. The exercise saw the first use of the C-17 Globemaster III as a strategic platform. The record-breaking flight began at Pope AFB, NC, on 14 Sep
when 500 82nd Airborne Div and 40 Central Asian soldiers boarded
six C-17s for the 19-hour flight.

Centurian Crusader: US–German special operations exercise. Centurion Crusader
01: 2nd Bn, 75th Ranger Regt, and the German Airborne Bde in a mass tactical
parachute assault originating in Washington and ending in Germany. The jump
was followed by three days of small-unit infiltration to the battalion assault objective, an inactive French caserne, and then training with the Belgian 1 Para Regt,

Portuguese Pathfinders, the Netherlands Airborne Bde, the Czech Republic 6th Special Forces Bde, and Fallschirmjaeger Bn 263 of the German Airborne Bde. Centurion Crusader 00: 13 Aug–21 Sep 2000.

CERCIS: Naval intelligence next-generation system replacing SIGINT Correlation of Recognized Emitters (SCORE) and SIGINT Universal Recognition Facility (SURF) analyst capabilities. In the late 1990s, CERCIS was installed at seven sites worldwide.

Ceroff: Navy anti-submarine-warfare command, control, and communications (C3), 1980s.

Certain Sage: National Guard mobilization to provide data for planning and implementing the recall of military retirees at the state level, 1986.

Certain Support/Force Projection Logistics Exercise 93: Joint theater-level combat support and combat service support command post exercise.

Chainwork: Air force and army AN/GSQ-237 cryptologic maintenance support system.

Chair: Office of Naval Research permanent first word, not currently in use.

Chalet: COMINT geostationary satellite follow-on to Canyon, first launched 10 Jun 1978. The satellite control system and downlinks were code-named Runway; the ground processing system at Menwith Hill, UK, was code-named Silkworth. After the name appeared in the news media, the name was changed to Vortex.

Chalice: U-2 R&D program, renamed from Aquatone.

Chalk: Navy (N89/N7SP) special access program first word, including Chalk Banyan, Chalk Eagle, Chalk Poinsettia, and Chalk Weed.

  + **Chalk Coral:** Strategic nuclear-related special access program; it goes back at least to 1985 and is included in the FY 2003 Defense Emergency Readiness Fund.
  + **Chalk Talk:** Chalk Talk communications network.

Challenge: Chief of Naval Operations (N6) first word.

Challenge Athena: Navy wide-band communications link capable of providing ships at sea with access to high-volume national-level imagery, intelligence databases, video teleconferencing, and telemedicine. Challenge Athena supports Tomahawk mission planning and Air Tasking Order transmissions. The Challenge Athena system uses commercial satellites to augment military satellite communications. It was first employed on the USS *George Washington* (CVN 73) in Desert Storm. The Challenge Athena II demonstration began during the *George Washington* fleet exercise in Mar 1994. The ship's intelligence center received more than 6,600 satellite images.

Chambered Round: Naval Space Command initiative to provide intelligence support to deployed forces by providing tip-offs of hostile satellite reconnaissance and assessments of reactions to US naval operations.

Champion Strike: Afghanistan operation conducted in the eastern Bermel Valley, Sep 2002. The operation involved 1st Bn, 504th Regt of the 82nd Airborne Div.

Channel: Navy (N89/N7SP) special access program first word, including Channel Finder (a navy surface warfare program, 1980s) and Channel Oak (Navy Project ZR2).

Chapel Gold: Australian–Thai interoperability army exercise. Chapel Gold 03: Jul 2003. Chapel Gold 02: Jul 2002. Chapel Gold 96: Aug 1996.

Charade: Chief of Naval Operations (N2) first word.

Charger: Former Chief of Naval Operations (N86) first word.

Chariot: Army tactical, manportable, receive-only S-band ELINT feed that provides users in the field with a means to receive large amounts of data. The Chariot receiver is capable of tracking and receiving signals from satellites in multiple orbits. Chariot was used during Agile Provider.

Check: Former Naval Crimnal Investigative Service permanent first word.

Checkboard: Air force direction finding system related to Host and Longroot.

Checkmate: 1. Headquarters air force operational planning organization, responsible for developing warfighting concepts and assisting in innovative and "think tank" work in support of air campaign formulation. Checkmate developed the original concepts for Desert Storm in Iraq and has been involved in developing the concepts of air operations ever since, working on special projects for the Air Force Director of Operations and the Air Force Chief of Staff.

2. **Checkmate:** Coast Guard special operations, Jul 1987–Jun 1990.

Cheese: Former Chief of Naval Operations permanent first word.

Chemwar 00: WMD response exercise, including Marine Corps NBC defense training.

Cherry: Former Chief of Naval Operations (N2) first word.

Chess: Compartment of early Talent Keyhole imagery intelligence (for instance, Top Secret Talent Keyhold Chess) derived from U-2 and SR-71 reconnaissance missions. *See also* Ruff.

Chicken Little: Joint munitions test and evaluation program office formed by the army and air force in 1984 to evaluate the performance of first-generation smart submunition systems. The program has now been institutionalized to assess all weapons systems performance.

Chinese Eye: Allied Command Europe Rapid Reaction Corps command post exercise, simulating deployment of a 100,000-strong European contingent, Oct 1994.

Chipped/Chocolate: Former Chief of Naval Operations (N2) first words.

Chrome Dome: Nuclear-armed B-52 airborne alert patrols, flown until one of the bombers crashed on the ice off Thule AB, Greenland, Jan 1968.

Church: Former Chief of Naval Operations (N095) first word.

Churinga: Five Power Defence Agreement (FPDA — Australia, Malaysia, New Zealand, Singapore, and the UK) air exercise, held in Singapore and Malaysia, Apr–May 1998, Sep 1997, Apr 1997, and Aug 1996.

CI Bilateral Exchange 1-99: US–Chilean exchange program to gain insight and knowledge of Chilean armed forces, cold-weather operations, and infantry training.

Cinnamon: Chief of Naval Operations (N2) first word.

Circuit: Chief of Naval Operations (N6) first word.

  ✦ **Circuit Mayflower:** Navy AN/BRT-2 Shore Automation System. Installed in at least nine shore receive sites. Located in Guam; Muscat, Oman; and RAF Croughton, UK.

Cirrus/Crystal Oak White: Navy TENCAP program, 1996.

Cirrus Wind: FEMA WMD consequence management exercise, Jun 1996.

Citadel: 1. Multi-service EOD special access program that enhances specialized render-safe, access, and disablement techniques employed against improvised explosives devices.

2. **Citadel:** Former Chief of Naval Operations (N09) first word.

3. **Citadel:** Australian operations in East Timor; replaced Tanager following East Timor independence in May 2002.

Clamp: Former Naval Criminal Investigative Service permanent first word.

Clarinet: Chief of Naval Operation (N61) first word, including Clarinet Pilgrim.

+ **Clarinet Merlin:** Shore-based receiving system that monitors transmissions from the Submarine Emergency Communication Transmitter buoys (AN/BST-1) launched from ballistic missile submarines. Six receiver sites, three covering the Atlantic Ocean and three covering the Pacific Ocean, receive emergency one-way transmissions used to report the loss of a submarine.

Classic: Naval Security Group permanent first word. Classic programs in the 1980s included Classic Ascot/Nomad; Classic Bulldog, Classic Bullseye (*see* Bullseye), Classic Coyote, Classic Flaghoist, Classic Fox, Classic Julep, Classic Mayflower, Classic Music, Classic Oracle, and Classic Seacoast. Current Classic programs include Classic Aerie, Classic Alpine, Classic Baritone, Classic Centerboard, Classic Opintel, and Classic Stevedore.

+ **Classic Erne:** AN/BRQ-2(V) navy electronic warfare system.
+ **Classic Outboard:** AN/SSQ-108 (V) shipboard direction finding system. Outboard provides electronic warfare signals acquisition and direction finding with the capability to detect, locate, and identify hostile targets at long range. The widely deployed system consists of VHF, mid- to high-frequency, and low-frequency direction finding. Outboard is particularly effective against emitters associated with counter-narcotics operations.
+ **Classic Owl:** SIGINT collection system, first deployed in the 1960s. Classic Owl operations continue at Naval Security Group activities at Camp Smith, HI; Classic Owl/Sensor Reach Facility, Eareckson AS, AK; JAC Molesworth, UK; Winter Harbor, ME; and Anchorage, AK.
+ **Classic Salmon:** AN/SLR-18 (V) submarine-based electronic warfare system.
+ **Classic Troll:** AN/ULR-21 ESM and information warfare exploitation system.

+ **Classic Trump:** Navy counter-narcotics SIGINT system.
+ **Classic Wizard:** White Cloud/Parcae ocean surveillance satellite system processors. *See also* Ranger.

Claymore: Former Chief of Naval Operations (N87) first word.

Clean Hunter: NATO Allied Air Forces Northern Europe live-fly air exercise (*see also* Central Enterprise) designed to demonstrate the ability to defend Europe. Participants include Belgium, Canada, the Czech Republic, Denmark, France, Germany, Italy, Luxembourg, the Netherlands, Norway, Poland, Spain, Turkey, the UK, and the US. US forces deployed for Clean Hunter may also participate in Baltops when the exercise dates overlap. The exercise replaced Brilliant Foil. Clean Hunter 05: Germany, Jun 2005. Clean Hunter 04/Combined Endeavor: 4–25 Jun 2004. Clean Hunter 03. Clean Hunter 02: 10–21 Jun 2002. Clean Hunter 01: UK, 18–29 Jun 2001. Clean Hunter 00: Northern France, 22 May–16 Jun 2000.

Clear/Elm Pine: Navy TENCAP program, 1996.

Clear Skies 02: NORAD homeland security air defense exercise, Sep 2002. Army Stingers and Avengers deployed to Washington, DC, the first time an air defense unit defended assets on US soil since the Cuban Missile Crisis.

Clear Vision: CIA program with Battelle Memorial Institute 1997–2000 to build and test foreign-designed biological weapons. Agency officials feared that Soviet-designed submunition weapons were being sold on the international market, and after attempting to obtain such weapons, the agency decided to fabricate and model the effects of prospective designs.

Clipper: Former Chief of Naval Operations (N3) first word, including Clipper Bow, a planned active radar ocean surveillance system in the 1980s.

Close Ties: Coast Guard special operation, 18 Feb–21 Apr 1991.

Cloud Gap: 1. Former air force special access program.
2. (**Project Cloud Gap**): Joint endeavor of the Arms Control and Disarmament Agency (ACDA) and DOD, Sep 1966.

Cloudy Call: NATO Central Europe exercise, 9–13 Oct 2000.

Cloudy Office: Exercise simulating a pro-Iraqi terrorist attack on the Office of the Secretary of Defense in the Pentagon, 30 May 1998. The exercise included the Defense Protective Service and involved more than 500 people from federal, state, and local agencies. It was a follow-on to exercise Crucial Office.

Clove: Army intelligence system, Bad Aibling, Germany.

Cluster: Naval intelligence first word. Cluster programs in the 1980s included Cluster Alpine, Cluster Baritone, Cluster Bay, Cluster Beaver, Cluster Black, Cluster Bright, Cluster Cactus, Cluster Chase, Cluster Chip, Cluster Cobb, Cluster Coral, Cluster Cord, Cluster Cotton, Cluster Cove, Cluster Digest, Cluster Dike, Cluster Dye, Cluster Easel, Cluster Echo, Cluster Elm, Cluster Fobia, Cluster Fortune, Cluster Gadder, Cluster Gambler, Cluster Geode, Cluster Gulf, Cluster Hatchet, Cluster Hawk, Cluster Hemlock, Cluster Hulk, Cluster Island, Cluster Knave, Cluster Knife, Cluster Lobster, Cluster Locust, Cluster Mackerel, Cluster Maid, Cluster Mail, Cluster Manager, Cluster Mango, Cluster Mantle, Cluster Maple, Cluster Marlin, Cluster Marsh, Cluster Mason, Cluster Match, Cluster Meter, Cluster Micron, Cluster Miracle, Cluster Mirage, Cluster Monster, Cluster Moon, Cluster Moss, Cluster Mound, Cluster Muff, Cluster Mug, Cluster Mullet, Cluster Mum, Cluster Muskie, Cluster Mute, Cluster Net, Cluster Noble, Cluster Note, Cluster Oak, Cluster Painter, Cluster Palace, Cluster Pansy, Cluster Peacock, Cluster Peak, Cluster Pearl, Cluster Pelt, Cluster Pride, Cluster Queen, Cluster Quick, Cluster Quid, Cluster Quiet, Cluster Quill, Cluster Rain, Cluster Raven, Cluster Ray, Cluster Razor, Cluster Rider, Cluster Ridge, Cluster River, Cluster Rose, Cluster Scatter, Cluster Shell, Cluster Spike, Cluster Star, Cluster Tear, Cluster Theresa, Cluster Thimble, Cluster Trace, Cluster Violet, Cluster Virtue, Cluster Watch, Cluster Yard.

+ **Cluster Ranger/Cast Glance:** P-3C electro-optical camera system, also used in the Precision Targeting Identification Advanced Concept Technology Demonstration.
+ **Cluster Robin:** Fleet Information Warfare Center airborne information warfare program, 1999.
+ **Cluster Snoop:** AN/USQ-149 (V) next-generation ELINT collection system, deployed in 2003.
+ **Cluster Spectator:** AN/WSQ-5 (V) and AN/WLR-8(V) submarine-based electronic-warfare-related intelligence system.

CMX (crisis management exercise): NATO procedural exercises that occur annually in spring. The exercises practice and test procedures for NATO crisis management response with emphasis on response options, the NATO Precautionary System, and the generation of forces with associated rules of engagement. The exercises include the staffs and senior representatives from the Department of State and the Office of the Under Secretary of Defense

(Policy). CMX 04. CMX 01. CMX 00/CRISEX 00: First-ever Western European Union (WEU)/NATO joint crisis management exercise, 17–23 Feb 2000. The exercise simulated a scenario calling for a UN-mandated complex humanitarian operation in a fictitious country, where NATO had agreed to support a WEU-led operation. CMX/CRISEX 98: 12–18 Feb 1998. CMX 97: 20–27 Feb 1997. CRISEX 95/96: 12–18 Dec 1995.

Coal/Frost Thunder: Navy TENCAP program, 1996.

Coal Warfighter: Air Force "operational warfighter" program initiated after OAF in 1999 to ensure that operational commanders have access to compartmented Special Technical Operations (STO) and special access programs. Allied Force revealed still too many planners and commanders without full "common" access to classified programs.

Coalition Flag: Red Flag exercise at Nellis AFB, NV, that emphasizes allied participation. The first coalition exercise was held 19 Aug–2 Sep 1995. Coalition Flag combined the Desert Storm allied forces into a similar wartime flying experience. Participants included Canada, Singapore, and Spain.

Coastal Carnage: Navy exercise series conducted by the aircraft carrier USS *Theodore Roosevelt* (CVN 71), 1996.

Cobalt: USAFE Emergency Action Message.

Cobalt Flash/Flexible Anvil: B-52/Conventional Air Launched Cruise Missile (CALCM) JTF operation in support of Joint Forge and Determined Force in the former Yugoslavia. On 9 Oct 1998, the US committed Cobalt Flash forces for possible attacks against Serb forces in Kosovo.

Cobb Ring: Special operations exercise series involving the 290th Joint Communications Support Sqn and the 224th Joint Communications Support Sqn (Georgia ANG). Cobb Ring 01: 1–23 Apr 2001. UK participation canceled. Cobb Ring 99.

Cobbler: Alaskan Air Command first word.

Cobra: 1. Navy continuity of intelligence transmitter program that provides for enhanced application of national satellite capabilities for Blue Force Tracking using Cobra transmitters. Additional funds for the program were included in the post-9/11 Defense Emergency Response Fund.

2. **Cobra:** Air Force TENCAP architecture program, aka Cobra Programs Pony Express.

3. **COBRA (Coastal Battlefield Reconnaissance and Analysis):** Passive multi-spectral sensor system capable of operating in a Pioneer UAV.

4. **Cobra:** OPLAN Cobra, the CENTCOM Coalition/Combined Force Land Component Commander plan for combat operations against the regime of Saddam Hussein in support of OPLAN 1003V. The air defense plan was called OPLAN Cobra II Blackjack.

Cobra: Air Force intelligence first word. Cobra programs in the 1980s included Cobra Ace (a special collection effort), Cobra Cage, Cobra Charm (a special collection effort), Cobra Chine (an intelligence collection system), Cobra Mist, Cobra Dice (a special collection effort), Cobra Ear (a DIA–Air Force project), Cobra Edge (a special collection effort), Cobra Foam (ELINT), Cobra Guard (an airborne ELINT platform), Cobra Jade (a special collection effort), Cobra Jean (use of Advanced Range Instrumentation ships for intelligence), and Cobra Nook (a special collection effort).

+ **Cobra Ball:** Specially configured RC-135S used for "airborne reentry data collection system" to collect optical and electronic data on ballistic missiles and their associated reentry vehicles The Cobra Ball mission transferred to the 55th Wing, Offutt AFB, NE, on 7 Jul 1992. On 1 Jul 1994, Cobra Ball operations ceased at Eareckson AS, AK, and started at Eielson AFB, AK. In 1996, Cobra Ball operated from Misawa and Kadena, Japan, carrying out 16 Pony Express deployments and a single domestic mission. In 1999, a third Cobra Ball aircraft was delivered. Cobra Ball aircraft deploy to Thailand for Cobra Gold exercises and for collection against Chinese missiles. Cobra Ball was involved in OIF.

+ **Cobra Brass:** National Air Intelligence Center space-based overhead nonimaging infrared MASINT system used in target tracking and aerosol discrimination.

+ **Cobra Dane:** AN/FPS-108 single-faced phased array radar at Eareckson AS, Shemya Island, AK. Located on the far end of the Aleutian Island chain and less than 500 miles from Kamchatka Peninsula, Cobra Dane collects technical intelligence and MASINT data on ICBM/SLBM test launches into the Kamchatka Peninsula and the Pacific Ocean. Cobra Dane's corollary mission is to provide warning of attacks on the US and southern Canada. Completed and turned over in Jul 1977, Cobra Dane underwent a system modernization program to update its hardware and software in the early 1990s.

+ **Cobra Eye:** Former RC-135X configured aircraft specializing in telemetry intelligence. The Cobra Eye mission was terminated in Jun 1993 and the RC-135X converted to a Cobra Ball configuration.

+ **Cobra Fang:** MASINT related.

+ **Cobra Gemini:** Sea- and land-based radar system under development in the mid-1990s that can detect, acquire, track, and collect high-precision data. While Cobra Judy looks at ICBMs, Cobra Gemini will look for "rest of world" missiles.

+ **Cobra Joe:** Far East "cooperative radar" deployed in the 1980s, possibly located in China.

+ **Cobra Judy:** AN/SPQ-11 ship-based phased array radar program installed on the USS *Observation Island* (AG 154) and first operational in 1981.

+ **Cobra Shoe:** Former over-the-horizon missile tracking and MASINT radar on Cyprus.

+ **Cobra Spot:** "Special collection effort."

+ **Cobra Talon:** 1. "Cooperative radar" in Thailand used to monitor Chinese missile launches, operational 1971–1976.

  2. **Cobra Talon:** 441D classified system, 1997.

Cobra Gold: US–Thai annual command post exercise/field training exercise, the centerpiece of US–Thai military relations, and the largest US exercise in Asia, launched in 1982. The 2004 exercise was the 23rd in the series and the 5th of the expanded program, making it PACOM's premier international event and the premier US military training opportunity in Southeast Asia. The exercise location rotates among the four Thai army regional commands, providing maximum US exposure to the Thai military and civilian community. While the focus is military training, there are several civic assistance projects involving construction and medical care. Cobra Gold 04/Team Challenge 04: 13–27 May 2004. Mongolia participated for the first time. Cobra Gold 03/Team Challenge 03: 15–29 May 2003. Phase I was Balikatan in the Philippines. Cobra Gold 00: Chuk Sa Met and Songkhla, 9–23 May 2000. First Cobra Gold in the expanded observer program, involving other nations. Singapore participated for the first time. 3rd Bn, 1st SFG, and 1st Bn, 19th SFG. Cobra Gold 99: May 1999. Cobra Gold 98: 3rd Bn, 1st SFG, Fort Lewis, WA, trained with 1st Special Forces Regt, Thai army, at Camp Pawai, Thailand. Cobra Gold 96: Utapao and Narathiwat, Apr 1996. USS *Fort McHenry* (LSD 43). Cobra Gold 95: May 1995. Cobra Gold 94: May 1994.

Cocked Pistol: Exercise term representing a simulated DEFCON 1 condition.

Coherent: JFCOM first word.

+ **Coherent Defense:** Theater missile defense computer-assisted demonstration, 1997–1998.
+ **Coherent Joint Fires 00 (CJF 00):** Project focused on "joint fires" in theater missile defense. The CJF 00 demonstration (formerly known as the Theater Missile Defense Initiative 99) was conducted during Roving Sands 00, 14–23 Jun 2000.

Coiled Cobra: Sixth Fleet Adriatic Sea operations involving the USS *Theodore Roosevelt* (CVN 71), commencing 7 Aug 1995.

Cold Fire: USAFE air defense exercise series, 1975–1990.

Cold Winter: Reagan-era exercise with NSC involvement, 15–21 Mar 1985.

Colossus (Project Colossus): Short-range, high-frequency, upward-looking sets of bottom-mounted ocean surveillance sensors, also called Jezebel, first installed in 1953.

Colt: Naval exercise. Colt 03: Hawaii. Colt 01: Thailand, 9–21 May 2001.

Combat: Air force operations first word, originating in the Vietnam War, with Combat Angel, Combat Apple, Combat Dawn, Combat Pink, and Combat Skyspot.

+ **Combat Archer:** 1. Special reconnaissance program.
   2. **Combat Archer:** Air Combat Command Weapons System Evaluation Program to test air-to-air employment skills, Tyndall AFB, FL, and Nellis AFB, NV. *See also* Combat Hammer.
+ **Combat Arrow:** Specially configured MC-130E special operations aircraft.
+ **Combat Challenge:** Worldwide C4 (command, control, communications, and computers) competition.
+ **Combat Hammer:** Air-to-ground Weapon System Evaluation Program (WSEP) run by the 86th FWS at Eglin AFB, FL, and Utah test ranges. Combat Hammer is sometimes combined with the Joint Camouflage, Concealment, and Deception exercise. The exercise provides the opportunity to employ live air-to-ground weapons in a variety of scenarios and provides data pertaining to the actual effectiveness of weapons.
+ **Combat Knife:** Specially configured MC-130E special operations aircraft.

+ **Combat Sent:** RC-135U airborne scientific and technical collection platform based at Offutt AFB, NE. The two Combat Sent configured aircraft collect precise data on the parameters of foreign antenna and electronics systems. Combat Sent also supports the air force National Air Intelligence Center's role as the ground processor for RC-135 collections supporting STRATCOM's "threat change validation and national precision polarization databases."
+ **Combat Shadow:** C-130 search and rescue aircraft with improved direction finding, observation, and rescue suites.
+ **Combat Spear:** Specially configured MC-130E special operations aircraft.
+ **Combat Talon:** MC-130E/H special operations aircraft equipped for low-altitude deep-penetration missions and used for infiltration and exfiltration.

Combat Track II: Low probability of intercept/low probability of detection satellite communications link between a command center (such as a CAOC) and combat aircraft. The system provides a capability that allows transfer of imagery files to aircrew while in flight and provides en route tracking of aircraft through periodic, secure feedback of GPS coordinates. B-2s, B-52s, and B-1s that participated in OEF had CT II installed. CT II was also demonstrated on two C-17s flying humanitarian relief missions from Ramstein AB, Germany, to Afghanistan. CT II enabled exchange of information such as drop zone changes and en route weather updates.

Combined Endeavor: EUCOM ISO/PfP annual communications interoperability command post exercise/field training exercise, held at Lager Aulenbach, Baumholder, Germany, and other locations. Participants include Albania, Armenia, Austria, Azerbaijan, Belgium, Bulgaria, Canada, Croatia, the Czech Republic, Denmark, Estonia, Finland, France, Georgia, Germany, Greece, Hungary, Ireland, Italy, Kazakhstan, Kyrgyzstan, Latvia, Lithuania, Macedonia, Moldova, the Netherlands, Norway, Poland, Romania, the Slovak Republic, Slovenia, Spain, Sweden, Switzerland, Ukraine, the UK, and Uzbekistan. Russia has also participated. Combined Endeavor 05: Germany and Romania, May 2005. Eleventh annual exercise. Combined Endeavor 04: Germany, Jun 2004. Combined with Baltops/Clean Hunter to test and execute command and control capability. Combined Endeavor 03: Germany, 8–22 May 2003. Portugal and South Africa observers. Combined Endeavor 02: Riga, Latvia, 16–21 Sep 2002. Combined Endeavor 01:

Germany, 10–24 May 2001. Combined Endeavor 00: Germany. Combined Endeavor 99: Germany, 6–20 May 1999. The Delaware ARNG provided cable and wire laying for the exercise and communications support personnel to the exercise. Combined Endeavor 98: Sembach, Germany, 7–20 May1998. The most extensive multi-national interoperability testing event ever conducted, including personnel and C4 equipment from 29 different countries. Combined Endeavor 97.

Comet (Project Comet): US–Japanese technical intelligence exchange arrangement.

Comet Spares: Air force Space Command logistics related.

Comfort: Air force reserve project code, including Comfort Arrow, Comfort Leap, and Comfort Steeple.

Comfy: Air Intelligence Agency (former Air Force Electronics Security Command) first word. Comfy programs in the 1980s included Comfy Bee (a high-altitude reconnaissance drone).

+ **Comfy Challenge:** Red and blue force command, control, and communications counter-measures teams used to test US C3 systems. Comfy Sword was the interim name during the transition from Constant Spur.

+ **Comfy Cobalt:** Specialized electronicd and technical analytical support by the 18th Intelligence Sqn to the Air Force Space Command deep-space surveillance mission. Comfy Cobalt missions include Sensor Shadow and Project Marty at Fort Meade, MD. In the 1980s, Comfy Cobalt referred to space-related ELINT collection from San Vito, Italy, and Edzell, Scotland.

+ **Comfy Exchange:** Cryptographic equipment replacement.

+ **Comfy Fix:** Upgrade to the direction finding data control section of the AN/FLR-9V (*see also* Enlarger).

+ **Comfy Harvest:** Tactical Information Broadcast System (TIBS).

+ **Comfy Levi:** ANG C-135 COMINT mission (now called Senior Scout), particularly active in Latin America starting in 1981 (*see* Coronet Guard). The last Comfy Levi system was decommissioned on 1 Jul 1991.

+ **Comfy Olympics:** *See* Sensor Olympics.

+ **Comfy Sabre:** Communications security monitoring system.

+ **Comfy Shire:** *See* Constant Web.

Command/Talon Command: Air Force Space Warfare Center TENCAP initiative to enhance warfighting C4I support.

Commando: Pacific Air Forces first word. The use of the name goes back at least to the Vietnam War with projects such as Commando Club and Commando Hunt. Other Pacific Commando programs included Commando Fox, Commando Pads, Commando Plug, Commando Port, and Commando Torii. A series of Commando "special plans" projects in Korea, Japan, and the Philippines were held in the 1980s–early 1990s, including Commando Arch, Commando Glimpse, Commando Handle, Commando Haven, Commando Pirate, Commando Rabble, and Commando West.

+ **Commando Escort:** HF/SSB communications network.
+ **Commando Mercury:** Air Force Materiel Command project, 1997.
+ **Commando Runner:** Command and control related.
+ **Commando Sling:** Air combat training deployments to Paya Lebar AB, Singapore. The exercises began with an agreement between the US and Singapore in 1990. The 497th Combat Training Sqn, which is based at Paya Lebar, provides coordination for three deployments per year of six fighter aircraft. In Commando Sling 98-4, Australia participated for the first time, flying F-18s.
+ **Commando Viking.**

Commando Look: Air force program to determine the suitability of prospective candidates for special operations missions.

Commando Peak: XVIII Airborne Corps and 10th Mountain Div exercise, 14–24 Sep 1998.

Commando Solo: EC-130E/J PSYOPs platform with worldwide color television and radio broadcast capability. The 193rd SOW of the Pennsylvania ANG operates Commando Solo.

Common Energy: NATO exercise to deploy Belgian F-16s and C-130s, with the help of US KC-10 tankers, to bases in Spain, 1994.

Companion Channel: Unknown program or operation, 1980s.

Compass: Hyperspectral MASINT sensor on Cyclops, developed by the Army Night Vision Electronics Sensor Directorate, to be integrated into the Predator UAV.

Compass: Air force R&D first word, particularly used for UAV and drone development. Compass programs in the 1980s included Compass Arrow, Compass

Bright, Compass Bin, Compass Cookie, Compass Cope, Compass Ears, Compass Dart, Compass Dawn, Compass Dwell, Compass Era, Compass Ghost, Compass Hammer, Compass Home, Compass Jade, Compass Lane, Compass Link, Compass Matrix, Compass Robin, Compass Sail, Compass Seven, Compass Sight, Compass Strike, and Compass Tie.

+ **Compass Bright:** Research program to develop advanced SIGINT capabilities to ensure that time-sensitive collection against emerging and future target signals occurs fast enough to be of immediate value in the conduct of military operations. It is the only air force program that pursues basic SIGINT research. Projects include Beamformer, Firehawk, Little Weasel, MUD, MPA, SWCR, and SUAVE-E.

+ **Compass Call/Rivet Fire:** EC-130H information warfare platform, currently being upgraded with Project Suter and upgrades enabling attack of IADS components.

+ **Compass Link:** Big Safari–managed special access program.

Concord/MC: *See* Talon Concord/MC.

Concordia: EU and NATO operation in Macedonia, the first collaborative effort of the two alliances, concluded in 2003.

Condor: 1. SOCOM command and control systems, including cell phones.

2. **Condor:** Boeing high altitude long endurance (HALE) UAV research effort.

3. **Condor (Operation Condor):** UK 45 Commando Group operation in Paktia Province in southeast Afghanistan to search and clear a significant area in remote mountains believed to be used as a base by al Qaeda and Taliban forces, 2–13 May 2002.

Condor Hawk: RC-135 direction finding and receiver system.

Condor Redoubt/Condor Samaritan: Exercises or operations including 622nd Aero-medical Evacuation Sqn, Macdill AFB, FL, 1981–1982.

Conga: Army intelligence system, Bad Aibling, Germany.

Conifer (UK Atomic Conifer): UK Secret or Top Secret information concerning details (quantities) of fissile, fissionable, fusion, or special materials as well as information on design of nuclear warheads.

Consequence Island 01: Puerto Rico local government–army reserve WMD exercise, Army Reserve Center, Fort Buchanan, Puerto Rico, 18–26 May 2001.

Consequence Management: Federal government WMD response exercise. Consequence Management 00: Fort Gordon, GA, 15–20 May 2000. More than 1,500 participants from local, state, and federal agencies in the largest WMD exercise of its kind to date. The scenario was a simulated terrorist attack on a federal building. Particpants included Department of Veterans Affairs, Public Health Service, state, and local government. Consequence Management 98.

Constant: Air force operations first word, often referring to Air Force Technical Application Center (AFTAC) and other reconnaissance missions. Constant programs in the 1980s included Constant Bore, Constant Dome, Constant Fish, Constant Globe, Constant Seek, and Constant Take.

+ **Constant Blue:** Presidential successor helicopter evacuation plan, part of the Joint Emergency Evacuation Plan.
+ **Constant Gate:** SOCOM-related program.
+ **Constant Help:** Special access program.
+ **Constant Phoenix:** Nuclear monitoring with specialized WC-135W aircraft of the 45th RS, 55th Wing, Offutt AFB, NE, 2002–present.
+ **Constant Pisces:** Former special access program.
+ **Constant Shotgun:** Cold War nickname identifying Soviet and Chinese aircraft entering the US under authorization.
+ **Constant Source:** Near-real-time dissemination of ELINT/tactical Electronic Order of Battle (EOB) data to theater and tactical units. Multi-source data is received from Tactical Digital Information Exchange System Broadcast/Tactical Receive Equipment (TADIXS B/TRE) as well as national and airborne ELINT broadcasts. Constant Source ties in with Sentinel Byte.
+ **Constant Spur:** Former Red Team that employed adversary C3 counter-measures actions against friendly operators (combat crews, weapons controllers, communications) and C3 facilities, activated 1980. Became Comfy Challenge.
+ **Constant Star:** Special access program.
+ **Constant Stare:** Air Intelligence Agency organizational entity.

Constant Harmony: NATO computer-assisted exercise/command post exercise focusing on intensive warfighting under an Article 5 crisis. Participants include Belgium, Canada, the Czech Republic, Denmark, France, Germany, Italy, the Netherlands, Norway, Poland, Spain, Turkey, the UK, and the US. Constant Harmony 01. Constant Harmony 00: UK, 2–17

Nov 2000. Exercise involved European real-world terrain with fictitious boundaries.

Constant Vigil (Laser Strike/Constant Vigil): SOUTHCOM counter-narcotics operations. Constant Vigil 98: Venezuela. Constant Vigil 97: Panama. Constant Vigil 96: Colombia. Constant Vigil 95: Panama. Constant Vigil 94: Panama.

Constant Watch: Korean peninsula air intelligence system, activated in 1981.

Constant Web: Air Force Information Warfare Center counter-measures/information warfare database that provides detailed all-source information on adversary military C3 structure. The database fuses general military intelligence with SIGINT technical information. The result shows "who is talking to whom" and how they are communicating. Details include network nodes, frequencies, radio equipment, signals, and other technical information related to networks. Constant Web started as Comfy Shire in 1979.

Contending Warrior: Air Combat Command security forces competition at Nellis AFB and Indian Springs, NV, 1996–1999.

Continue Hope: Somalia operation to support UNOSOM II and provide a Quick Reaction Force and logistics support, 5 May 1993–31 Mar 1994. On 14 Mar, eight men from the 16th SOS died when their AC-130 experienced a catastrophic failure while firing a 105mm cannon off the coast of Kenya. Operations were supported by the USS *Ranger* (CV 61), USS *Kitty Hawk* (CV 63), USS *Juneau* (LPD 10), USS *Tripoli* (LPH 10), and USS *Rushmore* (LSD 47).

Convoy: El Paso Intelligence Center–based domestic drug interdiction training program.

Cool: Alaskan Air Command first word, including Cool Barge (supply missions to AK) and Cool Ray (northern-latitudes experimentation), 1980s.

Cooperative (Coop): NATO PfP exercise first word. Exercises include Cooperative Advanced Exchange 02, Cooperative Advanced Express 00, Cooperative Aid 99, Cooperative Arcade 99, Cooperative Baltic, Cooperative Blend 99, Cooperative Express 00, and Cooperative From the Sea.

+ **Cooperative Adventure Exchange:** Joint Command Southeast command post exercise/CFX focused on interoperability of Allied Command Europe Mobile Forces, Land. Participants include Azerbaijan, Belgium, Bulgaria, Denmark, Georgia, Germany, Hungary,

Italy, Luxembourg, Macedonia, Moldova, Norway, Poland, Turkey, Ukraine, the UK, and the US. Cooperative Adventure Exchange 02: Yavoriv Training Center, Ukraine, 4–19 Oct 2002. Cooperative Adventure Exchange 01: 1–25 Oct 2001.

+ **Cooperative Adventure Express:** *See* Adventure Express.

+ **Cooperative Assembly 98:** Albania, 17–22 Aug 1998. Participants include Albania, Belgium, Canada, France, Germany, Greece, Italy, Lithuania, Netherlands, Russia, Spain, Turkey, the UK, and the US.

+ **Cooperative Associate:** Joint Command Southwest PfP command post exercise focused on brigade-level peacekeeping, humanitarian aid, and disaster relief operations. Beginning in 2002, Cooperative Dragon, Cooperative Determination, and Disciplined Warrior were integrated and renamed Cooperative Associate. Participants include Armenia, Azerbaijan, Austria, Bulgaria, France, Germany, Georgia, Greece, Hungary, Italy, Kyrgyzstan, Macedonia Moldova, Portugal, Romania, Slovakia, Switzerland, Turkey, Uzbekistan, the UK, and the US. Cooperative Associate 04: 16–30 Nov 2003. Cooperative Associate 03: G. S. Rakovski Defence and Staff College in Sofia, Bulgaria, 17–18 Mar 2003.

+ **Cooperative Aura:** Supreme Headquarters Allied Powers Europe (SHAPE) staff officer seminar series focusing on NATO higher-level staff and crisis management procedures and arrangements. Participants include Switzerland. Cooperative Aura 04. Cooperative Aura 00. Cooperative Aura 95.

+ **Cooperative Automation:** Netherlands-based SHAPE NC3A seminar series focused on technical aspects, features, and procedures in planning, preparing, conducting, and analyzing a computer-assisted exercise. Cooperative Automation 01: 10–14 Sep 2001. Cooperative Automation 99. Cooperative Automation 97.

+ **Cooperative Baltic Eye:** Joint Command Northeast biennal PfP search and rescue exercise in the Baltic Sea. Participants include Denmark, Estonia, Finland, France, Germany, Latvia, Lithuania, Poland, Russia, Sweden, the UK, and the US. Cooperative Baltic Eye 03: 13–15 May 2003. Cooperative Baltic Eye 01: 14–16 May 2001. Cooperative Baltic Eye 00. Cooperative Baltic Eye 99.

+ **Cooperative Banish 00:** NAVNORTH PfP maritime mine countermeasures exercise, Belgium, 19–30 Jun 2000.

+ **Cooperative Banners/Chance:** Joint Command Northeast quadrennial exercise focused on a NATO-led peacekeeping operation, held in

Norway. The exercise alternates every two years with Cooperative Jaguar/Chance. Participants include Azerbaijan, Bulgaria, Estonia, Finland, Latvia, Lithuania, Norway, Romania, Slovakia, and Sweden. Cooperative Chance is an air component part of each of these exercises. Cooperative Banners 04: Scheduled for Jun 2004 but canceled. Cooperative Banners 00: 29 May–10 Jun 2000. Cooperative Banners 97: 26 May–6 Jun 1997.

+ **Cooperative Bear:** Former exercise series (*see* Cooperative Casualty Bear). Cooperative Bear 99: Poland, 25 Sep–1 Oct 1999. Cooperative Bear 98: St. Mawgan, UK. Cooperative Bear 97: Såtenäs, Sweden, 1–5 Sep 1997.

+ **Cooperative Best Effort:** Joint Command South annual land field training exercise, the principal NATO and PfP land-based exercise in the alliance's Southern Region. The series focuses on improving and exchanging platoon-level light infantry skills while exercising in a variety of peacekeeping settings. Participants include Armenia, Austria, Azerbaijan, Bulgaria, Canada, Georgia, Greece, Hungary, Italy, Lithuania, Macedonia, Moldova, the Netherlands, Poland, Romania, Russia, Slovakia, Switzerland, Turkey, Ukraine, the UK, the US, and Uzbekistan. Cooperative Best Effort 05: Ukraine, Jun 2005. Cooperative Best Effort 04: Azerbaijan, 8–19 Sep 2004. Cooperative Best Effort 03: Yerevan, Armenia, 16–27 Jun 2003. First PfP exercise hosted by Armenia and the first time Russia participated in such a NATO exercise with staff officers and a fully integrated infantry squad. Cooperative Best Effort 01: Styria, Austria, 10–22 Sep 2001. Largest PfP exercise held on Austrian soil. Cooperative Best Effort 00: Cluj Napoca, Romania, 10–24 Sep 2000. Cooperative Best Effort 99: Canada. Cooperative Best Effort 98: Krivolak Training Area, Macedonia, 11–18 Sep 1998. Cooperative Best Effort 97: Latvia. Cooperative Best Effort 96: Czech Republic. First exercise of the series.

+ **Cooperative Binate:** AFNORTH workshop, Oct 2000.

+ **Cooperative Bridge 94:** Poznan, Poland.

+ **Cooperative Bright Eye:** *See* Bright Eye.

+ **Cooperative Casualty Bear:** Allied Forces Northern Europe (AFNORTH) annual medical exercise, a combination of Casualty Care and former Cooperative Bear series. Cooperative Bear 01: 29 Sep–5 Oct 2001. Canceled due to 9/11.

+ **Cooperative Chance:** Joint Command Northeast air force component of Cooperative Banners/Chance and Cooperative Jaguar/Chance.

Code Names

Participants include Austria, Bulgaria, Canada, the Czech Republic, Denmark, Finland, France, Hungary, Italy, Macedonia, Moldova, Germany, the Netherlands, Poland, Romania, the Slovak Republic, Sweden, Ukraine, the UK, and the US. Cooperative Chance 00: Bulgaria. Cooperative Chance 98: 31 AFB Sliac, Slovakia, 5–10 Jul 1998. Cooperative Chance 97: Hungary. Cooperative Chance 96: Kecskemet AB, Hungary, 18 Jul 1998.

+ **Cooperative Demand 97:** Joint Command Southwest exercise, Turkey.

+ **Cooperative Determination:** Joint Command Southwest computer-assisted exercise at multi-national brigade (MNB) level to familiarize partners with procedures related to peacekeeping and humanitarian assistance operations. Participants include Armenia, Austria, Azerbaijan, Bulgaria, Germany, France, Georgia, Greece, Hungary, Italy, Kyrgyzstan, Luxembourg, Macedonia, Moldavia, the Netherlands, Portugal, Romania, Slovakia, Switzerland, Spain, Turkey, the US, and Uzbekistan. Cooperative Determination 03. Cooperative Determination 01: Azerbaijan, 5–17 Nov 2001. Cooperative Determination 00: Swiss Armed Forces Training Center, Lucerne, 29 Oct–10 Nov 2000. First PfP exercise organized in Switzerland. Cooperative Determination 99: Bucharest, Romania. Cooperative Determination 98: Bulgaria. Cooperative Determination 97: Sibiu, Romania, 1–14 Nov 1997. The exercise scenario featured an armed conflict between two fictitious neighboring countries, Henan and Gobi, on a background of natural disasters and religious and social uprising that caused the UN Security Council to decide on deploying to the fictitious land. Cooperative Determination 95: Sibiu, Romania, 10–15 Sep, 1995. First NATO PfP land forces exercise scheduled for Romania.

+ **Cooperative Dragon:** Joint Command Southwest combination command post exercise/field training exercise. The exercise forms a multi-national HQ with up to two multi-national brigades and response cells. Participants include Albania, Austria, Azerbaijan, Bulgaria, the Czech Republic, Georgia, Greece, Hungary, Italy, Macedonia, Moldova, Poland, Romania, Slovakia, Spain, Turkey, Ukraine, and Uzbekistan. Cooperative Dragon 01. Cooperative Dragon 00: Tirana, Albania, 21 Jun–1 Jul 2000. Cooperative Dragon 99: Ohrid, Macedonia, 20 Jun–2 Jul 1999. Cooperative Dragon 96: Banska Bysticaa, Slovak Republic, Sep 1996. Cooperative Dragon-Esperia 95: Italy. Cooperative Dragon-Esperia 94: Cellina Meduna, Italy.

+ **Cooperative Engagement:** NAVSOUTH maritime exercise focused on coastal mine counter-measures and search and rescue operations. Cooperative Engagement 03: Split, Croatia, and in the Adriatic Sea, 13–20 Sep 2003. Cooperative Engagement 01: 17–23 Sep 2001.
+ **Cooperative Exchange:** 16th Air Force peacetime engagement exercise, 22–26 Jan 1996.
+ **Cooperative Guard:** Central Region annual command post exercise series. Cooperative Guard 01. Cooperative Guard 99: Vyskov military academy, Czech Republic, May–Jun 1999. Cooperative Guard 98. Cooperative Guard 97: Camp Trauen, Germany, 12–22 May 1997.
+ **Cooperative Jaguar/Chance:** Joint Command Northeast quadrennial combined computer-assisted exercise/command post exercise (alternating every two years with Cooperative Banners). Participants include Austria, the Czech Republic, Denmark, Estonia, Finland, France, Germany, Hungary, Latvia, Lithuania, Norway, Poland, Romania, Sweden, the UK, and the US. Cooperative Jaguar 06: Planned for Lithuania. Cooperative Jaguar 02/03. Cooperative Jaguar 99: Norway. Cooperative Jaguar 98: Grenaa, Denmark, 18–29 May 1998. The exercise scenario called for a NATO-led peacekeeping force to deploy to a country troubled by economic distress, ethnic tensions, and the breakup of its military forces. The two-week exercise culminated with an noncombatant evacuation operation exercise 24–29 May. Cooperative Jaguar 95.
+ **Cooperative Key:** AIRSOUTH combined command post exercise focused on practicing and refining no-fly-zone enforcement, close air support, search and rescue, and airlift. The exercise rotates between northern and southern regions. Participants include Austria, Azerbaijan, Bulgaria, the Czech Republic, France, Germany, Greece, France, Hungary, Italy, Latvia, Macedonia, Moldova, Norway, Poland, Romania, Slovakia, Slovenia, Sweden, Switzerland, Turkey, and the US. Cooperative Key 05: May/Jun 2005. Cooperative Key 04: Macedonia, 15–30 Sep 2004. Cooperative Key 03: Plovdiv, Bulgaria, 2–12 Sep 2003. The African scenario involved the fictitious countries of Peaceland, Dryland, and Toyland. About 20,000 refugees had been reported to have fled in the midst of a conflict between warring parties. Cooperative Key 02: Saint-Dizier, France, 22 Sep–4 Oct 2002. Cooperative Key 01: Bulgaria, 10–23 Sep 2001. Cooperative Key 00: Romania. Cooperative Key 99: Canceled because of OAF. Cooperative

Key 98: Turkey. Cooperative Key 97: 31 AFB Sliac and 32 AFB, Piestany, Slovakia, 13–18 Jul 1997. Cooperative Key 96: Nicolae Banciulescu Air Transport Base and 90th Otopeni AB, Romania, 15–18 Oct 1996. First of the series of NATO live-flying exercises. This was also the third multi-national exercise hosted by Romania.

+ **Cooperative Knowledge 04:** AFNORTH communications planning for NATO CJTF exercise. Helsinki, Finland.

+ **Cooperative Lantern:** AFNORTH PfP staff training conducted as a command post exercise to train comanders in staff procedures required to conduct peacekeeping operations in a multi-national brigade HQ. Cooperative Lantern 00: 14–17 May 2000. Cooperative Lantern 98: Lake Balaton and Taszar, Hungary, 11–16 May 1998.

+ **Cooperative Light 95:** Command post exercise, Hungary, 12–24 Oct 1995. Participants include Belgium, France, Germany, the Netherlands, the US, and 12 PfP nations.

+ **Cooperative Mermaid/Classica 95:** Ligurian Sea on the west coast of Italy, 17–19 Nov 1995. The exercise involved sea control and search and rescue. Participants included Bulgaria, France, Greece, Italy, Romania, Spain, Turkey, and Ukraine.

+ **Cooperative Meseta.**

+ **Cooperative Neighbor 97:** Aviv and Yavoriv Training Area, Ukraine, 1–14 Jul 1997. The command post and live exercise was attended by Secretary of Defense William Cohen.

+ **Cooperative Nugget:** JFCOM-designed computer-assisted exercise/command post exercise to train staff officers in component- and command-level tasks in a generic peacekeeping operation. In Aug 1995, Cooperative Nugget 95 became the first NATO PfP exercise ever held on US soil. Participants include NATO members and Kazakhstan, Macedonia, and Uzbekistan. Cooperative Nugget 04. Cooperative Nugget 03. Cooperative Nugget 02: Lisbon, Portugal; Fort Drum, NY; and Almnas, Sweden; 19–27 Jun 2002. Cooperative Nugget 01. Cooperative Nugget 00: Fort Carson, CO, 1–14 May 2000. Hosted by 3rd Bde, 4th Infantry Div. Cooperative Nugget 97: Fort Polk, LA, 11 Jun–3 Jul 1997. Cooperative Nugget 95: Fort Polk, LA, Aug 1995.

+ **Cooperative Ocean 00:** Passing exercise in the Baltic Sea, 20–27 Sep 2000.

+ **Cooperative Osprey:** JFCOM amphibious and peacekeeping operations exercise. Participants include Albania, Bulgaria, Canada, Estonia,

Georgia, Kazakhstan, Kyrgyzstan, Latvia, Lithuania, Moldova, Poland, Romania, Ukraine, the UK, the US, and Uzbekistan. Cooperative Osprey 03: Camp Lejeune, NC. Cooperative Osprey 01: Nova Scotia, Canada, Mar 2001. Cooperative Osprey 96: Camp Lejeune, NC, Aug 1996. Training included Military Operation in Urban Terrain, and civil disturbance operations.

+ **Cooperative Partner:** NAVSOUTH annual maritime and amphibious peacekeeping field training exercise. The exercise is focused on interoperability of the Black Sea region navies in convoy, embargos, and noncombatant evacuation operations. Participants include Azerbaijan, Bulgaria, France, Germany, Georgia, Greece, Italy, the Netherlands, Romania, Spain, Sweden, Turkey, Ukraine, the UK, and the US. Cooperative Partner 04: Bulgaria, Jun 2004. Cooperative Partner 03: Odessa, Ukraine, 20 Jun–5 Jul 2003. Cooperative Partner 02: Constanta, Romania, 21 Jun–6 Jul 2002. Cooperative Partner 01: Georgia, 11–24 Jun 2001. First full-scale NATO PfP exercise held in the South Caucasus. Cooperative Partner 00: Odessa, Ukraine, 19 Jun–1 Jul 2000. 24th MEU (SOC) and USS *Trenton* (LPD 14). Cooperative Partner 99. Cooperative Partner 98: Constanta, Romania. Cooperative Partner 97: Bulgaria, 22 Jun–5 Jul 1997. 22nd MEU. Cooperative Partner 96: Constanta, Romania. 22–28 Jul 1996. Second NATO exercise on Romanian territory. Cooperative Partner 95: Varna, Bulgaria.

+ **Cooperative Poseidon:** East Atlantic submarine safety seminar, tactical floor and computer-assisted training. Participants include Bulgaria, Canada, Denmark, France, Greece, the Netherlands, Norway, Poland, Sweden, Turkey, the Ukraine, the UK, and the US. Algeria serves as observer. Cooperative Poseidon 03: Turkey, Apr 2003. Cooperative Poseidon 00: Den Helder, Netherlands, 9–13 Oct 2000. Cooperative Poseidon 99.

+ **Cooperative Rescue 97:** Brasov, Romania.

+ **Cooperative Safeguard:** Supreme Allied Commander Transformation (formerly Atlantic) biennial PfP seminar/command post and live exercise based on a realistic natural disaster scenario, held in Iceland. Participants include Austria, Canada, the Czech Republic, Denmark, Estonia, Finland, Germany, Greece, Hungary, Latvia, Lithuania, Norway, Romania, Russia, Ukraine, and the US. The government of Iceland invites civil defense personnel from Sweden and Israel as well. Cooperative Safeguard 04: 24–30 Jun 2004. Cooperative Safeguard 03.

Cooperative Safeguard 02: 24 Jun–1 Jul 2002. The scenario shifted from search and rescue to maritime interdiction after 9/11. Cooperative Safeguard 00: 7–12 Jun 2000. Cooperative Safeguard 97: 22–31 Jul 1997. First PfP exercise held in Iceland.

+ **Cooperative Spider:** PfP exercise in the Netherlands, 1994.

+ **Cooperative Support:** Supreme Allied Commander Transformation (formerly Atlantic) PfP logistics desktop exercise. Observer countries included Algeria and Jordan. Cooperative Support 04. Cooperative Support 2003: Salzburg, Austria, 26 Nov–2 Dec 2003. Cooperative Support 02: 8–15 Oct 2002. Cooperative Support 00: Hungary, 25 Oct–2 Nov 2000. Cooperative Support 97: Constanta, Romania.

+ **Cooperative Telos 99:** Supreme Allied Commander Transformation (formerly Atlantic) JFCOM-led PfP mine counter-measures interoperability exercise exercise, Corpus Christi, TX, 18–29 Sep 1997.

+ **Cooperative Tide 01:** Supreme Allied Commander Transformation (formerly Atlantic) JFCOM-led exercise, Williamsburg, VA, 12–23 May 2001.

+ **Cooperative Venture:** North Sea/Norwegian Sea PfP exercise. Cooperative Venture 00. Cooperative Venture 99. Cooperative Venture 96: Baltic Sea, 26 Sep–11 Oct 1996. Cooperative Venture 94: 28 Sep–7 Oct 1994.

+ **Cooperative Zenith:** JFCOM-directed air-force-led PfP exercise designed to train in search and rescue operations. Participants include Albania, Armenia, Azerbaijan, Belarus, Bulgaria, the Czech Republic, Estonia, Georgia, Hungary, Kazakhstan, Kyrgyzstan, Latvia, Lithuania, Moldova, Poland, Romania, Russia, Slovakia, Ukraine, the UK, the US, and Uzbekistan. Began in 1996. Cooperative Zenith 00: Hurlburt Field, FL. Cooperative Zenith 99: NS Greenwood, Nova Scotia, Canada, 5–17 Oct 1999. Cooperative Zenith 98: 6–15 May 1998. Cooperative Zenith 97: Cornwall, Ontario; Trenton, Ontario; Sydney, Nova Scotia, Canada, 18–30 May 1997. Cooperative Zenith 96: Patrick AFB, FL, 7–16 May 1996.

Cooperative Thunder 99: AK-based exercise, element of the Cope Thunder series, including participants and observers from Australia, Brunei, Indonesia, Japan, Malaysia, South Korea, and Sri Lanka, Jul 1999.

Cope: Pacific Air Forces exercise first word.

+ **Cope Angel:** US–Japanese annual peacetime search and rescue exercise, held in Okinawa. Cope Angel 00: Dec 2000. Cope Angel 99: 12–16 Jul 1999.

+ **Cope Boomerang:** US–Australian training exercise.

+ **Cope Cage:** Hawaii-based quarterly exercise to test the air defense of the Hawaiian Islands. *See also* Cope Spade.

+ **Cope India:** US–Indian exercise and deployment to India. Cope India 04: Gwalior Air Force Station, India, 16–25 Feb 2004. F-15s from Alaska deployed to India for the first bilateral dissimilar exercise in more than 40 years. Cope India 02: Agra Air Station, India, 15–30 Oct 2002. More than 150 airmen from Yokota AB, Japan; Hickam AB, Hawaii; and Andersen AFB, Guam, deployed to the home of the Indian air force's 4th Wing and its parachute training school. Five US C-130s airlifted Indian paratroopers, continuing military-to-military contacts with India as the most active in 40 years.

+ **Cope Jade/CAPEX:** US–South Korean combined air defense exercise, held twice annually. The 7th Air Force activates its Combined Air Operations Center (CAOC) for the exercise. Cope Jade 99: 15–18 Jun 1999. Cope Jade 98: Feb 1998. Two B-1Bs of the 9th BS took off from Dyess AFB, TX, refueled over AK, joined up with six F-15Es deployed to Komatsu AB, Japan, and were to have conducted bombing at the Pilsung bombing range just south of the DMZ in South Korea, recovering at Andersen AFB, Guam. The mission was unsuccessful due to bad weather and poor communications; the bombers instead landed at Kunsan AB, South Korea.

+ **Cope North:** US–Japanese 5th Air Force/Japanese Air Self-Defense Force air defense exercise held twice annually. Includes Cope North 2002.

+ **Cope South:** US–Bangladesh annual humanitarian exercise, held since 1995. Cope South 03: Bangladesh Air Force (BAF) Base Bashar in Dhaka and Sylhet, 30 Sep–7 Oct 2003. Involved BAF and 1st Marine Air Wing. Cope South 98: 13–17 Sep 1998.

+ **Cope Spade:** Hawaii-based no-notice air defense exercise identical to Cope Cage. The 169th Aircraft Control and Warning orders a launch of the F-15s on alert, runs the weapons-safe checklist, and continues the intercept.

+ **Cope Taufan:** US–Malaysian annual airfield training exercise series, supported by the 497th Combat Training Sqn in Singapore. Deployment consists of up to 12 US F-15s/F-16s cross-training with Malaysian air force (TUDM) MIG-29s, F-5s, and Hawk fighter aircraft.

+ **Cope Thaw:** Hawaii deployments designed to enable Alaska-based, and Misawa, Japan, units off-station training opportunities during winter months.

+ **Cope Thunder/Cooperative Cope Thunder:** Pacific Air Forces' premier composite force air readiness exercise, held in Alaska. The exercise is designed to provide intense training with at least 10 sorties per aircraft in a realistic simulated combat environment. Cope Thunder exercises were first held in 1976 at Clark AB, Philippines, but moved in 1992 to Alaska after Mount Pinatubo erupted. Participants include Australia, Japan, Singapore, and the UK.

  Cope Thunder 01-4: 12–27 Jun 2001. Cooperative Cope Thunder 00: Largest air combat exercise in the Pacific. Representatives from Brunei, China, Malaysia, and Thailand observed the training areas and air maneuvers. Cope Thunder 99-4: Personnel recovery focus. Cope Thunder 98-4: 9–24 Jul 1998. The exercise represented the first time the five countries converged for Cope Thunder. Russia, China, Brunei, Malaysia, Thailand, and the Philippines sent observers. Cope Thunder 97-4: 10–14 Jul 1997. Cope Thunder 97 was the sixth Aerospace Expeditionary Force (AEF) deployment since Oct 1995 and the first no-notice, air tasking order-driven AEF exercise. Three B-52s from Barksdale AFB, LA, deployed to Eielson AFB, AK. Cope Thunder 96: 6–21 Jun 1996. Cope Thunder 93: 17 Apr–1 May 1993.

+ **Cope Tiger:** US–Thai annual field training exercise involving Australia, Indonesia, Malaysia, and Singapore. The exercise series started in 1978.

  Cope Tiger 03. Cope Tiger 98: Korat Royal Thai AFB (RTAFB), Thailand, 8–20 Feb 1998. Phase I was held at Paya Lebar AB, Singapore, 7 Nov 1997. Cope Tiger 97: Phase II, Korat RTAFB, Thailand, 16–29 Jan 1997. Phase I was held at Paya Lebar air base, Singapore, 29 Oct 1996. Cope Tiger 96: 26 Jan–12 Feb 1996. Cope Tiger 95: Korat RTAFB, Thailand, 5–16 Jan 1995. First exercise involving all three countries.

+ **Cope West:** Pacific Air Forces aircraft deployments to Southeast Asia providing combined training for countries that, for economical, political, or proficiency reasons, cannot participate in other combined exercises. Cope West 95: Butterworth AB, Malaysia, 11–28 Aug 1995.

Cope Max V: Reagan-era exercise with NSC involvement, 19 Nov 1985.

Cope Snapper 02: NAS Key West, FL, multi-aircraft dissimilar air combat training among air force F-15s and F-16s and navy F-18s and F-14s.

Copper Canyon: Former DARPA research program into hypersonic aircraft and vehicles.

Copper Cap: Air force intelligence intern program.

Copper Coast: Air force special access program.

Copper Green: Reported war on terrorism special access program. The *New Yorker* reported in May 2004 that Copper Green "encouraged physical coercion and sexual humiliation of Iraqi prisoners in an effort to generate more intelligence" and was at the root of the Abu Ghraib prison scandal in Iraq. The DOD vociferously denied that any such program existed, and when the Senate inquired about its existence, it was told no such program existed.

Coral: Air Force Materiel Command first word referring to maintenance and repair programs and base stand-up. General Coral names, such as Coral Airlift, Coral Avionics, and Coral Parts apply to logistical support. A number of Coral programs provide support to classified projects: Coral Abe, Coral Beam, Coral Legend, Coral Lift, Coral Orbit, Coral Raider, Coral Snow, and Coral Wind. Other logistical-related terms are grouped as follows: A-10: Coral Hog. Airlift: Coral Door, Coral Flame, Coral Flap, Coral Galaxy, Coral Gear, Coral Globemaster, Coral Jersey, Coral Source, Coral Strategic. Base support: Coral Catfish, Coral Drift, Coral Move, Coral Relief. Bombers: Coral Ace, Coral Bat, Coral Bearing, Coral Quest, Coral Taper. E-3 AWACS aircraft: Coral Eagle, Coral Icon, Coral Sentry. F-15: Coral Fire, Coral Hook, Coral Keek, Coral Main, Coral Screen, Coral Snout. F-16: Coral Comet, Coral Contender, Coral Falcon, Coral Fifty, Coral Heavy, Coral Lite, Coral Mako, Coral Phoenix, Coral Struts. F-22: Coral Prepare, Coral Wraith. Munitions: Coral Cas, Coral Glib, Coral Missile, Coral Nap, Coral Terminator, Coral Test. Training aircraft: Coral Burn.

+ **Coral Lease:** South Korean lease of T-38 training aircraft.
+ **Coral Rice:** Support for MH-60G activation at 33rd Rescue Squadron, Kadena AB, Japan.
+ **Coral Skies:** Support of Open Skies Treaty.

Coral Breeze: US Forces Korea WMD warfare seminar series examining the impact of North Korean use of chemical or biological weapons on US forces. Coral Breeze 97: Mar 1997.

Coral Fox: Classified air force special operations weapons evaluation, 1997.

Coral Mat/Sensor Ghost: Air Force foreign material exploitation, 1997.

Coral Sea: Reagan-era exercise with NSC involvement.

Corner Back: NORAD exercise that tests the command's detection and monitoring capabilities and interface with commands and agencies involved in the counter-narcotics effort.

Cornerstone: 1. DOD Counter-intelligence Field Activity (CIFA) foreign visitor tracking system.

2. **Cornerstone:** Scientific and technical intelligence production tool.

3. **Cornerstone:** Former EUCOM ISO/PfP engineering exercise. The 10th and final Cornerstone took place in 2003. Participants included Albania, Bulgaria, Estonia, Georgia, Greece, Latvia, Lithuania, Macedonia, Moldova, Romania, and Turkey. Cornerstone 03: Constanta, Romania, 15 May–15 Jul 2003. Cornerstone 01. Cornerstone 00-3: Macedonia, May–Jun 2000. First exercise conducted in support of the Southeast Europe Defense Ministerial (SEDM) objectives. Cornerstone 00-2: Tartu, Estonia, 17 Jul–16 Sep 2000. Cornerstone 00-1: Staseni, Moldova, Jul–Aug 2000. Cornerstone 99-2: Latvia, Jul–Aug 1999. Cornerstone 98: Bulgaria.

Cornet West: Transpacific ferry movement of Marine Corps aircraft.

Corona: 1. Original code word for imagery satellites KH-1 through KH-4.

2. **Corona:** Chief of Staff of the Air Force commanders' conference consisting of Corona Fall, Corona South, Corona Top.

Coronet: Air Combat Command (and former Tactical Air Command) first word designating a fighter or bomber deployment. Coronet is similar to the Air Mobility Command Phoenix first word, used to describe an operation with an unclassified nickname.

+ **Coronet Apollo:** RF-4C NV ANG deployment to Karup AB, Denmark, Jul–Aug 1994.
+ **Coronet Aspen:** 3rd Combat Communications Support Sqn and Red Horse deployments to Wadi Qena, Egypt, during Desert Storm and the 1990s.
+ **Coronet Astro:** Deployment for Central Enterprise, 1998.
+ **Coronet Bat:** 1995 nonstop, around-the-world flight by two B-1B bombers to demonstrate their ability to bomb in two hemispheres. Six refueling tracks were set up: off the coast of Maine, over the Mediterranean Sea, over the Middle East, east of Singapore, and in two regions over the Pacific Ocean. The 36-hour, 13-minute flight routed the two B-1Bs from Dyess AFB, TX, over the North Atlantic, through the Strait of Gibraltar, across the Mediterranean, south to the Indian

Ocean, north over the Pacific to the Aleutian Islands, southeast to the western coast of the US, and back to Dyess AFB.

+ **Coronet Blade:** 140th Wing, CO ANG deployment for Tactical Fighter Weaponry 97, Sep 1997.
+ **Coronet Bone:** Drawdown of B-1B bombers.
+ **Coronet Bugle:** B-2 deployment to Andersen AFB, Guam, 2004.
+ **Coronet Bunker:** Pre–Desert Storm "special activities" of the 9th Air Force, probably a classified base or deployment in the Middle East.
+ **Coronet Caretaker:** Air Combat Command.
+ **Coronet Chariot:** Wisconsin ANG deployment to Karup AB, Denmark, Aug–Sep 1994.
+ **Coronet Chest:** Pre–Gulf War "special activities" of the 9th Air Force, probably a classified base or deployment in the Middle East.
+ **Coronet Cove:** ANG regular deployment series to Panama. In 1978, Coronet Cove began a permanent rotation of four A-7 fighter aircraft to Howard AFB, Panama, to provide close air support to the 193rd Infantry Bde for defense of the Panama Canal and other SOUTHCOM-tasked missions. During Just Cause, Coronet Cove units (114th and 180th Tactical Fighter Groups) flew 34 missions, completed 34 sorties, expended 71.7 flying hours, and expended 2,715 rounds of ordnance.
+ **Coronet Dart:** South Dakota ANG deployment to Brustem AB, Belgium, for Central Enterprise, Jun 1993.
+ **Coronet Defender:** F-16 ANG deployment to Karup AB, Denmark, for Oksboel, Sep 1991.
+ **Coronet Dragoon:** Illinois ANG deployment to Karup AB, Denmark, Jul–Aug 1992.
+ **Coronet East:** A-7 Oklahoma ANG deployment to RAF Waddington, UK, for Central Enterprise, Jun 1991.
+ **Coronet Enterprise XIX:** B-52 deployments to Andersen AFB, Guam, 17–22 May 1995, including bombing at the Farallon de Medenilla range.
+ **Coronet Extent 97-1:** 4th Fighter Wing deployment to South Korea, 24–30 Oct 1997.
+ **Coronet Foil:** Pre–Desert Storm "special activities" of the 9th Air Force, probably a classified base or deployment in the Middle East.
+ **Coronet Freedom:** Georgia ANG deployment to Balikesir AB, Turkey, Oct 1991.

+ **Coronet Garrison:** Deployment to Sigonella, Italy, Oct 1992.
+ **Coronet Griffin:** Caribbean theater counter-narcotics operation, Aug 1992.
+ **Coronet Guard:** Comfy Levi missions flown from Howard AFB, Panama, in an attempt to expand SIGINT capabilities in the Central America area, 8 Oct–18 Dec 1981.
+ **Coronet Havoc:** F-117 deployment to Gilze-Rijen AB, the Netherlands, in support of Central Enterprise, Jun–Jul 1993.
+ **Coronet Independence:** 363rd Fighter Wing deployment to Ghedi Torre AB, Italy, for Dragon Hammer, Apr–May 1992.
+ **Coronet Lightning:** 1st Fighter Wing exercise to test the ability to support Commander Air Combat Command OPLAN 79 tasking. In 1981, eight F-15s deployed to Khartoum, Sudan, to respond to the Chad–Libya conflict in the first Coronet Lightning operations. The aircraft maintained an active air defense alert, becoming the first US air defense unit to do so in the Middle East.
+ **Coronet Macaw:** Caribbean counter-narcotics mission, Sep 1993–Sep 1994.
+ **Coronet Night:** B-52 5th BW operational readiness inspection and simulated deployments to U-Tapao, Thailand; Andersen AFB, Guam; and other contingency Pacific bases.
+ **Coronet Nighthawk:** Counter-narcotics deployment to Curaçao. Coronet Nighthawk was previously a Howard AFB, Panama, counter-narcotics operation using F-15 or F-16 aircraft.
+ **Coronet Nova:** Illinois ANG deployment to RAF Fairford, UK, in support of Resolute Response, Apr–May 1994.
+ **Coronet Oak:** Follow-on airlift support operation at Howard AFB, Panama, replacing Volant Oak, 20 May–03 Jun 1995. Relocated to Muniz ANGB in Puerto Rico in 1999, Coronet Oak began supporting counter-narcotics operations.
+ **Coronet Orion:** JCS-directed deployment by 1st FW to Jordan to participate in US–Jordanian military operations, 29 Apr–12 May 1994.
+ **Coronet Phoenix:** Giant Cave/Giant Dodge special access program established in Jan 1980.
+ **Coronet Portal:** Pre–Desert Storm "special activities" of the 9th Air Force, probably a classified base or deployment in the Middle East.
+ **Coronet Radar:** B-52 2nd BW deployment to Hickam AFB, HI, 2–9 Jul 1994.

+ **Coronet Rambler:** Coronet Rambler 3-5/Distant Thunder 98: May 1998. Two B-52H bombers from Minot AFB, ND, flew to the Konya Range, Turkey, bombed, exercised with Italian and Turkish aircraft, and recovered at Lajes AB, Azores. Coronet Rambler 4-5/RIMPAC 98: Jul 1998. On 20 Jul 1998, two B-52s departed Minot AFB and flew to the Hawaiian Islands, launched a Harpoon at a reusable target ship as part of a Combat Hammer evaluation, and recovered at Hickam AFB, HI.

+ **Coronet Regatta:** B-52 5th BW deployments to classified overseas locations. Coronet Regatta 95-2: Bombing at Pilsung Range, South Korea, and recovery to Guam. Coronet Regatta 95-1: UK, 18–24 Jul 1995.

+ **Coronet Saturn:** Iowa ANG deployment to Karup AB, Denmark, in support of Central Enterprise, Jun 1994.

+ **Coronet Save:** Pre–Desert Storm "special activities" of the 9th Air Force, probably a classified base or deployment in the Middle East.

+ **Coronet Scabbard:** Classified deployments to Wadi Qena, Egypt, 1970s–1990s. The 4401st Combat Support Sqn (Provisional) maintained a near-continual US presence at Wadi Qena called the CENTCOM "special support activity." Other names used include Coronel Aspen, Coronet Drake, and Coronet Mallard.

+ **Coronet Scorpion:** 388th FW deployment to Karup AB, Denmark, for Elder Joust, Sep 1993.

+ **Coronet Sentinel:** 302nd Tactical Fighter Wing deployment to Skrydstrup AB, Denmark, 1992.

+ **Coronet Sentry:** 552nd Aircraft Control and Warning (AC&W) airborne battle management tactics, techniques, and procedures exercise, Tinker AFB, OK. Coronet Sentry 00: 21–25 Aug 2000. Coronet Sentry 92-1.

+ **Coronet Soldier:** 419th Fighter Wing deployment to Aviano AB, Italy, Jun–Jul 1992.

+ **Coronet Spider:** Bomber "Global Power" deployments. Coronet Spider: Andersen AFB, Guam, 18 Jun 2000. Three B-2s deployed and tested the Combat Track II data link. Coronet Spider 28/Tiger Strike: Alaska Yukon Range, 14–18 Feb 2000. B-1 bombers provided support.

+ **Coronet Star:** 1st Fighter Wing deployment to Cambrai AB, France, in support of Central Enterprise, May–Jun 1994.

+ **Coronet Stroke:** 507th AC&W tactical communications exercise, Hunter Field, GA.

+ **Coronet Volunteer:** 33rd Fighter Wing deployment to Soesterberg AB, Netherlands, Jun–Jul 1992.

+ **Coronet White:** 1. Deployment to NAS Oceana, VA, May 1993.
  2. **Coronet White:** Air Combat Command operational readiness inspection.
+ **Coronet Wise.**
+ **Coronet Wrapper:** Pre–Desert Storm "special activities" of the 9th Air Force, probably a classified base or deployment in the Middle East.
+ **Coronet Yankee:** 27th Fighter Wing deployment to RAF Lakenheath, UK, for Central Enterprise, Jun 1992.

Coronet Prince: Electro-optical counter-measures aircraft pod canceled in 1991.

Cossack Express: NATO PfP exercise, France, involving the UK, May 2001.

Cossack Steppe: Ukraine–Poland–UK peacekeeping operation exercise. Cossack Steppe 03: 28 Aug–12 Sep 2003. Cossack Steppe 99 in Poland, Nov 1999, was canceled because of Kosovo operations.

Cotton Candy: Former RC-135D aircraft equipped with side-looking airborne radar.

Counter Guard 94: Multinational exercise with sites in Germany, France, the UK, and the Netherlands.

Country: Air Force Communications Command first word.

Country Mile: Air force subsistence stocks other than war reserve materials.

Courageous Bat: UK–Denmark exercise canceled Jun 1999 because of Kosovo operations, and canceled again in Sep 2002.

Courageous Channel: US–South Korean biennial noncombatant evacuation operation practice, held in spring and fall.

Cover All: Former SAC EC-135 airborne command post.

Covered Wagon: 1. Cold War RC-135 mission.
  2. **Covered Wagon:** Air force up-channel security police report informing higher headquarters that an unusual incident, probably or actually hostile, has occurred at an installation or dispersed site.

Crab Apple: UK–Kenyan exercise, 2000–2001.

Crackdown: CTF 180 coalition and 2nd Bn, 504th Parachute Infantry Regt operation near the village of Khar Bolah, Afghanistan, initiated 16 Apr 2003.

Crashpad: Defense Threat Reduction Agency ongoing demonstration of the Crash Prompt Agent Defeat modified Mk84 2,000-pound BLU-119/B thermobaric bomb intended for "agent defeat" in attacking WMD sites, initiated in 2002 for use in Afghanistan and Iraq.

Crazy: Army airborne intelligence collection program first word that goes back to the Vietnam era (Crazy Cat/Ceflien Lion).

+ **Crazy Dog:** RU-21A Army Reconnaissance Low (ARL) mission also called Cefirm Leader.
+ **Crazy Hawk:** RC-7B Army Reconnaissance Medium (ARL-M) mission integrating COMINT, Electro-Optical/Infrared imagery, and radar (Moving Target Indicator/Synthetic Aperture Radar) capability, replacing Grisly Hunter and Crazy Panther.
+ **Crazy Horse:** RC-12G Army Reconnaissance Low (ARL) mission, follow-on to Crazy Dog/Cefirm Leader.
+ **Crazy Panther:** Army Reconnaissance Low — COMINT (ARL-C) airborne radio direction finding platform. In Nov 1990, Congress mandated combining the Grisly Hunter program and Crazy Panther into a single program, which became ARL.

Credible: Air Force Materiel Command operational first word, including special projects from the 1980s. Credible Bear, Credible Cat, Credible Dove, Credible Eagle, Credible Hawk, Credible Pad, and Credible Theory are all 1990s classified projects that continue to the present.

+ **Credible Sport:** Test series to determine if modified MC-130 Combat Talon special operations aircraft could operate from very short runways, 1980–1982.

Credible Journey 89: Defense Nuclear Agency (now Defense Threat Reduction Agency) European theater nuclear air base survivability study to determine the ability of NATO nuclear forces to disperse to secondary bases and survive attacks, completed May 1990.

Credible Partner (Tayoreru): III MEF community relations projects in Okinawa and Ie Shima, Japan.

Credible Wolf: Military-deception-related SPECAT compartment. Credible Wolf information is transmitted via the Procomm communications system.

Creditable Dove (Project 202): Air Force Materiel Command classified project, 1997.

Creek: USAFE first word. The earliest known Creek nicknames were Creek Haven and Creek Dipper in Jun 1967, noncombatant evacuation operations from Libya and Jordan during the Arab–Israeli war. 1980s Creek intelligence programs included Creek Arch, Creek Aspen, Creek Beach, Creek Bramble, Creek Castle, Creek Chart, Creek Flush, Creek Misty, Creek Rib, Creek Slar, and Creek Spectre. Other Cold War–era Creek programs were Creek Cruiser, Creek Eagle, Creek Merlin, Creek North, Creek Party, Creek Plan, Creek Scope, Creek Sentry, Creek Splash, Creek Sweep, and Creek Willow.

+ **Creek Crab:** European HUMINT operations.
+ **Creek Defender:** USAFE security forces.
+ **Creek Distant:** U-2 European Southern Region Contingency Airborne Reconnaissance System (CARS) program or deployment, 1995.
+ **Creek Dragon:** U-2 operations at RAF Akrotiri, Cyprus.
+ **Creek Pegasus:** 1996 draft plan for the reorganization of USAFE.
+ **Creek Pinon:** Air Combat Command U-2 operation, 2002.
+ **Creek Quick:** U-2 European Southern Region program or deployment, 1995.
+ **Creek Sent:** Creek Sent 02: Jan 2002. Creek Sent 01: Jul 2001.
+ **Creek Standard:** Modernization and expansion of the USAFE command post.
+ **Creek Torch:** Air Combat Command 13th Intelligence Sqn and Air Intelligence Agency 48th Intelligence Sqn Deployable Ground Station (DGS-2) support for U-2 intelligence collection requirements of the NATO Stabilization Force (SFOR) in the Balkans. In 1997, the U-2 CARS DGS-2 station completed supporting its 400th Creek Torch mission.
+ **Creek Wind:** U-2 eastern Mediterranean reconnaissance missions flown in support of OEF.

Crescent Dagger: Southwest Asia reserve forces activation exercise, similar to Unified Charger.

Crescent Edge: OPREP-3CE report used to immediately notify the National Military Command Center of a compromise of, or an important development regarding, a special access program. The Crescent Edge report is the single reporting channel for all SAP units reporting incidents to higher headquarters.

Crescent Wind: Informal code name for early Iraq war planning, conducted by the air staff just days after 9/11. The Crescent Wind plan posited the capture of an air base inside Iraq and establishment of a US beachhead. The concept became the basis for establishment of FOB Rhino in Afghanistan during OEF and for the capture of H-2 in western Iraq during OIF.

Crested Cap: Former air force counterpart to the REFORGER exercise series. In 1969, US-based wings participated in their first dual-basing exercise, Crested Cap I, deploying to NATO bases in Europe. The redeployment from Germany was called Crested Cap II.

Crested Dove: Deception program of putting retired B-52s on active bomber bases to inflate the size of the US strategic bomber force, 1980s.

Crested Eagle: USAFE exercise series in Germany, ended in 1989.

Crested River 94: Army mortuary affairs exercise, Albany, GA, 14–22 Jul 1994.

Crew: Air Force Technical Application Center (AFTAC) first word referring to operations to detect and characterize nuclear testing. Programs include Crew Bravo (worldwide), Crew Cardnel, Crew Driver (South Pacific), Crew Light (advanced technology system development and testing), Crew Mark (surface collection worldwide), Crew Star (special operation), and Crew Valiant (advanced technology system acquisition programs).

Crimson: 1. USAFE Emergency Action Message.
2. **Crimson:** Air force first word for designated operational readiness inspections, including Crimson Hawk, Crimson Island, Crimson Sky, and Crimson Tide.

Crimson Cross: Army command and staff chemical and biological weapons seminar game series for senior- and executive-level officials to increase their awareness of issues, concepts, doctrine, and policies relating to the medical aspects of chemical and biological defense. A Crimson Cross seminar was held for the 3rd Medical Command, Sep 2000.

Croix Du Sud: France–Australia–New Zealand noncombatant evacuation operation exercise, including Tonga. Croix Du Sud 02: Feb–May 2003. Croix Du Sud 02: May–Nov 2002.

Crisis Decision Exercise (CDE): National War College war game series. CDE 00 was the capstone academic event for the Industrial College of the Armed Forces and the National War College, with 500 student players, supported by more than 100 faculty and staff.

Crisis Look 98: Travis AFB operation, CA.

CrissCross: DIA Transnational Warfare Group Program Office.

Croatian PHIBLEX: US–Croatian amphibious exercise, Sep 2000, involving the USS *Austin* (LPD 4) and 26th MEU.

Crocodile: Australian large-scale, air, land, and sea field training exercise series. The quadrennial exercise (99, 03) replaced the Kangaroo series in 1999. Crocodile forms part of the Australian Defence Force (ADF) theater exercise program and emphasizes the planning and conduct of combined operations. Starting in 2005, Crocodile will become part of Talisman Saber. Crocodile 03: Shoalwater Bay Training Area, Sep 2003. III MEF. Crocodile 99/Freedom Banner 99: Gladstone, Australia, Mar–Apr 1999. III MEF and an army brigade TF supported by Maritime Prepositioning Ships Sqn 3, as well as 1st Marine Air Wing, Naval Inshore Underwater Warfare Group, and an army field artillery battalion.

Cross Check: UK–Canadian exercise, 2000–2001.

Cross SKE 96: 110th FS, MD ANG A-10 deploying to RAF Lyneham, UK, Aug 1996.

Crossbolt: Navy Pioneer UAV test and evaluation, 1994, at Nellis AFB, NV.

Crossfire: Army intelligence Trojan Classic system.

Crosshair: *See* Unitary DF.

Crown: Air Combat Command (and former Tactical Air Command) first word.
+ **Crown Dust:** Luke AFB, AZ, semi-annual exercise involving personnel and equipment tasked to deploy to high-threat areas.
+ **Crown Royale:** Communications exercise.
+ **Crown Talon:** Luke AFB, AZ, quarterly exercise to assess a base's ability to effectively deploy in support of actual OPLANs.
+ **Crown Vigilance:** Nuclear weapons bomber generation exercise held in conjunction with Global Guardian.

Crown: White House Communications Agency program first word. Crown also informally refers to the White House switchboard.
+ **Crown Control:** White House communications tech control.
+ **Crown Helo:** Specially configured Marine Corps and air force helicopters for presidential use.

+ **Crown Shelter:** Reagan-era continuity of government program.

Crown Eagle: RAF exercise canceled because of Kosovo operations, Jun 1999.

Crucial Office: Pentagon exercise simulating a hostage situation in the defense secretary's office, 1997. *See also* Cloudy Office.

Crucial Player: DOD–FBI National Infrastructure Protection Center project focusing on predictive analysis of information warfare and terrorist threats to emerging technologies and the US critical infrastructure.

Crutch: Army intelligence system, Bad Aibling, Germany.

Crystal: 1. BYEMAN codeword for KH-11 and KH-12 imagery satellite program.
2. **Crystal:** JCS series of nuclear "battle staff" assessments testing mobile command center performance in a protracted nuclear war. Assessments include Crystal Monarch (NORTHCOM mobile command center) and Crystal Nugget (STRATCOM mobile command center).

Crystal Breakers: Naval Criminal Investigative Service exercise, Anacostia NS, Washington, DC, Sep 1999. The scenario involved a terrorist group seizing several hostages at the navy facility and threatening to kill them. To complicate the situation, the terrorists possessed a biological agent. Sixteen federal and military agencies were involved in the exercise, which featured hostage negotiations, terrorist engagement with SWAT teams, defusing of explosive devices, isolation and decontamination of infected personnel, and counterintelligence interviews of hostages and terrorists.

Crystal Fog: Air force classified special operations project started in 1983.

Crystal Sunset: Crisis management exercise for the Reserve Component National Security Course, National Defense University, Washington, DC, 2000.

Crystal Water: US–Albanian humanitarian assistance exercise, Jul 1995.

Curveball: Iraqi engineer purporting to have direct information on Iraqi biological weapons developments, and the principal source that the US used in 2000–2003 to conclude that Iraq had a mobile biological weapons program. The US had only one occasion of physical access to the source, who was being exploited and interrogated by German intelligence. The Defense HUMINT Service translated the reports and handled liaison with German intelligence. Though Curveball had provided some reliable intelligence prior to 2002, he was finally believed to be deceptive in claiming access to Iraq, and turned out to be the brother of a top aide of Ahmad Chalabi, the head of the Iraqi National Congress.

CUSEC: WMD response exercise using the Consequence Assessment Tool Set (CATS), a Geographic Information System–based application providing map-based hazard display and analysis.

Cyclops: Hyperspectral intelligence sensor developed by the Army Night Vision Electronics Sensor Directorate for integration on the Predator UAV with the ability to identify targets and pass location information for cross-cueing with other sensors.

Cygnet Globe: High-frequency communications exercise involving the 290th Joint Communications Support Sqn. Participants include Australia, Canada, Germany, New Zealand, and the UK. Cygnet Globe 98: Oct–Nov 1998. Cygnet Globe 97.

Cygnet: UK exercise series first word.

+ **Cygnet Goose:** Held in Belize and the Falklands. Cygnet Goose 02, Falkland Islands, Sep 2002, was canceled.
+ **Cygnet Spear:** Army exercise canceled because of Kosovo operations, Apr 1999.
+ **Cygnet Vine:** Army exercise in Cyprus. The Apr–May 2001 exercise was canceled due to other operational commitments. The May 99 exercise was canceled because of Kosovo operations.
+ **Cygnet Virgin:** British Virgin Islands.

— D —

Dacia 03: NATO civil emergency exercise to practice disaster relief after a terrorist attack, held in Pitesti, Romania, 7–10 Oct 2003. The exercise focused on the consequences of a radiological terrorist attack. It was the first NATO exercise to simulate a "dirty bomb" terrorist attack.

Particpants included Armenia, Austria, Azerbaijan, Belgium, Bulgaria, Croatia, Hungary, Italy, Moldova, Norway, Portugal, the Slovak Republic, Slovenia, Switzerland, Turkey, Ukraine, Uzbekistan, and the US. Observers included Albania, Belarus, Canada, the Czech Republic, Estonia, France, Germany, Greece, Serbia and Montenegro, and Sweden.

Damask: Australia operation in Afghanistan subsumed into Slipper.

Damsel Fair: NATO NAVSOUTH annual naval exercise held in the Mediterranean Sea. Damsel Fair 02: Aksaz, Turkey, May 2002. Damsel Fair/Linked Seas 00: Greece, May 2000. VP-8 from Sigonella employed MK-63 and MK-65 Quickstrike mines off the island of Peloponnisos. Damsel Fair 94: Italy. Damsel Fair 91.

Danger Storm 98: 1st Infantry Div intelligence exercise, 17–26 Feb 1998.

Dangerous Wind 01: Domestic federal government and army reserve WMD exercise, Fort Gordon, GA, 7–17 May 2001.

Daring Lion/Mountain Shield I: SETAF developed OPLAN and mission rehearsal to support extraction of UNPROFOR from Bosnia under hostile conditions. Mountain Shield exercises were held 30 May–26 Jun 1995 and Jun 1993.

Dark Eyes: Navy submarine based electro-optics intelligence system, 1980s.

Dark Portal: NDU National Strategic Gaming Center strategic policy forum examining responses to attacks on the US critical infrastructure, Feb 2004.

Dark Shadow: Coast Guard special operation, 15 Jan–27 Apr 2001.

Dark Star: Low-observable automated long-endurance UAV with electro-optical, Synthetic Aperture Radar (SAR), video and SIGINT capability, unveiled 1 Jun 1995 in a ceremony held at Lockheed's Skunk Works in Palmdale, CA. Dark Star was terminated in early 1999.

Dark Tea: Unknown classified air force system.

Dark Winter: Senior leader biological warfare response homeland security seminar co-sponsored by the Center for Strategic and International Studies and Johns Hopkins University, Jun 2001. The exercise simulated a smallpox attack on the US.

Darner (Project Darner): NSA support for Sentinel Bright, 1991.

DATEX: French air defense exercise with UK (and occasional US) involvement.

Dawn Panther 03: Australian–Thai special operations counter-hijack training exercise, Jun 2003.

Dawn Seagull 03: Australian–Singapore special operations counter-hijack training, May 2003.

Code Names

Day Anchor: Australia special operations recovery exercise.

Deadbolt: Coast Guard special operation, 31 Aug–15 Oct 1990.

Deadeye: *See* Deliberate Force.

Decisive: NATO former Yugoslavia operation first word.

  + **Decisive Edge:** AIRSOUTH plan in support of Joint Endeavor for the peace implementation force (IFOR) mission in Bosnia following Deny Flight, 21 Dec 1995–20 Dec 1996. Decisive Edge included maintaining a no-fly zone and air cover for peacekeeping forces. The operation was supported by the USS *America* (CV 66) and USS *George Washington* (CVN 73) Battle Groups. Continued as Deliberate Guard.
  + **Decisive Endeavor:** AFSOUTH support plan for peace implementation force (IFOR) mission in Bosnia. The 16th SOS (AC-130) deployed to Italy in support of the operation, 26 Apr–27 Sep 1996, until relieved by the 4th SOS (AC-130U).
  + **Decisive Enhancement:** Adriatic Sea maritime interdiction operation, 1 Jan 1996–1 Jan 1997. The operation was supported by the USS *America* (CV 66) and USS *George Washington* (CVN 73) Battle Groups, and the USS *Guam* (LPH 9) and USS *Wasp* (LHD 1) ARGs.
  + **Decisive Forge:** AFSOUTH Support Plan for follow-on to Joint Guard — NATO Stabilization Force (SFOR) in Bosnia — Jun 1998–present.
  + **Decisive Guard:** AFSOUTH support plan for follow-on to Joint Endeavor; NATO Stabilization Force (SFOR) operations in Bosnia, 20 Dec 1996–20 Jun 1998.
  + **Decisive Guardian:** AFSOUTH support plan for NATO peacekeeping operation in Kosovo, 11 Jun 1999–present.

Deep Look 97/Global Apache 97: Army Corps–level field training exercise, Utah Test and Training Range, Dugway, UT.

Deep Stare (Surveillance Technology Advancement and Replacement for Ebsicons): Replacement of unsustainable equipment in the 1970s Ground-based Electro-Optical Deep Space Surveillance System (GEODSS).

Deep Sea: Air Force 486L Mediterranean region communications system.

Deep Sea: Former Atlantic Command operations.

Deepwell: EP-3 AN/ALR-60 COMINT system, replaced by AIRES II.

Defense Challenge: Air force security forces combat training event, Camp Bullis, San Antonio, TX, Nov 1998, including the Canadian 15th Wing, Moose Jaw, Saskatchewan, Canada.

Delenda: Informal name for the NSC-created political–military plan to destroy al Qaeda, circulated in the Clinton administration in Sep 1998 following the military strikes against Afghanistan and Sudan in retaliation for the attacks on US embassies in Kenya and Tanzania. The strategy sought to combine four main approaches: diplomacy, covert action, financial measures, and military action. It was never formally adopted.

Deliberate: NATO former Yugoslavia operation first word.

+ **Deliberate Falcon:** Show of force, Jun 1998, to persuade Serbian President Slobodan Milosevic to ease up on his crackdown in Kosovo. USS *Saipan* (LHA 2) ARG.

+ **Deliberate Force/Deadeye:** NATO air strikes against Bosnian Serb forces threatening Muslim "safe areas" in Bosnia, 29 Aug–21 Sep 1995. NATO coalition forces flew 3,515 combat sorties and attacked 338 individual targets within 48 target complexes. Led to the Dayton Peace Agreement. Forces included the USS *Theodore Roosevelt* (CVN 71) Battle Group, USS *America* (CV 66) Battle Group, and USS *Kearsarge* (LHD 3) ARG.

+ **Deliberate Forge:** AIRSOUTH support to NATO Stabilization Force (SFOR) and enforcement of the no-fly zone in Bosnia–Herzegovina after Deliberate Guard, 20 Jun–Oct 1998.

+ **Deliberate Guard:** AIRSOUTH air support of SFOR Bosnia (Joint Guard), 20 Dec 1996–20 Jun 1998. The coalition flew more than 48,000 sorties.

Delphin: UK land-based SIGINT/electronic support measures equipment used in OEF/OIF.

Dense Crop 93: Air force reserve exercise including 622nd Aero-medical Evacuation Sqn, Macdill AFB, FL, and 810th Civil Engineer Flight, Fort Worth, TX.

Deny Flight: NATO enforcement of UN Security Council Resolution 816 no-fly zone over Bosnia, 12 Apr 1993–20 Dec 1995. Two USAFE F-16s (526th FS) shot down four Krajina-Serb Galeb jets violating the Bosnian no-fly zone, 28 Feb 1994. Cap. Scott O'Grady, 555th Fighter Sqn F-16 pilot, was shot down behind enemy lines on 2 Jun 1995. Six F-15Es (492nd FS) and six F-16CG (31st Fighter Wing) took part in NATO's first air strike, 21 Nov 1994; atacking Udbina airfield in Croatia. On 20 Dec 1995, Deny Flight became Decisive Edge. A total of 48,890 NATO sorties were flown. Nicknames initially considered included *Balkan Shield* and *Persuasive Force*.

Deprem: Turkey earthquake relief, 14–20 Mar 1992. An earthquake (6.8 on the Richter scale) near Erzincan, Turkey, killed nearly 500 people, injured more than 7,000, and left 19,000 homeless. The Provide Comfort TF delivered 95,000 pounds of food, water, clothing, tents, and medical equipment; helped search for survivors; provided medical care; and built a hospital annex.

Depus Romeo: Air force supply and requisition project code.

Desert: CENTCOM first word. "Iraq crisis" operations under Executive Order 13076, 24 Feb 1998, included Southern Watch, Northern Watch, Desert Spring, Desert Thunder, Desert Fox, Desert Falcon, and Desert Focus.

+ **Desert Aluminum:** Desert Iron strike operation with half the anticipated forces.
+ **Desert Badger:** Strike and combat search and rescue plan prior to OIF to respond to the loss of a no-fly-zone airplane inside Iraq.
+ **Desert Breeze:** WMD war game seminar series. Beginning in spring 1998, CENTCOM identified the need to address vulnerability of airfields and ports to chemical or biological attack.
+ **Desert Calm:** Air operations preceding Southern Watch, 1991–1992.
+ **Desert Crossing:** Planning effort, begun in 1999, for the possibility of occupying Iraq. The plan called for a nationwide civilian occupation authority, with offices in each of Iraq's 18 provinces.
+ **Desert Falcon:** Army show of force to deter continued Iraqi aggression in northern Iraq, 1997. The 1st Bn, 7th Air Defense Artillery (Patriot) from Germany deployed to Saudi Arabia in May 1997 and provided theater ballistic missile defense for about six months.
+ **Desert Farewell:** Redeployment of forces after Desert Storm.
+ **Desert Focus:** CENTCOM Force Protection Plan, Aug 1996–. After a truck bomb exploded outside the military compound at Khobar Towers in Saudi Arabia, killing 19 air force service members on 25 Jun 1996, Secretary of Defense William Perry and Saudi Minister of Defense and Aviation Prince Sultan agreed to move the JTF Southwest Asia from Riyadh and Dhahran to Prince Sultan AB. In four months, CENTCOM transferred nearly 5,000 people, 78 aircraft, and mainte-

nance facilities. Army forces moved to locations that were more defensible and deployed an infantry battalion to protect Patriot sites and other army facilities. *Desert Focus* then came to refer to the overall operations plan for defense of Saudi Arabia, 1 Jan 1998–2003, and the associated mission rehearsal exercises to validate deployment of forces.

+ **Desert Fox:** Four-day operation following Desert Thunder aimed at destroying installations associated with development of WMD, units providing security for those programs and Saddam Hussein, and Iraq's national command and control network. Officially 16–22 Dec 1998. During the course of four nights, American and British forces struck 100 Iraqi military targets. USS *Enterprise* (CVN 65) and USS *Carl Vinson* (CVN 70). Secretary of Defense William Cohen said at the Pentagon on 19 Dec: "We've degraded Saddam Hussein's ability to deliver chemical and biological weapons. We've diminished his ability to wage war against his neighbors."

+ **Desert Fury:** Two-day punative air operations strike plan around the time of Desert Fox.

+ **Desert Guard.**

+ **Desert Iron:** Air strike contingency plan around the time of Desert Fox.

+ **Desert Knight:** 1. Iraq OPLAN, 1990s.

  2. **Desert Knight:** Marine Corps I MEF field training exercise series and mission rehearsal using California and Arizona training areas to simulate the desert environment of Kuwait. Desert Knight/Steel Knight 01. Desert Knight 00. Desert Knight 99/Steel Knight: Yuma Proving Ground, AZ, and Twentynine Palms, CA, 2–12 Dec 1999.

+ **Desert Lightning:** 1. Iraq OPLAN for air strikes, called off Feb 1997.

  2. **Desert Lightning:** Pre–Desert Storm exercise, Jan 1991.

+ **Desert Run:** Program to improve command and control capabilities in the CENTCOM region.

+ **Desert Saber:** Planned amphibious assault of Kuwait during Desert Storm.

+ **Desert Sailor:** NAVCENT exercise series with counter-terrorism and chemical and biological weapons defense scenarios, held at Naval Support Activity Bahrain. Desert Sailor 04: Mar 2004.

+ **Desert Scorpion:** 1. Two-day punative air and cruise missile strike plan around the time of Desert Fox.

  2. **Desert Scorpion:** Army operation to root out Iraqi insurgents threatening coalition forces in and around urban areas, preceded Ivy

Cyclone II, Iraq, 2003. The operation followed Operation Peninsula Strike.

+ **Desert Shield:** Deployment of US forces to the Arabian Gulf in response to the Iraqi invasion of Kuwait, 7 Aug 1990–17 Jan 1991.

+ **Desert Spring:** Continuous deployment of combat forces to Kuwait, beginning 31 Dec 1998 following Desert Fox. Desert Spring replaced Intrinsic Action and formally established CTF Kuwait/JTF-KU, and authorized full-time staffing of C/JTF-KU (Fwd) at Camp Doha, Kuwait. In Aug 1999, all special operations Iris Gold exercises were incorporated under Desert Spring. Desert Spring expanded to include up to nine special forces teams and a special operations command and control (C2) element.

+ **Desert Sprint:** SOCOM operation.

+ **Desert Storm:** 17 Jan–28 Feb 1991. The 43-day first Gulf War, following a five-month Desert Shield.

+ **Desert Strike:** Operation to "suppress" Iraq's air defenses, 3–4 Sep 1996 (Desert Strike I), and continuing plans for strikes through 1 Feb 1997 (Desert Strikes II and III). On 31 Aug, Iraqi army units captured Erbil in the Kurdish autonomous region. A series of cruise missile attacks against surface-to-air missiles and command and control facilities were mounted in southern Iraq. The *Carl Vinson* (CVN 70) Battle Group was in the Arabian Gulf as part of a Rugged Nautilus show of force. Cruise missiles were launched from the USS *Laboon* (DDG 58), USS *Shiloh* (CG 67), and B-52 bombers. CENTCOM also deployed F-117 and F-16CJ aircraft, a heavy brigade TF, and a second aircraft carrier, the USS *Dwight D. Eisenhower* (CVN 69). The USS *Gettysburg* (CG 64), USS *Hewitt* (DD 966), USS *Russell* (DDG 59), USS *Jefferson City* (SSN 759), and USS *Pittsburgh* (SSN 720) supported the operations. The UN imposed additional sanctions; the no-fly zone was expanded to the 33rd parallel; and Operation Northern Watch was implemented, enforcing a new no-fly zone above the 36th parallel in northern Iraq.

+ **Desert Sword:** Early Desert Storm contingency planning for offensive operations.

+ **Desert Thunder:** Operations initiated when Saddam Hussein continued to defy UN resolutions by refusing to allow inspections of presidential facilities and by disallowing US members on the UN inspection teams, 11 Nov 1998–24 Dec 1998 (Desert Thunder I, 11 Nov–11 Dec, and

Desert Thunder II, 16–24 Dec). Kofi Annan traveled to Baghdad and on 24 Feb 1998 reached agreement with Saddam Hussein to comply fully with UN inspections. After the agreement unraveled, Desert Thunder was initiated. About 50 US ships and submarines and 200 aircraft surged into the region, including the USS *Nimitz* (CVN 68), USS *George Washington* (CVN 73), USS *John C. Stennis* (CVN 74), USS *Independence* (CV 62), USS *Guam* (LPH 9) ARG, and USS *Tarawa* (LHA 1) ARG. The Army Technical Escort Unit deployed a Chemical-Biological Response Team in support of Desert Thunder at Camp Doha, Kuwait. This highly visible deployment resulted in Iraq's eventual, but short-lived, compliance. *See also* Desert Fox.

+ **Desert Tighten:** Combined Desert Fury and Desert Scopion operations plan prior to Desert Fox.
+ **Desert Warrior 00-11:** CENTAF exercise, Prince Sultan AB, Saudi Arabia, Oct 2000. Tested the 363rd Air Expeditionary Wing's ability to respond to a chemical attack.

Desert Capture: Army intelligence experimentation series at the National Training Center (NTC) in Californa. Desert Capture I, conducted in late 1992, tested the All-Source Analysis System, the JSTARs Ground Station Module, and the Trojan SPIRIT. Desert Capture II, also held at Nellis AFB, NV, and the NTC in Apr 1994, included the Desert Hammer technology demonstration for a digitized maneuver force. Army Pioneer UAVs logged more than 70 flight hours, and the RC-135 participated. Desert Capture III was held in 1994.

Desert Fire: I MEF predeployment exercise series, Twentynine Palms, CA.

Desert Flag: Air force nickname for Red Flag flying operations, 1990–1991, in preparation for Desert Storm.

Desert Hammer: *See* Desert Capture.

Desert Lightning 99: Army TENCAP experiment, Feb 1999.

Desert Lion: CTF 180 coalition and 505th Parachute Infantry Regt, 82nd Airborne Div operation in the Kohe Safi Mountains near Bagram AB, Afghanistan, 27 Mar 2003.

Desert Peach: Air Force Fighter Weapons School exercise, Nellis AFB, NV, 1999. Five B-1Bs deployed from the GA ANG.

Desert Pivot: Air Combat Command Theater Air Command and Control Simulation Facility quarterly exercise in conjunction with Red Flag, Kirtland AFB, NM. The first Joint Synthetic BattleSpace Experiment, called JSB Desert Pivot Experiment (JDPE) Event 1, was conducted in Oct 2002.

Desert Predator: Navy TENCAP exercise, 1999, involving airborne testing of a time/frequency difference of arrival (T/FDOA) SIGINT geolocation receiver on board a Predator UAV. Ground emitter signals between 40 and 2,500 MHz were collected simultaneously by national, airborne and ground-based receivers. Various combinations of data were co-processed at Space and Naval Warfare Systems Command Systems Center, San Diego, to provide precise emitter geolocations at less than 500-meter accuracy.

Desert Rescue: Naval Strike and Warfare Center annual combat search and rescue (CSAR) exercise, NAS Fallon, NV, launched in 1991. Desert Rescue cross-trained on how to conduct CSAR in a GPS-jammed environment. Desert Rescue VIII: 8–18 Feb 2000. Desert Rescue VI: 28 Oct–6 Nov 1998.

Desert Scimitar: 1st Marine Div command and control field training exercise series, Twentynine Palms, CA. Desert Scimitar 02: 22 Apr–3 May 2002. Desert Scimitar 01: 1–12 May 2001. Desert Scimitar 99: Mar–Apr 1999. Desert Scimitar 98: Mar 1998.

Desert Thunder: UK–Jordanian air defense exercise. RAF Tornado and Hawk deployment to Azraq, Jordan, Nov 1999.

Desert Thunderclap: UK–Jordanian annual air exercise. Desert Thunderclap 03: Azraq, Jordan, Jan 2003. A task force of RAF Tornados, Harriers, and Jaguars conducted live fire with Jordanian counterparts.

Desert Victory: Army V Corps exercise series, Feb 1999.

Desert Warrior: UK 4 Armoured Bde field training exercise, held in Oman as part of exercise Saif Sarreia, Sep–Oct 2001. Desert Warrior replaced exercise Ulan Eagle 01.

Desperado: Ships Signal Exploitation Equipment (SSEE) Increment D sub-system upgrade. Includes Friar/Desperado, a Marine Corps system; and Wideband/Desperado, an EP-3E enhancement included in the FY 2003 Defense Emergency Readiness Fund for use in OEF and OIF.

Destined Glory: NATO AFSOUTH annual amphibious, maritime, and power projection exercise. Participants include France, Germany, Greece,

Hungary, Italy, the Netherlands, Portugal, Spain, Turkey, the UK, and the US. Destined Glory 04: 25 Nov–5 Dec 2003. Destined Glory 03: Italy. Destined Glory 02: Tyrrhenian and Ionian Seas, 5–15 Oct 2002. Destined Glory 01: Sep–Oct 2001. UK Royal Navy involvement was reduced because of post-9/11 exercise Saif Sareea in Oman. Destined Glory 00: Greece and Turkey, the Aegean and Eastern Mediterranean Seas, 9–25 Oct 2000. 26th MEU. Greece decided to withdraw from Destined Glory because it said Turkey did not abide by the rules. Destined Glory 98: 4–22 May 1998. Destined Glory 96: Central Mediterranean Sea near Sardinia and Tyrrhenian Sea and ashore at Capo Teulada, Sardinia, 13–26 Mar 1996. Destined Glory 95.

Determination: Canadian deployment to Arabian Gulf region in 1998 as part of show of force preceding Desert Fox.

Determination 84: Reagan-era exercise with NSC involvement, 17 Sep–15 Oct 1984.

Determined Falcon: NATO show of force to coerce Serbian forces to cease ethnic cleansing operations in Kosovo, 15 May–18 Jun 1998. Involved 13 countries and 85 NATO aircraft.

Determined Promise: NORTHCOM annual full-scale interagency field training exercise to train Joint Task Force — Civil Support (JTF-CS) and others on the military assistance to civil authorities mission. Determined Promise 03 was NORTHCOM's priority exercise for 2003 and the command's graduation to become a fully operational organization.

+ **Determined Promise 04:** 16–27 Aug 2004.
+ **Determined Promise 03:** Clark County, NV, 18–28 Aug 2003.
  Additional locations included Colorado Springs, CO; Washington, DC; Suffolk, VA; and Barkely Dam, KY. The two-week exercise began with local authorities dealing with a biological warfare incident involving terrorist release of pneumonic plague on the Las Vegas strip. The Nevada NG, FEMA, and JTF-CS all deployed to Clark County.
  NORTHCOM was also tasked with a simulated hurricane in the southeastern US, multiple simulated homeland security events, real and simulated wildland fires, and an airborne threat in Alaska.
+ **Determined Promise 01:** JFCOM-led exercise.

Determined Response: JTF efforts to respond to, and recover, the USS *Cole*

(DDG 67) in Yemen after the terrorist attack in the port of Aden, 12 Oct 2000. USS *Tarawa* (LHA 1) ARG, USS *Duluth* (LPD 6), and USS *Anchorage* (LSD 3) with the 13th MEU.

Devil Shock: CTF 180 operation, Naray, Afghanistan, Jan 2003.

Devils Hat: UK army exercise canceled because of Kosovo operations, May 1999.

Dewdrop: Targeting software that provides a method of precisely mensurating coordinates from the Digital Point Positioning Data Base (DPPDB). Replaced by Raindrop around 1999.

DFT (Deployment for Training).

+ **DFT AF-5006:** Search and rescue training, El Libertador AB, Maracay, Venezuela, 1–9 Sep 1995. The Air Force 71 Rescue Squadron (RQS) deployed one HC-130P and 19 personnel.
+ **DFT AF-6008:** Search and rescue training, Guayaquil, Ecuador, 9–17 Dec 1995. The Air Force 71 RQS deployed 1 HC-130P and 22 personnel.
+ **DFT 98:** Navy training, Ponte Delgada, Azores, Mar–May 1998.

Diagonal Glance: US–UK nuclear weapon accident exercise. Diagonal Glance 98: RAF Locking, UK, Sep 1998. The exercise tested the procedures in place for responding to the crash of a US transport aircraft carrying nuclear weapons. Ministry of Defence response forces were located at RAF Locking. Exercise activity also took place in Main Building, Whitehall, and at AWE Aldermaston. Approximately 300 personnel participated.

Dial Flinty: DOD-directed nuclear accident exercise. Includes Dial Flinty 96, involving 5th BW, Minot AFB, ND.

Diamond (Defense Incident Analysis and Monitoring Desk): DOD defensive information warfare program.

Diamond 1: Naval Research Laboratory–developed hyperspectral sensor similar to the Cyclops sensor, and intended as a prototype for UAV deployment.

Diamond Cutter: UK exercise, Botswana, 2000–2002.

Diamond Flame: Nuclear weapons accident and incident training.

DIAMONDS (Defense Integration and Management of Nuclear Data Services): Defense Threat Reduction Agency software for planning, programming, and budgeting nuclear weapons management, logistics planning, and component tracking.

Dice (Defense Interoperability Communications Exercise): Joint Interoperability Test Command exercise series. Dice 04. Dice 03.

Digger Shift: Nuclear weapons accident and incident training.

Digital Demon: Hostile penetration of US government computer networks, 1999 time frame. The DOD Computer Forensics Laboratory was involved in the counter-intelligence investigation.

Digital Storm: FBI system that controls Foreign Intelligence Surveillance Act (FISA) electronic surveillance activities and collects and transfers FISA information.

Dimming Sun: US–UK interagency nuclear weapons accident exercise. Dimming Sun 03: Wretham, Norfolk, UK, 16–20 Jun 2003. Exercise play was also conducted at the Ministry of Defence Nuclear Accident Response Organisation and the US embassy in London. Dimming Sun 03 was the largest combined nuclear weapon accident response exercise in UK history, featuring some 2,000 representatives from the UK and the US. The exercise scenario simulated the crash of a US C-17 aircraft carrying a cargo of four B-61 nuclear bombs while ferrying them from Germany to New Mexico. Local authorities and specialized military and civil agencies participated, including NNSA's Accident Response Group. The exercise was originally scheduled for 2001 but was canceled because of operations in Afghanistan. Dimming Sun 99, planned for 14–18 Jun 1999 at RAF Lakenheath, UK, was postponed because of operations in Kosovo.

Dipole: Defense Threat Reduction Agency counter-proliferation Advanced Concept Technology Demonstration program first word.

+ **Dipole Yukon:** Demonstration of the capability to plan and execute chemical/biological counterforce missions with the Joint Air-to-Surface Standoff Missile against a simulated biological weapons storage facility, 2003–2004.
+ **Dipole Zodiac:** Assessment of the suitability of the Conventional Air Launched Cruise Missile (CALCM) with a penetrating warhead and a Predator UAV-based standoff collateral effects assessment system, 2003–2004.

Direct Focus: Defense Threat Reduction Agency interagency WMD accident exercise. Direct Focus 98: Exercise involved four accident sites with aircraft debris and nuclear weapons. *See also* Dimming Sun.

Direct Support 97: Naval reserve DIA unit exercise to test the unit's ability to provide direct reachback support, Southwest Army Reserve Intelligence Support Center, Camp Bullis, San Antonio, TX. Reservists requested and received imagery, digital maps, and charts; retrieved secure and unsecure intelligence information from the Internet; accessed intelligence databases; and remotely provided direct, formatted inputs to update intelligence databases.

Disciplined Guard: NATO OPLAN completed in 1993 to support implementation of a UN Peace Plan for Bosnia-Herzegovina, never implemented because of unsuccessful negotiations.

Disciplined Warrior: NATO Joint Command South annual command post exercise. Disciplined Warrior 03: Verona, Italy, 24 Feb–7 Mar 2003. Disciplined Warrior 00: Disko Hit (Joint Command Southeast's wartime headquarters, east of Izmir, Turkey), 28 Feb–10 Mar 2000.

Disco Fun: Coast Guard special operation, 1 Apr–31 Aug 1995.

Discoverer II: DARPA, Air Force, and National Reconnaissance Office initiative to develop affordable space-based radar with Ground Moving Target Indication (GMTI) and Synthetic Aperture Radar (SAR) imaging capabilities. Discoverer II is the direct descendant of the DARPA Starlite initiative. In Jan 1998, the Defense Science Board TF on Satellite Reconnaissance recommended that a modified Starlite program be initiated, as a "Military Space Radar Surveillance Program," in an effort to achieve broad-area near-continuous radar integrated with military operations. The program was terminated by Congress in the FY 2001 DOD budget.

Discrete: SPECAT possibly associated with Defense Threat Reduction Agency and counter-proliferation weapons developments.

+ **Discrete Fortuna:** Thermobaric weapon demonstration, 2004.

Display Determination: Former NATO exercise series in Turkey, dating to the 1980s. Display Determination 92: 25 Sep–8 Oct 1992. Display Determination 91: SEABEEs built a Harrier takeoff and landing pad at Celibolu, Turkey, and simulated a raid at Kesan, Turkey. During Display Determination 90, F-16s and F-111s deployed to Turkey in anticipation of Desert Storm.

Display Deterrence: NATO Article IV operation in response to Turkey's request for assistance to deter an attack from Iraq, Feb 2003. NATO deployed AWACS aircraft and US and Dutch Patriot SAM batteries to eastern Turkey. The plan for Display Deterrence was approved on 13 Mar 2003. The operation was formally terminated 30 Apr 2003.

Display Select: Nuclear weapons accident response exercise, NWS Yorktown, VA, and Cheatham Annex, Williamsburg, VA, 18–27 Sep 1995.

Dissent: Air force special operations data collection program or foreign material exploitation, 1999.

Distant Frontier: Alaska-based air weapons training, precursor to Cope Thunder. Participants include UK Tornados and AWACS aircraft. Distant Frontier 01: Eielson AFB, AK, 25 Jun–7 Jul 2001. Distant Frontier 93: 1–28 May 1993. Distant Frontier 92 was the RAF's first major deployment to Alaska.

Distant Hammer: Reagan-era exercise with NSC involvement, 6–17 May 1985.

Distant Haven: SOUTHCOM JTF Suriname to provide safe-haven facilities for Haitian refugees on Suriname, 19 Aug–31 Oct 1994.

Distant Phoenix: Big Safari–managed special access program, probably the same as the Air Force Technical Application Center (AFTAC) air sampling operation involving WC-135 aircraft of 24th RS, 55th Wing, Jun 1994, in the Pacific. Those operations were terminated in Oct 1994.

Distant Runner: Noncombatant evacuation operation from Rwanda, 9–10 Apr 1994. Marines evacuated 148 Americans and 82 others from Rwanda after fierce fighting broke out between Hutus and Tutsis. Supported by the USS *Peleliu* (LHA 5) ARG. Marine Corps operations also took place in Bujumbura, Burundi.

Distant Sent: RC-135 operation, 82nd RS, Apr 1994.

Distant Shore: Nickname for the DOJ/IINS Mass Immigration Emergency Plan, Jun 1994.

Distant Star: RC-135 operation in support of PACOM, 45th RS, Sep 1994.

Distant Thunder: NATO AFSOUTH-led biennial (odd-year) large-scale air exercise. Participants include Belgium, the Czech Republic, Denmark, France, Germany, Greece, Hungary, Italy, the Netherlands, Portugal, Spain, Turkey, and the UK. Distant Thunder 04: 25 Nov–5 Dec 03. Distant

Thunder 03: Naples, Italy. Distant Thunder 01. Distant Thunder 99 canceled because of Kosovo operations. Distant Thunder 98: 11–13 May 1998. Distant Thunder 96: 16 Mar–5 Apr 1996. Distant Thunder 95: 7–21 Apr 1995. Six F-16Cs of the 555th FS deployed to Balikesir AB, Turkey.

Divine: Defense Threat Reduction Agency first word.

+ **Divine Canberra:** Counter-proliferation demonstration involving the Tactical Tomahawk penetrator variant and remote combat assessment using the Finder small expendable mini-UAV with a chemical point detector against a hard chemical production and storage facility, 2004–2005.
+ **Divine Invader:** Test series using Chemical Combat Assessment System.
+ **Divine Kingfisher:** Hard-target tunnel blast and overpressure experimentation and testing done for Afghanistan caves during OEF.

Diving 00: NATO PfP diving and rescue from submerged ship exercise, Spain, 27 May–2 Jun 2000.

Docklamp: Defense attaché communications system.

Dockmaster: NSA discussion board system used to informally exchange ideas related to computer security. Dockmaster supports a number of "forums."

Dobodan Lena 98: Slovenian-sponsored special operations exercise, 1998.

Dogfish: NATO submarine and anti-submarine-warfare exercise, the world's largest of its type, held in the Ionian and Mediterranean Seas. Participants include Canada, France, Germany, Greece, Italy, the Netherlands, Norway, Portugal, Spain, Turkey, the UK, and the US.

Dogfish 04: Ionian Sea, 19 Feb–3 Mar 2004. Largest-ever NATO anti-submarine-warfare exercise, and the 29th annual exercise of the series. USS *Thorn* (DD 988) and USS *Cole* (DDG 67). Dogfish 03: Waters of the Ionian Sea to east of Sicily, 20 Feb–5 Mar 2003. USS *Hawes* (FFG 53). Dogfish 02: Sigonella, Italy, 13–28 Feb 2002. Dogfish 01: Augusta Bay and Ionian Sea to the east of Sicily, Italy, 15–28 Feb 2001. USS *Norfolk* (SSN 714). Dogfish 00: 17 Feb–1 Mar 2000. Dogfish 98: USS *Boise* (SSN 764) participated with six NATO diesel-electric submarines and one other nuclear attack submarine. The exercise included search, localization, and prosecution of diesel-electric submarines. *Boise*'s AN/BSY-1 active sonar suite was tested in the winter Mediterranean environment. Dogfish 91.

Dogu Akdeniz: Turkish-sponsored naval exercise in the Mediterranean Sea. Participants include Argentina, France, Germany, Italy, the Netherlands, Spain, the UK, and the US. Dogu Akdeniz 03. Dogu Akdeniz 02: 18–28 Nov 2002. Dogu Akdeniz 98. Dogu Akdeniz 97: 10–23 Mar 1997. USS *Atlanta* (SSN 712).

Dole: Army National Ground Intelligence Center (NGIC) foreign material exploitation first word associated with equipment formerly owned by East German armed forces, including Dole Dart, Dole Dartington, and Dole Garden.

Dome Street: Army Foreign Science and Technology Center (FSTC)/National Ground Intelligence Center (NGIC) foreign material exploitation of a foreign tank, 1990.

Dominant Chronicle: DIA–FBI project that provides translation, exploitation, and dissemination of captured foreign records relating to the illegal drug business.

Double Eagle 95: US–Polish ground force exercise, Wedrzyn, Poland, 10–16 Jul 1995.

Double Take: Exercise term for a simulated DEFCON 4 condition.

Dragon Eye: "Backpack" mini four-pound UAV used by special operations forces in OIF.

Dragon Fury/ATHENA: DIA WMD threat database for all NBC and missile targets and capabilities outside the US.

Dragon Fury: US–Italian operation in the Showi Kot (Shahi Kot) mountains 85 miles southeast of Kabul, in Paktika Province, Afghanistan, initiated 2 Jun 2003.

Dragon Hammer: NATO Southern Region exercise series. Dragon Hammer 92: 6-20 May 1992. The prototype Theater Rapid Response Intelligence Package for counter-intelligence and HUMINT support was first deployed for Dragon Hammer. Dragon Hammer 90: 2–16 May 1990. The 22nd MEU and 77th TFS deployed to Aviano AB.

Dragon Lightning: US Army Europe information assurance emergency alert of a computer network compromise or intrusion.

Dragon Team 96: 101st Airborne Div seaborne emergency deployment readiness exercise.

Dragon's Thunder: National Defense University National Strategic Gaming Center strategic policy forum examining US responses to Chinese military action against Taiwan, Jul 2004.

Dragonfix: Army 525th MI Bde high frequency/direction finding (HFDF) system with a base station and two outstations, used during Desert Storm.

Dreamland: Nickname for "Area 51" Groom Lake, Nellis AFB, NV, restricted area.

Driver Fire: Coast Guard special operation, 31 Aug–30 Sep 1994.

Drug Market (Project Drug Market): DOD counter-narcotics information technology initiative dealing with money laundering investigative technologies, begun in 1999.

Druid: Former SIGINT compartment code word designating intelligence information derived from third parties. Subcompartments included Dikter (Norway), Dynamo (Denmark), Ishtar (Japan), Jaeger (Austria), Richter (Germany), and Setee (South Korea).

Druid Leader: DIA-led program that supplied intelligence information to the Iraqi military during the Iran–Iraq war, 1987–1988. The program later became Surf Fisher.

Druids Dance: UK field training exercise series on the Salisbury Plain designed to prepare armoured and armoured infantry battle groups for Medicine Man exercises. Normally, six are held each year.

Dual Eagle: 1st Infantry Div quarterly command post exercise. Dual Eagle 01, Sep 2001, included the command staff from the 21st Podhale Rifle Bde, Poland.

Dugong: US–Australian annual mining and explosive ordnance disposal exercise, held in Australia (*see also* Keen Edge). Dugong 02: 4–22 Nov 2002. Dugong 97: Nov 1997.

Dull Knife: NSA reconnaissance project to monitor a North Korean ground-based system, 2001.

Dull Sword: Flagword for a nuclear weapons incident.

Dunkal Hawk: Exercise or operation in Europe, 2001.

Dust Devil: 3rd Air Force local exercise practicing humanitarian assistance JTF roles.

Dynamic: NATO AFSOUTH exercise first word, including Dynamic Future 91.

+ **Dynamic Action:** Command post exercise/computer-assisted exercise. Dynamic Action 03. Dynamic Action 01. Dynamic Action 99. Dynamic Action 98. Dynamic Action 97: 23 Sep–7 Oct 1997.

+ **Dynamic Guard:** Amphibious and air land exercise series in Turkey. Participants include France, Germany, Greece, Italy, the Netherlands, Spain, the UK, and the US. Dynamic Guard 95?: B-1Bs conducted a 31-hour, 8,000-nautical-mile mission during the exercise. Dynamic Guard 94: 26 Sep–14 Oct 1994. The exercise was NATO's first major test of theater missile defense, linking German and Dutch Patriot units with airborne command post and ship-based radars. Dynamic Guard 93: Sep–Oct 1993. US Army Europe and 22nd MEU. The 55th FS deployed to Incirlik AB, the last operational deployment for the 20th FW while at RAF Upper Heyford, UK.

+ **Dynamic Impact 94:** Command post exercise/field training exercise, Capo Teulada, Sardinia, 4–18 May 1994. Participants included Belgium, France, Germany, Greece, Italy, the Netherlands, Portugal, Spain, Turkey, the UK, and the US. As part of the noncombatant evacuation operation scenario, 195 simulated evacuees were scattered throughout Capo Teulada's seven-mile peninsula. More than 70 surface and subsurface vessels and 4,250 amphibious troops participated in the amphibious assault phase. This was the first major NATO exercise in the western Mediterranean since 1992.

+ **Dynamic Mix:** Biennial multi-warfare exercise focused on sea control, power projection, and amphibious warfare. Participants include Belgium, Canada, the Czech Republic, Denmark, France, Germany, Greece, Hungary, Italy, the Netherlands, Portugal, Spain, Turkey, the UK, and the US. Dynamic Mix 04: Canceled. Dynamic Mix 02: Spain (including the Canary Islands), the Mediterranean Sea, and the southeast Atlantic, 21 May–6 Jun 2002. Dynamic Mix 01. Dynamic Mix 00: Capo Teulada, Sardinia, and Kyparissia, Greece, 20 May–10 Jun 2000. The UK withdrew because of operational commitments in Sierra Leone. Dynamic Mix 99. Dynamic Mix 98: Turkey, 1–21 Oct 1998. Largest exercise in the NATO Southern Region in 1998. Dynamic Mix 97: Greece. Turkey chose not to participate. Dynamic Mix 96: Saroz Bay, Turkey, Oct 1995. The USS *Firebolt* (PC 10) worked with Navy SEALs and the Turkish special action team. The 16th Air Force deployed to Turkish air bases, including Balikesir AB. Dynamic Mix 95: Canceled on 29 Jun 1995.

+ **Dynamic Response:** Operational rehearsal aimed to demonstrate NATO capability to deploy large numbers of forces into Bosnia and Kosovo. The exercises coincide with the rotations of forces. Dynamic Response 04: Bosnia, May 2004. Dynamic Response 03: Bosnia and Kosovo, 26 Aug–24 Sep 2003. Dynamic Response 00/Adventure Express was a mission rehearsal for initial Kosovo Force (KFOR) rotations, Mar 2000. Marines practiced riot control and nonlethal weapons use. Dynamic Response 98: Bosnia, 23 Mar–27 Apr 1998.

Dynamic Eagle: 1st FW Coronet Lightning inspection and combat search and rescue series.

— E —

Eager: CENTCOM first word.

+ **Eager Archer:** US–Kuwaiti air exercise series. Eager Archer 04. Eager Archer 99: Feb 1999. USS *Carl Vinson* (CVN 70). Eager Archer 98: Nov 1998. USS *Nimitz* (CVN 68) Battle Group, including USS *Olympia* (SSN 717). Eager Archer 95-1: USS *Constellation* (CV 64). Eager Archer 94/Native Fury 94: Apr 1994. USS *Constellation* (CV 64) and F/A-18s and KC-130s from the 3rd Marine Aircraft Wing. Eager Archer 92. USS *America* (CV 66).

+ **Eager Dancer 96:** US–Pakistani JCET between US and Pakistani special operations forces.

+ **Eager Express:** US–Kuwaiti explosive ordnance disposal exercise. Eager Express 94/Native Fury 94.

+ **Eager Glacier:** US–Iraqi intelligence cooperation during the Iran–Iraq war. Briefed to the pertinent congressional committees 5–6 Oct 1987, and again on 13 Oct 1987.

+ **Eager Initiative:** Classified NAVCENT exercise. Eager Initiative 04. Eager Initiative 03. Eager Initiative 01. Eager Initiative 97. Eager Initiative 94-1: The *USNS Narragansett* practiced survey of sunken LST and its cargo, followed by collection and disposal of ordnance, Mar–Apr 1994. USS *Grasp* and MV *Guiseppina*.

+ **Eager Light:** US–Jordanian ARCENT-executed biennial brigade-level training exercise. Prior to OIF, Eager Light supported ARCENT's objectives for Jordan: "expanding military relations and cooperation, encouraging participation in regional security programs, establishing access to

contingency required facilities, and improving ability to secure borders."
Goes back to at least Eager Light 87. Eager Light 04. Eager Light 03.
Eager Light 01/Eager Tiger/Infinite Moonlight: Simulation-focused seminars to prepare for a larger-scale exercise proposed for 2002. Eager Light
99: 2 Oct–19 Nov 1998. The 1st Bde, 3rd Infantry Div participated as
mentors and advisers to Jordanian units. Eager Light 98: Oct–Nov
1998. 3rd Infantry Div. Eager Light 95. Eager Light 94: Involved an airborne operation. Eager Light 87: 5-101st Aviation Regt.

+ **Eager Mace:** US–Kuwaiti naval exercise series, including Navy SEAL
activity. Eager Mace 03: Sep 2003. USS *Higgins* (DDG 76), USS
Chinook (PC 9), and USCGC *Aquidneck* (WPB 1309). Eager Mace 01:
May 2001. 11th MEU (SOC) urban warfare training on Falayka Island
and artillery firing at Udari Range. Eager Mace 00: Apr 2001. 15th
MEU (SOC). Eager Mace 99: 11th MEU (SOC). Eager Mace 98.
Eager Mace 95. Eager Mace 93: USS *Nashville* (LPD 13). Eager Mace
92: USS *Nashville* (LPD 13) and 22nd MEU.

+ **Eager Sentry:** US–UK–Kuwaiti trilateral naval surface exercise conducted in the northern Arabian Gulf. Eager Sentry 04. Eager Sentry 99:
Jan 1999. Eager Sentry 94/Native Fury 94: 4–25 Apr 1994. Largest
naval exercise ever conducted with Kuwait. USS *Paul Foster* (DD 964).
Eager Sentry 93-4: 22–26 May 1993.

+ **Eager Tiger:** US–Jordanian classified air exercise. Eager Tiger 03. Eager
Tiger 02. Eager Tiger 01: Merged with Eager Light. Eager Tiger 96:
May 1996. For Aerospace Expeditionary Force II, the 1st Fighter Wing
deployed 12 F-15s and more than 600 personnel to Shaheed Mwaffaq
AB, Jordan, 12 Apr–28 Jun 1996. The wing operated from the bare
base and provided support to Southern Watch. Eager Tiger 93. Eager
Tiger 92: The 27th FS, Langley AFB, deployed eight F-15Cs to al Jafr
AB, Jordan, 2–21 Sep 1992.

Eager Light: DIA imagery information code word used during Desert Storm.

Eagerness: Army intelligence system, Bad Aibling, Germany.

Eagle: CENTCOM first word.

+ **Eagle Arena:** US–Egyptian classified NAVCENT air exercise, including
US Marine Corps particpation. Eagle Arena 04. Eagle Arena 99. Eagle
Arena 98: 8–12 Aug 1998. USS *Dwight D. Eisenhower* (CVN 69).
Eagle Arena 94: 4–6 Apr 1994.

+ **Eagle Fury:** CTF 180 operation, Helmand and Uruzgan Province, Afghanistan, Feb 2003.
+ **Eagle Look** (Project 9AI): Show of force after an apparent Libyan bombing attack on Sudan, 15 Mar–15 Apr 1984. First deployment of CENTCOM's EC-135Y airborne command post (now retired).
+ **Eagle Resolve:** Gulf Cooperation Council annual senior leader seminar (replaced Ultimate Resolve). Eagle Resolve 04. Eagle Resolve 02/03. Eagle Resolve 2000: Le Royal Meridien Hotel, Manama, Bahrain, 7–9 May 2000. Seminar topics included defense against WMD, the Cooperative Defense Initiative, and consequence management. Amb. Michael Sheehan, Department of State counter-terrorism coordinator, and Lisa Gordon-Hagerty from the National Security Council participated. GCC Chiefs of Defense Staff and service chiefs, CENTCOM component commanders, US ambassadors from the GCC nations, and representatives from Egypt and Jordan attended. Eagle Resolve 99: CENTCOM HQ, Tampa, FL, Apr 1999.
+ **Eagle Response 04:** Classified exercise.
+ **Eagle Salute:** US–Egyptian naval exercise. Eagle Salute 03: USS *Vandergrift* (FFG 48). Eagle Salute 00: May 2000. USS *Samuel B. Roberts* (FFG 58).

Eagle: NATO Rapid Deployable Corps — Italy (NRDC-I) first word.

+ **Eagle Flight:** NRDC-I validation exercise series. Eagle Flight 03: Sep–Oct 2003. Eagle Flight 02: Sep 2002. Eagle Flight 00: Feb 2000.
+ **Eagle Landing:** NRDC-I mission preparation exercise, Mar 2004.

Eagle: 1. NSA FTP and Telnet capabilities server.

2. **Eagle:** Albanian–Italian–Macedonian search and rescue exercise series. Participants include Croatia and Greece. Eagle-SAR 04. Eagle 03: Albania, Jul 2003.

3. **Eagle (TF Eagle):** NATO implementation force (IFOR) for Bosnia–Herzegovina, 13 Dec 1996–present. Since Dec 1995, the US has provided forces. The Stabilization Force (SFOR) transitioned to a slightly smaller force 10 Jun 1998. Simultaneously, Joint Guard terminated and Joint Forge commenced.

Eagle (Aguila): SOUTHCOM operation and exercise series. Eagle III (Aguila III): Canceled US–Mercosur (Argentina, Brazil, Uruguay, Paraguay, and associate member Chile) air training exercise, planned for Oct–Nov 2003.

The exercise was canceled because Argentina would not approve an Article 98 exemption for US forces from prosecution in the International Criminal Court. Aguila: JTF operation, San Salvador, El Salvador, 10 Nov 1998–20 Feb 1999.

Eagle Assist: NATO air surveillance operations in the US as part of the Noble Eagle response to 9/11 attacks, 9 Oct 2001–16 May 2002. NATO AWACS aircraft were deployed to US bases; 830 crewmembers from 13 NATO countries flew more than 360 sorties.

Eagle Claw: Operation to rescue Iranian hostages, 12 Mar–3 Apr 1985.

Eagle Express: NIMA search engine for retrieval of imagery products ("NIMA-in-a-box"). Eagle Express is a customized Linux-based geospatial mass storage/server/search engine using ESRI's ArcView software. It provides a capability for easily storing and accessing imagery data.

Eagle Eye: 1. SACEUR OPLAN 10602, Operation Eagle Eye, the NATO Kosovo Verification Mission, 3 Nov 1998–23 Mar 1999.
   2. **Eagle Eye:** Big Safari–managed Bell HV-911 VTOL unmanned platform incorporating new airborne collection and ground processing capabilities.
   3. **Eagle Eye:** Strategic Insights International terrorist data mining tool.

Eagle Flag: Air Mobility Warfare Center flag-level combat support training program.

Eagle Look: Air Force Inspection Agency's assessment of munitions infrastructure and storage capability to support expeditionary operations, 2000.

Eagle Reach: Air Intelligence Agency link among ground collection units, aircraft, and the NSA CROFA located at Fort Meade, MD.

Eagle Talon: 101st Airborne Div command post exercise series held in preparation for deployment.

Eagle Thrust: 1st FW quarterly operational readiness exercise that tests the wing's ability to transition from peacetime to contingency and wartime posture.

Eagle Vision: Air Combat Command deployable ground receiver station, first deployed in Nov 1998 and able to merge commercial satellite imagery with national imagery for mission planning, intelligence, and topographic analysis. There are five downlinks. The systems can directly downlink: SPOT 10-Meter (France); LANDSAT 15-Meter (US); RADARSAT 8-Meter (Canada);

Quickbird 0.62-Meter (US); and India Remote Sensing (IRS) 5-Meter (India). Future capability planned have included IKONOS 1-Meter (US); and SPOT 5, 2.5-Meter (France). Eagle Vision I, located at Ramstein AB, Germany, collects and processes commercial and national imagery. Eagle Vision II, Fort Belvoir, VA, developed by the National Reconnaissance Office for the army, collects and processes commercial imagery. Eagle Vision III, or National Eagle, is an operational system that processes (no collection capability) national and commercial imagery at the 152nd Intelligence Sqn, Reno, NV. Eagle Vision IV is at McEntire Air National Guard Station, SC. Eagle Vision V is located at Hickam AFB, HI.

Eagle Vista (JTF Eagle Vista): JTF under the command of Maj. Gen. William S. Hinton Jr., 3rd Air Force commander, responsible for military support arrangements for President Clinton's 1998 Africa trip.

Eaglepipe: Army intelligence system, Bad Aibling, Germany.

Eagle's Talon 97: 183rd FW, IL ANG F-16 deployment to Powdiz, Poland, Sep 1997.

Early: CENTCOM first word.

+ **Early Call:** US response to a Libyan coup attempt against Sudan, Feb 1993. On 13–14 Feb 1983, four E-3A AWACS aircraft deployed from Tinker AFB, OK, to Cairo West AB, Egypt.
+ **Early Victor:** US–Jordanian SOCCENT annual readiness exercise. Participants also include Bahrain, Kuwait, Oman, UAE, and UK forces. The Early Victor communications network established in Jordan supports special operations in the country. Early Victor 04. Early Victor 02: 6–28 Oct 2002. Gen. Tommy Franks visited Jordan during the exercise. In Sep, the 112th Signal Bn (Special Operations) deployed to Jordan to activate the communications infrastructure. About 1,400 US SOF troops arrived for the exercise, a deployment that masked preparations for war in Iraq. Early Victor 01-2: Sep–Oct 2001. Elements of the 528th Special Operations Support Bn deployed. Early Victor 00/ Eastern Viper 00: Oct 2000. Early Victor 99: Sep 1999. The USS *Kamehameha* (SSN 642) became the first US submarine to visit a Jordanian port. King Abdullah visited the submarine while it was pierside in Aqaba. Early Victor 97: Jun 1997. 5th SFG and communications personnel activated an FOB in Jordan. Included a joint parachute jump. Early Victor 94: A JSOTF deployed with elements of 5th SFG,

160th SOAR, 75th Rangers, and Naval Special Warfare Task Group to an air base in eastern Jordan.

Earnest: CENTCOM first word.

+ **Earnest Leader:** US–Saudi Arabian annual Third Army ground forces exercise consisting of a series of seminars followed by a brigade level command post exercise. Earnest Leader 04. Earnest Leader 01: 11–17 Apr 2001. 3rd Infantry Div. Earnest Leader 00: Tabuk, Saudi Arabia, 1–3 May 2000. The three-day exercise used digitized terrain for the first time ever with Saudi land forces. 1st Cavalry Div.
+ **Earnest Will:** Reflagging of Kuwaiti oil tankers in the Arabian Gulf during the Iran–Iraq war, 1987.

Eastern: CENTCOM first word. Classified exercises include Eastern Angler, Eastern Falcon, Eastern Oryx, and Eastern Response.

+ **Eastern Action:** US–Qatar biennial Third Army–led field training exercise focusing on small-unit ground tactics. Eastern Action 03. Eastern Action 01.
+ **Eastern Castle:** Engineer readiness exercise that builds exercise-related construction projects for US use. Participants include Egypt, Jordan, Kenya, Oman, Qatar, and the UAE. Eastern Castle 04. Eastern Castle 01. Eastern Castle 97-7: UAE, Jul 1997. Construction of a military vehicle wash facility at the al Hamra training area base camp. Eastern Castle 97: Alexandria, Egypt. 416th Engineer Command, Darien, IL. Eastern Castle 96: Kenya, Jun–Jul 1996. TF 416/368th Engineer Bn built schools, maintenance facilities, and an infantry squad battle course. Eastern Castle 96?: Oman. Two men from the 823rd Red Horse Sqn died in a car accident during the exercise.
+ **Eastern Eagle:** Classified special operations exercise, including Eastern Eagle 99 and Eastern Eagle 95.
+ **Eastern Exit:** Noncombatant evacuation operation of the Somalian embassy, Mogadishu, 2–11 Jan 1991. USS *Guam* (LPH 9) ARG, USS *Trenton* (LPD 14) ARG, Marine force recon, and Navy SEALs.
+ **Eastern Leopard:** US–Qatar exercise, Apr 1994.
+ **Eastern Maverick:** US–Qatar amphibious exercise series. Eastern Maverick 01: Mar 2001. Eastern Maverick 00: May 2000. 15th MEU. Eastern Maverick 99. Eastern Maverick 98: 18–23 Apr 1998. USS *Tarawa* (LHA 1) and 11th MEU (SOC).

+ **Eastern Sailor:** US–UK–Qatar special operations and boarding exercise. Eastern Sailor 04: Apr 2004. USS *Bulkeley* (DDG 84) and USS *Firebolt* (PC 10), HMS *Grafton*, and two patrol boats from the Qatari Emiri Navy. The scenario involved defending a simulated oil platform from attack by fast boats. Eastern Sailor 94-1: 2–6 Jan 1994. Participants included the USS *Independence* (CV 62), USS *Gary* (FFG 51), and USNS Apache.
+ **Eastern Valor:** US–Oman classified special operations air exercise, including Eastern Valor 04 and Eastern Valor 01.
+ **Eastern Viper:** US–Qatar SOCCENT special operations exercise series. Eastern Viper 04. Eastern Viper 01: Qatar. Eastern Viper 00: 1st Bn, 5th SFG.
+ **Eastern Washdown:** US–Qatar amphibious exercise, 26 Mar–4 Apr 2001. The USS *Pearl Harbor* (LSD 52), USS *Bonhomme Richard* (LHD 6), and USS *Ogden* (LPD 5) discharged more than 200 vehicles via Landing Craft Air Cushion to a beach head four miles south of Mesaieed.

Eastern Access: Marine Corps operation on the Puerto Rican island of Vieques to remove trespassers from the live impact area of the training base, 2000.

Ebony Flame: US–Djibouti exercise, 1992. USS *America* (CV 66).

ECHELON: UK, US, Australia, Canada, and New Zealand signals intelligence requirements system of strategic (national-level) communications intercept. Each of the intelligence partners has stations that intercept a wide variety of communications, from point-to-point microwave and cell phone and satellite uplinks and downlinks where telephone and other communications travel. ECHELON allows Australia, as an example, to task (keyword) US collectors to watchlist information collected at the NSA station in Rosman, NC. Though ECHELON is often described as a global surveillance network, it is actually one US–UK requirements system.

Echo Mountain: Classified CENTCOM exercise involving the navy.

ECI: COMINT classification compartment designating a category of information similar to Gamma (such as Top Secret/Talent Keyhole ECI) derived from a highly sensitive source.

Edge: NSA "communications externals" database.

Edged Mallet: US–Kenyan annual combined arms exercise series, usually involving the 13th or 24th MEU (SOC). Edged Mallet 04: Lamu on the Kenyan–Somali border, 5–18 Jan 2004. Involved Expeditionary Strike Group One, a navy new force consolidated under one command that includes more powerful amphibious and operation capabilities than the traditional ARG. Edged Mallet 03: Manda Naval Base, Manda Bay, Kenya, Nov–Dec 2002. Edged Mallet 02: Manda Naval Base, Manda Bay, 4–21 Feb 2002. Edged Mallet 99: Mombasa, Kenya.

Eelpot: Unknown (possibly classified) air force system.

Effective Team 85: Reagan-era exercise with NSC involvement, Jul–Aug 1985.

Eidolon Lance: JCS TENCAP Special Project 93, 1993, executed during Tandem Thrust 93 to demonstrate methods by which tactical units could obtain access to operational intelligence databases by means of "user pull." The project was initiated to repair a Desert Storm shortfall where tactical units could not obtain current satellite imagery for strike planning and battle damage assessments. Eidolon Lance was a success, and "5-D" (Demonstration of Demand-Driven Digital Data) servers were installed in all theater intelligence centers.

El Dorado Canyon: Libya air strikes ostensibly as retaliation against the bombing of the La Belle discotheque in Berlin in which two US servicemen were killed and a number injured, 15 Apr 1986. Eleven USAFE F-111Fs, plus 15 navy A-6 and A-7 jets, hit terrorist-related targets in Benghazi and Tripoli. One F-111F was lost.

Elaborate Crossbow: JCS exercise addressing US global commitments in the war on terrorism. The Elaborate Crossbow I seminar was held 18–20 Mar 2003, just as OIF was starting, and the exercise was held 25–26 Mar 2003. Elaborate Crossbow II was held 7–8 May 2003.

Elaborate Journey: Joint Special Operations Command counter-terrorism training exercise, Reagan era.

Elaborate Maze: Contingency plan for a military operation in Panama, 1988.

Elang Ausindo 96: Australian–Indonesian air combat training. Elang Ausindo 97: Oct 1997. Elang Ausindo 96: Dec 1996.

Elder Brave 95: PACOM war game, War Gaming Facility, Camp Smith, HI, Aug 1995.

Elder Forest/Elder Joust: Former NATO biennial air defense exercise in the UK.

Elder Widow: Reagan-era exercise with NSC involvement, 30–31 May 1984.

Elegant Lady: SOCOM and air force special access program, 1991–present.

Elephant Grass: Initial name for DIA-led program to provide intelligence information to the Iraqi military during the Iran–Iraq war, 1987–1988. The program later became Druid Leader.

Elephant Herd: CIA and military covert operation to provide equipment to the Contras in Nicaragua, 1983.

Elf One: Aerial refueling aircraft deployments to Saudi Arabia (Project 9XX), 1980–1991.

Eligible Receiver: JCS No-notice Interoperability Exercises (NIEXs) associated with information warfare. Eligible Receiver exercise preparations are is very close hold to optimize realistic training among participants. Eligible Receiver 04. Eligible Receiver 03-1: 18–28 Oct 2002. Held by PACOM jointly with Thailand, the exercise focused on information warfare attacks associated with counter-terrorism. Participants included the CIA, Departments of Justice and State, the NSA, and the FBI. Eligible Receiver 02. Eligible Receiver 01. Eligible Receiver 00. Eligible Receiver 991/2. Eligible Receiver 97: Jun 1997. The Eligible Receiver highlighted indications and warning issues, as well as coordination of responses to cyber-warfare attacks upon the US. Eligible Receiver 97 was the first large-scale exercise designed to test DOD's ability to work with the federal government to respond to an attack on the national information infrastructure. During the exercise, an NSA Red Team was able, using open-source information and operating consistently with US law, to successfully penetrated DOD's networks. Eligible Receiver 92-1.

Ellipse: JCS-led highly classified interagency major crisis action and management exercise series held in each unified command, and involving WMD. Participants include Department of State, DOE, FBI, FEMA, the NSC, and the DHS: "Concept and location to be coordinated and announced through appropriate special category (SPECAT) communications channels."

+ **Ellipse Alpha:** JFCOM (formerly Atlantic Command). Ellipse Alpha/ Determined Promise 03: 1–15 Apr 2003. Ellipse Alpha/Determined Promise 02: 30 Oct–2 Nov 2002. Ellipse Alpha 01/Determined Spirit: 1–14 Sep 2001. Ellipse Alpha 99: Fort Monroe, VA, Aug 1999. Ellipse

Alpha 98: Norfolk and Virginia Beach, VA, Jun 1998. The scenario tested federal capabilities to respond to a domestic radiological WMD.

+ **Ellipse Bravo:** EUCOM. Some Ellipse Bravo exercises were held in Israel during the 1990s. Ellipse Bravo/Silent Guide 04. Ellipse Bravo 03: Mar 2003. Ellipse Bravo 01. Ellipse Bravo 99: Kelley Barracks, Stuttgart, Germany, 19–24 Sep 1999. Ellipse Bravo 98: Sep 1998. The scenario tested federal capabilities to respond to a radiological WMD in an overseas environment. USS *Anzio* (CG 68) in the Mediterranean and reportedly Polish special operating forces. Ellipse Bravo 95/Knotted Whip: 28 Sep–5 Oct 1995. Ellipse Bravo 92: Jun 1992. The exercise tested the ability to assemble a JTF to conduct a rapid emergency evacuation operation. Within 48 hours, a 22,000-strong JTF was relocated from land to sea. During the exercise, the USS *Detroit* (AOE 4) participated in the insertion and retrieval of army and navy SOF, and rescue efforts to a Turkish warship after it was struck by a missile. Ellipse Bravo 91: Oct 1991.

+ **Ellipse Charlie:** PACOM. Ellipse Charlie 04. Ellipse Charlie 03. Ellipse Charlie 01. Ellipse Charlie 00: Andersen AFB, Guam, Sep 2000. The scenario involved hostage rescue, vessel recovery, and SOF infiltration and exfiltration. Ellipse Charlie 99. Ellipse Charlie 92: During the period 10–24 Jun 1992, the 2nd Airborne Command and Control Sqn from Offutt AFB deployed an EC-135 airborne command post to PACOM to provide an airborne command post role in support of JTF-510 for Ellipse Charlie. Goes back at least to Ellipse Charlie 83: 1 Oct–30 Sep 1982.

+ **Ellipse Echo:** SOUTHCOM. Ellipse Echo 04: 16–18 Mar 2004. Ellipse Echo 02/03. Ellipse Echo 99: Feb–Mar 1999. Ellipse Echo 98: Dec 1997. Ellipse Echo 97: 16–28 Mar 1997.

+ **Ellipse Foxtrot:** CENTCOM. Ellipse Foxtrot 04. Ellipse Foxtrot 01. Ellipse Foxtrot 00: Tampa, FL. Ellipse Foxtrot 99. Ellipse Foxtrot/Gentle Plan 95: 18 Mar–8 Apr 1995.

ELMO: TENCAP system deployed in support of Northern Watch, used to update Imagery Communications and Operations Node (ICON) files from imagery satellites. Associated with Have CSAR/MATT/ELMO.

Eloquent Banquet: Deployment of US heavy weapons to Panama, Nov 1989.

Eloquent Nugget: JFCOM ISO/PfP political–military seminar designed to demonstrate civilian democratic control of the military and regional approaches and cooperation in combating transnational extremist groups. The exercise began in 1994. Participants include Albania, Algeria, Armenia, Austria, Azerbaijan, Bulgaria, Croatia, Egypt, Estonia, Finland, Macedonia, Georgia, Ireland, Israel, Jordan, Kazakhstan, the Kyrgyz Republic, Latvia, Lithuania, Mauritania, Moldova, Morocco, Romania, Russia, Slovakia, Slovenia, Sweden, Switzerland, Tajikistan, Tunisia, Turkmenistan, Ukraine, and Uzbekistan. Eloquent Nugget 03: 2–13 Jun 2003. Eloquent Nugget 02: 2–13 Jun 2002. The subtheme was crisis response to asymmetrical threats. Eloquent Nugget 01. Eloquent Nugget 97: Norfolk, VA, 15–27 Jun 1997.

Elusive Warrior: Air Combat Command exercise.

ELWELL: NSA communications security modernization program, begun in the 1980s.

Emerald: Coast Guard–DIA intelligence program.

Empire Med 00: New York ANG–Lithuania State Partnership exercise, held in Kaunus, Lithuania, Apr 2000.

Enable Freedom 02: USAFE computer-assisted exercise, Ramstein AB, Germany, May 2002. The exercise included testing of the Master Air Attack Planning (MAAP) Toolkit.

Encased Sword: Marine Corps Chemical-Biological Incident Response Force (CBIRF) deployment to Amman, Jordan, Sep 1999, involving the Joint Technical Augmentation Cell and navy entomologists.

Endrun (Project Endrun): USAFE program to provide secure, high-speed, wide-band, digital communications. Installation began in 1988.

Endseal: NSA special intelligence classification compartment designating a category of information similar to Gamma (such as Top Secret/Endseal).

Enduring Freedom (OEF): Overall name for the overseas US war against terrororism, evolved to apply mostly to operations in Afghanistan but officially applying to Philippines operations as well, initiated 20 Sep 2001.

Engraft: SIGINT system. *See also* Mailorder.

Enlarger: Upgrade to the AN/FLR-9 intelligence collection system.

Entgrou: UK–French exercise.

Epic Fury: NSA intelligence operation supporting OEF, Oct 2001.

Epic Goal: Special operations airborne communications system program.

Epic Mantle 04: CENTCOM exercise involving the navy.

Equus Red: DOD–DOE–FBI exercise, Kirtland AFB, Albuquerque, NM, 1983. The scenario involved terrorists with nuclear weapons, and demanded a simultaneous assault on two hostile positions. This was the first certification exercise for the FBI Hostage Rescue Team (HRT) and included the Department of Energy's Nuclear Emergency Search Team (NEST).

Errant Warrior: Guam-based exercise series.

Esperia: NATO Italy-based PfP company/platoon-level land-based exercise. Participants include Albania, Bulgaria, the Czech Republic, Hungary, Macedonia, Poland, Slovakia, and Spain. Esperia 99. Esperia 97. Esperia 95: Tor Di Nebbia Range, southern Italy, May 1995.

Essential Harvest (NATO TF Harvest): NATO operations to disarm the National Liberation Army (NLA) in Macedonia, 27 Aug–27 Sep 2001.

Eugenie: Classified EUCOM special operations exercise with the Groupe d'Intervention de la Gendarmerie Nationale (GIGN), the French counter-terrorism unit, and 13e Parachute Dragoons (13e RDP; Parachute Reconnaissance), French SOF. Eugenie 01. Eugenie 99. Eugenie 98. Eugenie 97: Dieuze, France, Apr–May 1997. Goes back to at least Eugenie 85.

European Mountaineer: UK–French mountaineering and infantry exercise, France, Feb 2002.

Even Stevens: Early code name for CIA U-2 operations.

Evident Surprise: JFCOM annual strategic-level information warfare exercise, begun in 1995. The exercise focuses on interagency coordination to decon-flict and execute offensive information warfare. Evident Surprise 98: 7–9 Apr 1998. The third annual forum focused on improving national information warfare capability. Participants included industry as well as 46 government agencies. The war game approach involved a Blue Team, a Red Team, and a Senior Oversight Group that debated 20 interaction points of physical, covert, technical, propaganda, and overt activities in an information warfare environment. Evident Surprise 97: Mar 1997.

Excalibur: Information warfare system.

Excalibur: USAFE semi-annual bombing competition at RAF Lakenheath,

UK, first held in 1987. Excalibur VII (00): summer 2000. Excalibur V (93): Jun 1993. Excalibur IV (92). Excalibur III (88): May 1988.

Excalibur: Army continuity of operations training event. Excalibur 98: 24–25 Jun 1998. Excalibur 96: Key offices within the Army Staff (the Emergency Relocation Group) were denied the use of their normal Pentagon work spaces and were directed to relocate to a relocation site.

Exercise 48 Hours: US Army Europe exercise.

Exodus (Project Exodus): Unknown, 1980s.

Expanded Sea: Worldwide merchant fleet readiness exercise, 5–13 Apr 1984.

EXTENDEX: US–Australian Royal Australian Air Force and Navy anti-submarine-warfare and maritime surveillance training against a US Navy submarine. Extendex 03-2: Jan–Mar 2003. Extendex 03-1: Oct–Dec 2002. Extendex 02-4: Jul–Sep 2002. Extendex 98-3: Involving VP-1.

Extract: UK airborne SIGINT/electronic support measures equipment used in OEF/OIF.

Eyecatcher: System for enhanced situational awareness of the battlespace.

— F —

Fabric/Factor/Faculty: Canadian NORAD Region first words.

Fade Out: Exercise flagword for simulated DEFCON 5.

Faded Giant: Message flagword to designate a nuclear reactor accident.

Fairwinds: Marine Corps operation to provide security for US forces in Haiti, Nov 1995–May 1996.

Falcon: NORAD CONUS Region first word.

Falcon (Forward Area Language Converter): Automated foreign-language document translation program, begun in 1994. The first version was used in Haiti to provide rough translations of French and Spanish. A Serbo-Croation version was deployed in Bosnia in May 1997. Additional languages include Arabic, German, Korean, and Russian. *See also* Gister.

Falcon: EUCOM Rwanda JCET 3rd SFG first word, including Falcon Gorilla (17 Jul–30 Aug 1996) and Falcon Racer (15 Jul–30 Aug 1997).

Falcon (TF Falcon): US forces assigned to Kosovo Force (KFOR). Since 11 Jun 1999, EUCOM has provided US forces and logistical support to Joint Guardian, the NATO-led peacekeeping operation in Kosovo, or KFOR.

Falcon 78: Classified US ammunition storage site in Qatar.

Falcon Nut: UK Royal Navy exercise planned for Nov 1999, canceled when ships redeployed with Amphibious Task Group to Mediterranean.

Falcon View: Portable flight planning system mapping application based on ArcView software. Falcon View can be loaded with a large number of overlay threat and cultural data, including intelligence data that can be displayed over any map background.

Falconer: 1. Nickname for the full-spectrum Air Operations Centers of the 7th Air Force (South Korea), 9th Air Force (CENTAF), 12th Air Force (SOUTHAF), USAFE, and PACAF.

2. **Falconer:** Australian defense force operations in support of OIF, with SOF and air deployments in Qatar and Jordan.

Falkland Sound: UK–Falklands exercise, 2000–2001.

Falling: NORAD CONUS Southwest Sector first word.

Fan: Air force Iceland first word, 1980s.

Fancy 98: US–French special operations exercise, Corsica, 23–26 Sep 1998.

Farrah: ELINT "ferret" satellite nickname, 1970s. *See also* Bridget, Marilyn, and Raquel.

Fast Falcon: Air Force Space Command logistical support for worldwide tracking stations.

Fast Pace: Exercise flagword for simulated DEFCON 2.

Fast Walker: Defense Support Program space surveillance system.

Fastlane: Cryptographic device that provides high-speed, transparent, low-latency security.

Fastner: Army intelligence system, Bad Aibling, Germany.

Code Names

Feathered: NORAD 23rd Region first word.

Federal: NORAD Southeast Sector first word.

Federal Spade: Exercises/operations involving the 290th Joint Communications Support Sqn, 1998–1999.

Felix: NORAD Northwest Sector first word.

Fencing: Alaskan NORAD Region first word.

+ **Fencing Brave:** Air surveillance/defense field training exercise held twice per quarter to deploy fighter assets and conduct air operations at King Salmon and Galena forward operating locations. *See also* Amalgam Fencing Brave.
+ **Fencing Indian:** Command post exercise held twice per quarter.

Ferghana 03: NATO PfP disaster preparedness exercise held in the Ferghana Valley region of Uzbekistan, Apr 2003. The exercise waas the first NATO-led civil emergency exercise held in Central Asia. Participants included Kyrgyzstan and Kazakhstan.

Fertile: NORAD Northeast Sector first word.

Fervent Archer (CTF Fervent Archer): EUCOM-led Joint Special Operation Command TF, 2001–present, headquartered in Sarajevo, Bosnia, and coordinated at the Joint Staff level. Fervent Archer is an element of Joint Forge, and is believed to be a continuation of Amber Star, the operation to apprehend war criminals in the former Yugoslavia. *See also* Justice Assured.

Feudal: Former NORAD 24th Region first word, 1970s.

Fiery Relief: Delivery of humanitarian supplies to Legaspi, Philippines, Mar 2000. The 353rd SOG and 1st SFG were supporting Balikatan 2000, when they received short-notice tasking to provide aircraft for disaster relief. Two MC-130H Combat Talon II aircraft from the 353rd SOG participated.

Fiery Vigil: Mount Pinatubo, Philippines emergency response, 10–28 Jun 1991. On 15 Jun 1991, Mount Pinatubo erupted and poured more than two cubic kilometers of ash and sand over a 30-mile radius, including the US naval base at Subic Bay and Clark AB. The eruption was followed by Typhoon Diding, whose torrential rains saturated the ash and sand, creating dangerous roof loads and many other problems. Thus began Fiery Vigil, including the provision of temporary shelter, emergency water and power, and clearance. The damage was so severe that 20,000 US military dependents were evacuated.

Fig Leaf: Air Combat Command crisis management and continuity of government exercise related to Polo Hat.

Final Nail: UK exercise, Jul 2001, canceled because of foot-and-mouth disease restrictions.

Fincastle: Australia anti-submarine-warfare competition. Participants include Canada, Indonesia, New Zealand, and the UK. Fincastle 02: Jul 2002. Fincastle 97: Oct–Nov 1997.

Fingel: UK name for support to the ISAF in Afghanistan.

Fingels Cave: UK–Canada exercise, 2000–2001.

Fireant: Big Safari–managed special access program.

Firebird: DEA global computer network and office automation infrastructure, including e-mail. Firebird serves as the backbone for Merlin, the DEA's intelligence network.

Fireboat: Naval Security Group and Marine Corps SIGINT system or operation.

Firehawk: Compass Bright language sorting project, 2003–2004.

Fireproof: NSA modernization program, 1999.

Firestarter: Air Force computer security R&D program.

Firm Response: Noncombatant evacuation operation from Brazzaville, Congo, 8–18 Jun 1997.

Flaming Arrow: 1. Europe-based dedicated nuclear weapons UHF communications network. Flaming Arrow Network — Europe (FAN-E) is installed at all main operating bases and munitions support squadrons were nuclear warheads are stored. *See also* Regency.

2. **Flaming Arrow 03:** Australian–Singapore field training exercise, Jun 2003.

Flank Thrust: US–Moroccan exercise series, including Flank Thrust/Aferdou 85.

Flash: SOCPAC special operations first word.

+ **Flash Iroquois:** Classified US–Indian special operations exercise.
+ **Flash Knife:** Classified US–South Korean special operations exercise.

Code Names

+ **Flash Piston:** US–Philippine Joint/Combined Exchange Training specializing in maritime operations and small-unit tactics conducted by the Navy Special Warfare Unit One and the Philippine Navy Special Warfare Group (SWAG), 2001–present.
+ **Flash Style:** US–Sri Lankan JCET, launched in 1994. Flash Style 00-1: 17 Jan–Feb 2000. SEAL Team 1 and its Special Boat Unit and the Sri Lanka navy's Special Boat Sqn (SBS) and Fast Attack Flotilla. A team from the 6th SOS also engaged in exercises with the Sri Lanka Air Force. A third team from the Army Psychological Operations Group trained personnel of the Sri Lanka Army Directorate of Psychological Operations. Flash Style 98-2: Oct 1997. 1st SFG. *See also* Balance Style.

Flash Burn: Presidential continuity of government related exercises, 1980s–early 1990s.

Fleet Battle Experiment (FBE): Naval Warfare Development Command exercise series designed to improve warfighting, doctrine, tactics, and techniques; validate requirements and define capability disconnects; explore technological, doctrinal, and organizational desired operational capabilities for the future; and exercise OPLANS.

+ **Fleet Battle Experiment Alfa (FBE-A):** Third Fleet, May 1997.
+ **Fleet Battle Experiment Bravo (FBE-B):** Third Fleet, Sep 1997.
+ **Fleet Battle Experiment Charlie (FBE-C):** Second Fleet, Apr 1998.
+ **Fleet Battle Experiment Delta (FBE-D):** Seventh Fleet, Oct 1998.
+ **Fleet Battle Experiment Echo (FBE-E):** Seventh Fleet, Mar 1999. The exercise involved use of the Counterproliferation Analysis and Planning System (CAPS) with real-time plume dispersal models in response to a terrorist chemical and biological attack. Also integration of high-powered microwave (HPM) weapons.
+ **Fleet Battle Experiment Foxtrot (FBE-F):** Fifth Fleet, Dec 1999. WMD scenario.
+ **Fleet Battle Experiment Golf (FBE-G):** Sixth Fleet, Apr 2000.
+ **Fleet Battle Experiment Hotel (FBE-H)/Millenium Dragon 00:** Second Fleet, Sep 2000.
+ **Fleet Battle Experiment India (FBE-I):** Third Fleet, spring 2001.
+ **Fleet Battle Experiment Juliet (FBE-J):** Seventh Fleet, fall 2001.
+ **Fleet Battle Experiment Kilo (FBX-K)/Tandem Thrust 03:** Guam and Northern Marianas Islands, May 2003. Participants included Australia. Information warfare and computer network defense experimentation.

Research vessel *Cory Chouest,* a low-frequency acoustic test platform, USS *Bremerton* (SSN 698), USS *Olympia* (SSN 717), and USS *City of Corpus Christi* (SSN 705).

✦ **Fleet Battle Experiment Lima (FBX-L):** Third Fleet, Sep–Nov 2004.

Fleetex (Fleet Exercise): 1. Pacific Fleet major exercise series in the northern Pacific during the Cold War and ending in 1991. *Fleetex* can also refer to internal naval training exercises at the fleet level.

2. **Fleetex:** US–Argentinian annual naval exercise series, held in 1994 and 1995.

Flexible Anvil (JTF Flexible Anvil): EUCOM JTF in support of NATO in the former Yugoslavia, 31 Aug 1998–20 Jul 1999. In Sep 1998, Sixth Fleet took on JTF Flexible Anvil aboard the USS *LaSalle* (AGF 3) to begin strike planning in support of UN Security Council Resolution 1199 and NATO efforts to establish the Kosovo Verification Mission. The JTF conducted continuous operations threatening Tomahawk cruise missile strikes, and planned and coordinated the first combined European cruise missile strike operational plan involving surface and submarine Tomahawks and B-52 bombers with Conventional Air Launched Cruise Missiles (CALCMs). *See also* Sky Anvil.

Flexible Leader 05: EUCOM-led Joint Interagency Coordinating Group war game, planned for 8–21 Nov 2004. The Army V Corps is to provide the core of the Joint Forces Land Component Commander (JFLCC) headquarters.

Flintlock: SOCEUR-led African-oriented special operations training events, held twice yearly since the 1980s. The 5th SFG combines JCET events in multiple countries along a common scenario. Flintlock 03: General De Wet Training Area (also known as De Brug), South Africa, 25 Jun–1 Aug 2003. 1st Bn, 75th Ranger Regt. Flintlock 01: Mali, Jun 2001. The army's 96th Civil Affairs Bn coordinated and executed the exercise. Flintlock 99 (IIB): Botswana, 1999. 3rd SFG. Flintlock 99 (IIA): Côte d'Ivoire, Mar–Apr 1999. The army's 96th Civil Affairs Bn coordinated and executed the exercise. Flintlock 98: Zimbabwe. Flintlock 96: Botswana.

Flowing Pen: Comfy Levi mission, first flown on 9 Jun 1989.

FLUENT: CIA program that can search foreign-language Web sites without requiring skills in the site's native language. FLUENT started in 1999 and searches materials in German, French, Portuguese, and Spanish on the Internet.

Fluvial: US–Argentinian peace enforcement riverine exercise series. Fluvial IV: Paraná River between Puerto Ibicuy and Campana, Argentina, 30 Jul–13 Aug 2000.

Flying Fish: Five Power Defence Agreement (FPDA — Australia, Malaysia, New Zealand, Singapore, and the UK) maritime and air defense exercise. Flying Fish 03: Jun–Jul 2003. Flying Fish 97: 13–30 Apr 1997.

Flying Rhino 02: UK–German exercise canceled because of operational commitments in OEF.

Foal Eagle: US Forces Korea full-scale annual field training exercise, initiated in the late 1970s. The exercise is the largest US force-on-force training exercise, is normally held in late Oct, and is about one month in length. Exercises simulate the increase in tensions on the peninsula prior to an opening of hostilities, including a noncombatant evacuation operation, reception, staging, onward movement and integration (RSOI) of forces, amphibious operations, anti-infiltration activities, and deep strike.

    Foal Eagle 04: 43rd annual exercise. Foal Eagle 02/03. Foal Eagle 00: 21 Oct–6 Nov 2000. USS *Essex* (LHD 2) ARG and 31st MEU (SOC). Foal Eagle 99/Turbo Intermodal Surge: Oct–Nov 1998. More than 1,000 army SOF soldiers from 1st and 19th SFGs and 75th Rangers deployed, making up nearly one-third of the army forces. The exercise included off-load of two MPS vessels in conjunction with Freedom Banner 99. Foal Eagle 98/Keen Sword 99: 29 Oct–17 Nov 1998. Four B-1s of the 34th Bomb Sqn deployed to Andersen AB, Guam, for bomber support. Foal Eagle 97. Foal Eagle 95.

Foam: US–South Korean first word.

Focal Point: JCS information compartment dealing with CIA support to the military, special technical operations (STOs), and military–CIA operations.

Focus Dragon Five: UNC/CFC exercise, South Korea. Focus Dragon Five 82: 25–29 May 1982.

Focus Relief: SOCOM involvement in the effort to train and equip West African battalions for deployment to Sierra Leone as part of the UN Mission in Sierra Leone (UNAMSIL). Operation Focus Relief took place in three phases; seven battalions were trained. Phase III was completed in 2002, and funding was reduced by Congress in the FY 2003 budget.

Focused Dispatch: Army Advanced Warfighting Experiment (AWE), follow-on to the Desert Hammer VI AWE conducted in Aug 1995. Focus Dispatch evaluated digital connectivity among fire support, intelligence, combat service support, and battle command in a mounted battalion TF.

Fog: US–South Korean first word.

Foil/Folder/Folio/Follow: US–Thai first words.

Fond/Food: US–Taiwanese first words.

Footlight: NSA communications system, 1980s.

Footprint: War on terrorism special access program associated with special operations.

Forage/Ford: US–Japanese first words.

Foreshadow: Army Special Operations Div code name, 1982.

Forest: US–Japanese first word.
  + **Forest Blade 85:** Reagan-era exercise with NSC involvement, 25–29 Mar 1985.
  + **Forest Light:** US–Japanese annual Marine Corps and Japan Ground Self-Defense Forces company-sized cold weather training exercise at the Dai maneuver area, Hokkaido, Japan. Forest Light 00.

Forest Green: 1. Sensors aboard the nuclear detonation detection system satellites.

   2. **Forest Green:** Possible clandestine air force intelligence program, a classified location of the DOD Intelligence Information System (DODIIS).

Forester: Foliage penetration reconnaissance, surveillance, tracking, and engagement radar.

Formal: US–Japanese first word.

Formation: Pacific Fleet first word.

Former: US–Taiwanese first word.

Formica: 1. HUMINT activity involving gathering information from military personnel and civilians employed by the US government.

   2. **Formica:** SOUTHCOM Foreign Military Intelligence Collection Activity.

Fortify Freedom: Pacific Fleet exercise.

Code Names

Fortress: Pacific Fleet first word.

Forward Challenge 04: FEMA interagency continuity of operations (COOP) exercise, 12–13 May 2004. Forward Challenge was the first-ever federal-government-wide COOP exercise held by the Department of Homeland Security. More than 40 federal agencies participated, testing procedures in response to a simulated terrorism-based scenario. Agencies established operational capabilities at alternate facilities and implemented succession and delegation of authority plans. *See also* Title Globe.

Forward Warrior 94: US Army Europe exercise.

Fracture/Frame: PACOM first words.

Franchise 85: Reagan-era exercise with NSC involvement, 20–24 May 1985.

Freedom: PACOM first word.
+ **Freedom Banner:** I MEF annual maritime pre-positioning force exercise, usually held in conjunction with another JCS exercise (such as Cobra Gold and Tandem Thrust) and dating to the 1970s. Freedom Banner 04: Pyongtaek, South Korea, Mar 2004. The exercise was the northernmost Marine Corps operation ever conducted on the Korean peninsula. Freedom Banner 03/Crocodile 03: Queensland, Australia, Oct 2003. Freedom Banner 02/Cobra Gold 02: Thailand, Apr–May 2002. Freedom Banner 01/Tandem Thrust 01: Australia, Jun 2001. Freedom Banner 00/Crocodile 99: Australia. Freedom Banner 98/Foal Eagle: Pohang, South Korea. Freedom Banner 95: Pohang, South Korea. Freedom Banner 94.
+ **Freedom Eagle:** Operations in the Philippines as part of the war on terrorism, 2003. Formally part of Enduring Freedom.

Freemont: Pacific Fleet first word.

Freeze/Freighter: PACOM first words.

Frequent Storm: Classified US–Thai major special operations exercise. Frequent Storm 04. Frequent Storm 01-1. Frequent Storm 01-2. Frequent Storm 00: 13–16 Mar 2000. Frequent Storm 99.

Fresh: PACOM first word.

Friar/Desperado: Marine Corps intelligence system.

Friartuck: Gulf War laptop-computer-based intelligence systems with a sensitive compartmented information classified hard drive used to identify selected enciphered signals.

Friday/Fried/Fringe: PACOM first words.

Frisian Flag: EUCOM Red Flag–like European exercise series, held at Leeuwarden AB, the Netherlands, and launched in 1992. Participants include Canada, Finland, France, Germany, the Netherlands, Norway, Sweden, the UK, and the US. Frisian Flag 02. Frisian Flag 01. Frisian Flag 00: 4–15 Sep 2000. Frisian Flag 99: 27 Sep–8 Oct 1999.

Front Burner: Flagword used on an OPREP-3 Pinnacle message alerting national authorities of a potential incident that could lead to the use of force.

Frontier: Coast Guard first word, including Frontier Saber II (special operation, 1–30 Mar 2000) and Frontier Shield (special operation, 1 Jan–30 Sep 1997).
+ **Frontier Lance:** Cooperative effort among the Coast Guard, the Dominican Republic, and Haiti to deny maritime smugglers sea routes into and around Hispanola, Jan–Jun 1998.

Frontier: PACOM Guam-related first word.
+ **Frontier Patrol 00-2:** Seventh Fleet exercise, Oct 2000.
+ **Frontier Scout:** Seventh Fleet exercise.

Frost: US–Taiwanese related first word.

Frosting: NSA program or system, 1980s.

Frown: US–Japanese first word.

Frozen: US–Taiwanese related first word.

Frugal: US–Japanese first word.

Fuerte Apoyo: *See* Strong Support.

Fuertes Caminos: SOUTHCOM engineer construction exercise conducted in Colombia, El Salvador, Honduras, and Guatemala, 1994.

Fuertes Defensas: SOUTHCOM major exercise held in Florida and selected locations in the South American region. The exercise practices crisis action planning procedures, application of common doctrine, and command and control. Fuertes Defensas 04. Fuertes Defensas 02: 29 Jan–1 Feb 2002.

Fuerzas Aliadas (Allied Forces): SOUTHCOM annual peacekeeping command post exercise and regional humanitarian exercise. Participants include

Argentina, Belize, Bolivia, Chile, the Dominican Republic, El Salvador, Guatemala, Honduras, Nicaragua, Panama, Paraguay, Uruguay, and the Caribbean Islands.

+ **Fuerzas Aliadas:** Humanitarian series.
+ **Fuerzas Aliadas Cabañas:** Crisis response exercise series.
+ **Fuerzas Aliadas Counter Drug:** Counter-narcotics series.
+ **Fuerzas Aliadas Humanitarias:** Disaster relief series.
+ **Fuerzas Aliades PKO:** Peacekeeping series.
+ **Fuerzas Aliadas Riverine.**

Fuerzas Commando 04: SOUTHCOM special operations exercise.

Fuerzas Defensas: SOUTHCOM seminar focused on defense of the trans-isthmian transportation systems of Panama against an insurgent force in Panama in a low-intensity environment. Fuerzas Defensas 02/03: Exercise introduces the updated Panama CONPLAN without the presence of US forces in Panama. In 2001–2003, the exercise was expanded to JTF exercise scale, in conjunction with Unified Endeavor.

Fuerzas Unidas (United Forces) Peacekeeping South (PKO SOUTHAM): SOUTHCOM annual regional peacekeeping exercise, rotating among host nations. Fuerzas Unidas 02: Montevideo, Uruguay. Fuerzas Unidas 00: Chile. Fuerzas Unidas 89: Bolivia.

Fulcrum: Desert Storm intelligence system, 1991.

Full Accounting: JTF Full Accounting, Vietnam, Laos, and Cambodia. The JTF, operational since 1992, is responsible for repatriation of the remains of prisoners of war/missing in action.

Full Moon: US–UK special operations reciprocal exercise series. Full Moon 00: Fort Bragg, NC. UK 3 PARA and 3rd Bn, 505th Infantry Regt. The UK-based exercise is called Winged Star.

Full Plate 84: Reagan-era exercise with NSC involvement, 10–14 Dec 1984 and 14–18 Jan 1985.

Full Provider: JTF Puerto Rico and Hispaniola, 25 Sep–1 Nov 1998.

Full Throttle: CTF 180 special operations covert reconnaissance and raid, Deh Rawod, Afghanistan, 30 Jun 2003. An AC-130 killed 34 civilians during the operation.

Fundamental Relief: Humanitarian assistance and disaster relief operation in response to Hurricane George, Puerto Rico Operating Area, 28 Sep–27 Oct 1998.

Fundamental Response: JTF Fundamental Response, Maiquetia, Venezuela, 27 Dec 1999–5 Mar 2000.

Furtive Bear: Air Force 430th Reconaissance Technical Group operation during Just Cause.

Future Look/Have Bridge: Air Force NAIC exercise, May 1997.

— **G** —

Gable: Air Force Special Operations Command first word.
+ **Gable Adder:** Contingency plan for operations in Panama, 1989.
+ **Gable Shark:** Deployment of two AC-130Hs of 16th SOS from Hurlburt, FL, 17 Jan 1991, on a Chairman JCS–directed, classified mission "of vital national importance" in direct support of Desert Storm.

Gabon 00: European exercise attended by members of the Western European Union (WEU) Secretariat General and Military Staff, 27–29 Jan 2000, an important precedent in the development of WEU's African peacekeeping policy.

Gadgeteer: Air Force SIGINT equipment.

Gaits: *See* Sentinel Aspen II.

Galaxy: Air Force special access program.

Gale (Generic Area Limitation Environment): National-level ELINT receiver and correlator. Gale is a replacement for JEAP/Sunshine. Gale Lite is a TENCAP application for field use.

Galidia: Unknown intelligence or communications system.

Gallant: CENTCOM (and predecessor Rapid Deployment Joint Task Force) first word.
+ **Gallant Eagle:** Former desert training exercise series held in various locations in California and Nevada, initiated in 1982.

+ **Gallant Knight:** Rapid Deployment JTF annual exercise series at Fort Bragg, NC, 1980–1988.

Gallant Warrior: Army 93rd Signal Bde exercise, 1998. The brigade deployed to "Georgina" to support a US Corps for routine peacetime training. Two terrorist organizations, upset by the US presence, began conducting small-scale terrorist attacks. The attacks' purpose was to disrupt theater command and control and to get US soldiers to overreact and escalate the violence, providing political capital to use against the US presence on the host country's soil.

Gambit: Former KH-7 and KH-8 imagery satellites.

Gambol Venture 95: US–Pakistani onetime special operations mobile training team that trained Pakistani SOF on static line and free-fall jumping.

Gamma: Classification compartment designating a COMINT subcompartment of Talent Keyhole satellite derived intercepts (for instance, Top Secret/Talent Keyhole Gamma). Similar sensitive COMINT categories include Endseal, ECI, and VRK. Gamma subcompartments previously designated specific country or operation sources. At one point, there were 20 Gamma designations, including Gilt, Goat, Gult, Gant, Gupy, Gabe, Gyro, and Gout. Delta designations referred to military information, and included Dace, Dice, and Dent.

Gangbusters: A subnet of the European nuclear weapons Cemetery Network.

Gangster: Navy shipboard software system.

Garden Plot: National civil disturbance response plan (NORTHCOM FUNC-PLAN 2502). The plan was implemented by JTF Los Angeles to support law enforcement authorities in Los Angeles during the Rodney King riots, 1–12 May 1992. The Military District of Washington conducted a Garden Plot Tabletop exercise, 6 Apr 1999. Garden Plot was originally under the purview of the army, but has now transitioned to Northern Command.

Gardenia: US–UK NAIC exploitation of a foreign aerospace system, 1997.

Garland:

+ **Garland Crown:** Multi-service crisis management exercise, 11–24 Jun 1995. Air Force EC-135 and RC-135 of the 55th Wing participated.
+ **Garland Green:** Multi-service crisis action exercise, 6–13 Feb 1995. Air Force EC-135 and RC-135 of the 55th Wing participated.

Gatchwork: Naval Security Group SIGINT system.

Gatekeeper: 1. Broadsword application.
    2. **Gatekeeper:** Counter-narcotics exercise, operation, or compartment.
    3. **Gatekeeper:** Tactical ballistic missile defense, Iceland related?

Gateway: 1. United Nations Special Commission–International Atomic Energy Agency intelligence and debrief operations in Bahrain, 1991–1998.
    2. **Gateway:** Australian cyclical maritime surveillance operations in the northern Indian Ocean and South China Sea.

Gateway Response: Full-scale multi-jurisdictional exercise involving chemical and radiological weapons, Port of Newark, NJ, 15 Nov 2003.

Gator Byte: Unknown exercise.

Gaulish: UK–French exercise series. Gaulish 4/02, Nov 2002, was canceled because of a UK firefighters strike. Gaulish Star 2/00, May 2000, was canceled because of Kosovo operations.

Gemini: NATO exercise, Norway, 1999.

Genesis II: Army intelligence project to provide lightweight, portable, advanced, one-of-a-kind or limited-production ELINT systems in support of the war on terrorism.

Genisys: DARPA Terrorism Information Awareness program to develop a mega-database to predict, track, and thwart terrorist attacks. The database would integrate all relevant existing intelligence databases and semi-structured information sources to automatically populate the new repository with many different and nontraditional data feeds.

Genoa: DARPA Terrorism Information Awareness project to develop the automated information technologies for use by intelligence analysts to process enormous amounts of electronic data, including intercepts and public and private transactions databases to identify and preempt terrorist activities.

Gentle Plan/Ellipse Foxtrot: CENTCOM crisis action exercise, 18 Mar–8 Apr 1995.

Gentry (Project Gentry): Former air force special access program.

Geronimo Thrust/Balance Iroquois 02-2: US–Indian exercise held in Alaska, 28 Sep–11 Oct 2002. The Army 1st Bn, 501st Parachute Infantry Regt hosted India's 50th Independent Parachute Bde, the first-ever live-fire exercise between American and Indian paratroopers. The Indian soldiers flew to Alaska in an Indian air force IL-76, and the exercise also marked the first time that an Indian combat aircraft has landed on US soil.

Ghost: 1. SAC code name referring to drone programs in the 1980s, including Ghost Echo, Ghost Game, and Ghost Rider.

    2. **Ghost:** US–Argentinian anti-submarine-warfare exercise. Includes Ghost 93.

Ghost Zone: Bolivia-based counter-narcotics operation, 1992.

Ghostrider II: JTF 6 counter-narcotics operation to stem the flow of drugs across the US–Mexican border.

Ghostwire: NSA SIGINT element of the Joint Deployable Intelligence Support System (JDISS).

GI Joe II/III: National Imagery and Mapping Agency (NIMA) coalition interoperability test including Australia, Canada, New Zealand, qualified NATO nations, and the UK.

Giant: STRATCOM (and predessesor SAC) first word. Cold War Giant programs include Giant Barnacle (SR-71 operations from Okinawa, Japan); Giant Moon (Emergency Rocket Communications System); Giant Pioneer (Cobra Ball mission communications system); Giant Reach (SR-71 operations at RAF Mildenhall, UK); Giant Sapphire (AN/GPS-10 radar, San Miguel, Philippines); Giant Star (Air Force Satellite Communications [AFSATCOM]); Giant Talk (HF/SSB radio network upgraded under Scope Signal).

+ **Giant Ball:** UHF communications reliability test series for strategic nuclear forces.
+ **Giant Drill:** Airborne command postbattle staff exercise.
+ **Giant Lance:** Exercise involving selective employment of bomber and tanker forces, including emergency loading of nuclear weapons.
+ **Giant Look:** Special exercise activities.
+ **Giant Net:** Air Combat Command support of the National Airborne Operations Center.
+ **Giant Pace:** Simulated electronic launch of Minuteman and Peacekeeper ICBMs. The results from SELM testing are used for predicting launch system reliability for war plans.

+ **Giant Shot:** Nickname used to notify air traffic control facilities of a no-notice operational airborne command post aircraft launch under peacetime conditions (*see also* Olympic Shot).
+ **Giant Sword:** Combat weapons loading competition.
+ **Giant Warrior:** B-52 deployments to Guam during Desert Shield, 1990.

Giant Cave/Giant Dodge: Air force special access program including Coronet Phoenix deployments.

Giant Shadow: STRATCOM and navy cruise missile submarine (SSGN) sea trial experiment involving converted strategic ballistic missile submarines firing Tomahawk sea-launched cruise missiles. Giant Shadow 04: Mar 2004. Giant Shadow 03: Bahamas, Jan 2003. The USS *Florida* (SSGN 728) launched two Tomahawk missiles, the first ever for a former Trident submarine. Onboard SEALs also conducted an ISR and NBC force protection mission experiment against a simulated terrorist chemical weapons site on a remote island. *See also* Silent Hammer.

Giant Voice: Loudspeaker system at Prince Sultan AB, Saudi Arabia, used to alert personnel of Scud missile or chemical weapons attack.

Gifted Eagle: SAC test series to improve attack of "strategic relocatable targets" in the Soviet Union and Russia, initiated in the 1980s. The initial test series took place over a military operating area of the Ottawa National Forest on Michigan's Upper Peninsula.

Gigster: NSA secure video-teleconference system and distance learning network.

Ginger: The battle of Takur Ghar during Anaconda in Afghanistan, Mar–Apr 2002.

Gister: Intelligence Advanced Concept Technology Demonstration to develop an optical character reading software system to recognize low-density scriptal languages, a part of Falcon. The initial languages of the experiment were Dari, Pashtu, and Thai.

Glacial Engima: UK exercise in Norway, Jan 2002, canceled because of operational commitments.

Glacier: Information warfare/information technology related, 2002.

Glad: Former SAC first word, including Glad Customer (B-52 operations in Darwin, Australia, during the 1980s).

Glass: Former SAC first word used starting in the 1960s. *Glass Eye* referred to reports submitted under the Continental US Airborne Reconnaissance for Damage Assessment (CARDA) OPLAN.

Global: Navy Title 10 War Game held each summer over a two-week period at the Naval War College, Newport, RI. The Global series (Global 95, Global 92) has focused on development of the Network Centric Warfare concept and other transformation issues.

Global: STRATCOM first word.

+ **Global Archer:** Twice-annual command post exercise conducted to validate and test battle staff, transition to war procedures, and test national nuclear adaptive planning procedures. Scenarios involve trans-/postexecution operations utilizing STRATCOM's ground and airborne mobile assets. STRATCOM conducts a Global Archer exercise each spring (Mar) and fall (Aug). The spring Global Archer is primarily a command post exercise conducted five to six months after Global Guardian to prepare for JCS inspections. The Global Archer each fall is an internal exercise to indoctrinate newly arrived personnel prior to their participation in Global Guardian. The exercises also link to Apollo Bronze, Vigilant Overview, Positive Force, and Crown Vigilance.

+ **Global Cajun:** Bomber exercise to prepare for conventional operational readiness inspections. Several Global Cajuns may be conducted each year.

+ **Global Cruise:** Nuclear and conventional air-launched cruise missile test series, held at the Utah Test and Training Range; Primrose Lake Evaluation Range, Canada; or Tonopah Test Range, NV.

+ **Global Guardian:** Single Integrated Operational Plan (SIOP) annual command post exercise/field training exercise to generate all US nuclear forces. The exercise evaluates command and control procedures and tactics in support of operations during a tran-/postattack nuclear environment, including reconstitution, redirection, and retargeting strategic nuclear forces. Held in cooperation with Amalgam Warrior, Apollo Bronze, Apollo Guardian, Crown Vigilance, Vigilant Guardian, and Vigilant Overview. After 1998, as a result of the assigning theater nuclear planning to STRATCOM in 1994, the Global Guardian exercises have been "dovetailed" with Pacific Command's Ulchi Focus Lens exercise on the Korean peninsula to practice adaptive nuclear planning against North Korea. Since Oct 1995, both Joint Staff and theater commands have participated. Several senior civilian and military leaders participate, including members from the Offices of the Secretary of Defense and Chairman of the JCS. Global Guardian 04: 20–29 Oct 2003. Global Guardian 03: 17–25 Oct 2002. Global Guardian 02: 22–31 Oct 2001. Global Guardian 01: 19–27 Oct 2000. Global Guardian 00: 25 Oct–3 Nov 1999. Global Guardian 99: 24 Oct–2 Nov 1998. To provide greater realism, Global Guardian 99 took place in conjunction with Amalgam Warrior, Apollo Guardian, and Vigilant Guardian. Global Guardian 99 also marked the first time that a Polo Hat connectivity test was integrated. The exercise practiced B-52 nuclear taskings in support of CENTCOM in the Middle East. The USS *Minneapolis–St. Paul* (SSN-708) fired a successful TLAM-N, the first since the end of the Cold War. Global Guardian 98: 27 Oct–5 Nov 1997. The exercise included a ballistic missile submarine (SSBN) Continuity of Operations (SCOOP) exercise (LANTSCOOPEX 1-98), involving the USS *Maryland* (SSBN 738) and USS *Emory S. Land* (AS 39) deploying to Roosevelt Roads, Puerto Rico; a nuclear Tomahawk regeneration with the USS *Atlanta* (SSN 712); and an SSBN security exercise, with the USS *Maryland*, USS *Atlanta*, and PATWING 11 participating. The exercise included a rigorous information warfare scenario of computer network attacks, and participation of the 4th FW, the first time a tactical-dual-capable aircraft unit participated. Global Guardian 97: 13 Oct–2 Nov 1996. Practiced implementation of SIOP-97, including theater nuclear options in the Middle East (CENTCOM) area. The exercise included cyber-warfare attacks on US systems for the first time, and the first deployment of STRATCOM's trailer-based Mobile Consolidated Command Center. It was also the last time B-1 bombers participated in the annual exercise. "Player cells" were located in Australia and the UK.

+ **Global Shadow:** Advanced Cruise Missile test series, held at the Utah Test and Training Range; Primrose Lake Evaluation Range, Canada; and Tonopah Test Range, Nevada. Global Shadows are sometimes combined with Busy Luggage drop tests of nuclear gravity bombs.
+ **Global Shield:** Former SAC annual nuclear exercise series held until 1991, when it was replaced by Global Guardian.

Global Apache 97/Deep Look 97: National Guard exercise building upon

Global Yankee 96 and incorporating land training in Deep Look, Dugway, UT, and Fort Drum, NY.

Global Engagement 97: Air force futures war game involving UK participation.

Global Hawk: RQ-4A UAV, called Tier II+ in development, with 24-hour loiter time at mission altitudes in excess of 60,000 feet. The UAV carries both an Electro-Optical/Infrared (EO/IR) sensor and a Synthetic Aperture Radar (SAR) with Moving Target Indicator (MTI) capability allowing day/night, all-weather reconnaissance. Global Hawk was first operationally deployed in support of OEF.

Global Lynx: SOCOM special operations exercise involving the 224th Joint Communications Support Sqn, 1999.

Global Mercury: Global Health Security Action Group bioterrorism tabletop exercise, Washington, DC, 8–10 Sep 2003. Participants included Canada, France, Germany, Italy, Japan, Mexico, the UK, and the US. The exercise scenario simulated a smallpox bioterrorism attack.

Global Patriot 99: Reachback training exercise, 10–27 Jul 1999. Principal locations included Utah Test and Training Range; Fort Drum, NY; and the Air Force Research Laboratory, Rome, NY. The exercise experimented with home station participation via computer data links.

Global Yankee: National Guard joint exercise. Global Yankee 96 evolved into Global Apache 97. Global Yankee 95: Fort Drum, NY, 17–30 Jun 1995.

Globus II: US–Norwegian Have Stare cooperative space tracking radar.

Glory Trip: ICBM test launch from Vandenburg AFB, CA.

Glow Worm/Rattlesnake: US–UK army exercise series. UK participation in the 9–23 Jun 2001 series was canceled due to foot-and-mouth disease restrictions. The Jun 1999 exercise was canceled because of Kosovo operations.

Goal Keeper: SOCOM operation, 2003–2004.

Gobi Dust/Steerspike: US–UK exercise series. Gobi Dust 2002 was canceled by the US because of OEF. The Nov 1999 exercise was canceled because of Kosovo operations.

Gold: Joint mobile/rapid targeting systems experiment series, begun after Desert Storm and hosted at the Naval Air Warfare Center — Weapons Div.

+ **Gold Pan:** F-15E Scud hunting experiments utilizing the Rapid Targeting Dissemination System with U-2 Advanced Synthetic Aperture Radar System (ASARS) and national imagery cueing.
+ **Gold Strike:** Joint F-16, F/A-18, and F-15E experiments.

Gold Coast: 51st FW combat effectiveness readiness exercise, 1999.

Gold Eagle: US–Australian amphibious field training exercise. Gold Eagle 03: Mar 2003. Gold Eagle 02: Jun–Jul 2002.

Gold Phone: White House–secretary of defense hotline for crises.

Gold Sword IV: 800th MP Bde prisoner-of-war exercise, Fort A. P. Hill, VA, Jun 1998. Included 33rd Interrogator-Translator Team, marine forces reserve.

Golden Cargo/Kastle: 1. Army Industrial Operations Command annual exercise incorporating ARNG combat service and combat service support organizations.

Golden Coyote 99: National Guard exercise focused on engineer projects, water purification, and maintenance in the Black Hills National Forest area and the surrounding recreational areas.

Golden Medic: Army reserve and local government medical exercise series to support natural disaster or WMD large casualty loads. Golden Medic 01: San Francisco Bay Area, 19–23 Jul 2001. Golden Medic 00: 10–14 Jun 2000. Golden Medic 99: Fort McCoy, WI (overall headquarters), Fort Gordon, GA, and Camp Parks, CA, Jul 1999.

Golden Pheasant: Honduras show of force no-notice deployment, 1988. The XVIII Airborne Corps operation was to counter a potential Nicaraguan incursion. It included an 82nd Airborne Div Bde TF of two battalions conducting a parachute insertion and air–land operation.

Golden Python: Army operation to remove more than 100,000 chemical munitions from Germany and transport them to Johnston Atoll, 1989–1990.

Golden Sands: UK–Jordanian exercise, 2000–2001.

Golden Spear: CENTCOM minister-/ambassador-level executive seminar for strategic-level security dialogue with the East African countries of Burundi, the DRC, Djibouti, Egypt, Eritrea, Ethiopia, Kenya, Rwanda, the Seychelles, Tanzania, and Uganda. Golden Spear 03: Addis Abba, Ethiopia,

Code Names

28–30 Jul 2003. Gen. John Abizaid, commander of CENTCOM, and Brig. Gen. Mastin M. Robeson, commander of CJTF — Horn of Africa, attended. Golden Spear 02: Nanyuki, Kenya, 23–25 Jul 2002. *See also* Neon Spear.

Golden Spike: Code name for emergency condition involving prisoners of war or other detainees in which military police are authorized to use deadly force.

Gondola (Project Gondola): Counter-narcotics communications project, mid-1990s.

Goodbye: High-powered microwave anti-personnel "active denial" technology development program. The weapon can be configured in a ground-mobile, airborne, or fixed-site system for single-person operation.

Goodwill 02: Australian–Japanese maritime exercise, Oct 2002.

Gotham Victory: V Corps urban warfare exercise in preparation for Operation Iraqi Freedom, held immediately following Victory Scrimmage. The 2nd Bde, 1st Armored Div tested the corps' newly developed tactics, techniques, and procedures for urban warfare against a "thinking" enemy.

Gothic Serpent: Somalia operation to free trapped Army Rangers in Mogadishu, 3–4 Oct 1993.

Gramophone Insult: Army Foreign Science and Technology Center Desert Storm project.

Granby: UK military operations during the 1991 Gulf War (equivalent of Desert Storm).

Grand Eagle: Army Intelligence Support Activity (Gray Fox) operation in the early 1980s to find remaining American POWs in Southeast Asia.

Grand Falcon/Great Falcon: Army Intelligence Support Activity (Gray Fox) operation during the Iran–Iraq war to attempt to acquire a Soviet T-72 tank from the Iraqi government.

Grand Prix: UK–Kenya Army Infantry Battle Group exercise series. Three are held each year. Grand Prix 3/02, 25 Oct–6 Dec 2002, canceled because of firefighters strike.

Grand Slam: FBI–San Diego local government "first responders" exercise, Aug

2000. The scenario involved the the release of an unknown chemical agent at Qualcomm Stadium during a public event.

Grandma Beguile: Army Foreign Science and Technology Center foreign material exploitation, 1992.

Grandslam: NSA initiative to improve near-real-time combat information for tactical military users. Grandslam II, Feb 1994, was run by NSA's Military Applications branch (G712), and was designed to document, examine, and improve the SIGINT system's capabilities to support tactical operations information requirements. Rivet Joint aircraft participated.

Granite: Army Foreign Science and Technology Center foreign material exploitation, 1989–1992. Includes Granite Diamond, Granite Eagle, Granite Key I/II, Granite Plane, Granite Rain, and Granite Wall.

Granite Sentry: NORAD air defense data and voice command, control, and communications network.

Grantor Shadow: Special access program compartment code name for the Army Intelligence Support Activity (Gray Fox); replaced Royal Cape and was replaced by Capacity Gear in 1989.

Graphic Book: Army Intelligence Support Activity (Gray Fox) SIGINT operation, 1980s.

Graphic Hand: Postal augmentation by military forces OPLAN.

Grass Blade: Former army special access program.

Gray Fox: Nickname for the clandestine Army Intelligence Support Activity (ISA) headquartered at Fort Belvoir, VA, and assigned to SOCOM since Jul 2002 (see part 1). It is currently controlled under the Titrant Ranger special access program.

Gray Herring: US–UK–Danish–German intelligence operation along the German border, 1985–1986.

Gray Pan: CIA–DIA project to acquire Soviet equipment from Iran, late 1970s.

Gray Star: Air force technical intelligence collection program involving installation of surveillance and tracking radar on the former ocean surveillance ship USNS *Invincible* (which was reclassified to T-AGM 24 in 2000 to better reflect the new mission). The S- and X-band acquisition and signature data collection radar monitors space, missile, or weapons test events, particularly theater ballistic missile testing. The DIA Central MASINT Office provides oversight and mission direction.

Grazing Lawn: Army Intelligence Support Activity (Gray Fox) low-profile clandestine airborne reconnaissance operation, conducted from Tegucigalpa, Honduras, 1983–1985. *See also* Canvas Shield.

Greater Slope: Army all-composite stealth helicopter special access program development program, contained in the FY 1983 defense budget and revealed in *Aviation Week and Space Technology*, 15 Nov 1982, p. 13.

Grecian Firebolt: Army Signal Command major regional contingency exercise, focused on homeland security and the war on terrorism since 9/11. Grecian Firebolt 03: Fort Meade, MD, 9–20 Jun 2003. The exercise connected service nodes, FEMA and other federal agencies, and South Korea. Grecian Firebolt 01: 16 Jun–6 Aug 2001. Grecian Firebolt 00: 3–25 Jun 2000. Grecian Firebolt 99: Connected units at 23 separate locations throughout the US. Grecian Firebolt 96: Jun 1996. Largest peacetime Army Signal Corps exercise, involving more than 4,000 soldiers and 33 satellite terminals across the US, Panama, Saudi Arabia, Kuwait, and South Korea. Grecian Firebolt 95. Grecian Firebolt 94: Exercise involving some 7,500 personnel communicating over voice and data networks at 40 sites in 17 states, as well as in Panama, Germany, and South Korea.

Greek Island: Former congressional emergency relocation site at the Greenbriar Hotel in West Virginia.

Greek Knights: US–Greek aircraft exchange, conducted at Anghialos AB, near Volos, 2000. Five F-16s deployed to Anghialos to fly with the Hellenic Air Force.

Green Clover: Counter-narcotics operations in Pucallpa, Peru, Oct–Dec 1995.

Green Flag: Air Combat Command annual electronic warfare/electronic combat field training exercise emphasizing electronic combat and command, control, communications, computers, and intelligence (C4I) awareness among aircrews, planning staff, and intelligence personnel. The Air Warfare Center at Nellis AFB, NV, is responsible for the planning and execution of Green Flag. The exercise emphasizes combat integration of fighter and bomber aircraft with EC/RC-135, JSTATRs, and reconnaissance platforms. One scenario is based on a fictitious Third World dispute over oil production and religious views. Despotia is an Islamic nation possessing 15 percent of the world's oil reserves. Petrolia possesses 30 percent of the world's oil reserves and is supported by the US. Numerous assassination attempts against the Petrolia royal family are undertaken by Despotia. Foziland, a democratic secular country also targeted by Despotia, is attacked, and Petrolia and Foziland request US military assistance. Participants include Canada, Germany, Italy, Spain, and the UK.

Green Light: US-only effort focused on apprehending Radovan Karadzic, the former Bosnian Serb political leader, as part of Amber Star (*see also* Buckeye).

Green Pine: Former air force Arctic early warning UHF radio network.

Green Quest: Post-9/11 US Customs Service financial anti-terrorism TF to identify, disrupt, and dismantle terrorist financial infrastructure. Green Quest is composed of investigators and analysts from customs, the IRS, the FBI, and the Treasury Department's Office of Financial Assets Control.

Green Sweep: Counter-narcotics operations in Bolivia, 1990.

Grenadier Bay: SOCOM program, 1991–present.

Grenadier BRAT (Blue Force Reporting and Tracking): Army and SOF beyond-line-of-sight transponder system that reports unit identification, location, and a short coded message, in the Low Probability of Intercept/Low Probability of Detection waveform, called the Cobra waveform. The transponder derives location information from GPS satellite broadcasts. Grenadier BRAT is one of the key elements of the blue force tracking (BFT), which allows equipped vehicles and aircraft to see (and be seen) by other forces. The BFT data is automatically fed to display a Common Operational Picture. Grenadier BRAT was used during OEF and OIF.

Greyhound: Big Safari–managed special access program.

Griffin: JCS coalition "Five Eyes" communications network to exchange Secret-level classified communications with Australia, Canada, New Zealand, and the UK. The initial Coalition Wide Area Network CONOPS was signed in Apr 2002. It is being expanded to include France and Germany. Griffin was used during OIF.

Grill Flame: CIA remote viewing program.

Grimace Monitor: Former army intelligence-related special access program.

Gringo-Gaucho: US–Argentinian situational air–naval exercise held during the transit of US Navy aircraft carriers.

Grisly Hunter: Former semi-clandestine Army Reconnaissance Low Imagery (ARL-I) Electro-Optical/Infrared mission, predecessor to the consolidated Army Reconnaissance Medium (ARL-M) program (Crazy Hawk). The Grisly Hunter program was originally based on CASA-212 aircraft flown out of Panama in the 1980s for support of Central American operations and counter-narcotics missions. *See also* Crazy Panther.

Grizzly Border Road: JTF-designed program to assist state and federal law enforcement efforts to decrease the flow of illegal drugs into the US along the Mexican border. National Guard engineer units construct barriers and access roads.

Grown Tall: Marine Corps civil disturbance exercise, 1980s.

Gryphon: 1. Survivable submarine communications, including ELF, TACAMO, Verdin, and Clarinet Pilgrim.
2. **Gryphon:** UAV made from special materials that make it resistant to destruction. Gryphon completed flight testing at Yuma, AZ, on 4 Dec 2003.

Guardian: Air Force Space Command, Vandenburg AFB, CA, first word.

+ **Guardian Challenge:** Space and missile competition, Vandenberg AFB, CA. Guardian Challenge 04: 2–7 May 2004. Guardian Challenge 03 canceled because of OIF. Guardian Challenge 97: 28 Apr–2 May 1997.
+ **Guardian Sword:** ICBM missile tactics development program.
+ **Guardian Tiger:** Forum to develop and refine doctrine and procedures supporting Spacelift, Space Surveillance, Satellite Command and Control, and Missile Warning mission areas.

Guardian Assistance: US support to international relief efforts in Rwanda/Zaire, 15 Nov–27 Dec 1996. USAFE deployed two C-130s 21 Nov; one returned 12 Dec, the other four days later.

Guardian Retrieval: EUCOM noncombatant evacuation operation from Zaire (now Democratic Republic of Congo), 15 Mar–5 Jun 1997. USS *Nassau* (LHA 4), USS *Kearsarge* (LHD 3), and 22nd MEU.

Guardian Shield 05: Army V Corps mass casualty evacuation training exercise.

Guardrail: Army airborne COMINT and ELINT system aboard a C-12 Super King (designated RC-12). Several generations are in service, each with different capabilities. All are remotely controlled collection and location systems backed by ground-based processing and analysis. The Guardrail Common Sensor (GRCS) combines the Improved Guardrail V COMINT package with advanced Quick Look ELINT and a Communication High Accuracy Airborne Location System (CHAALS). The first GRCS system was fielded to Europe in 1991, and the second was fielded to XVIII Airborne Corps in 1994.

Guestmaster: Navy SIGINT program.

Guidamakha 98: French West African peacekeeping exercise follow-on to Blue Hungwe in 1997. The US provided airlift and a participating Marine Corps platoon.

Guidepost: Scientific and technical intelligence processor/tool for missile analysis.

Guilder: Chief of Naval Operations (N2) first word.

Gulf: Navy (N89/N7SP) special access program first word.

Gulf Breeze: Air force–navy South Florida air combat exercise, 30 Apr–7 May 1999. The 94th FS deployed six aircraft and 71 personnel to conduct training with navy F-18s and F-16s from Homestead, FL.

GULFEX: Naval Forces Central Command (NAVCENT) exercise series held in the central Arabian Gulf. The 26th exercise in the series (GULFEX XXII) took place Feb–Mar 1994, and included France, Russia, the UK, and the US. The 1994 exercise was the third time Russia participated. Carrier Air Wing 5 from the USS *Independence* (CV 62) simulated strikes against the ships. French Mirage aircraft flew from Dhahran, Saudi Arabia.

Gulf Shield: Coast Guard operation, South Padre Island, TX.

Gumdrop: Possible classified clandestine military intelligence activity, part of the DOD Intelligence Information System (DODIIS).

Gun Runner 98: Australian strike and air reconnaissance exercise, Mar–Apr 1998.

Gunslinger: PACOM- and Office of Naval Research–related project.

Gunsmoke: Air Combat Command air-force-wide bombing competitition, Nellis AFB, NV.

Gusty: Navy special access program first word, including Gusty Yearling.

+ **Gusty Ant:** NRL ocean surveillance project.
+ **Gusty Oriole:** Information warfare computer algorithms for space applications, being conducted for the air force.

Gypsy: Navy (N89/N7SP) special access program first word, including Gypsy Dancer (Navy Project Code ZZ1-ZZ9).

Gypsy Bravo: Program to examine the impact of jamming and other electronic interference on GPS-guided precision weapons, also known as the Joint Global Positioning System Combat Effectiveness Joint Test and Evaluation. The first phase of Gypsy Bravo ran in Jan 2002 at NSA Fallon, NV. The test series runs for 51 months.

Gypsy Wagon: STRATCOM foreign material exploitation.

— H —

Hairspring: UK deployment to Norway. Hairspring 01: 5–16 Mar 2001. UK forces did not participate because of foot-and-mouth disease restrictions. The Mar 2000 deployment was canceled for lack of funding.

Hairy Buffalo: P-3 Orion fiber-optic backbone modification testbed allowing ground surveillance and real-time connections to ground forces, for use in time-sensitive targeting.

Hammer: Air force communications first word. Cold War and miscellaneous Hammer projects include Hammer Cable, Hammer Combat, Hammer Control, and Hammer Head.

+ **Hammer Ace:** Rapid response special-purpose communications team that provides communications in support of nuclear and aircraft mishaps, natural disaster civil relief operations, and other air force emergency operations. Activated in 1982, it is the only communications unit specifically to support nuclear weapons accidents.
+ **Hammer Rick:** AN/TSC-129 mobile secure satellite system used to establish a US–Israeli secure communications link during Desert Storm.
+ **Hammer Test:** Follow-on test and evaluation of communications equipment.

Hammer Focus: 3rd Infantry Div regular emergency deployment readiness exercise series, Fort Benning, GA.

Hammer Handle: Kuwait-based exercise, 8 Dec 1995–21 Mar 1996.

Hammerhead: Federal government interagency mass casualty WMD drill, Detroit, MI, Aug 1998.

Hammerlock 91: US–Greek naval exercise, Mediterranean Sea, Oct 1991. The USS *Forrestal* (CV 59) provided tactical air in support of and against an LHD Amphibious Task Group.

HANDA: US–Philippine annual seminar focusing on crisis action planning for coordinated and combined operations, 2001–present.

Harbor Shield: Federal and local government anti-terrorism exercise, Charleston Harbor, SC, 2002. Participants included the Coast Guard and marines from Camp Lejeune, NC.

Hard Flint: UK–Canadian air training exercise, Goose Bay, Canada. Hard Flint 01: 19 May–6 Jun 2001. The 13 May–8 Jun 2000 exercise was canceled because of UK operational commitments in Sierra Leone.

Hardfall: Former NATO Allied Command Europe (ACE) Mobile Force (Land) warfighting exercise in Norway. The exercises were held 1995–2002.

Hardlook: Naval Space Command special analysis intelligence product.

Haringaroo: Australian–Malaysian tropical field training exercise held in Malaysia. Haringaroo 02-2: Oct 2002. Haringaroo 97: Apr–Jun 1997. Haringaroo 96: Oct–Nov 1996.

Harmony (Project Harmony): Army National Ground Intelligence Center (NGIC)–managed database for foreign document exploitation (DOCEX) and translations management, begun in 1997. Harmony is the single, comprehensive bibliographic reference database for primary-source foreign technical and military documents and their translations. It is supplemented by the Deployable Harmony Application (DHA), a field system that facilitates management of foreign documents captured during operations. DHA was used in OEF and OIF. Same as FORMSS/Harmony network.

Harpoon: US–Canadian operation led by Canadian Light Infantry Battle Group, near simultaneous with Anaconda, in the eastern mountains of Paktia Province, Afghanistan, 13–19 Mar 2002.

Harvest: Air force civil engineer first word for engineering bare base mobility exercises and programs, including Harvest Bare, Harvest Eagle, Harvest Falcon, Harvest Stamp, Harvest Strapp. The Harvest Phoenix program was canceled.

Harvest Guard: NATO airborne early warning program.

Harvest Partner: Follow-on F-16 sales and support to Belgium, Denmark, and the Netherlands.

Hat Trick II: Narcotics interdiction operation in the Caribbean, 1986.

Hatchet: TF Hatchet, Bosnia, 5 Apr–21 Oct 1997.

Haunted Ramp: 74th Air Control Sqn exercise, Langley AFB, VA, 31 Oct 1997.

Have: Air Force Materiel Command (and previously Air Force Systems Command) first word. The *Have* first word can refer to innocuous communications systems, but it has also been consistently used to designate sensitive weapons systems and aircraft under development, and foreign aircraft exploitations. Cold War Have code names included Have Balance, Have Blinders, Have Canvas, Have Charity, Have Class, Have Claws, Have Dash, Have Doughnuts, Have Drag, Have Drill, Have Dungeon, Have Ears, Have Echo, Have Exit, Have Ferry, Have Field, Have Focus, Have Genesis, Have Glance, Have Knight, Have Lemon, Have Pole, Have Region, Have Rondo, Have Rose, Have Rust, Have Scoop, Have Siren.

+ **Have Blue:** Initial stealth fighter development program that resulted in the F-117A, first revealed in *Defense Week*, 25 Mar 1985. Have Blue developed a quarter-scale airplane, and Senior Trend developed the F-117A itself.
+ **Have Bunker:** Exploitation of missile system, 1989–1996. Have Bunker I evaluated RF Version.
+ **Have Charcoal:** Infrared counter-measures aboard airlift and VIP aircraft, including the National Airborne Operations Center.
+ **Have Cook:** Air Force Foreign Technology Division (now National Air Intelligence Center, NAIC) HUMINT activities covering command, control, and communications, 1980s.
+ **Have Crow:** Tactical electronics warfare system.
+ **Have CSAR:** Space Warfare Center Talon Knight TENCAP system deployed in support of Northern Watch. This included the Have

CSAR/MATT/ELMO systems and software to integrate daily flight plans, COMSEC and cryptographic systems, Iraqi ground and air electronic orders of battle, and "spider routes."

+ **Have Djinn:** Former special access program.
+ **Have Eagle:** Ballistic Missile Early Warning System (BMEWS) site upgrade at Fylingdales Moor, UK.
+ **Have Flag:** Tactical missile special access program, 1985–present.
+ **Have Flex:** Airborne Laser.
+ **Have Glib:** Exploitation of foreign ordnance.
+ **Have Gold:** NAIC threat assessments and evaluations of foreign ballistic missile and air-breathing platforms — aircraft, UAVs, unmanned combat aerial vehicles (UCAV), remote operating aircraft (ROA), micro aerial vehicle (MAV), and cruise missiles.
+ **Have Lite:** 1. Lightweight version of the Have Nap (AGM-142).
   2. **Have LITE:** Low Altitude Navigation and Targeting Infrared for Night (LANTIRN) pod.
+ **Have Mode:** F-22 supply.
+ **Have Nap:** B-52 (AGM-142) missile, a development of the Israeli Popeye missile.
+ **Have North:** North Warning System support.
+ **Have Note:** Ongoing electromagnetic vulnerability assessment program to test weapons systems and fuses.
+ **Have Quick:** Tri-service frequency-hopping anti-jamming radio system.
+ **Have Sabre:** Foreign material exploitation, 1992.
+ **Have Shade:** B-52 Common Strategic Rotary Launcher.
+ **Have Sight:** Ground-based Electro-Optical Deep Space Surveillance System (GEODSS) program support.
+ **Have Site:** Space Warfare Center Talon Knight program for support of special operations.
+ **Have Slick:** Low-observable, conformal-carried submunitions dispenser.
+ **Have Sound:** Supply support of special intelligence system.
+ **Have Star:** NAIC missile defense threat assessment.
+ **Have Stare:** AN/FPS-129 X-band space surveillance radar able to image geostationary satellites and detect extremely small particles of space debris. Activated in 1995 at Vandenberg AFB, CA, it was moved to Vardo, Norway, Oct 1998–May 1999.
+ **Have Terra:** RC-135 Combat Sent SIGINT mission.
+ **Have Trump:** Former air force special access program.

✦ **Have Union:** RC-135 Combat Sent SIGINT mission.

✦ **Have Void:** BLU-109/B special access program to develop a penetrating warhead.

✦ **Have Whip:** Foreign material exploitation, 1993.

Haven Denial: Coalition operation against Taliban remnants and al Qaeda fighters in southeast Afghanistan, Jul 2003.

Hawk: Noncommunications Signals Exploitation System. *See also* Phoenix, Raven, Merlin, Owl, and Mockingbird.

Hawkeye: 1. Proliferation Security Initiative airport-based ground interdiction training exercise, Germany, Mar 2004.

    2. **Hawkeye:** XVIII Airborne Corps disaster relief operations, St. Croix, US Virgin Islands, 1989.

Haystack: Long-range imaging radar located at Lincoln Laboratories and used for collection on geosynchronous satellite systems.

Hazarfend 97: NATO PfP exercise, Turkey. Participants included Macedonia.

HCS (HUMINT control system?): Classification compartment designating a subcompartment (such as Top Secret/HCS). HCS-P is also used.

Healthy: Air force communications-related first word.

Heart Ache: Army intelligence foreign material exploitation, 1993.

Heartleaf: Airborne reconnaissance SIGINT system.

Heavy: Air force operations first word. A series of PACAF "special plans" projects run out of HI in the 1980s were also called Heavy Door, Heavy Stone, and Heavy Sword.

✦ **Heavy Key:** Air Force Materiel Command (AFMC) operations support system, 1993–present.

✦ **Heavy Sword (Project 445):** AFMC-directed project, 1997.

Helicon Luk 02: Australian–Papua New Guinea air operations exercise, Nov 2002.

Helping Hand: Tactical report of possible hostile action, 1970s–present.

Herald: Air force weather-related first word. Includes Herald Stars, Herald Storm, Herald Switch, and Herald Weather.

Hercules: Space shuttle system of handheld photography coupled with a latitude, longitude, locator system able to accurately locate the pictures.

Heritage: Nonimaging infrared sensors aboard cooperative US satellites, including Jumpseat.

Hexagon: KH-9 "Big Bird" imagery satellite.

Hidden Treasure: Air Force Office of Special Investigations Det 106 counterintelligence operation that reportedly resulted in the savings of millions of dollars in protecting US research and development information.

HIDRAH (Handheld Integrated Directional Receiving and Homing System II): Marine Corps handheld tactical radio intercepts and signal-line-of-bearing/homing system.

High Flight: Search and rescue effort at Windhoek, Namibia, involving an MC-130P to locate an American C-141 and a German Tu-145 involved in a midair collision off the coast of Angola, 15 Sep–17 Oct 1997. Salvage operations continued until 28 Dec 1997.

High Point: Mount Weather High Point Special Facility, used during the Cold War for government relocation and continuity of government.

Highland Contact 99: Personnel recovery exercise, Brunswick, ME, 31 May–12 Jun 1999.

Highland Wind: RC-135 reconaissance missions flown during OEF.

Highport: UK Scotland-based exercise, 10 May 2001, canceled because of foot-and-mouth disease restrictions.

Hightop: NSA/Army INSCOM ELINT program.

HIJACK: Emissions security assessment that determines if counter-measures are required for cryptographic equipment. *See also* Nonstop.

HILEX (high-level exercise): Supreme Headquarters Allied Powers Europe HQ leadership seminar. During the Cold War, HILEX seminars were sponsored by the State Department and focused on plans, policies, and procedures for negotiations, consultations, and crisis escalation control within the NATO alliance. HILEX 00. HILEX 97: May–Jun 1997.

Himalayan Bluebell: UK–Nepal exercise, 2000–2001.

Code Names

Hip Pocket: 1. (**TF Hip Pocket**): Navy project to counter missile-armed or explosive-laden small-boat terrorist threats to US Navy vessels in port and at sea. Hip Pocket is evaluating defensive capability in the form of small arms and minor-caliber guns, surveillance systems, and nonlethal weapons such as prop fouling devices or anti-personnel acoustic weapons.

　　2. **Hip Pocket:** Evaluation of defense against cruise missiles, 1980s.

Holder: NSA program, 1980s.

Hollow Tile (HT): Air Intelligence Agency sensitive compartmented information or special access program.

Holystone: Special Naval Collection Program involving US submarine operations, begun in 1959. Holystone included covert submarine SIGINT and imagery collection to penetrate underwater communications cables. Aka Bollard and Pinnacle, and partially replaced by Barnacle. *See also* Ivy Bells.

Hombre: Army intelligence system, Bad Aibling, Germany.

HOMELINE: Flagword for mandated reports of incidents or events that do not merit HQ Air Force attention but may be of interest to the major command.

Honey Badger: Joint Special Operations Command program to develop a clandestine air capability, 1980s.

Hong Kong SAREX: PACOM annual search and rescue (SAR) exercise hosted by the Hong Kong Civil Aviation Department. Focus is on peacetime SAR and long-range overwater search.

Honor Guard: Air Combat Command–related SIGINT program, classified ACCHVTKCCJ (Air Combat Command handle via TK channels CJ?).

Hooker: Wideband electronic surveillance system, 1980s.

Hornet's Nest: Marine Corps exercise with air force participation, 1995.

Host (Project Host): Air force worldwide high frequency/direction finding (HF/DF) intelligence system upgrade, related to Longroot and Checkboard.

Hourglass: Coast Guard special operation, 1–27 Apr 1994.

House Call: Naval ECM equipment aboard ships, 1980s.

Hot Box: Exercise term to designate a defense emergency.

Hot Rock: Humanitarian assistance operation after the eruption of Mount Etna, Sicily, 13 Apr 1992. USS *Inchon* (LPH 12).

Hunter: 1. Army and Marine Corps RQ-5A 150–kilometer-range surveillance UAV.

2. **Hunter:** Kosovo defense campaign, 1 Apr 1999–1 Nov 1999.

3. **Hunter:** Australian–Thai maritime mine warfare and diving exercise series, including Singapore. Hunter 02: Aug 2002. Hunter 98: Apr 1998.

HyCAS (Hyperspectral Collection and Analysis System): CENTCOM Advanced Concept Technology Demonstration.

Hydra: 1. INTELINK-S related metadata search tool.

2. **CYCLOPS/HYDRA:** Suitcase-sized surveillance system with six TV monitors and fiber-optic links to 3.75 miles.

Hydrus: Navy submarine communications program that enables nuclear attack submarine (SSN) and ballistic missile submarine (SSBN) commanders to communicate with shore on a secure and reliable basis without compromising location or constrain operations. Includes Omen, Classic Mayflower, and Clarinet Merlin.

Hyperwide/Deltawing: EP-3E enhancements to the baseline COMINT, ELINT, and special signals collection capabilities included in the FY 2003 Defense Emergency Readiness Fund and used in OEF.

— I —

IADS ADEX: Five Power Defence Agreement (FPDA — Australia, Malaysia, New Zealand, Singapore, and the UK) air defense exercise. IADS ADEX 03: Apr 2003, canceled. IADS ADEX 01: Malaysia, Apr 2001. IADS ADEX 96-4: 14–21 Sep 1996.

Ibis: 1. NSA Integrated Battlefield Intelligence System?, also referred to as the IBIS/Gale system, 1990s–present.

2. **Ibis:** Foreign material exploitation first word, including Ibis Hammer (2002), Ibis Speed (2002), and Ibis Trough (1997).

Icarus: Sensitive compartmented information communications network.

Iceberg (Project Iceberg): Classified R&D project during OEF for forces in Afghanistan.

Iceshelf: US–Canadian Project Spinnaker experiments. Iceshelf 95: Testing of the Theseus Canadian Autonomous Undersea Vehicle (AUV). Iceshelf 96: Under-ice deployment of a complex acoustic array and 112 miles of small single-fiber cable in Arctic waters.

Icon: Army Foreign Science and Technology Center (FSTC)/National Ground Intelligence Center (NGIC) foreign material exploitation first word, including Icon Cache, Icon Chain, Icon Glass, Icon Opera, Icon Ports, and Icon Seal. Icon Glass was the exploitation of SA-8 SAMs from the former East Germany.

ICON (Investigations, Collection Operations Nexus): Post-9/11 Air Force Office of Special Investigations project to conduct tactical terrorist reporting, fusion, analysis, and production for analysis and dissemination.

ICON/PICON: Unknown intelligence analysis integration system.

ICSAS (Integrated Collection Situation Awareness System): *See* Battlescape.

Icthus Nickel: Air Combat Command Air Warfare Center classified project, Oct 1994.

Ictus: Army Foreign Science and Technology Center foreign material exploitation first word, 1993, including Ictus Jigsaw and Ictus Spade.

Idaho Thunder: *See* Midnight Stand.

Idealist: Early code name for air force U-2 program.

I'Les Dor: French-sponsored naval battle group training exercise in the Mediterranean, 1997, including USS *John F. Kennedy* (CV 67).

Ill Wind: National-level WMD response exercises using the Consequence Assessment Tool Set (CATS), a Geographic Information System–based application providing map-based hazard display and analysis, 1990s.

Immediate Response 04/05: US Army Europe demonstration of the ability to rapidly deploy a tailored immediate rapid reaction force.

Imminent Horizon: Worldwide counter-intelligence operation before and during OIF against Iraqi government intelligence agents and diplomats, and Iraqi exiles abroad. The US worked with foreign governments (reportedly including Australia, Hungary, Romania, and Sweden) to recruit, arrest, or expel potential sources, and to neutralize any Iraqi efforts to foment terrorism in response to military action.

Impelling Victory: US–Qatar classified bilateral tactical airfield training exercise. Impelling Victory 04. Impelling Victory 02/03. Impelling Victory 01. Impelling Victory 99. Impelling Victory 95. Impelling Victory 93: May 1993. USS *Nimitz* (CVN 68).

Impending Storm: Senior crisis simulation seminar, National Defense University, 23 Sep 2003. The seminar scenario was a major terrorist incident against maritime transportation systems in the US. Participants included 13 members of Congress, Secretary of Defense Rumsfeld, Deputy Secretary Paul Wolfowitz, the transportation security administrator, and representatives from the Department of Homeland Security, Coast Guard, FBI, Northern Command, and the JCS.

Impressive Lift I/II: Airlift of Pakistani forces to Somalia during the United Nations Operation in Somalia I (UNOSOM I), 13–29 Sep 1992.

Ince: UK land-based SIGINT/electronic support measures equipment used in OEF/OIF.

Indigo: 1. BYEMAN code word for digital imaging satellite, changed to LaCrosse.
   2. **Indigo:** SPECAT for Tomahawk cruise missile message format. An Indigo message tasks a firing unit, reports on a completed mission by the firing unit, and requests mission planning data. The launch message is referred to as an Indigo Strike.

Indigo: CENTCOM first word, including Indigo Response 04, a classified exercise.

+ **Indigo Anvil:** Classified US–Saudi Arabian air exercise. Indigo Anvil 00: 23–27 Jul 2000. USS *Dwight D. Eisenhower* (CVN 69). Indigo Anvil 99.
+ **Indigo Desert:** Classified US–Qatar special operations and amphibious exercise. JSOTF Indigo Desert and 5th SFG conduct regular operations at FOB 53, circa 1992–. Indigo Desert 01. Indigo Desert 99. Indigo Desert 96-1. Indigo Desert 95/Vigilant Sentinel 95: Sep–Oct 95. Indigo Desert 93.
+ **Indigo Musket:** Classified US–Saudi Arabian amphibious exercise. Indigo Musket 99. Indigo Musket 93: USS *Nashville* (LPD 13).

Indigo Serpent: US–Saudi Arabian Red Sea classified exercise series. Indigo Serpent 04. Indigo Serpent 96: USS *Tarawa* (LHA 1). Indigo Serpent 94-1: 22–27 Jan 1994.

Code Names

Indy: Air Expditionary Force deployment to South Korea, Jan–Jun 1998. 16th SOS (AC-130) deployed to Taegu AB.

Inferno Creek: US–Oman ARCENT biennial company-level infantry exercise conducted by 10th Mountain Div with Omani ground forces. The exercise goes back at least to Inferno Creek/Bright Star 85. Inferno Creek 04. Inferno Creek 01: 13 Apr–1 May 00. Inferno Creek 98: 8 Apr–5 May 1998.

Infinite: US–Jordanian CENTCOM first word.

+ **Infinite Acclaim:** Air training exercise. Infinite Acclaim 04. Infinite Acclaim 99. Infinite Acclaim 97: USS *John F. Kennedy* (CV 67). Infinite Acclaim 94: 1–3 Apr 1994. First-ever deployment of US fighter aircraft to Jordan, including Marine Corps F-18s. Activity included familiarization flights, dissimilar aircraft combat training, and fighter-on-fighter sorties with mixed sections of US and Jordanian aircraft.
+ **Infinite Anvil 02:** Marine Corps exercise, King Faisal AB, al Jafr, Mar 2002. Involved 22nd MEU (SOC), USS *Wasp* (LHD 1), and AV-8B Harrier IIs alongside Jordanian F-1s, F-5s, and F-16s bombing at Azraq range.
+ **Infinite Courage 95:** Naval exercise involving US, Italian, German, and UK forces in surface, undersea, and air warfare.
+ **Infinite Moonlight:** Amphibious exercise. Infinite Moonlight 00: 25 Jan–12 Feb 2000. 22nd MEU. Infinite Moonlight 99: 22nd MEU. Infinite Moonlight 98: 11th MEU. Infinite Moonlight 97: 15th MEU (SOC). Infinite Moonlight 96: 13th MEU in combined demolitions training in al Qatranah, Jordan. Infinite Moonlight 95: 22–28 Aug 1995. The USS *Theodore Roosevelt* (CVN 71) left Bosnia duty to speed to the Mediterranean Sea after a high-level Iraqi minister and two of Saddam Hussein's daughters fled to Jordan. CVW-8 aircraft flew combat air patrols over Jordan, and the aircraft carrier also visited Haifa, Israel.
+ **Infinite Shadow:** Navy exercise. Infinite Shadow: 03: USS *Vandergrift* (FFG 48). Infinite Shadow 00: May 2000. USS *Samuel B. Roberts* (FFG 58). Infinite Shadow 99: First military exercise with Jordan, Egypt, and the US participating together. Infinite Shadow 97: 11th MEU (SOC). Infinite Shadow 94-2: 3–6 Apr 1994.

Infinite Justice: Initial CENTCOM name for Enduring Freedom in Afghanistan after the 9/11 attacks. The name was changed on 25 Sep 2001 after a media uproar when Muslim scholars and clerics objected to the name on the grounds that infinite justice can only be dispensed by Allah.

Infinite Reach: CENTCOM operation, 20 Aug 1998, launching approximately 70 Tomahawk cruise missiles against a supposed al Qaeda–associated target in Khartoum (the al Shifa Pharmaceutical Plant) and in Khowst, Afghanistan (al Qaeda training camp), in response to bombings on 7 Aug of the US embassies in Nairobi, Kenya, and Dar es Salaam, Tanzania.

Infinite Resolve: JCS-led contingency planning for follow-on attacks on al Qaeda and Osama bin Laden, commencing in 1998. There were 13 options developed through 2001, including B-2 bombers, missiles, AC-130 gunships, armed Predator UAVs, and raids to capture and destroy al Qaeda leaders and targets. In Nov 2000, planners began developing a "phased campaign plan" in addition to the 13 options.

Inherent Fury: Classified SOCCENT special operations field training exercise, held with Bahrain and Kuwait. Inherent Fury 04. Inherent Fury 02/03. Inherent Fury 99/Eastern Viper 99: Army Rangers and air force MC-130s. Inherent Fury 98: Bahrain. Inherent Fury 97/Iris Gold: Oct–Nov 1997. 16th SOS (AC-130) deployed to Sheikh Isa AB in support of the operation.

Initial Link: CENTCOM fighter field training exercise series held among the Gulf Cooperation Council countries (Bahrain, Kuwait, Qatar, and the UAE), the US, and the UK, Sheikh Isa AB, Bahrain. Initial Link 02/03. Initial Link 01: 14–24 May 2001. Initial Link 00. Initial Link 99 was canceled because of OAF Initial Link 98. Initial Link 96..

Initiate Response: Marine Corps Chemical-Biological Incident Response Force deployment to Qatar, May 2001.

Inner Passage 04: Classified CENTCOM exercise.

Inspired: US–Pakistani CENTCOM first word.

+ **Inspired Alert:** Naval fixed-wing air-to-air and air-to-ground exercise conducted with the Pakistani air force. Inspired Alert 04. Inspired Alert 97-2: 8–12 Aug 1997. USS *Constellation* (CV 64). Inspired Alert 97. Inspired Alert 95: USS *Abraham Lincoln* (CVN 72).

+ **Inspired Gambit:** Third Army/ARCENT–executed biennial ground field training exercise conducted between a US light infantry company and a Pakistani conventional army battalion. Inspired Gambit 04. Inspired Gambit 01: 26 Apr–1 May 2001. 10th Mountain Div.

Inspired Gambit 99: 16 Apr–15 May 1999. 10th Mountain Div. Inspired Gambit 97. Inspired Gambit 95.

+ **Inspired Siren:** Naval surface and anti-submarine-warfare exercise, normally conducted two to three times a year. Inspired Siren normally includes two Pakistani destroyers and one to two US ships. Inspired Siren 97-2: USS *Constellation* (CV 64) Battle Group surface tactical maneuvering, electronic surveillance, gunnery events, air defense exercises, deck landing qualifications, and formation steaming among surface vessels from Pakistan and the US. Inspired Siren 96-3. Inspired Siren 94-1: 1–2 Feb 1994. USS *Helena* (SSN 725). Inspired Siren 93-2.

+ **Inspired Union:** Combined Inspired Siren and Inspired Alert exercise. Inspired Union 04. Inspired Union 97.

+ **Inspired Venture:** Special operations field training exercise. Inspired Venture 96. Inspired Venture 95. Inspired Venture 94.

Intelex 99-1: Personnel recovery and rescue exercise, Osan AB, South Korea, 23–26 Feb 1999.

Intense Look: Mine clearance in the Gulf of Suez and the Red Sea, 1984.

Internal Look: CENTCOM annual computer-assisted exercise/command post exercise to train headquarters and component staffs in warfighting doctrine and procedures pertaining to a Middle East major war. It is CENTCOM's number one training priority and the primary mission rehearsal vehicle for the theater level. The exercise has traditionally been held at Camp Blanding, FL, but is also executed via distributed operations at participants' home stations and forward CENTCOM bases and commands. Internal Looks 90–02 focused almost exclusively on Iraq. Internal Look 90, held 9 Jul–4 Aug 1990, was the first exercise to supplant the prevailing war against the Soviets in the Iran scenario. As the exercise unfolded, Iraq's forces invaded and captured Kuwait. Internal Look 03, 8–17 Dec 2002, extensively practiced the strategic and operational level of war implementation of OPLAN 1003V, the war plan for OIF. The exercise began with a "rock" drill 7–8 Dec 2002 and focused on joint and coalition operations specifically for the OIF campaign.

Interpret: UK airborne SIGINT/electronic support measures equipment used in OEF/OIF.

Intrinsic Action: Operation to keep a near-continuous presence of a battalion task force in Kuwait following Desert Strike (Sep 1996). US troops rotated to Camp Doha for four-month exercises with Kuwaiti forces through OIF.

Intruder: Next-generation SIGINT satellite development program, 1990s.

Iris Gold: Former US–Kuwaiti special operations training exercise series, 1992–1999. SOF created a permanent presence in Kuwait through the Iris Gold series. One SF company rotated every 120 days into Kuwait. In 1998, one SF company trained four Kuwaiti brigades, an asset that then became part of Desert Thunder. Iris Gold became Desert Spring in 1999. Inherent Fury 97/Iris Gold 97. Iris Gold 92: 22nd MEU.

Irish: CENTCOM classified reconnaissance operations first word. Irish Emerald, Irish Phoenix, and Irish Warrior are WC-135 sampling and reconnaissance missions, 2001–present. Irish Straw is a reconnaissance operation, possibly with Predator UAVs, 2001–present.

Iron: CENTCOM first word.

+ **Iron Cobra:** Classified US–Egyptian airborne operations exercise dating to the 1980s. Iron Cobra 04. Iron Cobra 00. Iron Cobra 99: Gebel Hamza drop zone southeast of Cairo, Egypt, 22 Oct–17 Nov 1998. 2nd Bn, 5th SFG. Iron Cobra 97: Oct–Nov 1996. 24th Infantry Div.
+ **Iron Falcon:** US–UAE ground exercise series. Iron Falcon 01/Iron Magic 101st Airborne Div. Iron Falcon 98. Iron Falcon 96: A company of equipment was unloaded from the *Cape Horn*, Mar–Apr 1996.
+ **Iron Fist 99:** US–UAE exercise, Apr 1999.
+ **Iron Magic:** US–UAE combined arms amphibious exercise series in the Arabian Gulf. Iron Magic 03/Iron Falcon: Jebel Ali and al Hamra, Dec 2003. 13th MEU (SOC). Iron Magic 01: Nov 2000. USS *Tarawa* (LHA 1) and 13th MEU (SOC), including Marine Corps M1A1 tank operations at the al Hamra Training Area. Marine Corps commandant Gen. James L. Jones visited the exercise and was briefed about new Marine Enhanced NBC equipment. Iron Magic 99. Iron Magic 97: Jebel Ali, 4 Aug 1997. USS *Boxer* (LHD 4), 11th MEU (SOC). Iron Magic/Iron Siren 96: Remote beach landing site, Feb 1996. USS *Peleliu* (LHA 5), USS *Anchorage* (LSD 36), USS *Denver* (LPD 9), and USS *Reuben James* (FFG 57), 15th MEU (SOC), Mobile Inshore Undersea Warfare Unit (MIUWU) 103, and Navy SEALs.
+ **Iron Siren:** US–UAE exercise series. Iron Siren 99/Iron Magic: Jan 1999. USS *Paul Foster* (DD 964). Iron Siren 94-2: 27–30 Mar 1994.

Iron: 1st Armored Div operation and exercise first word.

- **+ Iron Dragon:** Friedberg, Germany, Dec 1999. The exercise was first in Europe for Hungarian forces to practice in an Article 5 combat environment and included the 25th Hungarian Bde, 3rd Mechanized Div, along with Poland and the Czech Republic.
- **+ Iron Hammer:** Offensive operation in Iraq, 2003.
- **+ Iron Justice:** Operation in western Baghdad, Iraq, Dec 2003.

Iron Anvil: UK Army 3 Div field training exercise, British Army Training Unit Suffield, Sep–Oct 2001.

Iron Balance: *See* Balance Iron.

Iron Clad: Navy EP-3B special projects aircraft.

Iron Foray: UK exercise canceled because of firefighters strike, 5–11 Nov 2002.

Iron Gate: Continuity of government helicopter evacuation procedures associated with Site R (Raven Rock). *See also* Blue Light.

Iron Hare 99: PACOM and Joint Command and Control Warfare Center cyber-warfare exercise conducted at the CIA–NSA Information Operations Technology Center (IOTC). First-of-its-kind demonstration of offensive computer warfare capabilities.

Iron Lung: KC-135R and RC-135M aircraft ELINT configuration.

Iron Ram (Ferro Ariete): UK exercise, Italy. Iron Ram 02: 1–30 Nov 2002, canceled because of firefighters strike. Iron Ram 00, Mar 2000, and Iron Ram 99, Nov 1999, were canceled because of Kosovo operations.

Isaiah: Automated Web-based distribution program to disseminate satellite, UAV, and U-2 imagery. Isaiah was developed after 9/11 to assist in the accelerated development of target folders in support of OEF and Iraq mission planning. Isaiah stores information for approximately 45 days. The prototype was completed in Feb 2003.

Island Breeze: Grenada operation, 1984.

Island Crisis 99: WMD disaster response mass casualty exercise, Moanalua Medical Center, Honolulu, HI, 28 May 1999. The scenario involved toxic gas being released during a crowded event at Aloha Stadium.

Island Spell: UK exercise in the Falkland Islands, canceled Jun 2002.

Island Spirit: B-2 bomber deployment, Andersen AFB, Guam, 25 Mar 1998. Two B-2s deployed to Guam and conducted bombing at the Farallon de Medinilla islands north of Guam.

Island Sun: Special technical operations (STO) Planning and Decision Aids System (PDAS) used for compartmented communications and planning of clandestine military operations. (Officially, PDAS supports the planning and execution of "Integrated Joint Special Technical Operations.") Island Sun was formerly a DOD special access program. At least 10 separate sites have PDAS installed.

Island Thunder: US–Italian noncombatant evacuation operation (NEO) exercise, Capo Teulada training area, Sardinia. Island Thunder 97: 9–16 Feb 1997. USS *Nassau* (LHA 4), USS *Pensacola* (LSD 38), 26th MEU. Island Thunder 96: 1–17 Mar 1996. SETAF-led JTF scenario including an NEO with a follow-on UN peacekeeping force. The Italian Ministry of Defense raised concerns about the size of the exercise, and it was scaled down to 1,150 personnel, 24 helicopters, and 100 vehicles, with fixed-wing attack, airborne insertion, and amphibious landings canceled.

Istar: UK SIGINT/electronic support measures equipment used in OEF/OIF.

Ivy Bells: Holystone-related covert submarine project involving implanting a device to intercept the signals transmitted along a Soviet underwater cable in the Sea of Okhotsk. Submarines would penetrate the sea and implant and remove the devices. The operation continued until 1981, when former NSA employee Ronald Pelton compromised the program.

Ivy: 4th Infantry Div operation first word.

+ **Ivy Blizzard:** Operation in Iraq, 17 Dec 2003.
+ **Ivy Cyclone:** TF Ironhorse patrol operation to locate and detain or eliminate threats to coalition forces in Iraq, initiated 7 Nov 2003. Ivy Cyclone was the eighth postwar operation of the 4th Infantry Div/TF Ironhorse team.
+ **Ivy Cyclone II:** TF Ironhorse operation to root out and crush insurgents in north-central Iraq, initiated in Nov 2003. The operation combines "actionable intelligence" with close air support, army aviation, armor, artillery, mechanized infantry, and air assault operations for rapid deployment of dismounted artillery. It is the ninth postwar operation of the 4th Infantry Div/TF Ironhorse team.
+ **Ivy Focus:** Operation in Iraq, Oct 2003.

+ **Ivy Lightning:** Operation in Iraq, Aug 2003.

+ **Ivy Needle:** Operation in Iraq, Aug 2003.

+ **Ivy Serpent:** Operation in the "Sunni triangle" north of Baghdad to Tikrit and Balad, Iraq, part of operation Soda Mountain, 14–17 Jul 2003.

IWER 2003 (International Workshop for Emergency Response): Baton Rouge, LA, 18–25 May 2003. Workshop to practice response to a terrorist attack on a chemical production facility in a generic large city in Central Asia. IWER featured the efforts of four Central Asian nations (Kazakhstan, Kyrgyzstan, Turkmenistan, and Uzbekistan) and their four NG partner states (Arizona, Montana, Nevada, Louisiana) as they planned and executed responses to a simulated terrorist attack on a chemical production facility in Uzbekistan. Uzbekistan was the exercise co-host. Also participating were Tajikistan, Afghanistan, and Pakistan.

— J —

Jack Howl: USS *Dwight D. Eisenhower* (CVN 69) exercise.

Jackel Cave 01: SOCOM exercise involving more than 500 personnel, 62 aircraft, and 420 short tons of cargo, RAF Fairford, UK, 2001.

Jackpot (Joint Airborne Communications Center/Command Post): JCS mobile communications package used for disaster response and continuity of government.

Jade: Coast Guard special operation, 5 Feb–3 Mar 1992.

Jade Tiger: US–Oman exercise involving the 31st MEU, 29 Nov–8 Dec 1982.

Jagged Course: Corsica-based exercise. UK participation in the 16–27 Oct 2000 exercise was canceled due to operational commitments in Sierra Leone.

Jagged Wind: Air Force EC-135 airborne command post exercise, 19–25 Jun 1996.

Jaguar: Army intelligence system, Bad Aibling, Germany.

Javelin Maker 97: Pacific exercise involving USS *Curtis Wilbur* (DDG 54).

JEAP/Sunshine (joint electronic analysis program): DIA ELINT analysis suite and processing tool, being replaced by GALE-LITE.

Jedi Knight: Air Warfare Center program is to facilitate rapid responses to theater commander requests for solutions to immediate problems facing the warfighter.

JEEP/Joint Emergency Evacuation Plan: National-level continuity of government program to evacuate key government and military leaders. JEEP-1 card holders are provided 24-hour helicopter transportation to emergency relocation sites and alternate headquarters. JEEP is automatically implemented at declaration of DEFCON 2.

Jefferson (Project Jefferson): Research project, taken over by the DIA in 2001, to develop enhanced anthrax biological warfare agents using genetic modifications. Much of the project work was carried out by Battelle Memorial Institute. (*New York Times,* 4 Sep 2001).

Jester: Coast Guard special operation, 9 Sep–8 Nov 1989.

Jockey: Former NORAD 20th Region first word.

Jogger: Correlation of reconnaissance and early warning satellite- and ground-based over-the-horizon radar detections of space launches and missile firings. *See also* Fast Walker, Slow Walker.

Joint Anvil: Unknown special operations, 1999–2001.

Joint Endeavor: NATO operation to enforce the Dayton Peace Agreement in Bosnia–Herzegovina. The US 1st Armored Div commanded TF Eagle and the Implementation Force (IFOR) starting on 20 Dec 1995. Eleven other nations initially deployed to Multi-National Div (North): Estonia, Latvia, Finland, Poland, Denmark, Lithuania, Norway, Iceland, Sweden, Russia, and Turkey. Joint Endeavor was one of the largest peacetime operations since World War II, NATO's first operational commitment of forces, the first time US Army soldiers had served in Eastern Europe in substantial numbers, the first time American and Russian troops shared a common mission, and the first cold-weather combat operation since the Korean War. The operation was supported by the USS *George Washington* (CVN 73) and USS *America* (CV 66) Battle Groups, and the USS *Guam* (LPH 9) and USS *Wasp* (LHD 1) ARGs. In total, 50,227 sorties were flown in Decisive Edge 20 Dec 1995–20 Dec 1996. *See also* Joint Guard, Decisive Endeavor, Decisive Edge.

Joint Forge: NATO continuation of support for the Stabilization Force (SFOR) in Bosnia-Herzogivina at a lower level of forces, 1998–present. On 20 Jun 1998, the 1st Cavalry Div transitioned a smaller follow-on force, and Joint Forge supplanted Joint Guard. On 19 Feb 2001, SFOR was transferred to the operational control of NATO. Thirty-four nations were then contributing to SFOR, including 15 non-NATO nations (Albania, Austria, Argentina, Bulgaria, Estonia, Finland, Ireland, Latvia, Lithuania, Morocco, Romania, Russia, Slovakia, Slovenia, Sweden), for a total of about 20,000 troops. The NATO CJSTOF, which began operations in Bosnia on 13 Dec 1996, was also referred to as Joint Forge.

Joint Guard: NATO follow-on force to Joint Endeavor, supporting the Stabilization Force (SFOR) in Bosnia-Herzegovina, 20 Dec 1996–20 Jun 1998. On 20 Dec 1996, the IFOR mission concluded and the 1st Infantry Div/TF Eagle was selected to continue serving in Bosnia as part of the new Stabilization Force (SFOR). *See* Joint Forge.

Joint Guardian: NATO-led Kosovo Force (KFOR). US forces have supported the operation since 11 Jun 1999. Initially, the US agreed to provide approximately 7,000 personnel. The US sector (Multinational Bde East) is in southeast Kosovo, headquartered at Camp Bondsteel, near Urosevic. On 18 Jan 2001, NATO assumed operational responsibilities for the forces of Joint Guardian. KFOR at the time comprised forces from 39 nations, 20 of which were not part of NATO (Argentina, Austria, Azerbaijan, Bulgaria, Estonia, Finland, Georgia, Ireland, Jordan, Latvia, Lithuania, Morocco, Romania, Russia, Slovakia, Slovenia, Sweden, Switzerland, the UAE, and Ukraine).

Joint Spirit: NATO CJTF headquarters command post exercise/computer-assisted exercise. Joint Spirit 01/Cooperative Nugget 01: 1–30 Sep 2001. The exercise was designed as a building block for Strong Resolve, but was cut short because of 9/11. Formerly known as Unified Endeavor.

Joint Winter: NATO exercise held in Norway. Joint Winter 01: 5–16 Mar 2001. UK forces did not participate because of foot-and-mouth disease restrictions.

Joke/Jolly: Former NORAD first words.

Jolly Roger: UK national submarine exercise involving Canada, France, Germany, the Netherlands, and the US, 1995.

Joplin: Former NORAD 23rd Region first word.

JOPREP JIFFY: JCS message flagword that identifies electrically transmitted command-post-to-command-post messages and operational reports, and notifies communications centers to route a message directly to the command and control facility.

Jordan/Jorum: Former NORAD first words.

Joshua Junction: DOD–FBI exercise, Jackass Flats on the Nevada Test Site, 1979, the first exercise to certify the Joint Special Operations Command's "Delta" force in counter-terrorism operations and nuclear weapons recovery. The scenario involved Middle Eastern terrorists seizing an underground nuclear weapons site, along with several hostages (role-played by FBI agents).

JTFEX (Joint Task Force Exercise): JFCOM (formerly Atlantic Command) large-scale series to train deploying and surge-capable US-based forces in a littoral environment and to provide a venue for experimentation. The JTFEX is the culmination of predeployment training for carrier battle groups, ARGs, and MEUs. At least once per year a NATO exercise runs concurrently with JTFEX, with forces from Canada, Denmark, France, Germany, and the UK playing major roles. Other participants include Belgium, Brazil, Bolivia, and the Netherlands. JTFEX 04-1: Mar 2004. FORCEnet Spiral 3. JTFEX 03-3: Sep–Oct 2003. FORCEnet Spiral 2. JTFEX 02-1: 18–24 Jan 2002. JTFEX 01-3. 30 Jul–20 Aug 2001. JTFEX 01-2: 16–26 Mar 2001. JTFEX 01-1: 16–29 Oct 2000. JTFEX 99-2: 16–30 Jul 1999. JTFEX 99-1/TMDI 98: JTFEX 98-2: 30 Apr–13 May 1998. The USS *Dwight D. Eisenhower* (CVN 69) had an embarked Submarine Advisory Team (SAT) maintaining tactical control of USS *Atlanta* (SSN 712) and USS *Newport News* (SSN 750). JTFEX 98-1: 15 Jan–5 Feb 1998. Included Big Drop IV, a large-scale, airborne field training exercise with XVIII Airborne Corps. JTFEX 97-1. JTFEX 96: EX 8 Marine Mammal System (MMS) participated off the coast of Camp Pendleton, CA, undergoing minehunting feasibility demonstrations.

Jumbo: US–UK submarine burst transmission intercept program, 1980s.

Jumpseat: SIGINT satellite in highly elliptical orbit first launched 5 Mar 1975. Later became Trumpet.

Juniper: EUCOM US–Israeli first word. Juniper Control was a Reagan-era exercise with NSC involvement.

+ **Juniper Cobra:** V Corps–led theater missile defense exercise and operations series in support of OPLAN 4305, the contingency plan for the defense of Israel. The exercises involve deploying Patriot assets to Israel, set up at real-world battle positions, Patriot live fire, and the activation of a V Corps–led JTF that links into the Israeli and CENTCOM command and control systems. Juniper Cobra 05: Juniper Cobra 03: Dec 2002–Feb 2003. Deployment of Patriot missiles to Israel in anticipation of OIF. The exercise consisted of three phases: movement to occupy battle positions, command post exercise/computer-assisted exercise incorporating simulation of Iraq tactical ballistic missile threats, and Patriot live fire. Juniper Cobra 01: Southern Israel, 6–24 Feb 2001. The exercise included test-firing Patriot missiles, which evidently had been deployed in Israel to coincide with US–UK strikes on Iraq. The USS *Porter* (DDG 78) was stationed off the coast providing long-range radar support. MV *Bremer Saturn* loaded US equipment at Nordenham, Germany, in Jan, off-loading at Ashod, Israel.

+ **Juniper Falconry:** Command post exercise/field training exercise involving crisis resupply operations of Israel, also sometimes called Juniper Falcon. Juniper Faclonry 04. Juniper Falconry III/Noble Stallion 95: Mar 1995. 31st FW, 510th FS deployed to Site 53 in Israel. Juniper Falconry II/Juniper Fox.

+ **Juniper Fox:** Air Force field training exercise.

+ **Juniper Hawk:** Marine Corps and navy amphibious field training exercise. Juniper Hawk 98. Juniper Hawk 96/Noble Shirley 95: Aug 1996. USS *Enterprise* (CVN 65). Juniper Hawk 95/Noble Shirley 95/Noble Chris 95. Juniper Hawk 89: USS *John F. Kennedy* (CV 67).

+ **Juniper Stallion:** Air exercise involving air-to-air and air-to-ground live training. Juniper Stallion 04. Juniper Stallion 01: Mar 2001. 52nd FW exercise with Israeli air force, including activation of Site 53. F-16CJs of 22nd FS and KC-135s exercise with their F-15 and F-16 Israeli counterparts. This was reportedly the first time US aircraft operted in close formations with Israel from Israeli bases. Juniper Stallion 00: 19–26 Mar 2000. USS *Dwight D. Eisenhower* (CVN 69). An eight-plane detachment of CVW-7 aircraft flew out of Nevatim airfield, Israel, acting as opposition forces. Juniper Stallion 99: Mar 1999. USS *Enterprise* (CVN 65). Juniper Stallion 96: 7 Mar–1 Apr 1996. 16th Air Force. Juniper Stallion 95/Noble Stallion: 12–23 Mar 1995. 16th Air Force.

Just Cause: Panama operations to expel Manuel Noriega, 20 Dec 1989–11 Jan 1990. Just Cause was the first US combat operation after the Korean War whose nickname was designed "to shape domestic and international perceptions about the mission it designated," wrote army Lt. Col. Gregory Sieminski in "The Art of Naming Operations" in *Parameters*, the Army War College journal. Used instead of Blue Spoon, the planning nickname for the operation. ANG units participated in the operation under the cover of their regularly scheduled presence in Panama for Coronet Cove and Volant Oak.

Justice Assured (CTF Justice Assured): EUCOM-led Joint Special Operation Command TF, 2001–present, involved in apprehending war criminals in the former Yugoslavia. *See also* Fervent Archer.

— K —

Kalamazoo: US–Philippine first word.

Kalayaan-Aguila 02: US–Philippine military operations in the Basilan–Zamboanga area.

Kale: US–Philippine first word.

Kaleidoscope: USAFE system replaced at the Tactical Fusion Center, Boerfink, Germany, 1990.

Kangaroo: Former US–Australian exercise series. Participants included Indonesia, Malaysia, Singapore, Papua New Guinea, and the UK. The exercise was replaced by Crocodile in 1999.

Kansas: US–Philippine first word.

Kayo: PACOM Guam-related first word.

Kedge Hammer 04: US–Philippine command post exercise in support of OPORDER 0204-01.

Keelan: SIGINT maintenance system taught at Goodfellow AFB, TX.

Keen Edge/Keen Sword: US–Japanese command post exercise/field training exercise focusing on the defense of Japan, dating to 1986. Keen Edge is the command post exercise conducted every even-numbered fiscal year, and Keen Sword is the field training exercise held in odd-numbered years. Keen Edge is the primary training vehicle for the US Army Japan and I Corps staff to improve interoperability with Japanese forces, and is held with Yama Sakura. Keen Sword is an umbrella exercise amalgamating several service component exercises, such as Orient Shield. Keen Edge 04: 17–25 Feb 2004. Nearly

2,500 US and Japanese personnel participated in this first exercise ever to practice a scenario involving Situations in Areas Surrounding Japan. Keen Edge 02: 13–21 Feb 2002. Keen Sword 01/Orient Shield 01: Oct 2000. Keen Edge 00/Orient Shield 00. Keen Sword 99. Keen Edge 98: Jan–Feb 1998. Keen Sword 97. Keen Edge 94.

Keen Sage: USAFE C-130 Scathe Mean low-profile reconnaissance platform with an externally mounted electro-optical/infrared sensor pod, deployed at Ramstein AB, Germany.

Keens World: Classified Pacific Fleet exercise.

Kekoa 95: USS *Carl Vinson* (CVN 70) aircraft carrier exercise, Hawaii, Aug 1995.

Kelp: UK–Falklands exercise first word, including Kelp Drive and Kelp Fire.

Kendo Stream: B-2 deployment to Guam, Sep–Oct 1998.

Kennan: KH-11 imagery reconnaissance satellite.

Kennel: Pacific Fleet first word.

+ **Kennel Bear:** Naval Construction Bn field training exercise series. Kennel Bear 04: Okinawa, Feb 2004. Kennel Bear 00: Guam, Oct 2000. Kennel Bear 98: Okinawa, Jun1998. Kennel Bear 90-1: Tinian Island.

Kent: Pacific Fleet first word.

Keris Strike: US–Malaysian army exercise series.

Kernel: Third Fleet first word. Cold War Kernel exercises included Kernel Potlatch in the Aleutian Islands, 1982.

+ **Kernel Blitz:** Major fleet training exercise. Since 1997, this exercise has gradually grown into a venue for technical and doctrinal experimentation. Participants include Australia and Canada. Kernel Blitz 03: Jan–Feb 2003. Kernel Blitz 01/Capable Warrior 01: Mar–Apr 2001. The exercise simulated reestablishing freedom of navigation through the Straits of Catalina and clearing a conventional amphibious operating area. Included experimentation with the Dragon Eye UAV and the Extend Littoral Battlespace's Advanced Concept Technology Demonstration. Kernel Blitz 00: Jun 2000. USS *Nimitz* (CVN 68). Kernel Blitz 99/FBE-Echo/Urban Warrior: Mar 1999. I MEF. Kernel Blitz 97: Camp Pendleton, CA, Jun 1997. Using the Global Command

and Control System (GCCS) for the first time, all participating units received a common tactical and intelligence picture. Kernel Blitz 95.

+ **Kernel Raider:** Marine amphibious exercise, Sep 1993. USS *Gurnard* (SSN 662).
+ **Kernel Usher:** Former marine amphibious exercise, 1980s–1990s. Kernel Usher 90-2: Sep 1990. Kernel Usher 90-2.

Kerosene: Pacific Fleet first word.

Kerry: US–Australian first word.

Kestrel Phoenix: Special operations exercise, Hurlburt Field, FL, Aug 2000. The scenario involved a prisoner-of-war extraction mission similar to the "Son Tay Raid" and built around a real-world OPLAN. The 19th SOS, Army Rangers and SOF aviation, AC-130s, and a Navy recovery ship were all linked through Joint Synthetic BattleSpace mission rehearsal technology.

Ketchum: Unknown (possibly classified) air force system.

Key: Pacific Fleet first word.

Keyhole (KH): Nickname for imaging reconnaissance satellites, used since the first Corona (KH-1) satellites were launched in 1959. Each successive generation has been designated with a new number and a variety of additional code words. *See also* Talent Keyhole.

+ KH-1 Corona.
+ KH-2 Corona/Discoverer.
+ KH-3 Corona.
+ KH-4 Corona.
+ KH-5 Argon.
+ KH-6 Lanyard.
+ KH-7 Gambit.
+ KH-8 Gambit.
+ KH-9A/B "Big Bird" Hexagon.
+ KH-10 Dorian (Manned Orbiting Laboratory).
+ KH-11 Kennan /Crystal.
+ KH-12 Improved Crystal/Ikon?
+ KH-13?

Keystone: Marine Corps NBC defense training exercise involving military support to civil authorities. Keystone 01. Keystone 99. Keystone 2-98: Philadelphia, PA, 15–17 Sep 1998.

Khangar Hadd: Classified Arabian Gulf naval exercise, Oct 1996.

Kilting: NSA's national ELINT parametric data file, one of four major NSA military databases. Kilting is one of two key ELINT databases; the other is the National Air Intelligence Center's (NAIC) Electronic Warfare Integrated Reprogramming Data Base (EWIRDB). The Star Sapphire program will replace Kilting; NAIC's next-generation EWIR program will replace the current EWIRDB.

Kindle Liberty 85: Reagan-era exercise with NSC involvement, Panama, 23 Jan–20 Feb 1985.

King's Guard: US–Honduras exercise series dating to the early 1980s. King's Guard 92: Included the Marine Corps 30th Interrogator-Translator Team.

Kingfisher: 1. Classified PACOM command post exercise, including Kingfisher 02 and Kingfisher 99.
   2. **Kingfisher:** UK land-based SIGINT/electronic support measures equipment used in OEF/OIF.

Kinsfolk: AN/FLR-9 Circular Disposed Antenna Array.

Klieglight (KL): NSA SIGINT report format.

Klondike Key: Noncombatant evacuation operation plan for an evacuation of US citizens from Panama, 1989.

Knight: *See* Talon Knight.

Knob Key: SOCOM live-fire exercise, NAS Roosevelt Roads, Puerto Rico, Jan–Feb 1999.

Knockdown: Classified; possible intelligence system.

Knotted Whip/Ellipse Bravo: Classified EUCOM crisis management exercise, 28 Sep–5 Oct 1995.

Known Warrior: US–Thai special operations counter-terrorism exercise, Sep 2002.

Kodiak: Air force Minuteman II ICBM classified project, Sep 2000.

Kopeck Trade 92: 101st Airborne Div emergency deployment readiness exercise, 1992.

Krimson Sword: SOCOM classified ACTD, 2001–2002.

Kwik Link: SAC strategic reconnaissance satellite command and control net, 1980s.

— L —

LaCrosse/Vega: BYEMAN code name for Synthetic Aperture Radar (SAR) reconnaissance satellite. Formerly Indigo, later switched to Onyx.

Ladylove: NSA satellite communications intercept activities at Misawa AB, Japan, used to intercept Soviet/Russian communications. NSA assigned the Ladylove mission to the air force 31 Mar 1980.

Laf-: Former army intelligence letter block first word. Code words included Lafair Vite (La Faire Vite, a SIGINT system in the Harz Mountains, Germany, 1980s), Laffing Eagle (an RU-21D airborne radio direction finding mission, introduced in 1968), and Laffing Otter (an RU-1A airborne directing finding mission, also known as Café Girl).

Lakota: Army intelligence system, Bad Aibling, Germany.

Lancer: NSA project in the 1980s.

Lancer Growl: 68th FS F-16 deployment and operation to Savannah International Airport, GA, 12–19 Mar 1992.

Lanyard: Former KH-6 imagery satellite.

Lariat Response: US Army Europe emergency deployment readiness exercise, Kecskemet AB, Hungary, 6–12 Jun 2001.

Lark Song/Foxtrot: UK–Denmark army exercise series. Lark Song 02 canceled by Denmark. Lark Song 99 canceled because of Kosovo operations, May/Oct 1999.

Laser Strike/Constant Vigil: SOUTHCOM counter-narcotics surveillance operation based in Venezuela, and involving disrupting riverine and coastal drug smuggling. Laser strike involved sustained monitoring and tracking, including ground surveillance radar, as well as assessments and training, to support expanded interdiction and law enforcement efforts by nations of the source region. Followed Green Clover Laser Strike II in 1999.

Launch Relief 00: First US Army–FEMA–FBI disaster relief and counter-terrorism exercise. The scenario posited that after a storm wreaked havoc on Alabama, Georgia, and Florida, triggering a rash of tornadoes and flooding, a "militant group" put stolen chemical and biological substances into orange juice company distribution systems.

Lef-: Former army intelligence letter block first word. LeFox Gray and LeFox Purple were SIGINT systems in Germany, 1970s and 1980s. Left Bank, Left Foot, and Left Jab were Vietnam-era COMINT missions.

Legal Eagle I: Air force operational readiness inspection, Gulfport, MS, 31 Oct–03 Nov 1996.

Legation Quarter: Marine Corps information assurance (computer security) exercise.

Lemon Juice: Exercise term for simulated Air Defense Warning Yellow.

Lemonade: NSA special intelligence communications system.

LEO: Former strategic forces special access program.

Liberty: Former Chief of Naval Operations (N3) first word.

Liberty Shield: Department of Homeland Security operation to heighten security at the nation's airports, seaports, railways, borders, nuclear and chemical plants, and elements of the food supply and distribution system with initiation of OIF, commenced 18 Mar 2003.

Libertycap: NSA program to standardize all SIGINT software for airborne platforms.

Lifeman: *See* SEIGEL.

Light of Hope (Ashar Alo): US–Bangladesh humanitarian assistance and disaster relief command post exercise. Light of Hope 04: Oct 2003. Light of Hope 03: Oct 2002.

Lighthouse: 1. Cyber-security program to research network security management, malicious code analysis, and real-time intrusion detection.
    2. **Lighthouse:** Navy EW, ELINT, or COMINT program.

Lightning: Chief of Naval Operations (N2) first word.

Lightning Thrust: 25th Infantry Div Warrior training exercise, Hawaii. Lightning Thrust 03. Lightning Thrust 01: Feb 2001. Lightning Thrust 96: The scenario included a lodgment on the fictional island of "Cortina" and an air assault onto three landing zones, on treacherous mountain terrain marked by deep gullies and steep ravines, to defeat the "Cortinian Liberation Front."

Lilac: Former Naval Supply Systems Command first word.

Limit: Former Chief of Naval Operations (N09) first word.

LIMS: Counter-narcotics system.

Lincoln Gold: Department of Energy–DOD special operation capability involving the retrieval and neutralization of stolen nuclear weapons and improvised nuclear devices. The Joint Special Operations Command Lincoln Gold Augmentation Team (LGAT) provides expert technical advice concerning diagnostics, render-safe procedures, weapons analysis, and device modeling and effects prediction.

Linear: Former Chief of Naval Operations (N09) first word, including Linear Echo (1980s).

Linebacker: Air Force Materiel Command classified program established 20 Oct 1989.

Link: Navy (N89/N7SP) special access program first word, including Link Ash, Link Birch, Link Cedar, Link Cyprus, Link Dogwood, Link Evergreen, Link Hazel, Link Laurel, Link Plumeria, Link Saki, and Link Willow. Link Acorn is a SOCOM project.

Linked Seas: NATO small-scale triennial maritime training exercise that practices the Iberian Command's (IBERLANT) mission of protecting eastern Atlantic sea lines of communication. Participants include Canada, Denmark, Germany, the Netherlands, Portugal, Spain, the UK, and the US. Linked Seas 03. Linked Seas 00/Damsel Fair: Oeiras, Portugal, and the waters off the coast of Spain and Portugal, 2–16 May 2000. Six NATO submarines participated, including naval forces from 17 countries across an area stretching from the Gulf of Gascony to the island of Madeira. The scenario revolved around a border conflict between two non-NATO countries. Linked Seas 97: 22nd MEU. Linked Seas 95: Moron AB, Spain, 24 May–5 Jun 1995.

Lion Sun: UK army exercise series, Cyprus. The 23 Jul–20 Aug 2001, May–Jun 1999, and Oct–Nov 1999 series were canceled because of Bosnia and Kosovo operations and for lack of funding.

Lion's Pride: UK Territorial Army battalion-level overseas training exercise, Cyprus, Jun 2001.

Liquid: Former Navy Space and Warfare Systems Command first word.

Lisa Azul: Classified special operations exercise involving Naval Special Warfare Unit 2, possibly with Spain, 1990s.

Littar: Possible BYEMAN code word for imagery satellite (advanced KH-11?).

Little Picture (LITPIC): STRATCOM software program associated with nuclear weapons or information warfare planning, 2004.

Little Weasel: Compass Bright UAV ELINT project, 2003–2004.

Live Oak: Former Berlin-related NATO SPECAT used during the Cold War.

Livewire: DHS national-level cyber-warfare exercise, Oct 2003, the first exercise to baseline capabilities and communication paths for responding to hostile national attack. The exercise involved over 300 participants representing more than 50 organizations across federal, state, and local governments, as well as the private sector.

Lofty View: Gnat-750 CIA UAV program, also known as Tier I.

Log: Presidential continuity of government exercise first word, 1980s–early 1990s, including Log Horn and Log Tree.

LOMA: Possible nuclear-related classified information compartment.

Lone Eagle 01: UK–Slovakian air combat training, Sliac, Slovakia, 11–18 May 2001.

Lone Kestrel 01: UK–Finnish air combat training, Rovaniemi, Finland, 3–10 Aug 2001.

Lonely Ear: ELINT collection system, 1980s.

Lonestar: UK Scotland-based exercise, 31 May 2001, canceled because of foot-and-mouth disease restrictions.

Long Shot: Air Combat Command numbered air force bombing competition. Long Shot 95: Nellis AFB, NV, 27–29 Apr 1995.

Longlook: UK–Australian Seventh Fleet exercise, 2001–2002.

Longreach 02: Australian–New Zealand deployable joint force headquarters exercise, Oct–Nov 2002.

Longroot: Enhanced Automatic Direction Finding (EADF), an upgrade to current DF processors for approximately 24 intelligence collection sites worldwide. Related to Host and Checkboard.

Looking Glass: 1. STRATCOM airborne command post. Looking Glass was previously the SAC EC-135 Airborne Command Post, but on 1 Oct 1998, the navy's E-6B TACAMO Mercury aircraft replaced the air force EC-135 in the Looking Glass mission. Offutt AFB's new Looking Glass alert facility official opened on 4 Mar 1994.

2. **Looking Glass:** NSA SIGINT analysis and reporting software and workstation, RAF Mildenhall, UK.

Lost Source: Radiological response exercise, 1997.

Lucky: CENTCOM first word.

+ **Lucky Sentinel:** US–Kuwaiti battle staff land forces exercise. Prior to OIF, the exercise was conducted annually and was designed to train the CJTF-Kuwait staff, Kuwait armed forces staff, Ministry of Interior staff, and selected support unit staffs. Participants included the UK. Lucky Sentinel 04: 16–30 Apr 2004. The exercise was the number two priority for CENTCOM after Internal Look. Lucky Sentinel 03. Lucky Sentinel 02: 18–24 Apr 2002. Lucky Sentinel 01. Lucky Sentinel 00: 16–30 Mar 1999, Camp Doha, Kuwait. Lucky Sentinel 99.

+ **Lucky Warrior:** CENTCOM Coalition/Combined Force Land Component Commander (CFLCC) exercise series preparing for combat operations with Iraq under the OIF 1003V war plan. Lucky Warrior II: Kuwait, 8–12 Feb 2003. Real-time rehearsal of the first days of Phase III operations. Lucky Warrior I: Kuwait, 17–27 Nov 2002. The exercises focused on team building among V Corps, I MEF, and coalition forces and establishing standing operating procedures (SOPs) that would enable the CFLCC to integrate the operations of forces with differing capabilities, doctrines, languages, communications capabilities, and historical modes of operation. *See also* Internal Look, Victory Strike.

Lumbus 02: Australian–Philippines naval exercise, Oct 2002.

Lungfish: 1. Information warfare related program or capability.

2. **Lungfish:** US–Australian submarine operations exercise, held in Australia since 1990. Lungfish 03: USS *City of Corpus Christi* (SSN 705). Lungfish 02: Aug 2002. Lungfish 99: HMAS Stirling, Perth, Nov 1999.

USS *Los Angeles* (SSN 688). Lungfish 98: Jun 1998. Lungfish 97: Jul 1997. Lungfish 96: Oct 1996.

Lythia: Former DOD continuity of government code word (for example, Top Secret/Lythia).

— M —

M-22 (Mission 22): S-band satellite transponders on highly elliptical orbit SIGINT satellites, 1990s–present. *MTN* (often called "Mountain") refers to the M-22 Tactical Network, which is used to disseminate large files to tactical users, and possibly for covert communications. *See also* Jumpseat.

MACE: NATO electronic warfare interoperoperability exercise series. MACE XI: Eglin AFB, FL, Sep 2003. MACE XI included more than 10 NATO nations, each bringing aircraft outfitted with its latest airborne EW systems to operate against a sophisticated integrated air defense system. Participants include Canada, Denmark, France, Germany, Italy, the Netherlands, Norway, Spain, and the UK. *See also* Trial.

Magellan: 1. Office of the Secretary of Defense research project associated with future worldwide force structure bed down (overseas bases), completed 2003.

   2. **Magellan II:** Navy Surveillance Towed-Array Sensor System (SURTASS) and Low-Frequency Active (LFA) sonar at sea test series (Project M) associated with the submarine security and technology program. Series of tests have been held, in the Mediterranean, 1993; off the coast of California, Jun–Aug 1994; and off Oman, 1995.

Magic Carpet: UK–Oman live-fire aerial bombing exercise, Thumrait, Oman, 2–13 Feb 2002.

Magic Roundabout: UK–Oman maritime surveillance exercise, 2000–2001.

Magnum: SIGINT geostationary satellite, follow-on to Aquacade, first launched from the space shuttle *Discovery* on 25 Jan 1985. Name changed to Orion.

Mailorder: NSA SIGINT system. *See also* Engraft.

Maintain Democracy: Haiti peacekeeping operation, 1 Nov 1994–1 Mar 1995. USS *America* (CV 66) and USS *Dwight D. Eisenhower* (CVN 69) Battle Groups, and the USS *Inchon* (LPH 12) ARG. *See also* Uphold Democracy.

Majestic Eagle: CIA clandestine surveillance team involved in the hunt for Colombian drug lord Pablo Escobar. Majestic Eagle is similar to Gray Fox.

Majestran: Reported US–UK communications interception system, RAF Menwith Hill, part of ECHELON.

Major Manar: US–Tunisian annual exercise. Major Manar 01: USS *Harry S. Truman* (CVN 75) excrcised with Tunisian F-5s. Major Manar 00: 492nd FS deployed F-15Es to Sidi Ahmed AB and flew 144 sorties. Major Manar 98: The exercise was canceled with the 555th FS in Tunisia, and the unit returned to Aviano AB, Italy. Major Manar 96: Sidi Ahmed AB, Tunisia, 7–13 Sep 1996. Six F-16s from the 510th FS deployed to Tunisia. The exercise consisted of bombing at the Ben Ghilouf range and dissimilar air combat training with Tunisia's 15th Air Unit.

Makani Pahili: Pacific hurricane response exercise, 1996. Included use of the Consequence Assessment Tool Set, which assesses and predicts damage from natural and WMD disasters.

Malabar: US–Indian naval exercise series. Malabar 03: The largest naval exercise between India and the US since the countries resumed military training in May 2002. USS *Pasadena* (SSN 752). Malabar 02: Sep–Oct 2002. More than 1,500 American and Indian naval personnel participated, including flying operations, anti-submarine-warfare exercises, and replenishment at sea drills.

Mallard (Project Mallard): Former air force special access program.

Mallee Bull 96: Australian–Brunei army exchange, Oct 1996.

Mallet Blow: Air force 20th FW training exercise to test UK air defenses, 26–29 Mar 1990.

MALOLO: DIA sensitive compartmented information intelligence collection management tool for predicting collection operations, also informally called a "SCIF Fish Tool."

Manta: Unmanned underwater vehicle, deployed from a submarine to operate in shallow water and through minefields to track and destroy enemy submarines, under development at the Naval Undersea Warfare Center Div, Newport, RI. The first small-scale prototype was tested in 1999.

Maple Flag: US–Canadian air exercise in a simulated combat environment, CFB Cold Lake AB, Canada. Maple Flag comprises three two-week periods, normally executed May–Jun. Participants include the UK and other NATO countries. Maple Flag 34-3: 10–22 Jun 2001. Maple Flag 34-2: 27 May–8 Jun 2001. Maple Flag XXXI: 19 May–26 Jun 1998. Maple Flag XXIX: 5 May–15 Jun 1997.

Marathon: Contingency migrant operation involving Chinese migrants being smuggled into the US, Guantanamo Bay, Cuba, Oct 1996.

Marble Tor: UK Gibraltar-based exercise series. The 29 Apr–13 May 2000 Marble Tor was canceled due to other UK operational commitments.

MARCOT (Maritime Coordinated Operational Training): Canadian annual naval exercise series coordinated by the Canadian Forces Maritime Warfare Centre, Halifax, Nova Scotia. The exercise rotates between Atlantic and Pacfic, and is held in the Pacific during non-RIMPAC years. Participants include Australia, Chile, the UK, and the US. MARCOT 01: 9–16 Oct 2001. The scenario had the aggressive and unstable country Orange take over a strip of country Indigo, which has rich oil fields and a large population of ethnic Orangians on three islands off Indigo's coast. MARCOT/Unified Spirit 98: Newfoundland, Canada, 3–20 Jun 1998. Mine counter-measures experimentation focus involving USS *Inchon* (LPH 12). MARCOT 97-2: Oct 1997. MARCOT 96/ SHAREM 116: Jun 1996. MARCOT 76: Dec 1976.

Marilyn: ELINT "ferret" satellite nickname, 1970s. *See also* Bridget, Farrah, and Raquel.

Marine Interoperability Exercise (MIX): US–Philippine bilateral combat readiness and interoperability exercise. MIX 03/Philippine Interoperability Exchange (PIX) 03: Philippine marine base in Ternate, Cavite, Feb 2003. PIX 03 was the first marine-to-marine training exercise. About 700 marines from III MEF in Okinawa trained at the former Clark AB while SOF trained Filipino forces in counter-terrorism tactics in Zamboanga. Follow-on to Talon Vision.

Maritime Guard: NATO enforcement of the UN-sanctioned embargo against the former Republic of Yugoslavia, 16 Dec 1992–Jun 1993, followed by Sharp Guard.

Maritime Monitor: NATO surveillance of cargo being transported through the Adriatic to the former Republic of Yugoslavia, 15 Jun–Dec 1992, followed by Maritime Guard.

Market Square: 82nd Airborne Div emergency deployment readiness exercise, Fort Bragg, NC. The exercise goes back at least to exercise Market Square 88, and served as a preparation and proving ground for Just Cause and Desert Shield. Market Square 00: Sep 2000. Market Square 98: 11–30 Sep 1998.

Marlock: Guam-based SIGINT system.

Marne Focus: 3rd Infantry Div regular emergency deployment readiness exercise, Fort Stewart, GA. Marne Focus 03: Mar–Apr 2003. Marne Focus 00: 7–9 Feb 2000. Marne Focus 99: 6–27 Apr 1999.

Maroon: NSA first word, 1980s, including Maroon Archer I and II, Maroon Bowspirit, Maroon Sail, and Maroon Shield.

Marshland: Air force (probably classified) unknown system.

MARSURVEX (Maritime Surveillance Exercise): US–Philippine Seventh Fleet quarterly naval exercise involving P-3 Orion aircraft and focusing on improving over-the-horizon targeting and maritime operations with air and surface assets, 2001–present. MARSURVEX 99 was the first in the series since the closing of the US naval facilities at Subic Bay in 1991.

Martes: ELINT-related signals analysis database.

Marty (Project Marty): Air Intelligence Agency 18th Intelligence Sqn electronic, technical, and specialized analytical support to the Air Force Space Command deep-space surveillance mission. Marty allows for the accomplishment of Comfy Cobalt missions and Sensor Shadow projects.

Masked Dragon: National Defense University National Strategic Gaming Center strategic policy forum examining escalation options on the Korean peninsula, May 2004.

Mass Appeal: UK intelligence operation to make public the discovery of traces of the nerve agent VX on Iraqi missile warheads, 1998.

Masterkey: NSA modernization program.

Matador: EUCOM JTF exercise series involving strike operations and planning in the African littoral region. Matador 01: 17–25 May 2001. Matador 00: Stuttgart, Germany, and Gaeta, Italy, 10–25 Jul 2000. Matador 99: 22–30 Jun 1999. Matador 98: Sardina, 21–25 Jul 1998. 22nd MEU. Matador 96: Coast of Spain in the western Mediterranean, 10–25 May 1996. Six F-16s from the 555th FS took part, working with the Spanish air force.

Code Names

Matchlite: NSA specific emitter ID (SEI) ELINT/SIGINT database identifying platform, hull, and geographic area of emitting objects.

MAXCAP 05: FBI pre-9/11 plan to increase the counter-terrorism capability of the bureau, unveiled in 2000.

MCOP-EST: Estonian–Swedish mine clearing exercise, Nov 2001. Included the UK.

Measured Response: Army Chemical and Biological Defense Command domestic exercise series focusing on military support to civil authorities. The Measured Response Boston exercise, 7 Oct 1998, included a full-scale chemical disaster as part of the domestic preparedness program for the city of Boston. The exercise simulated the release of sarin nerve gas at a local gathering. Measured Response 97-2/97-1.

Med Shark (Mediterranean Shark): US–Moroccan Sixth Fleet naval exercise. Med Shark 02: 23 Sep 2002. The USS *George Washington* (CVN 73), USS *Mahan* (DDG 72), and USNS *Supply* (T-AOE 6) engaged in air maneuvers and surface maneuvering, boarding, and gunfire drills. Med Shark 01: May 2001. USS *Ponce* (LPD 15) and 24th MEU (SOC) conducted a helicopter insertion of a Moroccan naval infantry company.

MEDCEUR (Medical Exercise Central/Eastern Europe): EUCOM ISO/PfP semi-annual medical and disaster exercise. Participants include Albania, Azerbaijan, Bulgaria, Estonia, France, Georgia, Germany, Greece, Hungary, Italy, Macedonia, Moldova, Romania, Slovakia, and Turkey. MEDCEUR 04/Rescuer 04: Estonia, Latvia, and Lithuania, 15–29 Jul 2004. MEDCEUR 03/Rescuer 03: Vaziani Military Base, Georgia, Sep 2003. MEDCEUR 02: Estonia, 15–19 Jul 2002. MEDCEUR 01-2: Albania. MEDCEUR 01-1: Bulgaria. MEDCEUR 00-2: Romania, 11–20 Jul 2000. MEDCEUR 00-2/Rescue Eagle 00: Romania. MEDCEUR 99-2: Latvia. MEDCEUR 98-1: Slovakia, 1–15 May 1998. MEDCEUR 97-2F: Macedonia. MEDCEUR 96-1: Hissar, Bulgaria, 23–30 Mar 1996. MEDCEUR 95-1: Rinas AB, Tirana, Albania, 10–25 Mar 1995.

MEDFLAG/MEDCAP: EUCOM and CENTCOM African semi-annual medical exercise series. Exercises are called MEDFLAGs in the EUCOM area of operations, and MEDCAPs in the CENTCOM area. The exercises consist of training classes, a practical mass casualty exercise, immunizations, and health screenings in a local community. Participants outside Africa include Germany, the Netherlands, and the UK. MEDFLAG 04: South

Africa. MEDFLAG 03: Er-Rachidia, Morocco, 6–20 Sep 2003. MED-FLAG 02: Entebbe, Uganda, 10–25 Aug 2002. MEDFLAG 01-2: Nampula, Mozambique. MEDFLAG 01-1. MEDFLAG 00-2: Mauritania, 15–26 Sep 2000. MEDFLAG 99-2: Tanzania. MEDFLAG 97: Benin and Chad hosts. MEDFLAG 96-3: Mali, 7–17 Sep 1996. MEDFLAG 95-3: Harare, Zimbabwe, 27 Jul–18 Aug 1995. MEDFLAG 95: Côte d'Ivoire. MEDFLAG 94-3: Nigeria, 18–30 Aug 1994. MEDFLAG 94-1: Accra, Ghana, 17–28 Apr 1994. MEDFLAG 94: Bostwana. MEDFLAG 93-1: Niamey, Niger, 9–20 May 1993. MEDFLAG 93: Senegal. MEDFLAG 92: Zambia. MEDFLAG 92-2: Freetown, Sierra Leone, Apr–May 1992. Because of a coup, the team was evacuated early as part of Silver Anvil. MEDFLAG 91: Cameroon, Guinea-Bissau, Zimbabwe. MEDFLAG 90: Equatorial Guinea, Mauritania, Senegal, Tunisia. MEDFLAG 89: Botswana, Liberia. MEDFLAG 88: Cameroon, Gabon.

Medicine Man: UK army armoured/infantry battle group field training exercise, British Army Training Unit Suffield, Canada. The combined arms exercises are held four times a year.

Meditate: Former navy/NSA compartment dealing with submarine operations and an Ivy Bells–like operation. *See also* NASP.

MEDRETE (Medical Readiness Training Exercise): SOUTHCOM humanitarian and medical assistance exercise. The exercises are often combined with New Horizons. MEDRETE 00-3: Nicaragua, 13–25 Aug 2000. MEDRETE 00-2: Ecuador, 7–15 Mar 2000. MEDRETE 00-1: Peru, 5–19 Feb 2000.

Megas Alexandros: US–Greek air exercise series. Megas Alexandros 97: Volos region, Skyros, and Aghios Eustratios, Greece, 12–20 Jul 1997. Megas Alexandros 96: Magnisia-Skyros, Greece, 12–20 Jun 1996.

Mellin: Australian cyclical maritime surveillance operations in the Torres Strait and Timor Gap.

Mensa: Possible code word dealing with a satellite program.

Mercury: 1. **(Project Mercury):** Defense intelligence language "listening skills" initiative, 2003.

2. **Mercury:** SIGINT geostationary satellite, formerly Vortex.

3. **Mercury:** US–Singapore annual naval mine counter-measures training exercise. The Mercury series began with the US hosting the first in 1996.

Singapore hosts during alternate years. Mercury 2000: Gulf of Mexico and ashore at the Naval Station, Ingleside, TX, 10–21 Jul 2000.

4. **Mercury:** UK long-range communications exercise series named after Mercury (Plutonium Mercury, for instance, or Yttrium Mercury). Two annual exercises were reduced to one in 1999. Locations in the 1990s included the Turks and Caicos Islands, Florida, the Bahamas, the Cayman Islands, Trinidad and Tobago, Belize, Ascension Island, Kenya, Singapore, Nepal, and New Zealand.

5. **Mercury:** DEA message traffic system connecting offices worldwide.

Mergate: US–Singapore maritime patrol and anti-submarine-warfare exercise, 2002.

Meridian: Air force special access program.

Merino: Former code name for the CIA–National Reconnaissance Office Joint Defence Space Research Facility established at Pine Gap near Alice Springs, Australia, 1966.

Merlin: 1. DEA intelligence communications system that provides access to classified information and special reports, office automation capabilities, database information, and analytical tools.

2. **Merlin:** NSA Non-communications Signals Exploitation System. *See also* Hawk, Phoenix, Raven, Owl, and Mockingbird.

Merlion: US–Singapore naval exercise series, South China Sea. The exercise began in 1975. Merlion 01. Merlion 99: May 1999. USS *Kitty Hawk* (CV 63). Merlion 98. Merlion 97: May 1997, USS *Independence* (CV 62).

Merlynx: US–Singapore navy special operations exercises series.

Messiah: Army intelligence system, Bad Aibling, Germany.

Metropolis (Project Metropolis): Marine Corps military operations in urban terrain experimentation, George AFB, CA, 1999–2000. Follow-on to Urban Warrior.

Mica: Former SIGINT code word.

MICROWEB: Compass Call database.

MiDAS: S-band transceiver that communicates over the M-22 satellite network and serves as a downlink for real-time ELINT updates.

Midget Thrust 01: USAFE Air Operations Sqn crisis action team exercise, 25–26 Jul 2001. The exercise employed a notional scenario involving a non-combatant evacuation operation from Sierra Leone, with USAFE providing forces to a NAVEUR-led JTF and repatriating US citizens from Freetown Airport through a staging base in Senegal.

Midnight Express: Coast Guard exercise, Portland, OR, 1999.

Midnight Stand: STRATCOM offensive information operations Advanced Concept Technology Demonstration begun in 2003, formerly Idaho Thunder.

Midnight Trail: Munitions field training exercise as part of preparations under Desert Shield, Aug 1991.

Mighty Guardian: Defense Threat Reduction Agency (formerly Defense Special Weapons Agency)–funded "force on force" protection and physical security exercise, first held at Ellsworth AFB, SD, May 1994, and resulting in recommendations for improvements in nuclear weapons security and guard force training. On 30 Dec 1994, the chief of staff of the air force signed a memorandum emphasizing the need to enhance the security facilities and tactics used to secure nuclear weapons and air force bases. The formal Mighty Guardian series then started to focus on all aspects of nuclear weapons security. Mighty Guardian I, 1998, was conducted in response to lessons learned in the Khobar Towers bombing in Saudi Arabia and the Oklahoma City bombing in 1996. Mighty Guardian VII: 305th Air Mobility Wing, McGuire AFB, NJ, 2003. Mighty Guardian V: Naval Submarine Base, Kings Bay, GA, 26 Sep–8 Oct 2002.

Mighty Thunder: Air-force-sponsored exercise series. Mighty Thunder 96: Hill AFB, UT, Mar 1996. Mighty Thunder 95.

Milkyway: Air force special access program.

Mill Challenge: Naval surface exercise, Virginia, Sep 2000.

Millennium Challenge: JFCOM-sponsored operational-level joint experimentation series that combines live forces with simulation. It was the premier transformation event of the DOD, providing an overarching context for service experiments. Millennium Challenge 02: Jul–Aug 2002. The exercise was designed to assess the ability of a JTF to execute the rapid decisive operation (RDO) warfighting concept during the decade of the 2000s, as well as test the Standing Joint Force Headquarters (SJFHQ). More than 13,000 military personnel participated from eight live-training and 17 simulation locations. Millennium Challenge 02 focused on determining the extent to which the force could conduct an RDO without a major recapitalization of the force. Millenium Challenge 00: 14 Aug–13 Sep 2000. The exercise tested three different joint experiments: Precision Engagement, Joint Deployment Process Improvement, and Information Superiority/Command and Control. Training took place at 11 different sites. Millenium Challenge 99: Military Support to Civil Authorities for Y2K. Implemented Operations Order 5220-99, 30 Apr 1999.

Millennium Dragon: Marine Corps urban operations experiment testing the Dragon Eye backpack UAV, cellular staff structure standard operating procedures for the Joint Forces Land Component Commander, and the special operations mission planning environment — maritime.

Millennium Falcon: US–German weapons training deployment providing dissimilar air combat training. Millenium Falcon 01: Laage AB, Germany, 13–28 Apr 2001.

MINI–Noble Dina: *See* Noble Dina.

Mirrored Image: Defense Special Weapons Agency–hosted interagency command post exercise that involved incident response with an improvised radiological device, 1996.

Mistral: Australian operations to enforce an exclusive economic zone in the Southern Ocean, 1998–present.

Misty (Mysty?): Possible code word for possible stealth reconnaissance satellite.

Mobcap Apex: NSA and air force foreign material exploitation of a ground-based Asian system, 1995–2001, aka Sympton Zeus.

Mockingbird: Non-communications Signals Exploitation System. *See also* Hawk, Merlin, Phoenix, Raven, and Owl.

Monarch Eagle: DOD plan to consolidate service HUMINT organizations under DIA control, 1982–1983.

Mongoose: CTF 180 operation, Adi Ghar, Afghanistan, Jan 2003.

Monitor: Special operation including the 290th Joint Communications Support Sqn, 1999.

Mono Prix: UK–Kenyan exercise, 2000–2001.

Monticello: Army Foreign Science and Technology Center scientific and technical intelligence analyst tool/management system.

Moon Smoke: DIA Web-based information management system.

Moonlight Maze: Intrusions into DOD computer systems, Jun 1998–Feb 1999. Nineteen unclassified air force systems at Wright-Patterson AFB, OH, and elsewhere in the US were affected, and the air force claimed that data "equivalent to a stack of printed copier paper three times the height of the Washington Monument" was stolen. Reportedly, the US lodged a formal protest with the Russian government in 2000 after investigators from the FBI and DOD Computer Forensics Laboratory determined in their Storm Cloud investigation that the cyber-attacks appear to have originated from seven Russian Internet addresses.

Moonpenny: Reported satellite monitoring SIGINT system at RAF Menwith Hill, UK, 1980s–.

Moravian Shield: US–German military exercise. Moravian Shield 03 was canceled.

Moray: COMINT compartment (such as Top Secret/Moray) eliminated in May 1999, along with the code words *Umbra*, *Spoke*, and *Zarf*. Information previously classified Moray was subsequently designated Top Secret COMINT.

Moroccan Airex: Reagan-era exercise with NSC involvement, 3–4 Nov 1984.

Moroccan Phiblex: Reagan-era exercise with NSC involvement.

Mothia: Italy-hosted annual air exercise. Mothia 00: 17–19 Oct 2000. The Combined Air Operations Center 5 at Poggio Renatico directed participants from Austria, Belgium, France, Germany, Greece, the Netherlands, Spain, Turkey, the UK, and the US operating at 12 bases in Italy, 1 in France, and 1 in Greece.

Mount Hope III: Operation to recover a Soviet Mi-24 Hind attack helicopter. In Jun 1988, the 160th SOAR and other SOF received a short-notice directive to recover the Mi-24 from a remote location in Africa. The operation required two MH-47 crews to fly 490 miles at night without outside navigational aids, extract the Hind, and return.

Mountain: Mission 22 (M-22) Tactical Network.

Mountain: DIA code name for Israel-originated intelligence. Mountain Hall was an Israeli Iraqi source during the 1991 Gulf War. Mountain Ivy refers to a foreign material exploitation program involving Israel-acquired equipment. 2. **Mountain:** Combined Task Force 180 first word.

+ **Mountain Blizzard:** Jan–Feb 2004. Conducted 1,731 patrols, 143 raids, and cordons and searches, killing 22 enemy combatants. Followed by Mountain Storm.
+ **Mountain Lion:** Continuation of Anaconda, Apr 2002, looking for remaining pockets of al Qaeda and Taliban.
+ **Mountain Resolve:** US–Afghan and coalition operation in a remote northeastern region of Afghanistan bordering Pakistan, launched 7 Nov 2003. Followed by Avalanche.
+ **Mountain Storm:** Follow-on to Mountain Blizzard, beuan Mar 2004.
+ **Mountain Sweep:** 82nd Airborne Div and Ranger operation to capture cached weapons in southeast Afghanistan, 18 Aug 2002, the largest US offensive in Afghanistan since Anaconda. Follow-on to Mountain Lion.
+ **Mountain Viper:** US–Afghan and coalition operation begun in late Aug 2003 to drive Taliban and al Qaeda fighters from sanctuary in Zabul Province.

Mountain Air: DARPA ocean surveillance project.

Mountain Eagle III: US Army Europe exercise series. Mountain Eagle 95: Grafenwohr range, Germany, 27–31 Oct 1995. Two F-16Cs of the 510th FS participated while deployed to Spangdahlem AB. Marine Corps F/A-18Ds from VMFA 224 also participated.

Mountain Hawk: Army V Corps mission rehearsal training for TF Hawk possible deployment to support operations in Kosovo, 1999.

Moutain Mist: Emergency condition associated with North Korea and Pacific region airborne reconnaissance. *See also* Nickleback.

Mountain Peak: 10th Mountain Div emergency deployment readiness exercise, Fort Drum, NY.

Mountain Shield: NATO mission rehearsal for deployment to Bosnia. Mountain Shield II: 7–20 Sep 1995. The 16th SOS (AC-130) deployed to Germany. Mountain Shield I/Daring Lion: Germany, 12–24 Jun 1995. The 16th SOS (AC-130) deployed to Germany.

MTWS (Maritime Tactical Warfare Simulation): III MEF annual exercise, Philippines, 2001–present.

MTX 99 (Multinational Training Exercise 1999): Seventh Fleet live-fire exercise in the western Pacific in the vicinity of the Marianas Islands and involving USS *Kitty Hawk* (CV 63) and naval forces from Australia, Canada, Singapore, and South Korea. Ships, submarines, and maritime patrol aircraft from the five nations fired Harpoon, Penguin, and Maverick missiles, torpedoes, and shipboard guns at the ex-USS *Oklahoma City*, former Seventh Fleet flagship. The USS *Columbus* (SSN 762) and Korean submarine *Lee Chun* (SS 062) participated.

Mulberry Tree/Prickly Pear: US–UK exercise series. UK participation in the 2–15 Jun 2001 series was canceled due to foot-and-mouth disease restrictions.

Musketeer: NSA Special Signals Collection Organization (W23, formerly G81) going back to at least the early 1970s. Musketeer had devices installed in Wobeck, Germany. Musketeer Dixie II: ELINT-related SEI program. Musketeer Miko refers to a system aboard navy EP-3E aircraft.

Mustang: Big Safari–managed special access program.

Mystic Star: VIP computer-controlled electronic switching system that supports the president, vice president, and senior government and military officials while aboard Special Air Mission (SAM), VIP, or Command aircraft. The Mystic Star system consists of eight primary and nine secondary HF radio stations located in Ascension Island, Greenland, Guam, Japan, the Philippines, Portugal (Azores), Turkey, the UK, and the US. The Net Control Stations are at Andrews AFB, MD, and Offutt AFB, NE. *See also* Cartwheel, Scope Command.

— N —

NASP (Naval Activities Support Program): Sensitive-compartmented-information-level code word program associated with submarine intelligence and reconnaissance.

Narrow Passage 85: Reagan-era exercise with NSC involvement, 1–30 Nov 1984.

National Eagle: RADARSAT/LANDSAT/SPOT imagery downlink.

Nationwide: White House Communications Agency–operated presidential UHF radio communications network.

Native: CENTCOM/TRANSCOM first word.
+ **Native Atlas:** Joint Logistics Over the Shore exercise involving loading and unloading pre-positioned stocks from ships. Native Atlas 03: Qatar. Native Atlas 02: Camp Pendleton, CA, 29 Mar–15 Apr 2002. Supported a 3rd Infantry Div emergency deployment readiness exercise to the National Training Center. Native Atlas 00 was canceled.
+ **Native Fury:** Maritime pre-positioning force exercise series that transitioned from an Arabian Gulf scenario to an African regional response exercise in 2000 (*see* Natural Fire). Native Fury 99: Kuwait. Native Fury 98: Udairi Range, Kuwait, May–Jun 1998. The 1st Tank Bn, 7th and 11th Marine Regts downloaded approximately 400 pieces of equipment from the Diego Garcia–based *Corporal Louis J. Hauge*. The exercise was originally canceled when I MEF deployed to Kuwait for Desert Thunder. Native Fury 97: Qatar, Jan 1997. Native Fury 96: Kuwait, Oct–Nov 1996. Largest maritime exercise ever held in Kuwait. Native Fury 94: Kuwait, 4–25 Apr 1994. More than 2,000 Marines and sailors participated with the two MPF vessels MV *PFC James Anderson* and MV *Franklin J. Phillips*. Native Fury 93-1: Jun 1993. Native Fury 92/Eager Mace 92: Kuwait, Aug 1992.

Native Trail: UK exercise, Belize, 2000–2001.

Natural Fire: CENTCOM East African special operations exercise, held with Uganda, Kenya, and Tanzania. Natural Fire focuses on airborne operations, small-unit tactics, and refugee control. Natural Fire 04 canceled. Natural Fire/Native Fury 00: Kenya, 4 May–4 Jun 2000. 1st MEB deployed and then undertook humanitarian assistance and civic action projects. Participants included Kenya, Tanzania, and Uganda. MC-130E Combat Talon I aircraft of 919th SOW supported the missions. Natural Fire 98: Kenya. 5th SFG. Natural Fire 96: Kenya, Jul 1996. 5th SFG established a CJSOTF headquarters. 19th SFG, SEAL Team 3, and 16th SOW trained with Kenyan 20th Parachute Infantry Bn and Navy Clearance Dive Unit.

Natural River 86: Reagan-era exercise with NSC involvement, 18 Oct–15 Nov 1985.

Nautical: US–Saudi Arabian first word, including the classified exercises Nautical Fire and Nautical Sentry.

+ **Nautical Artist:** US–Saudi Arabian naval air exercise series. Nautical Artist 04. Nautical Artist 98: USS *Kitty Hawk* (CV 63). Nautical Artist 97: Dec 1997. USS *Nimitz* (CVN 68). Nautical Artist 95: Jul 1995. USS *Abraham Lincoln* (CVN 72). Nautical Artist 95-2: USS *Constellation* (CV 64). Nautical Artist 94: Jul 1994. USS *Constellation* (CV 64).

+ **Nautical Swimmer:** US–Saudi Arabian surface naval exercise series. Nautical Swimmer 04. Nautical Swimer 99: 8–9 Jun 1999. USS *Curtis Wilber* (DDG 54), USS *Ingraham* (FFG 61), USS *Ardent* (MCM 12), and USS *Dextrous* (MCM 13). Nautical Swimmer 95-2/Arabian Gauntlet: USS *Kinkaid* (DD 965). Nautical Swimmer 97: Mar 1997.

Nearland: Joint air defense and joint engagement zone test and evaluation project, Eglin AFB, FL, 17 Mar–2 Apr 1994.

Nebula: Zirconic subcompartment reportedly dealing with stealth reconnaissance satellites.

Nectar Bend: US–Ethiopian special operations exercise series, begun in 1992. Nectar Bend 04. Nectar Bend 01. Nectar Bend 00. Nectar Bend 99. Nectar Bend 94: 2 Jun–2 Jul 1994. 5th SFG surgical team. Nectar Bend 93: EOD training and preparations for Nectar Bend 94. Nectar Bend 93: Aug 1992. 5th SFG.

Nemean Lion: Fifth Fleet Tomahawk strike readiness exercise, northern Arabian Gulf, named for the mythical beast slain by Hercules as the first of his 12 labors. Nemean Lion 95: USS *Lake Champlain* (CG 57). Nemean Lion 94-2. Nemean Lion 94-1: 8–12 Jan 1994. The first day included strikes against five targets and involved the USS *Hayler* (DD 997) and USS *John Hancock* (DD 981) in the Red Sea, and USS *John Young* (DD 973), USS *Mobile Bay* (CG 53), and USS *Helena* (SSS 725) in the Arabian Gulf. The USS *Independence* (CV 62) acted as launch coordinator for the Arabian Sea with the USS *Hayler* as coordinator for the Red Sea. Nemean Lion 93-1: 1–5 Sep 1993. USS *Elliot* (DD 972). Nemean Lion IV. Nemean Lion I: Oct 1990. Tomahawk mission rehersal for Desert Storm, resulting in greater integration of missiles into the choreography of the strategic attack plan.

Neo Tapon: NATO Spanish-sponsored eastern Atlantic and Gibraltar Strait naval and anti-submarine-warfare exercise. Participants include Belgium, Canada, France, Germany, Greece, Norway, Portugal, Turkey, the UK, and the US. Neo Tapon 03: Jun 2003. Neo Tapon 02: Sep 2002.

Neon: US–Bahrain first word.

+ **Neon Arrow:** US–Bahrain naval exercise. Neon Arrow 95: USS *Constellation* (CV 64). Neon Arrow 94-1: 15–19 Jan 1994. A Carrier Air Wing Five detachment from the USS *Independence* (CV 62) went ashore for the exercise.

+ **Neon Falcon:** US–Bahrain major surface exercise with fully integrated chemical and biological warfare scenarios. Participants include France and the UK. Neon Falcon 04. Neon Falcon 03: Dec 2003. HMS *Norfolk* and USS *Philippine Sea* (CG 58). Neon Falcon 01: Apr–May 2001. Marine Corps Chemical-Biological Incident Response Force (CBIRF), Army 83rd Chemical Bn, Fort Polk, LA, with attachments from the 519th Military Police Bn and the 115th Field Hospital. The Center for Naval Analyses analyzed the implications of a biological attack against ships. Neon Falcon 00: Feb 2000. USS *Lake Champlain* (CG 57). Some 7,000 participants including a composite navy and Coast Guard harbor defense command, Mobile Inshore Undersea Warfare Unit 103, and the Marine CBIRF. HMS *Illustrious*, the nuclear submarine HMS *Triumph*, and the destroyer HMS *Gloucester*. Neon Falcon 99: Sep 1999. 13th MEU (SOC) and the Marine Corps CBIRF. Neon Falcon 97: Nov 1997. USS *Gary* (FFG 51), USS *Harry W. Hill* (DD 986), and HMS *Coventry*. Neon Falcon 96: Sep 1996.

+ **Neon Response:** US–Bahrain explosive ordnance disposal exercise. Neon Response 03: 5–15 Oct 2003. Navy and Bahraini EOD technicians trained on techniques used to defeat improvised explosive devices.

+ **Neon Spark:** US–Bahrain naval exercise series, including the UK. Neon Spark 98.

Neon Spear: Disaster response symposium with the East African countries of Burundi, Djibouti, Egypt, Eritrea, Ethiopia, Kenya, Rwanda, the Seychelles, Tanzania, and Uganda. Neon Spear 02: Nairobi, Kenya, 8–13 Jul 2002. *See also* Golden Spear.

Neptune Shield: Coast Guard special operation, 12 Sep 2001–31 Mar 2002.

Neptune Thunder: Seventh Fleet exercise to test the at-sea capability of the army Multiple Launch Rocket System and Army Tactical Missile System missiles, South Korea, Oct 2000.

Neptune's: UK army exercise series first word, including Neptune's Eagle, Neptune's Hawk.

New Horizon: Australian–Indonesian major maritime exercise series. Participants include Malaysia. New Horizon IX/98: May 1998, also May 1997, and Jul 1996.

New Horizons (Nuevos Horizontes): SOUTHCOM nation assistance and humanitarian exercise series used to train engineer, medical, and civil affairs units in austere tropical environments. In 2003, the New Horizon exercises completed 31 engineer projects consisting of schools, clinics, wells, and rudimentary road construction and repair. The 70 humanitarian medical deployments treated more than 300,000 patients, and veterinary teams treated approximately 57,000 animals. Belize, the Dominican Republic, Grenada, Panama, and St. Kitts hosted New Horizons exercises in 2004.

+ **New Horizons Antigua and Barbuda:** 12 Feb–14 May 2005 and 1 May–30 Jul 2000.
+ **New Horizons Bahamas.**
+ **New Horizons Bolivia:** 1 Jun 1999.
+ **New Horizons Dominica:** 15 Mar–15 Jun 2005.
+ **New Horizons Dominican Republic:** 15 Jun–15 Sep 2001.
+ **New Horizons Ecuador:** 1 Jun–1 Sep 2004.
+ **New Horizons El Salvador:** 14 Feb–15 May 2005 and Jan–Mar 1996.
+ **New Horizons Grenada:** 15 Sep–13 Nov 2003 and 1 May–30 Aug 2000.
+ **New Horizons Guatemala:** 15 Feb–15 May 2004 and 1 Feb–31 Apr 2001.
+ **New Horizons Guyana:** 2004.
+ **New Horizons Haiti:** 1 Jan–31 Mar 2001.
+ **New Horizons Honduras:** Feb–May 2004 and 1 Jan–30 Jun 2001.
+ **New Horizons Jamaica:** 2004. May–Aug 2000.
+ **New Horizons Nicaragua:** 16 Feb–15 May 2005.
+ **New Hoizons Panama:** 15 Feb–15 May 2005.
+ **New Horizons Paraguay:** 15 Mar–15 Jul 2001.
+ **New Horizons St. Lucia:** 15 Feb–15 May 2001.
+ **New Horizons St. Vincent:** 15 Mar–15 Jul 2001.
+ **New Horizons Suriname:** 2004.
+ **New Horizons Trinidad and Tobago:** 1 May–30 Jun 2000.

Newsdealer/Newstand: NSA Joint Worldwide Intelligence Communications System(JWICS) message handling system replacing Streamliner. The system includes Newsdealer Message Switch System, Newsdealer in a Box,

Newsdealer Automated Message Handling System, and Newsdealer Correction System.

Newsdealer/Seamark: SIGINT maintenance and operator training; taught at Keesler AFB, MS.

Nickel Grass: Operation to transfer equipment to Israel to compensate for losses in the Yom Kippur War, 1973.

Nickleback: Emergency condition associated with North Korea and Pacific region airborne reconnaissance. *See also* Mountain Mist.

NIEX (No-notice Interoperability Exercise): JCS highly classified exercise program that focuses on a chairman special interest, providing an opportunity to train key individuals, staff, and operational elements at the interagency, joint staff, and tactical levels in time-sensitive crisis action procedures. Normally, one to two NIEXs are conducted each year, lasting three to seven days each. In the 1990s, NIEX focused on the military's ability to respond to WMD incidents. In 1995, the NIEX required the interagency process to respond to a foreign nation's request to interdict and recover three stolen nuclear weapons. Joint Special Operations Command, Lincoln Gold, and other national-level forces were exercised. The 1996 NIEX tested the ability to respond to a crisis involving biological weapons. Other NIEXs focus on information warfare (Eligible Receiver) and national response and command and control (Positive Response).

Nifty Nugget/Rex 78: Nationwide mobilization exercise, 1978.

Nifty Package: Deployment of special operations forces to Panama for Just Cause, 1989.

Night: JCS TENCAP special project first word.

+ **Night Fury:** Special project to use SIGINT satellites to provide real-time tactical support, initiated 1988–1989. NSA resisted the project. The Night Fury Tactical Support Group activated at an NSA covert facility in the Pacific to influence collection, processing, and reporting for the benefit of combat units. Night Fury reporting was first used in Desert Storm to report Scud-related intelligence.
+ **Night Raider:** Special Project 84 with navy as exercise agent, used to demonstrate over-the-horizon targeting of Harpoon and Tomahawk anti-ship missiles.
+ **Night Slime:** Army intelligence.

✦ **Night Vector:** Special Project 95, a demonstration of the use of commercial Direct Broadcast Service (DBS) to deliver video and large databases to ships at sea, demonstrated during Roving Sands 95. DBS passed live video from Predator UAVs to ground forces.

Night: Australia special operations exercise first word.

✦ **Night Falcon 02:** Australian–Papua New Guinea special operations exercise, Nov 2002.

✦ **Night Kiwi:** Australian–New Zealand special operations exercise. Nov 2002 exercise canceled.

✦ **Night Leopard:** Australian–Brunei special operations exercise, renamed Star Leopard.

✦ **Night Lion 02:** Australian–Singapore special operations exercise, Aug 2002.

Night Blue: JCS and STRATCOM national-level continuity of operations exercise.

Night Camel: Desert Shield training exercise revealing that armored targets were visible at night when viewed through infrared sensors such as the F-111's Pave Tack laser designator. The discovery led to the development of "tank plinking" operations using laser-guided bombs against Iraqi armored vehicles.

Night Fist: Special operations counter-terrorism collaborative network-based fusion activity to improve the ability to detect and track difficult/time-fleeting and high-value targets, introduced in 2004. Night Fist is managed by the JCS Directorate of Operations (J-3), supports SOCOM's mission of strategic reconnaissance (SR), involves STRATCOM, and is budgeted under the PDAS program element (*see* Island Sun). According to the SOCOM budget, "SR complements National and Theater intelligence collection systems by obtaining specific and time sensitive information when other systems are constrained by weather, terrain masking, hostile countermeasures or conflicting priorities."

Nighthawk: Coast Guard special operation, 2 Jan 1992–2 Dec 1993.

Nightjar: US–UK exercise, Marine Corps Air Station Yuma, AZ, Apr 1993.

Nightwatch: E-4 National Airborne Operations Center, Offutt AFB, NE. The aircraft can be used as airborne command posts, for emergency relocation, or for executive transport (they can be refueled in the air). Nightwatch was also previously the code name for the EC-135J national airborne emergency command post, used by SAC. *See also* Rebound Echo.

Nike Air: Desert Shield/Desert Storm SPECAT relating to US chemical weapons.

Nimble Lion: Air force and SACEUR mission rehearsal exercise for possible operations in Kosovo, Warrior Preparation Center, Einsiedlerhof, Germany, 1998.

Nimble Vision: JCS war game series focusing on the impact of enhanced intelligence, surveillance and reconnaissance, and future C4I on warfighting. Nimble Vision IV: 6–10 May 1996. Nimble Vision III: Mar 1996. Nimble Vision II: Jan 1996. Nimble Vision I: Oct 1995.

Nimrod Dancer: SOUTHCOM operation to build up forces in Panama in the summer of 1989 before Just Cause.

Nine Lives: Presidential continuity of government exercise series.

Noble: US–Israeli first word.

+ **Noble Chris:** *See* Juniper Hawk 95.
+ **Noble Dina:** US–Israeli classified Sixth Fleet submarine and anti-submarine-warfare exercise. Noble Dina 04: USS *Thorn* (DD 988). Noble Dina 03: Jan 2003. USS *Deyo* (DD 989) visited Haifa, reportedly the first US combat ship to dock there in 10 years. The exercise was executed as part of preparations to defend Israel in Iraqi Freedom. Noble Dina 01. Noble Dina 99. *See also* Mini–Noble Dina.
+ **Noble Rose:** US–Israeli special operations exercise involving Naval Special Warfare Unit 2. Noble Rose 00. Noble Rose 99.
+ **Noble Safeguard:** No-notice deployment of V Corps air defense equipment to a classified Middle East country, probably Israel, 16 Feb–13 Apr 1998.
+ **Noble Shirley:** US–Israeli biennial Marine Corps live-fire training exercise. Noble Shirley 01 was canceled in May 2001 for "political reasons and military force protection reasons." Noble Shirley 00: 5–14 Jul 2000. USS *Wasp* (LHD 1), USS *Trenton* (LPD 14), and 24th MEU (SOC) calling in Haifa, with marines training in the southern Negev desert. Noble Shirley 99: 17 Dec 1998. USS *John F. Kennedy* (CV 67) air operations and movement of Patriot missiles to Israel. Noble Shirley 98

canceled Jun 1998. Noble Shirley 96: Feb 1996. USS *Wasp* (LHD 1), USS *Shreveport* (LPD 12), and USS *Whidbey Island* (LSD 41). Noble Shirley 95/Noble Chris/Juniper Hawk: 22nd MEU. Noble Shirley 93: 22nd MEU. Noble Shirley 89: 22nd MEU. Noble Shirley 87: 22nd MEU.

+ **Noble Stallion 94:** US–Israeli anti-air exercise.
+ **Noble Suzanne:** US–Israeli special operations exercise. Noble Suzanne 03. Noble Suzanne 00: USS *Dwight D. Eisenhower* (CVN 69), USS *Anzio* (CG 68), and USS *Cape. St. George* (CG 71). While the ships were transiting to Israel for the exercise, an Israeli Jericho I missile landed near the USS *Anzio* during a test launch. Noble Suzanne: Aug 1997. Noble Suzanne 96: Off the coast of Israel, Oct 1996. Air defense and surface warfare training took place with French and Israeli armed forces. USS *Anzio* (CG 68), USS *Firebolt* (PC 10), and USS *Chinook* (PC 9), along with the Israeli Nesher squadron of coastal patrol boats.

Noble Anvil: US-only JTF operations in support of the NATO Allied Force, Apr–Jun 1999. Noble Anvil supported air operations in France, Germany, Greece, Hungary, Italy, Turkey, and the UK.

Noble Obelisk: EUCOM noncombatant evacuation operation from Freetown, Sierra Leone, 27 May–7 Jun 1997. The USS *Kearsarge* (LHD 3), with the 22nd MEU staging from Guinea, evacuated 2,509 American citizens and foreign nationals.

Noble Piper: US–Kenyan special operations exercise series. Noble Piper 03. Noble Piper 01: Apr–May 2001. A Co, 3/5th SFG led the mission to train Kenyan infantry and provide medical and engineer assistance. Noble Piper 00: 21st STS, Pope AFB, NC. Noble Piper 99: Navy SOF and the 224th Joint Communications Support Sqn. Noble Piper 97.

Noble Response: JTF Kenya humanitarian assistance survey team that provided aid to victims of flooding in Mombasa and Garissa, Kenya, 21 Jan 1998–25 Mar 1998.

Nocona: Informal nickname for Air Intelligence Agency Detachment 1, 18th Intelligence Sqn. In mid-2001, the detachment was preparing to deploy a collection system to Southwest Asia in support of its Air Force Space Command mission of providing technical intelligence support. In the midst of preparing to deploy, Detachment 1 was diverted for OEF.

NOLES (Non-lethal Weapons Seminar): PACOM-funded Marine Force Pacific–coordinated initiative to improve nonlethal weapons and concept for use during missions where civil unrest may create a potential force protection issue. NOLES was first conducted in Indonesia in 2002. Particpating countries include Australia, Bangladesh, Brunei, India, Indonesia, the Maldives, Nepal, Philippines, Singapore, Sri Lanka, and Thailand. NOLES-01-03: Bangladesh, 9–11 Sep 2003. Special Operations Training Group and III MEF.

Nomad Vigil: Army bare base Predator UAV prototyype deployment to Gjader AB, Albania, 1 Jul–5 Nov 1995. Predator flew 130 sorties. Assets were then moved to Hungary in Feb 1996 for Joint Endeavor/Joint Guard.

NONSTOP: Emissions security assessment that determines if counter-measures are required for information systems that process classified national security information based on nearby receivers. *See also* Hijack.

Nordic Peace: NATO ISO/PfP Baltic exercise series. Participants include Finland, Norway, and Sweden. Nordic Peace 03: Finland, Sep 2003. Nordic Peace 02: Sweden. Nordic Peace 00: Aug 2000. Nordic Peace 98: Södertälje and Gotland, Sweden, 28 Sep–9 Oct 1998. Nordic Peace 97: Norway, May 1977.

Nordic Thrust: Air force early warning and missile defense Moving Target Indicator demonstration to detect Iranian ballistic missiles, integrating DSP, JSTARs, Predator UAVs, and MASINT sensors.

Norpac 85: Reagan-era exercise with NSC involvement, 9 Jul–27 Aug 1985.

North (Project North): ELINT system, part of the Tactical Data Processor Suite. Project North uses a Success radio to receive filtered enemy emitter data via TRAP, TIBS, or TADIXS-B.

North Wind: US–Japan Army and Japan Ground Self-Defense Force (JGSDF) company-level, cold-weather field training exercise. The exercise develops bilateral warfighting skills under extreme field conditions. The location rotates among the three northernmost regional armies of the JGSDF. North Wind 98: Feb–Mar 1998.

Northern Challenge: Former NORAD exercise relating to the air defense of North America.

Northern Edge: Alaska Command annual field training exercise involving Alaska-based forces and the Pacific Fleet in a state defense scenario. PACAF contributes the air component by scheduling a Cope Thunder in conjunction. Since 9/11, the exercise has rotated between supporting PACOM in even fiscal years and NORTHCOM in odd fiscal years (with a domestic security scenario). Northern Edge 04: Jun 2004. Northern Edge 01. Northern Edge 99: Feb–Mar 1999. USS *Alaska* (SSBN 732) conducted a ballistic missile submarine (SSBN) Continuity of Operations Exercise (SCOOPEX) during a visit to Seward during Northern Edge 99. Northern Edge 98: 17 Feb–6 Mar 1998. 4th Sqn, 3rd Armored Cavalry Regt.

Northern Light: NATO Supreme Allied Commander Transformation field training exercise designed to demonstrate and improve the readiness of NATO and national headquarters to conduct operations in a regional Article 5 crisis between two generic countries, both of which use NATO procedures. Northern Light 03: West coast of Scotland, UK, 15–26 Sep 03. Northern Light 01.

Northern Lights 99: French-sponsored exercise testing the counter-sea capabilities of the air force and the ordnance recovery capabilities of the navy. More than 11 countries participated, including the UK and France. Two B-52s from the 23rd Bomb Sqn deployed to the Bay De Quiberon, France, 12 Sep 1999; each B-52 dropped eight MK-62 quick strike training mines.

Northern Pike: US–Canadian mobility exercise that involved the largest-ever operational readiness inspection — 24 air force bases and six other locations — in 1995.

Northern Trilogy: Australia-based exercise, Jun 1996.

Northern Viking: Iceland-based EUCOM (formerly JFCOM) biennial command post exercise/field training exercise conducted in odd-numbered years to practice the warfighting capabilities of Iceland Defense Force, dating to the early 1980s. The New York ARNG provides command and control and operational support. Both ARNG and USAR units provide air support. Northern Viking 03: Jun 2003. Northern Viking 99: 23–27 Jun 1999. Northern Viking 97, 25 Jul–9 Aug 1997. During Northern Viking 97, two B-52H bombers deployed to NAS Keflavik.

Northern Watch: Follow-on operations to Provide Comfort II in Northern Iraq, 1 Jan 1997–30 Apr 2003. Northern Watch was charged with enforcing the no-fly zone north of the 36th parallel in Iraq and monitoring Iraqi compliance with the UN Security Council Resolutions 678, 687, and 688. The US, UK, and Turkey provided approximately 45 rotational aircraft at Incirlik AB, Turkey, with additional special operations, intelligence, and search and rescue forces in eastern Turkey.

NORTHPORT: Navy EW, ELINT, or COMINT system.

Northstar: 1. Office of Naval Intelligence internal LAN.

   2. **Northstar:** AT&T-operated ground entry points for E-4 National Airborne Operations Center presidential/VIP communications system and E-6 TACAMO Mercury force employment. There are 17 sites providing near coast-to-coast US coverage. The principal sites are in Waldorf, MD, Omaha, NE, and Lamar, CO, with the Special Government Operations Center at Waldorf, MD.

   3. **Northstar:** Former NATO Norway–based naval exercise held in waters above the Arctic circle. Northstar 91. Northstar 89: Feb 89.

Nova: Newsdealer/Newstand GENSER derivative software program.

Nova Light: Reagan-era NSC-related code word.

NTEX (National/Tactical Exploitation): DARPA "special project" involving automated exploitation of national reconnaissance and tactical assets to locate and identify air defense units. During OIF, NTEX screened Synthetic Aperture Radar (SAR) imagery to look for Iraqi air defense emplacements.

Nugget: US–Australian first word.

Nursery/Nutmeg: US military operations in Indonesia, 1980s.

— O —

Oak Apple: UK–Kenyan civic action exercise series.

Oak Tree: Detachment 421 AFTAC, Alice Springs ("Pine Gap"), Australia.

OASIS: P-3 aircraft tactical data processor used in the Precision Targeting Identification Advanced Concept Technology Demonstration.

Ocean Arium (Ocean Atrium?): NSA database search engine, accessed via Intelink, that allows analysts to search and retrieve the full text of messages, SIGINT products, and data from selected Intelligence Community databases. Ocean Arium adds a multi-media-based search to Anchory's text-only search capability, and will replace Anchory in 2005.

Ocean Safari: Cold War–era naval exercise series.

Ocean Venture: Former Atlantic Command (now JFCOM) exercise series. Ocean Venture 92 was the first exercise to use the intelligence-pull concept of operations with extensive deployment of Joint Deployable Intelligence Support System (JDISS) equipment to JTF commanders and components.

Ocean Wave 97: Australia air combat training, Jul 1997.

Oceanic: Atlantic Fleet naval control of shipping exercise. Participants include Argentina, Brazil, Chile, Ecuador, Paraguay, Peru, Uruguay, South Africa, and the US. Oceanic 98: Aug 1998. Active and reserve personnel were stationed at 75 naval ports in the western hemisphere and South Africa. Oceanic 98 established a new record with 69 merchant boardings and 409 reports. Oceanic XII-97: The exercise involved merchant ship routing, boarding, and tracking throughout a simulated crisis area in the Caribbean and South Atlantic.

ODANS: Sensitive compartmented information security advisory channel through Defense Special Security Communications System (DSSCS) called a DSSCS Address Group and used to disseminate special intelligence/Talent Keyhole sensitive compartmented information policy and guidance to special security offices.

Odette: UK maritime SIGINT/ESM equipment used in OEF/OIF.

Oilstock: NSA high-resolution Geographic Information System (GIS) plot record format that allows SIGINT track data to be viewed and manipulated in compatible formats with GIS industry standards. The system is used to store, track, and display near-real-time and historical intercept data over a map background.

Oilstone: Original air force code name for the U-2.

Olive: STRATCOM (and formerly SAC) first word for reconnaissance operations and other activities 1980s–present. Includes Olive Branch (radar bomb scoring practice low-level bombing routes), Olive Harvest (U-2 operations from RAF Akrotiri, Cyprus), and Olive Tree (U-2 operations and support).

Olympic: 1. Air force special access program.

2. **Olympic:** STRATCOM (and formerly SAC) first word for strategic forces and operations. Olympic programs associated with the U-2 have also been designated with the Olive and Senior first word since the 1960s. Includes Olympic Circle, Olympic Fire (Cuba), Olympic Game (North

Korea), Olympic Harvest, Olympic Jump, Olympic Race, Olympic Torch (Vietnam), and Olympic Winner.

+ **Olympic Aim:** Code changes associated with ICBM operations.

+ **Olympic Flare:** U-2 operations in support of Desert Shield and Desert Storm.

+ **Olympic Game:** On 25 May 1990, the 6903rd Expeditionary Strike Group and Detachment 2, 9th Strategic Reconnaissance Wing, flew U-2R Olympic Game mission sortie number 5,000.

+ **Olympic Play:** Monthly launch simulation that grades ICBMs in their ability to carry out their wartime nuclear missions. Test results supply the data used in developing the estimate of weapon system reliability that are, in turn, used in planning the SIOP. Olympic Play grades malfunctions or misconfigurations that could result in a "sortie" being incapable of successfully launching against its target.

+ **Olympic Shot:** Unclassified nickname used to notify NORAD and air traffic control facilities of airborne command post aircraft launches under emergency conditions.

Olympic Charlie: DOD, CIA, FBI, and Secret Service exercise held in preparation for the 1996 Summer Olympic Games in Atlanta, GA. It was the largest counter-terrorism exercise ever held in the US. The scenario involved the threat of a chemical weapons attack in the Atlanta subway.

Omar Response: FEMA–PACOM unknown JTF.

Omega: Air force special access program.

Omnibus: NSA program or system, 1980s.

One-Way: 16th Air Force annual two-week combat flying exercise at Zaragoza AB, Spain, and the nearby Bardenas range. One-Way 96: 28 Oct–19 Nov 1996. 555th and 510th FSs flew with F-18s and F-1s of the Spanish air force's 15th Wing. One-Way 95: 11 Oct–6 Nov 1995. 555th FS.

Ontario Water: Army intelligence offensive counter-intelligence operation (OFCO).

Onyx: BYEMAN code word for digital imaging and Synthetic Aperture Radar (SAR) reconnaissance satellite. Formerly LaCrosse/Vega.

Open Road: NATO SACLANT–sponsored PfP flag and senior officer operational seminar, Norfolk, VA. Participants include Switzerland. Open Road 04.

Open Road 03: Jan 2003. Open Road 02: Jan 2002. Open Road 99. Open Road 97.

Open Spirit: NATO Germany-hosted ISO/PfP mine counter-measures exercise and symposium. Participants include Estonia, Latvia, and Lithuania. Open Spirit 01: Sep 2001. Open Spirit 00: 5–21 Sep 2000. Open Spirit 99, planned for Aug 1999, was canceled when ships redeployed to NATO Standing Force (Mine Countermeasure Force North).

Opinion: Army Foreign Science and Technology Center foreign material exploitation, including Opinion Dirge, Opinion Monkey, and Opinion Wrench, all in the 1991–1992 time frame.

Optic: Army Foreign Science and Technology Center foreign material exploitation, including Optic Light, Optic Nerve, and Optic Star, all in the 1991–1992 time frame.

Optic Windmill (Joint Project Optic Windmill, JPOW): TMD exercise organized by the Netherlands air force, with EUCOM and NATO Supreme Headquarters Allied Powers Europe. Participants include Germany, the Netherlands, and the US. The first five JPOW exercises were held at De Peel AB, the Netherlands. JPOW VI: NAS Sigonella, Italy, Aug–Sep 2001. Optic Windmill 99: Mar 1999. The Alabama ARNG provided a Patriot missile cell as the only US contingent.

Optimal Focus 94: Department of the Army exercise designed to evaluate reserve unit ability to conduct home station mobilization tasks.

Opus: Coast Guard special operation, 20 May 1990.

Opus Willow: Army Foreign Science and Technology Center Type 1137C foreign material exploitation, 1993.

Oracle: UK "force integration training" involving naval forces, Mar–Apr 2002.

Orbit Comet: Chemical and biological weapons awareness seminar for senior- and executive-level officials. Orbit Comet 00: Fort Bragg, NC, and the communities of Spring Lake and Fayetteville, NC, 24–25 Oct 2000. The seminar considered the medical implications of a terrorist WMD attack on Fort Bragg and the impact on the XVIII Airborne Corps to sustain operations.

Ordeal Lancer (Project 932): Classified operation, 1 Mar 1985–present.

Ordinary Farm: Army Foreign Science and Technology Center foreign material exploitation, 1991.

Code Names

Ordway Grove: Army clandestine intelligence activity in Central America by the Cefirm Leader platform, 1980s, probably involving the Intelligence Support Activity (Gray Fox).

Orestes Bravo: Naval intelligence system or program.

Orient Classic: Imagery to support the ground force minefield breaching operation during Desert Storm.

Orient Express: 1. Army Foreign Science and Technology Center foreign material exploitation, 1991–1992.

    2. **Orient Express:** UK army series of Territorial Army battalion-sized exercises in Belgium. Two are held annually.

    3. **Orient Express:** US government plan to oust UN Secretary General Boutros-Ghali, 1996.

Orient Shield: US–Japan Army and Japanese Ground Self-Defense Force battalion-level field training exercise series. During odd-numbered years, Orient Shield is conducted as part of exercise Keen Sword. Orient Shield 99: Oct–Nov 1998.

Orion: SIGINT geostationary satellite, formerly Magnum. The Orion II satellite was code-named Trumpet. Name possibly changed to Omni.

Orlon Drum: Air force special operations foreign material exploitation or test, 1996.

Osprey: Navy (N89/N7SP) special access program first word.

OSSIZ: Sensitive compartmented information (SCI) security advisory channel through Defense Special Security Communications System (DSSCS) used to disseminate Bravo (BYEMAN) SCI policy and guidance to major command special security offices.

Osteal: Australian cyclical maritime surveillance operations in the Coral Sea.

Outboard: 1. Desert Storm intelligence system.

    2. **Outboard (Organizational Unit Tactical Baseline Operational Area Radio Detection):** Naval shipboard tactical signals exploitation and direction finding system. *See* Classic Outboard.

Outigui: US–Moroccan exercise, Sep 1985.

Outlaw: Office of Naval Research first word.

+ **Outlaw Bandit:** Command, control, and communications counter-measures signature reduction for surface ships, DDG-51 related.
+ **Outlaw Hawk:** Over-the-horizon target detection system installed on aircraft carriers.
+ **Outlaw Hunter:** P-3 avionics suite and over-the-horizon targeting enhancement prototype added to battle group support just prior to Desert Storm. Two Outlaw Hunter systems from VP-9 were used during Desert Storm.
+ **Outlaw Seahawk:** Radar evaluation special project conducted by Helicopter Anti-Submarine Sqn (Light) 49.
+ **Outlaw Shark:** Former over-the-horizon targeting system for Tomahawk using multi-source correlation techniques, terminated in 1980.
+ **Outlaw Viking:** S-3 modification program for integrated strike operations, tested in Joint Warfighter Interoperability Demonstration(JWID) 95.

Outlook: *See* Talon Outlook.

Outpost: Former Chief of Naval Operations (N09) first word.

Outrider: Tactical remotely piloted vehicle (RPV) development program in the late 1980s. The RPV became bogged down with proliferating require-ments from the army and navy, resulting in an expensive system that did not do any particular task well. It was canceled.

Overbid: Former Chief of Naval Operations (N3) first word.

Overtone: Former navy (N89/N7SP) special access program first word.

Overwatch: PACOM Advanced Concept Technology Demonstration to develop a system that helps detect, locate, and classify hostile artillery and missile firings and provides counter-fire targeting data, part of the Gunslinger project.

Owl: Non-communications Signals Exploitation System. *See also* Hawk, Phoenix, Raven, Merlin, and Mockingbird.

Oxen: Former Chief of Naval Operations (N87) first word.

Oxide/Ozone: Navy (N89/N7SP) special access program first words.

Pacer: Air Force Materiel Command (and former Air Force Logistics Command) code word involving a mind-boggling array of logistical-related terms, grouped as follows: Aerial refueling aircraft: Pacer Boom, Pacer Moss, Pacer Near, Pacer Quiet, Pacer Refuel, Pacer Rewire, Pacer Ridge, Pacer Tiara, Pacer Wire, Pacer Wizard. Aircraft engines: Pacer Activation, Pacer Assert, Pacer Case, Pacer Century, Pacer Core, Pacer Correct, Pacer Cruiser, Pacer Disc, Pacer Echo, Pacer Equal, Pacer Fleet, Pacer Growth, Pacer Handle, Pacer Health, Pacer Inspect, Pacer Move, Pacer Prove, Pacer Repair, Pacer Rhapsody, Pacer Rich, Pacer Savings, Pacer Squeeze, Pacer Transfer, Pacer Unique. Airlift aircraft: Pacer Arc, Pacer Air, Pacer Canal, Pacer Center, Pacer Dark, Pacer Deacon, Pacer Dixie, Pacer Doctor, Pacer Duke, Pacer Fatigue, Pacer Feathers, Pacer Gable, Pacer Hercules, Pacer Kitten, Pacer Lifter, Pacer Lock, Pacer Maintain, Pacer Out, Pacer Patch, Pacer Presto, Pacer Robot, Pacer Rock, Pacer Stinger, Pacer Wing. A-10: Pacer Controller, Pacer Convert, Pacer Fair, Pacer Kale, Pacer Kit, Pacer Pair, Pacer Palm, Pacer Panel, Pacer Pipe, Pacer Plus, Pacer Recall. Bombers: Pacer Action, Pacer Bat, Pacer Bee, Paper Boomerang, Pacer Buff, Pacer Light, Pacer Meter, Pacer Plank. C3, intelligence systems, and radar: Pacer Boost, Pacer Bounce, Pacer Execute, Pacer Four, Pacer Frontier, Pacer Joint, Pacer Link, Pacer Magic, Pacer Margin, Pacer Marsh, Pacer Mip, Pacer Progress, Pacer Provide, Pacer Recap, Pacer Sachem, Pacer Satellite, Pacer Scoop, Pacer Shot, Pacer Snow, Pacer Space, Pacer Speak, Pacer Stone, Pacer Strong, Pacer Summon, Pacer Surveillance, Pacer Turbo, Pacer Terminal. DEW line and other early warning radars: Pacer Alaska, Pacer Balance, Pacer Basin, Pacer Cap, Pacer Cedar III, Pacer Dew, Pacer Grab, Pacer Hall, Pacer Harmony, Pacer Mack, Pacer Provide III, Pacer Warning. F-15: Pacer Bake, Pacer Bayou, Pacer Corody, Pacer Fighter, Pacer Fly, Pacer Frost, Pacer Hay, Pacer Heath, Pacer Improve, Pacer Kaput, Pacer Modify, Pacer Pearl, Pacer Pecan, Pacer Pond, Pacer Probe, Pacer Retrograde, Pacer Role, Pacer Sacrament, Pacer Second, Pacer Site, Pacer Standard, Pacer Trainer, Pacer Vertical. F-16: Pacer Actuator, Pacer Adjust, Pacer Advocate, Pacer Aqua, Pacer Bird, Pacer Bond, Pacer Diode, Pacer Ferry, Pacer Flutter, Pacer Gem, Pacer Gyro, Pacer High, Pacer Loft, Pacer Mud, Pacer Oddity, Pacer Tiercel, Pacer Twin, Pacer Wedge. Foreign military sales: Pacer Agent, Pacer Escape, Pacer Sand. ICBMs: Pacer Blue, Pacer Cord, Pacer Peace, Pacer Safe, Pacer Seam. Munitions and missiles: Pacer Drop, Pacer Recoil, Pacer Shoot, Pacer Sparrow, Pacer Tamp, Pacer Widows, Pacer Winder. Special operations and rescue: Pace Adobe, Pacer

Bullet, Pacer Cagey, Pacer Chaser, Pacer Coin II, Pacer Durby, Pacer Enter, Pacer Gambler, Pacer Gas, Pacer Ghost, Pacer Glacier, Pacer Hawk, Pacer Hunt, Pacer Hurricane, Pacer Jolly, Pacer Learn, Pacer Petrol, Pacer Pueblo, Pacer Rescue, Pacer Salmon, Pacer Salt, Pacer Save, Pacer Sierra, Pacer Soc, Pacer Soffit, Pacer South, Pacer Spectre, Pacer Talon, Pacer Tomahawk. Training aircraft: Pacer Classic, Pacer Fad, Pacer Spur.

Pacer classified projects include Pacer Afford, Pacer Beam, Pacer Cape, Pacer Defense, Pacer Depth, Pacer Easy, Pacer Enlarger, Pacer Excite, Pacer Exploit, Pacer Ladder, Pacer Lane, Pacer Line, Pacer Log, Pacer Nine, Pacer Pack, Pacer Pebble, Pacer Point, Pacer Ray, Pacer Relent, Pacer Rib, Pacer Safari, Pacer Sight, Pacer Special, Pacer Spirit, Pacer Storm, and Pacer Vista.

+ **Pacer Bandit:** Support of counter-narcotics missions.
+ **Pacer Camel:** Merchant vessel Green Valley in support of CENTCOM.
+ **Pacer Chariot:** Support for Egyptian air force.
+ **Pacer Coin:** ANG C-130E/H IMINT aircraft, with all capabilities, supports SOF and counter-narcotics operations in the Western Hemisphere. The 152nd AW (ANG), Reno, NV, will replace two C-130H aircraft with two C-130E aircraft for a total of eight aircraft.
+ **Pacer Console:** Support for air force units operating at Incirlik AB, Turkey, for Provide Comfort.
+ **Pacer Crag:** KC-135 avionics (compass, radar, and GPS) overhaul project initially associated with Single Integrated Operations Plan (SIOP) alert duty, but now mandated for all air force KC-135s, meeting the congressionally mandated requirement to install GPS in all Defense Department aircraft. Pacer Crag aircraft were first deployed in 1999 in OAF.
+ **Pacer Forge:** Construction program for Egyptian air force.
+ **Pacer Goose:** The annual sealift resupply of Thule AB, Greenland.
+ **Pacer Griffin:** Support for Venezuelan F-5s.
+ **Pacer Lightning:** Communications and navigation program for the Egyptian Air force.
+ **Pacer Match:** Korea peninsula OPLAN 5027 munitions support.
+ **Pacer Mole:** Underground storage of nuclear weapons at Kirtland AFB, NM.
+ **Pacer North:** Airlift resupply of Greenland bases.
+ **Pacer Parts:** Support for Saudi Arabia aircraft engines.
+ **Pacer Reed:** Repair of a damaged C-130 for the Egyptian air force.
+ **Pacer Sentinel:** Support for Saudi Arabian E-3 AWACS aircraft.

+ **Pacer Ship:** Movement of assets to Israeli Aircraft Industries.
+ **Pacer Stable:** Tracking of nuclear weapons stored in Europe.
+ **Pacer Storage:** Storage of "frustrated explosive cargo" for Pakistan.
+ **Pacer Ware:** Serene Byte/Pacer Ware electronic warfare programming efforts to support exercises and real-world SOF activities.

Pacer One: Presidential support operations at Robins AFB, GA, during the Carter administration.

PACEX (Pacific Exercise): Pacific Fleet exercise series. PACEX 02. PACEX 89 was the largest peacetime naval exercise since World War II. Three aircraft carriers conducted operations in the Bering Sea, including operations inside the Aleutian Islands.

Pacific Bond: US–Australian army reserve exchange. Pacific Bond 02, Jul–Aug 2002.

Pacific Castle: Naval Pacific exercise.

Pacific Haven: Emergency evacuation of pro-US Kurds from northern Iraq to Anderson AFB, Guam, 15 Sep 1996–30 Apr 1997 (also called Quick Transit I). Beginning 16 Sep 1996, JTF Pacific Haven supplied shelter and care for 6,600 evacuees prior to their final relocation.

Pacific Horizon: WMD exercise using the new Consequence Assessment Tool Set (CATS), a Geographic Information System–based application providing map-based hazard display and analysis.

Pacific Kukri: UK–New Zealand exercise, 2000–2001.

Pacific Kukuri: Hawaii-based exercise, 2 Apr–7 May 2001, canceled by the US.

Pacific Look: US–Australian army reserve exchange, Jul–Aug 1997.

Pacific Nightingale: Pacific Air Force annual service-level aeromedical field training exercise, South Korea.

Pacific Protector: Proliferation Security Initiative (PSI) exercise held in international waters off northeastern Australia, 12–14 Sep 2003. The exercise was the first PSI exercise. Participants included Australia, France, Japan, and the US. Other PSI partners taking part as observers were Germany, Italy, the Netherlands, Poland, Portugal, Spain, and the UK. The scenario involved a Japanese-flagged merchant vessel suspected of carrying items related to WMD.

Pacific Reserve: US–Australian army reserve exchange. Pacific Reserve 03: Apr 2003. Pacific Reserve 02: Jul 2002. Pacific Reserve 97: Jul 1997.

Pacific Spectrum: PACOM one-day senior leadership tabletop seminar focusing on contingency planning in response to a cyber-warfare attack, 1999. Participants included the FBI, NSA, CIA, DIA, and Department of State. *See also* Saratoga Thunder.

Pacific Warrior 99: Space and Naval Warfare Systems Command telemedicine exercise connecting to US Forces Korea.

Pacific Wind: Desert Shield special operations plan to free American hostages being held in Kuwait, 1990.

Page One: Program for emergency relocation of key civilian officials, 1980s.

Palace: Air force first word nickname, including Palace Remote.

PALAH (Pang Lupa Alon Himpapawid—Sea Land and Air): US–Philippine semi-annual Seventh Fleet exercise focusing on small-unit tactics, marksmanship, and over-the-beach training. The exercise is conducted by Navy SEALs and the Philippine Navy Special Warfare Group (SWAG). A series of PALAH exercises was also held in the 1980s.

Pale Horse: Army Medical Department Center and School homeland security symposium and exercise, Fort Sam Houston, TX, 26–30 Aug 2002.

Pale Sky: Air Force Office of Special Investigations exercise.

Palladium: Canadian contribution to the NATO Stabilization Force (SFOR) in Bosnia–Herzegovina.

Pan II: Reagan-era exercise with NSC involvement, 23 Jan 1985.

Pangram: Former navy/NSA SIGINT compartment dealing with ocean surveillance.

Panther: Air force cyber-warfare first word.

+ **Panther Den:** Big Safari–managed air force information warfare program office, Hanscom AFB, MA. Panther Den provides program management of special access program information warfare projects, including Panther Den, Pirate Sword, and Steel Puma.
+ **Panther Leap:** Synthetic theater of war exercise related to Kestrel Phoenix, 2000.
+ **Panther Vision:** Big Safari–managed special access program.

Panther Cub: UK army infantry company group exercise series, Belize. Some seven Panther Cub deployments are held annually.

Paper Chase: Germany-based exercise. The 19–30 Jul 2001 exercise was canceled.

Paradise: 1. Australian–Papua New Guinea maritime surveillance training exercise, including Singapore. Paradise 02: Nov 2002. Paradise 97: Jul 1997. 2. **Paradise:** Air Force Electronic Systems Center exercise term, 1970s.

Parcae: Ocean surveillance satellite system that replaced White Cloud, launched in the early 1990s.

PARSEC/PARSEC II: Air force SIGINT analysis and reporting software.

Partner Challenge 00: First-ever trilateral National Guard exercise (GUARDEX) with Baltic militaries (Estonia, Latvia, and Lithuania) conducted by the Michigan NG, Camp Grayling, MI, Jun 2000. Partner Challenge 00 was a follow-up to Baltic Challenge.

Partnership Guard 98: US–Ukrainian special operations exercise conducted by the California NG, Ukraine, Aug 1998.

Paskal: US–Malaysian naval special operations exercise series with the Malaysian special "Paskal" unit, dating to the early 1980s.

Patch: Air force medical-related first word, including Patch Add, Patch Big, Patch Bite, Patch Collect, Patch Fixed, Patch Flight, Patch Great, Patch Huge, Patch Knife, Patch Little, Patch Long, Patch Medium, Patch Mod, Patch Move, Patch Noise, Patch Quick, Patch Reice, Patch Restore, Patch Safe, Patch Small, Patch Stage, Patch Type. Patch words associated with special operations include Patch Bare, Patch Dark, Patch Drop, and Patch Sneak.

+ **Patch Buggie:** War reserve biological/chemical defense materiel.
+ **Patch Control:** National emergency airborne command post.

Pathfinder: Army National Ground Intelligence Center (NGIC)–developed intelligence analyst tool designed to automate the labor-intensive management of digital intelligence data. Pathfinder provides the environment to integrate text, graphics, audio, video, and images. Pathfinder allows the analyst to index, search, visualize, sort, arrange, compare, group, match, and model large quantities of data. Pathfinder includes machine translation, format recognition and normalization, text extraction, text search and retrieval, tools for revealing relationships and links between data elements, visualization, plotting on maps, alerting features, annotation functions, and Web applications.

Patriot: Air force reserve aeromedical evacuation first word, including Patriot Dolphin, Patriot Medstar, Patriot Peach, and Patriot Samaritan.

Patriot Defender: Deployment of Patriot surface-to-air missiles to Israel during Desert Storm, 1991.

Patriot Excalibur: Air force special operations squadron-level, PC-based tool set to help aircrews conduct infiltration and exfiltration missions.

Patriot Thunder/Sentry Strike: Pacific Air Force–funded deployment of fighters to Hawaii in support of the 25th Infantry Division. Trainings are usually held three to four times a year.

Pave: Air force long-standing R&D first word that is applied to weapons and radar systems. Vietnam War–era names include Pave Aegis, Pave Arrow, Pave Claw, Pave Coin, Pave Gat, Pave Nail, Pave Onyx, Pave Pat III, Pave Phantom, Pave Pronto, and Pave Spectre. A number of Pave nicknames have to do with development of laser-guided bombs (Pave Knife, Pave Light, Pave Penny, Pave Spike, Pave Spot, Pave Storm, and Pave Tack) and drones and UAVs (Pave Cricket, Pave Deuce, Pave Eagle, and Pave Tiger).

+ **Pave Mover:** Joint Surveillance and Tracking System (JSTARS) development program.
+ **Pave Nickel:** Cold War RB-57F radar reconnaissance flights on the Warsaw Pact periphery.
+ **Pave Runner:** Former air force special access program.

Peace: Air force foreign military assistance first word. Use of the *Peace* first word goes back to at least Peace Wings, an exchange of the surviving Canadian F-101s for upgraded F-101B interceptors, 1970.

+ **Peace Alps:** F-5s to Switzerland.
+ **Peace Approach:** MPN-14 GCA radars to Taiwan.
+ **Peace Armangnac:** C-135Rs to France.
+ **Peace Atlantis:** F-16s to Portugal.
+ **Peace Atlas III:** Classified.
+ **Peace Bell:** F-5s to Yemen Arab Republic.
+ **Peace Bima-Sena:** F-16A/Bs to Indonesia, 1989–1990.
+ **Peace Bonito:** F-5s to Honduras.

+ **Peace Burgundy:** C-135s to France.
+ **Peace Caesar:** F-16s to Italy.
+ **Peace Carvin I/II/III:** F-16s and support to Singapore.
+ **Peace Chakri:** Military cooperation and assistance to Thailand.
+ **Peace Chellah:** F-16s to Morocco.
+ **Peace Corsair:** ALQ-131 pods to Portugal.
+ **Peace Crown:** F-16s to Bahrain. Under Peace Crown II, Bahrain was cleared to receive the AIM-120 air-to-air missile, the first gulf nation to be approved for foreign sales.
+ **Peace Cube:** Classified.
+ **Peace Delta:** F-16s to Venezuela.
+ **Peace Diamond:** F-4 Phantom IIs to Turkey.
+ **Peace Djem IV:** F-5Es to Turkey.
+ **Peace Dove:** AN/ALQ-131 ECM pods to Israel.
+ **Peace Eagle:** F-15s to Japan.
+ **Peace Echo:** RF-4E Phantom IIs to Israel.
+ **Peace Edge:** Installation of radars in Taiwan, 1998.
+ **Peace Falcon:** F-16s to Jordan.
+ **Peace Fenghuang:** F-16s to Taiwan.
+ **Peace Flame:** AIM-9 air-to-air missiles to Jordan.
+ **Peace Fox II/III/IV:** F-15s to Israel. Peace Fox II is F-15 support equipment. Peace Fox VI is F-15I program support.
+ **Peace Gate I/II/III/IV:** F-16A/Bs to Pakistan.
+ **Peace Guardian:** KC-135s to Singapore.
+ **Peace Haven:** Equipment support for the Berlin Air Route Traffic Control Centre (BARTCC), Germany.
+ **Peace Hawk:** RF-5Es to Saudi Arabia.
+ **Peace Icarus:** F-4Es to Greece.
+ **Peace Jack:** Development of the F-4 Phantom II, F-4E(S), intended as a reconnaissance aircraft for Israel.
+ **Peace Jolly:** HH-3 helicopters to ?.
+ **Peace Krypton:** Hawker 800XP Synthetic Aperture Radar (SAR) airborne intelligence system to South Korea.
+ **Peace Luxor:** ALQ 131 pods, likely to Egypt.
+ **Peace Marble:** F-16C/Ds to Israel. Peace Marble II is the follow-on sale.
+ **Peace Mate:** Classified.
+ **Peace Meadow:** Military cooperation and assistance to Thailand.
+ **Peace Menara:** T-38 trainer aircraft to Morocco.

+ **Peace Moon:** Classified.
+ **Peace Naresuan:** F-16C/Ds to Thailand.
+ **Peace Onyx:** F-16s to Turkey.
+ **Peace Pack:** Aircraft engines to Pakistan.
+ **Peace Panorama:** Air force command and control system to Colombia. Peace Panorama II, the upgraded surveillance system tied to US counter-narcotics radars, was delivered in Oct 2002.
+ **Peace Patch:** F-4Es to Israel.
+ **Peace Pearl:** Program to install Western electronics in the Chinese J-8B fighter, announced in Aug 1987. Technology transfers were terminated after the crackdown on pro-democracy protesters in Tiananmen Square in Jun 1989. China formally canceled participation in the program in 1990, citing technical difficulties, cost overruns, and a decline in US–Chinese relations.
+ **Peace Peek:** Installation of ELINT equipment in German Atlantic maritime patrol aircraft.
+ **Peace Pharaoh:** F-4 Phantom IIs to Egypt.
+ **Peace Pheasant:** F-4E Phantom IIs to South Korea.
+ **Peace Pioneer:** Hawker 800XP airborne intelligence (SIGINT/ELINT) system to South Korea.
+ **Peace Pulse:** AN/TPS-43E(V) radars to Saudi Arabia.
+ **Peace Puma:** F-16s to Chile.
+ **Peace Quiet:** Foreign military sales (FMS) Case SR-D-DGS.
+ **Peace Range:** AN/TPS-34 radars to Jordan.
+ **Peace Ranger:** KC-135s to Turkey.
+ **Peace Reed:** C-130s to Egypt.
+ **Peace Reef:** F-4E Phantom IIs to Australia.
+ **Peace Remo:** Turkey.
+ **Peace Sentinel:** E-3A AWACS and KE-3A to Saudi Arabia. Peace Sentinel VI is a Big Safari–managed special access program.
+ **Peace Shield:** Air defense and C4I high-speed network to Saudi Arabia. The program consists of 24 sites (1 command center, 5 sector command/operation centers, 17 radar/radio sites, and 1 C2 system support facility).
+ **Peace Spectator:** F-4D Phantom IIs to South Korea.
+ **Peace Stallion:** C-130s to Taiwan.
+ **Peace Station:** 707-3J9C tankers to Iran.
+ **Peace Sun:** F-15s and support to Saudi Arabia. Current program is Peace

Sun IX. The Peace Sun IX program is valued at approximately nine billion dollars, and is the largest air force FMS program. Originally established to support the acquisition and initial support of 72 F-15S aircraft, the Peace Sun Letter of Offer and Acceptance (LOA) has been amended or modified 14 times to broaden the program's scope.

+ **Peace Tornado:** Support of Tornado aircraft in Germany.
+ **Peace Trout:** Modification of a Luftwaffe RF-4E as electronic warfare aircraft.
+ **Peace Ultra:** Laser-guided bombs to Jordan.
+ **Peace Vang:** Classified.
+ **Peace Vector:** Sale of, and delivery of F-16s, built in Turkey, to Egypt.
+ **Peace Xenia:** F-16s to Greece.

Peaceful Bridge: NATO PfP peacekeeping exercise. Peaceful Bridge 98: Turkey, 29 Sep–5 Oct 1998. Participants included Georgia.

Peaceful Eagle: NATO PfP Southern Europe command post exercise series. Participants include Albania, Bulgaria, Greece, Italy, Macedonia, Romania, Slovenia, Turkey, and the US. Peaceful Eagle 99: Bulgaria. Peaceful Eagle 97: Larissa, Greece, and Sofia, Bulgaria. Peaceful Eagle 96: Rinas and Biza, Albania. Peaceful Eagle 96: Albania. This was the biggest exercise conducted in Albania to date as part of the PfP.

Peaceful Oriole 98: Search and rescue and medical evacuation command post exercise, Macedonia.

Peacekeeper: US–Russian exercise series. During Peacekeeper 95, Fort Riley, KS, 22 Oct–4 Nov 1995, Russian soldiers trained with American soldiers in the continental US for the first time. Peacekeeper 94: Totskoye, Russia. Four-day exercise with the 27th Guards Motorized Rifle Div.

Peaceshield: US–Ukrainian SETAF-led ISO/PfP brigade-level peacekeeping operations computer-assisted exercise/field training exercise, Yavoriv training area, approximately 37 miles northwest of L'Viv, Ukraine. The first Peaceshield took place in 1995, and it is now being combined with Cooperative Partner and Seabreeze. Participants include Azerbaijan, Belgium, Bulgaria, Belarus, Canada, Denmark, Estonia, Finland, Germany, Georgia, Greece, Italy, Kazakhstan, Latvia, Moldova, Norway, Poland, Romania, Russia, the Slovak Republic, Spain, Sweden, Turkey, Turkmenistan, and the UK. Peaceshield 05: Jun–Jul 2005. Peaceshield 04. Peaceshield 03: 10–25 Jul 2003. Peaceshield 01: Included a separate field training exercise to allow Polish certification of

Ukrainian soldiers for upcoming peacekeeping duties in Kosovo. Peaceshield 00: 8–22 Jul 2000. US–Ukrainian airborne insertion. The exercise included the first-ever use of distributed simulations and allowed participation from satellite training sites in Bulgaria and Estonia. Included the Illinois ARNG, the first time an NG unit was given responsibility for an exercise of this magnitude. Peaceshield 99: 1–14 Aug 1999. The California ARNG, Illinois ARNG, and Kansas ARNG all participated. Peaceshield 98. Peaceshield 97: California, 14–23 Nov 1997. Sponsored by the California ARNG.

Pearl: CIA classification compartment (for instance, Top Secret/Pearl) used for national-level intelligence findings and covert action.

Pecos Thunder: B-1B bomber and fighter air defense exercise.

Pegasus: DOD computer network detection mechanism that provides real-time alerting capabilities of system scans and intrusion attempts into military networks.

Penguin 97: Australian–Brunei maritime patrol and surveillance exercise. Penguin 02: Sep 2002. Penguin 97: Sep 1997.

Peninsula Falcon: Gulf Cooperation Council annual air training exercise. Peninsula Falcon 2: Ali al-Salem AB, Kuwait, Oct 1999.

Peninsula Shield: Gulf Cooperation Council (GCC) standing force and ongoing exercise program to protect Kuwait against external aggression. In Dec 2002, the GCC members agreed to increase the size of the standing force from 5,000 to 20,000, with a brigade of 6,500 stationed at Hafr al Batin in northern Saudi Arabia. The final anti-Iraqi Peninsula Shield deployment of GCC forces occurred in Feb 2003 when the UAE ship *Marrawah* (L81) off-loaded forces in Kuwait for possible future operations.

Peninsula Strike: TF Ironhorse operation to find Iraqi insurgents threatening coalition forces located on a peninsula along the Tigris River northeast of Balad, preceded Ivy Cyclone II, Jun 2003.

Penttbom: FBI investigation of the 9/11 attacks.

Perseous: Air force UAV assigned to SPACECOM (now STRATCOM), Sep 2000.

Pet Worth: US–UK program that involves observations of US flight trials identified to be of strategic importance to the UK, 1987–present.

PH: FEMA continuity of government compartment, initiated in 1983. *See also* ZH.

Phantom Menace: Pacific Ocean operation to locate and track a "real-world" submarine target, 1999.

Phantom Saber: Engineering and obstacle planning exercise series. Phantom Saber II: Fort Hood, TX, 1993. Phantom Saber: South Korea, 28 Jan–9 Feb 1996. 19th Theater Army Area Command, 13th Corps Support Command, and 416th Engineer Command.

Phazisi 2001: US–Georgian naval exercise, Black Sea near Poti and Kulevi, 8 Aug 2001. One US and six Georgian small craft practiced troop landings and other maneuvers. The exercise was led by Navy SEAL instructors.

Phoenix: Air Force Air Mobility Command (AMC) first word. Phoenix Eagle, Phoenix Hawk, and Phoenix Horizon are various career development programs. When operations, flight plans, and schedules are classified because of their association with the host nation and participating units, unclassified Phoenix nicknames are used to identify missions and programs belonging to AMC.

+ **Phoenix Ace:** Security forces exercise.
+ **Phoenix Alkali:** 349th Air Mobility Wing.
+ **Phoenix Allusion:** Fort Hood, TX, Aug 1995.
+ **Phoenix Ark:** Rhein-Main AB, Germany, operation.
+ **Phoenix Banner:** Airlift missions involving movement of the president.
+ **Phoenix Bunny:** McGuire AFB, NJ, mobility exercise, Apr 2000.
+ **Phoenix Castle:** Europe operation, 349th Air Mobility Wing.
+ **Phoenix Copper:** Airlift missions involving movement of the first lady.
+ **Phoenix Dagger:** Caribbean operation, 349th Air Mobility Wing.
+ **Phoenix Duke I/II:** Deployments of forces in preparation for OAF, primarily to Italy, 1998–1999. Phoenix Duke I involved the deployment of 150 tankers to locations in Europe to establish an air bridge, 11 Oct–Nov 1998. Phoenix Duke II again deployed 150 tankers on 18 Feb 1999.
+ **Phoenix Forge:** Aeromedical evacuation.
+ **Phoenix Gauntlet:** Operations in CENTCOM supporting OEF; involved 479 airlift sorties, Apr 2002–.
+ **Phoenix Jackal:** Contingency operation.
+ **Phoenix Jewel:** Single Integrated Operational Plan (SIOP) communca-

tions exercise designed to test generation and connectivity of aerial refueling assets.

+ **Phoenix Jomini:** Middle East operation, 349th Air Mobility Wing.
+ **Phoenix Moat:** 349th Air Mobility Wing.
+ **Phoenix Oasis:** Oman operation.
+ **Phoenix Onyx:** Somalia operation, 349th Air Mobility Wing.
+ **Phoenix Over:** Rhein-Main AB, Germany operation.
+ **Phoenix Pace:** Airlift of winter clothing and blankets to the Cheyenne River Sioux Indian Reservation at Eagle Butte, SD.
+ **Phoenix Partner:** Major USAFE exercise, Chievres AB, Belgium, 31 May–18 Jun 1994.
+ **Phoenix Perch:** Caribbean operation, 349th Air Mobility Wing.
+ **Phoenix Raven:** Air force anti-terrorism and security forces teams involved in base protection missions and operations at remote airfields and high-risk locations.
+ **Phoenix Readiness:** Travis AFB, CA.
+ **Phoenix Rook:** 349th Air Mobility Wing.
+ **Phoenix Sapphire:** Former Soviet Union operation, 349th Air Mobility Wing.
+ **Phoenix Scirocco:** Deployment of US forces to Jordan.
+ **Phoenix Scorpion I, II, III, IV:** Deployment of additional troops and equipment to Kuwait, Saudi Arabia, and the Arabian Gulf States in support of UN weapons inspectors and in response to threats from Saddam Hussein, Nov 1997–Dec 1998.
+ **Phoenix Shark:** Haiti operation, 349th Air Mobility Wing.
+ **Phoenix Silver:** Airlift missions involving movement of the vice president.
+ **Phoenix Stripe:** AMC open program.
+ **Phoenix Tent:** AMC exercise support.
+ **Phoenix Tusk:** Refugee relief effort in Rwanda and Zaire, 1996.

Phoenix: 1. Non-communications Signals Exploitation System. *See also* Hawk, Raven, Merlin, Owl, and Mockingbird.

2. **Phoenix:** South Florida counter-narcotics operations, 1996.

3. **Phoenix:** SAC SPECAT classification compartment (for instance, Secret/Phoenix) used for the strategic nuclear forces size review at the end of the Cold War, 1991–1992.

Phoenix Challenge: Air force and DOD initiative to identify state-of-the-art information warfare technologies, systems, and capabilities of industry and academia that could be leveraged and incorporated into current and future military systems. The 2002 Phoenix Challenge conference, scheduled 22–25 Apr, was the fifth in the series.

Phoenix Cooperative 98: First-ever US–French attack submarine exercise held in the Caribbean.

PI: Classified Advanced Concept Technology Demonstration, 2004.

Picket Fence: DOD classified intelligence initiative relating to the war on terrorism, 2004.

Piercer: SPECAT used for Grenada invasion, 1983.

Pilot Fish: Navy research, development, test, and evaluation program going back to the 1980s.

Pine Apple: UK–Kenyan exercise, 2000–2001.

Pine Cone: Classified "Technical Agreement" between the US and Belgium relating to the deployment of US nuclear weapons on Belgian soil.

Pine Ridge: Presidential continuity-of-government-related exercise series, 1980s–early 1990s.

Pinemartin: UK land-based SIGINT/electronic support measures equipment used in OEF/OIF.

Pinnacle: Submarine covert reconnaissance program, also known as Holystone.

Pinnacle: JCS-directed military-wide OPREP-3 report denoting an incident of potential national interest. A Pinnacle report is not restricted to operational information and covers a wide range of occurrences with actual or potential international repercussions or that could seriously change current operations.

+ **Pinnacle Broken Arrow:** Reports an accidental event involving nuclear weapons or nuclear components but does not create the risk of nuclear war.
+ **Pinnacle Empty Quiver:** Reports the seizure, theft, or loss of a nuclear weapon or nuclear component.
+ **Pinnacle Front Burner:** Reports any preconflict occurrence having the potential of escalating into a contingency or general war situation, such as armed attack on or harassment of US forces.
+ **Pinnacle Nucflash:** Reports actual or possible detonation of a nuclear weapon.

Pinnacle Exploit 95: III Marine Expeditionary Force (MEF) exercise, 1995.

Pinnacle Impact: JFCOM military transformation concept development exercise, formerly Olympic Challenge. Pinnacle Impact 04: 2–7 May 2004. Pinnacle Impact 03: Suffolk, VA, 12–21 May 2003. Pinnacle Impact used a detailed future scenario and involved some 110 players and 50 support personnel.

Pioneer: 1. White House Communications Agency post-9/11 project to modernize presidential communications infrastructure at 64 permanent "points of presence" and 10 temporary points of presence.

    2. **Pioneer:** Israeli UAV system based on DARPA's Praerie, procured in Dec 1985 for accelerated testing and subsequently deployed with the navy. The army fielded Pioneer in 1991 and flew nearly 300 reconnaissance sorties in Desert Storm.

Pirap Jabiru 02: Australian–Thai peacekeeping operations exercise, Sep 2002.

Pirate Sword: Panther Den special access program.

Pisces: Terrorist Interdiction Program (TIP) software, tailored to a country's specific needs. TIP provides border control and customs officials with information that allows them to identify and detain or track individuals of interest.

Pitch Black: US–Australian annual air combat training and air defense exercise, held in Australia. Participants include Australia, Singapore, the UK, and the US. Pitch Black 04: 19 Jul–10 Aug 2004. Pitch Black 02: Jul–Aug 2002. Pitch Black 97: Oct 1997. Pitch Black 96: Royal Australian Air Force Base Tindal, Australia, 13 Jul–3 Aug 1996.

PKO (Peacekeeping Operations) (Fuerzas Unidas Peacekeeping): SOUTH-COM exercise series in Central and South America. Ten nations participate in PKO South (including Argentina, Bolivia, Brazil, Chile, Colombia, Ecuador, Paraguay, Peru, and Venezuela) and 22 participate in PKO North (including Antigua and Barbuda, the Bahamas, Barbados, Belize, Dominica, the Domincan Republic, El Salvador, Grenada, Guatemala, Guyana, Honduras, Jamaica, Nicaragua, St. Kitts and Nevis, St. Lucia, St. Vincent and the Grenadines, Suriname, and Trinidad and Tobago).

   + **PKO North:** PKO North 04: Guatemala. PKO North 02: El Salvador, 18–28 Jun 2002. PKO North 01: Barbados, 27–31 Aug 2001. PKO North 99: Jamaica, 24–27 Aug 1999. PKO Guatemala, 1–16 May 1998.

+ **PKO South:** PKO South 04: Paraguay. PKO South 02: Uruguay, 6–10 May 2002. PKO South 01: Ecuador, 18–29 Jun 2001. PKO South 00: Chile, 26–30 Jun 2000. PKO South 99: Bolivia, 18–28 May 1999. PKO Bolivia, 2–6 Nov 1998. PKO Paraguay, 20–25 Apr and 10–25 Jul 1998.

Planet X: Army 4th Infantry Div operation in ad Dawr (Dour), Iraq, near Tikrit, which yielded the capture of an unidentified figure of the "top 55" list, May 2003.

PLANEX 96: NATO PfP emergency preparedness exercise, Ukraine. The exercise included emergency management personnel from Poland, Hungary, and Slovakia and the NG partner of each country. The exercise simulated a disaster in the western region of Ukraine of such a magnitude that Ukraine asked for assistance from other countries in the region.

Platform: Data connection between naval research and development organizations and NSA.

Platinum Rail: CIA laboratory established in 1999 to evaluate and better understand the functionality and interoperability of commercial collaborative tools to enhance the ability of analysts to share and produce better intelligence.

Platinum Wrench: Army reserve operation at Fort McCoy, WI, 13 May–8 Sep 1999.

Platypus: Army National Ground Intelligence Center (NGIC) national system secure server proof of concept.

Platypus Moon: Australian special operations submarine and swimmer exercise, canceled in 2002.

Plural Hemp: Air force special operation development program involving the 18th Flight Test Sqn.

Pointed Arrow: Army air defense exercise, Fort Bliss, TX, Oct 2002. The purpose of the exercise was to practice command and control of the theater air defenses for OIF.

Poise Talon: Classified special operation, 1995–present.

Poised Eagle: US–Tunisian combined JTF air exercise. Poised Eagle 95: Spain, Apr 1995. Poised Eagle 94: Tunisia.

Poker Buff I: Clandestine air force radar and SIGINT station deployed in the mountains near Tegucigalpa, Honduras, 1980s.

Polar Harpoon: 4th Bn, 31st Regt, 10th Mountain Div operation in Afghanistan during Anaconda, 2002.

Polar Moon: Classified special operation, 1995–present.

POLEX: Army FORSCOM quartermaster field training exercise.

Polo Hat: Worldwide nuclear C3 system operational assessment that evaluates the flow of information among sensors, command centers, and nuclear forces under conditions of a simulated nuclear war. Polo Hat assessments are run quarterly by STRATCOM and the JCS and test communications connectivity from the president and the secretary of defense, through the National Military Command System (including the Pentagon and Site R), to nuclear forces.

Polo Step: JCS "alternative or compensatory control measure" compartment for mid-1990s planning to undertake strikes in response to Iraqi provocations or terrorist incidents, including intelligence collection, targeting and offensive operations. The White House directed the military to keep a cruise missile capable submarine in the Arabian Sea, with the ability to undertake a quick reaction strike against Usama bin Laden. Polo Step then became the compartment used for Afghanistan planning after 9/11, and for national-level Iraq war planning in anticipation of OIF.

Pomelo: Australian contributions to UN peacekeeping efforts in Ethiopia/Eritrea, 2001–present.

Pond Jump West: UK–Canadian army infantry battle group training exercise series. Three are held annually. The Jul–Aug 2000 exercise was canceled due to operational commitments in Kosovo.

Ponte Vecchio: Italy-hosted joint NBC regiment exercise, canceled in 2002.

Pony Express: RC-135 reconnaissance and sampling missions collecting information about ballistic missile testing. Pony Express missions were flown to monitor Iranian missile activity during 2001. Pony Express operations guidance is provided by the DIA Central MASINT Office.

Poopdeck: Reagan-era exercise with NSC involvement.

Poor Debtor: Air force special operations exercise, Dec 1985.

Pop Fly: 16th Air Force Support Plan.

Poplar Tree: SOUTHCOM contingency plan for evacuation from El Salvador, 1989.

Poppy: Former SIGINT satellite.

Popular Forest: Army Intelligence Support Activity (Gray Fox) exercise, 1986–1987.

Port Call: Reagan-era command post exercise testing crisis management procedures, with NSC involvement.

Portal: 1. Open-source intelligence (OSINT) processor.
    2. **Portal:** Air Force National Air Intelligence Center foreign documents and translations database (being incorporated into Harmony).

Porthole: Navy SIGINT system.

Portico: Defense Counter-intelligence Information System (DCIIS) Investigative Information Management System used to standardize the collection, storage, and dissemination of investigative, intelligence, and operational reports, as well as source information, analysis, and production. Created by the Air Force Office of Special Investigations after 9/11, Portico is used by all US government agencies.

Poseidon 95: US–Romanian Sixth Fleet naval exercise, Constanta, Romania, Sep 1995.

Positive: Chairman, JCS worldwide national exercise series first word.

+ **Positive Deployment 95:** Exercise canceled.
+ **Positive Force:** Large-scale annual national command post exercise series, the highest priority of the JCS exercise program. The exercise focuses on DOD's ability to conduct large-scale military operations and to coordinate with the National Command Authorities (NCA), civil agencies (FEMA, Commerce, Homeland Security, Justice, and State), combatant commands, services, and defense agencies. The exercises normally last 7–15 days. The scenarios normally build from an ambiguous threat through surge and expanding industrial production. They are designed to evaluate deployment of US forces to a major theater war, noncombatant evacuation operation, relocation and continuity of operations for the Joint Staff, and support of a simultaneous small-scale contingency. Positive Force 04. Positive Force 03: Scheduled for

18–27 Mar 2003. Positive Force 01: 17–26 Apr 2001. Largest computer network defense exercise to date. Positive Force 98/99 — PF 98 (Mobilization) and PF 99 (Deployment): Oct 1997. This was the first command post exercise to test mobilization since 1989. Positive Force 97: Canceled. Positive Force 96: Postponed until FY 1997 due to real-world deployments to Southwest Asia in Oct 1996.

+ **Positive Leap 80:** First command post exercise of the Rapid Deployment JTF, Fort Bragg, NC, 10–15 Apr 1980.

+ **Positive Response:** Large scale No-notice Interoperability Exercises (NIEX) mini command post exercise linked to, and in preparation for, the Positive Force exercise. Positive Response normally considers strategic-level issues, including command and control of nuclear forces, test of backup national command and control, and continuity of government. Normally, three to five Positive Response exercises are conducted each year, lasting one to five days. Positive Response 04. Positive Response 03-3: National Strategic Gaming Center, Washington, DC, 16 Jul 2003. The interagency "strategic communication" exercise examined US government public relations and media performance during the war in Iraq. Positive Response 01: Two-part tabletop exercise that examined issues associated with noncombatant evacuation operation, foreign humanitarian assistance, and presidential reserve call-up authority. Phase 1, 3–5 Oct 2001 at the Marine Corps University, Quantico, VA. Phase 2, 12–15 Dec 2001, at the Army War College, Carlisle Barracks, PA. Positive Response Y2K-4 (PRY2K-4): 30 Aug–3 Sep 1999. The exercise was designed to test sustainment given a failure of mission-critical systems. Positive Response Y2K-2 (PRY2K-2): 3–7 May 1999. First national-level exercise conducted under the threat of multiple Y2K systems failures.

Potent: Coast Guard special operations first word, including Potent Archer (17–25 Aug 1988) and Potent Fencer (22–26 Aug 1987).

Potomac Sunrise: National Defense University strategy formulation exercise held for the reserve component National Security Course, Washington, DC, Jul 2000.

Powderblue: NSA program, 1980s.

Powder River 85: Reagan-era exercise with NSC involvement, 15–26 Oct 1984.

Power Drive: UK exercise in Gibraltar, canceled Nov 2002.

Power Hunter: USAFE intelligence network project, initiated Dec 1987.

Power Sweep 87: Reagan-era exercise with NSC involvement.

Powerful Gaze: Army Intelligence Support Activity (Gray Fox) exercise, 1986–1987.

Praerie: DARPA-developed mini remotely powered vehicle (RPV) program, canceled with the end of the Vietnam War.

Praetorian Guard: STRATCOM annual series of JCS-directed nuclear weapons "battle staff" fixed command center performance assessments to practice nuclear attack and response procedures. *See also* Crystal.

Prairie: Former naval intelligence first word, including Prairie Schooner (a submarine surveillance operation in the 1980s) and Prairie Wagon (a navy SIGINT program).

Prairie Dog: 1. Robot developed at the Air Force Research Laboratory Robotics Lab, Tyndall AFB, FL.
  2. **Prairie Dog/Prairie Dog II:** UAV deployment in support of a navy TENCAP experiment, MCAS Camp Pendleton, CA, 4–28 Jun 2001.

Prairie Fire: Libya operation, Mar 1986. Three aircraft carriers — USS *America* (CV 66), USS *Saratoga* (CV 60), and USS *Coral Sea* (CV 43) — entered the Gulf of Sidra, launching aircraft toward the Libyan coast, where they were fired on by Libyan SA-5 missiles. Navy A-7 aircraft fired anti-radiation missiles at the Libyan SAM site, which ceased operations. Two Libyan patrol boats were destroyed and one was damaged as they approached US ships.

Prairie Vigilance: Minot AFB, ND, local nuclear bomber generation exercise series. Prairie Vigilance 97-1: 31 Mar–7 Apr 1997. Prairie Vigilance 95-3: 13–15 Jul 1995. Prairie Vigilance 95-3: 26–30 Jun 1995. Nuclear weapons loading and mating included two nine-megaton B53 bombs. Prairie Vigilance 95-2: 17–21 Jan 1995.

Prairie Warrior: Advanced Warfighting Experiment (AWE), culminating the academic year at the Army Command and General Staff College (CGSC), Fort Leavenworth, KS, and held in May of each year. Prairie Warrior began in 1989. PW 93, based on a Southwest Asia scenario, was the largest in the series. More than 1,100 US and international students participated, and participants included France and the UK. PW 94 (May 1994) was a significant change, elevating above corps to incorporate the army's overall General Headquarters Exercise (GHQx). PW 95 (May 1995) became one of the first AWEs to evaluate military transformation. The scenario was Northeast Asia and included South Korea. PW 96 (May 1996) used a complex Joint Training Confederation linking 25 models, and included the air force and navy. Prairie Warrior exercises through PW 02 incorporated larger numbers of interconnected models.

Prayer Book: Set of CONPLANs for possible military operations in Panama, 1988.

Praying Mantis: Arabian Gulf "measured retaliatory response" operation, 18–19 Apr 1988, undertaken after the USS *Samuel B. Roberts* (FFG 58) struck an Iranian mine in the Arabian Gulf, 14 Apr 1988. US surface action groups destroyed two Iranian oil platforms and severely damaged two Iranian frigates and a missile patrol boat. Two A-6 aircraft from the USS *Enterprise* (CVN 65) sank a Swedish-built Boghammer speedboat and neutralized four more Iranian craft in the Mubarak oil field. US losses consisted of one AH-1T Sea Cobra.

Predator: RQ-1/MQ-1 UAV, Tier II under development, successfully employed by the air force in Bosnia and Kosovo operations, in surveilling Iraq as part of the no fly zone operations, and then procured by the CIA for operations over Afghanistan. In Sep–Oct 2000, CIA Predators operated from Uzbekistan while conducting surveillance of al Qaeda. The Predator was armed with the Hellfire missile, and was first employed in armed configuration after 9/11. CIA and air force Predators deployed to Shabbaz air base, Pakistan, during OEF.

Predominant Challenge: JCS war gaming exercise, 27–28 Jan 2003, to practice upcoming operations for OIF. *See also* Prominent Hammer.

Premier Gunner 96: Artillery field firing exercise involving Australia and New Zealand, Jul 1996.

Premier Link: Germany-based exercise, 19 Mar–1 Apr 2001. The UK canceled participation due to foot-and-mouth disease restrictions.

Premier Task 85: Reagan-era exercise with NSC involvement, 6–7 Feb 1985.

Present Arms 86: JCS national-level command post exercise evaluating selected Worldwide Military Command and Control System procedures and components, 1986.

Present Heaven: Marine Corps migrant operations at Guantanamo Bay, Cuba, Feb 1997.

Pressure Point 84: Reagan-era NSC exercise, 1984.

Prime Beef: Air Force Base Engineer Emergency Force (BEEF).

Prime Chance: Anti-Iranian operation initiated to protect ships passing through the Arabian Gulf, 1987–1989. The rmy's 160th SOAR conducted sustained nighttime helicopter strikes, operatng 30 feet above the water, using night vision goggles, engaging Iranian small boats.

Prime Directive: JCS national-level nuclear C3 exercise. Prime Directive 93 was canceled. Prime Directive 92.

Primed Pump: Special operation, Mediterranean Sea, 1987.

Principal (UK Atomic Principal): UK Secret or Top Secret information equivalent to Secret RD/FRD Sigma 1 and 2 or Critical Nuclear Weapon Design Information and dealing with the theory of operation and the internal design of a nuclear warhead and its unique components.

Prism: Former Air Force Electronics Security Command first word. In Feb 1991, Prism partially replaced Comfy.

Privateer: Navy special operations intelligence program, part of an evolutionary SIGINT system that provides a radar and communications early warning capability aboard *Cyclone*-class Patrol Craft and MK V special operations craft. Also known as the Mark V Patrol Coastal Threat Warning System.

Procomm: Special-access-required communications system used to transmit compartmented messages associated with special operations and military deception programs.

Proforma: Digital machine-to-machine unenciphered information that is tactically exploitable.

Project:
+ **Project 9A:** Former operations of the air force office of "special plans."
+ **Project 9GH:** PACOM counter-terrorism operations in a classified country (probably the Philippines), initiated 14 Jan 2002.
+ **Project 9GI/GK:** EUCOM counter-terrorism operations in two classified countries, initiated 13 Dec 2002.
+ **Project 19:** PACOM special access program war planning possibly associated with defending Taiwan.

+ **Project 33:** Former operations of the air force office of "special plans."
+ **Project 46:** SOCOM classified program, 1991–present.
+ **Project 101:** Air force (AF/XOXP) classified project.
+ **Project 341:** Air force special operations classified program support.
+ **Project 445:** Air Force Materiel Command classified project.
+ **Project 643:** Army special access program, 1996–present.
+ **Project 698AJ:** Air force classified project.
+ **Project 999:** Operations of the Air Force office of "special plans."
+ **Project 6404:** SOCOM counter-narcotics operation.
+ **Project 6415:** SOCOM counter-narcotics operation.
+ **Project 8407:** Operations of the air force office of "special plans."
+ **Project 9000:** Space-related special access program?
+ **Project 12108:** SOCOM operation.
+ **Project 24428:** SOCOM operation.
+ **Project 42134:** SOCOM tactical intelligence project.
+ **Project 42135:** SOCOM operation.
+ **Project 42562:** SOCOM operation.
+ **Project 47119:** SOCOM operation.
+ **Project 50348:** SOCOM operation.
+ **Project 53520:** SOCOM operation.
+ **Project 53527:** SOCOM operation.
+ **Project AII:** Air force operations (XOXP) classified project.

Prometheus: NATO southern region ISO/PfP exercise, held in Greece. Prometheus 99: Polykastro, Kilkis region, Greece, 12–22 Jun 1999. Participants included Albania, Bulgaria, Italy, the Netherlands, and Romania, with Turkey participating with staff officers only. Prometheus 98: Northern Greece, Jun 1998. Armenia participated. Prometheus 97: Kilkis region, Greece, 17–22 Nov 1997.

Prominent Hammer I: JCS exercise series to evaluate US global commitments in the war on terrorism and contingency planning for a prospective war with Iraq. Prominent Hammer I, Fort Belvoir, VA, 12–13 Mar 2002, was the first exercise of the Bush administration to formally include planning for potential war with Iraq. Prominent Hammer II, held 25–26 Sep 2002, included Australia and UK planners and forces, and incorporated new guidance from Secretary Rumsfeld and the White House.

Promise Kept: Special operation, 1995–present.

Promote Liberty: SOUTHCOM pacification operation in Panama after the completion of Just Cause, commencing 14 Jan 1990.

Prompt Response: JCS national-level Washington, DC, area mini command post exercise.

Proper Lady: Pacific Air Force "special plans" project, based in Hawaii, 1980s.

Prophet: 1. Army division-level SIGINT/EW suite, initiated in 2001. The High Mobility Multipurpose Wheeled Vehicle–based system is connected to helicopter and UAV extensions.

2. **Prophet/Cassandra:** Special operations SIGINT and DF system. The information warfare exploitation program is managed by Navy Space and Naval Warfare Systems Command.

Proteus: Collaborative effort of the Army Intelligence and Threat Analysis Center and the national Intelligence Community.

Proud: JCS national exercise series, 1980s, including Proud Eagle 89, Proud Saber 83, Proud Scout 88, Proud Saber/Rex-80 Bravo, and Proud Spirit 80.

Proud Flame: Intelligence assessment.

Proud Shield: Air Combat Command competition suspended in 1990.

Proven Force: Desert Storm "northern front" TF operating from Incirlik AB, Turkey, and other Turkish air bases, 17 Jan–28 Feb 1991.

Provide: EUCOM humanitarian intervention and assistance operations first word.

+ **Provide Assistance:** Zaire and Rwanda, 1994.
+ **Provide Comfort:** Kurdish assistance in northern Iraq under UN Security Council Resolution 688. JTF/CTF Provide Comfort formed and deployed to Incirlik AB, Turkey, after Desert Storm, 5 Apr–24 Jul 1991. By the end of the operation, the TF had delivered more than 17,000 tons of supplies to some 1.5 million refugees.
+ **Provide Comfort II:** Show of force to deter further Iraqi attacks on Iraqi Kurds, 24 Jul 1991–31 Dec 1996. The operation had only limited humanitarian objectives. US aircraft flew more than 42,000 fixed-wing sorties; the coalition flew nearly 62,000 fixed- and rotary-wing sorties. A USAFE F-16 shot down an Iraqi MiG-23 on 17 Jan 1993. Provide Comfort II was replaced by Northern Watch on 1 Jan 1997.

+ **Provide Hope I:** 10–26 Feb1992. Sixty-five C-5 and C-141 missions flew 2,363 tons of food and medical supplies to 24 locations in the former Soviet Union.

+ **Provide Hope II:** 15 Apr–29 Jul 1992. Transport shipment of excess food stocks from Europe to 33 cities in the former Soviet Union. Airlift missions began on 24 Apr where surface transportation was impractical (Minsk, for example).

+ **Provide Hope III:** 10 Jan–30 Apr 1994. USAFE mission to ship and install hospital equipment at Minsk, Belarus. Medical technicians from the 608th Contingency Hospital, RAF Upwood, UK, conducted the site survey, packed and shipped the materiel, installed the equipment, and provided technical training and assistance.

+ **Provide Hope IV:** 1 Jul–31 Aug 1994. Medical mission to deliver and install equipment and supplies in Chisenau and Beltsi, Moldova.

+ **Provide Hope V:** Airlift of hospital equipment to Kazakhstan, 15 Oct–19 Dec 1994. Technicians installed $12.5 million of supplies and equipment (equivalent to an 800-bed field hospital) in six medical facilities at Almaty.

+ **Provide Promise:** Bosnia relief following the disintegration of Yugoslavia, 3 Jul 1992–9 Jan 1996. USS *Dwight D. Eisenhower* (CVN 69) and USS *Theodore Roosevelt* (CVN 71). USAFE flew as many as six C-130 relief sorties per day from Rhein-Main AB, Germany, to Sarajevo. By the end of the operation, aircraft from 21 countries had flown 12,886 sorties into Sarajevo. The US performed 2,222 C-130 air drops.

+ **Provide Refuge:** Effort to airlift as many as 20,000 Kosovo refugees to safety in the US, 1999. The refugees arrived at Fort Dix, NJ where they stayed for about three weeks to complete legal processing before being placed with host families.

+ **Provide Relief:** Relief to Somalia and Somali refugees in northeastern Kenya, 14 Aug–7 Dec 1992. By the end of 1992, C-130 aircraft had flown 1,699 missions. The 2nd Bn, 5th SFG deployed to Kenya to provide security.

+ **Provide Transition:** Angolian demobilized soldier repatriation relief and support for Angolian national elections, 12 Aug–9 Oct 1992. Three C-130s deployed from Rhein-Main AB, Germany, to Luanda. The aircraft relocated government and rebel soldiers following 16 years of civil war in Angola.

Code Names

Provide Cover: ARCENT Saudi Arabia command and control network for the Patriot air defense artillery TF deployed in Kuwait and Saudi Arabia, 1996–2003.

Provide Relief: 1. Humanitarian operations in Kwajalein Atoll, 1993.

2. **Provide Relief:** Operation to rescue 525 Chinese nationals attempting to enter the US illegally on the ship *Eastwood*, 5 Feb 1993–6 Mar 1993.

Prowler: 1. Reported national stealth reconnaissance satellite. *See also* Misty.

2. **Prowler:** Australian domestic land surveillance and the collection of military geographic information.

Ptarmigan: UK 45 Commando Group OEF operation to clear a high valley in the Afghan mountains believed to have been occupied by al Qaeda and Taliban forces, 16–18 Apr 2002.

PUMA (Previously Unexploited MASINT Applications): Air force TENCAP program that exploits National Reconnaissance Office Synthetic Aperture Radar (SAR) data to detect moving ground targets.

Purple: 1. Air Mobility Command (and formerly Military Airlift Command) first word, since at least the 1970s.

2. **Purple:** UK Joint Force HQ annual exercise series (for instance, Purple Sound at Kinloss in 1998).

Purple Caduceus 00: Joint medical evacuation operations exercise, a component of Roving Sands, Camp Lejeune, NC, 13–25 Jun 2000. Participants included Canada.

Purple Dragon: Joint forced entry operations. Purple Dragon 00/Roving Sands 00: Fort Bragg, NC, and Puerto Rico, 2000. Exercise focused on emerging Third World threats with WMD capabilities and the conduct of near-simultaneous forceable entry operations (airborne, air assault, and amphibious). Purple Dragon 98/JTFEX 98-1: Fort Bragg, NC, Puerto Rico, and other locations in the eastern US, Jan–Feb 1998. Second largest airborne operation since World War II. The country of "Korona" invaded the pro-Western country of "Bragg Island," which dominated the air, land, and sea lines of communication. The invasion of Bragg Island was an indirect approach to distract attention from moves toward the disputed territory of "Khemis Province" on the borders of the pro-Western country of "Kartuna." Meanwhile, an insurgency was taking place in the pro-Western and poor island country of "Keeneland" (Vieques, Puerto Rico). Bragg Island asked for American assistance to defeat the occupying force.

Purple Flex I/II/III/Purple Flex Lite II: Sixth Fleet post-9/11 noncompliant maritime intercept operation in the Mediterranean Sea. Purple Flex Lite II: Dec 2003. *See also* Razor Sharp.

Purple Star: US–UK combined field training exercise. Purple Star 99/Neon Falcon: Bahrain, 1999. Purple Star 96: North Carolina and eastern seaboard of the US, 25 Apr–May 1996. The exercise involved a force of 45,000 US and 12,000 UK soldiers, the largest deployment of US and UK forces since Desert Storm. The scenario involved a CJTF deployed to provide assistance to a fictitious country invaded by a neighboring aggressor, and was the first test of the UK Permanent Joint Headquarters (PJHQ).

Purple Storm: Rehearsal conducted by US Army South (USARSO) to assert treaty rights and conduct tactical rehearsals for Just Cause, Panama, 1989.

Purple Strike: UK–Falklands exercise, 2000–2001.

— Q —

Quadrant Search: Army–CIA project to acquire and operate a clandestine vessel for mounting covert operations against Nicaragua, 1983–.

Quasar Talent: CIA (army?) Seaspray clandestine air unit.

Queen's Hunter: Army Intelligence Support Activity (Gray Fox) and CIA Seaspray Central America operation to monitor movements of Sandinista forces and Contra activities in El Salvador, Honduras, and Nicaragua, early 1980s.

Quick: EUCOM noncombatant evacuation operation (NEO) first word.

+ **Quick Lift:** NEO from Zaire (now Democratic Republic of Congo), 24 Sep–7 Oct 1991. A EUCOM JTF deployed French and Belgian troops to Zaire and evacuated 716 people following a mutiny by unpaid army troops.
+ **Quick Response:** NEO from the Central African Republic, 20 May– 22 Jun 1996, including the USS *Guam* (LPH 9) ARG.
+ **Quick Transit:** NEO of some 6,600 pro-US Kurds from northern Iraq to Guam (nicknamed Pacific Haven). Quick Transit III: 4–16 Dec 1996. Quick Transit II: 21–22 Oct 1996. Quick Transit I: 15–19 Sep 1996.

Quick Bolt: DOD Advanced Concept Technology Demonstration to develop technologies and methods in SIGINT to collect "short dwell" and "hard to get at" signals, started in 2001.

Quick Draw: 1. Air Intelligence Agency (AIA) information operations center (IOC) initiative, begun in 2000. The 9/11 terrorist attacks accelerated development efforts to establish an IOC for AIA similar to the Combined Air Operations Center. The IOC was completed several months ahead of schedule, and its first real-world operation took place during OEF.

2. **Quick Draw/Quickdraw:** Amphibious withdrawal of US forces from Somalia, 1994.

3. **Quick Draw 96-1:** Air Combat Command operation, Tyndall AFB, FL, 11–21 Nov 1995. The 27th FS deployed eight F-15s and 102 personnel to the Weapons System Evaluation Program.

Quick Fix: Army heliborne SIGINT and electronic warfare jamming system originally mounted on an EH-1 helicopter and introduced in 1979. Quick Fix II is an HF/VHF intercept and jammer, and a DF VHF interceptor mounted on an EH-60A; it was introduced in 1986.

Quick Force: 1. Air Combat Command 9th Air Force deployments to the western US for training, 1980s–1990s.

2. **Quick Force:** JFCOM movement exercise.

Quick Lift: Movement of UN Rapid Reaction Deployment Force to Croatia, 30 Jun 1995–11 Aug 1995. The MV *Cape Race* and MV *Cape Diamond* provided transport. In Jul, the air force airlifted 190 UK troops and cargo from RAF Brize Norton, UK, to Split, Croatia.

Quick Look: Army airborne ELINT platform, originally based on the OV-1 Mohawk and upgraded to the RV-1C/D aircraft. The last Quick Look was retired in 1996.

Quick Thrust: Air force special operations exercise, Apr–May 1985.

Quicksand: UK Middle East exercise, Apr 1993.

Quicksilver: Army intelligence system, Bad Aibling, Germany.

Quidditch: Army intelligence system, Bad Aibling, Germany.

Quiet Falcon: Clandestine airborne SIGINT operations, 1980s.

Quiet Knight: Air Force special operations helicopter threat detection/avoidance analysis system (SACM/MSIS++) that provides the means for covert ingress/egress of SOF by airborne insertion and extraction. The system includes the Constant Source Data Sub-system and access to TDDS, TOPS, and TIBS broadcasts.

Quiz Icing: Army Intelligence Support Activity (Gray Fox) exercise, 1986–1987.

— R —

Rabbit: Chief of Naval Operations (N2) first word.

Radiant: Navy TENCAP first word. Radiant Beryllium, Radiant Breeze, Radiant Crimson, Radiant Crystal, Radiant Frost, Radiant Pine, Radiant Thunder, and Radiant White are all classified TENCAP programs and experiments.

+ **Radiant Cirrus:** Transmission of imagery to ships using S-band weather antennas. Radiant Cirrus II was an operation demonstration during Tandem Thrust 92 to send images to USS *Coronado* (AGF 11). Radiant Cirrus III and IV in the Mediterranean supported Bosnia operations.
+ **Radiant Clear:** Minefield detection using national technical means.
+ **Radiant Coal/Town Crier:** Classified, 1995.
+ **Radiant Copper:** Navy Cryptologic Research Laboratory experiment, NAS Fallon, NV, 10-24 Sep 1999.
+ **Radiant Diamond.** NAWC classified experiment.
+ **Radiant Elm:** Demonstration associated with strike missile planning.
+ **Radiant Gold:** Demonstration associated with theater ballistic missile defense.
+ **Radiant Hail:** Deployable tactical information receiver in used in support of the 2nd Marine Aircraft Wing.
+ **Radiant Ivory:** Tactical detection and reporting system based on national satellites, projected for 2008.
+ **Radiant Jade:** Near-real-time Electronic Order of Battle updates to operational users via Joint Electronic Analysis Program (JEAP) and Sunshine systems. Radiant Jade I proved the concept in the Pacific area (seven sites); Radiant Jade II included the USS *Abraham Lincoln* (CVN 72); Radiant Jade III installed the capability to serve more than 20 users in Europe, Asia, and the US.
+ **Radiant Mercury:** First fully automated sanitization and downgrading system certified for use with formated intelligence information. Radiant Mercury allows release to coalition users not normally authorized access to sensitive compartmented information. Acquisition of Mercury terminals

began in 1997. After 9/11, the Joint Task Force — Computer Network Operations (JTF-CNO) was given responsibility for development of a rules-based system designed for rapid automatic sanitization and release of as much intelligence data as possible to allies. The hub is located in Tampa, FL.

+ **Radiant Mist:** Advanced electro-optical sensor for shipboard application, 1993–1996.
+ **Radiant Oak:** Exercise in which a navy aircraft was able to successfully destroy an over-the-horizon target using external targeting information received and processed by MATT.
+ **Radiant Outlaw:** Sister program to Radiant Mist, consisting of the same sensors packaged for airborne applications.
+ **Radiant Storm:** Commercial satellite (such as Direct Broadcast Satellite) broadcast demonstration to support military operations, Nov 1994. It was the precursor to the Joint Broadcast System.
+ **Radiant Tin:** Project investigating tactical uses of automated target recognition and image improvement software. The algorithm was developed by Texas Tech University.
+ **Radiant Topaz/Vista:** Classified, 1995.

Radiant Support: NATO PfP seminar developed as a maritime building block for Joint Search and Rescue Center (JSRC) North and JSRC Northeast exercises, 4–8 Dec 2000.

Radius: Navy (N89/N7SP) special access program first word.

Raging Bull 00-02: 72nd Air Base Wing and 32nd Combat Communications Sqn local exercise, Tinker AFB, OK, 2000.

Ragtime: Navy ballistic missile submarine code word/compartment (for example, Secret LIMDIS Ragtime) used when associating a submarine name with a particular project or operation.

Rainbow: Early U-2 code name.

Rainbow Maverick: Air force missile test series. The 307th FS deployed five aircraft and 49 personnel to Hill AFB, UT, Aug 1994, to participate in a Rainbow Maverick missile shoot, where they placed 23 of 23 functional Maverick AGM-65D/G missiles on target.

Rainbow Serpent: Australian-led command post exercise focused on peace-keeping operations, 1998.

Raindrop: Air force/Intelligence Community software tool used by mission planners and targeters to generate precise points. Raindrop was developed using commercial off-the-shelf software to replace Dewdrop. Raindrop utilizes overlapping stereo images with intuitive graphics-based tools to enable an operator to quickly identify, locate, and model objects. The mensurated coordinates derived are used as the foundation for creating Desired Mean Point of Impact (DMPI) and Desired Points of Impact (DPI) for targeting. Raindrop was designated the standard precise positioning system in Apr 02.

Rajawali Ausindo: Australian–Indonesian tactical air transport training series. Rajawali Ausindo 97: Nov 1997.

Rampart: Former Chief of Naval Operations (N3) first word.

Ramrod: ELINT satellite.

Ranch Hand: Ongoing Ranch Hand II Epidemiology Study to continue to evaluate the effects of Vietnam War defoliation and herbicide operations.

Ranger: Navy follow-on program to Classic Wizard.

Ranger (TF Ranger): Special operations support of UN operations in Mogadishu, Somalia. TF Ranger was led by JSOC, 22 Aug–25 Oct 1993.

Rapid Cheetah: Kosovo Force (KFOR) operation to locate and interdict contraband operations in the US-controlled sector of Kosovo, 2001.

Rapid Guardian: NATO exercise to support the ability to rapidly reinforce Kosovo Force in Kosovo.

Rapid Thunder: Combined Forces Command command post exercise series designed to exercise the CFC Crisis Action Team and Combined Battle Staff in South Korea. Participants normally include UN command, US forces, and service component command staffs. Rapid Thunder is conducted three times a year, preceding Ulchi Focus Lens, RSOI/Foal Eagle, and independently in fall.

Raptor Talon: BMDO Airborne Optical Surveillance System concept for detection of airborne rocket plumes from low altitudes (1.25 miles) through burnout, mid-1990s.

Raquel: ELINT "ferret" satellite nickname, 1970s. *See also* Bridget, Farrah, and Marilyn.

Code Names

Raven: 1. ELINT collection officer aboard Rivet Joint aircraft. Ravens operate the Automatic ELINT Emitter Location System (AEELS).

2. **Raven:** Navy (N89/N7SP) special access program first word.

3. **Raven:** Non-communications Signals Exploitation System. *See also* Hawk, Merlin, Mockingbird, Phoenix, and Owl.

Razor Sharp: Post-9/11 noncompliant maritime intercept operation in the Middle East region.

Ready: Air Force Space Warfare Center TENCAP program, 2000–present.

Rebound Echo: E-4 National Airborne Operations Center OPLAN designating a set of US dispersal airfields as NAOC support bases. The plan provides for ground support (such as vehicles, security forces, and after-hours base services) for E-4B crews in an emergency or nuclear war.

Red: Coast Guard special operations first word, including Red Fin (6 Jul–4 Aug 1989) and Red Herring (22 Sep–15 Oct 1988).

Red Dawn: Operation to capture Saddam Hussein, 13 Dec 2003.

Red Flag: Air Combat Command large-force tactical exercise that replicates the first 10 days of an air war, held four times a year at Nellis AFB, NV. Exercise duration may vary, but is normally composed of two or three two-week periods. Each period emphasizes electronic counter-measures, communications jamming, or Intelligence, Surveillance and Reconnaissance (ISR) collection and processing. Some periods are US only, allowing the integration of special access programs that cannot be used in conjunction with allied participation. The Blue forces use various tactics to attack Nellis range targets: mock airfields, vehicle convoys, tanks, parked aircraft, bunkered defensive positions, missile sites, et cetera. These targets are defended by a variety of simulated ground and air threats to give aircrews the most realistic combat training possible. Green Flag is similar to a Red Flag but emphasizes intelligence gathering, bomb damage assessment, and electronic warfare.

Red Force: Air Force Communications Data Link Jammer.

Red Reef: US–Saudi Arabian amphibious warfare and mine counte-rmeasures live-fire exercise, held in the Red Sea and on the Saudi coast. Red Reef 12: Southwestern shore of Saudi Arabia, 7–12 Jun 2001. 11th MEU (SOC). Red Reef 10: Jubail, Saudi Arabia, 2000. Red Reef 10 was the largest amphibious exercise in Saudi Arabia since Desert Storm. Participants included 13 US (navy and Coast Guard) and Saudi ships, a submarine, helicopters, and carrier airwing aircraft. Red Reef 99: USS *Constellation* (CV 64). Red Reef 97: Jul 1997. 11th MEU (SOC). Red Reef 5: Apr 1994. USS *Frederick* (LST 1184) with embarked marines detached from the USS *Peleliu* (LHA 5) ARG operating in Somalia. Red Reef 91: 22nd MEU and USS *Nashville* (LPD 13).

Red Rocket: Emergency Action Message (EAM) originating from the president, the secretary (or deputy secretary) of defense, or the chairman (or acting chairman) of the JCS and used for flash delivery of instructions to US forces. The unclassified flagword *Red Rocket* identifies the messages. Regulations require Red Rockets to be delivered in 20 minutes from the JCS to the commander officer in the field. White Rocket messages are exercise versions.

Red Snake: Australia special operations commando strike exercise.

Red Stripe: UK–Jamaica exercise, 2000–2001.

Red Tigress: Aries single-stage rocket booster (Minuteman 1 second stage) launches from Patrick AFB, FL, and Wallops Island, VA, in support of missile defense research, 1991–1995.

Reef. Chief of Naval Operations (N2) first word.

+ **Reef Point:** P-3B imagery and SIGINT aircraft used for littoral area surveillance in support of marines, employed during Desert Storm to collect bomb damage assessment on navy strikes on Iraqi ships. Probably changed to Storm Jib.

REFORGER (Return of Forces to Germany): Cold War exercise in Western Europe to test the readiness of reserve component units in reinforcing active components already engaged in a European conflict. The last REFORGER exercise was held in May 1993 in Germany.

Regal: Chief of Naval Operations (N2) first word.

Regency Network: Europe-based high-frequency nuclear weapons radio communications system used for transmission of Emergency Action Messages (EAMs). *See also* Flaming Arrow.

Regional Cooperation: CENTCOM ISO/PfP computer-assisted peace operations command post exercise replacing Centrasbat in 2001, and held at the Warrior Preparation Center, Einseidlerhof, Germany. Participants include

Kazakhstan, Kyrgyzstan, Uzbekistan, Turkey, Azerbaijan, Ukraine, and Mongolia. Observer nations include Germany, Jordan, Pakistan, and Turkmenistan. Regional Cooperation 04. Regional Cooperation 01, 17–28 Jun 2001.

Regs Ruby (Remote Operating Facility — Airborne, ROFA, ELINT Ground System Ruby): NSA ELINT processing station, Fort Meade, MD. *See also* Eagle Reach.

Reindeer Games: 101st Airborne Div operation in Mosul, Iraq, 10 Dec 2003.

Relex II: Australian operations to deter unauthorized boat arrivals, including air and surface patrols across the northern and western maritime approaches to Australia. Operation Relex I ceased and Relex II commenced on 14 Mar 2002.

Reliant Gorilla: 11th MEU (SOC) exercise, Arabian Gulf, 1995.

Reliant Mermaid: US–Israeli–Turkish Sixth Fleet naval exercise series focused on search and rescue. Reliant Mermaid VI: 13 Aug 2003. Reliant Mermaid V: Dec 2002–Jan 2003. Reliant Mermaid IV: Southern Turkey, 3–7 Dec 2001. Reliant Mermaid III: Off the coast of Haifa, Israel, 17 Jan 2001. Reliant Mermaid II: Off the Antalya coast, Turkey, 14–17 Dec 1999. Reliant Mermaid I: 7 Jan 1998. USS *John Rodgers* (DD 983) participated near Haifa, Israel. Turkish warships TCG *Yavuz* and TCG *Zafer* and Israel warships INS *La Hav* and INS *Nitzahon* participated in the first exercise of this type by the three nations. Jordan was an observer.

Reliant Rescue: Carrier Group 5 and 11th MEU (SOC) exercise, Arabian Gulf, 1995. This was the first exercise in the Arabian Gulf to practice procedures for future Fifth Fleet operations.

REMJA V: Inter-American Committee Against Terrorism seminar, Washington, DC, 26–30 Apr 2004.

Replicate: NSA National Cryptologic School training system.

Rescue 95: NATO PfP exercise, the first hosted by Romania, 1995.

Rescue Eagle: US–Romanian amphibious exercise series. Participants include Azerbaijan, Bulgaria, France, Georgia, Germany, Greece, Hungary, Italy, Moldova, Slovakia, Turkey, and Hungary. Rescue Eagle 01: Ground training was combined with the activation and deployment of hospital ship USNS *Comfort*. Rescue Eagle 00/MEDCEUR 00-2: Babadag and Vadu Beach,

Constanta region of Romania, 9–23 Jul 2000. MARFOREUR led the Alabama and Tennessee ARNGs for the first time in an exercise of this magnitude. Rescue Eagle 98: Babadag and Black Sea region, Romania, 5–12 Nov 1998. 22nd MEU. Rescue Eagle 97: Constanta, Romania, and Black Sea.

Rescue Eagle 96: US–Albanian special operations exercise, Durres, Albania, Jul 1996. This was the third US–Albanian post–Cold War exercise. USS *Kearsarge* (LHD 3) ARG and 24th MEU (SOC), and USS *Firebolt* (PC 10) with SEAL Team 2, embarked on USS *Austin* (LPD 4). Working closely with the Albanian SOF, the *Firebolt* provided command and control. Rescue Eagle evolved into a Romania-hosted exercise.

Rescuer/Medceur: EUCOM ISO/PfP regionally focused medical/crisis response training exercise. Rescuer/Medceur 05: Georgia, Jun 2005. Rescuer/Medceur 04: Lithania, Latvia, and Estonia, 16–30 Jun 2004. Rescuer/Medceur 02. Rescuer 01: Romania. Rescuer 99: 10–19 Sep 1999. Rescuer 97: Krivolak, Macedonia, 11–17 May 1997. Rescuer 96: Macedonia, 21–26 Oct 1996.

Resolute Barbara: Survey and stand-up of US air training activities at the Glamoc gunnery range, Croatia, 1996.

Resolute Response: Operation to improve force protection after the nearly simultaneous terrorist bombings at US embassies in Nairobi, Kenya, and Dar es Salaam, Tanzania, on 7 Aug 1998. The attacks killed more than 250 people, including 12 Americans, and injured about 5,000. JTF Kenya activated 7–31 Aug 1998. Fifth Fleet responded: In Nairobi: 1st Plt, Second Fleet Antiterrorism Security Team (FAST) Co; 2nd Plt, 1st FAST Co; MSG augments; 3rd Plt, Co G, BLT 2/1, 13th MEU (SOC); in Dar Es Salaam: 2nd Plt, 2nd FAST Co. The security mission continued in Nairobi during the construction of the new embassy.

Resolute Strike: Coalition and 82nd Airborne Div operation in Sangin, southern Afghanistan, 8–9 Apr 2003.

Response 95: WMD exercise using the Consequence Assessment Tool Set (CATS), a Geographic Information System–based application providing map-based hazard display and analysis.

Restore Democracy: Operations as part of United Nations Mission in Haiti (UNMIH), 31 Mar 1995–15 Mar 1996. USS *Dwight D. Eisenhower* (CVN 69), USS *America* (CV 66), and the USS *Wasp* (LHD 1) ARG.

Restore Hope: Somalia humanitarian relief operations, 4 Dec 1992–4 May 1994. President Bush pledged to provide security for the multi-national coalition originally known as the Unified Task Force (UNITAF). Joint Special Operations Forces — Somalia was activated on 12 Jan 1993, including 15th MEU, a SEAL platoon, a Special Boat Unit detachment, AC-130s, and army special forces. TF Ranger joined in Aug 1993 after 24 Pakistani soldiers were killed by Somali militia on 5 Jun 1993. In an operation on 3 Oct, TF Ranger captured six of Mohamed Farah Aideed's lieutenants and several militiamen, but two UH-60 helicopters were shot down ("Blackhawk Down") and US forces remaining on the ground came under heavy fire. During the intense firefight that followed, hundreds of Somalis were killed and hundreds more were wounded. A total of 16 Army Rangers were killed, and 83 were wounded. President Clinton then announced that all US forces would be withdrawn from Somalia, and withdrawal was completed on 25 Mar 1994. Operations were supported by USS *Ranger* (CV 61), USS *Kitty Hawk* (CV 63), USS *Juneau* (LPD 10), USS *Tripoli* (LPH 10), and USS *Rushmore* (LSD 47).

Retract: Navy (N89/N7SP) special access program first word, including Retract Amber, Retract Elm, Retract Juniper, Retract Larch, Retract Maple, Retract Oak, Retract Silver, Retract Violet, and Retract Yellow.

+ **Retract Barley:** Special access program included in the FY 2003 Defense Emergency Readiness Fund.
+ **Retract Heather:** Joint Warfare Analysis Center, Dahlgren, VA.

Retrofire: Naval Security Group sensitive compartmented information communications system. *See also* Newsdealer.

Reward: Navy (N89/N7SP) special access program first word.

Rex (Readiness Exercise): FEMA continuity of government and national preparedness exercise, 1980s.

Reynard Chase: UK exercise canceled because of resource constraints, 25 Nov–8 Dec 2002.

Rhino: UK army exercise series first word, including Rhino Charge, Rhino Holdfast, Rhino Spear. Rhino Charge 01, 6–22 Jan 2001, to be held in Germany, was canceled because of foot-and-mouth disease restrictions.

Rhyolite: SIGINT geostationary satellite first launched in 1970. The Rhyolite program was compromised by Soviet KGB spy and TRW employee

Christopher Boyce in 1975. The code name was changed to Aquacade, and Rhyolite was replaced by Magnum in 1985.

Rice Bowl: Iranian hostage rescue attempt, 1979.

Rifle Blitz: Army 3rd Armored Cavalry Regt offensive operation in western Iraq, 2003.

RIFT: Sensitive compartmented information security related.

RIGEL: Navy counter-narcotics information warfare exploitation system.

RIMPAC (Rim of the Pacific): PACOM large-scale biennial multi-phase, sea control, power projection fleet exercise held in the waters off Hawaii. RIMPAC is often the largest exercise conducted in PACOM and typically includes at least two carrier groups. RIMPAC 04 was the 20th RIMPAC conducted since its inception in 1971. Participants include Australia, Canada, Chile, France, Japan, Peru, South Korea, the UK, and the US. RIMPAC 02, 24 Jun–22 Jul 2002, was reduced in size by about 40 percent due to operational commitments in the war on terrorism. RIMPAC 00. RIMPAC 94: 4–12 Jun 1994. During the exercise, the navy operated two Mk-4 and four Mk-7 marine mammal systems (MMS) dolphins from the USS *Juneau* (LPD 10).

Ringgold: Counter-narcotics operation (Project Code 1295), 2000.

Rio Bravo: Army reserve chemical exercise held each year at Fort Bliss, TX.

Rio Grande 02: Coast Guard WMD exercise involving mock chemical agent attacks against a docked Coast Guard cutter, Alameda, CA, Jun 2002. Participants included the army reserve, California NG, and Alameda Fire Department.

Rio Lobo 2000: Chemical exercise hosted by the 415th Chemical Bde, Greenville, SC, 2000. The exercise evaluated the smoke and decontamination missions of active and reserve chemical units. Approximately 21,000 soldiers from 13 states participated.

River City: EPA led radiological incident tabletop exercise, Louisville, KY, 22–23 Jul 2003.

River Operation: US–Argentinian annual coastal environment training exercise, starting in the 1990s. River Operation IV: 30 Jul–13 Aug 2000.

Rivet: Air force intelligence first word. The original Rivet Joint RC-135E was designated Rivet Amber. Later models were designated Rivet Ball, Rivet

Brass, Rivet Card, and Rivet Quick. Rivet Ace, Rivet Bat, Rivet Cap, Rivet Switch, and Rivet Top were all Cold War programs.

+ **Rivet Fire:** EC-130H Compass Call aircraft modification that added an electronic counter-measures system (jamming system) for use against enemy command and control networks. Rivet Fire was employed in Just Cause and Desert Storm.

+ **Rivet Joint:** RC-135V/W aircraft assigned to the 55th Wing, Offutt AFB, NE. Rivet Joint is the primary airborne SIGINT platform of the US. The fleet consists of 14 aircraft, 10 primary and 4 backup. Primary missions are near-real-time COMINT and ELINT verification and update.

+ **Rivet Rider/Volant Solo:** EC-130E Commando Solo psychological operations variants.

Rivet Mile (Rivet Minuteman Integrated Life Extension): Minuteman ICBM program life extension and depot maintenance support, started in Apr 1985.

Roadrunner: Nickname for White House Communications Agency vans that provide presidential telecommunications support.

Roadwarrior: Army intelligence Trojan Classic system.

Robin Court: Reported Army Intelligence Support Activity (Gray Fox) code name.

Robin Sage: Army special forces large-scale field training exercise, held four times annually at the conclusion of the SF qualification course ("Q Course"), Fort Bragg, NC.

Rock and Roll: Federal government mass casualties WMD exercise, DC General and Bethesda Medical Hospitals, Washington, DC, 1998–1999.

Rock Work: UK–Gibraltar exercise series, canceled in 2002.

Rocketeer: *See* Wolfers/Rocketeer.

Rockingham: UK Defense Intelligence Staff support to the United Nations Special Commission (UNSCOM) and International Atomic Energy Agency, 1991–1998; and later support to UNMOVIC, 2002–2003. After OIF, Rockingham became the UK focal point for the work of the Iraq Survey Group.

Rocky Lance: UK–Oman exercise, 2000–2001.

RODCA: (Former?) HUMINT compartment (for instance, Top Secret/ RODCA) for information derived from non-US sources.

Rodent: Army Foreign Science and Technology Center foreign material exploitation first word, 1991–1993, including Rodent Denture, Rodent Exclaim, Rodent Hero, Rodent Motel, and Rodent Next.

Roiling Water (Project 931): Classified operation, 1 Mar 1985–present.

Roll Call 83: Pacific Fleet naval control of shipping exercise, 24 Apr–13 May 1983.

Roll-up: 4th Infantry Div operation in Iraq, 10 Dec 2003.

Roller Derby: ANG deployment, Azores, Portugal, 1995–1996.

Rolling Deep: UK–Netherlands amphibious force exercise. Rolling Deep 01, 8–21 May 2001, was canceled because of foot-and-mouth disease restrictions. Rolling Deep 95: Sep 1995.

Rolling Thunder: Army emergency deployment readiness exercise held in Kuwait, involving live-fire and close air support training for ground forces. Rolling Thunder 98: Camp Doha, Kuwait, Mar 1998. Rolling Thunder 93: 101st Airborne Div.

ROMO II: Air force unknown system.

Rook Knight: Air force special operations exercise in South Korea, Oct–Nov 1985.

Rook's Landing: CIA–army operation to monitor Nicaraguan flights, early 1980s.

Root Cellar: Army Foreign Science and Technology Center foreign material exploitation, 1992.

Rosetta Stone (Single integrated picture Topology-driven Optical Nonlinear Engine): Intelligence special access program integrating multi-source sensor data/track inputs, correlating the data and fusing it into a single integrated picture to reduce engagement decision time, improve target location estimates, and provide enhanced combat identification.

Roster: NSA–army INSCOM SIGINT program.

Rough and Ready: California NG–Ukraine State Partnership disaster relief and medical exercise, Ukraine, 1–7 Jun 2003. The CA NG deployed more than 200 soldiers to eastern Ukraine.

Round Gopher: Army Foreign Science and Technology Center foreign material exploitation, 1991–1992.

Round House: Simulated exercise DEFCON 3.

Rover: 1. **(Remote Operations Video Enhanced Receiver):** Real-time tactical video dissemination kit to feed video from a Predator UAV directly into ground stations. In Dec 2001, Rover was installed on AC-130 gunships for use in OEF.

2. **Rover:** HUMINT-related program.

Roving Sands: Army FORSCOM annual field training exercise, primarily using the White Sands Missile Range and Fort Bliss Ranges. The primary focus of Roving Sands is Joint Theater Air and Missile Defense and air operations. Roving Sands 02/03: 7–30 Jun 2002. Roving Sands 01: Jul 2001. Participants were to have included the 7 Air Defence Bde, but UK participation was limited to personnel only due to restrictions regarding importing equipment into the US. Roving Sands 00/Purple Dragon 00/Purple Caduceus 00/JLOTS/Coherent Joint Fires (CJF): Purple Dragon/Caduceus were conducted at Camp Lejeune, NC, and Fort Bragg, NC. JLOTS was at Fort Story, VA. CJF was at Barksdale AFB, LA, Fort Bliss, TX, and Nellis AFB, NV. The operating area was divided into two areas of hostility: in the west, Sabira versus Dahib and Karstan, and in the east Basa against Casma. The mission in the west was to defend and set conditions for offensive operations. Massive air and missile attacks were expected against US and coalition forces. The mission in the east was for the JTF to conduct forcible entry and decisive combat operations. Roving Sands 99: Largest air defense exercise held under the *Roving Sands* name. Roving Sands 97: CENTCOM scenarios. Roving Sands 96: 12–16 Jun 1996. Roving Sands 95: Mar 1995. CENTCOM Joint Project Optic Cobra to identify, target, and destroy mobile ballistic missiles. Roving Sands 94: Apr 1994. Roving Sands 92.

ROXAD: Sensitive compartmented information security advisory channel through Defense Special Security Communications System (DSSCS) called a DSSCS Address Group (DAG) and used to disseminate security education and awareness information to the field.

Royal: Army intelligence first word.

+ **Royal Cape:** Original special access program compartment for the Army Intelligence Support Activity (Gray Fox), replaced by Grantor Shadow in the mid-1980s.
+ **Royal Dragon 96:** Army TENCAP exercise to test passing real-time U-2 data to ground users, May 1996.
+ **Royal Duke:** Central America reconnaissance operation, probably of the Intelligence Support Activity (Gray Fox), 1980s. Included the Cefirm Leader platform.
+ **Royal Holiday:** Army Foreign Science and Technology Center foreign material exploitation, 1991–1992.

Royal Crown: White House secure communications switchboard. *See also* Crown.

Royal Patrol 96: US–UK special operations exercise, Gibraltar, 1996. The USS *Firebolt* (PC 10) provided support for Navy SEALs, RN Gibraltar Sqn, and Royal Marines. The ship conducted a clandestine recovery exercise linking with a P-3C maritime patrol aircraft, which monitored the progress of uploading data from an intelligence collection sonobuoy.

RSOI (Reception, Staging, Onward Movement and Integration): Combined Forces Command annual South Korean exercise to practice and improve the ability to receive reinforcements from US-based forces. RSOI is the second in the Korean command post exercise series (Foal Eagle is first) and occurs in Apr (sometimes in coordination with Foal Eagle). The exercise simulates a presidential reserve call-up and tests the ability to move troops and supplies from ports to the front. Each exercise includes a senior leader seminar where US and South Korean commanders discuss issues associated with OPLAN 5027. The exercise began in Apr 1994.

Rubble Pile: NCIS Mobile Crisis Response Team counter-terrorism exercise, Center for National Response, WV, May 2003. The scenario involved a mock car bombing at the former "Memorial Tunnel" training facility.

Rubicon: Navy FY 2003 Defense Emergency Readiness Fund program to integrate information warfare electronic support systems with electronic attack capabilities to provide a ship-based capability to disrupt radio-controlled weapons.

Ruby: Navy (N89/N7SP) special access program first word.

Ruff: Former compartment for early Talent Keyhole imagery intelligence (for example, Top Secret Talent Keyhole Ruff). *See also* Chess.

Ruffer: Ground processing station for Jumpseat.

Rugged: CENTCOM exercise and operations series first word.

+ **Rugged Arch:** CENTAF/9th Air Force show of force on the Arabian peninsula. Rugged Arch 03. Rugged Arch 02. Rugged Arch 00: 5–20 May 2000.
+ **Rugged Nautilus:** Short-notice show of force in the Arabian Gulf led by the USS *Carl Vinson* (CVN 70) Battle Group and including Aerospace Expeditionary Force III based in Qatar, 1 Jul–30 Aug 1996. The 13th MEU also conducted a landing in Kuwait. The *Vinson* Battle Group conducted Desert Strike during the deployment.
+ **Rugged Vortex:** Classified special operations repatriation exercise to practice recovery of downed air personnel and other repatriated military personnel, including Rugged Vortex 04, Rugged Vortex 02, and Rugged Vortex 00/01.

Ruler: National Sensor Model Integration software developed by the former National Photographic Interpretation Center to allow use of commercial imagery applications.

Rum Punch: Operation, Puerto Rico, 1996.

Rusher: NSA program, 1980s.

Russian BILAT (Torgau): US–Russian exercise to improve training and inter-operability. Russian BILAT 05: May 2005. Russian BILAT 04.

Rutley: SIGINT satellite ground processing system at RAF Menwith Hill, UK.

Rye: NSA program, 1980s.

— S —

Saber: 1. Navy submarine or anti-submarine-warfare equipment, space related.

2. **Saber:** Air force first word used beginning in the 1980s. The programs included Saber Executive (analysis of the airborne Emergency Action Message system for Single Integrated Operational Plan execution), Saber Penetrator (a B-2 early code name), and Saber Protractus, US capability in a protracted nuclear conflict.

Sable Tent: Air Combat Command Pacific basing of an intelligence asset, 2001.

Sabre (TF Sabre): Originally known as TF Able Sentry, the army's TF attached to the United Nations Preventive Deployment Force (UNPREDEP) in Macedonia. On 25 Feb 1999, the UN Security Council voted not to extend the UNPREDEP mandate; the mission was terminated 28 Feb 1999. UNPREDEP was renamed UN Skopje on 1 Mar 1999. DOD then modified the mission of Able Sentry, renamed TF Sabre, on 28 Mar 1999. Subsequently, TF Sabre became TF Falcon Rear.

Sacred Company: Europe special operations exercise. Sacred Company 01: Romania. Sacred Company 99: Marine Corps Force Reconnaissance platoon with SOF from Belgium and Greece.

Safe: 1. Air Force Security Police first word.

2. **Safe:** Coast Guard special operations first word. Safe Catch, 1 Nov 1999–6 Jun 2000. Safe River, 9 Mar–23 Apr 1997.

Safe Border (JTF Safe Border): US contribution to the UN Military Observer Mission in Ecuador and Peru (MOMEP), Patuca, Ecuador, 1 Mar 1995–9 Jun 1996. The operation included SOCOM counter-narcotics operations.

Safe Departure: Noncombatant evacuation operation from Asmara, Eritrea, to Amman, Jordan, 6–23 Jun 1998. The USS *Tarawa* (LHA 1) and 11th MEU (SOC) evacuated 105 Americans and 68 citizens of 10 other countries.

Safe Haven: Migrant camp operations conducted in Panama, 26 Aug 1994–1 Mar 1995.

Safe Passage: 1. Movement of Cuban migrants from Safe Haven in Panama to Guantanamo Bay, Cuba.

2. **(Safe Passage 94-1):** NAVCENT naval control of shipping exercise, Arabian Gulf.

Saffron Sands: UK–Jordanian ground forces live-fire exercise series. Saffron Sands 02: southern Jordan, 21 Aug–24 Sep 2002. Saffron Sands 99: 26 Sep–31 Oct 1999.

Saga: Air force unknown system.

Sage: Air force operations first word. Sage Scarab was a Pacific Air Force "special plans" projects run out Hawaii in the 1980s.

Sage Brush: Presidential continuity of government exercise series, 1980s–early 1990s.

SAGIP: PACOM annual humanitarian assistance and disaster response seminar, held in support of the Association of Southeast Asian Nations (ASEAN) Regional Forum (ARF). SAGIP began in 1999, and the seminars have been held in the Philippines, 2001–present.

Saif Sareea: UK–Oman large-scale exercise. Saif Sareea II/Argonaut 01: Aug–Nov 2001. Post-9/11 operation with significant participation from UK army formations, including HQ 1 (UK) Armoured Div, 4 Armoured Bde, and support units. Argonaut involved deployment of UK Amphibious Task Group 1.

Sailfish: UK exercise, Belize, 2000–2002.

Salitre 04: US–Chilean exercise, 20 Sep–12 Oct 2004.

Salty: Air force exercise first word. Cold War–era terms included Salty Bee and Salty Rooster.

+ **Salty Chase:** USAFE base-level chemical warfare exercise.
+ **Salty Demo:** Air base survival demonstration.
+ **Salty Gecko:** 613th Air Operations Sqn, Andersen AFB, Guam.
+ **Salty Hammer:** USAFE exercise.
+ **Salty Nation (Local Salty Nation):** USAFE local operational readiness exercise in preparation for a NATO tactical evaluation.
+ **Salty Script:** USAFE local quarterly unit evaluation in preparation for Nuclear Surety Inspections.

Salvation Eagle 96: US–Albanian special operations force exercise involving marines and the Albanian Zall Herr Commando unit, Aug 1996.

Sand Dollar: Cold War operation to retrieve Soviet test warheads from the ocean.

Sand Eagle: 101st Airborne Div emergency deployment readiness exercise, Egypt. Sand Eagle 92. Sand Eagle 89.

Sand Flea: SOUTHCOM rehearsal conducted by the 193rd Infantry Bde as part of preparations for Just Cause, 1989.

Sand Trap: Coast Guard special operation, 28 Jun–25 Jul 1991.

Sandbar: Command, control, and communications program, 1980s.

Sandcrab/Sand Scoop: Army HF intercept and jamming systems used during Desert Storm.

Sandgroper: US–Australian exercise held in alternate years, 1990s.

Sandkey: NSA counter-narcotics reporting system.

SANDS: Unknown ELINT system.

Sandy: Air force fighter aircraft support to combat search and rescue.

Sandy Coast 99: UK navy exercise planned for Sep 1999, canceled because ships were involved in ordnance clearance operations in the Adriatic Sea under NATO auspices.

Sanso 03: Proliferation Security Initiative maritime interdiction exercise, Mediterranean, 14–17 Oct 2003. Participants included France, Germany, Italy, Portugal, Spain, the UK, and the US. Australia, Japan, the Netherlands, and Poland participated as observers. *See* Pacific Protector.

Sapphire: 1. US–Canadian Surveillance of Space Project that is investigating activating three ground-based telescopes and placing in orbit a space-based visible sensor in order to conduct surveillance of space from space.

2. **(Project Sapphire):** Operations to remove fissile material from former Soviet republics.

SAR 2000: US–Argentinian search and rescue training exercise, 22–24 Aug 2000.

Sarah Lite: Message format software, Serene Byte/Pace Ware related.

Saratoga Thunder: PACOM cyber-warfare workshop, 1999, to validate policies, procedures, and processes developed since Eligible Receiver 97. Participants included the DIA and NSA.

SAREX: 1. NATO ISO/PfP search and rescue exercise series, held with Georgia, Albania, and Malta. SAREX 00: 28 Apr–5 May 2000. SAREX 95: Albania, 27–29 Jan 1995. This was the first exercise of Albania as part of the PfP.

2. **SAREX (South Asia Search and Rescue Exercise):** Seventh Fleet search and rescue exercise that includes India, La Reunion, Mauritius, the Maldives, Madagascar, Sri Lanka, and the US.

Satria Bhakti 97: Australian humanitarian assistance logistics war game, Nov 1997.

Sayers: Air force unknown (possibly classified) system.

Scarecrow: ECM unit developed for the Aquila remotely piloted vehicle, 1980s.

Scarlet Cloud: Department of Homeland Security–DOD–Health and Human Services homeland security exercise, Nov 2003. The scenario involved an anthrax attack in a number of cities.

Scarlet Hawk: Air force Major Accident Response Exercise (MARE) involving on base and civilian agencies, conducted regularly.

Scathe: Air force Big Safari program first word.

+ **Scathe Mean:** Special access program to convert air defense decoy drones used as targets into operational drones used to deceive Iraqi air defenses in Desert Storm. In the opening-night attacks on 17 Jan 1991, the drones were used to spoof Iraq radar and precede US attacking aircraft.
+ **Scathe View:** Special access program involving use of video recording cameras embedded in innocuous airlift aircraft. The program began to provide a tactical reconnaissance system for commanders during humanitarian and noncombatant evacuation operations, particularly in the former Yugoslavia. Scathe View has been used extensively after 9/11 for low-profile reconnaissance in the Middle East and South Asia. *See also* Keen Sage.

Scattered Castles: Intelligence Community database tracking personnel with sensitive compartmented information clearances, established Oct 2002.

Schriever: Air Force Space Warfare Center war game intended to provide a platform to investigate issues associated with the role of space systems in military transformation. The Schriever wargames are tied in with the air force's Global Engagement and Futures Game, the navy's Global, the army's After Next, and other transformation exercises.

Science: Air force space-related first word.

+ **Science Dust:** Defense Meterological Satellite Program tactical support.
+ **Science Flash:** Defense Dissemination Program.
+ **Science Media:** Classified R&D project.
+ **Science Realm:** Special access program established in May 1985.
+ **Science Streak:** Defense Meterological Satellite Program strategic support.

Scope: Air force communications-related first word. Cold War programs included Scope Dawn, Scope Dial, Scope Exchange, Scope Premise, and Scope Saint.

+ **Scope Axis:** Upgrade of backbone communications in Greece and Turkey, 1980s.
+ **Scope Command:** High-frequency communications modernization, completed in 1997, replacing Scope Control, Scope Pattern, and Scope Signal III equipment to support Mystic Star, tactical army and marine commanders, and Spanish/US/Canadian networks. Scope Command modernized the worldwide network of high-power stations as part of the Global HF System. *See also* Commando Escort and Giant Talk.
+ **Scope Eagle:** Air Force Executive Course for colonels, colonel selects, and civilian equivalents on command and control systems.
+ **Scope Force:** EUCOM nuclear communications modernization, 1980s.
+ **Scope Light:** LANTCOM (now JFCOM) EC-135 airborne command post, 1980s.
+ **Scope Response:** Communications for European Collocated Operating Bases.
+ **Scope Sand:** Communications link among Diyarbakir, Turke,y and command centers in Germany and the UK, 1980s.
+ **Scope Shield II:** AN/PRC-139 handheld radio used by security police. *See also* Have Quick, Pacer Speak.
+ **Scope Signal I/II/III/IV/V:** High-frequency communication networks. Scope Signal III replaced Giant Talk in the 1976–1986 time frame. Replaced by Scope Command.
+ **Scope Warrior:** Air force annual communications summit initiated in Oct 1984.

Scorpion Wind: Marine Corps air exercise series held at MCAS Yuma, AZ, and NAS Fallon, NV. Scorpion Wind 95-2. Scorpion Wind 94-1. Scorpion Wind 93-1. Scorpion Wind 91-2.

SCWS (Senior Commander Warfighting Seminar): EUCOM exercise series. SCWS 04. SCWS 02.

Sea Angel (Operation Sea Angel): PACOM disaster relief operation in Bangladesh. Sea Angel II: 1992; Sea Angel: 10 May–13 Jun 1991. The Sea Angel JTF was formed in May 1991, the first time a Marine Air Ground Task Force (MAGTF) was used as a JTF nucleus. The JTF included the 5th MEB, an army SOF team (1st Bn, 1st SFG), and Navy SEALs.

Sea Bass: Office of Naval Research special access program.

Sea Breeze: EUCOM PfP biennial naval and amphibious command post exercise/field training exercise focused on peacekeeping and disaster relief, usually held in Ukraine. Participants include Bulgaria, Canada, France, Georgia, Germany, Greece, Italy, the Netherlands, Romania, Russia, Turkey, the UK, and Ukraine. The exercise will be combined with Peaceshield and Cooperative Partner in 2005. Sea Breeze 99: Bulgaria participated for the first time. Sea Breeze 98: 22nd MEU. Sea Breeze 97.

Sea Dagger: UK–UAE amphibious exercise series, Feb 2002, postponed from Oct 2001 after 9/11.

Sea Eagle: US, Japanese, Australian, and New Zealand exercise, 1981.

Sea Ferret: Program to develop a small sea-launched cruise missile capable of coastal surveillance. *See* Bold Rapier.

Sea Horse Wind: Marine Corps air insertion and heliborne assault exercise. Sea Horse Wind is the only major rotary-wing-led exercise where marine air elements conduct a large-scale, battalion-sized lift over a significant distance. Sea Horse Wind 02: Twentynine Palms, CA, 19 Sep 2002. Sea Horse Wind 00: 3–11 Sep 2000, Fort Hunter Liggett, CA.

Sea Link: Coast Guard special operation, 13–27 Jul 1994.

Sea Nymph: Former navy AN/WLQ-4 submarine ELINT program (Project Code ZC3). Sea Nymph was phased out and replaced by Cluster Spectator. *See also* Barnacle.

Sea Saber: Proliferation Security Initiative exercise in the Arabian Sea, 11–17 Jan 2004. The USS *Enterprise* (CVN 65) led the 12-nation exercise, including Australia, France, Italy, Singapore, Spain, and the UK, with Denmark, Germany, Japan, Portugal, and Turkey observing.

Sea Shadow: DARPA Lockheed Skunk Works program begun in 1978 to leverage F-117A stealth developments for a stealth ship. Lockheed developed a scale model of a stealth surface ship, and DOD ordered the navy to develop a full-sized ship. Sea Shadow was built and tested for two years. The navy leadership terminated further investment, believing that it competed with the DDG-51 destroyer program.

Sea Signal: USS *Tripoli* (LPH 10) ARG operation to interdict Haitian migrants and transport them to Guantanamo Bay, Cuba, 20 May 1994–15 Apr 1996. *See also* Support Democracy.

Sea Soldier: US–Oman live-fire amphibious exercise series. Sea Soldier 02: 30 Mar–10 Apr 2002. 13th MEU (SOC) trained with the Western Frontier Regt (WFR) of the army of Oman. Sea Soldier 99. Sea Soldier 98. Sea Soldier 93: 22nd MEU. In preparation for Desert Storm, the 4th MEB conducted four Sea Soldier amphibious exercises in southern Oman: Sea Soldier IV: 19 Jan–2 Feb 1991; Sea Soldier III: 8–9 Dec 1990; Sea Soldier II: 1–9 Nov 1990; and Sea Soldier I: 29 Sep–4 Oct 1990.

Sea Spider: Hydrophone array around the Hawaiian Islands.

Sea Star: Anti-submarine-warfare sensor advanced development.

Sea Trout: UK–Falklands exercise, 2000–2001.

Sea Viking 04: Navy FORCEnet and Marine Corps transformation and Advanced Warfighting Experiment, Dec 2003–Oct 2004.

SEACAT (Southeast Asia Cooperation Against Terrorism): PACOM exercise involving CARAT participants (Thailand, Philippines, Singapore, Malaysia, Brunei, and Indonesia) centered on international cooperation in an information gathering/sharing effort.

Seafox: Navy surface warfare program, 1980s.

SEAL Orca: Pacific Fleet special operations exercise.

Seamark: *See* Newsdealer.

Seaspray: CIA–army clandestine air unit developed after the failure of Eagle Claw, the mission to rescue Iranian hostages in 1980, and formally activated on 2 Mar 1981. Seaspray was involved in airborne intelligence collection and support for a wide variety of covert operations with JSOC and Gray Fox in the 1980s. It operated under the cover of a front company, Aviation Tech Services, at Fort Eustis, VA; MacDill AFB, FL; and Maxwell AFB, AL. The army's 160th SOAR evolved as a "white" counterpart of Seaspray.

Seawatch: Naval global maritime movement current intelligence processor.

Security Force: Reinforcement of US housing complex in Tirana, Albania, Aug–Oct 1998.

Seek: Air force R&D first word. At one time, nuclear programs (such as Seek Bang, development of a nuclear Walleye capability for the F-4D, and Seek Straw, planning and preparation support for nuclear weapons tests) also had

Seek code names. Various Cold War names include Seek Axle, Seek Bat, Seek Dawn, Seek Frost, Seek Igloo, Seek Skyhook, Seek Spinner, and Seek Talk.

+ **Seek Clock:** Strategic nuclear-related special access program.
+ **Seek Eagle:** Program for aircraft stores certification at Eglin AFB, FL, involved in the incorporation of every new weapon and pod onto air force aircraft.
+ **Seek Gunfighter:** Aggressor space applications project initiative to obtain and analyze commercial space imagery and open-source information to assess the vulnerabilities of US operations and facilities. In 1997, the ASAP Team demonstrated its ability to track a deploying Aerospace Expeditionary Force and produce target intelligence from commercial satellite imagery (tracked the 366th Air Expeditionary Wing to Sheikh Isa, Bahrain, and monitored its operations Oct–Dec 1997).
+ **Seek Score:** Weapon delivery offset radar scoring system, located at Nellis AFB, NV.
+ **Seek Smoke:** Counter-proliferation Advanced Concept Technology Demonstration involving laser detection of biological and chemical weapons and aerosols. The Seek Smoke laser-based perimeter was installed in 1995 as an evaluation program at Osan AB, South Korea.

Semester: Army intelligence system, Bad Aibling, Germany.

Seminole (TF Seminole): 5th SFG and FL ARNG contingent in western Iraq for OIF, staged out of Jordan.

Senator: UK nuclear weapons accident exercise. Senator 00: Northern UK, Jul 2000. Senator 97: Prince William of Gloucester Barracks, Grantham, with the Strategic Coordination Group meeting at Lincolnshire Fire Brigade HQ, Lincoln, 22–25 Sep 1997. Senator 96: Otterburn Army Training Area, 20–24 May 1996.

Senior: Air force special-access-program- and reconaissance-related first word. Historically, it has included code names for foreign operations such as Senior Book (Taiwanese U-2 operations over China), Senior Look (U-2 operations in Europe), and various Cold War reconnaissance programs: Senior Bowl, Senior Crown, Senior Echo, Senior Guardian, Senior Ice, Senior Lance, Senior Monk, Senior Open, Senior Prom.

+ **Senior Blade:** Senior Year ground station consisting of a forward exploitation van capable of exploiting U-2R digital imagery.

+ **Senior Chevron:** Senior Year–related project, 1995–present.
+ **Senior Citizen:** Aurora high-speed reconnaissance aircraft or other low observable system.
+ **Senior Club:** Low observable anti-tamper advanced technology systems assessment.
+ **Senior Glass:** U-2 SIGINT sensor package upgrade combining Senior Spear and Senior Ruby.
+ **Senior Hawk:** Global Hawk.
+ **Senior High:** Classified R&D program.
+ **Senior Hunter:** EC-130E (SH) and newer EC-130J aircraft flown by the 193rd SOW, Harrisburg IAP, PA.
+ **Senior Jade:** Senior Jade "segment" (TREDS) that correlates surveillance tracking information.
+ **Senior Keystone:** Classified information warfare related.
+ **Senior Mace:** SIGINT exploitation system related to Oilstock and Sunshine.
+ **Senior Needle:** Program support for the Advanced Cruise Missile special access program.
+ **Senior Nike:** Big Safari–managed special access program.
+ **Senior Ruby:** U-2R ELINT radar emission monitoring sensor package, 1980s to present. Being integrated into Senior Glass.
+ **Senior Scout:** Tactical airborne intelligence system made up of a collection capsule (or "modular" SIGINT package) designed for insertion and removal in any C-130E/H aircraft. ANG C-130 Senior Scout aircraft are heavily involved in support of counter-narcotics and special operations. The Airborne Collection Electronic Signals II (ACES II) capsule has 12 operators sampling COMINT and ELINT bands. Antenna arrays are temporarily fitted to tail, parachute doors, main gear deflector panels, and main gear doors. On 26 May 1989, Senior Scout made its first test flight. On 16 Mar 1990, the first Senior Scout system arrived in Panama, replacing Comfy Levi.
+ **Senior Sky:** Development of the F-22 Raptor fighter.
+ **Senior Smart:** DOD unified SIGINT system and advanced tactical architecture for the Joint Signals Intelligence Avionics family.
+ **Senior Span:** Senior Span "segment" U-2 (CARS) COMINT configuration, first flight-tested in Mar 1989 and scheduled to be replaced by Global Hawk.
+ **Senior Spear:** U-2R COMINT system, being integrated into Senior Glass.

+ **Senior Spur:** U-2 beyond-line-of-sight configuration, part of Senior Year.
+ **Senior Stretch:** U-2 COMINT configuration. Now Senior Span.
+ **Senior Surprise:** Conventonal Air Launched Cruise Missile (CALCM) special access program development.
+ **Senior Suter:** Big Safari–managed special access program. *See* Suter.
+ **Senior Trend:** F-117A special access program development, formerly Have Blue.
+ **Senior Troupe:** System that transmits, receives, sanitizes, and disseminates intelligence information. On 23 Aug 1991, the first Senior Troupe system was assigned. The only remaining unit is maintained by the Utah ANG.
+ **Senior Year (SYERS):** U-2 Contingency Airborne Reconnaissance System (CARS) Electro-Optical/Infrared (EO/IR) reconnaissance system. The Senior Year program was a special access program until Jul 1999.

Senior Warrior: Marine Corps radio signal monitoring sensor package used during Desert Storm.

Sensor: Air force intelligence first word.

+ **Sensor Ace:** Proforma research and development program. Sensor Ace procures specialized signals processing equipment and computer hardware for testing software algorithms designed to detect and analyze foreign air and air defense command and control networks. It provides detailed signals and network analysis, recordings, training, operational expertise, and developmental testing for deployment of quick reaction equipment and collection analysis in support of computer network attack.
+ **Sensor Aspen:** National Air Intelligence Center (NAIC) former Soviet Union guided missile exploitation, 1998.
+ **Sensor Beam:** The US and Friendly Parametric and Signatures Database, which develops and/or acquires, measures, analyzes, stores, and distributes US and coalition parametric and signature data for worldwide military use. Databases include parametric information of US and friendly radar, Electro-Optical/Infrared (EO/IR), electronic counter-measures (ECM), electronic counter-counter-measures (ECCM), and communications systems, as well as signatures information on aircraft and missile IR, radar cross section (RCS), and related equipment antenna patterns. Includes the US Electromagnetic Systems Database (USELMSDB), which provides blue radar system data to the Electronic Warfare Integrated Reprogramming Database (EWIRDB),

the Blue Airborne Target Signatures (BATS) database, and the US Non-Communications Support Database (USNCSDB).

+ **Sensor Box:** Air Intelligence Agency imagery data warehousing capability on Intelink.

+ **Sensor Bus:** Air Intelligence Agency command, control, and communications infrastructure program.

+ **Sensor Chief:** NAIC MiG-29 ECM exploitation.

+ **Sensor Dark:** Classified MASINT capability.

+ **Sensor Eyes:** Foreign material exploitation of an airborne system. In Feb 1995, Combat Sent participated in a test of Sensor Eyes components.

+ **Sensor Fir/Flam:** DIA-led classified program, 1994.

+ **Sensor Flower:** NAIC Russian radar interference exploitation, 1998.

+ **Sensor Guard:** Deployable intelligence reachback capability that allows users to access national- and theater-level intelligence databases. The 820th SFG used Sensor Guard for intelligence and counter-intelligence reachback capabilities during Shining Hope.

+ **Sensor Harvest:** Air Force Information Warfare Center information warfare target analysis application used to create "Country Builds." Data combined from national intelligence agencies and other sources creates multidimensional computer overlays and textual windows, providing facility/geographic targeting support. Sensor Harvest facilitates planning related to OPSEC, deception, PSYOP, destruction, electronic warfare, and information attack. Each Sensor Harvest Country Build product represents an individual data set on one country. Used in OEF for Afghanistan.

+ **Sensor Heart:** R&D system supporting RC-135s and STRATCOM, 1999.

+ **Sensor House/Fix:** Air Intelligence Agency SIGINT related.

+ **Sensor Loop:** Handheld camera carried on RC-135 Rivet Joint missions.

+ **Sensor Mace:** Air Force Information Warfare Center mission support system that provides real-time message handling, correlation of multiple disciplines of intelligence data, and automatic database updating. Sensor Mace is capable of secondary imagery analysis through the use of ELT or 5-D imagery applications.

+ **Sensor Olympics:** Air Intelligence Agency awards program to recognize its best technicians.

+ **Sensor Pacer:** Ground communications system and processor, used to relay information from airborne platforms, including the EP-3. Sensor Pacer is installed in Bahrain and the UK.

✦ **Sensor Shadow:** Information prediction and analysis tool that allows analysis of all-source intelligence to assess and report the current and projected worldwide threat to command, control, communications computer systems and operations. Capabilities include categorizing hostile presence on the Internet, modeling adversary processes, and developing analytical systems to predict attacks.

Sent Ranger: Combat Sent emitter locator.

Sentinel: Air Intelligence Agency training first word. *Sentinel* refers to a weapons and tactics team approach to upgrade the competence of intelligence and mission planners who support strike operations. Development was accelerated after 9/11.

✦ **Sentinel II:** Software integration contract to develop and field common intelligence software functions on both Sentinel Aspen II and Sentinel Bright II.
✦ **Sentinel Aspen I:** General imagery intelligence training system.
✦ **Sentinel Aspen II:** General applications intelligence training system.
✦ **Sentinel Bright I:** Voice processing training system used to train linguists.
✦ **Sentinel Bright II:** Intelligence training system.
✦ **Sentinel Byte:** Data automation and mission planning training system for intelligence staffs of operational units. *See also* Constant Source.
✦ **Sentinel Concho:** Program to merge Sentinel Aspen and Sentinel Bright into a single, integrated intelligence training system at Goodfellow AFB, TX.

Sentinel Lifeguard: Contingency response buildup in response to a civilian aircraft shot down by Cuban fighters on 24 Feb 1996. The operation was supported by the USS *Nassau* (LHA 4) ARG, USS *Mississippi* (CGN 40), USS *Ticonderoga* (CG 47), and USS *John L. Hall* (FFG 32).

Sentinel Torch: Airborne reconnaissance mission over the former Yugoslavia.

Sentry: ANG exercise and deployment first word. Sentry Aloha, Sentry Combat, Sentry Endurance, Sentry Independence, Sentry Keystone, Sentry Oasis, Sentry Readiness, Sentry Sand.

✦ **Sentry Corsair:** A-7D/K deployments to Spangdahlem AB, Germany, Jun–Jul 1991.
✦ **Sentry Eagle:** Biennial air-to-air exercise. Sentry Eagle 03, Kingsley

Field, Klamath Falls, OR, 14–17 Aug 2003, was the first Sentry Eagle since 9/11.

+ **Sentry White Eagle 02:** Powidz AB, Poland, Jun 2002.

Sentry Husky: Exercise to demonstrate DOD's ability to switch from dedicated communications systems to public-switched networks in an emergency, 1990.

Sentry Strike 03: Close air support exercise involving 25th Infantry Div (Light), 25th Air Support Operations Sqn, 162nd FW, and a SEAL team, Pohakuloa Training Area, HI, Feb 2003.

Serene: Air Force Materiel Command (and former Air Force Logistics Command) first word. Serene Fox, Serene Response, and Serence Robins are base-level operational readiness inspections and exercises.

+ **Serene Byte/Pacer Ware:** Electronic warfare/counter-measures reprogramming, both real world (Pacer Ware) and test (Serene Byte). The Serene Byte/Pacer Ware process reprograms electronic warfare systems rapidly to meet changing electronic threats.
+ **Serene Response:** Aerospace Fuels Management Directorate, San Antonio Air Logistics Center exercise to handle accidents or incidents involving the bulk transportation of N_2O_4 liquid oxidizer over national highway and railway systems.

Service Star: Air force reliability assessments of ICBM reentry vehicles.

Seven: Air Force Office of Special Investigations (AFOSI) first word. A series of 1980s Caribbean and Central American counter-intelligence and security operations was code-named Seven Cays, Seven Gamblers, Seven Grand, and Seven Mayas.

+ **Seven Acres:** CENTCOM area counter-intelligence and security operation.
+ **Seven Citadels:** AFOSI adversary threat "red teaming" to acquisition programs.
+ **Seven Doors:** AFOSI offensive counter-intelligence operation (OFCO).
+ **Seven Hunters:** Post-9/11 initiative to track counter-terrorism investigative leads and collection efforts.
+ **Seven Phoenix:** AFOSI Research and Technology Protection Program that provides counter-intelligence and investigative services to safeguard air force technologies, programs, critical program information, personnel, and facilities.

+ **Seven Seekers:** AFOSI/FBI investigation into the leak of classified information (presumably Polo Step), 2002–2003.

Shadow: Army and special operations RQ-7A Shadow 200 UAV. Shadow was employed by SOF in OEF. The Shadow 200 serves as the Stryker Bde commander's tactical UAV.

Shadow Express: Noncombatant evacuation operation in Monrovia, Liberia, Sep–Oct 1998. On 18 Sep, government forces fired on Krahn leader Roosevelt Johnson and his entourage at the US embassy. The attack wounded two US personnel and killed four Krahn; an extended siege followed. SOCEUR dispatched a 12-man survey and assessment team (ESAT). The ESAT team planned to move Johnson to a third country, coordinated logistical support, and provided security for the Johnson group's departure. SOCEUR dispatched the USS *Chinook* (PC 9) from NSWU-10, Rota, Spain, and moved a NSWU-2 element via MC-130 to Freetown, Sierra Leone. SOF maintained a highly visible maritime presence 29 Sep–7 Oct off the embassy's coast. A second patrol coastal vessel, the USS *Firebolt* (PC 10), also arrived.

Shadow Hawk: US–Jordanian special operations exercise, beginning in 1984, including Shadow Hawk 85 (1–15 Jul 1985) and Shadow Hawk 84 (10–25 Jul 1984).

Shaker Support: AK-based homeland security military support to civil authorities exercise. Shaker Support 04: Sep 2004. Shaker Support 03: Elmendorf AFB, AK, Sep 2003.

Shant Doot ("Messenger of Peace," MPE): US–Bangladesh peacekeeping exercise series. MPE 2, held at the Bangladesh Institute of Peace Support Operation Training (BIPSOT) at Rajendrapur cantonment, commenced 14 Sep 2002. Participants included Bangladesh, India, Mongolia, Nepal, and Sri Lanka. Egypt, Madagascar, the Maldives, and Mauritius were minor participants. Canada. Japan, Malaysia, the Philippines, Russia, Thailand, and the UK took part as observers.

Shanti Path 03: US–Indian peacekeeping operation exercise, commencing 10 Feb 2003. Shanti Path 03 was the seventh US–Indian military exercise since 9/11. The exercise involved battalion staffs from Bangladesh, India, Nepal, Sri Lanka, and the US, and civil police and other staff officers from Madagascar, Mauritius, Fiji, Mongolia, Malaysia, Thailand, the Philippines, and Tonga.

Shared Accord 02/03: US–Tunisian exercise deploying medical forces to conduct peacekeeping and humanitarian assistance, Tanga AB, Tanzania, 14–28 Feb 2002.

Shared Endeavor: EUCOM exercise. Shared Endeavor 01. Shared Endeavor 00. Shared Endeavor 99: Botswana, 1–20 Aug 1999. Shared Endeavor 95.

SHAREM (Ship Anti-submarine-warfare Readiness Effectiveness Measuring): Navy exercise series. SHAREMs are numbered and are generally held twice a year in each forward fleet's area of responsibility.

+ **SHAREM 146:** Off the coast of Okinawa, Sep 2003. "The most complex and tactically challenging SHAREM ever attempted in Seventh Fleet." A special project team from Naval Rotary Wing Aircraft Test Sqn (HX 21), NAS Patuxent River, MD, tested and evaluated new anti-submarine-warfare technologies for possible future use. USS *Olympia* (SSN 717).
+ **SHAREM 143/KEFTACEX:** Denmark Straits, late summer 2002.
+ **SHAREM 141:** Mediterranean, Jul 2002.
+ **SHAREM 140/Show Force/Arabian Shark:** Arabian Gulf, Mar 2002. USS *Lake Champlain* (CG 57) and USS *Decatur* (DDG 73) with the Bahrain navy.
+ **SHAREM 138:** East China Sea, 23 Jul–2 Aug 2001, US–Japan Maritime Self Defense Force, including attack submarine USS *Buffalo* (SSN 715).
+ **SHAREM 137:** Mediterranean Sea, Apr 2001. USNS *Bold* conducted Navy Surveillance Towed-Array Sensor System (SURTASS) operations.
+ **SHAREM 136:** Hong Kong — Korea West Sea, 24 Jan–2 Feb 2001.
+ **SHAREM 134:** Aug 2000. USS *Vincennes* (CG 49) exercise conducted with several Japanese ships and other US participants.
+ **SHAREM 133:** Sixth Fleet, 11–18 Jun 2000. The UK withdrew because of operational commitments in Sierra Leone.
+ **SHAREM 130/Distant Thunder:** Japan, 13 Aug–8 Sep 1999. USS *Cushing* (DD 985), USS *Vincennes* (CG 49), USS *John S. McCain* (DDG 56), and USS *Buffalo* (SSN 715).
+ **SHAREM 128:** North Arabian Sea and Gulf of Oman, Jun 2000. USS *David R Ray* (DD 971), USS *Curtis Wilbur* (DDG 54), USS *Halyburton* (FFG 40), and USS *Cheyenne* (SSN 773).
+ **SHAREM 127:** Sea of Japan, 21 Feb–2 Mar 1999. US–Korea.
+ **SHAREM 126:** South Korea, 8–21 Sep 1998. USS *Columbia* (SSN 771).

- **SHAREM 125:** Italian naval base at Panteleria Island and Mediterranean Sea, 9–15 Jul 1998. Test of Automatic Radar Periscope Detection and Discrimination.
- **SHAREM 124:** Arabian Gulf, 1–10 May 1998. USS *Cole* (DDG 67) with US and UK submarines.
- **SHAREM 122:** Western Pacific.
- **SHAREM 120:** Korea and Yellow Sea, Apr 1997. USS *Topeka* (SSN 674).
- **SHAREM 119:** Arabian Gulf and Bahrain. USS *Kitty Hawk* (CV 63) Battle Group.
- **SHAREM 118:** Ligurian Sea and Sigonella, Italy. Including USS *Newport News* (SSN 750), USS *James K. Polk* (SSN 645), French and Italian submarines, and maritime patrol aircraft from Canada, Italy, Germany, and the Netherlands.
- **SHAREM 116/MARCOT 96:** Jun 1996. USS *Cole* (DDG 67) with Canadian navy.
- **SHAREM 114/INVITEX 1-96:** Gulf of Valencia, 23–29 Feb 1996.
- **SHAREM 110:** Gulf of Oman, 5–19 Feb 1995. The last three days were spent participating in free-play sub hunting events. A *Los Angeles*–class submarine simulated a diesel submarine trying to carry out port breakouts and attacks on the USS *David R Ray* (DD 971) Surface Action Group.
- **SHAREM 108:** Japan, 22–31 Jan 1998.
- **SHAREM 102 PHASE II/AIREM-B-93P:** Off the coast of Iran, 23–29 Aug 1993. USS *Elliot* (DD 967), USS *Ingraham* (FFG 61), USS *Pasadena* (SSN 752), and USNS *Silas Bent* (T-AGS 26).

Shark: Morse code intercept system introduced in 1999. Playback software allows immediate playback of collected data while still in collection mode.

SHARP (Sharpening Hyperspectral imagery And Reprojection Project): Air Force TENCAP project that fuses panchromatic imagery (black and white) with spectral imagery (multi-spectral) for a high-accuracy image.

Sharp Dagger: NATO exercise at the German army's Warfighting Simulation Center, Wildflecken, 23 Apr–2 May 2003.

Sharp Eagle 01: Naval Forces Europe–led JTF computer-assisted exercise, Kelley Barracks and Ramstein AB, Germany, and aboard the USS *La Salle* (AGF 3), 15–30 Aug 2001. The scenario included peacekeeping and the formation of a civil–military operations center.

Sharp Edge: Noncombatant evacuation operation from Liberia, 5–21 Aug 1990. USS *Nashville* (LPD 13).

Sharp Focus 05: Sixth Fleet–led JTF practicing a noncombatant evacuation operation.

Sharp Guard: NATO maritime interdiction operations in the Adriatic Sea enforcing the UN embargo against the former Yugoslavia (amended to exclude Bosnia in Nov 1994), 17 Jun 1993–. Operations were supported by USS *Dwight D. Eisenhower* (CVN 69), USS *America* (CV 66), USS *Theodore Roosevelt* (CVN 71), USS *Wasp* (LHD 1), USS *Kearsarge* (LHD 3), and USS *Nassau* (LHA 4). Sharp Guard was renamed Decisive Enhancement after the Dayton Peace Agreement.

Sharp Point: UK–Kenyan exercise, 2000–2001.

Sharp Reply 02: USAFE field training exercise.

Sharp Wedge: Naval Mobile Construction Bn annual exercise. Sharp Wedge 03: Camp LeJeune, NC.

Sheepskin: Code name for the classified Technical Agrement allowing for the deployment of US nuclear weapons in Greece. The last B61 nuclear bombs, based at Araxos air base, were withdrawn in 2003.

Shepherd Sentry: Noncombatant evacuation operation from the Central African Republic, 2 Nov 2002.

Shepherd Venture (JTF Sepherd Venture): SOCEUR JTF deployment to Dakar, Senegal, 10 Jun 1998, as part of contingency planning in response to the deteriorating situation in Guinea-Bissau. The total force consisted of about 130 personnel. With the final US citizens safely evacuated, EUCOM ordered JTF Shepherd Venture to redeploy on 15 Jun 1998. The JTF was disestablished on 17 Jun 1998.

Sherman: NSA program, 1980s.

Shield: Space Command R&D testbed using real-time satellite data to provide operational warning of missile launches. *See also* Alert.

Shielded Shark 98: Naval special operations and harbor security exercise, Key West, FL.

Shin Kame: US–Japanese submarine exercise series. Shin Kame 96: 3–5 Sep 1996. USS *Hawkbill* (SSN 666).

Code Names

Shining: EUCOM first word.

+ **Shining Express:** Noncombatant evacuation operation in Liberia, 2003. USS *Kearsarge* (LHD 3).

+ **Shining Hope/Sustain Hope:** JTF deployment to Kosovo, 4 Apr–10 Jul 1999, now designated Allied Harbour/Shining Hope. The Warrior Preparation Center, Einsiedlerhof, Germany, set up the rear operation of the JTF in May 1999, providing administrative and logistical support. President Bill Clinton visited the WPC on 5 May to observe the JTF in progress, accompanied by Secretary of State Madeleine Albright, Secretary of Defense William Cohen, and Chairman of the JCS Gen. Henry H. Shelton.

+ **Shining Presence:** Operation to augment air and theater missile defense of Israel, Dec 1998, during Desert Fox. JTF Shining Presence Commander was Major Gen. Julian H. Burns Jr., deputy commanding general, V Corps.

Shoaling Waves: Navy test conducted in Duck, NC, Nov–Dec 1999.

Shooter: Air Force Space Warfare Center TENCAP program, 2000–present.

Short Haul: Australian–New Zealand tactical air transport exercise, Nov 1997.

Short Sprint: 20th Air Force ICBM missile launch crew exercise series. Short Sprint exercises are scheduled three times per year (one each in Jan–Apr, May–Aug, and Sep–Dec).

Short Swing: Navy Ships Signal Exploitation Equipment "Increment D" subsystem upgrade, 2001. *See also* Desperado.

Shortroot: Automatic high frequency direction finding for short-duration and wide-band signals. *See also* Longroot, Taproot.

Sidearm (Secondary Imagery Dissemination Environment and Resource Maneuver): TENCAP program to transmit and receive standard formatted imagery products, initiated in 1989. Used during Desert Storm (then called FAISS SID System) and deployed with a wide variety of imagery users at low levels.

Sidewinder: 4th Infantry Div operation to apprehend Iraqi insurgents threatening coalition forces in the "Sunni triangle" north of Baghdad, supporting operation Desert Scorpion, preceded Ivy Cyclone II, Iraq, 29 Jun–7 Jul 2003.

Sierra (Project Sierra): Former army special access program.

Sigma: Department of Energy nuclear weapons data compartment dealing with the workings of nuclear warheads. Sigma numbered categories designate different levels of sensitivity. In Jun 1994, Sigmas 14 and 15 were established to protect "use control" information, the knowledge of which could significantly enhance circumvention of use control features in nuclear weapons.

Silk Purse: Former EUCOM EC-135 airborne command post.

Silent: EUCOM first word.

+ **Silent Guide 04:** Exercise held in conjunction with Agile Response 04, a training opportunity to prepare for crisis management in preparation for the Summer Olympics in Greece.
+ **Silent Horse 03:** Exercise.
+ **Silent Lance:** Sixth Fleet Adriatic Sea presence operations, 2000–2001.
+ **Silent Promise:** Relief operations in Mozambique and South Africa, renamed Operation Atlas.
+ **Silent Warrior 04:** Exercise, canceled.

Silent Assurance: 1. US–Saudi classified exercise, May 1997.
2. Silent Assurance. Arabian Gulf exercise, Doha, Qatar, Nov 1997, involving 13th MEU (SOC) and USS *Peleliu* (LHA 5) ARG enhancing security during the Middle East/North Africa (MENA) Economic Conference.

Silent Breeze II: Chemical and biological defense exercise, 1998–1999.

Silent Fury: US–Japanese submarine and anti-submarine-warfare exercise, 2003.

Silent Hammer: Navy proof-of-concept test of the cruise missile submarine (SSGN) program, Third Fleet, Jun 2004.

Silent Knight: AN/WLQ-4 (V) ESM system on SSN-21 attack submarine class. *See also* Cutty Sark.

Silent Pearl 98-1: Anti-submarine-warfare exercise involving the US, Australia, and Chile, Apr–Jun 1998.

Silent Shield: AFSOC program in support of PSYOPS, gunship air interdiction, search and rescue, noncombatant evacuation operations, and support to special access programs. One Silent Shield effort is the Joint Threat

Warning System, which provides threat warning and enhanced situational awareness to SOF aircrews at the Secret level. Direct support operators (airborne "crypto-linguists") at Hurlburt Field, FL; Kadena AB, Japan; and RAF Mildenhall deploy onboard SOF aircraft to provide threat warnings. Silent Shield is also installed on AC-130 gunships. *See also* Privateer.

Silent Vector: Senior national security leader homeland security seminar conducted by the Center for Strategic and International Studies and ANSER Institute for Homeland Security, Oct 2002.

Silent Viper: AFSOC intelligence and surveillance demonstration, also called SOFSTARS.

Silver Anvil: Noncombatant evacuation operation in Sierra Leone, 2–5 May 1992. Following a coup that overthrew the president, a JSOTF evacuated 438 people (including 42 third-country nationals). Two C-141s flew 136 people from Freetown, Sierra Leone, to Rhein-Main AB, Germany; nine C-130 sorties carried another 302 to Dakar, Senegal. Silver Anvil was supported by 7th SOS MC-130E Combat Talons.

Silver Compass: Noncombatant evacuation operation, 22–25 Oct 1992.

Silver Dollar: Former call sign for the national airborne emergency command post.

Silver Eagle: EUCOM JCET in Botswana and Malawi. Silver Eagle 04. Silver Eagle 01. Silver Eagle 99: 3rd SFG in Malawi, Aug 1999. Silver Eagle 92: Botswana, Jan 1992.

Silver Flag Alpha: Air force security police training exercise series.

Silver Knight: Marine Corps exercise and preparation for possible noncombatant evacuation operation from Tirana, Albania, 22 Sep–29 Oct 1998.

Silver Scimitar: Army reserve exercise, Jackson, MS, 29 Jul–11 Aug 2000.

Silver Sword 99: Army reserve Military Police biennial Enemy Prisoners of War (EPW) exercise, Fort McCoy, WI, and Fort Dix, NJ, 31 Jul–14 Aug 1999.

Silver Wake: Noncombatant evacuation operation in Albania, 12 Mar–14 Jul 1997. The operation involved SOF, 22nd MEU, and the USS *Nassau* (LHA 4) ARG. In total, 808 people (390 US, 418 other nationals) were evacuated.

Silverfish: Army intelligence system, Bad Aibling, Germany.

Silverweed Ruckus: Reported UK SIGINT system at RAF Menwith Hill, UK.

Sinbad: Coast Guard special operation, 15 Sep–30 Oct 1991.

Singaroo: Australian–Singapore maritime exercise. Singaroo 03: May 2003. Singaroo 96: Oct.

SIT-II: US–UK Missile and Space Intelligence Center "dynamic test series" special access program database being developed by Summerfield Atlantic Research Limited, 2001–.

Six: System for enhanced situational awareness of battlespace.

Six Pack: Marine Corps CMS-7706 SIGINT receiver.

Ski Jump: Presidential continuity of government exercise, 1980s–early 1990s.

Skilled Anvil: CJTF Skilled Anvil, Mannheim, Germany, 1999–2001. In Oct 1999, SETAF was tasked with providing the core of a JTF to plan for potential operations in the EUCOM theater.

Skivvy 9: North Korea and Chinese Morse code intercept operations at Osan AB, South Korea, 1981–present.

Sky Anvil: EUCOM strike planning for Kosovo operations, beginning Oct 1998. Sky Anvil was the 16th air-force-led counterpart to the navy-led Flexible Anvil, a cruise-missile-only strike contingency similar to that undertaken in Desert Fox. Sky Anvil planned for a gradually escalating air operation, targeting Yugoslavia's air defense system, command and control sites, fielded forces, and targets of military significance first in Kosovo, then in the rest of Yugoslavia.

Skybird: STRATCOM call sign for all command posts, launch control centers, HF stations, air traffic control towers on host tenant bases, and air defense sites in Canada.

Skyking: STRATCOM call sign associated with Single Integrated Operational Plan (SIOP)–committed forces. Its meaning is "all SIOP committed aircraft and missile crews copy the following message."

Skylink: Diplomatic Telecommunications Services Satellite System.

Skymaster: STRATCOM call sign associated with airborne command posts.

Slammer (Project Slammer): Oral history project originally begun in the mid-1980s consisting of voluntary interviews with incarcerated spies. The effort was de-funded in the early 1990s and consequently lost impetus, with several Slammer papers and tapes unprocessed. In 1998, the government looked at reviving Slammer, establishing a database as a resource for security and counter-intelligence professionals.

Sling Dolorose: Reagan-era exercise with NSC involvement. Sling Dolorose 85: 6 Nov 85. Sling Dolorose III.

Slipper: Australian contribution to OEF and the war on terrorism.

Slovak Express: UK Territorial Army battalion-level training exercise in Slovakia, Sep 2001.

Slow Walker: Detection and tracking of aircraft and missile afterburner emissions by Defense Support Program (DSP) satellites, initiated in 1982. Slow Walker was used in Desert Storm to detect Iraqi Scud missile launches. Naval Space Command Detachment ECHO provided personnel for Slow Walker operations at DSP ground stations in Australia and Colorado. *See also* Fast Walker.

Slunj 2000: US–Croatian exercise, Nov 2000. The 26th MEU participated.

Sly: First word associated with a set of clandestine surveillance prototypes that have been deployed with SOF in the war on terrorism.
- + **Sly Boulder:** Remote sensor controller with suite of special optical sensors.
- + **Sly Pirate:** Remote sensor controller with day and night cameras.
- + **Sly Stone:** Remote sensor controller with suite of sensors.
- + **Sly Viper:** Suite comprised of remote sensor camera controller and associated optical and unattended ground sensors.

Snake Bite: Air defense operations in Florida, 1995–1996.

Snipe: UK 45 Commando Group operation to clear a significant area in the remote southeast Afghan mountains believed to be used as a base by al Qaeda and Taliban forces, 2–13 May 2002.

Snow: FEMA presidential continuity of government exercise first word, 1980s–early 1990s. The exercises included Snow Fall, Snow Storm, and Snow Time.

Snow Eagle: CTF Provide Comfort delivery of more than 100 tons of blankets, medical supplies, and food to 110 villages in the area around Gormec, Turkey, after avalanches, 2–9 Feb 1992.

Snow Falcon: NATO cold-weather training, Norway, followed by Venture Express or Joint Winter. The exercise has been ongoing since at least 1988. Snow Falcon 02: Bardufoss, Norway, 21 Jan–1 Feb 2002. UK participation in the 25 Sep–6 Oct 2000 exercise was canceled due to operational commitments in Sierra Leone.

Snow Man: Exercise term for simulated Air Defense Warning White.

Snow Shoe: UK–Canadian exercise series. The Jan–Mar 2000 series was canceled due to other UK operational commitments.

Snow Storm: Air force program, 1997.

Snowbird: ANG training program, Tuscon, AZ.

Snowdrop: French special operations exercise, with UK involvement.

Soda Mountain: Army operation in Iraq ranging from Samawah in the south to Tall Afar in the north to secure lines of communication for US and coalition forces, 12–17 Jul 2003.

Softring (Project Softring): Technical and engineering services associated with possible special access program, late 1990s.

Solania: Australian cyclical maritime surveillance operations in the southwestern Pacific.

Solar Sunrise: Hostile penetration of US military networks. As the US was preparing to take military action against Iraq in Feb–Mar 1998, military computer systems were scanned by an unknown entity that appeared to originate from the UAE. Shortly after the scans, unauthorized hackers compromised several DOD machines. This series of attacks became known as Solar Sunrise. The intruders penetrated at least 200 unclassified military computer systems, including seven air force bases and four navy installations, Department of Energy National Laboratories, NASA sites, and university sites. *See also* Digital Demon and Moonlight Maze.

Solid Citizen: DOD–FEMA military support to civil authorities exercise. Solid Citizen 01: Great Lakes, IL, 21–25 May 2001. Solid Citizen 99. Solid Citizen 94.

Solid Curtain: Fleet Forces Command anti-terrorism/force protection exercise. Solid Curtain 04: 3–6 Aug 2004. Solid Curtain 03: Scenario involved 15 simultaneous attacks across the country including NAS Corpus Christi, NS Ingleside, local shipyards, and other targets of attack in the coastal bend of southern Texas, 4–7 Nov 2003. Solid Curtain 02: NS Newport, RI, 22–26 Jul 2002. Solid Curtain 01: 30 Jul–2 Aug 2001.

Soothsayer: UK maritime SIGINT/ESM equipment used in OEF/OIF.

Sorbet Royale: NATO submarine search and rescue exercise series. The first Sorbet Royale took place in 1986 off Stavanger, Norway, and the second took place in 1992 in the Mediterranean. Participants include France, Italy, the Netherlands, Norway, the UK, and the US. Sweden, which has signed a bilateral submarine rescue agreement with Norway, participated in 1996. Sobet Royale 02. Sorbet Royale 00: 4–13 Sep 2000. Sorbet Royale 99. Sorbet Royale 96: Vestfjorden, Norway, 4–14 Jun 1996. Included the USS *Sand Lance* (SSN 660), which then went on to make an under-ice transit to the North Pole.

Sound Shake: Coast Guard exercise, Port Angeles, WA, 1999.

Southern Breeze: TRANSCOM chemical weapons protection field test series. Southern Breeze 02: NWS Charleston, SC, Jun 2002. The test evaluated internal contamination allowed by ventilation systems of a ship when contaminated with a simulated chemical agent and evaluated the effectiveness of decontamination procedures. Southern Breeze 01: NWS Charleston, SC, May 2001. The test objective was to determine how covering versus not covering cargo affected the level of contamination and the amount of time needed to decontaminate items.

Southern Crusade: French airborne forces exercise with UK involvement.

Southern Focus: CENTCOM air operations under the cover of Southern Watch in preparation for OIF. During Southern Focus, coalition air forces dropped 606 bombs, responding to 651 Iraqi "attacks" from Jun 2002 until OIF began 19 Mar 2003.

Southern Frontier: US–Australian semi-annual marine air–ground training exercise. Southern Frontier 02: Royal Australian Air Force Base Tindal and Darwin, Jun–Sep 2002. Southern Frontier 99. Southern Frontier 2-96: 23 May–8 Jul 1996.

Southern Knight: Interrogation exercise at Fort Dix, NJ, conducted by the 202nd Military Intelligence Bn and hosted by the Northeast Army Reserve

Intelligence Support Center. Southern Knight 99: Jun 1999. Southern Knight 97: 1–13 Jun 1997. The 33rd Interrogator-Translator Team, marine forces Reserve, and military intelligence interrogators from the Netherlands and UK participated.

Southern Pine: Presidential continuity of government exercises, 1980s–early 1990s.

Southern Tiger 97: Australian–Malaysian army training, including Singapore, Oct 1997.

Southern Vigilance 96: Army TENCAP exercise, Jul 1996.

Southern Warrior: SOUTHCOM anti-terrorism/force protection exercise based on a Colombia scenario, 20 Sep 2000.

Southern Watch: Iraqi no-fly-zone operation to prohibit Iraqi air activity south of 32 degrees, initiated 26 Aug 1992. The US established a no-fly zone south of the 32nd parallel to monitor Iraqi compliance with UN Security Council resolutions and established the combined US–UK–Saudi JTF — Southwest Asia to command the operation at Prince Sultan AB, Saudi Arabia. The mission was formally concluded on 30 Apr 2003, with a total of 286,000 missions flown.

Space 7: Air Intelligence Agency Advanced Programs Division, Directorate of Information Operations.

Spanish Phiblex: Reagan-era exercise with NSC involvement.

Spartan: Navy multi-mission deployable battlespace awareness and force protection Advanced Concept Technology Demonstration, 2001–present. Spartan is an unmanned surface vehicle that can be used in protection of ports and ships in port against terrorist threats, or converted for anti-submarine warfare or mine avoidance during chokepoint transits. The covert intelligence potential could also be applied to counter-narcotics operations. Singapore and South Korea are involved in the development.

Spartan Challenge: Army chemical response exercise, Bamberg, Germany, Apr 2000.

Spartan Focus: 3rd Infantry Div regular emergency deployment readiness exercise.

Speak Easy: Air force program supported by Pacer Easy, 1994.

Spear: Jamming system on B-52 bomber, a Big Safari–managed special access program.

Speckled Minnow: Air force project similar to Speckled Trout.

Speckled Trout: Air force heavily modified NC-135 aircraft used by the 412th Flight Test Sqn at Edwards Air Force Base, CA, as a testbed for avionics and communications systems, and for executive transport and emergency communications. Speckled Trout aircraft also fly out of Andrews AFB, MD. Gen. Richard Myers, chairman of the JCS, was flying aboard a Speckled Trout on 9/11.

Spectre: Counter-terrorism-related compartment, probably no longer in use.

Spectrum: Unknown exercise, 1996–1997.

SPECTRUM RISC: TENCAP maintenance course taught at the army intelligence school, Fort Huachuca, AZ.

SPECWAR SUBEX 00-3 (T): Pacific Fleet/Seventh Fleet exercise, May 2000.

Spiderweb: Army intelligence system, Bad Aibling, Germany.

Spinnaker (Project Spinnaker): US–Canadian program to develop lightweight, low-power, low-cost ocean surveillance arrays for quick, covert deployment. The immediate goal of Project Spinnaker in the 1990s was the deployment of arrays in the Arctic.

Spirit Hawk: Air exercise mission rehearsal, Mountain Home AFB, ID. On 14 Oct 1999, four B-2 bombers supported Spirit Hawk II flying 12 sorties as part of composite strike packages.

Spirochaete: UK exercise, 8–26 Oct 2001, canceled because of OEF operational commitments.

Spoke: COMINT compartment (for example, Secret/Spoke) eliminated in May 1999, along with the code words *Umbra*, *Moray*, and *Zarf*. Information previously classified Spoke was subsequently to be designated Top Secret COMINT.

SPONTEX: French maritime exercise with UK (and occasional US) involvement.

Spotlight: Naval intelligence element of the Integrated Undersea Surveillance System.

Spray Paint: Biological weapons sensor.

Spring's Wind: Unknown exercise, including Spring's Wind 98 and Spring's Wind 97.

Stabilise: East Timor and Philippine Sea operation to provide communications and logistics support for peacekeeping missions in East Timor, Sep 1999–. Initially included the USS *Mobile Bay* (CG 53), *USNS Kilauea* (T-AE 26), USS *Belleau Wood* (LHA 3), USS *Peleliu* (LHA 5), 11th MEU, and 31st MEU.

Stadium Clock: Army Foreign Science and Technology Center foreign material exploitation, 1990–1991.

STAFFEX 92-3: STRATCOM nuclear weapons exercise, Aug 1992.

Stalker: Software program that supports area limitation and movement modeling for planners. Stalker assists in determining locations that vehicles cannot access due to terrain limitations.

Standoff Four: 68th FS deployment of six F-16s to Homestead ARB, FL, following the downing of an American aircraft by Cuba, Mar 1996.

Star Eagle 03: US–Australian engagement exercise between the 75th Ranger Regt and the 4th Bn, Royal Australian Regt, Apr–May 2003.

Star Gate: DIA–army intelligence remote viewing program.

Star Leopard: Australian–Brunei special operations exercise, formerly Night Leopard, Nov 2002.

Star Safire: AN/AAQ-22 programmable electro-optical camera system evaluated as part of the Precision Targeting Identification Advanced Concept Technology Demonstration.

Star Sapphire: NSA program to develop the Advanced Electronic Signals Database, a database to store all future ELINT data, which is scheduled for activation first quarter 2005. Star Sapphire will replace Wrangler and reengineer and unify the Kilting and ELINT Parameter Limits databases into a single database featuring a new ELINT signal representational model, modern multi-media and digital content, a fully relational database structure, and customer, producer, and user tools.

Stardex: Five Power Defence Agreement (FPDA — Australia, Malaysia, New Zealand, Singapore, and the UK) maritime-oriented air defense exercise, Singapore and Malaysia. Stardex 02: Sep 2002. Stardex 01: 3–15 Sep 2001.

Starfish 96: Five Power Defence Agreement (FPDA — Australia, Malaysia, New Zealand, Singapore, and the UK) maritime exercise, Malaysia, Sep 1996.

Starhouse: Army intelligence system, Bad Aibling, Germany.

Starlite/Discoverer: DARPA 24 LightSAT constellation development program. *See also* Discoverer II.

Starquake: Army intelligence system, Bad Aibling, Germany.

Starwindow: UK SIGINT/electronic support measures program.

Steady State: South American counter-narcotics operation (formerly Support Justice).

Steal Puma: 12th Air Force exercise, 28 Feb–4 Mar 2000.

Steamroller: Army intelligence Trojan Classic system.

Steel Box: Operation to move chemical weapons from Germany to Johnston Island, 26 Jun–22 Sep 1990. Some Pentagon planners suggested that the chemical munitions be sent to Saudi Arabia for use against Iraq instead of to Johnston Island. *See also* Nike Air.

Steel Eagle: Advanced remote ground unattended sensor (ARGUS) that operates in the same manner as Steel Rattler but can be air-deliverable, including by most tactical aircraft (such as F-15Es and F-16s). *See also* Steel Rattler.

Steel Eye: DIA electro-optical viewing system, 1980s.

Steel Knight: I MEF desert training exercise. Desert Knight/Steel Knight 01: Sep 2001. Steel Knight 00: Included the use of Pioneer UAVs. Steel Knight 99. Steel Knight 96: Dec 1996.

Steel Puma: Panther Den special access program "full-spectrum" information warfare exercise including SOUTHCOM, the Joint Staff, CIA–NSA Information Operations Technology Center, DIA, and Joint Information Operations Center, 1999.

Steel Rattler: Advanced remote ground unattended sensor (ARGUS) man-portable unattended seismic and acoustic sensor carried into the operating area, typically by SOF. It is used to identify targets and report their presence to a remote workstation.

Steel Trap: Theater missile defense ground-based radar program with a corollary capability of MASINT data collection.

Steeplebush/Steeplebush 2: Magnum/Trumpet/Vortex satellite operations system and downlink, associated with RAF Menwith Hill, UK.

Stingray: Predator UAV Moving Target Indicator (MTI).

Stock Deal I/II/III: Army Foreign Science and Technology Center foreign material exploitation program, 1992.

Stone Ax: Code name for classified Technical Agreement allowing the deployment of US nuclear weapons in Italy.

Stone Ghost: DIA Intelink C classified Web-based network capable of allowing access to sensitive compartmented Modernized Integrated Database (MIDB) and other order of battle information by CENTCOM and other coalition users at lower levels of classification.

Stoney Run/Mill Race: UK army exercise canceled because of Kosovo operations, May–Oct 1999.

Storm Cloud: FBI and DOD law enforcement and counter-intelligence investigation of the Moonlight Maze penetration of US government computer networks.

Storm Jib: Navy P-3 VPU program, formerly Reef Point.

Story: Navy EP-3 reconnaissance and communications/electronics intercept package first word under the AIRES II program.

- **Story Book:** EP-3 special signal (proforma) acquisition, data processing, and data fusion system that provides situation awareness based on special signals exploitation. Works with Windjammer.
- **Story Classic:** EP-3 system that provides operators with an upgraded search and acquisition system for low-band signals.
- **Story Finder:** EP-3 enhancement included in the FY 2003 Defense Emergency Readiness Fund for OEF.
- **Story Teller:** EP-3 system that provides the capability to manipulate collected data and external intelligence input to view a composite tactical situation display.

Straight Arrow: Navy unknown program, Project Code ZC7.

Strain Drum: Army Foreign Science and Technology Center foreign material exploitation of an unknown helicopter, 1991–1992.

Streamliner: Automated digital system for compartmented sensitive information message traffic. *See* Newsdealer.

Strong Resolve: NATO bi-command quadrennial major composite force field training exercise. The exercise involves deployment of a NATO CJTF in the Supreme Allied Transformation (formerly SACLANT) and Supreme Allied Europe (SACEUR) command regions to exercise NATO's ability to cope with multiple, simultaneous crises in separate geographic regions. Particpants include Belgium, Canada, the Czech Republic, Denmark, France, Germany, Greece, Hungary, Italy, Lithuania, Macedonia, the Netherlands, Norway, Poland, Portugal, Romania, Slovakia, Slovenia, Spain, Sweden, Spain, Turkey, the UK, and the US. Strong Resolve 06: Planned for the Southern Region and subsuming exercises Dynamic Mix, Cooperative Partner, and Cooperative Key. Strong Resolve 02: Norway and Poland, 1–25 Mar 2002. UK participation scaled back due to OEF. Unified Endeavor 01-4/Joint Spirit served as a building block for the exercise, which engaged SACLANT in a crisis response operation scenario with Poland as the host nation. Strong Resolve 98: Norway and Portugal, 3–21 Mar 1998. CJTF HQ trial involving some 50,000 military personnel and consisting of two halves; exercise Crisis North, in Norway, and exercise Crisis South, in Portugal. Pretraining took part in France. The USS *Mount Whitney* (LCC 20) operated off the Iberian coast, while amphibious vehicles landed in Sierra del Retin. Strong Resolve 95.

Strong Support: JTF Bravo/Aguila humanitarian assistance and disaster relief operations in response to Hurricane Mitch, Honduras, El Salvador, Guatemala, and Nicaragua, Nov 1998.

Success: Radio SIGINT system.

Succumbios: 7th SFG counter-narcotics operation, Ecuador, 5 May–9 Jun 1997.

Sudden Dawn: DIA assessment of unusual phenomena uncovered during MASINT efforts using reconnaissance satellites, 1982–1983.

Suman Warrior: Five Power Defence Agreement (FPDA — Australia, Malaysia, New Zealand, Singapore, and the UK) annual land defense command post exercise. Suman Warrior 02: Sep–Oct 2002. Suman Warrior 01: Australia, Oct 2001. Suman Warrior 97: Oct 1997. Suman Warrior 96: Malaysia and Singapore, 17–28 Oct 1996.

Summit Cap: US–Czech fighter air cover of NATO summit in Prague, Czech Republic, 20–23 Nov 2002.

Sumo Tiger 03: US–Bangladesh air exercise, Dhaka, Bangladesh, Sep 2003.

Sun City: STRATCOM-initiated alternative nuclear force structure study, 1993. Sun City predated the 1994 Nuclear Posture Review and analyzed the number and combinations of forces required for START II implementation and beyond. It also focused on the amount of capability and flexibility that would be lost at different levels of funding and arms control reductions. A Sun City Extended study in 1994 looked at Russian and Chinese nuclear war scenarios that might require increases in nuclear forces and new targeting schemes.

Sunburst: Cryptographic system used on STICS.

Sundowner (Project Sundowner): Air force special operations and 18th Flight Test Sqn involvement in an Advanced Concept Technology Demonstration, 1999.

Sunny Hope/Sunny Relief: Humanitarian operations in Jordan in support of OIF. Belgium deployed a C-130 to Kuwait on 22 Apr 2003 to execute humanitarian missions for the International Committee of the Red Cross (Sunny Hope) and the UN (Sunny Relief). The Belgian detachment continued operations from Amman airport, Jordan, after the end of OIF major combat operations.

Sunshine: Air Force SIGINT system, related to Wrangler.

Sunshine/Surf: E-3 AWACS ELINT collection system used for air and maritime emitter collection.

Sunstreak: Former CIA remote viewing program.

Superbad: Army intelligence system, Bad Aibling, Germany.

Support Democracy/Sea Signal: Operations in and around Haiti to enforce UN sanctions on the Cedras regime, 18 Oct 1993–19 Sep 1994. Operations were supported by the USS *Nassau* (LHA 4), USS *Yorktown* (CG 48), USS *Conolly* (DD 979), USS *Bradley* (FFG 49), USS *Morrison* (FFG 13), USS *Fahrion* (FFG 22), and USS *Jack Williams* (FFG 24). Followed by Restore Democracy.

Support Hope: JTF operations to provide aid to refugees from Rwanda following the massacre of civilian Tutsis, 22 Jul–6 Oct 1994 (initial name Quiet Resolve). Army troops deployed to Rwanda on 17 Jul 1994. By 26 Jul, a

EUCOM TF organized around a heavy maintenance battalion was providing clean water to combat outbreaks of cholera, assisting in the burial of the dead, and integrating transportation and distribution of relief supplies. The JTF secured the Kigali International Airport and established a civil–military operations center. By the end of Sep, the JTF turned over operations to the UN High Commission for Refugees and NGOs. The peak army strength reached 2,415 on 23 Aug 1994. Two C-130s and four crews deployed to Entebbe, Uganda, flew 65 sorties. Supported by the USS *Tripoli* (LPH 10) ARG.

Support Justice: Counter-narcotics operations in Peru, 1990s (later called Steady State). Support Justice IV/Steady State, Yurimaguas, Peru, Feb 1994–Dec 1995.

Support Sovereignty: Deployment to Swan Island, Honduras, Apr 1992.

Surf Board: Presidential continuity of government exercises, 1980s–early 1990s.

Surf Fisher: DIA-led program that provided intelligence information to the Iraqi military during the Iran–Iraq war, 1987–1988. Formerly Druid Leader.

SURGEX 02: Naval submarine exercise involving the USS *Emory S. Land* (AS 39), 2002.

SURIOT/NORMINEX: French mine counter-measures exercise, with UK and US involvement.

Suspect Stole/Suspect Runaway: Army Foreign Science and Technology Center foreign material exploitations, 1991–1992.

Sustain Hope/Shining Hope: EUCOM JTF for Kosovo, 4 Apr–10 Jul 1999. Sustain Hope built three camps (Hope, Eagle, and Liberty) in Albania to house approximately 60,000 refugees.

Suter (Project Suter): Air Intelligence Agency airborne capability for cyber-warfare attack of time-critical targets and integrated air defense systems involving remote penetration of enemy computer systems, manipulation of information and databases, and the planting of false targets and messages. Suter was the first operational remote computer network attack capability in the US military. Suter 1 was practiced by a combination of RC-135 Rivet Joint, EC-130 Compass Call, and F-16CJ aircraft during Joint Expeditionary Force Experiment (JEFX) 00. Suter 2 was exercised during JEFX 02, working in unison with the special access program Panther Den. Big Safari–managed program under Senior Suter.

Swabian Crusade: Germany-based exercise. For the 12–20 Mar 2001 exercise, UK participation was canceled due to foot-and-mouth disease restrictions.

Swamp Box: Marine Corps CS-2001 SIGINT receiver.

Swamp Fox: Naval special operations submarine exercise. Swamp Fox 93-1: Oct 1993. USS *Sturgeon* (SSN 637). Swamp Fox 92: Cape Canaveral, FL. USS *Sturgeon* (SSN 637). Swamp Fox 91: Roosevelt Roads, Puerto Rico, Jan 1991. USS *Sturgeon* (SSN 637).

Swarmer: Presidential continuity of government exercises, 1980s–early 1990s.

Sweeney: US–UK anti-smuggling and humanitarian assistance operation on the al Faw peninsula in southern Iraq, 2003–2004.

Sweepstakes: Shemya, AK–based operation, 1970.

Swift Freedom: OEF operation of the 15th MEU (SOC) seizing the forward operating base Rhino in southern Afghanistan, south of Kandahar, 25 Nov 2001.

Swifthawk: Collection Requirements Management System developed by the DIA, used by the Marine Corps in Desert Storm.

Swinger: NSA program, 1980s.

Symphony: DARPA Terrorism Information Awareness language translation project.

Sympton Odin: Air force special-operations-related test program, possibly a foreign material exploitation.

Sympton Zeus: *See* Mobcap Apex.

— T —

Taa Nok In Sii: Australian–Thai surveillance training operation. Taa Nok In Sii 03-1: Apr 2003. Taa Nok In Sii 02-2: Dec 2002.

Tabler: Army intelligence system, Bad Aibling, Germany.

Tacit: Air force first word.

+ **Tacit Blue:** Prototype stealth aircraft (the "Whale") publicly unveiled in May 1996. Tacit Blue was built by Northrop Grumman at its

Hawthorne, CA, facility and was the first aircraft to use streamlined curved aluminum and composite surfaces to scatter and absorb radar. The program began in 1978; the plane made its last flight in 1985.

+ **Tacit Rainbow:** Loitering anti-radiation missile/lethal UAV (AGM-136). The first Tacit Rainbow air launch occurred 30 Jul 1984, and 30 test launches were made before the program was canceled in 1991.

Tackle: PACOM first word.

Tactical Fighter Weaponry (TFW): Danish annual field training exercise conducted in western Denmark, the North Sea, and Baltic approaches with emphasis on conventional defense. TFW 02/03: Aalborg, Denmark, 16 Aug–4 Sep 2002. TFW 01: 19–31 Aug 2001.

Talent Keyhole (TK): Classification compartment designating information derived from COMINT satellites (for instance, Top Secret/Talent Keyhole or TS/TK). Talent Keyhole information can be further designated with a BYEMAN, Gamma, or H category (such as Top Secret/Talent Keyhole Gamma). In May 1999, NSA eliminated use of the code words *Umbra*, *Spoke*, *Moray*, and *Zarf* to designate COMINT. Any Talent Keyhole information previously protected as Zarf became merely Talent Keyhole.

Talisman Saber: US–Australian exercise merging Tandem Thrust, Kingfisher, and Crocodile, and using training areas in Australia. The Seventh Fleet organizes as a coalition TF in a short-warning, power projection, forcible entry scenario. Each exercise includes a command post exercise and field training exercise module.

Talon: 1. Post-9/11 AFOSI process to monitor and report suspicious activities that fall below the threshold of DOD collection requirements. Talon reporting is posted on the restricted Eagle Watch Web site.

2. **TALON (TACSIM Analysis Operations Node):** TACSIM subsystem that aggregates intelligence information for exercises.

Talon: Air Force Space Command Space Warfare Center (SWC) TENCAP first word.

+ **Talon Abbacus:** 2003–2005.
+ **Talon Aura:** 2003–2004.
+ **Talon Beowolf:** 2003–2004.
+ **Talon BRITE (Broadcast Request Imagery Technology Experiment):** *See* BRITE.

+ **Talon Chamelion:** 2004–2005.
+ **Talon Charm:** 2003–2005.
+ **Talon Command:** SWC program office responsible for enhancing warfighting support.
+ **Talon Concord/MC:** TENCAP multi-channel tactical receiver for HC-130 aircraft and HH-60 helicopters for enhanced situational awareness in search and rescue by providing blue force tracking data, TIBS, TDDS, and TADIX-B.
+ **Talon E-FASSR:** TENCAP support to air force command and control.
+ **Talon Flash:** 2003–2005.
+ **Talon FOGLITE:** Congressionally mandated evaluation of laser imaging capability.
+ **Talon Gateway:** TENCAP information distribution system providing fighter aircraft links to the time-critical targeting cell. Tested in Joint Expeditionary Force Experiment (JEFX) 00 onboard a modified KC-135.
+ **Talon Granite:** 2003–2004 project that transitioned outside the air force.
+ **Talon HP/Elwood:** 2003–.
+ **Talon IMOEN/Dirty Sally:** 2003–2004.
+ **Talon Jake:** 2004–.
+ **Talon Knight:** SWC program office responsible for enhancing special operations support. Projects include Talon MASTT, Talon BRITE, Have Site, and Talon Concord/MC.
+ **Talon Lance:** Real-time information in the cockpit.
+ **Talon MASTT (Multi-mode Air and Space Tagging and Tracking):** Talon Knight project support to JSOC and the CIA in providing low probability of intercept/low probability of detection (LPI/LPD) tagging, tracking, and locating solutions to SOF using active (Cobra line-of-sight receiver) and semi-active (radar responsive) tagging technologies. This enabled aircraft and satellites to identify tagged US personnel on the ground during close air support and other covert operations.
+ **Talon Mini-Cobra:** TENCAP support to special operations.
+ **Talon MREC:** 2003–2004.
+ **Talon Music:** TENCAP support to air force command and control.
+ **Talon Outlook:** SWC program office responsible for identifying warfighting enhancements and operational technology deficiencies that might be resolved with future national satellite initiatives.

Code Names

+ **Talon Pole Vault:** 2003–.
+ **Talon Radiance:** TENCAP support to EUCOM requirement for foliage penetration imagery, a Big Safari special access program. Talon Radiance provides near-real-time anomaly detection capability using hyperspectral sensing on a Predator UAV.
+ **Talon Reach:** 2003–2004.
+ **Talon Ready:** SWC program office responsible for enhancing national systems products for mission planning, preparation, rehearsal, and combat execution support.
+ **Talon Ready Sharp:** Classified TENCAP project, 1999–present.
+ **Talon SACM:** TENCAP classified support to special operations.
+ **Talon Seeker:** 2003–2004.
+ **Talon SEII/Precise:** 2003–2004.
+ **Talon Shield:** System to supply attack and early reporting to theater users.
+ **Talon Shooter:** SWC program office responsible for enhancing sensor-to-shooter support.
+ **Talon SIMPL-ASE:** Classified TENCAP program.
+ **Talon Suter:** *See* Suter.
+ **Talon Sword/Global Sword:** Post–Desert Storm program to improve mobile targeting by bringing information into the cockpit. In 1994, Pioneer UAVs participated in Talon Sword/Global Sword at NAS Fallon, NV. Pioneer proved the ability to use existing commercial satellite links to securely broadcast video and data.
+ **Talon Threads:** 2003–2004.
+ **Talon TSP:** TENCAP support to AFIWC and Air Intelligence Agency.
+ **Talon Vision:** SWC program office responsible for enhancing future warfighting support.
+ **Talon Warrior:** TENCAP training centers, including the Air Combat Command command and control Warrior Center Facility and Aerospace Integration Center, PACAF Cope Thunder Facility, USAFE Special Applications Employment Facility, Air Mobility Warfare Center, and Special Operations Forces Space Center. The Talon Warrior Space Information Distributed Architecture (SPIDAR) connects the facilities and delivers space information to battle staffs.

Talon Gold: Pointing and tracking telescope experiment to evaluate the ability of a satellite-borne low-energy laser to track potential targets accurately, terminated in Jan 1985.

Talon Sabre: Navy-led Advanced Concept Technology Demonstration to develop a sensor network to enhance the effectiveness and reduce the vulnerability of Marine Corps and SOF in high-risk urban environments, during airfield seizures and other highly coordinated, fast-paced operations. Wearable computers or other hand-portable devices will provide interface between individual operators and supply a common operational picture.

Talon Vision: US–Philippine air–ground integration exercise. Talon Vision 04: 2003. Talon Vision 02: Former Clark AB. Included airborne operations by US and Philippine Marines, and live-fire AH-1 Cobra training.

TAMEX: New Zealand–hosted submarine and anti-submarine-warfare maritime surveillance exercise involving Australia and the US. Tamex 03-2: Apr–Jun 2003. Tamex 03-1: Jan–Mar 2003. Tamex 02-4: Oct–Dec 2002. Tamex 02-3: Jul–Sep 2002. Tamex 98-1: Australia, Mar 1998.

Taming the Dragon/Dalmatia 02: NATO ISO/PfP exercise, Makarska, Croatia, 16–18 Apr 2002.

Tanager: Australian operations in East Timor, replaced by Citadel.

Tandem: PACOM first word.

+ **Tandem Orbit 85:** Reagan-era exercise with NSC involvement, 1–30 Sep 1985.
+ **Tandem Thrust:** US–Australian biennial (odd-year) field training exercise, historically held on Guam, launched in 1997. It was held in Australia in 1999 and 2001. Starting in 2005, Tandem Thrust will become part of Talisman Saber. Tandem Thrust 03/Fleet Battle Experiment Kilo: May 2003. Information warfare and computer network defense experimentation including USS *Olympia* (SSN 717). Tandem Thrust 00: Pearl Harbor, HI, and Brisbane, Australia, 3–7 Apr 2000. Tandem Thrust 99: Orate Airfield, Guam. Tandem Thrust 99 saw the first live-fire Maverick missile shot from a P-3 aircraft and the first P-3 Maverick shot in Seventh Fleet. Participants included Canada, Australia, Singapore, and South Korea. USS *Albuquerque* (SSN 706). Tandem Thrust 97: Northeast Australia, 1–22 Mar 1997.

Tangent Flash: Former US–Philippine exercise, dating to the early 1980s.

Tapestry: Special access program relating to security clearance sharing among Joint Personnel Adjudication System (DOD), Security/Suitability

Investigations Index (Office of Personnel Management), and Scattered Castles (Intelligence Community) databases.

Tapioca: PACOM first word.

TAPON: French anti-submarine-warfare exercise. Participants include Greece, Spain, the UK, and the US. TAPON 96: Alboran Sea, Gulf of Cadiz, and the eastern Atlantic Ocean, Jun 1996. USS *Grayling* (SSN 646).

Tarmacq: Homeland security operation to capture illegal immigrants posing as airport security workers in the US, 2002–2003.

Tarpaulin/Tartan: PACOM first words.

Tartan Eagle: US–UK exercise series. Tartan Eagle 01: Sep 2001. UK forces did not participate due to operations in Sierra Leone. In 2000, the US reduced the annual commitment to one reciprocal exercise a year. Two exercises, one in the UK and one in the US, were canceled as a result.

Tartan Venture: UK–Netherlands amphibious force exercise, Jun 1995.

Tasman: Australian–New Zealand exercise series first word, including Tasman Eagle, Tasman Exchange, Tasman Link, and Tasman Reserve.

Tasmanex 03: Australian–French–New Zealand maritime surveillance, anti-submarine-warfare, and maritime interception operations, Feb–Mar 2003.

Tassel: US–Thai first word.

Tasty: US–Philippine first word.

Taxi/Teacher: PACOM first words.

Teak: PACOM JCET series first word.

+ **Teak Piston:** US–Philippine JCET focusing on air operation and maintenance conducted by the 353rd SOG and the Philippine air force, 2001–present.
+ **Teak Torch:** US–Thai JCET series.

Teal: Cold War DARPA program first word, utilized 1970s–1980s, including Teal Amber and Teal Blue (space surveillance programs), Teal Cameo (high-altitude remotely piloted vehicle follow-on to U-2/TR-1), Teal Dawn, Teal Emerald (a post–Teal Ruby generation of stabilized sensor platforms), Teal Parrot, Teal Rain (a High Altitude Long Endurance UAV), and Teal Ruby (an optical system for infrared detection of air vehicles from space).

Team: PACOM first word.

+ **Team Challenge:** Southeast Asia umbrella exercise to train a contingency JTF. The series links existing bilateral exercises with Australia, Thailand, the Philippines, and Singapore using a UN Chapter VII and noncombatant evacuation operation scenario. Phase I provides JTF training for the Seventh Fleet during Tandem Thrust. Phase II provides JTF training for III MEF and I Corps (in alternating years) in Balikatan, Cobra Gold, Cope Tiger, and Commando Sling. Team Challenge 04: May 2004. Team Challenge 03/Cobra Gold 03: Satahip, Thailand, May 2003. III MEF, Thai Supreme Command, and Singaporean army. Team Challenge 02/Cobra Gold 02: 21–28 May 2002. III MEF Team Challenge 01.

+ **Team Spirit:** Former US–South Korean exercise, now Ulchi Focus Lens. The exercises were initiated in 1976 and conducted annually until 1994. Team Spirit 94 was postponed and later canceled as a confidence building measure while negotiations with North Korea on compliance with the Nuclear Non-proliferation Treaty were ongoing. The option remains open to conduct the large-scale demonstrations of South Korean and US resolve to defend against North Korean aggression if needed.

Teamwork: Former major NATO exercise series. Teamwork 92 was the largest NATO exercise in more than a decade.

Telephone Booth (TB): Sensitive compartmented information program associated with unified command operations.

Telic: UK military operations coinciding with the US Operation Iraqi Freedom.

Tel-Scope (Telescope): Air Force National Air Intelligence Center telecommunications modeling program used in information warfare planning. Tel-Scope models adversary telecommunications links and nodes and shows physical routes for telecommunications traffic, allowing for interactive C3 targeting to determine if prospective targets will affect traffic.

Tempest Express: PACOM computer-assisted exercise to train the CINCPAC staff to function as a JTF headquarters. The exercise is held as often as needed, three to seven times per year.

Tempest Rapid: Employment of military resources in natural disaster emergencies within the continental US, Puerto Rico, the Virgin Islands, Alaska, and Hawaii.

Temple Jade: Australian–UK triennial (97, 00, 03) army exchange.

Tempo: SOCOM classified activity in the FY 2003 budget.

Tempo Brave: Former PACOM exercise, Camp Smith, HI, and Fort Lewis, WA, to train a contingency JTF staff in crisis planning and execution, replaced by Terminal Fury. Tempo Brave 01-1: I Corps acted as PACOM's JTF for consequence management in the chemical and biological defense scenario. Tempo Brave 00: Jul 2000. Tempo Brave 99: Sep 1999. Tempo Brave 98-1/Trailblazer 97: Tempo Brave concentrated on humanitarian assistance/disaster response, while Trailblazer worked with synthetic terrain. Tempo Brave 96. Tempo Brave 95.

Tender/Tennis: PACOM first words.

Terminal: Pacific counter-terrorism and force protection exercise series.

Terminal Breeze 96: Chemical defense exercise providing an opportunity for law enforcement, health and medical, fire, environmental, and emergency management agencies of Virginia, Maryland, and Washington, DC, to work with DOD on plans, policies, and procedures for crisis and consequence management in response to a WMD terrorist attack.

Terminal Fury: PACOM high-level exercise series involving activation of JTF headquarters and future innovation. Terminal Fury 04/Cobra Gold: 3–14 Dec 2003. Terminal Fury 03: Camp Smith, HI, and Okinawa, Japan, 1–13 Dec 2002. Replaced Tempo Brave.

Terrace/Terrier: PACOM first word.

TESON: Counter-narcotics compartment or codeword?.

Thai Boomerang 96: Australian–Thai air defense exercise, Aug 1996.

Theme Castle: Former air force (mobility forces?) special access program.

Theorem: UK information compartment dealing with nuclear weapons.

Thermal: PACOM first word.
  + **Thermal Gale:** Former PACOM triennial special operations exercise in Hawaii.
  + **Thermal Vicar:** DOD special access program.

Thirst Watcher: DOD special access program.

Thirsty Panther: UK exercise, Belize, 2000–2002.

Thirsty Saber: Former DARPA special access program, 1998–1991, known as Multi-Sensor Target Recognition System (MUSTRS). MUSTRS attempted to develop a sensor that would replicate human reasoning.

Thirsty Warrior: DARPA research program to integrate precision submunitions into a cruise missile for use in attacks on mobile targets, linked to Thirsty Saber. The impetus was Desert Storm, where Iraqi Scud missiles could not be found and destroyed with manned aircraft despite a massive sortie rate. The impetus for deployment waned rapidly after the war.

Thor/Odin: Denmark-hosted UK reciprocal training series. Two two-week reciprocal exercises planned for Mar–Dec 2000 were canceled by Denmark.

Thor's Hammer 04: JFCOM, SOCOM, STRATCOM, National Reconnaissance Office, CIA, and Department of Homeland Security interagency space simulation involving space and the exchange of intelligence information through the Joint Interagency Coordination Group in a preconflict scenario set in a global crisis in the next decade, 23–27 Feb 2004.

THREADS (Threat HUMINT Reporting, Evaluation, Analysis, and Display System): National Reconnaissance Office and Air Force Information Warfare Center effort supporting the war on terrorism.

Throttle Car: Counter narcotics program, 2000.

Thundercloud: Information-warfare-/information-technology-related location or activity, 2002.

Tide: NSA code name used in the 1980s.

Tidytips III: SIGINT collection and electronic warfare system, 1990s.

Tier I: 1. CIA Gnat 750 UAV program.
2. **Tier I:** Short-range, conventional (not stealthy) UAV such as Outrider or Hunter.

Tier II: Conventional, low- to medium-altitude UAV. *Tier II* is often used to refer to the improved version of the Amber UAV, ultimately called Predator.

Tier II+: Conventional, high-altitude UAV, often used to refer to the program initiated to replace the terminated Tier III, ultimately called Global Hawk.

Tier III: 1. Classified, stealthy, long-range UAV terminated in favor of a Tier II+.
2. **Tier III:** US–UK nuclear accident exercise.

Tier III–: Stealth-configured, high-altitude UAV, often used to refer to Dark Star.

Tiger Balm: US–Singapore command post exercise series, partially held in Alaska, including Tiger Balm 03, Tiger Balm 00, Tiger Balm 91, and Tiger Balm 89.

Tiger Lake: UK–US biological warfare effects special access program.

Tiger Rescue: Noncombatant evacuation operation of several hundred American citizens during the civil war in Yemen, 1994.

Tiger Response: Office of the Secretary of Defense/Special Operations and Low-Intensity Conflict noncombatant evacuation operation interagency crisis management war game, War Gaming and Simulation Center, National Defense University, 2000.

Tight Door: Desert Storm army counter-intelligence program, 1991.

Timber Line: Presidential continuity of government exercise, 1980s–early 1990s.

Timber Wind: Former Strategic Defense Initiative Organization (SDIO) special access program involving development of a nuclear propulsion system for a rocket that would intercept ballistic missiles, 1987–1992.

TIMBUKTU: Army intelligence collaborative tool used during OIF.

Tin Shield: Army Foreign Science and Technology Center foreign material exploitation program, 1992.

Tipster: Intelligence Community text processing initiative, begun in 1981 and including at least 15 industy and university research projects aimed at improving text processing.

Title Globe: Interagency communications exercise series associated with continuity of operations (COOP) and continuity of government (COG). Title Globe 04: 12 May 2004.

Titrant Ranger: Special access program compartment code name for the Army Intelligence Support Activity (Gray Fox), used during the war on terrorism, replacing Capacity Gear.

Toltec Spear: Army counter-intelligence program.

Tomcat: Signals intelligence system used by the Marine Corps in Desert Storm.

Tonal Key: Army intelligence cover program.

Toolchest: Code word for the classified Technical Agreement relating to the deployment of US nuclear weapons in Germany.

Top: Army Single Source Processor — SIGINT (SSP-S), including Top Gable (AN/TSQ-163), delivered in Jul 1990, upgraded in Jun 1996; Top Gallant (AN/TSQ-156), delivered in Oct 1998, upgraded in Feb 1996; and Top Graphic (AN/TSQ-163), delivered in Mar 1990, upgraded in Oct 1995.

Top Dollar: Air-force-sponsored tri-service operations other than war competition and chemical warfare protective exercise, Fairchild AFB, WA, 1990s.

Top Hand: Peacekeeper and Minuteman ICBM ongoing readiness evaluation program, Vandenburg AFB, CA.

Top Hunter: Marine Corps SIGINT and electronic attack suite based on the AN/PRD-12 Teammate system used by the army.

Top Scene (Tactical Operational Preview Scene): 3-D strike planning system. In the late 1980s, the navy began to install Top Scene systems aboard aircraft carriers. Loaded with a database that combined high-quality satellite imagery with Digital Terrain Elevation Data, Top Scene permits strike planners to "rehearse" missions by "flying" through 3-D depictions of intended strike routes.

Top Spin: Coast Guard special operation, 3 Jun–12 Jul 1991.

Tophat: 1. Navy AN/BQR-19 submarine system.

2. **Tophat:** Nickname for the president's daily briefing during the Reagan era.

Topic 700/Topic 900: Missile-defense-related Airborne Surveillance Testbed sensitive program associated with reentry objects, 1999–present.

TOPOFF (Top Officials): Federal government NSC-coordinated interagency WMD terrorism response exercise involving actual top officials, mandated by Senate Report 105-235. In this report, "the Committee commends the administration for its efforts to enhance our ability to prevent and respond to chemical, biological, and cyber-weapon attacks. The Committee is aware that numerous exercises are conducted each year to practice operations in the event of a terrorist incident. The Committee understands that few of the top officials of agencies have ever fully participated in these exercises. The Committee directs that an exercise be conducted in fiscal year 1999 with the participation of all key personnel who would participate in the consequence management of such an actual terrorist event." TOPOFF III: Scheduled for Apr 2005 in Connecticut and New Jersey. Department of Homeland Security–led homeland defense exercise coordinated with NORTHCOM's planned Ardent Sentry exercise, and involvement by JTF-Civil Support (CS) and JTF-Consequence Management (East). TOPOFF III planning anticipates participation by Canada and the UK. TOPOFF II: 12–16 May 2003. The Department of Homeland Security and Department of State, in cooperation with federal, state, local, and Canadian partners, undertook the full-scale simulation of response in the event of a WMD attack. The scenario involved attacks in the Chicago and Seattle metropolitan areas. The state of Washington, King County, and the city of Seattle responded to an explosion containing radioactive material. The state of Illinois, Cook, Lake, DuPage and Kane Counties, and the city of Chicago responded to a covert release of a biological agent. Nineteen federal agencies and the American Red Cross were involved. TOPOFF I/National Capital Region 00: 20–24 May 2000. Conducted under the direction of the Department of Justice Office of State and Local Domestic Preparedness Support and FEMA, TOPOFF I was the largest exercise ever of its kind, involving three separate locations. The exercise simulated simultaneous chemical, biological, and radiological attacks. The scenario included a small explosion with a mustard gas chemical release in Portsmouth, NH, a biological attack involving release of plague in Denver, CO, and two small explosions with radiation releases on consecutive days in the metropolitan Washington, DC, area. The radiological release was actually run as a "concurrent" exercise, National Capital Region 00. Though TOPOFF was intended to be a "no-notice" exercise, almost everyone involved knew the general exercise time frame weeks in advance.

Topsail: Intelligence community program to develop predictive analysis tools for intelligence analysts to be able to better anticipate and preempt terrorist threats to the US.

Topsight: Synthetic Aperture Radar (SAR)–related development program.

Torch Light III: Reagan-era exercise with NSC involvement, 15 Jun 1984.

Torii: Canadian-led coalition operation in the Tora Bora region, Afghanistan, 4–7 May 2002. The mission was to find Taliban and al Qaeda cave complexes, gather information about terrorist operations, and destroy cave complexes to prevent future use.

Torn Victor: Intelligence Support Activity (Gray Fox) support for Buckeye, the effort to apprehend war criminals in the former Yugoslavia. Covert intelligence efforts in support of Amber Star and Green Light and involving the Special Collection Service of the CIA and NSA and Torn Victor.

Torpedo Focus: US–UK live-ordnance exercise supplementing Red Flag, Davis-Monthan AFB, AZ, 25 Mar–5 Apr 2002.

Torpid Suction: Army Foreign Science and Technology Center foreign material exploitation program, 1991–1992.

Tossing: Army foreign material exploitation first word, 1990–1992, including Tossing Mister, Tossing Quick, Tossing Sundae, and Tossing Wind.

Total Defender: Army-led joint collaborative planning process for Integrated Missile Defense, a set of experiments involving integration of space and missile defense component systems. The focus of the ongoing program is to integrate army and other service air defense, missile defense, space operations, and information operations.

Totaliser: Reported UK SIGINT system at RAF Menwith Hill, UK.

Touchback: E-mail and database security system, under development in 1991.

Touted: Air force foreign material exploitation of a missile system, 1991–1992, including Touted Cousin and Touted Gleam, an air force project involving acquired Scud missiles.

Town Crier: *See* Radiant Coal/Town Crier.

Toy: Army intelligence foreign material exploitation first word, 1989–1993, including Toy Bean, Toy Blister, Toy Result, Toy Store, and Toy Train.

Toy Chest: Code word for the highly classified "Technical Agreement" allowing the deployment of US nuclear weapons in the Netherlands.

Tracker: Coast Guard special operation, 30 Jun–18 Jul 1993.

Trackwolf: Army AN/TSQ-152 SIGINT system.

TRACS (triangulation ranging and crossfix system): Big Safari–managed program.

Tractor: Army special access program first word, including Tractor Bird, Tractor Gage, Tractor Card, Tractor Dirt, Tractor Dump, Tractor Earl, Tractor Field, Tractor Gem, Tractor Heavy, Tractor Helm, Tractor Hike, Tractor Hip, Tractor Hole, Tractor Jewel, Tractor Pull, Tractor Red, Tractor Rose, Tractor Rut, Tractor Tire, Tractor Trailer, and Tractor Tread.

Tradewinds: SOUTHCOM exercise conducted annually in the Caribbean, initiated in 1986. The two-phase land and maritime exercise is traditionally designed to test the defense of the lower Caribbean Islands, but since 9/11 has concentrated on counter-terrorism, counter-narcotics, and disaster preparedness. Participants include Antigua and Barbuda, the Bahamas, Barbados, Belize, Canada, Dominica, the Dominican Republic, Grenada, Guyana, Haiti, Jamaica, the Netherlands, Netherlands Antilles, St. Kitts, St. Lucia, St. Vincent, Trinidad and Tobago, and the UK.

+ **Tradewinds 05:** Maritime phase in the Dominican Republic; ground phase in St. Vincent, 4–22 Apr 2004.
+ **Tradewinds 04:** Maritime phase in St. Vincent, 26 Mar–2 Apr 2004; combined phase in the Dominican Republic, 10–27 Apr 2004. The exercise simulated a response to a terrorist bombing in Port Kingstown, St. Vincent, and airfield attacks in the Dominican Republic. Elements of the 4th MEB (Anti-Terrorism) and Marine Corps Security Force Bn deployed, joined by UK and Dutch marines.
+ **Tradewinds 03:** Jamaica and Barbados.
+ **Tradewinds 02:** Maritime phase in the Bahamas 6–13 Apr 2002; land phase in Antigua and Barbuda, 6–26 Apr 2002.
+ **Tradewinds 01:** Maritime phase in the Dominican Republic, 2–8 Apr 2001; land phase in Trinidad and Tobago, 17 Apr–5 May 2001. The 1st Bn, 20th SFG.
+ **Tradewinds 00:** Maritime phase in Jamaica and St. Lucia; land phase at Camp Santiago, Puerto Rico, 26 Mar–2 Apr 2000. The maritime phase included Haiti.
+ **Tradewinds 99:** Maritime phase in the Dominican Republic, St. Lucia, and Trinidad and Tobago, 12–30 Apr 1999; land phase in Guyana, 16–26 Apr 1999. Navy SEALs trained at Takama waterfront, Guyana.
+ **Tradewinds 98:** Maritime phase in Antigua and Barbuda and Trinidad and Tobago, 2–14 Mar 1998; combined land and maritime phase in Belize, 5–20 Apr 1999.

Trafficjam: Army AN/TLQ-17 Sandcrab jammer.

Trailblazer: 1. 3rd Air Force–led annual JTF computer-assisted exercise exercising FUNCPLAN 4269-96 and CONPLAN 4250-96 to provide a USAFE-led JTF, Warrior Preparation Center, Einsiedlerhof, Germany. Participants include the UK and South Africa. Trailblazer 01/Sharp Eagle 01: 5–15 Oct 2001. The exercise was scaled back due to 9/11. The 32nd Air Operations Group provided an air operations center with augmentation from the 152nd Air Operations Group in a Balkans-based scenario that utilized real-world terrain. Trailblazer 00: 18–29 Oct 1999. Peace enforcement and humanitarian assistance scenario in North Africa. Trailblazer 98: 19–30 Oct 1998. Trailblazer 97. Trailblazer 96: 2–10 Aug 1996. Activities included theater missile defense, neutralization of WMD, and "special capabilities." Trailblazer 95.

2. **Trailblazer:** Army AN/TSQ-138 semi-automatic high-frequency/very high-frequency communications intercept and direction finding system used in Desert Storm.

Transoceanic Exercise XV: Multi-national maritime traffic control communications exercise, Argentina, 7–18 Aug 2000. Participants included Argentina, Brazil, Chile, Ecuador, Paraguay, Peru, South Africa, Venezuela, and the US.

Treetop: "Presidential Successor Emergency Support Plan," jointly managed by FEMA and the JCS. Treetop plans are numbered (for instance, TREETOP IX) provide for the maintenance of emergency kits that include war plans, regulations, and instructions, and outline procedures for the establishment of Treetop teams consisting of civilian and military advisers to presidential successors. The NSA prepares unique authenticators for each potential successor, and a system of code words and tools used to confirm proper succession. The Treetop plan was originally meant to ensure that if both the president and vice president were killed in a nuclear attack, the presidency would survive through a statutory presidential successor. Treetop is practiced through highly classified exercises (such as Nine Lives).

Tri-City Sweep: Army 87th Infantry Regt operation to confiscate weapons and suspected Taliban members in Say Khan, Gulmani Kot, and Pir Kowti, Afghanistan, 29 Sep 2003.

Tri-Crab: US–Australian–Singapore annual naval exercise designed to test and evaluate explosive ordnance disposal and improvised explosive device disposal operations, Andersen AFB, Guam. Tri-Crab 03: Apr 2003. Tri-Crab

02: Sep 2002. Tri-Crab 99: Explosive Ordnance Disposal Mobile Unit 5, the Australian navy's Clearance Diving Team One, and the Singapore Naval Diving Unit. Tri-Crab 98: Apr 1998. Tri-Crab 97: 31 Mar–13 Apr 1997. Helicopter Combat Support Sqn Five, air force controllers from the 320th Special Tactics Sqn, and C-130s from the 1st SOS.

Trial: NATO coalition electronic warfare interoperability trials, held since 1978. Participants include Canada, Denmark, France, Germany, Italy, Netherlands, Norway, Portugal, Spain, and the UK. Every three years, an infrared (Trial Embow) or a radio frequency (Trail Mace) test is held. *See also* MACE.

Triangle 1, 2, 3: NSA-related program, 1980s.

Tributary: Scalable Transportable Intelligence Communications System (STICS) application, a mobile intelligence communications system allowing field interfaces with national and NSA time-sensitive systems. STICS II is known as Tributary and is used for indications and warning missions.

Trident Arch: Navy operation involving the swap-out of pre-positioned fleet hospital units between US and overseas storage locations. Trident Arch 03 (X): Bjugn caves, Norway. Trident Arch 02: Okinawa, Japan. Trident Arch 01 (VIII): Bogen Bay and Osmarka Cave Warehouse, Evenes, Norway, Sep 2001. Trident Arch 00 (VII): Pohang and Taegu, South Korea, May 2000. Trident Arch 95 (II): South Korea, Jun 1995.

Trident D'Or: French-sponsored naval exercise, Sardinia, 21 May–1 Jun 2001. Participants included more than 15,000 personnel and 50 warships from Belgium, Denmark, Germany, Greece, Italy, Portugal, Spain, Turkey, the UK, and the US.

Trident Warrior 04: Navy transformation warfare, Jul 2004.

Tridente: Italian maritime invitational exercise. Tridente 95.

Trilateral War Game (TWG 2000): US crisis management war game with Argentina, Brazil, and Canada, 10–14 Apr 2000.

Trilogy: FBI telecommunications and computer network upgrade, precipitated and spurred on by 9/11. The system provides the FBI the ability to collect, store, search, retrieve, assess, and disseminate investigative and intelligence information throughout the bureau and with the Intelligence Community. In Nov 2000, Congress approved $379 million for Trilogy. In Mar 2003, the FBI announced that it had completed the Trilogy network at 591 sites.

Trinity: SOCOM classified project.

Trisetia: Australian–Indonesian army training. Trisetia 96: Oct 1996. Trisetia 97: Nov 1997.

Trojan: Army and Marine Corps intelligence program first word. The Trojan system is a family of remotely controlled SIGINT collection systems used extensively in OEF and OIF.

+ **Trojan Bare:** Trojan Baseline Architecture Receive Element.
+ **Trojan Classic:** AN/FSQ-144 (V) family of systems, subsystems, and support equipment, including Crossfire, Roadwarrior, Steamroller, TATERS, and Trojan Lite.
+ **Trojan Lite (Lightweight Integrated Telecommunications Equipment):** Provides a dedicated sensitive compartmented information (SCI) communications system to disseminate and access SCI data/information and provide shared ground-mobile forces bandwidth for tactical units.
+ **Trojan Spirit I/II (Special Purpose Integrated Remote Intelligence Terminal):** Communications terminal used to provide connectivity to the national SIGINT database as well as to units worldwide. The SPIRIT I/II terminals receive, process, and transmit on 14 channels of medium-capacity multi-plexed voice and data circuits over commercial and military satellites.

Trojan: Continuity of government network control center operating in support of OEF and WMD Civil Support Teams.

Trojan Footprint: JCS classified exercise. Trojan Footprint 04. Trojan Footprint 01. Trojan Footprint 00. Trojan Footprint 99. Trojan Footprint 96.

Trojan Horse: Coast Guard special operation, 15–29 Sep 1987.

Trojan Warrior: 1st Bn, 10th SFG land and water movement stamina exercise and competition, held on the Danube River in southern Germany, 22–24 May 2000.

Trophy: DARPA foreign material equipment exploitation with Israeli cooperation, 1997.

Troutman: Reported UK SIGINT system at RAF Menwith Hill, UK.

True: Naval Forces Marianas recurring exercise, Guam.

True Blue: Army intelligence involvement in the Classic Wizard high frequency/direction finding program.

Trump: Navy Ship's Signals Exploitation Equipment.

Trumpet: Orion II SIGINT satellite. Possible follow-on to Jumpseat.

Trumpet Dance: British small-unit infantry deployment to the US, 1998.

TSARINA (Tracking Simulation and Real-World IADS Network Analysis): Targeting-and-effects-based operations project that teaches planners to treat Integrated Air Defense Systems as coherent systems rather than as gatherings of stand-alone radars, SAM sites, communications, and so on).

Tumbril: Army intelligence system, Bad Aibling, Germany.

Turbo: TRANSCOM exercise first word.

+ **Turbo Activation:** Exercise that evaluates the readiness of the Ready Reserve Fleet.
+ **Turbo Cads (Containerized Ammunition Distribution System):** Live ammunition containerization exercise involving the relocation, retrograde, and forward deployment of theater ammunition stocks. Turbo Cads 04. Turbo Cads 01/JLOTS 01: Pacific. Turbo Cads 00: Saudi Arabia, Qatar, Oman, and Kuwait. Turbo Cads 99: The MV *Chesapeake Bay* lifted 940 containers of ammunition to South Korea and Guam. Turbo Cads 98.
+ **Turbo Challenge:** Exercise providing collective training in wartime logistical tasks. In alternate years, Ultimate Caduceus is held in conjunction with Turbo Challenge. Turbo Challenge 04. Turbo Challenge 01.
+ **Turbo Intermodal Surge:** Container exercise that practices contractor ability to move cargo. Turbo Intermodal Surge 01. Turbo Intermodal Surge 00/Foal Eagle 00: Aug–Dec 1999. In four phases, the contractor (DynCorp) transported/loaded equipment from the 4th Infantry Div's 2nd Bde (164 shipping containers at Fort Hood, TX) onto the *Cape Knox* (29 Aug–11 Sep 1999), transported containers to Pusan, South Korea, to a tactical assembly area, redeployed to Pusan, and then returned to Fort Hood 18 Dec 1999.
+ **Turbo Patriot:** On-load and off-load during 25th Infantry Div National Training Center rotation, Camp Pendleton, CA, 6–10 Sep 2000.

Turtle Heritage/Turtle Truss: UK exercise on Ascension Island, 2001–2002.

Twin Ears: Army and national intelligence agencies technical intelligence exploitation.

TX Thunder: Tomahawk missile firing during RIMPAC 00.

Tyne Tease V: UK-hosted exercise, 1999, involving the 33rd Interrogator-Translator Team, marine forces reserve.

— U —

U-125: *See* Peace Krypton.

Uje Krystal 96: US–Albanian exercise to construct and repair the Tirana Military Trauma Hospital, Albania, 1996.

Ulan Eagle: UK–Polish ground forces annual exercise series at the Drawsko Pomorski training area, Poland. Ulan Eagle 01 was canceled and replaced by Desert Warrior. Ulan Eagle 03: Jan 2003. Ulan Eagle 02: 26 Aug–21 Sep 2002. The exercise was downsized due to resource constraints. Ulan Eagle 00: Sep–Oct 2000. Ulan Eagle 98. Ulan Eagle 97: Oct 1997. Ulan Eagle 96: 30 Aug–20 Sep 1996. First NATO field training exercise in Poland. Participants included Ukraine.

Ulchi Focus Lens: US Forces Korea (USFK) major exercise, the largest command post exercise in the JCS exercises program and the largest computer modeling and simulation command post exercise in the world, dating to the early 1980s and always in the Aug–Sep time frame. Focus Lens is the last in the Korean command post exercise annual series (the Foal Eagle and RSOI exercises take place first), and is conducted in conjunction with South Korea's national-only mobilization exercise "Ulchi." The exercise allows USFK to practice implementation of OPLAN 5027 with the scenario of response to North Korean aggression, and includes distributed participation from worldwide US forces. Ulchi Focus Lens 04: Aug 2004. Ulchi Focus Lens 03:10 Aug–10 Sep 2003. Ulchi Focus Lens 02: Aug 2002. Ulchi Focus Lens 01: 20–31 Aug 2001. 3rd Infantry Div and 101st Airborne Div. Ulchi Focus Lens 00: Aug 2000. Ulchi Focus Lens 99: During the exercise, the DIA Missile and Space Intelligence Center developed a virtual Intelligence Preparation of the Battlespace site tailored to dynamically support this exercise's stringent theater missile defense intelligence support requirements.

Ultimate Caduceus: TRANSCOM aeromedical command post exercise, with some field training, held in alternating years in conjunction with Turbo Challenge.

Ultimate Resolve: CENTCOM–Gulf Cooperation Council command post exercise/field training exercise emphasizing the defense of the Arabian peninsula and Kuwait. Ultimate Resolve 00. Ultimate Resolve 99: Aug–Sep 1999. XVIII Airborne Corps. Ultimate Resolve 96: Apr 1996. Ultimate Resolve 95. Ultimate Resolve 93: The first exercise, held late in 1993, brought nearly all of the coalition members together for the first time since Desert Storm, including Egypt and Syria.

Ultrapure: Reported UK SIGINT system at RAF Menwith Hill, UK.

Ulu Rajah: UK–Brunei exercise, 2001–2002.

Umbra: COMINT compartment (for example, Top Secret/Umbra) eliminated in May 1999, along with the code words *Moray, Spoke,* and *Zarf.* Information previously classified Moray was subsequently to be designated Top Secret COMINT.

Umbrella: DOD special access program, 1997–.

Underseal: US–Thai naval unconventional warfare and special operations exercise.

Unified Charger: Military Sealift Command Europe annual exercise to allow naval reserves to activate, deploy, and support large-scale contingency movements in Belgium, Germany, Italy, the Netherlands, Spain, and the UK, begun in 1994. Unified Charger 02: May 2002. Unified Charger 01. Unified Charger 00: Dec 1999. Unified Charger 99: Also supported real-world operations in Kosovo.

Unified Defense: NORTHCOM (formerly JFCOM) interagency homeland security and continuity of operations exercise. Unified Defense 04: 19–25 Feb 2004. The exercise tested the Initial National Response Plan, its modifications and revisions. When approved, the final plan will replace the 1992 Federal Response Plan. Participants included more than 50 federal, state, and local agencies in a series of events. Scenarios included a terrorist nuclear attack in Texas, simulated hijackings of commercial airliners, a cyber-attack against DOD computers, and attacks against maritime and port security assets in Alaska. Participants included the Canadian NORAD Region in

Winnipeg, Canada; FEMA Region VI in Denton, TX; JTF AK; and the Terrorist Threat Integration Center in Washington, DC. Mexico sent observers to the exercise. The exercise incorporated Vigilant Overview 04-2. Unified Defense 03-1: Feb 2003. Unified Defense 02-2: Sep 2002. JFCOM conducted exercise to help NORTHCOM assess its organizational structure, operating procedures, and command and control capabilities.

Unified Endeavor: JFCOM semi-annual JTF exercise. The JTF develops an OPORDER and then conducts operations based on that order. The primary purpose is to exercise crisis action planning procedures, application of doctrine, and command and control procedures. Unified Endeavor 04: Sep 2004. Unified Endeavor 03-2: Sep 2003. Unified Endeavor 01-4: 10–17 Sep 2001. Unified Endeavor 01-3: Apr 2001. Unified Endeavor 01/Fuertas Defensas 01: Feb–Mar 2001. Unified Endeavor 99. Unified Endeavor 98-1. Unified Endeavor 98: 27 Oct–4 Nov 1997. The scenario was a Southwest Asia deterrent operation that was a show of force transitioning into a defense. XVIII Airborne Corps, 10th Mountain Div, and 44th Med Bde. Unified Endeavor 98-3: The Joint Information Operations Center (JIOC) country team produced an extensive command and control capabilities study that combined real-world and notional data for information warfare planning. A JIOC red team was also integrated and assisted in developing a credible enemy cyber-threat throughout the exercise. A team of JIOC technicians worked with Joint Warfighting Center personnel to run the "J-quad IO model" and supported both intelligence- and information-warfare-specific battle damage assessment. Unified Endeavor 97: Dec 1996. Unified Endeavor 96-1: Apr 1996. Unified Endeavor 95-2: Oct 1995. Unified Endeavor 95-1: May 1995.

Unified Quest 03: Army-sponsored transformation war game, Carlisle Barracks, PA, 27 Apr–2 May 2003. The exercise was the first to be held after OIF and attempted to define the operational level of war to determine how well army capabilities slated to be deployed after 2008 with the Future Combat Systems might work within a multi-national environment. The scenario was set in 2015 and posited a nuclear-armed Middle Eastern country (Iran) and an insurgent group threatening a Southeast Asian ally (Philippines).

Unified Resolve: Coalition and Afghan series of movements throughout the eastern province of Nangarhar around Jalalabad, Afghanistan, initiated 18 Jun 2003.

Unified Spirit/Trace Record: NATO naval exercise series held in the western Atlantic off the coast of North Carolina and Virginia. Unified Spirit 03: Sep 2003. Unified Spirit 00/JTFEX 01-1: 5–27 Oct 2000. The UK withdrew because of operational commitments in Sierra Leone. Unified Spirit 00/JTFEX 01-1: 18–27 Oct 2000. Unified Spirit 98/MARCOT 98: 6–26 Jun 1998. Unified Spirit 97: 12–29 Aug 1997.

Unified Vision: JFCOM future warfare capabilities experiment series used to prepare for Millenium Challenge. Unified Vision 03: 1–15 Apr 2003. Unified Vision 01: Suffolk, VA, 7–24 May 2001. The exercise developed concepts for a Standing Joint Task Force Headquarters. Unified Vision 00: The focus was "shaping the battlespace," introduced in the Rapid Decisive Operations white paper in a circa-2010 coercive campaign using a Balkans terrain base.

Union Flash: 16th Air Force led Joint Forces Air Component Commander (JFACC) computer-assisted exercise, Warrior Preparation Center, Einsiedlerhof, Germany. Union Flash is the only full-up JFACC training event held in Europe. Union Flash 02/Agile Lion 02/Warfighter Exercise (WFX) 02: Linked through a common scenario and planning process resulting in a new JTF exercise named Urgent Resolve 02. Union Flash 01: Apr 2001. The 32nd Air Operations Group practiced the establishment of an air operations center. The US-only exercise featured a Balkans-based scenario developing around CONPLAN 4601E-00 (Scarlet) with real-world target sets, order of battle, terrain, and expected opposing force reaction. Union Flash 00: 1–5 May 2000. Union Flash 98: 20–30 Apr 1998. Union Flash 97: May 1997. Union Flash 96: 3–4 Oct 1996. The exercise scenario called for a simulated JFACC deployment to a fictional country called "Blueland," which requested aid in response to pressures from neighboring "Orangeland" aimed at overthrowing Blueland's government.

Unitary DF: Project to determine all-service direction finding requirements and to develop a course of action to satisfy those requirements, resulting in a system called Crosshair. *See also* Centerboard.

Unitas: SOUTHCOM Western Hemisphere annual naval exercise series involving the deployment of a navy TF that visits a variety of Latin American and Caribbean nations and exercises with their maritime forces. The Unitas deployment began in 1959 as strictly a navy operation. In 1981, Unitas was expanded to include amphibious operations with the marines.

The exercise typically runs each year between Jul and Dec and is four months in duration. Participants include Argentina, Brazil, Chile, Colombia, Ecuador, Paraguay, Peru, Uruguay, and Venezuela. Typical is Unitas 04, where Peru hosted the Unitas Pacific and amphibious phases, while Uruguay hosted the Unitas Atlantic phase. In Unitas 38-97, attack submarine USS *Sand Lance* (SSN 660) conducted a six-month deployment. During Unitas 30-89, VP-5 participated in anti-submarine-warfare training in which the squadron operated from nearly every South American country over a five-month period.

United Orbit: 332nd Expeditionary Air Support Operations Sqn and army special forces close air support exercise at Udairi Range, Kuwait, 9 Aug 2000.

United Shield: Support to UN withdrawal from Somalia, 22 Jan–25 Mar 1995. The CTF under Lt. Gen. Anthony C. Zinni, commander of I MEF, included Italian, Pakistani, French, Malaysian, and UK forces. USS *Essex* (LHD 2) and *Belleau Wood* (LHA 3) ARGs.

Universal Trek 85: Reagan-era exercise with NSC involvement, 12–28 Apr 1985.

Uphold Democracy: Permissive entry stability operation in Haiti to restore and support the legitimate government of President Aristide, 26 Sep 1994–30 Mar 1995. Lt. Gen. Hugh Shelton, commander of XVIII Airborne Corps, commanded the JTF. Army troops, including the 3rd Bn, 75th Rangers, deployed on 15 Sep 1994. Peak Army strength reached 18,401 on 13 Oct 1994. The 16th SOS (AC-130) deployed to Cuba in support of the operation. The last SOF elements departed Haiti in Feb 1996. The army also provided a quick reaction force and trained more than 5,000 Haitian national police at Fort Leonard Wood, MO, Jun 1995–early 1996. The navy provided USS *Wasp* (LHD 1) and USS *Inchon* (LPH 12) ARGs. Followed by Maintain Democracy.

Upward Key 86: Reagan-era exercise with NSC involvement, 6–22 Nov 1985.

Urban Encounter: Naval Forces Europe Fleet Antiterrorism Security Team (FAST) training exercise with the UK army's Northern Ireland Training Advisory Team (NITAT) at its urban training facility.

Urban Warrior: Marine Corps urban warfare advanced warfighting experiment. Urban Warrior 99: During 1999, the National Reconnaissance Office provided technology, systems, and training. Urban Warrior 98: 7–23 Jan 1998.

Urgent Fury: Invasion of Grenada, 1983.

Urgent Resolve 02: US Army Europe (USAREUR) JTF exercise, planned for 10 Feb–6 Mar 2002 in Italy and Germany, and canceled because of OEF. The exercise was USAREUR's number one exercise priority for the year, and was linked Union Flash 02, Agile Lion 02, and Warfighter Exercise (WFX) 02 in a common scenario and planning process.

Urgent Response: I Corps medical exercise, Thailand, Apr 2001. The exercise centered on the deployment of a JTF for consequence management to provide medical assistance in response to the use of a smallpox biological weapon.

Urgent Thunder: Army V Corps classified global war on terrorism operation.

Urgent Victory: US Army Europe (USAREUR) V Corps warfighter exercise, Germany. Urgent Victory 04/Agile Leader 04: 21–27 Apr 2004. Urgent Victory was the USAREUR number one exercise priority for FY 2004. The exercise goal was to train and certify V Corps headquarters as a fully trained and operational JTF. Urgent Victory 01: Apr 2001. Urgent Victory 00: Apr–May 2000.

Ursa Minor: Bulgaria-hosted exercise. UK forces did not participate in Oct 2001 due to operational commitments.

Utah: UK classified information compartment dealing with nuclear weapons.

Utopian Angel: SOCOM project, 1996–present.

— V —

Vacant/Vagabond/Valentine: PACOM first words.

Vacation: Pacific Air Forces first word.

Valiant: PACOM first word.
  + **Valiant Blitz:** III MEF amphibious training exercise based on a Korean peninsula scenario, dating to the 1980s, and including Valiant Blitz 94 and Valiant Blitz 91.
  + **Valiant Brave:** JTF command and control training exercise. Valiant Brave 96: Mar 1996.
  + **Valiant Mark:** US–Singapore special operations training exercise. Valiant Mark 02. Valiant Mark 95: Guam and Tinian, 20–25 Sep 1995.

+ **Valiant Usher:** Pacific Fleet major exercise with Korea peninsula scenario, dating to the 1970s. Valiant Usher 98. Valiant Usher 90-3.

Valiant Strike: Major coalition and 82nd Airborne Div operation in southern Afghanistan and along the Pakistani border, launched 19 Mar 2003 in coordination with OIF. Valiant Strike was aimed at villages and cave complexes east of Kandahar in the Sami Ghar Mountains.

Valid Shot: Pacific Fleet exercise.

Valor: Naval Forces Marianas Guam exercise first word, including Valor Gable and Valor Skyhook.

Vampire: UK maritime SIGINT/ESM equipment used in OEF/OIF.

Vanguard: Navy War College and Naval Medical Research Developoment Command science and technology wargame. Vanguard 98: 7–20 Jun 1998. Vanguard 97. Vanguard 96 focused on the future of biomedical research, development, testing, and evaluation requirements.

Varnish: NSA program, 1980s.

Varsity: Pacific Fleet first word.

VATOS: Sensitive-compartmented-information-policy-related message traffic.

Vaudeville: Pacific Fleet first word.

Vector: SOCPAC first word designating JCET "Balance" events as counter-terrorism related.
+ **Vector Balance Mint:** US–Malaysian national police exercise series.
+ **Vector Balance Piston:** US–Philippine JCET series focused on close-quarters battle and marksmanship skills, and serving as a cover for real-world counter-terrorism operations, 2001–present. The exercise is conducted by the 1st SFG and the Philippine Army Special Operations Command.
+ **Vector Balance Torch:** US–Thai JCET series.

Vector South 84: Reagan-era exercise with NSC involvement, 17–24 Aug 1984.

Vega (LaCrosse/Vega): BYEMAN code word for MASINT applications aboard the KH-12? digital imaging and Synthetic Aperture Radar (SAR) satellite. Later swtched to Onyx.

Veneto Rescue: US–Italian SETAF-sponsored noncombatant evacuation operation exercise. Veneto Rescue 01: Northern Italy and Slovenia, May–Jun 2001. Veneto Rescue 00: Northern Italy and Slovenia.

Venture: PACOM first word.

Verdant: Former navy and NSA SIGINT compartment.

VERDIN (Very Low Frequency Digital Information Network): Navy VLF/LF program. An enhanced VERDIN system is the receive terminal for submarine and the airborne relay (TACAMO) platforms.

Veritas: British military operations during OEF in Afghanistan, 2001–2002.

Veritas II: NATO diesel submarine exercise, Norway, 1999.

Victor Squared: Contingency plan for possible noncombatant evacuation operation from Haiti, Sep 1991.

Victory: US Army Europe V Corps operation and exercise first word.

+ **Victory Bounty:** Operation in Iraq to track down midlevel Ba'ath Party operatives, former regime bodyguards, and aides and Saddam Fedayeen who might provide intelligence about the whereabouts of Saddam Hussein and other former senior leaders, begun Jul 2003. In the first week, Victory Bounty netted nearly 70 former Fedayeen fighters, including several general- and field-grade officers.

+ **Victory Cobra:** Original V Corps plan based on OPLAN 1003V to assault Iraq with five divisions in OIF.

+ **Victory Focus:** V Corps training exercise. Victory Focus 02: Grafenwohr, Germany. Rehearsal of Victory Cobra war plan. Victory Focus 00: Nov–Dec 1999. Victory Focus 95: 6–10 Feb 1995.

+ **Victory Scrimmage:** V Corps computer-assisted exercise/command post exercise, Grafenwoehr, Germany, Jan–Feb 2003 preparing for OIF. Victory Scrimmage's primary purpose was team building among units that would be employed in the coming campaign. All of the subordinate divisions and separate brigades were represented, and the units "fought" a campaign similar to the one that would shortly unfold. The army's Opposing Force portrayed Iraqi armed forces.

+ **Victory Strike:** V Corps force-on-force deep-strike exercise at the Drawsko Pomorskie training area, Poland. The Poland-based Victory Strike exercises have been some of the largest deep-strike training events since the Cold War. The first exercise in 2000 was the first time major

US forces operated on Polish soil since World War II. Victory Strike 05: 25 May–24 Jun 2005. Victory Strike 04 was to have been held 1 Sep–1 Oct 2004, but was canceled because of the demands of OIF. Victory Strike 02: In Sep 2002, V Corps and selected subordinate command posts deployed to Poland to practice planning, preparing, and executing corps operations with a focus on the deep fires and maneuver that would be critical to the coming OIF campaign. Victory Strike 02 enabled the corps to train with the air force in a "live" environment. Victory Strike 02 led the way for a series of exercises through the fall and winter of 2002–2003 that resulted in completed and rehearsed plans for OIF. *See also* Lucky Warrior. Victory Strike 01: 13–23 Oct 2000. More than 2,000 V Corps soldiers took part in the attack helicopter and long-range artillery operations. Victory Strike 00: The first exercise of the series involved the movement of a brigade TF using more than 50 trains with 1,400 railcars carrying nearly 1,700 pieces of equipment and over 3,000 passengers, the largest troop movement by train since World War II. The exercise also involved air deployments and convoys movements across the German–Polish border.

+ **Victory Warrior:** Command post exercise preparing for OIF.

Vigilant: US–Australian intelligence exercise with Canadian and UK involvement, held since 1995, testing doctrine for counter-intelligence and HUMINT support to combined multi-national TFs. The exercises alternate each year between Hawaii (Vigilant Shield) and Australia (Vigilant Blade). Vigilant Shield 03: 16–30 Jun 2003. 205th Military Intelligence Bn and the 75th Ranger Regt. Vigilant Blade 02: Jul–Aug 2002. Vigilant Blade 97. *See* Vigilant Shield.

Vigilant: NORAD and Air Force Space Command (AFSPC) first word.

+ **Vigilant Eagle:** AFSPC leadership screening board.
+ **Vigilant Guardian:** NORAD command post exercise involving headquarters, Continental NORAD Region, Alaskan NORAD Region, Canadian NORAD Region, and supporting units, conducted in conjunction with Global Guardian (STRATCOM) and Apollo Guardian (STRATCOM). One Vigilant Guardian is scheduled each year; the length varies depending on the exercise scenario and objectives. Vigilant Guardian: Sep 2001. The exercise was several days under way on 9/11, and the North East Air Defense system (NEADS) was fully staffed. The scenario postulated a bomber attack from the former Soviet Union. Vigilant Guardian 99.
+ **Vigilant Hawk:** AFSPC personnel program.

+ **Vigilant Overview:** NORAD systems and readiness command post exercise involving headquarters, Alaskan NORAD Region, Canadian NORAD Region, and supporting units. The series began in the 1970s; the emphasis is on nontraditional threats, such as counter-narcotics, terrorism, and WMD. Vigilant Overview 04-2/Unified Defense 04: Feb 2004.
+ **Vigilant Virgo 99-1:** NORAD Integrated Tactical Warning/Attack Assessment warning exercise in preparation for Y2K, 2–4 Dec 1998.

Vigilant Guardian: 82nd Airborne Div preparations for the first Afghan military operations in urban terrain (MOUT) training site, 23 Apr 2003.

Vigilant Hammer: CENTCOM operations to download prepositioned afloat (APS) stocks in anticipation of war in Iraq, 2002–2003. A combat brigade of equipment and a division base were moved from Um Sa'id, Qatar, to Kuwait in Jul 2002, and an additional two brigades were moved in Jan 2003.

Vigilant Hawk (TF Vigilant Hawk): New Jersey NG post-9/11 TF providing security at airports.

Vigilant Lion: PA Emergency Management Agency — DOE WMD incident exericse involving a simulated radiological material release, Fort Indiantown Gap, PA, 29–30 Sep 1999.

Vigilant Sentinel: CENTCOM show of force to deter Iraqi aggression, Aug 1995–Feb 2000, after two of Saddam Hussein's sons-in-law defected with their families to Jordan. Vigilant Sentinel involved increasing alert of US-based units, an accelerated scheduled military exercise with Jordan, extension of the USS *Abraham Lincoln* (CVN 72) in the Arabian Gulf, deployment of air and ground forces to Kuwait, Bahrain, and Saudi Arabia, support by the USS *America* (CV 66), USS *Dwight D. Eisenhower* (CVN 69), and USS *Theodore Roosevelt* (CVN 71), and moving pre-positioned equipment from Diego Garcia to Kuwait and Saudi Arabia. Followed Vigilant Warrior.

Vigilant Shield: 1. **Vigilant Shield 03:** PACOM counterintelligence and force-protection exercise, Hawaii, 16–30 Jun 2003, with participants from Australia, Canada, the UK, and the US. The 205th Military Intelligence Bn hosted the exercise, which included intelligence personnel from throughout the Pacific and Army Rangers from the 75th Ranger Regt. *See also* Vigilant.

2. **Vigilant Shield 06:** National homeland defense exercise planned for Nov 2005 involving NORTHCOM and the Department of Homeland Security.

Vigilant Warrior: CENTCOM response to the Iraqi buildup along the Kuwaiti border, Oct–Dec 1994. The USS *George Washington* (CVN 73) and the USS *Tripoli* (LPH 10) ARG deployed. By the end of Oct, CENTCOM had deployed more than 28,000 troops and over 200 additional aircraft to Saudi Arabia, Kuwait, Oman, Qatar, Bahrain, and the UAE. Vigilant Warrior was the first time CENTCOM headquarters deployed to the region since Desert Storm. Iraq pulled its forces north of the 32nd parallel.

Viking: Sweden-hosted ISO/PfP peacekeeping computer-assisted exercise. Participants include Albania, Austria, Azerbaijan, Bulgaria, Croatia, Denmark, Estonia, Finland, France, Germany, Greece, Ireland, Italy, Latvia, Macedonia, Norway, Poland, Romania, Russia, Switzerland, Turkey, Ukraine, the UK, the US, and Uzbekistan. Viking 03: Enköping, Sweden, 2–12 Dec 2003. Remote sites participating over the Internet include Estonia, Ireland, Romania, and Uzbekistan. NGOs participating include Amnesty International, the International Committee of the Red Cross, and the UN High Commission for Refugees. Viking 01: 3–14 Dec 2001. Viking 99: 23 Nov–2 Dec 1999.

Vinson: TSEC/KY-57/58 encrypted VHF/UHF wide-band communications system.

Viper: OEF operation, Kalata, Baghni Valley, Afghanistan, Feb–Mar 2003.

Vision/Talon Vision: Air Force Space Warfare Center TENCAP program to influence the design of space architectures/systems to optimize their ability to support conventional operations.

Vista: *See* Radiant Topaz/Vista.

Volant: Air Mobility Command (and former Military Airlift Command) first word. Volant Chuck, Volant Cross, Volant Curry, Volant Eye, Volant Fish, Volant Ghost, Volant Met, Volant Miss, Volant Splash, and Volant Weather were associated with nuclear, weather, and special reconnaissance missions. Other Cold War programs included Volant Boom, Volant Cat, and Volant Clear.

+ **Volant Banner/Volant Silver:** Air missions that support the president.
+ **Volant Dew:** Supply missions to the radar line in Greenland, flown by ski-equipped LC-130H aircraft.
+ **Volant Oak:** ANG and air force reserve C-130 operations initiated in 1978 at Howard AFB, Panama, and conducted through 1994. Operation Volant Oak provided airlift and search and rescue support to

SOUTHCOM. The guard and reserves shared this mission by rotating six C-130 aircraft and ground and aircrews each week at Howard AFB. Volant Oak then flew regularly scheduled missions to support the US military and embassies throughout Latin America. During Just Cause, Volant Oak C-130 aircrews flew 22 missions.

+ **Volant Partner:** Volant Partner 92: Belgium, 1992. Volant Partner 91: Aviano AB, Italy, 11–30 Sept 1991. Volant Partner 86: Zaragosa, Spain, 13 May–1 Jun 1986.

+ **Volant Pine:** Contingency operation to supplement tactical airlift in Europe in support of Desert Shield/Desert Storm, 1990–1991.

+ **Volant Scorpion:** Air force security forces course/exercise at Little Rock AFB, AR.

+ **Volant Sierra:** Foreign material exploitation, 1994.

+ **Volant Silver:** Air missions that support the vice president or Secret Service. *See also* Volant Banner.

+ **Volant Solo/Rivet Rider:** EC-130 psychological warfare version fitted with VHF/UHF communications equipment including AM/FM radio and color TV broadcasting equipment.

+ **Volant Wind:** Airlift operations during Desert Shield.

Vortex/Vortex II: SIGINT geostationary satellites, launched 1979–1984. The name was used after *Chalet* was mentioned in the press. When the name *Vortex* was itself published in 1987, the name was changed to Mercury.

VRK (Very Restricted Knowledge): Classification compartment designating a COMINT category similar to Gamma (for instance, Top Secret/Talent Keyhole VRK). The VRK system was established by NSA in Nov 1974 to limit access to uniquely sensitive COMINT activities and programs. VRK is normally cited along with a category number (such as, VRK 7), further designating the sensitivity of the information.

— W —

Wagonload: Equipment suites for cryptologic maintenance training, Keesler AFB, MS.

Walburn: Digital family of cryptographic keys for microwave trunks, high-speed circuits, video teleconferencing, and satellite channels.

Wantok Warrior 03: Australian–Papua New Guinea army civil support exercise, Apr 2003.

War Steed: 2nd Infantry Div annual combat exercise, South Korea.

War Wagon 00-09: 72nd Air Base Wing and 32nd Combat Communications Sqn local exercise, Tinker AFB, OK.

Warbreaker: DARPA time-sensitive targeting research effort initiated after Desert Storm and focused on intelligence. The original objective was to be able to monitor an area of a million square kilometers, conduct mission planning in 10 minutes, and find 1-square-meter targets in a 10,000-square-kilometer search box. Warbreaker would build the capability to maintain a real-time database of all vehicles and mobile weapons. Warbreaker then focused foliage penetration using Synthetic Aperture Radar (SAR) image formation algorithms and automatic target recognition.

Warlord: Army intelligence Automated Intelligence Processing System application used at the division level (also called All Source Analysis System-Warlord). Warlord is used to create a tactical picture of the battlefield and disseminate in overlay format to command centers.

Warlord 2: Army reserve and NG intelligence interrogation and linguist exercise, Devens Reserve Forces Training Area, MA, 10–23 Aug 1996. Participants included a contingent of UK RAF reservists from Flight 7630.

Warrior: *See* Talon Warrior.

Warrior Bravo: CENTAF move from Prince Sultan AB in Saudi Arabia to the CENTCOM Combined Air Operations Center in Qatar, 2003.

Warrior Flag 97: Air force command and control exercise, 25–28 Jul 1997.

Warrior Focus: Army Advanced Warfighting Experiment, Nov 1995, that established the baseline for digitization of dismounted battalion TFs and continued the exploration of dismounted "own the night" issues.

Warrior Sweep: US–Afghan military operation begun 23 Jul 2003 to drive Taliban and al Qaeda fighters from sanctuary in the Ayubkhel Valley, southern Afghanistan. Warrior Sweep was the largest and longest combat operation in Afghanistan since Anaconda in Mar 2002 and the first major military operation conducted by the Afghan National Army.

Warstock: Army intelligence system, Bad Aibling, Germany.

Wasatch Slapper: Deployment of F-15s to Hill AFB, UT, to support the B-1 Weapons School, 8–23 Oct 1999.

Water Pitcher: Humanitarian assistance operation, May–Jun 1992.

Waterboy: AN/WLR-6 SIGINT system aboard attack submarines, 1980s, and replaced by Sea Nymph.

Wedding Ring: Army missile-related intelligence program, 1980s.

West African Training Cruise (WATC): EUCOM engagement program with African coastal nations. During Phase I, a navy flag officer and selected staff members visit nations and plan humanitarian construction or medical projects. During Phase II (odd years), a combat vessel visits. Training is focused on improving host nation arms and drug smuggling interdiction capabilities, small-unit operations, and amphibious and riverine training. WATC began in 1978; starting in 1998, the focus expanded from West Africa to alternate with southern Africa. WATC 04: South Africa, Nov 2003. High Speed Vessel *Swift* (HSV 2). WATC 03: Ghana. WATC 02: South Africa, Togo, 31 Oct–7 Dec 2001. WATC 01: Cape Verde Islands and Gabon, May 2001. WATC 00: Ghana, Mar–May 2000. WATC 99: South Africa, Namibia, Nigeria, Ghana, and Côte d'Ivoire.

West Axe: P-3 deployment to Keflavik, Iceland, 1997.

West Eagle: US–Belgian patrols in the western and central Caribbean on routes from Colombia to Jamaica and Haiti, 2002.

West Wind 99: FBI WMD terrorist incident exercise, Van Nuys airport, CA, Feb1999. This was the largest state-level WMD training exercise to date, involving more than 2,000 participants from local and federal organizations. Westwind 99 simulated a chemical attack on a local air show by a fictional domestic terrorist group, resulting in the simulated deaths of 2,000 victims.

West Wing: Informal code name for the two US air bases in Jordan during OIF — Shaheed Mwaffaq AB (Azraq) and Prince Hussein AB (H-5), Safawi (25 miles northeast of Azraq). The bases accommodated A-10 and F-16 aircraft, as well as SOF personnel.

Western Response 04: CENTCOM unknown exercise.

Western Vortex: UK–Canadian low-flying exercise, Goose Bay, Canada. Western Vortex 01: May–Oct 2001. Western Vortex 99 was canceled because of Kosovo operations.

Westpac MCMEX/DIVEX (Western Pacific Mine Counter Measures and Diving Exercise): Seventh Fleet exercise series. The inaugural exercise was held in Singapore in 2001, and included six navies and 15 ships in the MCMEX and 64 divers from eight countries in the DIVEX. The second MCMEX, held 21 May–6 Jun 2003, was co-hosted by Indonesia and Singapore, and included eight navies and 18 ships in the MCMEX and 78 divers from nine navies in the DIVEX. Participants include Australia, Indonesia, Malaysia, New Zealand, Philippines, Thailand, the UK, and the US.

Wet Gap: Germany-based exercise series. UK participation in the 1–15 Oct 2001 exercise was canceled because of foot-and-mouth disease restrictions.

Wheelhouse: Presidential/VIP communications circuit, originally based on the 1960s JCS "tactical switchboard"and used as part of the Joint Emergency Evacuation Plan. Today it supports president/VIP helicopter coordination in the local Washington, DC, area.

White Alice: Cold War Arctic communications system.

White Cloud: Naval ocean surveillance satellites consisting of multiple low-earth-orbit satellites able to triangulate ELINT signals, first launched in 1976. A second generation was launched in the early 1990s, and the replacement Space-Based Wide Area Surveillance System was launched 8 Sep 2001. *See also* Parcae and Classic Wizard.

White Dot: Former SAC Emergency Action Message (EAM).

White Horse: Los Alamos National Laboratory neutral particle beam demonstrator, tested in the 1980s, part of the Strategic Defense Initiative (SDI) program.

White Knight: Communications/encryption system used for special access program material.

White Pinnacle: Exercise flagword for simulated OPREP-3 Pinnacle reporting.

White Rocket: Exercise flagword for a Red Rocket Emergency Action Message (EAM).

White Truck: Army operations plan, first published 1988.

Wild Cherry: US–Japanese map exercise series, 1980s.

Wiley: Army intelligence system, Bad Aibling, Germany.

William Tell: Air force air defense fighter competition based at Tyndall AFB, FL.

Willoh: Australian–New Zealand air combat training, May 1998, Jul 1997, and Aug 1996.

Willow: DIA foreign material exploitation program. Willow Dune was a short-range ballistic missile thermal response and infrared signatures exploitation, 1998. Includes Willow Sand.

Windjammer: Navy EP-3 fusion engine, part of the Story Book tactical signals exploitation system that enabled a collector to sort out the dense signal environment. Windjammer is able to fuse together diverse data streams received simultaneously from multiple-signal sources into a cohesive tactical picture.

Winged Star: US–UK special operations reciprocal exercise series. The US-based exercise is named Full Moon. Winged Star 02 was canceled because of a British firefighters strike. Winged Star 00: C Coy 3 PARA hosted 120 US soldiers at training areas in Kent and Norfolk. The Dec 1999 exercise was canceled because of Kosovo commitments.

Winter Forest: NATO Baltic exercise. Winter Forest 97. Winter Forest 96.

Winter Harvest: Joint Special Operations Command and Army Intelligence Support Activity (Gray Fox) operation to rescue Army Col. James Dozier, kidnapped in Italy by members of the Red Brigade terrorist faction on 17 Dec 1981.

WIPEOUT: DEA–PACOM marijuana eradication effort in Hawaii.

WISE (WMD Interagency Support Exercise): FBI- and DOE-funded interagency WMD terrorist incident exercise held for the 1996 presidential inauguration. WISE included a crisis response tabletop seminar and a field training exercise to rehearse procedures for terrorist incident response.

Wolf Hunt: Navy anti-submarine-warfare "Rodeo" competitition held at NAS North Island, CA.

Wolfers/Rocketeer: Intelligence-related AN/FTC-54 telephone connection/switch equipment and support equipment (Rocketeer).

Woodpecker: Army communications exercise conducted by the 442nd Signal Bn, Fort Gordon, GA, 20–21 May 1998. The exercise validated the Secure Mobile Anti-Jam Reliable Tactical Terminal (SMART-T).

Wrangler: NSA operated large-scale database management system that houses the national ELINT database, one of four major NSA military databases. Wrangler receives, processes, stores, and disseminates ground-, airborne-, and satellite-derived data in support of worldwide missions. Included are the ELINT Intercept Database (EIDB) and several ELINT-related reference file databases including Kilting, ELINT Parameter List (EPL), Distributed Common Ground System (DCGS), a copy of Electronic Warfare Integrated Reprogramming Data Base (EWIRDB), and a copy of the DIA Electronic Order of Battle (EOB). Wrangler is slated to be replaced by Star Sapphire.

Wyvern Sun 02: Australian–Thai SOF training, Jul 2002.

Wyverin Trail: Marine Corps exercise, 1999.

— X-Y-Z —

XDAMO: Air Force Defense Special Security Communications System (DSSCS) Address Group used by special security officer to generate cross talk about sensitive compartmented information communications and security policy.

Yama Sakura: Japanese–US annual US Army Japan (USARJ) and Japanese Ground Self-Defense Force (JGSDF) command post exercise designed to enhance bilateral contingency planning and interoperability. Distributive simulation networks include I Corps at Fort Lewis, WA; 25th Infantry Div at Schofield Barracks, HI; and the III MEF in Japan. The annual exercise is held during Jan; the location rotates among the five co-hosting regional armies of the JGSDF. Yama Sakura is typically the second largest command post exercise conducted in the Pacific theater. Yama Sakura 04 was the 45th exercise in the series.

Yankee (Operation Yankee): FEMA federal and state government regional preparedness emergency response exercise series. Yankee 04 was canceled due to the Democratic National Convention, and plans were made to combine it with TOPOFF III in 2005. Yankee 03: Naval War College, Newport, RI, 6–8 Aug 2003. The exercise scenario included a hurricane approaching New England with a simultaneous biological attack.

Code Names

Yankee/Zulu: White House Communications Agency VHF network used for encrypted presidential and VIP limousine communications.

Yankee White: Security clearance compartment associated with White House presidential support duties.

Yellow Fruit: Army highly classified clandestine intelligence unit during the Reagan era, likely predecessor to the Intelligence Support Activity (Gray Fox). After financial improprieties were uncovered in 1983, Yellow Fruit was disestablished.

Yolkos 99: European exercise, Bulgaria participating.

Yudh Abyas 04-1: US–Indian training exercise, Counter Insurgency Jungle Warfare Center, Mizoram, 28 Mar–16 Apr 2004. Alaska-based 172nd Stryker Bde.

Zarf: Subcompartment of Talent Keyhole–derived satellite ELINT (for example, Top Secret/Talent Zeyhole Zarf) eliminated in May 1999, along with the code words *Umbra*, *Moray*, and *Spoke*.

Zenith Star: BMDO space-based chemical laser program.

Zenith Star 99-1: JTF computer network defense (CND) exercise, Oct 1999. The exercise examined interagency working-level coordination using a computer network defense scenario similar to Eligible Receiver 97. The exercise demonstrated how little it would take for hackers or terrorists to trigger "blackouts" in regions with military bases or shut down 911 emergency systems.

ZH: FEMA continuity of government compartment, initiated in 1983. *See also* PH.

Zhardem: CENTCOM classified exercise series with Kazakhstan. Zhardem 04. Zhardem 03. Zhardem 02. *See also* Balance Zhardem.

Ziffer: Nickname for an informal SIGINT administrative message sent via Operational Communications (OPSCOMM), Critical Information Communications System (CRITICOMM), or Defense Special Security Communications System (DSSCS) systems.

Zircon: Internet relay chat interface used in US military command posts, allowing planners, targeters, and intelligence analysts to informally communicate. Used extensively during OIF. Zircon over the Joint Worldwide

Intelligence Communications System (JWICS) intelligence network is called Chatterbox.

Zirconic: Former BYEMAN subcompartment (for example, Top Secret/Talent Keyhole BYEMAN Zirconic) that reportedly referred to stealth reconnaissance satellite programs under the names *Misty* and *Prowler*.

Zodiac Beauchamp: Suborbital rocket launch program from Barking Sands, HI, for missile-defense-related research purposes, 1990–present.

PART IV

ACRONYMS
AND GLOSSARY

5D: Demand Driven Direct Digital Dissemination. Digital imagery product storage and retrieval capability, replaced by IPL on 31 Mar 2002.

AB: Air Base.

ABM: anti-ballistic missile.

ACBA: Airborne Communications Bus Architecture. C-135 Speckled Trout system.

ACC: Air Combat Command (air force).

ACCM: alternative or compensatory control measure.

ACE: analysis and control element; Allied Command Europe (NATO).

ACIC: Army Counter Intelligence Center.

ACINT: acoustic intelligence.

ACIS: Arms Control Intelligence Staff (CIA).

ACO: Allied Command Operations (NATO) (formerly ACE).

ACOTA: *See* African Contingency Operations Training and Assistance.

Acquisition and Cross-Servicing Agreement (ACSA): Also called Mutual Logistic Support Agreements (MLSA). Agreements for the provision of reimbursable logistics support, supplies, and services, including food, medical services, dental support, force protection, transportation and material handling equipment, billeting, vehicle/equipment maintenance, and fuel.

ACRI: African Crisis Response Initiative.

ACSA: *See* Acquisition and Cross-Servicing Agreement.

ACSI: Assistant Chief of Staff, Intelligence (air force and army term).

ACT: Allied Command Transformation (NATO) (formerly SACLANT).

ACTD: Advanced Concept Technology Demonstration.

ACTTA: *See* Anti-Crime Training and Technical Assistance.

ACVOP: Advanced COMINT Voice Processor.

ADARS: Airborne Digital Audio Recording System. RC-135 recording system.

ADCI: Assistant Director of Central Intelligence.

ADCI/C: Assistant Director of Central Intelligence for Collection.

ADDI: Associate Deputy Director for Intelligence.

ADNET: Anti-Drug Network (DOD).

AEAO: Airborne Emergency Action Officer.

AEELS: Automatic Electronic Intelligence Emitter Location System. RC-135 system.

AEF: Aerospace Expeditionary Force.

AEN: arbitrary ELINT notation.

AFB: Air Force Base.

AFIWC: Air Force Information Warfare Center.

AFMC: Air Force Materiel Command (formerly Air Force Logistics Command).

AFNORTH: Allied Forces Northern Europe (NATO).

AFOSI: Air Force Office of Special Investigations.

African Contingency Operations Training and Assistance (ACOTA): US program that trains and equips African military units so that they are better able to deploy and operate in peace support operations and other complex humanitarian situations.

AFSOC: Air Force Special Operations Command.

AFSOUTH: Allied Forces Southern Europe (NATO).

AFSPC: Air Force Space Command.

AFTAC: Air Force Technical Application Center.

AIA: Air Intelligence Agency.

Air Defense Warning:
- Air Defense Warning Red: Attack by hostile aircraft/missiles is imminent or under way. Synonymous with Civil Defense Attack Warning Signal.
- Air Defense Warning Yellow: Attack by hostile aircraft/missiles is probable. Synonymous with Civil Defense Attack Warning Signal.
- Air Defense Warning White: Attack by hostile aircraft/missiles is not considered probable or imminent.

AIRES: Advanced Imagery Requirements and Exploitation System. EP-3E mission subsystems including Story Finder, Story Teller, Story Book, Story Classic, and an unnamed AN/ULQ-16.

AIRSOUTH: Allied Air Forces Southern Europe, now Air Component Command.

AJ: anti-jam.

AJCC: Alternate Joint Communications Center.

ALCOR: army radar located on Kwajalein Atoll.

AMB: Automated M-22 Broadcast. Satellite communications system designed primarily for the dissemination of large imagery files to tactical users.

AMC: Air Mobility Command.

AMHS: Automated Message Handling System (now M3).

AN/ALQ-151(V)2: Nomenclature for Quick Fix IIB.

AN/BQR-19: Nomenclature for Tophat.

AN/BRQ-2(V): Nomenclature for Classic Erne.

AN/BRT-2: Nomenclature for Circuit Mayflower.

AN/FQQ-1/2/3/9: Nomenclature for Caesar/SOSUS/IUSS.

AN/TRQ-152: Nomenclature for Trackwolf.

AN/ULR-21(V): Nomenclature for Classic Troll.

AN/URC-119: Nomenclature for Pacer Bounce.

AN/USD-9A/B: Nomenclature for Guardrail.

AN/USQ-149(V): Nomenclature for Cluster Snoop.

AN/WLQ-4(V)/(V): Nomenclature for Cutty Sark and Silent Knight.

AN/WLR-8 (V)2/(V)5: Nomenclature for Cluster Spectator.

AN/WLR-18(V): Nomenclature for Classic Salmon.

AN/WSQ-5(V): Nomenclature for Cluster Spectator.

ANA: Afghan National Army.

ANG: Air National Guard.

ANGB: Air National Guard Base.

ANMCC: Alternative National Military Command Center (Site R).

Anti-Crime Training and Technical Assistance (ACTTA): US security assistance programs to support improvements in foreign criminal law, prosecutorial procedures, law enforcement, and counter-narcotics activities.

Antiterrorism Training Assistance (ATA): Primary provider of US government anti-terrorism training and equipment to the law enforcement agencies of friendly countries and the first specific counter-terrorism program funded by the Department of State, authorized in late 1983.

AO: area of operations.

AOC: air operations center.

AOR: area of responsibility.

Acronyms and Glossary

AQF: Advanced Quick Fix.

AQL: Advanced Quick Look.

ARCENT: Army Forces Central Command.

ARFOR: Army Forces.

ARG: Amphibious Ready Group.

ARGUS: advanced remote ground unattended sensor.

ARIES: airborne reconnaissance integrated electronic warfare system.

ARL: Army Reconnaissance Low. Army-operated "low-profile" airborne SIGINT system aboard commercial-appearing modified DeHavilland Dash-7 four-engine turpoprop aircraft (designated RC-7), first deployed in 1993. ARL aircraft look like civilian commuter planes and make relatively little noise. ARL is a multi-function, day/night, all-weather reconnaissance asset. It consists of communications intelligence (COMINT), imagery intelligence (IMINT), or Moving Target Indicator/Synthetic Aperture Radar (MTI/SAR) mission payloads. The COMINT subsystem on the ARL-M, called Superhawk, provides an electronic support measures (ESM) capability for intercept, identification, and location of both conventional and Low Probability of Intercept (LPI) communication signals in the HF, VHF, UHF, and SHF frequency bands. ARL was used in Desert Storm and is used extensively in South America for counter-drug intelligence collection. ARL-Cs and ARL-Ms are stationed at Fort Bliss, TX, and primarily support SOUTHCOM requirements; ARL-Ms provides support to PACOM (Korea).

ARL-C: Army Reconnaissance Low — COMINT.

ARL-M: Army Reconnaissance Low — Multifunction.

ARNG: Army National Guard.

Article 98 Agreement: Bilateral accord pledging that US persons will not be surrendered to the International Criminal Court (ICC) for prosecution. The American Service Members Protection Act, passed by Congress in 2002, requires the freezing of US military assistance to non-NATO countries that decline to enter into bilateral agreements under Article 98 of the Treaty of Rome establishing the ICC, which allows countries to make bilateral arrangements to exempt each other's citizens from being extradited for prosecution by the ICC. As of 2004, the United States had signed bilateral "nonsurrender" agreements with 81 countries. Under the provisions of the American Service Members Protection Act, NATO members as well as some US-designated

"Major Non-NATO Allies" were exempted from sanctions. The US suspended more than $47 million in military aid to 35 countries that failed or refused to grant US citizens immunity from the ICC, including Colombia, South Africa, Bulgaria, Croatia, Slovakia, and Slovenia.

AS: Air Station.

ASARS: Advanced Synthetic Aperture Radar System.

ASAS: All Source Analysis System.

ASCI: Assistant Chief of Staff, Intelligence (now DCSI).

ASCIET: All Service Combat Identification Evaluation Team.

ASW: anti-submarine warfare.

ASWEX: anti-submarine-warfare exercise.

ATA: Anti-Terrorism Training Assistance

ATAC: Anti-Terrorism Alert Center (NCIS).

ATO: air tasking order; Advanced Technology Office.

AWACS: Airborne Warning and Control System (air force).

AWE: Advanced Warfighting Experiment.

B: BYEMAN (also Bravo).

B-NICE: Biological, Nuclear, Incendiary, Chemical, or Explosive.

BAT (Bahamas and Turks and Caicos): Multi-agency, international operation based in Nassau, Bahamas. The mission is to stop the flow of cocaine and marijuana originating in South American source countries, transiting the Bahamas and destined for the US.

BCO: BYEMAN Control Officer.

BCTP: Battle Command Training Program.

BDA: Bomb Damage Assessment; Battle Damage Assessment (aka combat assessment).

Bde: Brigade.

BFE: Blacker front end.

BGIXS: battle group information exchange system (navy).

BGPHES: Battle Group Passive Horizon Extension System (navy).

BL: Blue Lightning.

Bn: Battalion.

BRIGAND: Bi-static Radar Intelligence Generation and Analysis Display.

BPRP: Bioterrorism Preparedness and Response Program.

BRITE: Basic Rate Interface Transmission Extension (Air Force Space Command Knight project).

BS: Bomber Squadron.

BSLE: Border Security and Law Enforcement. US security assistance program to improve the capabilities and interoperability of the border guards, customs, and other security forces.

BW: biological weapons; Bomber Wing.

C2: command and control.

C2W: command and control warfare (replaced by information warfare).

C3I: command, control, communications, and intelligence.

C3ISR: command, control, communications, and intelligence, surveillance, and reconnaissance.

C4I: command, control, communications, computer, and intelligence.

C4ISR: command, control, communications, computer, and intelligence, surveillance, and reconnaissance.

CABIN: Chemical and Biological Information Network.

CACTIS: Community Automated Counter-Terrorism Intelligence System. Sensitive compartmented information (SCI) network.

CAMH: Commander-in-Chief Alternate Mobile Headquarters (replaced by MCCC).

CAMPS: Compartmented ASAS [All Source Analysis System] Message Processing System.

CAOC: Combined Air Operations Center.

CAR: Central African Republic.

CARS: Contingency Airborne Reconnaissance System (replaced by DSS).

CARVERS: Criticality, Accessibility, Recuperability, Vulnerability, Effect on Enemy, Recognizability, Survivability (targeting term).

carve out: A classified contract issued in connection with a special access program (SAP).

CASIAT: National Center for the Analysis of Violent Crimes Computer Assisted Security Investigative Analysis Tool.

CATIS/IESS: Computer-Aided Tactical Information System/Imagery Exploitation Support System.

CAX: computer-assisted exercise; combined arms exercise.

CBDCOM: Chemical-Biological Defense Command (army).

CBIRF: Chemical-Biological Incident Response Force (Marine Corps).

CBQRF: Chemical-Biological Quick Response Force.

CBRN: Caribbean Basin Radar Network.

CBRNE: Chemical, Biological, Radiological, Nuclear, and High-Yield Conventional Explosive.

CBRNE-CM: Chemical, Biological, Radiological, Nuclear, or High-Yield Conventional Explosive — Consequence Management.

CBS: Corps Battle Simulation.

CCP: Consolidated Cryptologic Program (part of the classified defense budget).

CDAA: Circular Disposed Antenna Array.

CDE: collateral damage estimation.

CDL: Common Data Link.

CENTAF: Central Air Forces.

CENTCOM: Central Command.

CENTRIX: Originally Central Region Information Exchange; now Combined Enterprise Regional Information Exchange. Communications network by which US intelligence can be fused and sanitized through Information Support Server Environment [ISSE] and Radiant Mercury for dissemination to allies. CENTRIX originated as a US–Saudi "community of interest" network at Prince Sultan AB, Saudi Arabia, in Apr 2001 to run the Iraqi no-fly-zone operations. After 9/11, a new project sought to establish a global CENTRIX Secret releasable-level network to support the war on terrorism, including e-mail, chat, common operational, and intelligence picture. CENTRIX Tier 1 (Global Counter-Terrorism Force, formerly known as COWAN C) was activated in Oct 2002 and constituted a 50-plus nation CENTCOM network. CENTRIX-J was tested with the Japan Maritime Self-Defense Force during ANNUALEX in Nov 2003 and has a built-in language translator.

CERT: Computer Emergency Response Team.

CFACC: Coalition/Combined Force Air Component Commander.

CFB: Canadian Forces Base.

CFC: Combined Forces Command (South Korea).

CFLCC: Coalition/Combined Force Land Component Commander.

CFMCC: Coalition/Combined Force Maritime Component Commander.

CFSOCC: Coalition/Combined Force Special Operations Component Commander.

CFX: command field exercise.

CGS: Joint Surveillance and Tracking System (JSTARS) Common Ground Station.

CHAALS: Communications High Accuracy Airborne Location System. Army COMINT/direction finding system.

CHATS: Counterintelligence/HUMINT Automated Tool Set (formerly TRRIP).

CHIMS: Counter Intelligence/Human Intelligence Information Management System.

CI: counter-intelligence.

CI&SCM: counter-intelligence and security counter-measures.

CIA: Central Intelligence Agency.

CIALink: Classified computer intranet at CIA headquarters.

CICTE: Organization of American States (OAS) Inter-American Committee Against Terrorism (Spanish-language acronym). In Jul 2003, the convention entered into force after six countries deposited their instruments of ratification (Antigua and Barbuda, Canada, El Salvador, Mexico, Nicaragua, and Peru). In 2004, Panama and Venezuela ratified the convention.

CIDCON: Civil disturbance condition. There are five conditions of increasing preparedness of military forces to prepare for deployment in response to an actual or threatened civil disturbance:
+ CIDCON 5: Normal training and preparedness status.
+ CIDCON 4: Increased monitoring and analysis, initiation of detailed planning; 12-hour response time and airlift prepared.
+ CIDCON 3: Increase in designated Garden Plot force preparedness; pre-positioning of forces.
+ CIDCON 2: Movement of Garden Plot forces.
+ CIDCON 1: Maximum force preparedness; deploy within 1 hour.

CIF: CINC In Extremis Force. Special operations protective guard force for unified commanders and other VIPs.

CIMEX: civil military exercise (aka WINTEX/CIMEX).

CIO: Central Imagery Organization.

CIRVIS: Communications Instructions for Reporting Vital Intelligence Sightings.

CIS: Commonwealth of Independent States.

CJCS: Chairman, Joint Chiefs of Staff.

CJSOTF: Combined Joint Special Operations Task Force.

CJTF: Combined Joint Task Force; commander, joint task force.

CLIPR: Cryptologic Linguist Program. Air force linguist foreign-language proficiency maintenance, enhancement, and sustainment.

CM: consequence management.

CMO: Central MASINT [Measurement and Signature Intelligence] Organization (former DIA organization).

CMS: Community Management Staff (DCI, replaced the IC staff in 1992).

CMX: crisis management exercise.

CNC: Crime and Narcotic Center (CIA).

CNIPS: Caribbean Narcotics Interdiction and Planning System.

CNMC: crosshair net management center.

Co: Company.

COA: courses of action.

Coalition Warfare Program (CWP): Program begun in 2001 to provide research and development, testing and evaluation (RDT&E) funding to improve coalition interoperability. CWP surveillance projects were funded with Canada, France, Germany, Italy, Norway, Saudi Arabia, and the UK.

COBLU: Cooperative Outboard Logistics Update. The AN/SSQ-108 (V) COBLU is a joint US–UK program to modernize the detection, location, and analysis capability of US and UK Outboard systems.

code word: A single word assigned to a classified meaning to ensure security concerning intentions and to safeguard information pertaining to real-world military plans or operations classified as Confidential or higher.

COG: *See* continuity of government.

COLISEUM: Community On-Line Intel System for End-Users and Managers. DIA automated Intelligence Community production and requirements management system. It provides the mechanism for registering and validating intelligence requirements, for deconfliction of collection requirements, for assigning and scheduling production, and for managing overall production activities.

collateral information: National Security Information (such as Top Secret, Secret, and Confidential) under the provisions of Executive Order 12958 but not subject to the enhanced security protection required for special access program (SAP), sensitive compartmented information (SCI), or special intelligence (SI) information.

COLT: Contingency Operations Liaison Team. CIA Office of Military Affairs reachback system used in Operation Enduring Freedom and Operation Iraqi Freedom.

COMINT: communications intelligence.

COMIREX: Committee on Imagery Requirements and Exploitation.

compartmentation: Formal system of restricted access, normally for intelligence operations. Such systems are established to protect the sensitive aspects of specific sources, methods, and analytical procedures of foreign intelligence programs. The information is then held within a named compartment and classified by the classification level (such as Top Secret, Secret, and Confidential) as well as the compartmented name.

COMPTUEX: composite training unit exercise (navy).

COMSEC: communication security.

CONPLAN: Operations Plan in Concept Form, also commonly called contingency plan.

CONR: Continental US NORAD Region.

Container Security Initiative (CSI): Department of Homeland Security (DHS) initiative that aims to protect containerized shipping from exploitation by terrorists. Several CSI ports are operational: Halifax, Montreal, and Vancouver, Canada; Göteborg, Sweden; Le Havre and Rotterdam, Netherlands; Bremerhaven and Hamburg, Germany; Antwerp, Belgium; Singapore; Yokohama, Japan; Hong Kong; and Felixstowe, UK. Taiwan has also been identified by DHS as one of the top 20 foreign ports for implementation of the initiative. CSI requires bilateral agreements to be created with other governments to target and prescreen high-risk containers in overseas seaports before they are shipped to the United States. Customs inspectors (prescreeners) are also stationed in CSI ports to work with their overseas counterparts.

continuity of government (COG): The program to ensure that the executive, legislative, and judicial branches can continue to discharge minimal essential responsibilities in a catastrophic emergency. The Top Secret Presidential Decision Directive 67, "Enduring Constitutional Government (ECG) and Continuity of Government (COG) Operations," 21 Oct 1998, requires plans and programs for Continuity of the Presidency (COP), COG, and Continuity of Operations (COOP).

Continuity of Operations (COOP): The program that provides for a coordinated internal effort within federal and local government branch components to ensure the capability to continue essential functions across a wide range of potential emergencies, including localized acts of nature, accidents, and technological or attack-related emergencies.

CONUS: continental United States.

COOP: *See* Continuity of Operations.

COS: Chief of Station (CIA).

COSMEC: Common Spectral MASINT Exploitation Capability.

COSMIC: NATO term, always capitalized to designate Top Secret information.

Counterdrug Surveillance and Control Systems (CSCS): Program that encompasses the activities from the Caribbean Basin Radar Network (CBRN) and SOUTHCOM Counterdrug Surveillance (SCDS) Programs. CSCS provides air surveillance information to SOUTHCOM and seven participating host nations. Long-range radar sites throughout the Caribbean, Central America, and South America are integrated into the system. The radar sites pass information to the Southern Regional Operations Center (SROC) in Panama and the Caribbean Region Operations Center (CARIBROC) in Key West, FL. Four additional sites in Puerto Rico provide information to the Puerto Rico Operations Center (PROC).

Counter-Terrorism Action Group (CTAG): In Jun 2004, the G-8 leaders established the CTAG to expand counter-terrorism capacity building assistance. The CTAG will include the G-8 as well as other states, mainly donors.

COWAN: Combined Operations Wide Area Network connecting the UK, Canada, New Zealand, Australia, Japan, South Korea, and the US. COWAN A supports information exchange solely among Australia, Canada, the UK, and the US at a higher level of classification.

CPA: Coalition Provisional Authority.

CPX: command post exercise.

CRITIC: Critical Information. Highest-urgency warning message containing critical information concerning foreign situations or developments that affect the security or national interests of the US.

CRITICOMM: CRITIC Communications System. NSA-managed portion of the Defense Special Security Communications System (DSSCS) used to transmit and deliver CRITIC message traffic. The secondary function is to support routine sensitive compartmented information (SCI) traffic requirements.

CROFA: Cryptologic Remote Operations Facility, Airborne. Located at Fort Meade, MD. U-2 system that provides tactical and strategic information to both national-level and theater commanders as well as actionable intelligence to tactical operators without a new footprint in theater.

CSAR: combat search and rescue.

CSCS: *See* Counterdrug Surveillance and Control Systems.

CSG: Counterterrorism Security Group.

CSI: *See* Container Security Initiative.

CSIDS: CENTCOM–SOCOM Intelligence Database System.

CSL: Cooperative Security Location (formerly forward operating location).

CSO: Center for Special Operations (SOCOM).

CSS: Communications Surveillance System (Silent Shield).

CSTARS: Combat Sent Technical Acquisition Receiver System.

CT: counter-terrorism.

CT Fellowship: Regional Defense Counter-terrorism Fellowship Program (DOD).

CTAG: *See* Counter-Terrorism Action Group.

CTAPS: Contingency Theater Automated Planning System (air force).

CTC: Counterterrorism Center (CIA).

CTF: Combined Task Force.

CTOC: Cryptologic Telecommunications Operations Center. NSA 24-hour operation primarily responsible for management and operation of the NSAnet that includes worldwide telecommunications assets, messaging and data systems, and all network interconnections supporting the US Cryptologic Systems.

CTS: COSMIC Top Secret (NATO).

CTSA: COSMIC Top Secret ATOMAL (NATO).

CTT: Commander's Tactical Terminal. AN/TSC-125 system used to disseminate intelligence data collected from multiple airborne systems.

CTT/H: Commander's Tactical Terminal/Hybrid.

CTT/H-R: CTT/H-Receive.

CVBG: CV [Aircraft Carrier] Battle Group.

CVIC: CV [Aircraft Carrier] Intelligence Center.

CW: Constant Web.

CWP: *See* Coalition Warfare Program.

DARO: Defense Airborne Reconnaissance Office.

DARPA: Defense Advanced Research Projects Agency.

DAT: Defense Attaché (DIA).

DCGS: Distributed Common Ground System.

DCI: Director of Central Intelligence.

DCID: Director of Central Intelligence Directive.

DCIIS: Defense Counter-intelligence Integrated Information System.

DCSINT. Deputy Chief of Staff, Intelligence (army)

DCTN: Defense Commercial Telecommunications Network. Collateral video teleconference (VTC).

DCTS: Defense Collaboration Tool Suite.

DDCI: Deputy Director of Central Intelligence.

DDDS: Defense Data Dictionary System.

DDI: Deputy Director for Intelligence (analytical part of CIA).

DDO: Deputy Director for Operations (covert part of CIA).

DDS: Defense Dissemination System.

DEA: Drug Enforcement Administration (Department of Justice).

DEFCON: Defense Readiness Condition. Defense Readiness Conditions are the uniform system of progressive alert postures identified by the short titles DEFCON 5, 4, 3, 2, and 1, with DEFCON 5 being normal readiness posture and DEFCON 1 being maximum readiness of military forces.
+ DEFCON 1: General Alert, Maximum Force Readiness.
+ DEFCON 2: Reinforced Alert.

- **DEFCON 3:** Simple Alert, Increased Force Readiness.
- **DEFCON 4:** Military Vigilance, Increased Intelligence Collection.
- **DEFCON 5:** Normal Readiness.

DEFSMAC: Defense Special Missile and Aeronautics Center (DIA).

DEW: Distant Early Warning.

DF: direction finding.

DGS: Deployable Ground System. DGS-1 (30th Intelligence Squadron, Langley Air Force Base, VA) supports Predator in CENTCOM; DGS-2, Beale Air Force Base, CA, supports U-2 and Global Hawk; DGS-3, Osan air base, Korea, supports the Pacific; DGS-4, Ramstein air base, Germany, supports Europe.

DHS: Department of Homeland Security; Defense HUMINT Service (DIA).

DI: Directorate of Intelligence (analytical part of CIA).

DIA: Defense Intelligence Agency.

DIAC: Defense Intelligence Analysis Center (DIA).

DICE: Distributed Information Warfare Constructive Environment of the Air Force Information Warfare Center (AFIWC).

digraph and/or trigraph: A two- and/or three-letter acronym for an assigned code word or nickname (such as *TK* for "Talent Keyhole" or *GCO* for "Gamma Control Office").

DII COE: Defense Information Infrastructure Common Operating Environment.

DIN: Defense Intelligence Network. DIA internal classified television network.

DIOBS: Defense Intelligence Order of Battle System.

DIRNSA: Director of NSA.

DISA: Defense Information Systems Agency.

DISN: Defense Information Systems Network.

Div: Division.

DMPI: Desired Mean Point of Impact (now Desired Point of Impact, DPI).

DO: Directorate of Operations. CIA, sometimes DDO.

DOCEX: document exploitation.

DOD: Department of Defense.

DODIIS: Department of Defense Intelligence Information System.

DOE: Department of Energy.

DOJ: Department of Justice.

DPI: Desired Point of Impact.

DPPDB: Digital Point Positioning Database.

DRC: Democratic Republic of the Congo.

DSNET: Defense Secure Network. The network consists of three subnetworks, DSNET1: Secret; DSNET2: Top Secret; and DSNET3: sensitive compartmented information (SCI) level.

DSP: Defense Support Program (early-warning satellite).

DSS: Defense Security Service; Deployable Shelterized System (formerly the Contingency Airborne Reconnaissance System, CARS).

DSSCS: Defense Special Security Communications System. Worldwide, special-purpose communications system for processing formatted SIGINT and CRITIC messages, sensitive compartmented information (SCI) traffic, and the personal communications of general officers and other senior officials. DSSCS uses terminals and relay facilities of NSA and DIA (such as CRITICOMM and SPINTCOMM).

DSSS: Defense Sensitive Support System.

DSWA: Defense Special Weapons Agency (now DTRA).

DTRA: Defense Threat Reduction Agency.

DTS: Deployable Transit-cased System.

EA: engagement area; electronic attack (formerly electronic counter-measures, ECM).

EACIC: Echelons Above Corps Intelligence Center.

EACTI: Eastern Africa Counterterrorism Initiative. In Jun 2003, President Bush announced a $100 million EACTI to expand and accelerate counterterrorism efforts with Kenya, Ethiopia, Djibouti, Uganda, Tanzania, and other countries. The EACTI provides training and some equipment for special counter-terrorism units for senior-level decision makers and for legislators who are concerned with drafting legislation on terrorist financing and money laundering.

EADF: Enhanced Automatic DF [direction finding]. High frequency direction finding (HF/DF) processor upgrade, part of Longroot.

EAGLE: Evolutionary Air and Space Global Engagement Relay Mirror System.

EAPC: Euro-Atlantic Partnership Council.

EASI: Expert Analysis System for Intelligence.

EBO: effects-based operations.

ECCM: electronic counter-counter-measures.

ECG: *See* Enduring Constitutional Government.

ECI: unknown codeword classification.

ECM: electronic counter-measures.

ECOWAS: Economic Community of West African States.

EDA: *See* Excess Defense Articles.

EIFEL: *Electronisches Informations Und Fuhrung System Fur Die Einsatzbereitschaft Fur Der Luftwaffe* (NATO C2 System in Germany).

EIJ: Egyptian Islamic Jihad.

EIPC: Enhanced International Peacekeeping Capabilities. US security assistance grants for training.

ELINT: electronic intelligence.

ELNOT: ELINT notation.

ELVIS: Enhanced Link Virtual Info System.

EMCON: emission control.

Enduring Constitutional Government (ECG): Executive, legislative, and judicial branch efforts, coordinated by the president, to preserve the capability to execute constitutional responsibilities in a catastrophic emergency.

ENTICED: Enhanced National Tactical Imagery and COMINT Externals Dissemination.

EO: Executive Order.

EOB: Electronic Order of Battle.

EOBS: Electronic Order of Battle System.

EPDS: Electronic Processing and Dissemination System.

EPL: electronic parameter listing; ELINT Parameter List.

EPLRS: Enhanced Position Location Reporting System.

EPPIC: Enhanced Precise Positioning Integrated Capability. Precision-point targeting and electronic light table software, and integration of hardware, software, and training.

ER: Eagle Reach.

ESI: extremely sensitive information.

ESM: electronic support measures.

ETHICS: European Theater High Capacity Intelligence Communications System. European subset of the Joint Worldwide Intelligence Communications System (JWICS).

ETIBS: Enhanced Tactical Information Broadcast System.

ETUT: Enhanced Tactical Users Terminal. ARCENT's central database for ELINT and primary collection management automation tool.

EU: European Union.

EUCOM: European Command.

EW: electronic warfare.

EWIRDB: Electronic Warfare Integrated Reprogramming Data Base. The DIA database that contains parametric data describing electronic warfare systems, used for mission and reprogramming data.

EXBS: Export Control and Related Border Security Assistance. US security assistance program to improve border control, prevent weapons proliferation, and fight narcotics trafficking and financial crimes.

Excess Defense Articles (EDA): Defense articles owned by the US and not procured in anticipation of military assistance or sales requirements, or pursuant to a military assistance or sales order, which are in excess of DOD components at the time such articles are dropped from inventory by the supplying agency for delivery to countries or international organizations.

exercise term: A combination of two words, normally unclassified, used exclusively to designate a test, drill, or exercise. An exercise term is employed to preclude the possibility of confusing exercise directions with actual operational directives.

F3S: Field Station Support System. One of four major NSA military databases.

FAA: Federal Aviation Administration.

FAISA: FORSCOM Automated Intelligence Support Activity (army).

FAISS: FORSCOM Automated Intelligence Support System (army).

FAST: Forward Area SIDS [Secondary Image Dissemination System] and TRE [Tactical Receive Equipment]; Forward Area Support Terminal. Army SIGINT processor that gathers both national and theater ELINT.

FATF: *See* Financial Action Task Force on Money Laundering.

FBI: Federal Bureau of Investigation.

FEMA: Federal Emergency Management Agency.

fence: National Foreign Intelligence Program funds that are buried within the defense budget and are protected from reprogramming (spent on anything other than what it was approved for and across-the-board or fair-share cuts applied to military service budgets).

FIDNET: Federal Intrusion Detection Network (NSA-managed network).

Financial Action Task Force on Money Laundering (FATF): Established at the G-7 Economic Summit in 1989, FATF is an intergovernmental body whose purpose is the development of international standards aimed at combating money laundering and the financing of terrorism. The FATF Eight Special Recommendations on Terrorist Financing are widely acknowledged as the international standards. FATF members include Argentina, Australia, Austria, Belgium, Brazil, Canada, Denmark, the European Commission, Finland, France, Germany, Greece, the Gulf Cooperation Council, Hong Kong, China, Iceland, Ireland, Italy, Japan, Luxembourg, Mexico, the Netherlands, New Zealand, Norway, Portugal, Russia, Singapore, South Africa, Spain, Sweden, Switzerland, Turkey, the UK, and the US.

FINCEN: Financial Crimes Enforcement Network. A Treasury Department intelligence clearinghouse on money laundering.

FIRESTORM: Federation of Intelligence, Reconnaissance, Surveillance and Targeting Operations, and Research Models.

FISA: Foreign Intelligence Surveillance Act.

FISINT: Foreign Instruments Signals Intelligence (also TELINT).

Five Power Defence Agreement (FPDA): Arrangement that commits Australia, New Zealand, and the UK to consult on a response to any armed attack or threat against Malaysia or Singapore and provides a framework for training exercises and other contacts. It was formally established in 1971 specifically to defend Malaysia and Singapore against external attack at the time of the UK withdrawal "east of Suez." FPDA celebrated its 30th anniversary at Butterworth air base in Malaysia in Nov 2001.

FIWC: fleet information warfare center.

FLEETEX/FLTEX: fleet exercise.

FMF: *See* Foreign Military Financing.

FMS: *See* foreign military sales.

FOB: forward operating base.

FOL: forward operating location.

Foreign Military Financing (FMF): Funds provided in the Foreign Operations, Export Financing and Related Appropriations Act and emergency supplementals to deliver military articles, services, and training to support the efforts of US friends and allies.

foreign military sales (FMS): US security assistance authorized by the Arms Export Control Act (1976), as amended, and conducted on the basis of formal contracts or agreements between the US government and an authorized recipient government or international organization. FMS includes government-to-government sales of defense articles or defense services, from DOD stocks or through purchase under DOD-managed contracts, regardless of the source of financing.

FORMICA: Foreign Military Intelligence Collection Activity.

FORSCOM: Army Forces Command.

FOUO: For Official Use Only.

FPC: Federal Preparedness Circular.

FPCON: Force Protection Condition.

FPDA: *See* Five Power Defence Agreement.

FRD: Formerly Restricted Data.

FRIAR: Fast Response Intelligence Analyst Resource. COMINT analytical equipment.

FS: Fighter Squadron.

FSA: Freedom Support Act. The Freedom for Russia and Emerging Eurasian Democracies and Open Markets (FREEDOM) Support Act (FSA), enacted in Oct 1992, is the basis for assistance to nations of the former Soviet Union, particularly Ukraine.

FSTC: Foreign Science and Technology Center (now National Ground Intelligence Center, NGIC).

FTD: Air Force Foreign Technology Division (now the National Air and Space Intelligence Center, NASIC).

FTX: field training exercise.

FUNCPLAN: Functional Plan. Military plan for operations in a peacetime or permissive environment.

FWS: Fighter Weapon Squadron.

FY: fiscal year.

G-7: Group of Seven (Canada, France, Germany, Italy, Japan, UK, US).

G-8: Group of Eight (major industrialized nations — Canada, France, Germany, Italy, Japan, UK, US, Russia).

GALE: Graphic Area Limitation Environment.

GAT: Guidance Apportionment and Targeting Cell.

GBCS: ground-based common sensor.

GBS: Global Broadcast Service.

GCC: *See* Gulf Cooperation Council.

GCCS: Global Command and Control System.

GCCS-M: Global Command and Control System — Maritime.

GDIP: General Defense Intelligence Program (now Joint Military Intelligence Program, JMIP).

GEDA: gaining, exploiting, defending, and attacking activities. A space and information domain doctrinal term.

GENSER: General Service. A worldwide communications system for processing unclassified and collateral (up to Secret-level) classified information.

GEO: Geosynchronous Earth Orbit.

GEP: Ground Entry Point.

GIS: Geographic Information System.

GMI: General Military Intelligence. Substantive intelligence products produced by national-level intelligence agencies and theater Joint Intelligence Centers (JICs). Topics include foreign military capabilities, Order of Battle (OB), installations, organizations, training, tactics, doctrine, strategy, area and terrain intelligence (such as urban areas and landing beaches), transportation systems, military material production and support industries, military and civilian command, control, and communications (C3) systems, and other sociological, political, economic, and military subjects.

GRASP: Graphic SIGINT Products (NSA).

GRCS: Guardrail Common Sensor.

GRIFN: Guardrail Information Node.

GRSOC: Fort Gordon [GA] Regional SIGINT Operations Center. Primary NSA MASINT support site.

GSE: Ground Support Equipment.

GSM: ground station module.

GSR: ground surveillance radar.

GTEP: Georgia Train and Equip Program.

GTMO: Guantanamo Bay.

Gulf Cooperation Council (GCC): Six-member Arabian Gulf cooperative council, founded in 1981 and comprising Bahrain, Kuwait, Oman, Qatar, Saudi Arabia, and the UAE. The GCC signed a defense agreement in Dec 2000 in which every member country must come to the defense of any other member country. The GCC has taken common decisions, such as that in 1994 to drop secondary and tertiary boycotts against Israel. The GCC also has a collective defense force called Peninsula Shield that deployed to Kuwait in 2003.

GWEN: Ground Wave Emergency Network.

GWOT: Global War on Terrorism.

HAE: high altitude endurance.

HALE: high altitude long endurance.

HAT: HUMINT Augmentation Team.

HDBT: Hard Deeply Buried Targets.

HEO: Highly Elliptical Orbit.

HFAC: Human Factors Analysis Center (DIA).

HF/DF: high frequency direction finding.

HILEX: high-level exercise (FEMA).

HIRIS: Hyperspectral InfraRed Imaging System.

HOCNET: HUMINT Operational Communications Network.

HQAN: Have Quick A-Net.

HSC: Homeland Security Council.

HSI: Hyperspectral Imagery.

HSI/SAR: Hyperspectral Imagery/Synthetic Aperture Radar.

HSPD: Homeland Security Presidential Directive.

HT: Hollow Tile (Air Intelligence Agency).

HUMINT: human intelligence.

HVCCO: Handle Via COMINT Channels Only.

HVSACO: Handle Via Special Access Channels Only.

HVT: high-value target.

HYDICE: Hyperspectral Digital Imagery Collection Experiment.

HYDRA: Hyperspectral Day/Night Radiometry Assessment.

HYMSMO: Hyperspectral MASINT Support to Military Operations.

I&W: indications and warnings.

IAP: International Airport.

IAS: Intelligence Analysis System (Marine Corps).

IBS: Integrated Broadcast System.

IC: Intelligence Community.

ICARIS: Intelligence Communications and Requirements Information System.

ICC: International Criminal Court.

ICEX: interrogator counter-intelligence exercise.

ICON: Imagery Communications and Operations Node.

ICR: Intelligence Collection Requirement.

ICS: Interagency Communications System; Incident Command System. During the Cold War, ICS was a system for communications between the FEMA Special Facility and Site R, and between civilian and military relocation sites in the "federal arc." ICS was also possibly a FEMA special access program compartment dealing with continuity of government.

ICTT: Improved Commander's Tactical Terminal (army).

IDB: integrated database.

IDEX: Imagery Digital Exploitation System.

IDHS: Intelligence Data Handling System.

IDSF: Intelligence Defector Source File.

IES: Imagery Exploitation Station.

IESS: Imagery Exploitation Support System.

IEW: intelligence and electronic warfare.

IEWSE: IEW Support Element.

IFF: Identification Friend or Foe.

IFOR: Implementation Force.

IFR: indigo firing report (navy).

IGRV: Improved Guardrail V.

IGSM: Interim Ground Station Module.

IMET: International Military Education and Training. US security assistance program that provides training to selected foreign-military- and defense-associated civilian personnel on a grant basis. IMET is authorized by the Foreign Assistance Act of 1961, as amended.

IMINT: imagery intelligence.

IMOM: improved many-on-many.

IMPACTS: IW [Information Warfare] Mission Planning Analysis and C2 [Command and Control] Targeting System.

INCA: Intelligence Communications Architecture.

INCLE: International Narcotics Control and Law Enforcement. US security assistance funding for counter-narcotics, law enforcement, border control, anti-money-laundering, and judicial reform programs.

INR: Bureau of Intelligence and Research (Department of State).

INSCOM: Army Intelligence and Security Command.

International Traffic in Arms Regulation (ITAR): Manual prepared by the Bureau of Politico-Military Affairs, Department of State, providing licensing and regulatory provisions for the export of defense articles, technical data, and services.

INTSUM: intelligence summary.

IO: information operations.

IOB: Intelligence Oversight Board (subunit of the President's Foreign Intelligence Advisory Board, PFIAB).

IOSS: NAVCENT Genser Intelligence Broadcast.

IOTC: Information Operations Technology Center (CIA–DOD).

IPB: intelligence preparation of the battlefield.

IPDS: Imagery Processing and Dissemination System.

IPL: Image Product Library.

IR: infrared; information requirements.

IRISA: Intelligence Information Index Summary.

IROF: Imagery Reconnaissance Objective File.

IS: intelligence squadron (air force).

ISAF: International Security Assistance Force (Afghanistan).

ISAR: Inverse Synthetic Aperture Radar.

ISG: Iraq Survey Group.

ISO/PfP: In support of [NATO] Partnership for Peace.

ISR: Intelligence, Surveillance, and Reconnaissance.

ISSE Guard: Information (or Imagery) Support Server Environment.

ITAR: *See* International Traffic in Arms Regulation.

I-TRAP: Interagency Terrorism Response Awareness Program.

ITDB: Intercept Tasking Database.

IUSS: Integrated Undersea Surveillance System.

IW: information warfare.

IWPC: Information Warfare Planning Capability. An automated set of tools to integrate information warfare capabilities into the overall targeting and weaponeering effort of a campaign.

J2X: Formerly Joint Operational Support Element (HUMINT Assets).

JAC: Joint Analysis Center (the European Command Joint Intelligence Center).

JAIEG: Joint Atomic Information Exchange Group (US–UK).

JBS: Joint Broadcast System.

JCAPS: Joint C4ISR [Command, Control, Communications, Computer, and Intelligence, Surveillance, and Reconnaissance] Architecture Planning/Analysis System (replaces Intelligence Communications and Requirements Information System, ICARIS).

JCET: Joint/Combined Exchange Training Program.

JCMEC: Joint Captured Enemy Material Exploitation Center.

JCMT: Joint Collection Management Tool.

JCS: Joint Chiefs of Staff.

JCSAN: Joint Chiefs of Staff Alert Network. Point-to-point, on-call, secure voice communications between the National Military Command Center (NMCC)/Alternative National Military Command Center (ANMCC) and command centers of each unified command.

JDEC: Joint Document Exploitation Center.

JDISS: Joint Deployable Intelligence Support System. Sensitive compartmented information (SCI) communications.

JDS: Joint Dissemination System.

JEAP: Joint Electronic Analysis Program.

JEEP: Joint Emergency Evacuation Plan.

JFACC: Joint Forces Air Component Commander.

JFC: Joint Force Command (NATO).

JFC-N: Joint Force Command North (NATO) (formerly AFNORTH).

JFC-S: Joint Force Command South (NATO) (formerly AFSOUTH).

JFCC: Joint Force Component Commands (NATO).

JFCOM: Joint Forces Command.

JFLCC: Joint Forces Land Component Commander.

JFMCC: Joint Forces Maritime Component Commander.

JFSOCC: Joint Forces Special Operations Component Commander.

JHQ: Joint Headquarters (NATO).

JI: Jemaah Islamiyah.

JIACG: Joint Interagency Coordination Group.

JIATF: Joint Interagency Task Force.

JIC: Joint Intelligence Center.

JICPAC: Joint Intelligence Center Pacific.

JIOC: Joint Information Operations Center.

JIPTL: Joint Integrated Prioritized Target List.

JIVA: Joint Intelligence Virtual Architecture.

JLENS: Joint Land Attack Cruise Missile Defense Elevated Netted Sensor System.

JLOTS: Joint Logistics Over the Shore (TRANSCOM).

JMCIS: Joint Maritime Command Information System.

JMIP: Joint Military Intelligence Program. Part of the National Foreign Intelligence Program (NFIP) classified budget, formerly part of Tactical Intelligence and Related Activities (TIARA).

JOSE: Joint Operational Support Element (now called J2X).

JPAS: Joint Personnel Adjudication System (replaces Sentinel Key).

JPOTF: Joint Psychological Operations Task Force.

JRC: Joint Reconnaissance Center.

JRTC: Joint Readiness Training Center.

JSIPS: Joint Service Imagery Processing System.

JSIPS-N: Joint Service Imagery Processing System — Navy.

JSOC: Joint Special Operations Command.

JSOTF: Joint Special Operations Task Force.

JSOTFC: Joint Special Operations Task Force Commander.

JSTARS: Joint Surveillance and Tracking System.

JTA: Joint Technical Architecture.

JTF: Joint Task Force.

JTF-HOA: Joint Task Force — Horn of Africa.

JTF-SWA: Joint Task Force — South West Asia.

JTFEX: joint task force exercise.

JTT: Joint Tactical Terminal. Integrated UHF/VHF/S-band national and theater communications receiver that provides tactical users the capability to receive, decrypt, process, correlate, format, and distribute data from the Integrated Broadcast System (IBS).
  + **JTT/H3:** Joint Tactical Terminal/Hybrid 3-Channel.
  + **JTT/H-R:** Joint Tactical Terminal/Hybrid — Receive Only.
  + **JTT/H-R3:** Joint Tactical Terminal/Hybrid — Receive Only 3-Channel.

JTT: Joint Targeting Toolbox. A Joint Chiefs of Staff initiative to incorporate a suite of interoperable targeting tools.

JTTF: Joint Terrorism Task Force (FBI).

JTWS: Joint Threat Warning System.

JWAC: Joint Warfare Analysis Center (JFCOM).

JWICS: Joint Worldwide Intelligence Communications System. JWICS is the sensitive compartmented information (SCI) component of the Defense Information Systems Network (DISN). The JWICS architecture is designed to provide secure, high-capacity communications to handle data, video, voice, imagery, and graphics. JWICS supports intelligence production and dissemination as well as crisis management operations for the Office of the Secretary of Defense, the Joint Staff, combat support agencies, all combatant command Joint Intelligence Centers and tactical components, the service intelligence departments, scientific and technical intelligence production centers, and selected military and civilian federal executive agencies. JWICS is the primary interactive video teleconferencing system connecting indications and warning centers and the Washington-area Secure Video Teleconferencing System. JWICS is used to "broadcast" daily and/or crisis intelligence briefings from any one site to one or more sites.

JWID: Joint Warfighter Interoperability Demonstration.

KCOIC: Korean Combat Operations Intelligence Center.

KFOR: Kosovo Force.

KH: Keyhole.

KISS: Korea Intelligence Support System.

KL: Klieglight (NSA).

KRSOC: Kunia [HI] Regional SIGINT Operations Center (NSA).

LEASAT: Leased Satellite.

LIVEX: live exercise.

LIVID: Language Identification and Voice Identification Device (SOCOM).

LIWA: Land Information Warfare Activity (army).

LLSO: low-level source operations.

LO: Low Observable.

LPI: Low Probability of Intercept.

LRS: long-range surveillance.

LRSU: long-range surveillance unit.

M3: Multimedia Message Manager. Standard message handler for the DOD Intelligence Information Center community. M3 provides real-time dissemination of incoming message traffic, retroactive search of an archive message database, and message composition, coordination, release, and validation. Formerly Automated Message Handling System (AMHS).

MAC: Military Airlift Command (now Air Mobility Command, AMC).

MAGIC: Marine Air–Ground Illusion Capability (Deception); Maritime Air–Ground Intelligence Cell (now called Strike Amphibious Warfare Intelligence Cell, SAWIC).

Major Non-NATO Ally: Provision of law that allows special benefits, including eligibility for priority delivery of Excess Defense Articles (EDA), stockpiling of US defense articles, purchase of depleted uranium shells, participation in cooperative research and development programs, and eligibility for the Defense Export Loan Guarantee program. The secretary of defense may loan to a country that is a NATO ally or Major Non-NATO Ally materials (other than strategic and critical materials), supplies, or equipment for the purpose of carrying out a program of cooperative research, development, testing, or evaluation. In addition, the secretary may accept as a loan or gift from such allies materials, supplies, or equipment for similar purposes. Major Non-NATO Allies include Argentina, Australia, Bahrain, Egypt, Israel, Japan, Jordan, Kuwait, New Zealand, the Philippines, and South Korea. With 30 days prior notification to Congress, the president can either add or delete a country to this listing. Under law (§1206, PL 107-228), Taiwan is treated as though it was designated as a Major Non-NATO Ally.

MANTIS: Manpack Tactical Intelligence System.

MARCENT: Marine Forces Central Command.

MARDEZ: Maritime Defense Zone.

MARFORPAC: Marine Forces Pacific.

MASINT: measurements and signatures intelligence. MASINT capabilities include radar, laser, optical, infrared, acoustic, nuclear radiation, radio frequency, spectroradiometric, and seismic sensing systems as well as gas, liquid, and solid materials sampling and analysis.

MASTT: Multi-mode Air and Space Tagging and Tracking. *See* Talon Knight in part 3.

MATINT: materials intelligence. One aspect of MASINT.

MATRIX: Multi-source Automatic Target Recognition and Interactive Exploitation.

MATT: Multi-mission Advanced Tactical Terminal.

MAXI: Modular Architecture for Exchange of Intelligence.

MCAS: Marine Corps Air Station.

MCIA: Marine Corps Intelligence Activity.

MCM: mine counter-measures.

MDCI: multi-discipline counter-intelligence.

MDIDTS: Migration Defense Intelligence Threat Data Systems.

MDITDS: Modernized Defense Intelligence Threat Data System (DIA/ HUMINT).

MEDINT: medical intelligence.

MEF: Marine Expeditionary Force.

MEK: Mujahedin-e Khalq.

MEMS: Micro Electro Mechanical Systems.

MERIT: Marine Corps Military Exploitation of Reconnaissance and Intelligence Technologies.

METOC: Meteorology and Oceanography Command (navy). An unclassified LAN.

MEU: Marine Expeditionary Unit.

MEWS: MASINT Exploitation Workstation. MEWS is capable of processing, exploiting, and producing special Synthetic Aperture Radar (SAR), radiometric, and spectral MASINT products. Some of the products include but are not limited to Coherent Change Detection, Two-Color Multi-View, Dynamic Imaging, and Terrain Elevation Modeling.

MEWSS: Mobile Electronic Warfare Support System.

MI: military intelligence.

MIB Military Intelligence Board.

MIDAS: Miniature Data Acquisition System (MiDAS). S-band transceiver that communicates over the M22 satellite network and serves as the Technical Data Processor Suite (TDPS) Direct Down Link.

MIDAS-T: Miniature Data Acquisition System — TERPES [Tactical Electronic Reconnaissance Processing and Evaluation System].

MIDB: Modernized Integrated Database. Worldwide DIA General Military Intelligence (GMI) database that provides intelligence on locations and military forces order of battle. It contains retrieval and maintenance capabilities to manage military forces, installations, and facilities, population concentrations, command and control (C2) structure, significant events, and equipment database information. It includes the Electronic Order of Battle System (EOBS).

MIES: Mobile Imagery Exploitation System.

MIIDS: Military Intelligence Integrated Data System.

MILSATCOM: Military Satellite Communications.

MINEX: mine warfare exercise.

MIO: maritime interdiction operations.

MISSI: Multi-level Information System Security Initiative (NSA).

MMSK: Multi-Mission Search Kit (COMINT Search System).

MNC: Multi-National Coalition.

MNNA: *See* Major Non-NATO Ally.

MOAB: Mother of All Bombs; Massive Ordnance Air Blast.

MOB: Main Operating Base.

MOU: memorandum of understanding.

MPA: Multi-Protocol Architecture (Compass Bright).

MRDBS: MASINT Requirements Data Base System.

MRSOC: Medina [TX] Regional SIGINT Operations Center (NSA).

MSC: Military Sealift Command.

MSCA: Military Support to Civil Authorities.

MSIC: Missile Space Intelligence Center (DIA).

MSIS: Multi-Source Intelligence System. E-2C, JSTARS, SOF-IV, and Quiet Knight system.

MTIX: Moving Target Indicator/Indication Exploitation.

MTMC: Military Traffic Management Command.

MTS: Man Transportable SOCRATES [Special Operations Research, Analysis, and Threat Evaluation System].

MUCELS: Multiple Communications Emitter Location System.

MUD: Multi-User Detection (Compass Bright).

MUSIC: Multi-User Special Intelligence Communications System.

NACIC: National Counterintelligence Center.

NADR: Nonproliferation, Anti-terrorism, Demining, and Related Programs.

NAIC: National Air Intelligence Center (air force) (now the National Air and Space Intelligence Center, NASIC).

NAOC: National Airborne Operations Center.

NAS: naval air station.

NASA: National Aeronautics and Space Administration.

NASIC: National Air and Space Intelligence Center (formerly National Air Intelligence Center, NAIC).

NAVCENT: Naval Forces Central Command.

NAVEUR: Naval Forces Europe.

NAVFOR: Naval Forces.

NAVNORTH: Allied Naval Forces Northern Europe.

NAVSOUTH: Allied Naval Forces Southern Europe (now Maritime Component Command).

NBC: nuclear, biological, chemical.

NC: NATO Confidential.

NCA: NATO Confidential ATOMAL; National Command Authorities.

NCIS: Naval Criminal Investigative Service.

NCS: naval control of shipping.

NCWR: non-code-word reporting.

NDP-1: National Policy and Procedures for the Disclosure of Classified Military Information to Foreign Governments and International Organizations.

NDU: National Defense University.

NEO: noncombatant evacuation operation. Movement of DOD-sponsored personnel, Department of State personnel, other US-government-sponsored personnel, and US citizens and designated aliens from a threatened geographic area or theater of operations.

NES: National Exploitation System.

NF: *See* NOFORN.

NFIB: National Foreign Intelligence Board.

NFIP: National Foreign Intelligence Program (intelligence budget, minus Tactical Intelligence and Related Activities, TIARA).

NG: National Guard.

NGA: National Geo-spatial Intelligence Agency.

NGIC: National Ground Intelligence Center (army).

NIC: National Intelligence Council.

nickname: A combination of two separate unassociated and unclassified words assigned to refer to a classified program, activity, exercise, or special access program.

NIE: National Intelligence Estimate.

NIMA: National Imagery and Mapping Agency.

NIO: National Intelligence Officer.

NIPC: National Infrastructure Protection Center (FBI; established 1997 by Presidential Decision Directive 63).

NIPRNET: Non-secure Internet Protocol Router Network.

NIPS: Navy Intelligence Processing System.

NIST: National Intelligence Support Team.

NIWTWG: National Information Warfare Threat Working Group (formerly Joint Information Warfare Threat Analysis Working Group).

NL-PRIME: NIMA [National Imagery and Mapping Agency] Library Pathfinder Information Management Environment.

NMCC: National Military Command Center (in the Pentagon).

NMIC: National Military Intelligence Center (former designation of NMJIC).

NMJIC: National Military Joint Intelligence Center (in the Pentagon).

NNSA: National Nuclear Security Administration.

NOC: non-official cover.

NOFORN: Not Releasable to Foreign Nationals (sometimes NF).

NOIWON: National Operational Intelligence Watch Officer's Network. A secure teleconference among intelligence duty officers at the White House, Pentagon, State Department, NSA, and CIA.

NORAD: North American Aerospace Defense Command.

NORTHCOM: Northern Command.

NPC: Nonproliferation Center (CIA, now Center for Weapons Intelligence, Nonproliferation and Arms Control, WINPAC).

NPIC: National Photographic Interpretation Center (formerly CIA, now part of National Geo-spatial Intelligence Agency/National Imagery and Mapping Agency).

NR: NATO Restricted.

NRF: NATO Response Force.

NRL: Naval Research Laboratory.

NRO: National Reconnaissance Office.

NRP: National Reconnaissance Program.

NRTD: Near Real Time Data. An integrated NSA SIGINT source data broadcast service system, formerly Binocular.

NS: NATO Secret; Naval Station.

NSA: National Security Agency; NATO Secret ATOMAL.

NSC: National Security Council.

NSDD: National Security Decision Directive.

NSG: Naval Security Group.

NSOC: National Security Operations Center (NSA) (formerly National SIGINT Operations Center).

NSTL: National Security Threat List. A road map for FBI counter-intelligence resources, especially as pertains to industrial espionage.

NSTL: National Strategic Target List.

NSTS: NSA Sensitive Telephone System.

NSWU: Naval Special Warfare Unit.

NUCEX: nuclear exercise.

NUCLEX: nuclear load-out exercise.

NUDET: Nuclear Detonation Report.

NULKA: Active Electronic Decoy.

NWARS: National Wargaming System.

OADR: Originating Agency's Determination Required.

OAF: Operation Allied Force.

OB: Order of Battle.

OBP: On Board Processing.

OCMC: Overhead Collection Management Center (NSA).

OEF: Operation Enduring Freedom.

OFAC: Office of Foreign Assets Control (Department of Treasury).

OGS: Overseas Ground Station.

OIF: Operation Iraqi Freedom.

OL: Operating Location.

OMA: Office of Military Affairs (CIA).

OMEGA: Operational Model Exploiting GPS Accuracy.

ONI: Office of Naval Intelligence.

OOTW: operations other than war.

OPAL: Office of the President Alternate Location.

OPLAN: Operations Plan.

OPORDER: Operations Order.

OPR: Office of Primary Responsibility.

OPREP: operations report.

OPSCOMM: Operational Communications.

OPSEC: operational security.

ORCON: Originator Controlled.

ORD: Office of Research and Development (CIA).

OREB: Orestes Bravo.

OSCE: Organization for Security and Cooperation in Europe.

OSD: Office of the Secretary of Defense.

OSIS: Ocean Surveillance Information System; Open Source Information System.

OST: Office of Special Technology (Office of the Secretary of Defense).

OTCIXS: Officer-in-Tactical-Command Information Exchange System.

PACAF: Pacific Air Forces.

PACOM: Pacific Command.

Pan Sahel Initiative (PSI): Multi-year effort to wage the war on terrorism and enhance regional peace in the Sahel region of Africa. PSI aims to assist the countries of the Sahel — Chad, Niger, Mauritania, and Mali — in controlling their borders, countering traffickers and smugglers, and monitoring the trafficking of people and illicit material. The program, funded by the State Department, was announced in 2002 but not funded and operated until Nov 2003. The initiative received $6.5 million in fiscal year 2004.

PARPRO: Peacetime Aerial Reconnaissance Program.

PASSEX: passing exercise (navy).

PDAS: Planning and Decision Aid System (pronounced *p-das*). *See* Island Sun in part 3.

PDB: Presidential Daily Brief.

PDD: Presidential Decision Directive.

PE: Program Element.

PEAD: Presidential Emergency Action Document.

PELVIS: Palm version of ELVIS [Enhanced Link Virtual Info System].

PEOC: Presidential Emergency Operations Center.

PFIAB: President's Foreign Intelligence Advisory Board.

PfP: Partnership for Peace (NATO).

PHIBLEX: amphibious exercise.

PID: *See* Plan Identification.

PIJ: Palestinian Islamic Jihad.

PKO: peacekeeping operations.

Plan Identification (PID): Command-unique four-digit number that identifies deliberate plans of the US combatant commands. A two-digit suffix indicates the Joint Strategic Capabilities Plan (JSCP) year for which the plan is written (such as 1003–98), and a one-character alphabetic suffix indicating the Operations Plan (OPLAN) option (such as 1003V-98). The four-digit number in the PID does not change when the OPLAN is revised or converted into an Operations Order (OPORDER) and is not reused when the requirement for the plan is canceled. Supporting plans are assigned a PID identical to that of the supported plan. PIDs are assigned by number blocks:

NUMBER BLOCK	COMMAND OR AGENCY
0001 through 0999	Joint Chiefs of Staff
1000 through 1999	CENTCOM
2000 through 2999	JFCOM
3000 through 3399	NORAD
3400 through 3999	NORTHCOM (formerly SPACECOM plans)
4000 through 4999	EUCOM
5000 through 5999	PACOM
6000 through 6999	SOUTHCOM
7000 through 7999	SOCOM (7000–7499; formerly FORSCOM plans)
8000 through 8999	STRATCOM
9000 through 9599	TRANSCOM
9600 through 9699	Reserved
9700 through 9799	Coast Guard

Acronyms and Glossary

Plt: Platoon.

PME: Professional Military Education.

PRCSO: Peacetime Reconnaissance and Certain Sensitive Operations.

PRIME BEEF: Prime Base Engineer Emergency Force (air force).

PRIME RIBS: Prime Readiness In Base Services (air force).

PRISM: EUCOM Intelligence, Surveillance and Reconnaissance (ISR) planning tool for resource integration, synchronization, and management.

PROFTAR: Probable Friendly Targeted Area.

Proliferation Security Initiative (PSI): Unveiled by President Bush in a 31 May 2003 speech. The initial 16 PSI participants were Australia, Canada, Denmark, France, Germany, Italy, Japan, the Netherlands, Norway, Poland, Portugal, Singapore, Spain, Turkey, the UK, and the US.

PSI: *See* Pan Sahel Initiative; *see* Proliferation Security Initiative.

PSM: Presidential Support Mission.

PSYOP: psychological operations.

PUMA: Previously Unexploited MASINT Applications.

QC LITE (Quantum Cascade Interrogation of Target Effluents): MASINT application to detect chemical agents on Unmanned Aerial Vehicles (UAVs) or helicopter dispensing.

RAPIDS: Sensitive compartmented information (SCI) communications network.

RD: Restricted Data.

READIEX: readiness exercise (navy). The series is usually numbered 90-1, 90-2, and so on.

RECCEXREP: Reconnaissance Exploitation Report (navy).

Regt: Regiment.

RELROK: Releasable to the ROK (South Korea).

RF: Radio Frequency.

RINT: Unintentional radiation intelligence.

RMS: Sensitive compartmented information (SCI) communications network.

ROTHR: Relocatable Over-the-Horizon Radar.

RPV: remotely piloted vehicle.

RS: Reconnaissance Squadron.

RSN: Red Switch Network. An automated secure-voice service to users at the National Military Command Center, Site R, and command centers worldwide.

RSOC: Regional SIGINT Operations Center.

SABI: Secret and Below Interoperability.

SAC: Supreme Allied Command.

SACEUR: Supreme Allied Command Europe (NATO).

SACLANT: Supreme Allied Command Atlantic (NATO).

SACT: Supreme Allied Commander Transformation (NATO).

SAFE: Support to the Analysts' File Environment.

SALUTE: Size, Activity, Location, Unit, Time and Equipment.

SAM: Surface-to-Air Missile.

SAP: *See* special access program.

SAPCO: Special Access Program Coordinating Office.

SAPOC: Special Access Program Oversight Committee.

SAPF: Special Access Program Facility.

SAPWG: Special Access Program Working Group.

SAR: Special Access Required; Synthetic Aperture Radar; search and rescue.

SARK: Saville Automatic Rekeying (cryptographic equipment).

SART: Strategic Aircraft Reconstitution Team.

SATAN: Security Administrator's Tool for Analyzing Networks.

SATRAN: Satellite Reconnaissance Advance Notice.

SAWIC: Strike Amphibious Warfare Intelligence Cell (formerly Marine Air–Ground Illusion Capability, MAGIC).

SBS: Senior Blade Segment.

SBU: Sensitive But Unclassified.

SCAMPI: SOCOM and other government agency (CIA) field telecommunications system. SCAMPI provides satellite service for voice, data, facsimile, and video teleconferencing. A deployable SCAMPI capability provides small teams with connectivity to national links.

SCARS: Signal Classification and Recognition Subsystem.

SCG: Security Classification Guide.

SCI: sensitive compartmented information.

SCIF: sensitive compartmented information facility (pronounced *skiff*).

SCN: Satellite Control Network.

SCO: *See* Shanghai Cooperation Organization.

SCOOP: Submarine Continuity of Operations. Contingency plan for the creation of temporary homeports and logistics support stations for ballistic missile submarines during generated alert and in the trans- and postnuclear war phases. SCOOP planning and exercises in the Pacific have included the creation of Trident support facilities in Alaska, Hawaii, and Guam; and in the Atlantic in Puerto Rico.

SCS: Special Collection Service (joint CIA–NSA).

SEABASS: Sea Based Assets Security System. A current intelligence processor.

SEAL: sea–air–land.

SECC: Survivable Endurable Command Center.

SECEX: ballistic missiile submarine (SSBN) security exercise.

SEI: specific emitter identification. SEI provides ELINT signal collection platforms with the capability to uniquely identify a radar transmitter accurate enough to make it possible to assign a "fingerprint" to the particular signal.

sensitive compartmented information (SCI): Classified information concerning or derived from intelligence sources, methods, or analytical processes, which is required to be handled exclusively within formal access control systems established by the Director of Central Intelligence (DCI). Foreign disclosure of SCI is governed by DCI Directive 5/5, Conduct of SIGINT Liaison with Foreign Governments and the Release of US SIGINT to Foreign Governments.

SETAF: Southern European Task Force (army).

SEWS: Satellite Early Warning System.

SEXTANT: Signals Exploitation Tactical Network.

SF: special forces (army).

SFG: Special Forces Group (army).

SFOR: Stabilization Force (Bosnia).

Shanghai Cooperation Organization (SCO): China and Russia joined with the Central Asian nations of Kazakhstan, Kyrgyzstan, Tajikistan, and

Uzbekistan to establish the SCO in Jun 2001. The SCO is designed to promote regional stability and cooperate to combat terrorism in the region.

SHAPE: Supreme Headquarters Allied Powers Europe (NATO).

SHAREM: Shipborne Anti-submarine Warfare (ASW) Readiness Effectiveness Measuring.

SHD: special handling designator.

SI: special intelligence.

SICG: Senior Interagency Coordination Group. Counter-WMD.

SIDEARM: Secondary Imagery Dissemination Environment and Resource Maneuver (army Tactical Exploitation of National Capabilities program).

SIDS: Secondary Image Dissemination System.

SIGINT: signals intelligence. The terms SIGINT and cryptology are essentially the same. SIGINT is intelligence information comprising Communications Intelligence (COMINT), Electronics Intelligence (ELINT) and Foreign Instrumentation Signals Intelligence (FISINT). The term cryptology refers to SIGINT functions and incorporates information security functions.

SINKEX: sink exercise; target/hull sinking destruction exercise.

SIOP: Single Integrated Operational Plan (OPLAN 8044),

SIPRNET: Secret Internet Protocol Router Network.

SITGO: Special Intelligence Task Group Orestes.

SMASHEX: search for simulated submarine casualty exercise.

SMDC: Army Space and Missile Defense Command.

SMU: *See* Special Mission Unit.

SNIE: Special National Intelligence Estimate. Fast-track NIE.

SOAR: Special Operations Air Regiment.

SOC: special operations capable (Marine Corps).

SOCCENT: Special Operations Central Command.

SOCEUR: Special Operations European Command.

SOCEX: Special Operations capability exercise.

SOCOM: Special Operations Command.

SOCPAC: Special Operations Command Pacific.

SOCRATES: Special Operations Research, Analysis, and Threat Evaluation

System. A SOCOM Intelligence Data Handling System (IDHS) that provides automated intelligence and imagery support.

SOCSOUTH: Special Operations Southern Command.

SOF: special operations forces.

SOFA: Status of Forces Agreement.

SOG: Special Operations Group.

SOIS: Special Operations Intelligence System.

SOS: Special Operations Squadron.

SOSUS: Sound Surveillance System. The name was changed to Integrated Undersea Surveillance System (IUSS) in 1985.

SOTA: SIGINT Operational Tasking Authority.

SOUTHAF: Southern Air Forces.

SOUTHCOM: Southern Command.

SOW: Special Operations Wing.

SPACECOM: Space Command (now part of STRATCOM).

SPAWAR: Space and Naval Warfare Systems Command.

SPEAR: Strike Protection Evaluation Anti–Air Warfare Research (navy).

SPECAT: special category. SPECAT messages are classified messages identified with specific projects or subjects that require special handling procedures supplemental to those imposed by the security classification. The special handling procedures ensure that the message will be handled and viewed only by properly cleared and authorized personnel. SPECAT messages must be classified at least Confidential. Control of SPECAT messages during electronic transmission is done through assignment of a special handling designator (SHD). The three types of messages associated with the SPECAT caveat are SIOP-ESI, SPECAT (Code Word), and Exclusive For.

special access program (SAP): Classified research and development effort, acquisition program, operation, intelligence activity, or plan that is so sensitive or critical that the value of the information warrants enhanced protection beyond that normally provided for access to Confidential, Secret, or Top Secret information. SAPs include formal additional controls limiting the number of persons authorized access, nondisclosure agreements, and physical security and communications standards. SAPs may only be approved by the secretary or deputy secretary of defense. Information about SAPs is marked

"Special Access Required" or with an assigned nickname or code word. Annually, the DOD provides Congress with a report on existing SAPs.

special activities: Military and intelligence activities planned and executed so that the role of the US government is not apparent or acknowledged publicly. By regulation, these cannot include activities intended to influence US political processes, public opinion, policies, or media; nor do they include collection and production of intelligence.

Special Arabic: Hebrew.

Special Mission Unit (SMU): A group of operations and support personnel from designated organizations that is task-organized to perform highly classified activities.

SPECTRA: Standardized Production Environment for Classification of Terrain and Resource Analysis.

SPECWEPS LOADEX: special (nuclear) weapons loading exercise.

SPNF: Special Project Night Fury.

SRIG: Surveillance, Reconnaissance, Intelligence Group (Marine Corps).

SPINTCOMM: Special Intelligence Communications Network. The DIA-managed portion of the Defense Special Security Communications System (DSSCS).

SPIRIT: Special Purpose Intelligence Remote Integrated Terminal — Trojan (army).

Sqn: Squadron.

SRF: SIGINT readiness facility.

SSEE: Ship's Signals Exploitation Equipment (navy).

SSES: Ship's Signals Exploitation Space (navy, aboard aircraft carriers).

SSO: special security office.

SSP-S: single source processor — SIGINT.

ST: special tactics (air force).

STAR: Sensitive Target Approval/Review. Joint Chiefs of Staff process for secretary of defense and presidential approval for attack of "sensitive" targets.

STAR: S-band Tactical Automated Receivers (Chariot/Tactical Electronic Reconnaissance Processing and Evaluation System).

STARS: Special Tactics and Rescue Squad.

State Partnership Program (SPP): National Guard bilateral state-to-country partner program with militaries and civil security agencies. The SPP was established in 1993 to pair state National Guards with Estonia, Latvia, and Lithuania. State Partners actively participate in bilateral training and familiarization events, exercises, exchanges, fellowship-style internships, and civic leader visits. In 2004, a total of 30 states and 1 territory were partnered with 29 countries around the world.

STE: Secure Terminal Equipment cryptographic product.

STICS: Scalable Transportable Intelligence Communications System. An intelligence support communications system usually deployed to support a Joint Task Force/J2 with hardware and software capable of interfacing with national tactical systems, NSA time-sensitive systems, and the US Customs Service.

STO: Special Technical Organization/Operation.

STON: Special Technical Operations Network. Classified Command, Control, Communications network with 12 operation centers connected by 24 data circuits; being upgraded to a distributed network with 18 sites.

STRATCOM: Strategic Command.

STREDS: Standard TRE [Tactical Receive Equipment] Display. National ELINT system used by navy and air force.

STS: Special Tactics Squadron.

SUAVE: Small UAV [Unmanned Aerial Vehicle] Experimental Payload (Compass Bright).

SUCCESS: Synthesized Ultra-High Frequency Computer Controlled Equipment Subsystem.

SURTASS: Surveillance Towed–Array Sensor System.

SUSLAK: Special US Liaison Advisor — Korea.

SVN: Secure Voice Nestor.

SVTS: Secure Voice Teleconferencing System. Executive-level (president/White House to secretaries) data network.

SWCR: Superwideband Compressive Receiver (Compass Bright).

SYERS: Senior Years Electro-optical Reconnaissance System (U-2).

TACELINT: tactical electronic intelligence.

TACLANE: ATM/IP (KG-175) crytographic device.

TACSIM: Tactical Simulation. A system that provides interactive computer-based simulation to support intelligence training. TACSIM simulates the spectrum of intelligence operations.

Tactical Analysis Team (TAT): SOUTHCOM counter-narcotics intelligence team located in Western Hemispheric embassies. The TAT is able to receive near-real-time intelligence from the US system and transmit that information to foreign military and security services. There are total of 18 TATs, including the Bahamas, Belize, Bolivia, Brazil, Colombia, the Dominican Republic, El Salvador, Guatemala, Honduras, Jamaica, Mexico, Panama, and Peru.

TADIXS: Tactical Data Information Exchange System.

TADIXS-B: Tactical Data Information Exchange System — Broadcast. Collateral broadcast of nationally derived (satellite) ELINT.

TAREX: target exploitation.

TARPS: Tactical Air Reconnaissance Pod System (navy F-14).

TAT: *See* Tactical Analysis Team.

TATERS: Trojan Air Transportable Electronic Reconnaissance System.

TCAC: Tactical Control and Analysis Center.

TCIM: Tactical Communication Interface Module (Hadron replacement).

TCS: Talent Keyhole Control System.

TDDS: Tactical Receive Equipment (TRE) and Related Applications (TRAP) Data Dissemination System (TDDS).

TDE: Tactical Data Exploitation.

TDG: Tactical Dissemination Group.

TDN: Trojan Data Network.

TDPS: Tactical Data Processor Suite. Modular electronics intelligence and communications suite of equipment capable of receiving national-level and theater-originated threat data at the collateral or sensitive compartmented information (SCI) level.

TECHINT: technical intelligence.

TEG: Tactical Exploitation Group.

TENCAP: Tactical Exploitation of National Capabilities. An air force TENCAP program whose first names include Outlook, Knight, Vision, Command, Ready, and Shooter.

TERPES: Tactical Electronic Reconnaissance Processing and Evaluation System.

TERS: Tactical Event Reporting System.

TES: Tactical Exploitation System.

TEXIS: Theater Exercise and Intelligence Simulation.

TEXTA: Technical Extracts of Traffic Analysis database.

TF: task force.

TGO: Task Group Orestes.

THREATCON: Threat Condition

+ ALPHA condition applies when there is a general threat of possible terrorist activity directed against units and personnel, the nature and extent of which are unpredictable, and the circumstances do not justify full implementation of the measures of THREATCON BRAVO. However, it may be necessary to implement certain selected measures from THREATCON BRAVO as a result of intelligence received or as a deterrent. The measures in this THREATCON must be capable of being maintained indefinitely.

+ BRAVO condition applies when an increased and more predictable threat of terrorist activity exists. The measures in this THREATCON must be capable of being maintained for weeks without causing undue hardship, without affecting operational capability, and without aggravating relations with local authorities. All previous measures remain in effect.

+ CHARLIE condition applies when an incident occurs or when intelligence is received indicating that some form of terrorist action against units and personnel is imminent. Implementation of this measure for more than a short period will probably create hardship and will affect the peacetime activities of the unit and its personnel. All previous measures remain in effect.

+ DELTA condition applies in the immediate area where a terrorist attack has occurred or when intelligence has been received that terrorist action against a specific location is likely. Normally, this THREATCON is declared as a localized warning.

+ NORMAL condition applies when a general threat of possible terrorist activity exists but warrants only routine security posture.

TIARA: Tactical Intelligence and Related Activities. A defense budget category for military sensor systems that are considered by the US military to belong to operations rather than to military intelligence.

TIBS: Tactical Information Broadcast Service.

TIDAT: Target Intelligence Data.

TIDES: Threat Intelligence Data Extraction System.

TIDS: Tactical Information Distribution System.

TIE: Tactical Information Element.

TIGER: Tactical Intelligence Gathering and Exploitation Relay.

TIP: Terrorist Interdiction Program. The TIP enhances the border security of participating states by providing them with a computerized database system that allows border control officials to quickly identify and detain or track individuals of interest. The project began in Pakistan; Middle Eastern and East African countries were candidates for early installations. The US has installed the TIP in Cambodia.

TIU: TIBS [Tactical Information Broadcast Service] Interface Unit. A self-contained, highly mobile system that can transmit and receive TIBS messages, data files, or query messages.

TK: Talent Keyhole.

TOM: TDDS [Tactical Receive Equipment and Related Applications Data Dissemination System] Operational Manager.

TOPINT. Technical Operational Intelligence.

TOPS: Tactical Onboard Processing System (DIA).

TOPSCENE: Tactical Operations Preview Scene. Mission rehearsal program that generates high-quality, free-roam perspective views in 3-D and in real time, allowing views of the terrain at high and low altitudes while the user maneuvers through the high-resolution terrain and among the 3-D cultural features.

TRANSCOM: Transportation Command.

TRANSEC: Transmission Security.

TRAP: Tactical Receive Equipment and Related Applications. The TRAP broadcast provides global surveillance information in time for sensor cueing, and indications and warnings.

TRAT: TACAMO Regeneration Assurance Team.

TRE: Tactical Receive Equipment.

TRIXS: Tactical Reconnaissance Intelligence Exchange System.

TRRIP: Theater Rapid Response Intelligence Package (replaced by Counter-intelligence/HUMINT Automated Tool Set, CHATS).

TRS: Tactical Receive System.

TRUMPS: Transportable Reconnaissance U-2 Mission Planning System.

TS: Top Secret.

TSA: Transportation Security Administration.

TST: time-sensitive target.

TTIC: Terrorist Threat Integration Center (Department of Homeland Security).

UAE: United Arab Emirates.

UAV: Unmanned Aerial Vehicle.

UBL: Usama bin Ladin.

UCA: Unified Cryptologic Architecture.

UCIRF: US Army Europe combat intelligence readiness facility, Augsburg, Germany.

UK-C: United Kingdom Confidential.

UK-R: United Kingdom Restricted.

UNC: United Nations Command (South Korea).

UNMOVIC: United Nations Monitoring, Verification, and Inspection Commission.

UNOSOM: United Nations Operation in Somalia.

UNPROFOR: United Nations Protection Force.

UNSC: United Nations Security Council.

UNSCOM: United Nations Special Commission.

UNSCR: United Nations Security Council resolution.

USAFE: US Air Forces in Europe (EUCOM).

USAREUR: US Army in Europe (EUCOM).

USCS: US Customs Service; US Cryptologic Systems.

USD: undersecretary of defense.

USG: US government.

USIGS: US Imagery and Geospatial Information System.

USIS: US Imagery System.

USSID: US Signal Intelligence Directive.

USSS: US SIGINT System.

VETRETE: veterinary readiness training exercise.

VTC: video teleconference.

WASHFAX: Washington Area Secure Facsimile. Secure fax capability for the National Military Command Center (NMCC) and surrounding area.

WATCHCON: Watch Condition. National indications and warnings.

WIMEA: Wiretapping, Investigative Monitoring, and Eavesdropping Activity.

WINPAC: Center for Weapons Intelligence, Nonproliferation and Arms Control (CIA).

WISE: WMD interagency support exercise.

WMD: weapons of mass destruction.

WOT: war on terrorism.

WOTS: Worldwide Origin Threat System. A tactical ballistic missile defense information system in Southwest Asia.

XOI: Operations Deputy for Intelligence, Surveillance, and Reconnaissance (ISR) (air force intelligence chief).

ABOUT THE AUTHOR

William M. Arkin (warkin@igc.org) is an independent journalist and consultant and a long-time military analyst for NBC News. He was a military columnist for the *Los Angeles Times* from 2001 to 2004, and from 1998 to 2002 he was a columnist for the *Washington Post*'s on-line service, writing the biweekly column *DOT.MIL*. From 1985 to 2002, he wrote *Last Word*, a column in the *Bulletin of the Atomic Scientists*, and coauthored "Nuclear Notebook," a bimonthly publication of the National Resources Defense Council that is the standard accounting of the world's nuclear arsenals. Recently, he has been a Senior Fellow at the Center for Strategic Education at the Johns Hopkins University School of Advanced International Studies (SAIS) in Washington, DC, and an Adjunct Professor at the School of Advanced Air and Space Studies, US Air Force, Maxwell AFB, Alabama. He previously served as Senior Military Adviser to Human Rights Watch, the largest international human rights and law organization in the United States.

Arkin served in the US Army as an intelligence analyst in West Berlin from 1974 to 1978. He wrote a groundbreaking book in 1981 on how to do research on military and national security affairs, and he coauthored the first volume of the Natural Resources Defense Council's *Nuclear Weapons Databook* series, the first comprehensive unclassified reference book on nuclear weapons. He then coauthored *Nuclear Battlefields,* a 1985 bestseller that revealed locations of all US and foreign nuclear bases worldwide.

Throughout his career, Arkin's research and writing has resulted in the first public disclosure of numerous military and nuclear weapons programs, plans, and practices. In the late 1980s, he conceived Greenpeace International's Nuclear Free Seas campaign, which was successful in facilitating the removal of tactical nuclear weapons from ships and submarines during the first Bush administration. His revelation of "mini-nuke" research efforts in 1992 led to a subsequent 1994 congressional ban on such research. In 1994, an op-ed piece he wrote for the *New York Times* that revealed US efforts to produce blinding lasers led to a Defense Department decision to agree to an international ban on such weapons. More recently, he was the first to write about the current Bush administration's Nuclear Posture Review, and was the first to write authoritatively about the war plan for Operation Iraqi Freedom. In 2003, he revealed the extreme religious views of Gen. William "Jerry" Boykin, one of the nation's top terrorist hunters.

Bill Arkin doesn't just sit behind a desk. He toured Europe to research the presence of US nuclear weapons in the 1980s. He was a member of the first-ever private delegation to observe Soviet nuclear warheads as part of the NRDC–Soviet Academy of Sciences' Black Sea experiment in June 1989, and two years later he was one of the first westerners to visit a Soviet nuclear weapons storage site. Arkin headed Greenpeace International's war response team in the Persian Gulf during Operation Desert Storm, and he visited Iraq to evaluate civilian damage as part of the Harvard Study Team in 1991, conducting one of the most methodical on-the-ground bomb damage assessments after the war. Since then, Arkin has also conducted bomb damage assessments on the ground in Lebanon, Yugoslavia, Afghanistan, and Eritrea. He is well known as a pioneer in independent fieldwork and research methods used to investigate the effects of weapons and warfare on civilian populations. Gen. Charles A. ("Chuck") Horner, the commander of air forces during the first Gulf War, said in a 10-year anniversary Desert Storm interview in US Naval Institute *Proceedings* that the briefing Arkin gave him on the air war and its civilian effects in Iraq was the best he'd received after the war.

Arkin is author or coauthor of 10 books, and has authored or co-authored more than 500 articles and conference papers on military affairs, as well as chapters in more than two dozen compilations. His books have been translated into Chinese, German, Russian, Spanish, and Japanese. He lives in South Pomfret, Vermont.

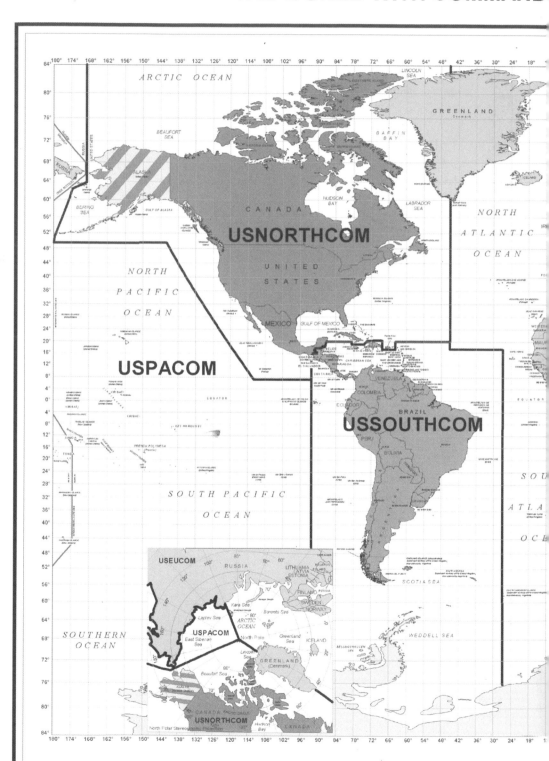